ISRAEL
AT VANITY FAIR

BRILL'S SERIES
IN JEWISH STUDIES

VOL. II

ISRAEL AT VANITY FAIR

*Jews and Judaism in the
Writings of W.M. Thackeray*

BY

S.S. PRAWER

E.J. BRILL
LEIDEN · NEW YORK · KØBENHAVN · KÖLN
1992

The paper in this book meets the guidelines for permanence and durability of the Commit-
tee on Production Guidelines for Book Longevity of the Council on Library Resources.

Library of Congress Cataloging-in-Publication Data

Prawer, Siegbert Salomon, 1925-
    Israel at Vanity Fair: Jews and Judaism in the writings of W.M.
Thackeray / by S.S. Prawer.
      p.   cm.—(Brill's series in Jewish studies, ISSN 0926-2261;
vol. 2)
    Includes bibliographical references and index.
    ISBN 90-04-09403-2 (cloth)
    1. Thackeray, William Makepeace, 1811-1863—Criticism and
interpretation. 2. Jews in literature. I. Title. II. Series.
PR5642.J48P73   1991
823'.8—dc20   91-25465
                                          CIP

ISSN 0926-2261
ISBN 90 04 09403 2

Dedicated to the memory of
my revered teacher
Dr E.M.W. TILLYARD
of Jesus College, Cambridge:
lover of English literature
and
unprejudiced friend to generations
of students from many lands and of
the most varied ethnic provenance

CONTENTS

ACKNOWLEDGMENTS

I am grateful to Professor Fritz Stern and the Director of the Russell Sage Foundation, New York, for hospitality enabling me to consult important manuscript material in the USA, and to the British Academy for a travel grant to the same end. The Librarians of the Bodleian Library and the English Faculty Library, Oxford, the British Library in Bloomsbury and Colindale, the Berg Collection of the New York Public Library and the Pierpont Morgan Library generously opened their precious holdings to my scrutiny; the last-named also allowed me to reprint an excerpt from Thackeray's manuscript of his lecture on George I. Excerpts from Thackeray's letters and journals are reprinted by kind permission of his great-granddaughter, Mrs. Belinda Norman-Butler. Among experts who allowed me access to their greater and deeper knowledge pride of place must go to Professors Kathleen Tillotson and Robert Colby; but I have also incurred obligations to many others, notably Dr George Rowell, Dr Russell Stephens, and Professor Jeffrey L. Sammons.

When the manuscript of this book was completed, the critical edition of Thackeray's works undertaken by the Garland Publishing Company had not progressed beyond its first two volumes. I have therefore confined my references, in the main, to the Oxford Thackeray, edited by George Saintsbury—an edition which is cited, in the pages below, with volume and page numbers only. References to Gordon Ray's edition of Thackeray's Letters and Private Papers, and Philip Collins's edition of Interviews and Recollections, are cited as LPP and IR respectively. These and other editions used are listed in the Select Bibliography, which also contains a check-list of critical writings consulted with profit in the course of the present book's gestation. I have kept references to secondary literature to a minimum in the body of the book, and hope that the Select Bibliography may be taken as an acknowledgment of my debt to generations of previous scholars.

INTRODUCTION

> "I can't help telling the truth as I view it, and describing what I see. To describe it otherwise than it seems to me would be falsehood in that calling in which it has pleased Heaven to place me . . ."
> Thackeray: "Charity and Humour" (X, 625).

Among the great Victorian novelists none is more apt to disconcert the reader than William Makepeace Thackeray. His dark vision of society and its vanities co-exists with an artist's delight in the rich glitter of its superficies and a *bon viveur*'s pleasure in the comforts and amenities it offers those who can afford them. His ready adoption of stereotypes, from grinning child-like blacks to the saintly well-bred English ladies of his later work, must disappoint those who have come to admire the keen sense of complex motivation, complex thought and feeling, shown by the author of *Vanity Fair*. Prejudices instilled by education and confirmed, in later life, by a narrowly circumscribed social set co-exist with a keen consciousness of how unjustified a Victorian English gentleman's pride often turned out to be, and with a realist's tendency to allow characters clogged with authorial approval to perform actions or exhibit sentiments which are less than admirable. Such co-presences, contradictions and disconcerting developments make Thackeray's presentation of Jews—which has never been fully examined and chronicled—at once fascinating and disturbing. As one of the few novelists who illustrated their own work, Thackeray was able to reinforce and supplement the mental imagery conveyed by his texts with powerful visual images that have profoundly affected generations of readers—not least through his work for *Punch*, whose early attitudes and representations he helped to shape. The present book seeks to document and analyze Thackeray's pen-and-pencil portrayal of Jews, exhibiting both its evolution and its permanent features and setting it in the context of his developing art and world-view. It hopes in this way to highlight, not only a significant aspect of Thackeray's art of "a thousand little touches" (the phrase is Chesterton's), but also an important chapter in the way British society perceived, or was made to perceive, the Jews at its periphery and in its midst.

Between 1811, the year of Thackeray's birth, and 1863, the year

of his death, the Jewish community of Britain increased from under
10 000 to some 40 000 men, women and children. Even with this
fourfold increase, Jews remained a tiny part of the total population
of these islands—less than half a percent. They divided into a small
but prestigious group of Sephardim (families like the Montefiores,
who traced their ancestry back to Mediterranean countries) and a
much larger group of Ashkenazim, whose family origins lay in
Germany and Eastern Europe. In this period, a few wealthy and
increasingly cultured families became part of the British establishment, either through intermarriage and baptism, or through acceptance into the dining and club circuit of fashionable London;
scholars and *littérateurs* like Isaac D'Israeli and musicians like
Ignaz Moscheles gained society's respect; in industries like ready-
made clothing Jews made themselves more and more felt as a social
force to be reckoned with; and the small traders, pedlars, money-
lenders and dealers in old clothes which were so conspicuous in the
East End of London moved increasingly outwards into other London districts and into the British provinces. Though they aroused a
certain amount of xenophobic resentment they were not subjected
to physical violence, they were left free to practice their religion,
and many Gentiles of good will, including such figures as Hazlitt
and Macaulay, agitated for the removal of the civic disabilities that
still prevented professing Jews from entering the public service and
hindered many kinds of professional advancement. The chief cause
of such disabilities were Corporation and Test Acts that imposed
upon candidates for office or admission an oath "on the true faith of
a Christian". The House of Commons passed a Jewish Emancipation Bill in 1833, but in that year, and many times hereafter, the
House of Lords prevented its passage. The office of Sheriff, however, and other municipal offices, were opened to Jews in the
eighteen thirties and forties, other restrictions were removed by the
Religious Opinions Relief Bill of 1846, and only membership of the
British parliament was denied to Jews who had not, like Benjamin
Disraeli, been baptized. This exclusion was challenged by the City
of London in 1847, when Lionel Rothschild was elected to the
House of Commons; his admission was blocked, however, on this
and subsequent occasions, by his inability, in conscience, to swear
"on the true faith of a Christian". A compromise formula was
found in 1858, when each House of Parliament was empowered to
determine its own form of oath, and Lionel Rothschild was at last
able to take his seat in the House of Commons. Wider educational
opportunities were offered to Jews by the founding of new universities, particularly the non-sectarian University College, London,

which opened its doors in 1836. The older universities, however, continued making matriculation (in the case of Oxford) and proceeding to a degree (in the case of Cambridge) conditional on religious tests that excluded professing Jews; a galling disability which was not removed until eleven years after Thackeray's death, when the University Test Acts gave Jews the same educational opportunities as members of the Church of England.

If one looks at Disraeli's many pronouncements about Jews, one soon discovers that what he stresses is racial origin rather than religious adherence. Pride of race was something many Englishmen could understand—particularly Anglo-Indians like Thackeray, who was inclined to see the dark-skinned peoples of Asia and Africa as the white man's burden, and whose visits to the American South made him more inclined to insist on qualitative differences between himself and the black man than on the common brotherhood stressed by the contemporary anti-slavery movement. On the whole, however, Britons tended to pooh-pooh the "purity of race" fanatics of Continental Europe, ridiculed by *Punch* in a splendid piece published in 1848 (Vol. XV, p. 93);[1] and whenever violence was offered to Jews abroad (whether to British subjects, like Don Pacifico, or to subjects of the Czar and of Eastern potentates) British Gentiles joined their Jewish fellow citizens in condemnation and demands for redress. Nor did the British government seek to treat Jews living under its jurisdiction as lesser breeds whose community relations should be subject to interference. Sephardim and Ashkenazim were left free to regulate their own modes of worship and seek accommodation with Jews who were anxious to reform some of the traditional ritual; to establish their own free and uncensored press (the *Jewish Chronicle*, which is still going strong, began publication in 1841); to develop educational institutions of its own (from Hyman Hurwitz's fashionable Jewish school at Highgate to Jews' College, the theological seminary founded in 1855, alongside Hebrew-teaching establishments ranging from the elementary *kheder* to the sophisticated Talmud-studying *yeshiva*); and to set up its own Welfare Board, the Board of Guardians which regulated many community affairs from 1859 onwards.

In a valuable compilation entitled *Victorian Jews Through British Eyes* (Oxford 1986) Ann and Roger Cowan have demonstrated how the image of the Jew conveyed by British periodicals progresses, in Thackeray's life time, "from a collection of stereotypes—the finan-

---

[1] See Appendix.

cier, the pedlar, the old clothesman, the sharp entrepreneur, the rather shady ancillary of the machinery of the law—to a more accurate representation of a Victorian bourgeois with distinctive religious practices and traditions" (p. xi). That quotation comes from V.D. Lipman's Introduction to the Cowans' book; an Introduction that usefully compares the image of Jews propagated by the writers and illustrators of Victorian illustrated magazines with the image a modern sociologist would recognize as true. The latter would point to the beginnings of a Jewish industrial proletariat in the clothing and tobacco trades at a time in which, on the whole, Jewish occupational patterns changed " from hawking and general dealing to middle class occupations like shopkeeping, manufacturing and commerce", concentrating especially in "sectors like clothing and footwear, food (especially fruit), jewellery and watchmaking, furniture and tobacco." (p. xii). Lipman also describes assimilation to the British way of life in the upper social regions, among the Rothschilds, Goldsmids, Montefiores and Salomons, and shows how growing affluence and respectability in less exalted social strata often brought with it a change of name. Moses became Marsden, Hyam became Halford, when the firms they had built up "moved up-market" in the eighteen fifties (loc. cit.).

Thackeray's English vantage point was London rather than the provinces. Here the processes Lipman describes and the Cowans document could be observed more fully and clearly than elsewhere—as could the progress of Jewish emancipation marked by such events as the admission of Jews to the freedom of the City of London in 1831 (with attendant privileges in retail as well as wholesale trade); the election of David Salomons as a sheriff of the City in 1835, as alderman in 1847, and as Lord Mayor in 1855; and Lionel Rothschild's long progress towards a seat in the House of Commons, which culminated in his admission in 1858. The present book seeks to trace, in chronological narrative, Thackeray's limited contact with Jews at home and abroad; the image of Jews past and present which he formed from such contact and from his reading; and the way in which that image emerges and develops in his published writings, his drawings, and his more private jottings and communications.

Two points calling for especial mention may be indicated by quoting from an essay on "National Character" which Thackeray accepted for publication during his brief but highly successful tenure of the editorship of the *Cornhill Magazine*.

> We always invest the the Jews, whether ancient or modern, with a few striking but most unpleasant attributes, such as stubborn obsti-

nacy, intense national and religious feeling, somewhat narrow
shrewdness, and an unsocial exclusive zeal for themselves and their
own modes of thought and conduct; and no doubt, if we view them in
their corporate capacity we have a right to paint them in these
colours; but we ought to remember that in doing so we paint only
those features which the net result of their history has impressed on
our minds.

(*Cornhill Magazine*, November 1861, p. 592)

What is so striking here is that every single one of the attributes the
writer lists were thought applicable, by contemporary observers, to
the British; and that British Victorians therefore had some grounds
for feeling an affinity with Jews. Feelings of that kind could find
ample nourishment in memories of earlier identifications with the
Israelites of Bible times, which had led John Lyly, for instance, to
speak of his country "as of a new Israel, His chosen and peculiar
people"—a sentiment often echoed afterwards. It is not surprising,
therefore, to find the writer in the *Cornhill* continuing his reflections
on a presumed "national character" of the Jews by pointing to the
influence of the Bible.

We think of the Jews as the recipients of the revelation on which
Christianity was founded, and as the people amongst whom the
transactions recorded in the Old Testament took place.
    It is not only a natural, but almost an unavoidable error, to
identify them so completely with their and with our own religious
belief, as to suppose that their religion coloured and almost absorbed
the whole of their life, and that the harsh and solemn features of the
portrait which we draw present not only a faithful, but a complete
resemblance to the original. It requires little reflection to see how far
this impression is from the truth . . .

(ibid., pp. 592–3)

It is obvious that the sight and sound of humble Jewish old clothes
men haggling over pennies would conflict with memories of the
dignified utterances of Biblical prophets; it is equally obvious,
however, that no examination of how a Victorian writer depicted
medieval and modern Jews could be deemed complete without
taking into account that writer's attitude to the Bible and the use he
makes of figures, incidents and formulations from the Old Testament.

In *T.S. Eliot and Prejudice*, a study published in 1988 which
established new parameters for discussions of stereotyping and
classifying in literature, Christopher Ricks distinguished four ways
in which an author's attitude to Jews and Judaism could be viewed.
One is the *biographical*, which takes account of that author's private
utterances, experiences and directly expressed or deduced opinions. Another is the *historical*—a description of the times in which

the author lived and the changes he experienced along with his contemporaries. The third way Ricks names the *dissociated*, by which he means careful distinction between what occurs in a work of literature and the author's personal or political doings and sayings. The fourth, by contrast, is the *continuous*, which sets an author's dealings with a particular group or set of problems in the context of larger issues raised by the whole body of his literary work, cultural tradition, and contemporary ways of thinking and feeling. (op. cit., p. 61). The present study attempts to do justice to all four of these points of view. Its central concern is Thackeray's literary work, including essays, lectures, poems, comic squibs and parodies as well as novels and stories, along with the graphic work which accompanied all these. At the same time, however, it seeks, in separate sections introduced at chronologically appropriate moments, to document Thackeray's privately expressed opinions on Jews and Judaism and to adduce comparative material from Thackeray's writings as well as the writings of others, in order to provide a meaningful context for the central texts examined. Since many of these texts have not been available in print for a long time, full quotation will be necessary. It is hoped that this will make *Israel at Vanity Fair* an anthology of unfamiliar texts by one of the great Victorian novelists as well as a work of interpretation in which due weight is given to that "frailty of prejudice" which Hazlitt thought "the unavoidable consequence of the frailty and imperfection of reason", along with struggles to counteract it; to the pull of literary and social stereotypes, along with their use and occasional subversion by a major English writer; and to the interplay of ironic distancing and passionate self-projection in the work of a man who thought he was speaking for his contemporaries when he said, in his late essay "De Finibus", that "our books are diaries, in which our own feelings must of necessity be set down."

CHAPTER 1

QUEER GRACES
(1811–1836)

O, Plutus! your graces are queerly bestowed! . . .
(I, 17)

i

Born in Calcutta in 1811, into an English family that had done well out of its connection with the East India Company, Thackeray was sent to England in 1817 to be inducted into the code and the life of a nineteenth-century English gentleman, first in a horrible school at Southampton, then in a somewhat better one at Chiswick, and finally at Charterhouse, where he stayed from 1822 to 1828. In his earliest years, as he later recalled, he had learnt to associate Old Testament stories with a mother's love:

> When as a child I used to sit on my mother's knee and hear her tell the story of Joseph & his brethren, I received her ideas with her embraces Heaven bless them & their sacred memory! . . .
> (to Mrs. Carmichael-Smith, 26 February 1853—LPP III, 217);

but at Chiswick the Old Testament connected itself, in his mind, with pompous and unloved authority. "I myself remember", his daughter Anne tells us, "hearing it said in the family, that when Dr. --- used to read the Ten Commandments of a Sunday to his boys and the rest of the people assembled, his wife and several members of the congregation had been heard to declare, that to hear his resounding tones reminded them of Mount Sinai itself!" (*Biographical Edition*, I, xv). At Charterhouse Bible instruction was, if anything, even more dispiriting. The chief teaching method Thackeray remembered was to make each boy read out a single verse from the Authorized Version; if the headmaster thought the emphasis wrong, he would roar at the unfortunate in question just as he did when a pupil misplaced a stress in the Greek or Latin classics. School chapel services were boring; and when Thackeray's mother, who had remarried after the death of her first husband and now bore the name Carmichael-Smyth, returned from India, she brought into her son's life an image of the Old Testament God which served to alienate him even further from the Judaic part of the Christian religion. Henrietta Corkson, who knew her well, recalled in later years that "when Mrs. Carmichael-Smyth talked about God to me, she always made me think that he was an angry, harsh old gentleman, who saw every little act of mine, and would eventually punish me." (IR, I, 62). Thackeray came to associate the image Henrietta Corkson here evokes with the Old Testament, and we shall later see how he tried to confront his mother with a different image culled wholly from the New.

Though Charterhouse, known to Thackeray as "Slaughter-house" before time and distance lent a spurious enchantment to his view, came to accept Jewish pupils in the course of the nineteenth century, there is no record of any social contact he may have had with Jewish boys of his own age. What he glimpsed or heard of the presence of Jews in contemporary English society seems to have constituted a source of superior amusement—Thackeray's school-fellows long remembered a series of pen-and-ink caricatures he had drawn for their delectation, one of which illustrated the idea of "Carving" by means of a drawing that represented "a pimple-faced man with strong Jewish features, going in with a huge knife and fork at a similarly exaggerated ham." (IR, I, 89). That drawing is lost; but the theme of Jews breaking the strict religious taboo on pig-meat is a traditional one, exemplified by an anonymous eighteenth-century cartoon entitled "Jews at Luncheon, or a Peep into Duke's Place" (Duke's Place housed London's principal Ashkenazi Synagogue, also known as the "Great Synagogue").

Cartoons of this kind offered budding artists like Thackeray a number of welcome stereotypes: physical stereotypes of strongly marked features in which the nose—that favourite organ of all cartoonists—played a prominent part; cultural stereotypes of changing mores and of practice defying precept.

If the cartoon which depicts "Carving" has been lost, that depicting "Speculation" has been preserved, thanks to a posthumous publication entitled *Thackerayana* (London 1875) which brought before the public a generous selection of Thackeray's earliest drawings. "Speculation" (op. cit., p. 16) depicts a Jewish old clothes man bargaining for a pair of superannuated trousers while his boy is directing a defiant, mocking gesture towards the world at large.

The old clothes dealer is here realistically depicted in a London street; but a marginal illustration in Thackeray's copy of Rollin's *Ancient History*, purporting to depict the Saracen conqueror of Rhodes selling the remains of the famous Colossus to a Hebrew merchant who carried it off on 500 camels, precipitates him into the year 672 of the Christian era and ornaments his head with that

JEWS AT A LUNCHEON.
Or a peep into Dukes Place

Illustration 1

Illustration 2

multiplicity of hats piled one on top of the other which was to
become the caricature attribute of Jewish old clothes men in the
columns of *Punch*. This drawing too found its way into *Thackerayana*
(p. 45).

Illustration 3(a)

The contrast of the fat Saracen and the lean Jew, the liveliness of
gesture and posture, and the suggestion of a line of camels stretch-
ing out to the crack of doom, make this one of the most accomplished and amusing of all Thackeray's drawings.

The same multiple hats also appear in a little caricature which
puns on the name of a now defunct office of the English Chancery
Court: "Clerk of the Petty Bag":

Clerk of the Petty Bag.
Petty Bag Office, Rolls Yard

Illustration 3(b)

In a public school in which flogging and fagging were familiar
parts of daily life, Thackeray stood out by the kindliness and good

temper that went with his tall stature. Where others would send their fags on errands with a blow or a threat, Thackeray would say to a younger boy: "Hooky, . . . go up and fetch me a volume of *Ivanhoe* out of my drawer, that's a good fellow; in the same drawer you will, perhaps, find a penny, which you may take for yourself." (Recollections of John Frederick Boyes, quoted in G.N. Ray's *Thackeray: The Uses of Adversity*, London 1955, p. 95). The mention of *Ivanhoe* is not fortuitous. This was indeed the young Thackeray's favourite novel, and it did two things for his conception of Jews and Jewishness: it provided historical explanations for the usual stereotype, when it traced the comic and grasping qualities exhibited by the ever trembling Israelite Isaac of York to the persecutions to which his people was subjected in medieval times; and it implanted in his imagination the alluring image of a *belle Juive* constantly menaced by spoliation and rape from which a valiant Christian knight might rescue her. The dark beauty of Rebecca of York was to haunt Thackeray's writings; it was the nearest he ever came to the Romantic Agony.

ii

During the year he spent at Trinity College, Cambridge (1829–1830), Thackeray discovered a passion for gambling which led him and his fellow-addicts into occasional dealings with money-lenders and bill-discounters, some of whom may well have been Jewish; but such dealings have left no discoverable traces in his correspondence or in the recollection of his college friends. Two other contacts with Jews have left such traces, however. The first was due to his delight in theatrical entertainments of almost every kind. On his forays to London he sought out performances by a Jewish improviser of verses and songs named Charles Sloman, whose art Thackeray relished particularly because he was himself, in the circle of his friends, a notable *improvisatore*. "Thackeray", Henry Silver wrote in 1860, "tells of his asking Sloman to dine with him and feeling hurt at ye great man's refusal on the plea of a previous engagement. This was when T. used to come up to ye Bedford from Cambridge." (Ray, *The Uses of Adversity*, p. 134). The smart of Sloman's refusal, it would seem, was still felt some thirty years after the event.

Thackeray's second contact with a Jewish fellow-citizen at this time may be glimpsed in one of his letters. Mrs. Carmichael-Smyth had been told by some tattle-tale that her son had given offence with a libellous caricature—a charge to which Thackeray replied on 18

January 1831: "I drew a caricature of Mr. Harte, it is true, but as for publishing it it never entered my head.—The said Mr. Harte is a Jew, who wanted to persuade George [Carmichael-Smyth] to try for some borough, & pay all the expenses of it—with the merit of having dissuaded him from this very hazardous project I 'must gild my humble name.'" (LPP, I, 141). A letter to the same correspondent dated 25 January 1931 calls the Harte caricature affair "a romance founded on fact." Here Thackeray clearly takes credit for having counteracted the wiles of a Jewish political agent who sought to entice one of Thackeray's relatives into a dubious electoral contest just before the Reform Act diminished the number of rotten boroughs and easily manipulable constituencies.

As for his spiritual welfare—Thackeray had been able to allay Mrs. Carmichael Smyth's understandable anxieties soon after his arrival in Cambridge by assuring her of the respect with which her beloved Old Testament was treated in that seat of learning: "We had a beautiful sermon at St. Mary's to-day about the undesigned coincidences wh. occur in the books of Moses, & thereby strengthen their authority." (May 1929—LPP I, 73). The good effect wore out a week later, however, when Thackeray attended another in the same series of addresses by J.J. Blunt, the Lady Margaret Professor of Divinity. In a letter to his mother dated 11–17 May 1829 he acknowledges hearing "a good sermon on the undesigned coincidences in Scripture" in which Professor Blunt showed himself "very ingenious *almost too much so*" (LPP 1, 78—my italics). Attendance at acts of worship became more and more boring to him, and the chanted Psalms proved an especial trial. His mother can hardly have been pleased by the Scriptural parody in which he communicated his weariness on 1 November 1829: "Sunday Chapel is a great Lion—it is rather too tedious for us who hear it so often. The anthems are rather long-winded, & the chant of the Psalm taketh up a long time" (LPP I, 105).

The sceptical temper which asserted itself during Thackeray's year or so at Trinity College, Cambridge, even led him to doubt, for a time, the divinity of the Jewish-born founder of Christianity; but a devout fellow-student, John Allen, who was later to lend traits to the character of Dobbin in *Vanity Fair*, was able to enter into his diary under the date 7 February 1830: "Thackeray came up— expressed some doubts of X^t being = with God, read over St Matthew together & he was convinced thank God for it" (IR, I, 21). No-one who scans Thackeray's letters and diaries can long remain in doubt that he retained Christian beliefs throughout his life which enabled him to remain, without difficulty, a member of the Church of England, and that his devotion to the person and teaching of Jesus was matched only by his abhorrence of much of the dogma that later ages had erected on Gospel foundations— especially if rigid adherence to such dogma led to persecution of others. He had read a horrifying account of the tortures devised by the Inquisition, which he ironically describes as "delectable" in a letter to his mother (12–21 February 1828—LPP I, 22), and he came to share his mother's anti-Catholicism to the extent of affixing his signature to a petition of Trinity College undergraduates against the Catholic Emancipation Bill of 1829 (to Mrs Carmichael-Smith, 22 March 1829—LPP I, 47). When the Bill became law, however, he confessed to his mother: "I am glad of it, for a refusal [by the King to sign the bill] would have only I think created disturbance, and have done no good" (13–19 April 1829—LPP I, 57). He had taken the first step towards a pragmatic and tolerant attitude which some ten years later caused him to tell his mother that he was in no danger of converting to Roman Catholicism, but that they should both "remember that it was *the* church for 13 hundred years, and that it produced, Saints and Sages, who is to doubt." "Are we", he continues, "to cry fy at such a respectable old family because we happen to be born out of it [?]" (23–31 December 1839—LPP I, 405). In the conditions of nineteenth-century England such favourable attitudes to the civic emancipation of Catholics was likely to foster favourable attitudes towards the civic emancipation of Jews as well.

During his brief stay at Cambridge Thackeray first saw his writings in print. He contributed pieces to the undergraduate journals *The Snob* and *The Gownsman* which include a mock prize-poem entitled *Timbuctoo* in which he pokes equal fun at colonial exploitation and its victims:

At home their lives in pleasure always flow,
But many have a different lot to know!
They're often caught, and sold as slaves, alas!
Thus men from highest joy to sorrow pass.
Yet though thy monarchs and thy nobles boil
Rack and molasses in Jamaica's isle!
Desolate Afric! thou art lovely yet!!
One heart yet beats which ne'er shall thee forget.
What though thy maidens are a blackish brown,
Does virtue dwell in whiter breasts alone?
Oh no, oh no, oh no, oh no, oh no!
It shall not, must not, cannot, e'er be so.
The day shall come when Albion's self shall feel
Stern Afric's wrath, and writhe 'neath Afric's steel.
I see her tribes the hill of glory mount,
And sell their sugars on their own account;

While round her throne the prostrate nations come,
Sue for her rice, and barter for her rum!

(I, 2)

Is it fanciful to hear, beneath the banter, serious fears about revenges brought in by the whirligig of time, when the valleys will be exalted and the mountains and hills made low? The poem found a good deal of favour among the university men who read it when it appeared in the *The Snob* on 30 April 1829. Hearing it praised by those who had no idea that the author was within earshot, Thackeray felt a pride that he sought to temper, in a letter to his mother, by quoting what was to become his favourite quotation from Ecclesiastes 1, 2: "The men knew not the Author, but praised the Poem, how eagerly did I suck it in!—"All is vanity—" (11–17 May 1829—LPP I, 76).

The Snob soon expired, but its successor, *The Gownsman*, also attracted a contribution from Thackeray. This took the shape of a "Letter from Mrs. Ramsbottom"—a lower class Mrs Malaprop invented by Theodore Hook. Thackeray's piece introduced a word-game which he was to play over and over again in his published works and private writings: "I must", writes Mrs Ramsbottom, "bid you a jew, my dear Jemima ..." (I, 11–12 November 1829). The substitution of "jew" for "dieu" had overtones to which Thackeray, whose addiction to puns and double meanings is as well documented as his dislike of what he conceived to be the Old Testament conception of God, could hardly have remained deaf. It is to be found in his letters no less than his publications.

After five terms at Cambridge, more remarkable for gambling losses than academic achievements, Thackeray left without a degree and travelled to the Continent, spending the winter of 1830–1831 in Weimar, where he met Goethe, joined the entourage of Goethe's daughter-in-law Ottilie, and enchanted everyone with his ability and readiness to draw caricatures. Some of his sketches, made at home and abroad during this period, have been preserved by his friend Edward FitzGerald, who was later to achieve literary fame of his own with the *Rubáiyát of Omar Khayyám*. They include one of a "Miss Absaloms", a pupil at a finishing school, of which Thackeray said: "I trust her appearance will explain her acquirements character fortune &c—I think her one of my masterpieces" (LPP, I, 503).

Masterpiece or not, the caricature certainly shows that Thackeray's image of Jewish girls was not wholly dictated by Scott's Rebecca. FitzGerald's collection also contains an impression of Ludwig Devrient, whose performance as a hook-nosed Shylock,

Miss Absaloms.

Illustration 4

money bag at his belt, scales for weighing Antonio's flesh in his left
hand while his right rests on the hilt of his knife, Thackeray was
able to see during his stay at Weimar (ill.5).

Another drawing, from the same period, shows Devrient's Shylock in a more apprehensive, shrinking posture (ill. 6).

This was by no means the first of Thackeray's encounters with
impersonations of Shylock. At Cambridge he had attended a reading by the actor Charles Reece Pemberton; but all he could find to
say about that worthy's "delineation of the character of Shylock"
was: "I could have done it as well myself" (to Mrs Carmichael-
Smith, 22–29 March 1829—LPP I, 48). A year later he made
plans to attend Edmund Kean's farewell performance, which included Act IV of *The Merchant of Venice* (to Mrs Carmichael-Smith,
16 July 1830—LPP I, 110); but if he carried this out he has left
record of what he thought and felt on that occasion. Now, in
Weimar, he saw Devrient give a series of performances—as Hamlet
and Falstaff as well as Shylock—which imprinted themselves indelibly on his memory. "I have done nothing but practise drawing his
face since I saw it", he wrote on 18 January 1831 (LPP I, 142). It is
not, therefore, surprising to find that when Thackeray came to
depict Shylock in one of the emblematic capitals of his later work he
should show himself influenced by Devrient's account of the role
rather than Kean's softer, more sympathetic one. These later works

Illustration 5

Illustration 6

sympathetic one. These later works also transmute into fiction some of the adventures, amatory and otherwise, he had during his stay in Germany. If, as several biographers surmise, "Miss Löwe" had an autobiographical substratum of this kind, then Thackeray's attempt to find a real-life embodiment of Scott's Rebecca proved sadly unsuccessful.

Returning to London in 1831, Thackeray entered the Middle Temple, but seems never to have taken his Law-studies at all seriously. An opportunity arose in 1832 to become part-owner of an ailing cultural journal—an opportunity he readily seized as an outlet for the practice of journalism and for seeing his writings in print. The purchasing arrangements included negotiations with a financier called Goldshede of whom nothing else is known; but a passage in Thackeray's later novel *Lovel the Widower*, which is clearly based on this incident in the novelist's life, suggests that he may have been one of the originals of the Jewish financier Sherrick. While negotiations for the purchase of the grandiloquently titled *National Standard of Literature, Science, Music, Theatricals, and the Fine Arts* were still going on, Thackeray again felt himself drawn to the Continent, particularly to that city of Paris in which he had first stayed in 1829 and which became a second home too him in the period that extends from 1832 to 1837.

The *National Standard* was eventually acquired, and Thackeray contributed verse, prose-pieces, and sketches during the brief period it lasted (1832–1833). That it was not financially viable became apparent all too soon, and for a short time Thackeray tried to find an additional source of income by joining a firm of bill-discounters in Birchin Lane. For historically understandable reasons bill-discounting was an activity in which many Jews were involved in Thackeray's London. His account book for 1833 contains the cryptic entry "unveiling Mosaic" and references to clients and business partners (Bronatte, Meyer, Phillips) who may have been Jewish. That this episode, of which he hated to be reminded in later years (see LPP, II, 103–5) did not make him well-disposed towards Jewish financiers comes out clearly in his contribution to the *National Standard* of 18 May 1833.

N.M. ROTHSCHILD, ESQ.

HERE'S the pillar of 'Change! Nathan Rothschild himself,
   With whose fame every bourse in the universe rings;
 . The first[1] Baron Juif; by the grace of his pelf,

---

[1] Some years ago, shortly after the elevation (by the Emperor of Austria) of one

Not 'the king of the Jews,' but 'the Jew of the kings.'

The great incarnation of cents and consols,
    The eighths, halves, and quarters, scrip, options, and shares;
Who plays with new kings as young Misses with dolls;
    The monarch undoubted of bulls and of bears!

O, Plutus! your graces are queerly bestowed!
    Else sure we should think you behaved *infra dig.*,
When with favours surpassing, it joys you to load
    A greasy-faced compound of donkey and pig.

Here, just as he stands with his head pointed thus,
    At full-length, gentle reader, we lay him before ye;
And we then leave the Jew (what we wish he'd leave us,
    But we fear to no purpose), *a lone* in his glory.

N. M. ROTHSCHILD, ESQ.

Illustration 7

of the Rothschilds to the rank of Baron, he was present at a soirée in Paris, which he entered about the same time as the Due de Montmorenci. 'Ah!' said Talleyrand, 'Voici le premier baron Chrétien, et le premier baron Juif.' The Montmorencies boast, and we believe justly, that they are the first Christian barons. We all know that the Rothschilds may make the same claim of precedence among the Jews.

(I, 17–18)

Thackeray's attack on the head of the English branch of the Rothschild family as an uncouth incarnation of money-power, as the engineer of social upsets that place kings at the mercy of stock exchange manipulators, articulates resentments felt by many upholders of an established order which the Rothschilds themselves were always concerned to prop up. Such resentments were felt in France more fiercely than in England—they were to be given their fullest expression by Toussenel and Leroux in the 1840s. Thackeray's poem shows the familiarity he had gained with scrips, options, shares and consols and indulges in a crudity of invective ("greasy-faced compound of donkey and pig") that is fortunately never paralleled in his later writings. The poem ends with a characteristic pun which asks Rothschild to "leave us alone" while indicating, at the same time, that "a loan" would be welcome—a *double entendre* that Rothschild would have been entitled to counter with Shylock's words, slightly amended to fit his case:

> Hath a pig monies? Is't possible
> An ass can lend three thousand ducats?

The illustration accompanying and supplementing these verses is obviously based on a contemporary print showing Rothschild standing before his favourite pillar in the London Stock Exchange, himself, as Thackeray says, a "pillar of 'Change". Here is the anonymous print:

Illustration 8

In Thackeray's variation Rothschild holds his hands behind his back instead of in his pockets, and his head, with its jutting lower lip, tilts haughtily upwards. The poem draws attention to this alteration("with his head pointed thus"), suggesting that Thackeray may actually have observed Nathan Rothschild when visiting the Stock Exchange. Rothschild's snub-nosed features are only moderately porcine and not at all donkey-like in Thackeray's drawing; but the association of Jew and pig, so persistent in caricature ever since the *Judensau* representations of the Middle Ages, recurs in the mock coat of arms he provides for his "premier baron Juif". This shows two curled pigtails flanking a blank shield surmounted by a coronet. The background of Thackeray's drawing suggests an affinity between Rothschild's large-scale dealings and the small-scale dealings of humbler co-religionists: it shows a bearded Jew persuading a (presumably non-Jewish) colleague or customer to close a deal. To depict Rothschild in association with a humbler bearded Jew is again traditional: a caricature of the Duke of Wellington's financial policy, published in 1828 under the title "An Untoward Event or a Tory Triumph", had shown Nathan Rothschild with a bearded Jew who urges him to "take care of de monish". We shall find the conventional "Jew-speak" illustrated by these words imitated and developed in Thackeray's later writings. Is Thackeray here taking out on the Jews his uneasiness about his own bill-discounting activities, which he clearly thought beneath his dignity, which did not even bring him any profit, and which were in fact to be brought up against him by a contributor to *Fraser's Magazine*, some ten years later, in a lampoon to which he took great exception?

> The first person we met in the coffee-room was Bill Crackaway, one whom we have always looked upon as a bird of ill omen. His long ungainly person is crowned with a face which Dame Nature must have fashioned just after making a bad debt, and, therefore, in the worst of tempers. A countenance of preternatural longitude is imperfectly relieved by a nose on which the partial hand of Nature has lavished every bounty—length, breadth, thickness, all but a—bridge; a mouth that seemed suddenly arrested in the act of whistling, and, from its conformation, could only eliminate a sinister sneer, but was physically incapable of the candour of an honest laugh, which, with a most inhuman squint, gave a rare finish to the *os frontis* of this Corinthian capital of our club.
>
> The first question this worthy lispingly asked of us was, 'Have you heard the news?' To which, answering in the negative, he proceeded to inform us that Lord Edward Softhead had, to use our informant's expression, 'cut his stick and bolted.'
> 'On what account?'
> 'Oh! the bums are making some kind inquiries after him.'

'And how much does he owe?' we asked.

'Only 300,000*l*.' was the answer; 'but then, it is to the discounters, and I suppose, as he is rather green, he will not have touched more than 30 or 40,000*l*.'

Now, as Crackaway added to the occupation of editor of a pseudo-philosophical magazine the business of a bill-broker in the City, we take it for granted he knew something about these matters. (*Fraser's Magazine*, April, 1843, pp. 399–400)

Thackeray protested to the editor of *Fraser's* about "the libel on me" which he thought "unworthy of an honest man". If the author, he continued with heavy irony, were to "let it be publicly known that it is his intention to abuse in the public prints any private individuals, whose personal appearance and qualities may be disagreeable to him, it is surprising how popular he will become, how his society will be courted, and his interests in life advanced" (LPP, II, 102–3; to G.W. Nickisson, 8 April 1843). By then he may well have reflected that his own early sally against Nathan Rothschild was open to exactly the same objections; he certainly never republished the Rothschild poem and drawing in any subsequent collection.

The piece on Rothschild was one of a number of such pen-and-pencil portrayals in the *National Standard*, the first of which had caricatured yet another Jewish figure in public life: John Braham, whom Charles Lamb characterized, in one of his letters, as "that glorious singer . . . a rare combination of the Jew, the gentleman, and the angel." (*The Letters of Charles and Mary Lamb*, ed. E.V. Lucas, London 1935, II; 91). Braham was one of several synagogue choristers and cantors who made the transition to the operatic and concert stage in the nineteenth century. In his mock-eulogy Thackeray indulged his fondness for parody by adopting what he conceived to be the style of William Wordsworth, while his drawing took off from Braham's celebrated performances of his own composition "The Death of Nelson".

MR. BRAHAM

SONNET. By W. WORDSWORTH

SAY not that Judah's harp hath lost its tone,
Or that no bard hath found it where it hung,
Broken and lonely, voiceless and unstrung,
Beside the sluggish steams of Babylon;

Sloman![1] repeats the strain his fathers sung,

---

[1] It is needless to speak of this eminent vocalist and improvisatore. He nightly delights a numerous and respectable audience at the Cider-cellar; and while on

MR. BRAHAM

Illustration 9

And Judah's burning lyre is Braham's own!
Behold him here. Here view the wondrous man,
Majestical and lovely, as when first
In music on a wondering world he burst,
And charmed the ravished ears of sov'reign Anne![2]
Mark well the form, O! reader, nor deride
The sacred symbol—Jew's harp glorified—
Which circled with a blooming wreath is seen
Of verdant bays; and thus are typified
The pleasant music and the baize of green
Whence issues out at eve, Braham with front serene!

---

this subject, I cannot refrain from mentioning the kindness of Mr. Evans, the
worthy proprietor of that establishment. N.B.—A *table d'hôte* every Friday.—*W.
Wordsworth.*

 [2] Mr. Braham made his first appearance in England in the reign of Queen
Anne.—W.W.

(*National Standard*, 11 May 1833—I, 16–17)

Wordsworth probably earned the place among philo-Judaic eulogists which Thackeray here assigns him by a poem entitled "A Jewish Family", written in 1828, which ends with the words:

> Mysterious safeguard, that, in spite
>   Of poverty and wrong,
> Doth here preserve a living light,
>   From Hebrew fountains sprung;
> That gives this ragged group to cast
>   Around the dell a gleam
> Of Palestine, of glory past,
>   And proud Jerusalem!

As befits a parody, the brazen insult of "greasy-faced compound of donkey and pig" gives way, in Thackeray's piece on Braham, to mock-praise of "the wondrous man / Majestical and lovely"—a description hardly borne out by the drawing of a bulbous-nosed, thick-lipped, podgy-handed and pot-bellied figure incongruously dressed in a Jack Tar outfit, with the English coast-line, a castle, and a sailing boat filling in the background. "In person", the *Dictionary of National Biography* informs its readers, "Braham was short, stout and Jewish-looking"—and this is clearly the aspect Thackeray's caricature seeks to bring out. He adds, once again, the figure of a bearded Jew, marked out by the multiple hats and the shouldered sack as a seller of old clothes; he varies the image, however, by making the topmost hat an admiral's, as a tribute no doubt, to Braham's celebrated composition "The Death of Nelson". The first line of the poem built around this drawing speaks of "Judah's harp"—a reference, it might seem at first sight, to the harp of the psalmist, of *David rex et poeta*, or to the harps hung on the willows during the Babylonian exile; but Thackeray undercuts these exalted associations by suspending above Braham's head a humbler instrument, the "Jews' harp", surrounded by a mocking chaplet of laurel. The text of the poem also goes on to deflate Braham's claims to high art by associating his performances with those of Charles Sloman, whom Wordsworth is made to praise in a footnote that sounds like a paid puff, and who is said to "repeat the song his fathers sung". In this way Sloman is not only reminded of his Jewish ancestry but also associated, in Thackeray's drawing, with humbler Jews—in much the same way as Rothschild is associated with the bearded Jewish businessman in the caricature already discussed. The elaborately emblematic "cut" of Braham in the *National Standard* is matched by simpler sketches Thackeray executed for his own amusement and that of his friends. He caricatured the famous singer's unimpressive appearance in many different ways: showing him as Sir Huon with sword and feathered headdress, placing him on a tabouret (which emphasises his squat stature) and giving him an imperious gesture which a tall Englishman answers with a sunny smile while he points to a page in a book, or "immortalizing" Braham in a framed portrait which shows him singing from a musical score.

Illustration 9(a)

Illustration 9(b)

These drawings probably came into existence in 1831–2, when Thackeray lived in chambers at 1 Hare Court, The Temple. In the columns of the *National Standard* the published caricature of Braham was joined by another of Jewish entertainers in a savage review, dated 15 June 1833, of a performance of Mozart's *The Magic Flute* which Thackeray had witnessed at Covent Garden Opera House, then under the management of the much-ridiculed Alfred Bunn.

Illustration 9(c)

Papageno omitted his songs (for which we were sorry, for he sang and acted very well): would to heaven Papagena had done the same! Madame Meissinger is a nuisance so intolerable, that positively she ought to be indicted. She is not, however, paid above fifty pounds a week, so that we have not much reason to complain. The three boys, who advise and instruct, and lead Tamino in his wanderings, and who, whenever he is in doubt or fear, inspire him by their presence, and console him with their sweet minstrelsy, were enacted by a round-faced old woman and two Jewesses—Behold their likenesses!

They stuttered under their songs, and staggered under the weight of their enormous palm-branches, vying in discord with the 'attendants of the Queen of Night.' For the rest, the house was nearly empty; and if, as was the fact, the discord was horrible, there were very few to be affected by it.

(I, 30–31)

Illustration 10

Like all these contributions, the review of *The Magic Flute* was anonymous; Thackeray attributed it to "a gentleman whose opinion we asked with regard to the opera" and added, again anonymously:

> Having attended ourselves at Covent Garden, we are compelled to say that we fully agree with our correspondent, though we should not have spoken quite so freely regarding the personal defects of the ladies of the chorus. Bunn 'Maximus' must resort to some other method of filling his benches and his treasury.
>
> (I, 31)

This suggests that Thackeray, who was himself highly sensitive to criticism, did not feel altogether easy about his caricatures of recognizable Jewish contemporaries, though he was as yet unwilling to suppress the more malicious sallies of his pencil and his pen.

In the circumstances it is not without piquancy to find, in the columns of the *National Standard*, Thackeray's first reference to the novels of Benjamin Disraeli, which he was later to review and parody in a way Disraeli himself found offensive. After retelling the plot of one of the more horrifying stories in Petrus Borel's *Immoral Tales*, Thackeray adds: "My dear young ladies, who are partial to Lord Byron, and read Don Juan slyly in the evening; who admire French fashion, and dishes, and romances—it is for your profit and amusement that this summary has been made. You will see by it how far this great nation [i.e. France] excels in genius and imagination, even though Bulwer and Disraeli still live and write" (*National Standard*, 29 June 1833). The irony is patent; but nothing is made of Disraeli's Jewish origin, and he is paired with the impeccably Gentile Bulwer Lytton. An equal reticence marks Thackeray's diary-entry for Monday, 11 June 1832:

> Curzon came in the morning & sat for a couple of hours   Then we went to see the Steam Gun & then to his house where I sat drawing till 6. dined at Woods & went to see the authorized version of Robert le Diable—it was admirably played & sung & danced, but did not strike me as being anything super-excellent—The first drinking & gaming choruses were very pretty, & the resuscitation of the nuns very awful. The scenery was admirable—The nun scene the finest I ever saw on the stage.
>
> (LPP, I, 208)

Thackeray was sufficiently impressed by *Robert le Diable* to base several drawings on its characters and plot; but neither in the early thirties, nor in later years, when he came to think more highly of Meyerbeer's art, does he ever refer to that composer's unbaptised Jewishness.

When Thackeray left London to become the *National Standard's*
Paris correspondent, the harps he had apostrophized in the piece
on Braham pursued him. On 6 July 1833 he reported ironically on
a production at the *Ambigu comique* which seems to have discovered
the Cecil B. de Mille combination of sex, spectacle and religion a
century before that master of high kitsch began his operations.
Shapely ladies stepping out of baths and theatrical tableaux based
on popular paintings (in this case the grandiose works of John
Martin) tart up the Bible, titillate the spectators, and make a
strange setting for a depiction of the sorrows of exiled Israelites.

> At the *Ambigu Comique* is an edifying representation of "Belshazzar's
> Feast". The second act discovers a number of melancholy Israelites
> sitting round the walls of Babylon, with harps on the willows. A
> Babylonian says to the leader of the chorus, "Sing us one of the songs
> of Zion"; the chorus answers, "How can we sing in a strange land?"
> and so on; the whole piece is a scandalous parody of the Scripture,
> made up of French sentiment and French decency. A large family of
> children were behind me, looking with much interest and edification
> at the Queen rising from her bath! This piece concludes with a
> superb imitation of Martin's picture of Belshazzar.
>
> (I, 37)

After this reminder of the Babylonian exile it is hardly surprising
that the harp image should spring to mind again when the *National
Standard's* Paris correspondent saw the melancholy remnants of a
tribe of American Indians on the Champs Élysées:

> . . . a year ago this tribe was destroyed, and they fled into the desert,
> bearing with them, not their harps, like the Hebrews, but the skulls of
> their enemies, the ornaments of their cabins . . .
>
> (*Stray Papers*, ed. L. Melville, London 1901,
> p. 41—*National Standard*, 13 July 1833)

The erstwhile warrior fierceness brought out by the contrast between harps and skulls makes the spectacle of these subjugated
Indians sadder to contemplate; but Victorian readers would surely
have felt, too, that civilization was well served by the taming of
those who ornamented their dwellings in so gruesome a way.

Two other contributions to the *National Standard* are relevant to
the subject of the present book. The first of these appeared on 8
June 1833 and bears the title:

LOVE IN FETTERS

A TOTTENHAM COURT ROAD DITTY

*Showing how dangerous it is for a Gentleman to fall in love with an
'Officer's Daughter'*

The heroine of this mock balled, sub-titled "An Ower True Tale", turns out to be a *belle Juive*

> Whose cheeks would beat the rose;
> The raven tresses of her hair
> In blackness could with night compare,
>   Like Venus's her nose:
> Her eyes, of lustre passing rare,
>   Bright as the diamond glowed

Her father, the "officer" of the title, soon reveals himself as a bailiff with powers to arrest the would-be swain:

> By a parchment slip I could discern
> That by me stood a bailiff stern,
>   My Rosamunda's sire!
> I served the daughter with verse and wit,
> And the father served me with a writ,
>   An exchange I don't admire:
> So here in iron bars I sit
>   In quod securely stowed,
>
> Being captivated by a she,
> Whose papa captivated me;
>   All at the back
>   Of the Tabernác
> In Tottenham Court Road.

(I, 22, 25)

Bailiffs, sheriff's officers and the keepers of debtors' lock-ups—those instruments of financial nemesis who are here seen thwarting a romance—are frequently portrayed as Jewish in Thackeray's writings.

The last of Thackeray's appearances in the columns of the *National Standard* of which notice must be taken here is perhaps the most significant of all. On 16 August 1833 he reviewed a book entitled *Le Népenthès. Contes nouvelles et critiques* by a writer whom he calls "M. Weimar", but who is better known to posterity as François Adolphe Loève-Veimars (1801–1854). In this collection one piece of translation from the German so took his fancy that he was moved to render it into English and reprint it in full under the title "An Evening at the Brocken Inn." This is, in fact, a chapter from Heinrich Heine's *Die Harzreise*; and after translating it, Thackeray adds: "The works of M. Heine are at present very popular in Germany. We have received a pamphlet lately published by him, on modern German literature, the greater part of which we hope to transfer to this paper." (*The National Standard*, Volume II, No. 33, pp. 100–101). The pamphlet in question must have been either an offprint of a series entitled "État actuel de la littérature allemande", published in *L'Europe littéraire* between March and May 1833, or a copy of its German original, *Zur Geschichte der neueren schönen Literatur in Deutschland* (Paris and Leipzig, April 1833). The former is more likely, since when Thackeray quotes Heine again in later years, he does so in French; but though Loève-Veimars was not the most accurate of translators, he had enabled Thackeray to make contact with the mind of a great writer of Jewish origin with whom he felt an affinity. The *National Standard*, alas, did not survive long enough to introduce Heine's thoughts on German literature and culture to English readers under Thackeray's sponsorship; it folded early in 1834.

Thackeray's respectful treatment of Heine and Meyerbeer shows clearly that the *National Standard* did not see attacking and ridiculing Jews as part of its programme. On the contrary: it had reviewed *Alroy*, Disraeli's novel with an explicitly Jewish theme, with an enthusiasm only mildly tempered by strictures on its florid style (30 March 1833) and had devoted a good deal of space, in a review of I.F.C. Hecker's *The Black Death in the Fourteenth Century*, to deploring the sufferings of medieval Jews who were unjustly held responsible for that scourge. "One of the principal causes of these persecutions", the reviewer comments, "was the plunder to be obtained from the unhappy Israelites" (7 September 1833). It is refreshing to find so clear-eyed a view of the economic mainsprings of a persecution which was all too often dressed up a justifiable religious zeal or as due revenge for fancied injuries.

iii

In the private correspondence he conducted in the early thirties Thackeray also reveals that for all his acceptance of a number of unfriendly stereotypes he was not a programmatic anti-Semite. A letter to Edward FitzGerald, dated 8–9 September 1831, shows that he had been reading Maria Edgeworth's *Harrington* (1816)—a novel specifically designed to atone for earlier unsympathetic portrayals of Jews, though the "Jewish" heroine has to turn out to be really a Christian before she is allowed to marry the non-Jewish hero—and that he found it "very good" (LPP I, 158). In the same letter he expresses his sympathy with "the poor Poles" whose revolt had been crushed by the Russians by comparing "the massacres at Warsaw" with "the siege of Jerusalem" (ibid). Such shorthand from Jewish history is matched elsewhere by similar shorthand from the Old Testament: a diary entry of 5 April 1832 says of James Galt, whose *Stanley Buxton* Thackeray had been reading: "a man

may write very wisely and be no Solomon" (LPP I, 187). Another
letter to Edward FitzGerald show Thackeray about to sample the
art of Jacques François Halévy by going to see Marie-Louise
Duvernay in the opera-ballet *La Tentation* (8 October 1834—LPP I,
276). As for the "Jewish" facial traits that he so loved to
caricature—he learnt very soon that these could appear on non-
Jewish faces too, for a young man called Barwick, "a pleasant
fellow enough" from an English Christian family seems to have "a
strange Israelitish look" that Thackeray seeks to capture in a rapid
sketch (to Mrs Carmichael Smith. 23 December 1833—LPP I,
271).

Illustration 11

The swarthy chin and long nose which constitute the "Israelitish
look in Thackeray's eyes here appear in a portrait that could do
duty for a young Mr Dombey.

Just before embarking on his *National Standard* adventure, Thackeray had taken part in an election campaign designed to get his
friend Charles Buller into parliament. His humorous account of
this campaign in letters to Edward FitzGerald describe how Buller's Christian supporters mingled texts taken from the Psalms (in
particular Psalm 19) with others from Thomas Moore's *Sacred
Songs*, which had drawn on the same venerable source:

> . . . a waggon load of young ladies of all denominations of Christians
> who from their seat wh. was all covered with laurels chanted the
> heavens declare the Glory of God, Sound the loud timbrel & other
> godly and appropriate airs . . .
>
> (5–7 July 1832—LPP I, 248)

Buller's opponent was a wealthy aristocratic Tory; in combating
him, Buller promised—with Thackeray's support—to lessen taxes,

provide for the agricultural and commercial interests of Cornwall (where the election was fought), and to combat "that infamous traffic, which at present legalizes the West Indian slave". The campaign gave Thackeray "parliamentary visions" of a "Tory knight with his country as his mistress", who would "eternally descant on old times & old glories" and "enlist all the romance of the nation on his side." (Ray, *The Uses of Adversity*, p. 158—LPP, I, 114–5). This clearly anticipates the appeal of Disraeli's "Young England" programme; but for all his conservative instincts, Thackeray never joined the Tory party and kept aloof from the Whigs too. Nor could he afford trying out his ideas on the electorate on his own behalf; for the Calcutta agency house in which the bulk of Thackeray's family fortune had been invested collapsed in 1833, followed by the démise of the *National Standard* early in the next year. Henceforward he had to think of some way to earn his own living; he could no longer hope to live the life of a gentleman *rentier*, and such parliamentary ambitions he had conceived had to be deferred until a much later day.

The writings and drawings surveyed in this chapter showed Thackeray taking cognisance of contemporary Jews, or men and women of Jewish origin, as financiers great and small, as composers, as singers, as novelists, as irregular political agents, as old clothes men, and as gourmands indulging in forbidden food. He took up, and played variations on, a number of well-known topoi: the *Judensau* association of Jew and pig; Rothschild as "Jew of the Kings" (a deliberate inversion of the Biblical "King of the Jews"); the Jews' harp as a symbolic instrument—a caricature, as it were, of the harps of David and the Babylonian exile; the dangerous attraction of raven-haired beauties; and physical features attributed to Jews which Gentile Englishmen found rather less alluring. Behind it all loomed the conception of the Old Testament God as a sternly threatening force rather than a loving father. Thackeray had experimented with a variety of forms ranging from crude invective to ironic praise, from straight-forward review to literary parody. He had tried out a number of ways in which text and picture might combine: the graphic representation of Braham undercut the pseudo-Wordsworthian paean while the caricature of Covent Garden singers supplemented and supported the text. He had also used his graphic work to make connections his text only hinted at—the link between Rothschild and humbler Jewish bargainers, for instance, or that between Braham and old clothes men, suggesting that Jew is Jew, and that differences in fortune and fame counted little in that context. He had also, however, taken delight in the wit of Heinrich Heine, whose Jewish origins were no secret in Paris although Thackeray does not allude to them. The crude invective of the Rothschild piece would disappear from his published writings after the *National Standard* days; but the other features we have noticed would recur, with significant additions, variations and disclaimers, in his later work, along with a new note heard most clearly in his savage anecdote about an upstart colonel given a baronial title and summary powers by Napoleon:

> There was a certain jeweler of the Israelitish persuasion who had been doing business at Dresden, and was returning home with his papers properly signed, when he came to the frontier place where Champignon commanded. The gallant colonel was living at the time with a lovely lady from the Académie de Musique, who took the title of Madame la Baronne for the time being, and to whom her temporary husband was the most generous of masters.
>
> Hearing that the Jew had diamonds with him, Colonel Champignon said he wished to make a handsome present to Madame la Baronne: and the merchant was directed to come to the commandant's quarters with several sets from which the Baronness might choose. The poor fellow brought his precious wares—and while showing them to Madame la Baronne, was seized as a spy, and shot in ten minutes. The serjeant who commanded the party employed to shoot him died that night, and the men were drafted into another regiment. Colonel Champignon covered himself with glory at the next general action, and his bravery was mentioned in terms of the highest encomiums in the proclamation after the victory.
>
> The little trait will serve to show the Colonel's character and genius.
>
> (transcribed from Ms. by R.W. Oram in "Catalogues of War": Thackeray's "Essay on Pumpernickel", *Victorian Institute Journal* 15 (1987), p. 132).

In this fragmentary piece, probably intended for *Fraser's Magazine* in the early 1840s, Thackeray conveys his sense of the vulnerability of Jews—his realization that they could fall innocent victims to predators as easily in nineteenth-century wars as in the medieval conditions depicted in Scott's *Ivanhoe*.

CHAPTER 2

SHADOWS AT FOLLY'S HEELS
(1836–1840)

> Wherever shines the sun, you are sure to find Folly
> basking in it; and knavery is the shadow at Folly's
> heels.
>
> (I, 540).

i

When he lost the bulk of his income in the crash of a Calcutta agency-house towards the end of 1833, Thackeray at first thought that he might be able to make a living as a painter and illustrator; but three years of desultory attempts to obtain an adequate professional training in Paris convinced him that he would never be more than a highly gifted amateur. In a letter to Frank Stone he expressed his frustration in characteristic Biblical pastiche: "The sun riseth upon my efforts and goeth down on my failures . . . O God, when will Thy light enable my fingers to work, and my colours to shine?" (LPP I, 279–17 April 1835). The very first book he published did, however, consist of a series of pictures with a minimum of caption. Under the pseudonym "Théophile Wagstaffe" he brought out *Flore et Zéphyr. Ballet mythologique*: a Daumieresque skit on classical ballet performed by dancers portrayed as angular and less than beautiful bourgeois. By using lithographic techniques Thackeray entered into competition with Parisian lithographers who, under the leadership of Charles Philipon, were raising the art of political and social caricature to new heights. Some of the dancers so unflatteringly depicted were recognizable contemporarics; thc frontispiece of *Flore et Zéphyr* is an unmistakable caricature of A.E. Chalon's lithograph of Taglioni in the role of Flore. The final plate in Thackeray's series entitled "Les Délassements de Zéphire", show the principal male dancer after the performance, accepting a pinch of snuff from a well-dressed patron whose features suggest that he is to be thought of as Jewish—the first of Thackeray's verbal and graphic representations of Jews as patrons or hangers-on behind, and as spectators in front, of the theatrical scene (ill. 1).

Thackeray also tried his hand at cartoon stories in the manner of Rodolphe Toepffer, one of which, *The History of Dionysius Diddler*(ca. 1838; published posthumously in *The Autographic Mirror*, 1864)

Illustration 1

featured a cheerful representation of a bulbous-nosed Jewish pawn-broker (ill. 2).

1836, the year that saw Thackeray's first publication in book form, was also the year of his marriage to Isabella Shawe, who bore him three daughters (one of whom died in infancy) before sliding into the insanity that clouded her and her husband's life from 1840 onwards and led to the wholly unjustified supposition that Thackeray had served as a model for Charlotte Brontë's Rochester. The consequent lack of a settled home life ensured that Thackeray was drawn more and more into the life of the gentlemen's clubs which were so prominent a feature of the London scene; a life for which his public school, university and Middle Temple experience fitted him, in which he felt comfortable, though he had an artist's insight into its narrownesses and weaknesses and snobberies, and though his comparative indigence made him something of an outsider until *Vanity Fair* ensured his celebrity and his financial future.

The income on which he and his family depended derived, mainly, from his hard work as a journalist; and this meant, under nineteenth-century conditions, that his writings appeared anonymously or under a pseudonym. Some of these pseudonyms—notably that of Michael Angelo Titmarsh—soon became transparent to many of his readers, for literary gossip travelled fast. In

The first thing he does is to take his wig out of pawn.

Illustration 2

1836 and 1837 he contributed notes on Parisian politics to a short-lived radical journal, *The Constitutional and Public Ledger*, one of the planks of whose platform was religious liberty and toleration. He thought of himself as a Republican in those days, who scorned Whigs and Tories alike; but what he saw of government by the moneyed bourgeoisie under Louis Philippe seems to have appalled him more than the inherited privilege of the British aristocracy.

"He was groping", Ray has rightly said in *The Uses of Adversity*, "towards an ideal of gentlemanliness which would adapt it to an age of middle-class dominance" (Op. cit., p. 215); and he found neither this nor true liberty in Louis Philippe's France. "I am afraid I am growing a Tory, in France that is, or rather a Tiers–parti man", he wrote to his mother; "the Republican party is the most despicable I ever knew: they are bigoted and despotic." (quoted Ray, op. cit., p. 191).

Thackeray's contributions to *The Constitutional and Public Ledger* contain passages in praise of enlightened modern times in which "there is no opportunity for showing Christian zeal by burning a Jew or shooting a heretic; but there are plenty of opportunities for true believers to show their faith and exercise their good works" (26 November 1836). It is an age, however, which is prone to worship the most unlikely "heroes"; in which a journey to Africa by Louis Philippe's son, the Duc de Nemours, becomes a parody of the heroic progress of an Old Testament prophet and liberator:

> This puny lad becomes the head and front of an expedition . . . He goes abroad with marshalls and generals at his back, and extends his patronage to mayors, pious Turks call down benedictions on his head, and grateful Jews look up to him as a second prophet—a little beardless Moses.

Thackeray goes on to quote an account in the *Moniteur Algérien* which tells how "the Prince terminated his visits to the religious establishments by one to the synagogue of the Jews, which was decorated with the greatest luxury. His entry into the temple was saluted by a psalm in Hebrew." This roused the satirist in him and stimulated a parodic fleshing out of the *Moniteur*'s bare statement, incorporating the young Jewish orange sellers and dealers in pencils and sealing wax which were a common sight in Victorian London.

> The writer in the *Moniteur algérien* conceals the particulars of the Royal Duke's festive visitation; but a very common imagination can easily supply the details. Is this Titus or Vespasian coming in triumph among the Jews, that they receive him with such respect? They who refused to take down their harps for the great Assyrian conqueror, strike up a Hebrew melody at the approach of the noble Nemours; dark-eyed Hebrew maidens throw oranges at the feet of the young warrior; bushels of sealing wax, and black lead pencils, are burned in his honour; the temple is filled with grateful believers, and festooned with old clothes—who does not honour the prince receiving such honour, and admire the stiff-necked Hebrews who bend before him?

> (23 December 1836)

The Duke's triumph, and Thackeray's piece, do not end here, for the Turks are shown to be "every whit as tender as the Jews" towards him; and dropping the ironic mask, Thackeray protests that "the actions and sufferings of thousands of brave men are set aside to make ways for the triumphs of this paltry lad."

The contrast drawn in this characteristic satire is not only between the Duc de Nemours and the heroic figures of the past, from Moses to Titus and Vespasian, but also between apparently sycophantic Jews of modern times and their more stiff-necked Biblical ancestors. Between these Biblical figures on the one hand, and the petty traders of London and the servile worshippers in Algeria or France on the other, stands the figure of Shylock, to which Thackeray so often felt driven to return. In *The Constitutional and Public Ledger* he used Shakespeare's Jew as an image for Louis Philippe, but only in order to point out what he saw as an all-important difference: no Portia comes to judgment to thwart him, the pliant judges of the French courts are all on his side: "henceforth His Majesty has justice in his own hands, the law allows it and the court awards it." (31 December 1836).

Besides working for *The Constitutional and Public Ledger*, Thackeray contributed pieces to *Galignani's Messenger* and *The Paris Literary Gazette*; wrote book-reviews and art-criticism for *The Times*, *The London and Westminster Review*, the American magazine *The Corsair* and others; and produced humorous narratives and sketches for *Bentley's Miscellany*, *The New Monthly Magazine*, and *Britannia: A Weekly Journal of News, Politics and Literature*. *Bentley's Miscellany* printed his first published piece of fiction, "The Professor. A Tale of Sentiment", in July 1837. This features a Seminary for Young Ladies situated in Hackney, whose pupils include a Miss Jacobs "who could very nearly climb through a ladder (Jacob's ladder [Professor Dandolo] profanely called it)" and who retires "to her relations in Houndsditch"—a London district inhabited by many Jews—when scandal injures the Seminary's reputation (I, 113, 118). Thackeray's most distinctive contributions, however, in these years before the founding of *Punch*, were reserved for *Fraser's Magazine*, which published "The Memoirs of Mr. Charles J. Yellowplush, Sometime Footman in Many Genteel Families" from November 1837 to August 1838, with a postscript in 1840, and also Thackeray's first novel, *Catherine*, in instalments that ran from May 1839 to February 1840.

The Yellowplush Memoirs draw much of their humour from the eponymous author's pronunciation-based spelling—a device that leaves ample room for Joycean puns and introduces a sub-text of which the fictional writer is presumed to be unaware. The joke first tried out in *The Gownsman* is pressed into service once again when Yellowplush mocks Frenchmen for their "O mong Jews" (I, 219); Greek mythology is ludicrously Hebraized in "Jewpeter" and "Jewno" (I, 325); and stern duty is provided with a caricatured Old Testament context in such coinages as "jewty" and "jewty-ful". That Yellowplush's first-hand acquaintance with both Testaments is not extensive may be gathered from such malapropisms as "as old as Jerusalem" (for "Methuselah") and "a sneaking, double-faced Jonas" (for "Judas", I suppose). Without benefit of Yellowplush's malapropisms and metonymic substitutions Thackeray plays a naming game of his own when he introduces, into "Dimond Cut Dimond", a firm of attorneys named "Screwson, Hewson, and Jewson" (I, 191)—a Gentile partnership, no doubt, whose name, however, brings a suggestion of "Jewish" practices into a company joined, in Chapter V of "The Ravenswing", by "Blunt, Hone, and Sharpus". Yellowplush takes temporary leave of his readers in a chapter headed "MR. YELLOWPLUSH'S AJEW" (I, 300). He is nothing of the kind, of course, nor do his adventures take him at all deeply into the tents of Israel; but in the employ of Mr. Deuceace, a gambler and financial *Luftmensch*, he does encounter "old Solomon, a money-changer" who authenticates some English bank-notes, which enable Deuceace to buy his way out of a Parisian debtors' prison, and offers what seems a fair price for them. (I, 289).

The illustrations with which Thackeray accompanied Yellowplush's account of his adventures contain one very striking one in which Yellowplush himself, depicted on shipboard en route for "foring parts", is upstaged by a heavily wrapped, swarthy, hook-nosed, thick-lipped, wide-eyed figure stretched at full length on the planks (ill. 2(a)).

Neither Yellowplush's narration nor the text beneath the engraving (THE CALAIS PACKET—MR. YELLOWPLUSH'S EMOTIONS ON FIRST GOING TO SEA—I, 221) identify this prominent figure, which is clearly not Yellowplush's master Deuceace, whose likeness appears elsewhere (I, 238). It may well be Thackeray's first impression of one of those sea-sick Jews whom he introduced into *Notes of a Journey from Cornhill to Grand Cairo* and other later works.

A more vivid and detailed view of nineteenth-century Jews is offered by the author of a twopenny newssheet called *The Town* to which Thackeray introduced the readers of *Fraser's Magazine* in the course of a review published in March 1838 under the title "Half-

Illustration 2(a)

a-Crown's Worth of Cheap Knowledge.'' The passage Thackeray thinks interesting enough to deserve quotation reads as follows:

BELILO'S.

Near unto Aldgate is situated a place called the Orange Market; and in the Orange Market stands Howard's Assembly Rooms, and there doth the great Belilo hold regnant sway. He is the presiding deity,—in common *parlance*, the master of the ceremonies; and, to do him justice, we must observe that he is a most perfect master of every ceremony attendant on the ball-room. The weekly assemblies of Mr. Belilo are held every Saturday night, from eight till twelve o'clock.

Before the Christian adventurer profanes the temple of Belilo with his presence, it is necessary that he pay the sum of one shilling, and sixpence extra for the privilege of wearing his hat. This custom, we are sorry to say, is very prevalent, and we confess ourselves surprised at a man of Mr. Belilo's acknowledged politeness permitting such a gross breach of etiquette within the rooms governed by his mighty self; but so it is.

Having complied with these enactments, you enter a square room, capable of holding four sets of quadrilles, and numerous spectators. The walls are decorated with landscape paintings, and the temple is illuminated with lamps of ground glass. On the right of the door sits a little Jew boy with a basket of 'suth nith cakes'; and on the left sits a full-blown Jewess behind a bar, the administering angel to the wants of Jew and Gentile, in the way of refreshments. Nearly facing the door, the band is stationed, consisting of a violin, a trumpet, and a harp; the latter instrument may be properly denominated the Jew's-harp, for all the musicians are of that persuasion.

Having described the room and its appointments, we will now proceed to give some few critical remarks upon the company who frequent it. They are for the most part Jews and Jewesses. The men are great nobs in their way; it is surprising to witness with what elegance they smoke their cigars whilst whirling in the dizzy mazes of the waltz; and it is even more so to observe the fortitude with which their partners endure the horrid nuisance of their repeated puffs of smoke slap in their pretty faces. Boots are the order of the night, and it would be considered a mark of effeminacy to sport pumps. Hats, as we have said before, are worn in the dance; they appear to be generally of the tall silk description, and as we like to assign reasons for absurdities, we believe them to be worn by the Hebrew lads because they imagine that they give a dignified cast to the Jewish phiz. The wit of some of these *sparks* is exceedingly *bright*; for example, to a gentleman lighting a cigar,—'By Cot, sir, if you don't take care, you'll burn that cigar.' This piece of imagined humour we have heard repeated half a dozen times in one evening. There is one little chap, a Jew, who stands about four feet nothing, who is frequently exceedingly rude and impertinent, and very fond of dispossessing strangers of their places in the dance, by stating that he had previously taken them. Belilo should see to this insufferable little monkey; if he does not, we shall, most certainly, in a future number. We shall now go into the ladies, dear creatures!

(I, 149–50)

Here the reviewer tactfully breaks off: "Perhaps the reader thinks we have carried him far enough, and has no disposition to listen to any further description from the lips of this exquisite writer of the *Town*, whose observations, when he does get among the 'dear creatures', are not exactly such as would bear repetition in this Magazine." (I, 150). The main point, indeed, of this piece about *The Town* and similar publications, is to fulminate against literature which is likely to familiarize servant maids, footmen, apprentices and schoolboys with haunts once known only to rakes and intrepid explorers of London's underworld. Thackeray's conclusion begins with a pseudo-Biblical flourish.

> Blessed, then, be the press and the fruits thereof! In old times (before education grew general), licentiousness was considered as the secret of the aristocracy. Only men enervated by luxury, and fevered by excess of wealth, were supposed to indulge in vices which are now common to the meanest apprentice or the poorest artisan. And, as mystery in those bigoted days accompanied all knowledge, the science of wickedness was as occult as any other,—only followed by the practitioners in silence and darkness. When the people lighted on one of them, they hunted him down, like a Jew, or an alchymist, or a witch; witness poor old sainted Charteris, well-nigh a martyr to the foul-mouthed illiberality of the bigots of his day! But the schoolmaster is abroad, and the prejudices of the people disappear. Where we had one scoundrel, we count them now by hundreds of thousands. We have our penny libraries for debauchery as for other useful knowledge; and colleges like palaces for study—gin-palaces, where each starving Sardanapalus may revel until he die.
>
> (I, 151)

The passage is characteristically double-edged. On the one hand, the reviewer has no sympathy with the bigotry that instituted Jew-hunts and witch-hunts in the Dark Ages; on the other, however, he seems anything but convinced of the blessings of the new literacy and inclined to take a gloomy view of moral progress: "Where we had one scoundrel, we count them now by hundreds of thousands."

Thackeray was clearly fascinated as well as repelled by *The Town*'s vivid description of the Jewish clientèle of an Aldgate dance-hall; and this mingled fascination and repulsion carried over into his own journalistic depictions of the activities of contemporary Jews. There was the "Gold Dust" case, for instance, in which a number of Jewish defendants were accused of receiving and processing one hundredweight of gold dust stolen from a ship berthed in London at Easter 1839. Despite the intervention of a large number of character witnesses, including the Chief Rabbi, the trial went ahead at the Central Criminal Court Old Bailey, and the jury found the defendants guilty—a verdict which caused "a sensation in Court, which was crowded chiefly by persons of the Jewish persuasion, many of whom had been present during the whole of the trial" (*The Times*, 3 July 1839). Some of this was in Thackeray's mind when he promised readers of the American journal *The Corsair* reports from Paris on the state of the theatre in France: "when, if you are anxious to know, you shall hear . . . in what happy provinces the fair Jewess Mademoiselle Rachel proposes to teach the true manner of declaiming Racine and Corneille." "By the way", he continued, "what a noble subject for a tragedy is that conspiracy of three hundred Jews, to put down the piece at the London theatre, about Gold-Dust—the French would have made a dozen vaudevilles of it before this!" (*The Corsair*, No. 475, 5 October 1839). The precise events behind this account have been described by M.J. Landa:

> Jews began to display fierce resentment against the ruthless treatment of them on the stage. Following the deluge of Fagins in theatrical adaptations and imitations of *Oliver Twist*, the production at the Garrick Theatre, Goodman's Fields, on July 24, 1839, of *Gold Dust*, based on the robbery of two boxes of gold dust from the neighbouring St. Catherine's Docks in the preceding February, led to a remarkable scene. Disturbance broke out immediately the curtain rose, and was maintained with such persistence that not a word was heard: the whole of the play was performed in dumb show, according to a contemporary report. Neither the play, nor any record of the plot, nor even the name of the author, has survived.
> (*The Jew in Drama*, London 1926, p. 169)

I have not been able to trace the "contemporary report" to which Landa refers; it may well have been the very one which provoked Thackeray's ironic account.

When it came to the graphic or pictorial representation of Jews, no-one, in Thackeray's eyes could rival his erstwhile teacher George Cruikshank. His "Essay on the Genius of George Cruikshank", first published in the *London and Westminster Review* in June 1840, hymns the "grotesque beauty" of Cruikshank's drawings and admires that artist's ability to evoke a whole world "with a few strokes on a little block of wood not two inches square". Cruikshank's ability to mingle "the awful and the ridiculous" appears with particular force, so Thackeray believed, in his depictions of Fagin. "For Jews," he says, " . . . Mr Cruikshank had a special predilection. The tribe of Israelites he has studied with amusing gusto; witness the Jew in Mr. Ainsworth's 'Jack Sheppard' and the immortal Fagin of 'Oliver Twist'." (II, 434). And again, a little later: "We must not forget to mention 'Oliver Twist', and Mr. Cruikshank's famous designs to that work . . . the Jew—the dreadful Jew—that Cruikshank drew." (II, 488). When Thackeray

comes to speak, in this same essay, of the difficulties faced by
engravers who are furnished designs by artists less careful of their
needs than Cruikshank, he skips from thoughts of Fagin to
thoughts of another fictional Jew celebrated in English literature:

> The engraver . . . receives these little dots and specks, and fantastical
> quirks of the pencil, and cuts away with a little knife round each, not
> too much nor too little. Antonio's pound of flesh did not puzzle the
> Jew so much; and so well does the engraver succeed at last, that we
> never remember to have met with a single artist who did not vow that
> the wood-cutter had utterly ruined his design.
>
> (II, 463–4)

The image of "the Jew" wielding a knife designed to cut flesh has
entered deep into Thackeray's consciousness; it has here been
brought to the surface by thoughts of Fagin closely followed by
thoughts of the wood-engraver's tool.

Thackeray had, in fact, collaborated with Cruikshank in the
Comic Almanach for 1839, and had taken care to give the artist scope
for drawing what a Victorian readership would recognize as "Jewish" faces. The tale he wrote for Cruikshank is entitled "Stubbs's
Calendar, or The Fatal Boots"; it is interesting as a first exercise in
the device he was to employ so brilliantly in *Barry Lyndon*: the
self-revelation, in first person narrative, of a thorough scoundrel.
Stubbs relates his adventures with self-approval and self-pity; but
everything he tells us only serves to confirm that he is a heartless,
conscienceless, mercenary, swindling, sneaking, cowardly rogue.
Not, however, a successful rogue—for he lacks the intelligence and
empathy needed to take in more honest people for any length of
time and to avoid falling victim to more skilful rascals than himself.
Though Stubbs tells his own story, Thackeray makes sure we do
not give him too much credit for the liveliness and skilful organization of his narrative by overtly introducing, at the end of the tale, a
professional writer to whom Stubbs has been pouring out his story
and who then sets it down, edits it, and sells it to a publisher.

The instruments that defeat Stubbs's schemes include, besides
the German shoemaker whom Stubbs has tried to cheat over the
boots named in the subtitle, the Jewish characters Thackeray
introduced for Cruikshank's sake. Stubbs's great ambition, for
which he will sacrifice all honest affection, is to marry money; and
Thackeray provides him with a lady who figures prominently in
instructions he sent to the artist on 4 December 1838: "Make her a
Jewish looking woman; and the bailiff another. The children likewise with a Hebrew look. Make Timms a very military looking man

SEPTEMBER.—PLUCKING A GOOSE

Illustration 3

in an immense braided frock coat: the children round him & their mother, he starting from the bum." (LPP, I, 371–2). Illustration 3 shows how Cruikshank acquitted himself of that task.

By the time this drawing reached Thackeray, "Timms" had already become Bob Stubbs, whom the plot introduces to one Mrs. Manasseh, rumoured to be a very wealthy widow.

> 'Look at that Mrs. Manasseh,' said a gentleman (it was droll, *he* was a Jew, too), sitting at dinner by me; 'she is old, and ugly, and yet, because she has money, all the men are flinging themselves at her.'
> 'She has money, has she?'
> 'Eighty thousand pounds, and twenty thousand for each of her children; I know it *for a fact*,' said the strange gentleman. 'I am in the law, and we, of our faith, you know, know pretty well what the great families amongst us are worth.'
> 'Who was Mr. Manasseh?' said I.
> 'A man of enormous wealth—a tobacco-merchant— West Indies; a fellow of no birth, however; and who, between ourselves, married a woman that is not much better than she should be. My dear sir,' whispered he, 'she is always in love—now it is with that Captain Dobble; last week it was somebody else—and it may be you next week, if—ha! ha! ha!—you are disposed to enter the lists. I wouldn't, for *my* part, have the woman with twice her money.'
> What did it matter to me, whether the woman was good or not, provided she was rich? My course was quite clear. I told Dobble all that this gentleman had informed me, and, being a pretty good hand at making a story, I made the widow appear so bad, that the poor

fellow was quite frightened and fairly quitted the field. Ha! ha! I'm dashed if I did not make him believe that Mrs. Manasseh had *murdered* her last husband.

I played my game so well, thanks to the information that my friend the lawyer had given me, that in a month I had got the widow to show a most decided partiality for me; I sat by her at dinner, I drank with her at the Wells—I rode with her, I danced with her, and at a pic-nic to Kenilworth, where we drank a good deal of champagne, I actually popped the question, and was accepted. In another month Robert Stubbs, Esq., led to the altar, Leah, widow of the late Z. Manasseh, Esq., of St. Kitt's!

The self-styled lawyer, needless to say, is in cahoots with the widow; it is even suggested that he is really her husband; and Stubbs, who had married her under the pretence that his wealth extended to far more than the patrimony out of which he had cheated his own mother and sister, finds himself pauperized by attachment for her debts. This brings in yet another Jewish figure, briefly foreshadowed in "Love in Fetters", but from now on a perennial apparition in Thackeray's fiction: the sheriff's officer who conducts debtors to a lock-up which is usually located in Cursitor Street, a shabby thoroughfare off Chancery Lane, in the heart of London's legal quarter.

My own estate had been sold, and the money was lying at a bank in the city. About three days after our arrival, as we took our breakfast in the hotel, previous to a visit to Mrs. Stubbs's banker, where certain little transfers were to be made—a gentleman was introduced, who, I saw at a glance, was of my wife's persuasion.

He looked at Mrs. Stubbs, and made a bow. 'Perhaps it will be convenient to you to pay this little bill, one hundred and fifty-two poundsh.'

'My love,' says she, 'will you pay this—it is a trifle which I had really forgotten.' 'My soul!' said I, 'I have really not the money in the house.'

'Vel, denn. Captain Shtubbsh,' says he, 'I must do my duty—and arrest you—here is the writ! Tom, keep the door!'—My wife fainted—the children screamed, and I—fancy my condition, as I was obliged to march off to a spunging-house, along with a horrid sheriff's officer!

(I, 469)

Here Thackeray employs for the first time conventional notations of "Jewish" speech that add to the common cockney substitution of "v" for "w" the distortion of "s" into "sh" and "th" into "d" as well as some queer vowel-sounds exemplified in the bailiff's later announcement, on being called a rogue and extortioner by the irate Stubbs: "'Oh no, Mishter Shtubbsh', says he grinning still, 'dere is som greater roag dan me—mosh greater.'" (I, 470). Such

notations draw on stage convention more than on actual experience; but Thackeray rejects the convention that gives Jewish characters a lisp, exemplified by Barney in Dickens's *Oliver Twist*, and
in the "Belilo" piece from *The Town*: "suth nith cakes".

The Cursitor Street establishment into which Mr Nabb—as the
Jewish bailiff is here called, with obvious reference to his prescribed
task—introduces the wretched Stubbs provides a setting that is
destined to become more and more familiar to readers of Thackeray's fiction.

> What a palace!—in an odious, dismal street, leading from Chancery
> Lane,—a hideous Jew boy opened the second of three doors; and shut
> it when Mr. Nabb and I (almost fainting) had entered: then he
> opened the third door, and then I was introduced to a filthy place,
> called a coffee-room, which I exchanged for the solitary comfort of a
> little dingy back-parlour, where I was left for a while to brood over
> my miserable fate. Fancy the change between this and Berkeley
> Square!
>
> (I, 469)

The "hideous Jew Boy" of that description, along with other such
expressions ("Israelitish brood", "hideous Jew monster"), must be
credited to the awful Stubbs, of course, not to the author; but while
we can have little sympathy with Stubbs, the revelation of the
manner in which he was fleeced is not likely to induce admiration
for those who did to him what he would have done to them.

> In the fullness of my heart I told him [the Commissioner who
> examined Stubbs's financial affairs] how Mr. Solomonson the attor-
> ney had introduced me to the rich widow, Mrs. Manasseh, who had
> fifty thousand pounds, and an estate in the West Indies. How I was
> married, and arrested on coming to town, and cast in an action for
> two thousand pounds brought against me by this very Solomonson
> for my wife's debts.
>
> 'Stop,' says a lawyer in the court, 'Is this woman a showy black-
> haired woman, with one eye? very often drunk, with three children—
> Solomonson, short, with red hair?'
>
> 'Exactly so,' said I, with tears in my eyes.
>
> 'That woman has married *three men* within the last two years. One
> in Ireland, and one at Bath. A Solomonson is, I believe, her husband,
> and they both are off for America ten days ago.'
>
> (I, 474)

Thackeray has provided Stubbs with a double nemesis: the honest
though vindictive German shoemaker, whom Stubbs had cheated
and who now thwarts his projects at every turn; and the dishonest
Jewish couple whose unattractive appearance is here described and
which is shipped off to America when it has fulfilled its plot-

function of rooking the would-be rook. But Thackeray's last page, and Cruikshanks' last illustration, bring in yet another Jewish nemesis. Stubbs, we learn, has himself become assistant to an officer of the Sheriff of Middlesex, and finds himself dismissed and kicked out by young Nabb, who has succeeded his father as master of the Cursitor Street lock-up.

> It's a thing that has very seldom happened to a gentleman, to be kicked out of a spunging-house; but such was my case. Young Nabb . . . drove me ignominiously from his door, because I had charged a gentleman in the coffee-rooms seven-and-sixpence for a glass of ale and bread and cheese, the charge of the house being only six shillings. He had the meanness to deduct the eighteenpence from my wages, and because I blustered a bit, he took me by the shoulders and turned me out—me, a gentleman, and, what is more, a poor orphan!
>
> How I did rage and swear at him when I got out into the street! There stood he, the hideous Jew monster, at the double door, writhing under the effect of my language. I had my revenge! Heads were thrust out of every bar of his windows, laughing at him. A crowd gathered round me, as I stood pounding him with my satire, and they evidently enjoyed his discomfiture. I think the mob would have pelted the ruffian to death (one or two of their missiles hit *me*, I can tell you), when a policeman came up, and, in reply to a gentleman, who was asking what was the disturbance, said, 'Bless you, sir, it's Lord Cornwallis.' 'Move on, *Boots*,' said the fellow to me, for, the fact is, my misfortunes and early life are pretty well known—and so the crowd dispersed.
>
> (I, 484)

Stubbs has remained self-righteous to the last, blustering on happily unconscious of his own meanness and nastiness, and attempting to divert popular ridicule and hostility from his own person to that of the "hideous Jew monster". The reader, however, helped not only by the text but also by Cruikshank's lively and amusing illustration, knows very well that it is not the Jew who is being jeered at, and feels satisfaction at seeing the egregious Stubbs soundly kicked by a man he feels entitled to despise (ill. 4).

The Jewish characters in *Stubbs's Calendar* do what is necessary to see that he gets his just deserts—they are his nemesis in the same way that Becky Sharp will be the nemesis of corrupt members of the society within which she operates. Unlike Mrs. Manasseh and her red-haired accomplice, however, whom Thackeray takes care to ship out of England, Nabb junior is left to continue his legally sanctioned if unpopular tasks in a dismal street off Chancery Lane.

Stubbs's Calendar is one of Thackeray's "rook and pigeon" tales, in which great satisfaction is derived from the spectacle of seeing

DECEMBER.—'THE WINTER OF OUR DISCONTENT'

Illustration 4

would-be rooks become pigeons under the spell of sharper rooks than themselves. It is, indeed, essential for a proper understanding of the Jewish characters introduced into Thackeray's fiction to see them in the context of the less than admirable Gentile-dominated society in which they live and work. In *Thackeray's Literary Apprenticeship*, H.S. Gulliver quotes a review in *The Times* of 7 September 1838 in which Thackeray overestimates the prosperity Jews were able to achieve in the dominions of the Czar while forcibly making the point, in a Russian setting, that there was not much to choose between a Jewish rascal and a Gentile one.

> At the entrance to the capital, in order, as we suppose, to give the newcomer an idea of the high state of civilization of the place, somebody dexterously cut away Mr. Raikes's portmanteau. A knowledge of this excellent natural disposition on the part of his subjects probably induced Peter the Great, when asked to expel the Jews from his dominions on account of their cunning, to say, "Let them alone, my Russians are a match for them." And the Hebrews have remained prospering and multiplying on pretty equal terms with the rest of the Emperor's subjects. It is only in a republic that civilization has reached to such heights as to place the Christians on a level with the Jews, as the profound Mr. Slick, or some other equally veracious historian, avers, that in certain provinces of the States Scotchmen in mercantile concerns are as simple as babes, and Jews starve.
>
> (op. cit., Valdosta 1934, p. 219)

If Haliburton's Sam Slick is to be believed, the rooks that out-rooked the wretched Stubbs are themselves likely to become pidgeons when they step off the boat in the United States.

ii

The "rook and pigeon" theme is taken up again in *Catherine*, which began its career as a serial in *Fraser's* (May 1839—February 1840) and was not published in book-form until 1869, six years after its author's death. In this tale, the inn whose landlord is a notorious fence and in which John Hayes and his newly-wedded wife are held for ransom by two other rogues, bears the symbolic name "The Three Rooks". This is no humorous tale of biters bit, however; it is, rather, a dark story of murder and dismemberment followed by a horrific judicial execution, with gory details derived from the *Newgate Calendar* and contemporary newspaper reports. The book version of *Catherine* omits some of these details; but readers of *Fraser's Magazine* got the beauty of it hot, with graphic accounts of criminal decapitation and judicial burning alive.

Burning alive was no longer a legally sanctioned punishment in Thackeray's day; his tale is of the early eighteenth century (it begins in 1705 and ends in 1726, when the historical Catherine Hayes was executed), but it is told by a nineteenth-century narrator who is anxious to produce a more authentic picture of criminal mentality and behaviour than could be gathered from such fashionable "Newgate novels" as Bulwer's *Eugene Aram* and Ainsworth's *Rookwood* and *Jack Sheppard*, or from the Nancy sections of *Oliver Twist*. This narrator, whose voice is only occasionally interrupted by an editorial footnote, is named below the title of the work:

CATHERINE

A STORY

BY IKEY SOLOMONS, ESQ., JUNIOR

Ikey tells us of his intention to "tread in the footsteps of the immortal Fagin" (III, 4), but he will do so without transforming criminals into highfalutin' philosophers, glamourizing them, or sentimentalizing their nature and their plight. Criminals are to be shown in their true sordid colours:

> And if the British public (after calling for three or four editions), shall give up, not only our rascals, but the rascals of all other authors, we

> shall be content—we shall apply to the government for a pension, and think that our duty is done.
>
> (III, 32)

The reference to the "immortal Fagin" is not fortuitous; for even though Dickens may not have had the career of the original Ikey Solomons—Ikey Senior, as it were—foremost in mind when creating his Fagin, the two figures were soon associated in the popular imagination. A pamphlet published in 1829 and ascribed to one Moses Hebron, "formerly a Jewish Rabbi, but now a Christian" enumerates in its title the chief exploits with which Ikey senior was credited.

> The Life and Exploits of Ikey Solomons, Swindler, forger, fencer, and brothel-keeper. With accounts of flash and dress houses, flash girls and Coves of the Watch, now on Town; With instructions how to guard against Hypocritical Villains, and the lures of abandoned Females. Also, particulars of Mrs. Ikey Solomons, and the Gang who infested London for Nineteen Years.

The narrator of *Catherine*, Ikey junior, dates his story from "Cold Bath Fields" (III, 32), where the Middlesex House of Correction was situated; a footnote signed "O.Y." tells us that he "has his lodgings and food provided for him by the government of his country" (III, 79)—a polite way of indicating that he is in prison. He is thus likely to be more intimately acquainted with criminal mentality than Bulwer or other "Newgate" novelists, and he presents his credentials by showing his familiarity with thieves' slang. At one point a footnote has to explain that "the Stone Jug" is "a polite name for her Majesty's prison of Newgate"; but at other times terms like "topping prigs" are left unglossed, leaving the reader unversed in such "polite" locutions to deduce from the context that what must be meant is "expert thieves" (III, 105). Ikey has been, among other things, a "prig" of this kind; and he tells us something of his family history when he seeks to disprove what he thinks Maria Edgeworth's "doctrine" that all criminals are made, not born.

> A celebrated philosopher, I think Miss Edgeworth, has broached the consolatory doctrine, that in intellect and disposition all human beings are entirely equal, and that circumstance and education are the causes of the distinctions and divisions which afterwards unhappily take place among them. . . . . . I, Ikey Solomons, once had a dear little brother who could steal before he could walk (and this not from encouragement,—for, if you know the world, you must know that in families of our profession the point of honour is sacred at home,—but from pure nature)—who could steal, I say, before he could walk, and lie before he could speak; and who, at four and a-half years of age,

having attacked my sister Rebecca on some question of lollypops, and smitten her on the elbow with a fire-shovel, apologized to us, by saying, simply, '———her, I wish it had been her head!' Dear, dear Aminadab! I think of you, and laugh these philosophers to scorn. Nature made you for that career which you fulfilled; you were from your birth to your dying a scoundrel; you *couldn't* have been anything else, however your lot was cast; and blessed it was that you were born among the prigs,—for had you been of any other profession, alas! alas! what ills might you have done!

(III, 98–100)

Thackeray here raises, within a Jewish context, the more general problem of innate disposition. The knowledgable reader will perceive irony, of course, in the application of the term "celebrated philosopher" to the author of *Castle Rackrent*, *Moral Tales*, and *Tales of Fashionable Life*, though Ikey may be thought anxious to minimize his criticism of the views he ascribes to Maria Edgeworth because of her amends for earlier depictions of Jewish bugbears in the saintly Montenero of *Harrington* (1817). But though the proposition "that in intellect and disposition all human beings are entirely equal" flies in the fact of all experience, the reader need not side with Ikey in believing that an apparently "innate disposition" remains wholly uncorrectable in a favourable environment. Unlike little Aminadab, whose youthful exploits he describes with such graphic reference to lollipops and fire-shovels, Ikey himself seems well on the way to reformation and respectability. An epilogue dated "Horsemonger Lane, January 1840" suggests that he has been released from prison, and that when he says: "Be it granted Solomons is dull, but don't attack his morality" (III, 187) he has taken the first steps on a road which may lead to a coat of arms and eventual ennoblement:

> Sir Ikey Solomons would not sound badly; and who knows whether, some day or other, another batch of us literary chaps may not be called upon by a grateful sovereign to kneel gracefully on one knee, majesty waving over our heads a glittering cut-and-thrust, and saying with sweet accents, 'Rise up, Sir Something Whatdyecallum!' —who knows?

(III, 32)

Ikey is also, we learn, something of a ladies' man: "I do believe", he tells us, "after a reasonable degree of pressing, any woman will capitulate to any man; such at least, has been my experience" (III, 96); and his origins and experiences make him aware of affinities between a Jew's emotional life and that of his Gentile neighbour.

> Love, like Death, plays havoc among the *pauperum tabernas*, and sports with rich and poor, wicked and virtuous alike. I have often fancied,

for instance, on seeing the haggard, pale, young old-clothesman, who
wakes the echoes of our street with his nasal cry of 'Clo:' I have often,
I say, fancied that, besides the load of exuvial coats and breeches
under which he staggers, there is another weight on him—an *atrior
cura* at his tail—and while his unshorn lips and nose together are
performing that mocking, boisterous, Jack-indifferent cry of 'Clo,
Clo;' who knows what woful utterances are crying from the heart
within? There he is chaffering with the footman at No. 7, about an old
dressing-gown, you think his whole soul is bent only on the contest
about the garment. Psha! there is, perhaps, some faithless girl in
Holywell Street who fills up his heart; and that desultory Jew-boy is a
peripatetic hell!

(III, 21–2)

John Loofbourow, in a justly famous passage of his book *Thackeray
and the Form of Fiction* (Princeton 1963), has analysed the style of the
extract from *Catherine* which has just been quoted, and has related it
to an "ethical ambiguity" found in two authors whom Thackeray
detested: Byron and Bulwer Lytton.

The controlled development of this passage is based on the juxtaposition of elevated classical phrases with realistic images—"pauperum
tabernas" with "old-clothesman," "*atrior cura*" with "at his tail"—
and poetic amplification as in "haggard pale young old" contrasted
with satirical diminution in "exuvial coats and breeches." This is one
of Thackeray's typical methods: the integration of the lyric rhythms
and images of fashionable fiction with the harsher rhetoric of neoclas-
sical satire and contemporary realism. Through such expressive
interaction he is able to introduce a phrase that retains the emotional
intensity of the fashionable mode but transmutes its insincere ideal-
ism into a valid insight—"who knows what woful utterances are
crying from the heart within?" Separated from its context, this
sounds like a Victorian truism; its quality is altered by the insistence
that love sports not only with "rich and poor" but with "wicked and
virtuous alike." Wordsworth and Dickens had proclaimed the power
of love among the poor, but they did not like to suggest that love
might be experienced by a reprobate without modifying his moral
character—where his personality remained vicious, the amorous
impulse must be no more than animal lust. Lord Byron and Bulwer
Lytton, despite their artistic insincerities, were the Victorian pioneers
in this area of ethical ambiguity, where an increasing interest in
subjective experience adumbrated the explorations of modern psychology.

(op. cit., p. 18)

What needs to be added is that there is no suggestion that the
chaffering old clo' man is wicked as well as poor. By letting Ikey
speculate on the agonies behind the pale face, the beard, the nasal
cry, the body bent under its heavy load, and the necessary haggling
about pennies, Thackeray leads his readers to a more sympathetic

and empathetic view of a Jew's inner life than his previous writings could have led them to expect.

The allusion to Horace's *atra cura* in the passage just cited is entirely characteristic of the vast array of allusions to, and quotations from, the Greek and (especially) the Roman classics, as well as a variety of English authors, with which Ikey's narrative is studded. Together with his splendid parodies of sensational dramatists and sentimental novelists, and his close acquaintance with the manners and the speech of the eighteenth century, these citations and allusions bespeak a gentlemanly education that would have been exceedingly rare in a Jewish "prig" of Holywell Street. Ikey even quotes accurately from Goethe's *Faust*—a feat well beyond cultivated Englishmen of the day who had not, like Thackeray, spent time in Weimar, in the ambience of Goethe himself. Ikey tries to account for all this by claiming that he had been a "gyp" or College servant at Cambridge (III, 116); but that is hardly enough to make us believe in Ikey's authorship of such Thackerayan flights as the opening of Chapter VIII:

> We are obliged, in recording this history, to follow accurately that great authority, the *Calendarium Newgaticum Roagorumque Registerium*, of which every lover of literature in the present day knows the value; and as that remarkable work totally discards all the unities in its narratives, and reckons the life of its heroes only by their actions, and not by periods of time, we must follow in the wake of this mighty ark—a humble cockboat. When it pauses, we pause; when it runs ten knots an hour, we run with the same celerity; and as, in order to carry the reader from the penultimate chapter of this work unto the last chapter, we were compelled to make him leap over a gap of five blank years, ten years more must likewise be granted to us before we are at liberty to resume our history.
>
> (III, 113–114)

As an independent narrative voice Ikey Solomons junior never comes alive, however carefully Thackeray plots his life-history, his confusions about narrative authority, his obvious self-contradictions, his shifting sense of audience, his empathies, and his distancings. The considerable narrative skills exhibited in the elaboration of a case-history recorded in the *Newgate Chronicle* are the developing skills of a major English novelist, not those of the Jewish narrator he has invented.

One of these skills is the emblematic or symbolic use of Biblical incidents; and here Thackeray does seem to consider Ikey's religious persuasion by making him link the tale of Catherine Hayes and her husband, in which a severed head plays a gruesome part, with the Old Testament story of Judith and Holofernes rather than the Christian legend of Salome and John the Baptist. The image is first introduced in Chapter III ("By heavens! the woman means murder! I would not be the Holofernes to lie by the side of such a Judith as that . . ."—III, 45) and is then reintroduced in Chapter XI, where we find Judith and Holofernes depicted on a tapestry above John Hayes's bed. Its sombre warning is reinforced by an ill-omened clock.

> Against this tapestry, and just cutting off Holofernes's head, stood an enormous ominous black clock, the spoil of some other usurous transactions . . . It was just upon six, and presently the clock began to utter those dismal grinding sounds which issue from clocks at such periods, and which sound like the death-rattle of the departing hour. Then the bell struck the knell of it; and with this Mr. Hayes awoke, and looked up, and saw Catherine gazing at him.
>
> Their eyes met for an instant, and Catherine turned away burning red, and looked as if she had been caught in the commission of a crime.
>
> (III, 154)

The master-stroke here is surely the "cutting off" of Holofernes's head, not by Judith (who, we have learnt earlier, is also represented on the tapestry) but by the clock. "Cutting off", in that context, is synonymous with "hiding"; and the problem of hiding Hayes's head will prove more insuperable to Catherine and her co-conspirators than the problem of severing it. That Ikey cannot claim a monopoly of Old Testament references goes without saying; Thackeray remains as fond as ever of such references as a means of conveying his meaning picturesquely and economically. Reviewing the speeches of Lord Brougham, for instance, in *The British and Foreign Review* (for April 1839), he tells his readers that Brougham

> loves himself ten times more than party or principle; and if they should thwart him, he is man enough to fight against the two, and, like Samson, to pull the house about his enemies' ears, though his own should be damaged by the fall.
>
> (*Stray Papers*, ed. L. Melville, London 1901, p. 119)

The better known the story, the more effective the communication.

The "Catherine cathartic", as Ikey calls his tale (III, 184), was intended to purge the public of sentimental sympathy with criminals; but at least one of the rogues it presents turned out to be rather engaging, and the author himself came to have a "sneaking kindness" for his eponymous heroine which served to deepen rather than palliate his dislike of the "disgusting subject" he had chosen (to Mrs. Carmichael-Smyth, 11–15 February and 20 (?) March

1840—LPP I, 421, 433). That he also felt dissatisfied with the narrative voice he had adopted in *Catherine* may be deduced from his later preface to *Pendennis*, where he speaks of abandoning a plan to introduce "exciting" criminals and criminal action: "I found that I failed from want of experience of my subject; and never having been intimate with any convict in my life, and the manners of ruffians and jail-birds being quite unfamiliar to me, the idea of entering into competition with M. Eugène Sue was abandoned." (XII, xxxvi). To have sustained a believable "Jewish" voice throughout a piece as long as *Catherine*, Thackeray would have needed more intimate contact with Jews than he was willing to seek out. In the event, he did not even try, and the life-experience with which Ikey Solomons junior is credited seems constantly at logger-heads with his manner of speech and his width of reference.

iii

The horrific punishments described at the end of *Catherine* in its first, unrevised version belong to the eighteenth century; but public hangings still went on in Thackeray's own day, and in his essay "Going to See a Man Hanged" (*Fraser's Magazine*, August 1840) he portrays such an occasion in a way that leaves little doubt of his revulsion.

> But murder is such a monstrous crime (this is the great argument),—when a man has killed another it is natural that he should be killed. Away with your foolish sentimentalists who say no—it is *natural*. That is the word, and a fine philosophical opinion it is— philosophical and Christian. Kill a man, and you must be killed in turn; that is the unavoidable *sequitur*. You may talk to a man for a year upon the subject, and he will always reply to you, it is natural, and therefore it must be done. Blood demands blood.
>
> Does it? The system of compensations might be carried on *ad infinitum*,—an eye for an eye, a tooth for a tooth, as by the old Mosaic law. But (putting the fact out of the question, that we have had this statute repealed by the Highest Authority), why, because you lose your eye is that of your opponent's to be extracted likewise? Where is the reason for the practice? And yet it is just as natural as the death dictum, founded precisely upon the same show of sense. Knowing, however, that revenge is not only evil, but useless, we have given it up on all minor points. Only to the last we stick firm, contrary though it be to reason and to Christian law.
>
> (III, 204)

" . . . we have had this statute repealed by the Highest Authority": Thackeray firmly believed, and maintained against his mother, that the "old Mosaic law" was no longer binding on Christians.

His letters to Mrs. Carmichael-Smyth bear witness to the same belief; one of these even links his repudiation of the Judaic basis of Christianity to the absurd contention that Israel had no conception of a spiritual God: "The God believed in by all rude nations, the Jews as much as any other, has been material" (LPP, I, 404). How such a belief could survive a reading of the Old Testament is inconceivable. In a letter dated 3 March 1840, Thackeray describes to his mother how his little daughter reacted to a book of Bible illustrations: "a great scene took place when she came to Abraham sacrificing Isaac: she cried and screamed and said, 'No, he should not kill the little boy', and tried to pull Isaac off the altar. Truly, out of the mouths of babes and sucklings comes wisdom. I don't like to show her these pictures, for they are almost all of them painful, and relating to some scene of death or punishment." (LPP, I, 424). It does not seem to have occurred to Thackeray to explain to his daughter that Isaac was not, in fact, killed—that God stopped the sacrifice, and that Isaac lived on to become the father of Jacob and Esau.

Thackeray has been portrayed, by John Sutherland and others, as what is nowadays termed a "racist"; and it is indeed possible to extract from his writings a florilegium of remarks about Jews, blacks and half-castes which could easily lead to his condemnation by a modern race relations board. His animadversion on Jews must, however, be seen in a threefold context. The first is that of his own time and class, of beliefs instilled in him by the educational system which had formed him, and confirmed by much of the company he was predisposed to keep. The second, underlined by the construction of the present book, is that of his own later development and the increasing integration of Jews into British society. The third context is provided by the way in which he presented his own kind, middle and upper middle class Englishmen, whose actions are often made to appear as bad as—and not infrequently worse than—any he attributes to individuals outside that charmed circle. Major Goliah Gahagan, for instance, whose first name is intended to recall the gigantic Philistine warrior of the Book of Samuel while his surname places him firmly in Thackeray's gallery of grandiloquent and tale-spinning Irishmen, leaves the British Raj little justification for complaint about the barbarous behaviour of "lesser breeds" when he describes what the British could get up to in the territories they administered. Take Gahagan's chronicle of the exploits of Captain Julius Jowler, C.B. and of the men under his command:

Some influence, equally melancholy, seemed to have fallen upon poor old Jowler. About six months after we had left Dum Dum, he received a parcel of letters from Benares (whither his wife had retired with her daughter), and so deeply did they seem to weigh upon his spirits, that he ordered eleven men of his regiment to be flogged within two days; but it was against the blacks that he chiefly turned his wrath: our fellows, in the heat and hurry of the campaign, were in the habit of dealing rather roughly with their prisoners, to extract treasure from them. They used to pull their nails out by the root, to boil them in kedgeree pots, to flog them and dress their wounds with cayenne pepper, and so on. Jowler, when he heard of these proceedings, which before had always justly exasperated him (he was a humane and kind little man), used now to smile fiercely, and say, 'D—— the black scoundrels! Serve them right, serve them right!'

(I, 347)

One must allow for Gahagan's Münchhausen-like exaggerations and distortions, of course; but the attitudes Thackeray pillories here, and the kinds of action to which they may give rise, are terrifyingly true to life. The opening of the significantly titled "Captain Rook and Mr. Pigeon" introduces Jews alongside "Turks, Quakers, Methodists, Catholics and Church of England men" in a way that leaves little to choose between these groups:

The statistics mongers and dealers in geography have calculated to a nicety how many quartern loaves, bars of iron, pigs of lead, sacks of wool, Turks, Quakers, Methodists, Jews, Catholics, and Church of England men, are consumed or produced in the different countries of this wicked world: I should like to see an accurate table showing the rogues and dupes of each nation; the calculation would form a pretty matter for a philosopher to speculate upon. The mind loves to repose, and broods benevolently over this expanded theme. What thieves are there in Paris, oh, heavens! and what a power of rogues with pigtails and mandarin buttons at Pekin! Crowds of swindlers are there at this very moment pursuing their trade at St. Petersburg: how many scoundrels are saying their prayers alongside of Don Carlos! how many scores are jobbing under the pretty nose of Queen Christine! what an inordinate number of rascals is there, to be sure, puffing tobacco and drinking flat small beer in all the capitals of Germany; or else, without a rag to their ebony backs, swigging quass out of calabashes, and smeared over with palm oil, lolling at the doors of clay huts in the sunny city of Timbuctoo! It is not necessary to make any more topographical allusions, or, for illustrating the above position, to go through the whole Gazetteer; but he is a bad philosopher who has not all these things in mind, and does not in his speculations or his estimate of mankind duly consider and weigh them. And it is fine and consolatory to think, that thoughtful nature, which has provided sweet flowers for the humming bee; fair running streams for glittering fish; store of kids, deer, goats, and other fresh meat for roaring lions; for active cats, mice; for mice, cheese, and so on; establishing throughout the whole of her realm the great doctrine that where a demand is, there will be a supply (see the romances of Adam Smith, Malthus, and Ricardo, and the philosophical works of Miss Martineau): I say it is consolatory to think that, as nature has provided flies for the food of fishes, and flowers for bees, so she has created fools for rogues; and thus the scheme is consistent throughout. Yes, observation, with extensive view, will discover Captain Rooks all over the world, and Mr. Pigeons made for their benefit. Wherever shines the sun, you are sure to find Folly basking in it; and knavery is the shadow at Folly's heels.

(I, 539–40)

No religious or ethnic group, no nation and no people is exempt from folly and knavery, nor has any a monopoly of rogues and dupes. Indeed, the survey of national rogueries undertaken by the narrator of "Captain Rook and Mr. Pigeon" reaches the lapidary conclusion that

there is no cheat like an English cheat. Our society produces them in the greatest number as of the greatest excellence. I defy you to point to a great city on the Continent where half a dozen of them are not to be found: proofs of our enterprise and samples of our home manufacture . . .

(I, 540)

The bird-of-prey image embodied in the "Captain"'s name is elaborated in such locutions as "is Captain Rook the kind of fellow to give up a purse when his hand has once *clawed* hold of it" (I, 545—my italics)—it is well to keep this in mind when we hear similar images used to characterize Jews in Thackeray's later fiction. The account given of Rook's formal and informal education shows him, at one time, pretending to read for the bar while leading a "fast" life his purse cannot sustain. We find him, therefore, falling "into the hands of the Jews" and landing in that "spunging-house in Cursitor Street" of which Thackeray's later fiction will allow his readers more intimate views, and which constitutes, in Rook's case, "the nearest approach he has made to the Temple"—where, of course, his law studies should have taken him—during his three years' residence in London.

"Captain Rook and Mr. Pigeon" is the first of a number of "Character Sketches" (modelled on the popular French "physiologies" of the day) which Thackeray contributed to a collaborative venture called *Heads of the People* in 1840 and 1841. Another of his contributions to *Heads of the People* invites the reader to take a walk around Soho:

Look at Newman-street. Has earth, in any dismal corner of her great round face, a spot more desperately gloomy? The windows are spotted with wafers, holding up ghastly bills, that tell you the house is 'To Let.' Nobody walks there—not even an old clothesman; the first inhabited house has bars to the windows, and bears the name of 'Ahasuerus, officer to the Sheriff of Middlesex'; and here, above all places, must painters take up their quarters,—day by day must these reckless people pass Ahasuerus's treble gate. There was my poor friend, Tom Tickner (who did those sweet things for 'The Book of Beauty'). Tom, who could not pay his washerwoman, lived opposite the bailiff's; and could see every miserable debtor, or greasy Jew writ-bearer that went in or out of his door. The street begins with a bailiff's, and ends with a hospital. I wonder how men live in it, and are decently cheerful, with this gloomy, double-barrelled moral pushed perpetually into their faces. Here, however, they persist in living, no one knows why; owls may still be found roosting in Netley Abbey, and a few Arabs are to be seen at the present minute in Palmyra.

("The Artists"—I, 76–79)

To call the Jewish writ-bearer who furnishes Ahasuerus with tenants "greasy" is obviously offensive; but if one collects together the many instances in which Thackeray applies the same adjective to non-Jewish characters—including, prominently, a Christian clergyman in *Philip*—one may regain a sense of proportion, and see the greasy writ-bearer in context, as staffage for the dreary townscape which the author is attempting to paint in appropriately gloomy colours. Since artists make up a large part of the population of the Victorian Soho here described, it is not surprising to find Jews in the role of artists' models. Old-clothesmen, we are told, are impressed for sittings as Jewish high priests, just as guardsmen do duty as Roman conquerors and "blackamoors" (crossing-sweepers, perhaps?) represent Othello on canvas (I, 595). In this same sketch of the life led by struggling artists in London Thackeray introduces a novel way of using the concept of race: to denote the individual look portrait painters working in one and the same period impart to their subjects. Thomas Lawrence and Joshua Reynolds, he declares, "seem to have painted different races of people" (I, 588).

The section of *Heads of the People* devoted to "The Fashionable Authoress' (a lady presented, ironically, as a compound of Delilah and Circe) takes us into more exalted regions, allowing us to hobnob with the likes of Prince Scoronconcolo "who had married a Miss Solomonson with a plum" (I, 564). A "plum" was £100 000—a sum which enabled this Jewish heiress to win the grotesquely named Prince away from Lady Fanny Foxy, daughter of Pitt Castlereagh, second Earl of Reynard, Kilbrush Castle, County Kildare.

In 1840 Thackeray seized another opportunity of collaborating with Cruikshank: "Cox's Diary, or, Barber Cox and the Cutting of his Comb" appeared in Cruikshank's *Comic Almanach* of that year, with chapter headings running from January to December just as those of "Stubbs's Calendar" had done. Cruikshank introduced some peripheral Jewish figures identified by hand gestures as well as physiognomies:

APRIL.—THE FINISHING TOUCH

Illustration 5

Thackeray matched these pictorial characterizations with caricatures of "Jewish" speech, suitably relativized by being set amid similar caricatures of French and German distortions of the English language. A dubious German baron introduces Mr Abednego, the Jewish keeper of a lodging house and billiard room with which His Excellency is evidently satisfied.

> 'Gut,' says he, 'gut; I lif, you know, at Abednego's, in de Quadrant; his dabels is goot; ve vill blay dere, if you vill;' and I said I would: and it was agreed that, one Saturday night, when Jemmy was at the Opera, we should go to the Baron's rooms, and give him a chance.
>
> We went, and the little Baron had as fine a supper as ever I saw; lots of champang (and I didn't mind drinking it), and plenty of laughing and fun. Afterwards, down we went to billiards. 'Is dish Mishter Coxsh, de shelebrated player?' says Mr. Abednego, who was in the room, with one or two gentlemen of his own persuasion, and several foreign noblemen, dirty, snuffy, and hairy, as them foreigners are. 'Is dish Mishter Coxsh? blesh ma hart, it is a honer to see you, I have heard so much of your play.'

'Come, come,' says I, 'sir;' for I'm pretty wide awake; 'none of your gammon; you're not going to hook *me.*'

'No, begar, dis fish you not catch,' says Count Mace.

'Dat is gut! haw! haw!' snorted the Baron; 'hook him! lieber himmel, you might dry and hook me as well. Haw! haw!'

Well, we went to play. 'Fife to four on Coxe,' screams out the Count.—'Done and done,' says another nobleman. 'Ponays,' says the Count.—'Done,' says the nobleman. 'I vill take your six crowns to four,' says the Baron.—'Done,' says I; and, in the twinkling of an eye, I beat him;—once making thirteen off the balls without stopping.

We had some more wine after this; and, if you could have seen the long faces of the other noblemen, as they pulled out their pencils and wrote I.O.U.'s for the Count. 'Va toujours, mon cher,' says he to me, 'you have von for me three hundred pounds.'

'I'll blay you guineas dis time,' says the Baron. 'Zeven to four you must give me though;' and so I did: and in ten minutes *that* game was won, and the Baron handed over his pounds. 'Two hundred and sixty more, my dear, dear Coxe,' says the Count; 'you are mon ange gardien!' 'Wot a flat Mishter Coxsh is, not to back his luck,' I heard Abednego whisper to one of the foreign noblemen.

'I'll take your seven to four, in tens,' said I to the Baron. 'Give me three,' says he, 'and done.' I gave him three, and lost the game by one. 'Dobbel, or quits,' says he. 'Go it,' says I, up to my mettle; 'Sam Coxe never says no;'—and to it we went. I went in, and scored eighteen to his five. 'Holy Moshesh!' says Abednego, 'dat little Coxsh is a vonder! who'll take odds?'

'I'll give twenty to one,' says I, 'in guineas.'

'Ponays, yase, done;' screams out the Count.

'*Bonies*, done,' roars out the Baron; and, before I could speak, went in, and, would you believe it?—in two minutes he somehow made the game!

.   .   .   .

Oh, what a figure I cut when my dear Jemmy heard of this afterwards! In vain I swore it was guineas: the Count and the Baron swore to ponies; and when I refused, they both said their honour was concerned, and they must have my life, or their money. So when the Count showed me actually that, in spite of this bet (which had been too good to resist) won from me, he had been a very heavy loser by the night; and brought me the word of honour of Abednego, his Jewish friend, and the foreign noblemen, that ponies had been betted:—why, I paid them one thousand pounds sterling of good and lawful money;—but I've not played for money since: no, no; catch me at *that* again if you can.

(III, 229–30)

A pigeon has evidently been rooked; but Thackeray's treatment of Mr. Abednego is no more and no less unfavourable than that of the dubious baron, and among the figures in Cruikshank's lively drawing Abednego and his coreligionists seem by no means the most disreputable.

Very soon after this episode Barber Cox is taken behind the scenes of an opera house. The crowd he sees there includes "young and old gents, of the fashion, crowding round and staring at the actresses practising their steps"; "yellow, snuffy foreigners, chattering always, and smelling fearfully of tobacco"; old men in nightgowns, troops of girls, and: "scores of Jews, with hooked noses, and black muzzles, covered with rings, sham diamonds, and gold waistcoats" (III, 235–6). The vision is Cox's, of course, who had recently spent a day with the Surrey hounds and is therefore ready to see "muzzles" instead of mouths; but it is somewhat disturbing to find this dehumanizing locution applied to Jews rather than any of the other characters. Jewish love of the theatre, in Victorian times, is well attested; and the flamboyance of dress and ornamentation which Cox here describes may well be seen as a phenomenon closely related to that fascination.

"A Shabby Genteel Story", which appeared in *Fraser's Magazine* in the same year as "Cox's Diary", occupies a special place in the Thackeray canon: for it was destined to become the prelude, an introductory section as it were, of his later novel *The Adventures of Philip*. Some of its characters travel on a steamer from London to Margate and observe that at Gravesend "a wandering Jew or two were set down" (III, 351)—thus bringing together Jewish traders who help the flow of goods from the English capital to the provinces with the legendary figure which had fascinated the English Romantic poets and which had recently been brought before the novel-reading public by Eugène Sue's sensational best seller. When the travellers arrive at Margate, they toil up its deserted High Street,

> by gaping rows of empty bathing-houses, by melancholy Jolly's French bazaar, by mouldy pastry-cooks, blank reading-rooms, by fishmongers who never sold a fish, mercers who vended not a yard of riband—because, as yet, the season was not come,—and Jews and Cockneys still remained in town.
>
> (III, 354)

How much livelier and more delectable the place will be, we are made to feel, when "Jews and Cockneys" arrive, and the season gets under way!

The villain of "A Shabby Genteel Story" is George Brandon, who will later metamorphose into the Dr Firmin of *Philip*. Brandon is a "getting-and-keeping scoundrel" rather than an extravagant and careless one (III, 300); and when he decamps from London to Margate, he leaves behind debts which he undertakes to discharge after "my marriage with Miss Goldmore, the great Indian heiress"—a marriage that never takes place. Among his unsatisfied creditors are "Mr. Snipson the tailor, Mr. Jackson the boot-maker" and a man whom Brandon calls "honest Solomonson the discounter of bills" (III, 296). How ironic the adjective "honest" is meant to sound in this context, every reader must decide for himself; what is crystal clear, however, is that Solomonson is very unlikely to see Brandon's bill honoured.

"A Shabby Genteel Story" once again introduces Thackeray's favourite spelling game—a stout lady at Margate is made to exclaim: "O mong jew, mong jew! c'est André—c'est lui!—(III, 355); but at this period he shows little inclination, when not stimulated by Cruikshank's lively drawings, to allow Jewish characters into the centre of his stage. He does, however, introduce the name "Rothschild" as a personification of wealth into an essay on his favourite novelist, Henry Fielding, which he published in *The Times* in 1840—the year that had also seen the appearance of "Cox's Diary" and "A Shabby Genteel Story". When Fielding, he writes,

> had spent his little fortune, and saw that there was nothing for it but to work, he came to London, applied himself fiercely to the law, seized upon his pen again, never lost heart for a moment, and, be sure, loved his poor Amelia as tenderly as ever he had done. It is a pity that he did not live on his income, that is certain; it is a pity that he had not been born a lord, or a thrifty stockbroker, at the very least; but we should not have had *Joseph Andrews* if this had been the case, and indeed it is probable that Amelia liked him quite as well after his ruin as she would have done had he been as rich as Rothschild.
>
> (III, 387)

Nathan Mayer Rothschild, of whom the young Thackeray had written in such scathing terms, was dead by 1840, and the passing reference just quoted is a mere statement of fact about the Rothschilds' reputed wealth, unaccompanied by the vulgar abuse that had marked Thackeray's poem in the ill-fated *National Standard*.

iv

By no means all of Thackeray's contributions to *Fraser's Magazine* have been traced back to him. "Elizabeth Brownrigge: A Tale" (1832), with its "Jew slopseller in the neighbourhood of Rag Fair", has been attributed to his authorship by Leslie Stephen and others; this attribution has been rejected, however, on valid stylistic grounds, by most modern authorities. Another very doubtful case is that of "The Jew of York" (1836), a story that stands halfway between *Ivanhoe* and *Rebecca and Rowena* with its horrified description of a medieval pogrom by "bloodthirsty savages" bent on murder and pillage who call themselves Christian, and its loving presentation of a *belle Juive* who, in the end, converts to Christianity. We are on somewhat surer ground with "Our Batch of Novels for Christmas, 1837", which commends Mrs. Trollope's *The Vicar of Wrexhill* for its "capital burlesque of a Jew-Missionary to Washebo" and its "most unwomanlike genius for slang and drollery" (*Fraser's*, January 1838); but doubts remain, and we leave the subject quickly, noting only that Frances Trollope's Mr Isaacs goes to Fababo, and that the "slang and drollery" she introduces burlesques, not Jewish speech, but that of born-again Christians. What can be ascribed to Thackeray with absolute certainty is the campaign, in *Fraser's*, against the insipid Orientalism of many plates in contemporary annuals and keepsakes, "the endless Zuleikas and Isidoras of the Book of Beauty" (II, 354):

> oh ye of the taper fingers and six-inch eyes! shut those great fringes of eyelashes, close those silly coral slits of mouths. Avaunt, ye spider-waisted monsters! who have flesh, but no bones, silly bodies, but no souls . . .
>
> (II, 378)

These creatures have their male counterparts too; a plate in *The Keepsake* for 1838 is said to depict a "strange creature of a Turk" who wears what seems to be Persian rather than Turkish costume:

> We fancy the figure to be neither Turk nor Persian. There is a Jew model about town, who waits upon artists, and is very like Mr. Herbert's Sooliman . . .
>
> ("A Word on the Annuals", December 1837—II, 341)

The "Orientalist" taste which provides employment for Jewish models has invaded the Royal Academy too; Titmarsh notes "numerous Zuleikhas [sic] and Lalla Rookhs, which are hanging about the walls of the Academy and the New Water-Colour Gallery . . . such handsome Turks and leering Sultanas; such Moors, with straight noses and pretty curled beards!" (II, 401). This comes from a piece entitled "A Second Lecture on the Fine Arts. By Michael Angelo Titmarsh, Esq. The Exhibition", which *Fraser's* printed in June 1939. In this same lecture Titmarsh objects to the academically lifeless manner in which a well-known painter has tackled a specifically Jewish subject:

> Mr. Charles Landseer's 'Pillage of a Jew's House' is a very well and carefully painted picture, containing a great many figures, and good points; but we are not going to praise it: it wants vigour, to our taste, and what you call *actualité*. The people stretch their arms and turn their eyes the proper way, but as if they were in a tableau and paid for

standing there; one longs to see them all in motion and naturally, employed.

(II, 388–9)

What is clearly missing is the horror and despair evoked in the pogrom scene of "The Jew of York" which Fraser's had printed some three years earlier. Nor is Titmarsh at all impressed by the achievements of the Jewish painter Solomon Alexander Hart (1806–1888), who was to be elected to the Royal Academy in 1840:

> I would just as soon have Mr. Hart's great canvas of 'Lady Jane Grey' (which is worth exactly twopence-halfpenny) as Sir David Wilkie's poor picture of 'Seringapatam'.
>
> (II, 395)

Wilkie and Hart alike paint historical pictures which Titmarsh finds "poor, feeble, theatrical" (ibid.): A year after this "Second Lecture", Titmarsh returns to the charge in a piece entitled "A Pictorial Rhapsody . . . With an Introductory Letter to Mr. Yorke" (*Fraser's Magazine*, June 1840).

> . . . painters will do well to try their powers, and, if possible, measure and understand them before they use them. There is Mr. Hart, for instance, who took in an evil hour to the making of great pictures; in the present exhibition is a decently small one; but the artist has overstretched himself in the former attempts; as one hears of gentlemen on the rack, the limbs are stretched one or two inches by the process, and the patient comes away by so much the taller: but he can't *walk* near so well as before, and all his strength is stretched out of him.
>
> (II, 510)

Titmarsh never refers to the well-known fact of Hart's Jewish origins; he judges him as a painter, and finds him as wanting as most of his Gentile contemporaries who exhibited their work in London at the end of the third decade of the nineteenth century.

A taste for the Oriental and exotic blends easily with a taste for Biblical subjects. Titmarsh's art-criticism takes note of this and frequently pinpoints the failure of contemporary painters to match the vigour and poetry of the Old Testament. Francis Danby's *The Deluge*, though not exempt from similar strictures, is praised beyond what post-Victorian observers would think its deserts and judged superior to treatments of the same subject by Poussin and Turner; Etty is accused of using Biblical subjects as pretexts for the otherwise proscribed exhibition of luscious flesh. But Titmarsh's art-criticism remains delightfully informal and playful, and never betrays the kind of animus against certain Old Testament stories that comes out in some of Thackeray's letters.

v

In the summer of 1840, it would appear, Mrs. Carmichael-Smyth, in the course of one of her periodic attacks on the Church of Rome, again tackled her son about his negative attitude to the Jewish bases of Christianity, quoting Job 19, 25–27 in support of her contention that ancient Israel believed in a future state beyond the grave, and pointing to the great philanthropist Sir Moses Montefiore as an example of someone sustained by a worthy faith. Her son replied, on 1 September 1840:

> Concerning Judaism, I believe it is pretty generally allowed that the doctrine of a future state did not obtain among the Jews till they learned it in the Babylonish captivity. Except that passage in Job, w^h has nothing to do with the matter, being applied by J to his own bodily condition find another in the O.T.—one that says expressly there is a Heaven for the good & something else for us wicked ones. Such a doctrine of such importance ought to be taught by something more than implication, & should not be left to honest persons to decide whether it is so or no. . . . I should like to show you how the assertion that every word of the Bible from Genesis to Malachi proves Jewish belief in the immortality of the Soul cant be supported, and the argument about Moses Montefiore is beside the question. But by Jupiter-Ammon, as I go through the world it seems to me that I am the single person in it, who am always right. People will not look dispassionately, but never mind God's sun shines over us all Jews, Heathen Turks, Methodists, Catholics, Church-of-England men, but this is an old story that I have often told. It seems to me blasphemy to say that out of a certain sect there is no salvation, Heaven forbid say you: well then one sect is as good as another, and as men have different eyes noses and we sh^d be monstrously bigotted if we were to say that such and such a hook or such and such a swivel shd be damned—in like manner let us accord the same charity to men's minds w^h are all different & must all worship God their own way. Indeed it is something noble I think to think even of this difference: that God has a responding face for every one of these myriad intelligences, and a sympathy with all. Why then be anxious that those we love should cast their religious thoughts precisely in our mould?

> (LPP, I, 466–7)

There is an obvious conflict here between Thackeray's prejudgment of Jews and his plea for universal tolerance, between his strictures on his mother's sectarianism and his own insistence on views that conflict with the opinion of people who had read the Bible with greater attention, and more profound theological understanding, than he could lay claim to. He must himself have been aware of this, for he introduces an element of amused self-persiflage: "But by Jupiter-Ammon, as I go through the world it seems to me that I am the single person in it, who am always right." No-one knew better than Thackeray the proneness to error which afflicts all human beings—and the plea for tolerance with which the passage just quoted concludes is surely addressed to himself as well as his mother. Nor could anyone as sensitive to the associations of words and images as Thackeray fail to notice how often, when he looked for the neatest and fullest formulation of what he wanted to say, he found himself impelled to use phrases from the Old Testament. This is true of *The Second Funeral of Napoleon*, for instance, which contains a letter dated "Paris, December 16, 1840" in which readers are introduced to "the great HUMBUG-PLANT" that shelters all the generations of men:

> Cowards fig themselves out fiercely as 'salvage men', and make us believe that they are warriors . . . men have, as it were, entered into a compact among themselves to pursue the fig-leaf system *à outrance*, and to cry down all who oppose it. Humbugs they will have. Humbugs themselves, they will respect humbugs . . .
>
> (III, 369)

Thackeray's own characteristic invention, the humbug-plant, can only flourish in symbiosis with the fig-leaves of Genesis.

The writings examined in this chapter are centrally concerned with what Thackeray called the "rook and pigeon" theme; and the Jewish characters he introduces usually belong to the rooks rather the pigeons. He treats the affair of the stolen gold dust as cause for amusement rather than indignation, and suggests that the activities of London Jews rallying round coreligionists accused of dishonest dealings might make a good vaudeville. In his fictional presentations of dishonest Jews he never shows them up as worse rooks than dishonest Gentiles; they mainly harm the greedy, and often act as a nemesis which overtakes those who try to rook others. They also appear as unloved agents of an unloved law that decrees imprisonment for debt. If "greasy Jew writ-bearer[s]" constitute an unattractive part of an unattractive townscape, the absence of lively "Jews and cockneys" makes for dullness and desolation in a seaside resort out of season. With the help of a contemporary journalist Thackeray leads his readers into East End places of amusement, with a Jewish staff and largely Jewish clientèle. He takes us behind the scenes of a theatre to show Jewish hangers-on whose flashy ways of dressing seem less out of place in a theatrical atmosphere than in the more sober streets of London; but he also recognizes, not without irony, how important the "fair Jewess" Rachel Felix has become as a trendsetter in the interpretation of French classical drama. He introduces Jewish gamblers, and a (self-styled) Jewish attorney operating on the fringes of the law. His assumption of a Jewish persona in *Catherine* is unconvincing, but it does lead him to make a sympathetic attempt to fathom the emotional life of a poor Jewish old clothes man. We meet a Jewish painter, and Jewish artists' models. The name "Rothschild" ceases to be an automatic target for anti-capitalist abuse; it has become a characterizing and comparative term like "Croesus", to denote an apogee of riches. Other wealthy Jewish families appear on the periphery, including one that is able to hook a prince by means of a dowry of a hundred thousand pounds. Thackeray's admiration for Cruikshank's caricatures of Jews leads to collaborative ventures in which Cruikshank's drawings are supplemented by Thackeray's verbal thumb-nail sketches ("a showy black-haired woman with one eye"; "Solomonson, short, with red hair") and by experiments with the notation of a variety of Jewish accents that range from Solomonson's successful adoption of standard English to the sheriff's officer's "Vel denn. Captain Shtubsh". Cruikshank's amusing depictions of what Thackeray calls "a Hebrew look" bring more terrifying images to mind: ". . . the Jew—the dreadful Jew, that Cruikshank drew"—a formulation that recalls Dickens's Fagin along with Shakespeare's vision of the Jew with knife and money-bag, for "This is the Jew / That Shakespeare drew" is, of course, Pope's famous salute to Macklin's performance in *The Merchant of Venice*. Behind Fagin, and behind Shylock, stands what Thackeray saw in the God of the Old Testament—the God who put a knife in Abraham's hand to test his obedience. In "Going to See a Man Hanged—Thackeray's most powerful blast against capital punishment—may be found an uncompromising contrast between Old Testament and New Testament justice, which takes no account of the enlightened social legislation of the Mosaic code or of the way in which Jesus's humane ideas and attitudes are anticipated there.

None of this, however, shakes Thackeray's confidence in the virtues of religious toleration or leads him to advocate a return to a medieval practice of "hunting down" Jews; nor does it make him at all reluctant to show, in one formulation and one image after another, how indelibly the Old Testament, in its King James version, formed part of his cultural heritage.

CHAPTER 3

WANDERING RACE
(1840–1843)

Who ever travelled by steamboat, coach, diligence,
eilwagen, vetturino, mule-back, or sledge without meeting some of the wandering race?

(II, 3)

It was in Paris I saw this man. Where else have I not
seen him? In the Roman Ghetto—at the Gate of
David, in his fathers' once imperial city . . . Enough!
You know his name.

(XVII, 636)

i

In 1840 Thackeray collected some stray pieces together to help
make up his first full-length book in the English language. He
called it *Paris Sketch Book* and assigned it to his alter ego Michael
Angelo Titmarsh, who was named as author on the title page
and who signed the "Dedicatory Letter" to a "M. Aretz"—a
Parisian tailor who had treated him with kindness and generosity
but who is not otherwise known to fame. Thackeray had found the
name "Tidmarsh" vaguely comic when he came across it in a book
("Titmarsh" had even more comic possibilities, of course, if—like
Thackeray—one was given to puns); he combined it with "Michael
Angelo" because the Renaissance figure these names recalled had
not only united the practice of the visual art with literary activities,
but had also shared a physical peculiarity with Thackeray: they
both had a broken nose.

It is once again Titmarsh, then, who signs as author and illustrator of the *Paris Sketch Book*; but the portrait of the author which
adorns the opening chapter—a portly gentleman gazed at by two
wondering urchins—is unmistakably a caricature of Thackeray
himself (ill. 1).

This opening chapter, which describes the boat-journey from
London Bridge to Boulogne, mentions Jews in its very first sen-
tence, as Thackeray transfers onto the larger and more crowded
European stage the wanderers whom the narrator of "A Shabby
Genteel Story" had observed on the steamer that plied between
London and Margate.

Illustration 1

> ... the bell has tolled, and Jews, strangers, people-taking-leave-of-
> their-families, and blackguard boys ... are making a rush for the
> narrow plank which conducts from the paddle-box of the "Emerald"
> steamboat onto the quai ...
>
> (II, 1)

And again, a little later:

> There are, of course, many Jews on board. Who ever travelled by
> coach, diligence, eilwagen, vetturino, mule-back, or sledge, without
> meeting some of the wandering race?
>
> (II, 3)

When Thackeray speaks of "race", he usually means the ramifica-
tions of a family (eg. "the race of Thackeray", LPP I, 322). This
notion could be expanded, as in the passage from the *Paris Sketch
Book* which has just been quoted, to denote an ethnic group, people
believed to be connected by common descent or origin. Disraeli
commonly spoke of the Jews from whom he was descended, and to
whom he still felt himself linked even after his baptism, as a race, or
part of a race, in this sense. In the *Paris Sketch Book* passage Thackeray
adopts Disraeli's usage, without, however, adopting the high valua-

tion which Disraeli had placed on belonging to this particular
branch of the human family; and he combines it with an oblique
reference to the Wandering Jew, who was rapidly becoming a
generally recognized symbol for the whole of post-exilic Jewry.
This is the only instance in the *Paris Sketch Book* in which Titmarsh
speaks of "race" in this Disraelian way; elsewhere we find him
speaking of the "foolish race" of all mankind (II, 46); of Napoleon's
"race" (II, 136)—meaning his family, and the dynasty he hoped to
found; of "simple legends . . . handed down by the people, from
race to race" (II, 308—meaning "from generation to generation"
as well as across ethnic and national boundaries); and of the "blind
race" of modern painters whose ambition takes them away from
quotidian reality in pursuit of opportunities to exhibit their "genius" in a great 'historical picture'" (II, 54).

A little later this opening chapter of the *Paris Sketch Book* homes in
on one representative figure: "The Jewish gentleman, who has been
so attentive to the milliner during the journey, and is a traveller
and bagman by profession, gathers together his various goods" (II,
8). Whether such attentiveness is due to professional interest (the
goods in which the bagman deals may well appeal to a milliner),
flirtatiousness, the natural courtesy of a gentleman, or perhaps a
mixture of all three, the reader must decide for himself. We lose
sight of the bagman in the disembarking crowd; but in Paris one of
his English co-religionists, who practises a profession familiar, by
now, from Thackeray's writings, is seen hobnobbing with the
highest, and the most respectable, of his Christian fellow-
countrymen. "The last time we dined at 'Meurice's'", Titmarsh
tells us, towards the end of this opening chapter, "we hobbed and
nobbed with no less a person than Mr. Moses, the celebrated bailiff
of Chancery Lane; Lord Brougham was on his right, and a clergyman's lady, with a train of white-haired girls, sat on his left,
wonderfully taken with the diamond rings of the fascinating stranger" (II, 12). Titmarsh's caricature of the bailiff's flashy finery, and
the fascination it exerts on these well-brought-up girls, is good-
natured; he makes his readers feel that he was by no means
uncomfortable in the mixed company he describes. On the contrary: meeting Mr Moses in such circumstances is a pleasurable
diversion delightfully different from a forced encounter in Cursitor
Street. A later piece ("The Fêtes of July, in a letter to the Editor of
the 'Bungay Beacon'", dated "Paris, July 30th, 1839") even allows
a glance into a Jewish house of prayer.

> Today (Saturday), funeral ceremonies, in honour of the victims of July,
> were held in the various edifices consecrated to public worship . . . The

> Synagogue of the Israelites was entirely hung with black; and a great concourse of people attended. The service was performed with the greatest pomp.
>
> (II, 34–5)

This passage is translated from an unnamed French source, however; there is no evidence that either Titmarsh or his creator had ever witnessed a synagogue service, in Paris or anywhere else. What is more, Titmarsh clearly regards his French sources as sycophantic stuff worthy of being treated with withering sarcasm and scorn—a scorn heightened by the parody of Genesis with which he opens his commentary.

> And the evening and the morning were the first day.
> There's nothing serious in mortality: is there, from the beginning of this account to the end thereof, aught but sheer, open, monstrous, undisguised humbug? I said, before, that you should have a history of these people by Dickens or Theodore Hook, but there is little need of professed wags;—do not the men write their own tale with an admirable Sancho-like gravity and naïveté, which one could not desire improved? How good is that touch of sly indignation about the *little catafalques!* how rich the contrast presented by the economy of the Catholics to the splendid disregard of expense exhibited by the devout Jews! and how touching the *"apologetical discourses* on the Revolution," delivered by the Protestant pastors!
>
> (II, 36)

That Jews should be solemnly presented as exhibiting "splendid disregard of expense" seems to Titmarsh part of the humbug he associates with the France of Louis Philippe.

One Jew who might well have been thought capable of such disregard is Baron James Rothschild, the head of the Paris house who had become, after the death of his brother Nathan, the leading spirit of the famous family. It is no wonder, therefore, that in Paris Titmarsh's thoughts should, once again, turn to the Rothschilds. In the essay "On the French School of Painting" we hear of "a palace which all the money of the Rothschilds could not buy" (II, 54); and the particularly important piece on "Caricature and Lithography in Paris" asks, rhetorically, "whether *all* the persons whose names figure at the head of announcements of projected companies [in England] are as rich as Rothschild or quite as honest as heart could desire." (II, 188) Thackeray's letters of this period introduce the Rothschilds, not just as a thermometer of riches, but also as a by-word for rock-solidity: the writer clearly does not believe in the possibilities he describes when he says that "Mr. Rothschild might want a shilling if the bank broke, or the Duke of Devonshire be begging for a dinner if there were a revolution . . ." (to Mrs.

Carmichael-Smyth, April 1841—LPP, II, 18–19). In Thackeray's England, the Rothschilds and the Dukes of Devonshire are equally solid and equally safe.

The *Paris Sketch Book* introduces English readers to a figure that had become familiar to Frenchmen of Thackeray's generation through Daumier's *Caricaturiana* and through theatrical performances starring the actor Frédéric Lemaître: the swindler and confidence trickster Robert Macaire, to whom Titmarsh gives a dubious—and presumably Jewish—associate who calls herself "Mdlle. Eloa de Wormspire" (II, 191). This Balzacian figure is joined elsewhere in the *Sketch Book* by a more ancient stereotype; in "The Painter's Bargain" the imp Diabolus, offering a diabolic contract, tells his intended victim: "I ask the easiest interest in the world: old Mordecai, the usurer, has made you pay twice as heavily before now . . ." (II, 65). The old association of devil and usurer here serves to conjure up the atmosphere of medieval superstition the story demands. A more modern colouring, however, is introduced by another Jewish figure flashed onto the reader's consciousness when Gambouge, the painter of the title, appropriates a meal originally ordered by "old Simon, the Jew dandy, who was mad after an opera girl, and lived on the floor beneath" (II, 66). That transposes into a Parisian theatrical setting an image of "the Jew Protector" familiar from Plate II of Hogarth's *A Harlot's Progress*. "The Devil's Wager", a later story also centering on a diabolic bargain, again introduces the Jew as lover, though this time the social positions are different. The Comte de Chauchigny, we learn, has hanged one of the lovers taken by his niece, the Lady Mathilde, but has spared another who, the Devil tells him,

> will assassinate your successor, the lady Mathilde's brother; and, in consequence, will be hanged. In the love of the lady he will be succeeded by a gardener, who will be replaced by a monk, who will give way to an ostler, who will be deposed by a Jew pedlar, who shall, finally, yield to a noble earl, the future husband of the fair Mathilde. So that, you see, instead of having one poor soul afrying, we may now look forward to a goodly harvest for our lord the Devil.
>
> (II, 217)

Here the amorous "Jew Pedlar"—familiar from English cartoons with such titles as "Moses in the Bulrushes"—forms but one *bonne bouche* in the banquet of lovers of varying provenance to which noble Lady treats herself.

Among other tales drawn from contemporary French sources Titmarsh retells and elaborates a Hoffmannesque story about a grotesque dwarf made the subject of practical jokes by friends who play on his vanity and credulity. One of these jokes involve introducing the eponymous hero of this tale, "Little Poinsinet", to a pretended miracle-worker, "a man who understood a little of the noble art of conjuring, and performed some clever tricks on the cards." (II, 205). He is presented to the credulous Poinsinet as a kind of Cagliostro:

> you will hear that man—that wonderful man—called by a name which is not his; he is a Portuguese Jew, a Rosicrucian, and Cabalist of the first order, and compelled to leave Lisbon for fear of the Inquisition . . .
>
> (II, 205)

The tricks this "Portuguese enchanter" plays on Poinsinet are made possible by the covert co-operation of the little man's friends; and whether we are really meant to take him for a Jew named Acosta (a famous name in the history of the Sephardic branch of Judaism), or whether he assumes that identity in order to make his victim believe in his command of cabalistic magic, Thackeray's adaptation of his French source does not reveal.

A story of the robber Cartouche, which Thackeray had encountered in France, fascinated him because of its double "rook-and-pigeon" theme, and he therefore retells it in the *Paris Sketch Book*. It concerns a confidence trick by means of which a womam tries to inveigle Cartouche, whom she takes for the immensely rich Comte de Griche, into marriage. She brings into the room where the marriage contract is to be signed a number of witnesses whom she presents as her respectable relatives, "persons of the *finance* or the *robe*", including the president of the court of Arras. Before the contract is signed, however, one of Cartouche's associates whispers to him:

> Captain, do you know who the president of the court of Arras, yonder, is? It is old Manasseh, the fence, of Brussels. I pawned a gold watch to him, which I stole from Cadogen, when I was with Malbrook's army in Flanders.
>
> (II, 91)

The other witnesses turn out to be equally far from what they pretend to be, but none of them is identified as Jewish. The Jewish fence is only a minor player in a cozening game planned and executed by a pack of Gentile rogues; he seems a more harmless character than his confrère in "The Painter's Bargain", about whom there are no suggestions of Jewishness and who combines fencing with blackmail of his suppliers: "Will you have half the money?—Speak, or I'll peach" (II, 67–8).

In the course of the *Paris Sketch Book* Thackeray refers repeatedly to what he calls "Catholic reaction" in France; a fashion like other French fashions, in his view, but one that had significant repercussions in the repertoire of the Parisian theatre. In a piece entitled "French Dramas and Melodramas" he writes:

> As, in this happy country, fashion is everything, we have had not merely Catholic pictures and quasi religious books, but a number of Catholic plays have been produced, very edifying to the frequenters of the theatres or the Boulevards, who have learned more about religion from these performances than they have acquired, no doubt, in the whole of their lives before. In the course of a very few years we have seen—*The Wandering Jew*; *Belshazzar's Feast*; *Nebuchadnezzar*; and the *Massacre of the Innocents*; *Joseph and his Brethren*; *The Passage of the Red Sea*; and *The Deluge*.
>
> (II, 293)

The subjects of all but two of the plays here adduced to demonstrate "Catholic reaction" derive from the Old Testament; and of the two exceptions one is based on that legend of the Wandering Jew which fascinated the whole of Europe even before Eugène Sue's *Le Juif errant* made it the starting point of one of the nineteenth century's most sensational best sellers.

Some of the ways in which figures from Biblical history were presented on the French stage strike Titmarsh as distinctly grotesque:

> In the Festin de Balthasar, we are . . . introduced to Daniel, and the first scene is laid by the waters of Babylon, where a certain number of captive Jews are seated in melancholy postures; a Babylonian officer enters, exclaiming, "Chantez nous quelques chansons de Jerusalem," and the request is refused in the language of the Psalm. Belshazzar's Feast is given in a grand tableau, after Martin's picture. That painter, in like manner, furnished scenes for the *Deluge*. Vast numbers of schoolboys and children are brought to see these pieces; the lower classes delight in them. The famous *Juif Errant*, at the theatre of the Porte St. Martin, was the first of the kind, and its prodigious succcss, no doubt, occasioned the number of imitations which the other theatres have produced.
>
> The taste of such exhibitions, of course, every English person will question; but we must remember the manners of the people among whom they are popular; and, if I may be allowed to hazard such an opinion, there is, in every one of these Boulevard mysteries, a kind of rude moral. The Boulevard writers don't pretend to "tabernacles" and divine gifts, like Madame Sand and Dumas before mentioned. If they take a story from the sacred books, they garble it without mercy, and take sad liberties with the text; but they do not deal in descriptions of the agreeably wicked, or ask pity and admiration for tender-hearted criminals and philanthropic murderers, as their betters do.
>
> (II, 302–5)

Thackeray is here reusing a description he had already vouchsafed
to the readers of the short-lived *National Standard*. The exchange
between the Babylonian officer and the captive Jews continued to
afford him amusement, and we have contemporary testimony that
he delighted in guying it. Major Frank Dwyer recalled in later
years how in 1842, at Temlogue, Thackeray

> came out with a strong bit of humorous representation, which con-
> vulsed us with laughter. It had reference to some drama or opera, I
> forget what, in which the principal male character comes on the stage
> with a pirouette, and waving his hand in a majestic manner to a
> chorus representing Jews in exile at Babylon, says, 'Chantez nous
> une chanson de Jérusalem.' Thackeray rose from his seat and did the
> thing, pirouette and all, most inimitably: by the way, he was fond of
> exhibiting his French pronunciation, also of caricaturing very clev-
> erly that of his own countrymen.
>
> (IR, I, 66)

Fun poked at pseudo-Jewish accents and movements is here robbed
of any sting it might have had by being joined to equal fun at the
expense of Frenchmen and true-blooded Englishmen.

Since much of the *Paris Sketch Book* is concerned with theatrical
representations of one sort or another, it is not surprising that it
contains an impression of the Jewish actress Rachel Félix, who was
then at the height of her fame. Thackeray himself, it seems, had not
at that time seen her in any of the performances of classical French
tragedy which had made her reputation. He had watched her only
in what he thought "an atrocious piece called Marie Stuart; she
made the most . . . of that unfortunate but deservedly decapitated
sovereign." (to Mrs. Procter, 28 May–5 June 1841—LPP, II, 23).
Titmarsh, however, does appear to have seen Rachel (the most
celebrated *belle Juive* or *belle-laide Juive* of the day) in classical
tragedy; that, at least, is the impression conveyed by the very
beginning of the piece on "French Dramas and Melodramas" from
which I have already quoted, where France's "old classical drama"
is declared "well-nigh dead, and full time too: old tragedies, in
which half-a-dozen characters appear, and spout sonorous Alexan-
drines for half-a-dozen hours":

> The fair Rachel has been trying to revive this *genre*, and to untomb
> Racine; but be not alarmed, Racine will never come to life again, and
> cause audiences to weep as of yore. Madame Rachel can only
> galvanize the corpse, not revivify it. Ancient French tragedy, red-
> heeled, patched, and be-periwigged, lies in the grave; and it is only
> the ghost of it that we see, which the fair Jewess has raised.
>
> (II, 291)

"The fair Rachel", "the fair Jewess"—Titmarsh is clearly impressed by her appearance and bearing, which he later pronounces difficult to depict: a portrait of Rachel by Chalon is judged "quite curious for its cleverness and unlikeness." (II, 578). But however fascinating he may have found Rachel herself, Thackeray, like his Titmarsh, never learnt to relish the classical French tragedies to whose performance she dedicated so much of her public life. In this as in other respects, he resembled Heinrich Heine, who was living in Paris at the same time as Thackeray. The two men never met; but the *Paris Sketch Book* affords further evidence that Thackeray knew Heine's work, and that he read it in French rather than German. Titmarsh presents Heine as one of the godfathers of a pantheistic "French party" that seeks to supersede Christianity. Though out of sympathy with this Saint-Simonian movement of thought and feeling, he calls Heine "a great genius" and quotes from the French version of *Zur Geschichte der Religion und Philosophie in Deutschland* which appeared in the *Revue des deux mondes* under the title "De l'Allemagne depuis Luther" (November–December 1834): "'Dieu est mort', says another writer of the same class, and a great genius too.—'Dieu est mort' writes Mr. Henry Heine, speaking of the Christian God; and he adds, in a daring figure of speech,— 'N'entendez-vous pas sonner la clochette?'" (II, 231). Titmarsh may be out of sympathy with the "French party" that counted Heine among its adherents for a short while; but he cannot conceal his respect for powerful qualities of his prose which even translation cannot muffle.

The quotation from Heine forms part of an essay entitled "Madame Sand and the New Apocalypse" in which Titmarsh examines a work of fiction whose central protagonist begins life as an Austrian Jew, passes through Protestantism and Catholicism, and after enduring a "dark night of the soul" embraces a new pantheistic faith akin to that of the Saint-Simonians. The work in question is George Sand's *Spiridion*, of which Titmarsh says:

> For anything he learned, Samuel-Peter-Spiridion-Hebronius might have remained a Jew from the beginning to the end. Wherefore be in such a hurry to set up new faiths? Wherefore, Madame Sand, try and be so preternaturally wise? Wherefore be so eager to jump out of one religion, for the purpose of jumping into another? See what good this philosophical friskiness has done you, and on what sort of ground you are come at last. You are so wonderfully sagacious, that you flounder in mud at every step; so amazingly clear-sighted, that your eyes cannot see an inch before you, having put out, with that extinguishing genius of yours, every one of the lights that are sufficient for the conduct of common men. And for what?
>
> (II, 240–1)

For what indeed? The "Manuscript of Spiridion", in which the erstwhile Samuel has laid down the truth he has discovered (*"the* truth, what a wise Spiridion!"*) is characterized, by Titmarsh, with the words: "Of all the dull, vague, windy documents that mortal eye ever set eyes on, this is the dullest." (II, 243). Titmarsh's conclusion is a thoroughly conservative one:

> It is a pity that this hapless Spiridion, so eager in his passage from one creed to another, and so loud in his profession of the truth, wherever he fancied that he had found it, had not waited a little, before he avowed himself either Catholic or Protestant, and implicated others in errors and follies which might, at least, have been confined to his own bosom, and there have lain comparatively harmless. In what a pretty state, for instance, will Messrs. Dr—d and P—l have left their Newman Street congregation, who are still plunged in their old superstitions, from which their spiritual pastors and masters have been set free! In what a state, too, do Mrs. Sand and her brother and sister philosophers, Templars, Saint Simonians, Fourierites, Lerouxites, or whatever the sect may be, leave the unfortunate people who have listened to their doctrines, and who have not the opportunity, or the fiery versatility of belief, which carries their teachers from one creed to another, leaving only exploded lies and useless recantations behind them! I wish the State would make a law that one individual should not be allowed to preach more than one doctrine in his life; or, at any rate, should be soundly corrected for every change of creed. How many charlatans would have been silenced,—how much conceit would have been kept within bounds,—how many fools, who are dazzled by fine sentences, and made drunk by declamation, would have remained quiet and sober, in that quiet and sober way of faith which their fathers held before them.
>
> (II, 241–2)

In Spiridion's case, that "quiet and sober way of faith" would have been Judaism. Titmarsh, it would seem, and his creator along with him, sets little store by the efforts of the many conversion societies that tried, in Victorian times, to turn Jews into Christians, and even less store by those who tried to formulate new doctrines designed to shake men out of whatever religious faith they had inherited from their fathers. In a passage that greatly disturbed Thackeray's anti-Catholic mother, Titmarsh fulminates against Protestant proselytism, ridiculing the author of tracts like "Father Clement, a Roman Catholic Story" who

> demolishes the stately structure of eighteen centuries, the mighty and beautiful Roman Catholic faith, in whose bosom repose so many saints and sages,—by the means of a three-and-sixpenny duodecimo volume, which tumbles over the vast fabric, as David's pebble-stone did Goliath . . .
>
> (II, 232)

It is once again an image from the Old Testament which helps Thackeray convey his Titmarsh's meaning economically, graphically and poetically.

The Old Testament figure which inspired Thackeray with truest respect was that of Moses; and he found his encounter with Michelangelo's sculpture of the great lawgiver of the Jews (in a replica exhibited in the École des Beaux Arts) an overpowering experience.

> There is the "Moses", the grandest figure ever carved in stone. It has about it something frightfully majestic, if one may so speak. In examining this, and the astonishing picture of "The Judgment", or even a single figure of it, the spectator's sense amounts almost to pain. I would not like to be left in a room alone with the "Moses". How did the artist live amongst them, and create them? How did he suffer the painful labour of invention? One fancies that he would have been scorched up, like Semele, by sights too tremendous for his vision to bear. One cannot imagine him, with our small physical endowments and weaknesses, a man like ourselves.
>
> (II, 48)

The Biblical paintings of Horace Vernet, by contrast, may be violent or pretty—but they have nothing tremendous about them.

> . . . he is so clever a man, that all he does is good to a certain degree. His "Judith" is somewhat violent, perhaps. His "Rebecca" is most pleasing; and not the less for a little pretty affectation of attitude and needless singularity of costume . . .
>
> (II, 51)

Vernet, Thackeray judges, is "clever"—the word recurs three times in six lines; and his readers can hardly have missed the pejorative suggestion such apparent praise contains. He would never have thought of insisting on Michelangelo's "cleverness" in this way!

An aspect of the story "A Gambler's death", included in the *Paris Sketch Book*, deserves some notice in the context of the present book. This tale, not culled from a French source but based on an incident in Thackeray's own life, shows its narrator meeting up again with an old schoolfriend, Jack Attwood, and being appalled by the vulgarity of his appearance: "His hair was dripping with oil; his hands were covered with rings . . ." (II, 115) A few years later he encounters him once more. Attwood is now wearing "a greasy well-cut coat, with a shabby hat cocked on one side of his dirty face . . . he thrust a great greasy hand across the table . . . a dirty fist . . . [clutched] greasy, dusky bank notes . . ." (II, 117–118). Attwood is an Englishman of undoubtedly Gentile ancestry, who has received a gentleman's education at C- (Charterhouse) and has held a commission in a cavalry regiment. His greatest passion is gambling—a ruinous passion Thackeray knew all too well from personal experience. Titmarsh's fastidious recoil from Attwood's oily hair, ringed hands, greasy coat and dirty fist should be remembered when Thackeray introduces Jewish characters that fail to meet his standards of hygiene. Some of his descriptions of "sales Juifs" which will be found on later pages are undoubtedly offensive; but when we come to such pages we should remember Attwood and the many other dirty and greasy but undoubtedly Gentile Britons that flit through Thackeray's writings from "Yellowplush" to *Philip*. Conversely, perhaps, one should also recall that when that most sympathetic of observers, George Eliot's Daniel Deronda, first enters Ezra Cohen's shop, he notes that Mrs. Cohen "had that look of having made her toilet with little water, and by twilight"!

Of greater importance for the 'placing' of Thackeray's references to Jews, however, is Titmarsh's constant criticism, in the *Paris Sketch Book*, of French humbug, braggadocio and Robert Macairism in the age of Louis Philippe, and of such English expatriates and travellers as those encountered in Paris and Boulogne:

> Believe me, there is on the face of this world no scamp like an English one, no blackguard like one of these half-gentlemen, so mean, so low, so vulgar,—so ludicrously ignorant and conceited, so desperately heartless and depraved.
>
> (II, 7)

Nowhere, in all the published works, will we find a passage on Jews as unequivocally condemnatory as this attack on Gentile Englishmen. There are, of course, more complimentary passages to offset such indictments: descriptions of cheerful English travellers and artistically gifted Frenchmen; but nothing could be more unjust than a presentation of Thackeray's references to Jews without siting them in the context of his frequent censure, satire and caricature of the conduct, the taste, and the morals, of French and English men and women amid the Macairism that he finds on one side of the Channel, and "the clank of steam-engines . . . the shouts of politicians . . . the struggle for gain and bread, and the loud denunciations of stupid bigots" (II, 173) that confront him on the other, the English, side.

The *Paris Sketch Book* contains, among its "Imitations of Béranger", a poem entitled "Jolly Jack" whose overt purpose is to show the way to achieve contentment in the midst of political and social strife—and one of the chief means to this end, it turns out, is religious toleration (VII, 128). Jews are not specifically mentioned

in this poem; but what Jack proclaims has clear affinities with what
we have just heard Titmarsh say about sensible men who keep to
"that quiet and sober way of faith which their fathers held before
them". Jack himself, we are assured, could never embrace any faith
that obliged him to "see the smiling earth / And think there's hell
hereafter."

Jews do appear, briefly, in some poems of this period which did
not rate inclusion in the *Paris Sketch Book*. In December 1839 *Fraser's
Magazine* published a ballad which renewed that combination of
verse with marginal prose with which Thackeray had experimented
in his early mock prize poem "Timbuctoo", and suffused it with
the manner of R.H. Barham, whose *Ingoldsby Legends* had begun to
appear. Originally entitled "The Great Cossack Epic of Demetrius
Rigmarolovicz", "The Legend of St. Sophia of Kioff" mocked
traditional stories of a saint "whose statue is said to have walked, of
its own accord, to take its station in the church of Kiew":

> Ding-dong, ding-dong, ding-ding-a-ring-ding,
> The bells they made a merry, merry ring,
> From the tall, tall steeple; and all the
>   people
> (Except the Jews) came and filled the pews—
>   Poles, Russians and Germans,
>   To hear the sermons
> Which Hyacinth preached to those Germans and Poles,
>   For the safety of their souls.
>
> (VII, 75)

The context hardly suggests that the Jews are to be blamed for
absenting themselves from worship in a Russian Orthodox church.
More significant is a poem published just two years later, in
December 1841, in Cruikshank's *Omnibus*. "The King of Brent-
ford's Testament. By Michael Angelo Titmarsh", tells an inverted
Sandford and Merton story in which we are made to sympathize
with the improvident Ned rather than the prudent Tom:

> While Tom frequents his banker,
> Young Ned frequents the Jews.
>
> (VII, 17)

"The Jews", of course, are money-lenders; but what makes the
poem so significant in our context is that the Gentile Tom is as
ready to lend out money at high interest as any Jew—or, indeed, as
Thackeray himself in his bill-discounting days.

> . . . Young Thomas lent at interest
> And nobly took his twenty-five per cent.
>
> (VII, 22)

This shows again how important it is to look at Thackeray's Jews, not in isolation, but in the wider context he has himself so carefully and deliberately provided.

Another work of 1841, one of Thackeray's most accomplished essays, can help provide such a context. *The Second Funeral of Napoleon, in Three Letters to Miss Smith, of London, by Mr. M.A. Titmarsh* speculates on what it is that makes the "gentleman"; and while Titmarsh readily admits that "nature's gentlemen" do exist—"a few here and there"—he believes that far more gentlemen are made by art and good fortune than by nature.

> Good birth, that is, good, handsome, well-formed fathers and mothers, nice cleanly nursery maids, good meals, good physicians, good education, few cares, pleasant easy habits of life, and luxuries not too great or enervating, but only refining—a course of these going on for a few generations are the best gentleman-makers in the world, and beat nature hollow.
>
> (III, 439)

Even if one allows for different judgments of what is "handsome" and "good", the majority of Jews Titmarsh might encounter in the London of 1841 was hardly likely to have enjoyed the advantages which make for the gentility he here describes.

ii

When Thackeray's next serial narrative ran in *Fraser's Magazines* from September to December 1841, it was found to feature two Titmarshes: Michael Angelo as editor and illustrator, and Samuel as central protagonist. "The History of Samuel Titmarsh and the Great Hoggarty Diamond" is another rook-and-pigeon tale; and since a diamond is involved it was to be expected that Jews, dealers in diamonds and precious stones the world over, would figure in the story. And so, indeed, it turns out. As George Saintsbury has pointed out (IV, xiii), "diddling" here moves onto a larger stage, in the guise of "commercial fraud which, never unknown, was becoming commoner than ever in consequence of the mania for companies." Samuel Titmarsh himself is an honest young clerk drawn into the fashionable world of London's West End by an accidental meeting with an eccentric old lady, who claims a relationship with him on the basis of a diamond ornament given to him by his Irish aunt Hoggarty. He works for a bubble company symbolically named "The Independent West Diddlesex Fire and Life Insurance Company" run by a swindler named John Brough who never tires of referring to his country-house, significantly named "The Rookery", as "a happy, humble, Christian home."

The men at the head of this and other bubble companies are all professing Christians—as are Aunt Hoggarty and other dislikable characters, including a dissenting clergyman convicted of fraud who ends up on the bottle after marrying the odious aunt for her money. The tale does introduce a few sympathetic characters: Sam Titmarsh himself, his sweet-natured wife, and some members—by no means all!—of the aristocratic family that befriends him when he first sports the Hoggarty diamond, and then offers him employment after the diamond, and all Sam's savings, have lost in the Diddlesex Company's inevitable crash.

The England in which the Jewish characters of "The Great Hoggarty Diamond" have to make their way is animated by greed and selfishness, in which men mouth words of Christian charity while worshipping Mammon and ruthlessly ruining those who trust them. Among those who learn these lessons from their masters is a young clerk in the West Diddlesex Company whom we first meet as the managing director's yes-man and informer and who is marked out as a Jew by the name "Abednego". Abednego's father, we learn, is "a mock-jewel and gold-lace merchant in Hanway yard" (IV, 28), and when Sam Titmarsh becomes an object of his young fellow-clerks' flattering attention by reason of his possession of the Hoggarty diamond and his newly acquired aristocratic friends, Abednego informs him that "the jewel was worth at least ten poundsh, and that his governor would give me as much for it"—a speech which makes the other clerks hazard a guess that "Tit's diamond is worth at least thirty" (IV, 45). It is noteworthy that before this scene Abednego had spoken impeccable English; but now, all of a sudden, when pricing the diamond below its worth, he is made to use the distorted forms ("poundsh") that Thackeray uses, on occasions, to suggest "Jewish" speech.

Young Abednego—we soon learn that his given name is Moses—makes himself a news-gatherer on behalf of his chief, who also uses him as the Diddlesex Company's maid of all work; and he rises in rank and salary as more respectable members of the firm prudently get out. Just before the inevitable crash he advances to head clerk: but when the crash comes, he moves into the background while his father, hitherto a shadowy presence in his Hanway Yard shop, moves forward along with associates whose names Thackeray derives, like that of Abednego, from the Book of Daniel.

> Not only did Roundhand leave, but Highmore went away. Abednego became head clerk: and one day old Abednego came to the place, and was shown into the directors' private room; when he left it, he came trembling, chattering, and cursing downstairs; and had begun,

'Shentlemen—' a speech to the very clerks in the office; when Mr.
Brough with an imploring look, and crying out, 'Stop till Saturday!'
at length got him into the street.

On Saturday, Abednego junior left the office for ever and I became
head clerk with 400l. a year salary. It was fatal week for the office,
too. On Monday when I arrived and took my seat at the head desk,
and my first read of the newspaper, as was my right, the first thing I
read was, 'Frightful fire in Houndsditch! Total destruction of Mr.
Meshach's sealing-wax manufactory, and of Mr. Shadrach's adjoin-
ing clothing dépôt. In the former was 20,000l. worth of the finest
Dutch wax, which the voracious element attacked and devoured in a
twinkling. The latter estimable gentleman had just completed 40,000
suits of clothes for the cavalry of H.H. the Cacique of Poyais.'
Both of these Jewish gents, who were connexions of Mr. Abednego,
were insured in our office to the full amount of their loss. The
calamity was attributed to the drunkenness of a scoundrelly Irish
watchman, who was employed on the premises, and who upset a
bottle of whisky in the warehouse of Messrs. Shadrach, and incau-
tiously looked for the liquor with a lighted candle. The man was
brought to our office by his employers; and certainly, as we all could
testify, was *even then* in a state of frightful intoxication.

(IV, 99–100)

Titmarsh calls these suspicious conflagrations "the Jewish fires";
but Thackeray is careful, once again, to put them into perspective:

The Jewish fires were the heaviest blows we had had; for though the
Waddingley Cotton-mills had been burnt in 1822, at a loss to the
Company of 80,000l., and though the Patent Erostratus Match
Manufactory had exploded in the same year at a charge of 14,000l.,
there were those who said that the loss had not been near so heavy as
was supposed—nay, that the Company had burnt the above-named
establishments as advertisements for themselves. Of these facts I
can't be positive, having never seen the early accounts of the concern.

(IV, 100)

There is nothing to suggest that the Patent Erostratus Match
Manufactory (how good Thackeray is at creating these ominous
names!) is not run by Christians as respectable as those who run
the Independent West Diddlesex Fire and Life Insurance Company. Nor do Shadrach and Meshach get away with anything; in
court

the two gentlemen from Houndsditch were present to swear to their
debts, and made a sad noise, and uttered a vast number of oaths in
attestation of their claim. But Messrs. Jackson and Paxton produced
against them that very Irish porter who was said to have been the
cause of the fire, and I am told hinted that they had matter for
hanging the Jewish gents if they persisted in their demand. On this
they disappeared altogether, and no more was ever heard of their
losses.

(IV, 114)

The financial connection of Old Abednego with the West Diddlesex Company—among whose directors he had figured alongside Mr Mull, General Sir Dionysius O'Halloran, Mr Macraw, M.P., Q.C., Mr Manstraw and Mr Shirk, none of whom is ever likely to have any connections with the synagogue—remains obscure.

When the Diddlesex Company collapses, Sam Titmarsh is left to face the music, and is arrested by (who else?) Mr Aminadab the Sheriff's Officer, who carries him away to his lock-up off Chancery Lane, at which we now take a harder look than in any previous Thackeray fiction.

> The house before which the coach stopped seemed to be only one of half a dozen in that street which were used for the same purpose. No man, be he ever so rich, can pass by those dismal houses, I think, without a shudder. The front windows are barred, and on the dingy pillar of the door was a shining brass plate, setting forth that "Aminadab, Officer to the Sheriff of Middlesex,' lived therein. A little red-haired Israelite opened the first door as our coach drove up, and received me and my baggage.
>
> As soon as we entered the door, he barred it, and I found myself in the face of another huge door, which was strongly locked; and, at last, passing through that, we entered the lobby of the house.

Here Thackeray is entering into competition with Dickens, who had introduced the same Cursitor Street establishment into one of the *Sketches by Boz* (1836): the one entitled "A Passage in the Life of Mr. Watkins Tottle". Dickens's description begins as follows:

> At length Mr. Gabriel Parsons turned into Chancery Lane, and having enquired for, and been directed to, Cursitor-street (for it was a locality of which he was quite ignorant), he soon found himself opposite the house of Mr. Solomon Jacobs. Confiding his horse and gig to the care of one of the fourteen boys who had followed him from the other side of Blackfriars-bridge on the chance of his requiring their services, Mr. Gabriel Parsons crossed the road and knocked at an inner door, the upper part of which was of glass, grated like the windows of this inviting mansion with iron bars—painted white to look comfortable.
>
> The knock was answered by a sallow-faced red-haired sulky boy, who, after surveying Mr. Gabriel Parsons through the glass applied a large key to an immense wooden excrescence, which was in reality a lock, but which, taken in conjunction with the iron nails with which the panels were studded, gave the door the appearance of being subject to warts.
>
> "I want to see Mr. Watkins Tottle," said Parsons.
>
> "It's the gentleman that come in this morning, Jem," screamed a voice from the top of the kitchen-stairs, which belonged to a dirty woman who had just brought her chin to a level with the passage-floor. "The gentleman's in the coffee-room."

What renders this so unmistakably Dickensian is the fantastic, anthropomorphizing description of the front door, whose lock, "an immense excrescence", makes the door appear subject to warts. Thackeray is more sparing than Dickens with anthropomorphizations of this kind, which he professed to dislike; but they do, occasionally, occur in his work too. The house at 120 Fitzroy Square, which we shall see Sherrick leasing to Colonel Newcome, has a "moaning" cistern and a front-door that bears the "scar" left by a previous tenant's brass plate. That tenant was one Madame Latour, whose care-worn face, made more ghastly by rouge, is reflected in the appearance of the house she had occupied when it has received a lick of paint. (cf. John Carey, *Thackeray: Prodigal Genius*, London 1977, p. 131). In "The Great Hoggarty Diamond", Dickens's evocations of the interior and exterior of the sponging-house, as well as his characterizations of its voluntary and involuntary inhabitants, are matched remarkably closely. They had a common model, of course; the house in Cursitor Street actually existed, and was run for a time by a Jewish family named Sloman. "There is no need to describe it", Thackeray makes his Titmarsh continue;

> It is very like ten thousand other houses in our dark city of London. There was a dirty passage and a dirty stair, and from the passage two dirty doors let into two filthy rooms, which had strong bars at the windows, and yet withal an air of horrible finery that makes me uncomfortable to think of even yet. On the walls hung all sorts of trumpery pictures in tawdry frames (how different from those capital performances of my cousin Michael Angelo!); on the mantelpiece, huge French clocks, vases, and candlesticks; on the sideboards, enormous trays of Birmingham plated-ware; for Mr. Aminadab not only arrested those who could not pay money, but lent it to those who could; and had already, in the way of trade, sold and bought these articles many times over.
>   I agreed to take the back-parlour for the night, and while a Hebrew damsel was arranging a little dusky sofa-bedstead (woe betide him who has to sleep on it!) I was invited into the front parlour, where Mr. Aminadab, bidding me take heart, told me I should have a dinner for nothing with a party who had just arrived.
>
>   (IV, 104–5)

Though to the shocked Titmarsh Aminadab seems a "grinning wretch", it soon appears that he is not unkindly; he spares Sam what shame he can by keeping shut the windows of the coach in which the debtor is conveyed to Cursitor Street and sees to it that he has dinner at someone else's expense on his first night. Titmarsh's description, though understandably unconcerned with his gaoler's feelings, brings home forcibly the depressing surroundings

in which such bailiffs had to bring up their families—here represented by "a little red-haired Israelite" and a "Hebrew damsel". A
later scene introduces another depressing feature of the house in
Cursitor Street: a courtyard railed in atop like a cage, with great
iron bars, beneath which "Mr. Aminadab's jailbirds took the air."
(IV, 108). The new life Thackeray here manages to give to the
apparently so dead metaphor of "jailbirds" is highly characteristic
of his best writing. His Aminadab family, like that of Solomon
Jacobs in *Sketches by Boz*, does not spend much time or money on
keeping its depressing quarters clean; but the Aminadabs make
themselves as comfortable as their income (supplemented by pawn-
broking on the side) will allow. It is no surprise, therefore, to
discover Mr Aminadab "in a room blazing with gilt lamps",
drinking claret in the company of Mr Jehoshaphat, "another rich
gentleman of his trade and religious persuasion", and a non-Jewish
sherriff's officer, a Mr Lock from Brighton. They are "rich" in the
impoverished Sam Titmarsh's eyes, of course, but might not seem
so to a more affluent observer.

The presence of Mr Lock is characteristic—Thackeray conti-
nually makes sure that his readers understand his Jews to have
Gentile colleagues who are no better and no worse. "Chirping as
merrily and [looking] as respectable as any noblemen in the land"
the three of them invite Sam to join their potations; and it soon
appears that they are all under the false impression that Sam has
secretly salted away some of the money that ought to have gone to
the bankrupt West Diddlesex's creditors.

> 'A deep file,' said Aminadab, winking and pointing me out to his
> friend Mr. Jehoshaphat.
> 'A good one,' says Jehoshaphat.
> 'In for three hundred thousand pound,' says Aminadab; 'Brough's
> right-hand man, and only three-and-twenty.'
> 'Mr. Titmarsh, sir, your 'ealth, sir,' says Mr. Lock, in an ecstasy of
> admiration. 'Your very good 'ealth, sir, and better luck to you next
> time.'
> 'Pooh, pooh! he's all right,' says Aminadab; 'let him alone.'
> 'In for *what?*' shouted I, quite amazed. 'Why, sir, you arrested me
> for 90l.'
> 'Yes, but you are in for half a million,—you know you are. *Them*
> debts I don't count—them paltry tradesmen's accounts. I mean
> Brough's business. It's an ugly one; but you'll get through it. We all
> know you; and I lay my life that when you come through the court,
> Mrs. Titmarsh has got a handsome thing laid by.'
> 'Mrs. Titmarsh has a small property, sir,' says I. 'What then?'
> The three gentlemen burst into a loud laugh, said I was a 'rum
> chap'—a 'downy cove,' and made other remarks which I could not
> understand then.
>
> (IV, 107)

Mr Lock, we see, expresses his admiration in much the same terms
as the other two; nothing, at this point, differentiates his idiom from
that of his Jewish companions. This changes with the entrance of
Sam's friend Gus, who now joins a party that also includes Mr B.-,
one of Sam's fellow-prisoners. Gus has not had opportunities to
drink Burgundy before—he calls it "Bergamy" and it seems to Sam
that in putting him right Aminadab allows himself a sneer at such
innocence. The "Herr von Joel" named in the passage that follows
was famous for his barn-yard and bird imitations; Thackeray had
heard him perform at Evans's supper club.

> It was in the midst of this conversation that, as I said, Gus came in;
> and whew! when he saw what was going on, he gave *such* a whistle!
>   'Herr von Joel, by Jove!' says Aminadab. At which all laughed.
>   'Sit down,' says Mr. B.,—'sit down, and wet you whistle, my piper!
> I say, egad! you're the piper that played before Moses! Had you
> there, Dab. Dab, get a fresh bottle of Burgundy for Mr. Hoskins.'
> And before he knew where he was, there was Gus for the first time in
> his life drinking Clos Vougeot. Gus said he had never tasted Bergamy
> before, at which the bailiff sneered, and told him the name of the
> wine.
>   '*Old Clo*! What?' says Gus; and we laughed, but the Hebrew gents
> did not this time.
>   'Come, come, sir!' says Mr. Aminadab's friend, 've're all shentle-
> men here, and shentlemen never makish reflexunsh upon other
> shentlemen'sh pershuashunsh.'
>
>   (IV, 107–8)

Young Moses Abednego had also been ribbed about his Jewishness, but had not dared exhibit sensitivity on that score; the Jewish
bailiffs, however, plainly take offense at the reference to "Old Clo"
so soon after Mr. B-'s Old Testament joke, and as they do so, one of
them suddenly drops into conventional "Jew-speak". Is he mocking the image that Gentiles have of Jews? Or has Sam Titmarsh
suddenly become sensitized to differences in speech patterns that
he had earlier ignored? Be that as it may, the atmosphere becomes
less cordial and the parting from Cursitor Street is considerably less
friendly than the arrival had been.

> 'Will you pay my bill, Mr. What-d'ye-call'em?' here cried
> Mr. Aminadab, flinging open the door (he had been consulting with
> Mr. Blatherwick, I suppose)—'I want the room for a *gentleman*. I
> guess it's too dear for the like of you.' And here—will you believe
> it?—the man handed me a bill of three guineas for two days' board
> and lodging in his odious house.

Titmarsh lands in the Fleet, a debtor's prison at which Aminadab
often has to call in the exercise of his profession; but friendly

relations are never restored, and the bailiff fades out of the story "saying that I was a poor-spirited creature, a mere tool in Brough's hand, and had not saved a shilling." (IV, 113). If Aminadab, for all his kindly instincts and conviviality, turns out, in the end, to value men according to the amount of shillings they can salvage for themselves out of other men's financial wreckage, he is, in Thackeray's world, in good Christian company.

We have not yet done, however, with the Jewish interest of this tale of the Great Hoggarty Diamond. Throughout, the name "Rothschild" has once again been invoked, as shorthand not only for a truly rich man but also for a solidly based financial house, a standard by which other institutions are judged. "A man as well known as Mr. Rothschild in the City of London" is the highest recommendation Brough can think of. (IV, 57); and this name of "Rothschild" appears in as strange a context as I have found anywhere in one of Brough's addresses to Samuel, who has now become the head clerk on whose innocent head responsibility for settling the bankrupt company's debts is designed to fall.

> 'Titmarsh, my boy,' said he one day to me, after looking me hard in the face, 'did you ever hear of the fate of the great Mr. Silberschmidt of London?' Of course I had. Mr. Silberschmidt, the Rothschild of his day (indeed I have heard the latter famous gent was originally a clerk in Silberschmidt's house)—Silberschmidt, fancying he could not meet his engagements, committed suicide; and had he lived till four o'clock that day, would have known that he was worth 400,000l. 'To tell you frankly the truth,' says Mr. B., 'I am in Silberschmidt's case.
>
> (IV, 101)

The tale of Silberschmidt is Brough's whistle in the dark, as he feels his financial edifice crashing about his ears; but it has a force and point of its own, showing that Jewish financiers are not omniscient manipulators, that they can miscalculate to their own disadvantage, that they can fatally misinterpret their own situation and achievement.

It would be idle to pretend that the picture of British Jews that Samuel and Michael Angelo present in "The Great Hoggarty Diamond" is a favourable one; but the context in which Thackeray has here placed his Jewish protagonists allows the right reader to understand and to make allowances, and warns him not to be too hasty in supposing the commercial dealings of professing Christians, and even the moral characteristics of a worldly Christian clergyman like Mr. Wapshot, are intrinsically superior to those of the Jews they despise or use as convenient instruments. Samuel Titmarsh himself, on whose testimony we have to rely, does not

escape censure; the reader can only agree with the Bankruptcy
Commissioner who says to Sam: "Look you sir, if you had not been
so eager after gain, you would not have allowed yourself to be
deceived, and you would have kept your relative's money, and
inherited it . . . one day or other. Directly people expect to make a
large interest, their judgment seems to desert them." (IV, 117). In
this atmosphere of greed Jews have to make their way as best they
can; and Thackeray disdains playing the anti-Jewish game of
shifting the blame for that atmosphere onto them.

Michael Angelo Titmarsh does not try, in his illustrations for
"The Great Hoggarty Diamond", to vie with Cruikshank in the
pictorial representation of Jews. We have to make our own mental
picture of the Jewish characters, building on whatever hints Sam
Titmarsh gives us. But when he draws Sam's wife Mary for us,
after she has lost her own baby and won a post as wetnurse for
which another, less loving and sensitive woman had applied, he
lifts his picture into an archetypal realm by giving it a title drawn
from the Old Testament: "The Judgment of Solomon" (ill. 2).

The Old Testament here supplies a parable which illuminates
the meaning of one of the more solemn and serious moments in
Thackeray's tale.

iii

While "The Great Hoggarty Diamond" was still wending its way
through *Fraser's Magazine*, Thackeray had yet another chance to
work with Cruikshank. This time his tale, first published in Cruikshank's *Omnibus* in October 1841, surrounded just a single picture:
but two of the main characters which it presents to us are, once
again, marked out as Jewish (ill. 3).

The story is called "Little Spitz", and subtitled "A Lenten
Anecdote from the German of Professor Spass"; and it turns out to
be the nearest Thackeray has yet come to acquainting his readers
with some of the quaint mechanisms of anti-Jewish prejudice. He
does so in a German setting—indeed, his sub-title suggests that the
little work is a translation from the writings of a German professor
whose name signifies "joke"; but the name of the central character—
Lorenzo, "Signior Lorenzo", or "Signior Lorenz"—deliberately
recalls *The Merchant of Venice*. Like his Shakespearean counterpart,
this Lorenzo has been enchanted by the "beautiful eyes" of a
Jewish maiden, whose name, Rebecca, recalls Scott's *Ivanhoe* as
forcibly as Lorenzo recalls Shakespeare's play. Unlike Shylock,
however, her father—once again called "Abednego"—is willing to
accompany his daughter to the house of Christians and partake of

The Judgment of Solomon

Illustration 2

Illustration 3

food there. Indeed, the plot is set in motion by Rebecca's longing for a delicacy sold by a Christian master butcher of the town of Krähwinkel in which all the characters live.

> 'I THINK,' said Rebecca, flinging down her beautiful eyes to the ground, and heaving a great sigh,—'I think, Signor Lorenzo, I could eat a bit of—sausage.'
>
> 'Of *what?*' said Lorenzo, bouncing up and forgetting all sense of politeness in the strange demand. 'My dearest madam, *you* eat a sausage?'
>
> 'Ha, ha, I'm blesht,' shouted Abednego, Rebecca's papa, 'I'm blesht, if Signor Lorenz does not think you want to eat the unclean animal, Rebecca, my soul's darling. These shtudents are dull fellows, look you, and only know what's in their books. Why, there are in dis vicked vorld no less than four hundred kindsh of shausages, Signor Lorenz, of which Herr Bürcke, the court butcher, will show you the resheipts.—Confess, now, you thought my darling wanted to eat pig—faugh!'

The speech of two Jewish generations is sharply differentiated here: while Rebecca's differs in no way from that of her Christian swain, Abednego's once again has all the features of what readers had learnt to accept as "Jew-speak" in Thackeray's fiction. Every wish of what the story calls "the fair Jewess" and "the lovely Israelite" is her Lorenzo's command:

> Lorenz opened his window, looked into his little garden, whistled, and shouted out: 'Hallo! *Spitz!*'
>
> 'Now,' said he, 'you shall see my familiar;' and a great scratching and whining was presently heard at the door, which made Rebecca wonder, and poor old fat Abednego turn as yellow as a parsnip. I warrant the old wretch thought that a demon with horns and a tail was coming into the room.
>
> (IV, 104)

The familiar spirit, of course, is a dog, who is sent out with a note to the court butcher demanding beef-sausages; but poor, superstitious, parsnip-yellow Abednego is clearly no super-Jew, even though he is a banker, commands a factotum of all work called Israel Löwe (a name Thackeray may well have found in Heine's *Pictures of Travel*), and runs a carriage he had taken in settlement of a bad debt. While the dog is out on his errand, we are told how the three characters encountered at the opening had come together. Thackeray has a good deal of fun here with the medieval attitudes of Professor Spass, whose German narrative he pretends to be translating.

> Lorenzo was allowed a handsome income of a hundred rix-dollars per year by his parents, and used to draw this at the house of Mr. Abednego, the banker. One day, when he went to cash a draft for five

dollars, the lovely Miss Rebecca Abednego chanced to be in the
room. Ah, Lorenzo, Lorenzo! better for you to have remained at
home studying the Pons Asinorum; better still for you to have been at
church listening to the soul-stirring discourses of Father Windbeutel;
better for you to have been less learned and more pious: then you
would not have been so likely to go astray, or allow your fancy to be
inflamed by the charms of wicked Jewesses, that all Christian men
should shun like poison. Here it was Lent season—a holiday in Lent,
and Lorenzo von Tisch knew nothing about the matter, and Rebecca
Abednego and her father were absolutely come to breakfast with him!

                                                           (IV, 156)

"Windbeutel" signifies "windbag", and tells us something of the
preacher whose teachings Spass so earnestly commends. He turns
up again, *in absentia* as it were, in a passage that describes the court
butcher's wife watching Abednego and his daughter driving out to
keep their appointment with Lorenzo—a passage which acquaints
us further, by means of Thackeray's well-known method of adding
successive little touches in the course of a narrative that gradually
build up our impression of a character, with the attractions of the
belle juive Rebecca. It also mocks anti-Jewish prejudice by having it
extended to a horse.

> Now, on this day in Lent, it happened that Frau Bürcke was looking
> out of her windows instead of listening at church to Father Wind-
> beutel, and she saw at eleven o'clock Mr. Israel Löwe, Herr Abedne-
> go's valet, porter, coachman, gardener, and cashier, bring round a
> certain chaise that the banker had taken for a bad debt, into which he
> stepped in his best snuff-coloured coat, and silk stockings, handing in
> Miss Rebecca in a neat dress of yellow silk, a blue hat and pink
> feathers, and a pair of red morocco slippers that set off her beautiful
> ankle to advantage.
> 'Odious people!' said Mrs. Bürcke, looking at the pair that Mr.
> Löwe was driving; 'odious, vulgar horse!' (Herr Bürcke kept only
> that one on which his lad rode;) 'Roman-nosed beast! I shouldn't
> wonder but that the horse is a Jew too!'—and she saw the party turn
> down to the left into Bolkum-Strasse, towards the gate which I have
> spoken of before.
> When Madame Bürcke saw this, she instantly flew from her front
> window to her back window, and there had a full view of the Bolkum
> Road, and the Abednego chaise jingling up the same. Mr. Löwe,
> when they came to the hill, got off the box and walked; Mr. Abednego
> sat inside and smoked his pipe.
> '*Ey, du lieber Himmel!*' screamed out Mrs. Bürcke, 'they have
> stopped at the necromancer's door!'

                                                           (IV, 157)

Hating Spitz, who had once bitten her, fearing Lorenzo, whom she
thinks a sorcerer, and hating Jews, Frau Bürcke (whose name is
surely meant to recall the murderer Burke, of Burke and Hare

fame) cuts off poor little Spitz's tail and lays it in his basket instead of the beef sausages that Rebecca, shooting seductive glances from what Professor Spass calls "her great wicked black eyes", had demanded in this Lenten period. She was, the Professor adds, "a sad gormandizer for so young a woman" (IV, 158, 159). Spass then concludes his story:

> What took place during the rest of the entertainment, I have never been able or anxious to learn; but this I know, that there is a single gentleman now living with Madame Konisgunda von Speck, in the beautiful town of Polkwitz, a gentleman, who, if he has one prejudice in the world, has that of hating the Jewish nation—a gentleman who goes to church regularly, and, above all, never eats meat in Lent.
>
> He is followed about by a little dog—a little ugly dog—of which he and Madame Von Speck are outrageously fond; although, between ourselves, the animal's back is provided with no more tail than a cannon-ball.
>
> (IV, 160)

Lorenzo, it would appear, blames Jewish "gormandizing" for the mutilation of his beloved dog effected by the Jew-hating Frau Bürcke. Could any reason for "hating the Jewish nation" be more absurd than this? Is there anywhere, in English literature before the twentieth century, a passage that more effectively derides the irrational prejudice to which Germans were prone even before the advent of Hitler? And are such prejudices confined only to Germany? The pointers towards Shakespeare and Scott which Thackeray embedded in the very names "Lorenzo" and "Rebecca" may well suggest otherwise.

That the story invites a Freudian analysis is patent. I shall not attempt it here, but confine myself to remarking that the cutting off of poor little Spitz's tail and the consequent passage from infatuation with a *belle Juive* to revulsion against her and her whole "nation" make a pattern few amateur psychoanalysts could resist. That Thackeray had anything like this consciously in mind is more than doubtful; but it strengthens the aura of irrationality, of subconscious, hardly acknowledged motivation, which pervades this slight story told by a professor whose name means Joke.

iv

In June 1842 Thackeray introduced the readers of *Fraser's Magazine* to a new persona: George Savage Fitz-Boodle, second son of a baronet, ex-officer of the Lancers, bachelor clubman, gambler, despiser of mere *literati*, lover of a good cigar, a passionate traveller (when he can afford it) who "can order a dinner in every language in Europe", indefatigable raisonneur and story-teller. Among the towns he has visited are Cologne and Bonn; and there, he tells us, he had in his youth been entranced by a *belle Juive*, Minna Löwe, whom even in his later days, after severe disenchantment, he recalls in such terms as these:

> Minna was the most beautiful creature that my eyes ever lighted on. Sneer not, ye Christian maidens; but the fact was so. I saw her for the first time seated at a window covered with golden vine-leaves, with grapes just turning to purple, and tendrils twisting in the most fantastical arabesques. The leaves cast a pretty chequered shadow over her sweet face, and the simple, thin, white muslin gown in which she was dressed. She had bare white arms, and a blue riband confined her little waist. She was knitting, as all German women do, whether of the Jewish sort or otherwise; and in the shadow of the room sat her sister Emma, a powerful woman with a powerful voice. Emma was at the piano, singing, 'Herz, mein Herz, warum so trau-au-rig?'—singing much out of tune.
>
> I had come to change one of Coutts's circulars at Löwe's bank, and was looking for the door of the *caisse*.
>
> '*Links, mein Herr!*' said Minna Löwe, making the gentlest inclination with her pretty little head; and blushing ever so little, and raising up tenderly a pair of heavy blue eyes, and then dropping them again, overcome by the sight of the stranger. . . . 'Links, mein Herr,' said lovely Minna Löwe.
>
> That little word *links* dropped upon my wounded soul like balm. There is nothing in *links*; it is not a pretty word. Minna Löwe simply told me to turn to the left, when I was debating between that side and its opposite, in order to find the cash-room door. Any other person might have said *links* (or *rechts* for that matter), and would not have made the slightest impression upon me; but Minna's full red lips, as they let slip the monosyllable, wore a smile so tender and uttered it with such inconceivable sweetness, that I was overcome at once.
>
> (IV, 223–4—"Fitz-Boodle's Confessions)

The sensuality of these "bare white arms" emerging from a "thin, white muslin gown", "heavy blue eyes" and "full red lips" is palpable; a slight blush and a quick raising and lowering of the eyes add piquancy, while the domestic activity of knitting counteracts a sense of danger. Fitz-Boodle completes his picture by encircling a "little waist" with a blue riband and framing the whole with vine-leaves, grapes just turning purple, and tendrils forming fantastic arabesques. That the powerful voice singing about a sad heart is felt to be "much out of tune" introduces a sobering, anti-sentimental touch and hints at discords to come.

Minna's father, the banker Moses Löwe, we are told in this Fitz-Boodle Paper, was later imprisoned for forgery and fraudulent bankruptcy; and Fitz-Boodle remarks, tantalizingly, that he him-

self was only saved from marrying the Jewish siren by his addiction
to tobacco. We leave Minna, for the present,

> blushing under the vine-leaves positively, whilst I was thanking my
> stars that she never became Mrs. George Fitz-Boodle. And yet who
> knows what thou mightst have become, Minna, had such a lot fallen
> to thee? She was too pretty and innocent-looking to have been by
> nature that artful, intriguing hussy that education made her, and that
> my experience found her. The case was simply this, not a romantical
> one by any means.
>
> (IV, 226)

This takes up a theme already broached by Ikey Solomons junior,
the narrator of *Catherine*: are there innate dispositions to evil which
are bound to lead to evil deeds, or may such dispositions be
deflected by virtuous upbringing in a good and loving environment? Ikey, with his experience of criminals both in and out of
prison, inclined to the first supposition; Fitz-Boodle favours the
second, more benevolent one. The Löwe family constitute the
unfavourable environment that makes of Minna a creature belied
by her "pretty and innocent" look. It is marked out as Jewish by
the given names of the banker and his son (Moses and Solomon
respectively), and by the reader's reflection that "Löwe" not only
takes its place in a series of heraldic names that includes "Wolf"
and "Hirsch" but that it could also stand as a Germanization of
the name "Levi". "Löwe" and "Hirsch" frequently functioned,
moreover, as emblems of the tribes of Judah and Naphtali. These
cases are clear—but what were Thackeray's readers to make of a
name like Frank Leveson? In June 1842 Fitz-Boodle is made to
introduce subscribers to *Fraser's Magazine* to a character so named,
in the course of a passage which begins, significantly, with the
Burkean observation that "the age of chivalry is passed."

> No, no; the age of chivalry is passed. Take the twenty-four first men
> who come into the club, and ask who they are, and how they made
> their money? There's Woolsey-Sackville; his father was Lord Chan-
> cellor, and sat on the woolsack, whence he took his title: his grand-
> father dealt in coal-sacks, and not in wool-sacks,—small coal-sacks,
> dribbling out little supplies of black diamonds to the poor. Yonder
> comes Frank Leveson, in a huge broad-brimmed hat, his shirt cuffs
> turned up to his elbow. Leveson is as gentlemanly a fellow as the
> world contains, and if he has a fault, is perhaps too finikin. Well, you
> fancy him related to the Sutherland family: nor, indeed, does honest
> Frank deny it; but *entre nous*, my good sir, his father was an attorney,
> and his grandfather a bailiff in Chancery Lane, bearing a name still
> older than that of Leveson, namely, Levy. So it is that this con-
> founded equality grows and grows, and has laid the good old nobility
> by the heels. Look at that venerable Sir Charles Kitely, of Kitely

Park: he is interested about the Ashantees, and is just come from Exeter Hall. Kitely discounted bills in the City in the year 1787, and gained his baronetcy by a loan to the French princes. All these points of history are perfectly well known; and do you fancy the world cares? Psha! Profession is no disgrace to a man: be what you like, provided you succeed. If Mr. Fauntleroy could come to life with a million of money, you and I would dine with him: you know we would; for why should we be better than our neighbours?

Put, then, out of your head the idea that this or that profession is unworthy of you: take any that may bring you profit, and thank him that puts you in the way of being rich.

(IV, 239–40)

Here Thackeray shows again how far he is from the vulgar Jew-hatred which loads onto Jews all the blame for capitalism and money-worship. Leveson is no better and no worse than Lord Woolsey-Sackville or Sir CharlesKitely, of Kitely Park, though unlike them his family's rise in the world has brought him no title; and no fit reader of Thackeray will accept without question Fitz-Boodle's denigration of "confounded equality" coupled with exaltation of "the good old nobility". Much of Thackeray's later fiction, as well as his lectures on the Four Georges, will be dedicated to ensuring that his readers do not share Fitz-Boodle's sentimental delusion. Who could prefer the Marquis of Steyne to the gentlemanly, "finikin" Frank Leveson? And if "honest Frank" is not altogether frank and honest about his ancestry, he is no worse in that respect than the "most respectable"— and impeccably English—Newcome family whose fortunes Thackeray will chronicle in one of his later works.

The story of "Miss Löwe", which had been held in abeyance while Frank and other characters are introduced and placed, was continued in *Fraser's Magazine* of October 1842. Though it is "neither very romantic in itself in its details, nor very creditable to myself", Fitz-Boodle interjects, it insists on being told:

Let us take her where we left her in the June Number of this Magazine, gazing through a sunny cluster of vine-leaves, upon a young and handsome stranger, of noble face and exquisite proportions, who was trying to find the door of her father's bank. That entrance being through her amiable directions discovered, I entered and found Messrs. Moses and Solomon Löwe in the counting-house, Herr Solomon being the son of Moses, and head-clerk or partner in the business. That I was cheated in my little matter of exchange stands to reason. A Jew banker (or such as I have had the honour to know) cannot forgo the privilege of cheating; no, if it be but for a shilling. What do I say—a shilling?—a penny! He will cheat you, in the first place, in the exchanging your note; he will then cheat you in giving gold for your silver; and though very likely he will invite you to a splendid repast afterwards that shall have cost him a score of thalers to procure, he will have had the satisfaction of robbing you of your *groschen,* as no doubt he would rob his own father or son.

Herr Moses Löwe must have been a very sharp Israelite, indeed, to rob Herr Solomon, or vice versa. The poor fellows are both in prison for a matter of forgery, as I heard last year when passing through Bonn; and I confess it was not without a little palpitation of the heart (it is a sausage-merchant's now) that I went and took one look at the house where I had first beheld the bright eyes of Minna Löwe.

For let them say as they will, that woman whom a man has once loved *cannot* be the same to him as another.

(IV, 261–2)

Here Fitz-Boodle, repeating typical nineteenth-century travellers' talk, makes the kind of anti-Jewish generalization which is all too common even today; but he puts it into perspective soon afterwards, when he spells out what his younger self remained blissfully unaware of:

upon my word, the bragging of the Frenchman is not so conceited or intolerable as that calm, silent, contemptuous conceit of us young Britons, who think our superiority so well established that it is really not worth arguing upon, and who take upon us to despise thoroughly the whole world through which we pass. We are hated on the Continent, they say, and no wonder. If any other nation were to attempt to domineer over us as we do over Europe, we would hate them as heartily and as furiously as many a Frenchman and Italian does us.

(IV, 265)

Even his courtship of Minna is now seen in a light which Fitz-Boodle's brash young self could not perceive: "The easy vulgar assurance of victory with which I, a raw lad, from the stupidest country in Europe, assailed one of the most beautiful women in the world!" (IV, 271). The generalization which makes Britain "the stupidest country in Europe" is on a par with that which draws universal inferences about Jews from a few over-reaching money-changers "such as I have had the honour to know".

Of Minna Löwe's attractions Fitz-Boodle leaves us in no doubt; unlike her sister and sister-in-law she is graceful, beautiful and elegant, and enchants Fitz-Boodle sufficiently to want to marry her and to fight a duel on her behalf. In depicting his own personal appearance in a narcissistic way satirized by the older and somewhat wiser Fitz-Boodle by means of such pulp-fiction phraseology as "a young and handsome stranger, of noble face and exquisite proportions" (IV, 261), he leaves little doubt about his ideals of male handsomeness:

I was a sight worth contemplating then,—I had golden hair which fell gracefully over my shoulders, and a slim waist (where are you now, slim waist and golden hair?), and a pair of brown moustachios that curled gracefully under a firm Roman nose, and a tuft to my chin that could not but vanquish *any* woman.

(IV, 224)

To this ideal the physical appearance of the Jewish men introduced to us in "Miss Löwe" signally fail to correspond. In describing one of them, the factotum Hirsch who later turns out to be Minna's "affianced husband", Fitz-Boodle reveals preconceptions that extend beyond his impression of one particular individual to the appearance of other Jewish men.

This Hirsch was a little albino of a creature with pinkish eyes, white hair, flame-coloured whiskers, and ear-rings. His eyes jutted out enormously from his countenance, as did his two large, swollen red lips, which had the true Israelitish coarseness. He was always, after a short time, in and out of my apartments. He brought a dozen messages and ran as many errands for me in the course of the day. My way of addressing him was 'Hirsch, you scoundrel, get my boots!' 'Hirsch, my Levite, brush my coat for me!' 'Run, you stag of Israel, and put this letter in the post!' and with many similar compliments. The little rascal was, to do him justice, as willing as possible, never minded by what name I called him, and above all—came from Minna. He was not the rose; no, indeed, nor anything like it; but as the poet says, 'he had lived beside it'; and was there in all Sharon such a rose as Minna Löwe?

(IV, 264–5)

The arrogance Fitz-Boodle here exhibits is compounded later, when he seeks to make Hirsch a go-between between himself and Minna while constantly ridiculing him; a mode of behaviour which the older Fitz-Boodle once again "places" for the reader:

Now when I went abroad I fancied myself one of the finest fellows under the sun. I patronized a banker's dinners as if I did him honour in eating them; I took my place before grave professors and celebrated men, and talked vapid nonsense to them in infamous French, laughing heartily in return at their own manner of pronouncing that language. I set down as a point beyond question that their customs were inferior to our own, and would not in the least scruple, in a calm way, to let my opinion be known. What an agreeable young fellow I must have been!

With these opinions, and my pleasant way of expressing them, I would sit for hours by the side of lovely Minna Löwe, ridiculing with much of that elegant satire for which the English are remarkable, every one of the customs of the country,—the dinners, with the absurd un-English pudding in the very midst of them; the dresses of the men, with their braided coats and great seal-rings. As for little

Hirsch, he formed the constant subject of my raillery with Mademoiselle Minna; and I gave it as my fixed opinion, that he was only fit
to sell sealing-wax and oranges to the coaches in Piccadilly.

'Oh, fous afez tant d'esprit, fous autres jeunes Anglais,' would she
say; and I said, 'Oui, nous avons beaucoup d'esprit, beaucoup plus
que les Allemands,' with the utmost simplicity; and then would half
close my eyes, and give her a look that I thought must kill her.

(IV, 265–8)

Is it any wonder that towards the end of the sorry tale Hirsch turns
on the man who thought he could insult him with such impunity?

'You coward!' roared Hirsch, 'coward as well as profligate! You
communicated to me your lawless love for this angel,—to me, her
affianced husband; and you had the audacity to send her letters, not
one of which, so help me Heaven, has been received. Yes, you will
laugh at Jews—will you, you brutal Englishman? You will insult our
people,—will you, you stupid islander? Psha! I spit upon you!' and
here Monsieur Hirsch snapped his fingers in my face, holding Minna
at the same time round the waist, who thus became the little monster's buckler.

(IV, 278)

The "little monster" spoils the effect, alas, by offering later on to do
business with the man who had so insulted him—but he does
acquire a degree of dignity when he at last snaps his fingers at the
man who could see nothing in him but an ugly instrument to
compass his own ends. Fitz-Boodle's one reason for associating
with Hirsch, we learn, had been that "in comedies and romances
that I had read the hero has always a go-between—a valet, a
humble follower who performs the intrigue of the piece." (IV, 270).
At the climax of the tale, Hirsch refuses to play Leporello any
longer; and Minna leaves Fitz-Boodle in no doubt that when it
came to a choice between himself and Hirsch, she would stand by
the latter. Hirsch bravely challenges Fitz-Boodle to a duel; but
Fitz-Boodle finds that the man who brings the challenge has "the
air of an old-clothesman", declines fighting a duel with a Jewish
opponent and second, and decamps the next morning.

The contrast Fitz-Boodle perceives between the ugly male Jew
and the beautiful Jewess, strengthened by everything he tells us
about the appearance of Solomon and Moses Löwe, is a familiar
one in European literature: we find it in *Ivanhoe*, in Grillparzer's *Die
Jüdin von Toledo*, and in many other, lesser works. In "Miss Löwe",
however, this contrast is made to serve a sinister purpose—for the
beautiful girl allows herself to be used by her father, her brother,
and what Fitz-Boodle calls "her filthy little bridegroom", as a
mantrap, inducing the swains attracted to her to swell the family

coffers by buying inferior goods at inflated prices. The *belle Juive* becomes a *Juive fatale*. The conspiracy comes out when Fitz-Boodle discovers how he had been cheated over the purchase of tobacco—a weed to which he is hopelessly addicted. The plot reaches its climax at a dance, at which Hirsch rounds on Fitz-Boodle in a way already described, aided and abetted by the beauteous Minna; and when, many years later, Fitz-Boodle catches sight of her once more, in a front box at the Frankfort theatre, she is married to Hirsch who has purchased the Austrian title Baron Hirsch von Hirschenwald, she appears "loaded with diamonds, and at least sixteen stones in weight." But Fitz-Boodle adds, in a last access of gallantry:

> Ah! Minna, Minna! thou mayest grow to be as ugly as sin, and as fat as Daniel Lambert, but I have the amber mouthpiece still, and swear that the prettiest lips in Jewry have kissed it!
> The MS. here concludes with a rude design of a young lady smoking a pipe.
>
> (IV, 280)

Thackeray does not in fact supply the "rude design" he here attributes to Fitz-Boodle; but he has reminded his readers forcibly enough of an earlier incident which had brought Minna, Fitz-Boodle and tobacco together in a context that seemed at first to have no more than a loose connection with the Löwe family's trading interests.

> 'Get his lordship a pipe, Minna, my soul's darling!' exclaimed the banker.
> 'Oh yes! the beautiful long Turkish one,' cried Minna, springing up, and presently returned bearing a long cherry-stick covered with a scarlet and gold cloth, at one end an enamelle damber mouthpiece, a gilded pipe at the other. In she came dancing, wand in hand, and looking like a fairy!
> 'Stop!' she said; 'I must light it for Herr George.' (By Jupiter! there was a way that girl had of pronouncing my name 'George,' which I never heard equalled before or since.) And accordingly, bidding her sister get fire, she put herself in the prettiest attitude ever seen: with one little foot put forward, and her head thrown back, and a little hand holding the pipe-stick between finger and thumb, and a pair of red lips kissing the amber mouthpiece with the sweetest smile ever mortal saw. Her sister, giggling, lighted the tobacco, and presently you saw issuing from between those beautiful, smiling, red lips of Minna's a little curling, graceful, white smoke, which rose soaring up to the ceiling. I swear, I felt quite faint with the fragrance of it.
>
> (IV, 267–8)

The image of Minna's red lips sucking at a long gilded pipe with an amber mouth-piece has a sexual charge that is unmistakable even to those who have not marked the "association of amber-colour with sex" documented by John Carey in *Thackeray: Prodigal Genius* (p. 46). The satisfaction derived from that charge is what is really being traded when Moses Löwe sells Fitz-Boodle the pipe and its mouthpiece at an exorbitant price.

> When the pipe was lighted, she brought it to me with quite as pretty an attitude and a glance that—Psha! I gave old Moses Löwe fourteen pounds sterling for that pipe that very evening; and as for the mouthpiece, I would not part with it away from me, but I wrapped it up in a glove that I took from the table, and put both into my breast-pocket; and next morning, when Charley Wilder burst suddenly into my room, he found me sitting up in bed in a green silk nightcap, a little apricot-coloured glove lying on the counterpane before me, your humble servant employed in mumbling the mouthpiece as if it were a bit of barley-sugar.
>
> (IV, 268)

This is the true heart of the tale; and Thackeray makes sure we realize this by causing his Fitz-Boodle to refer back to it in the very last sentence of the tale of "Miss Löwe".

It will have been noticed that when Moses Löwe calls to his "soul's darling", his speech-patterns suggest no deviation from the conventions of pronouncing vowels and consonants which operate in his society. Elsewhere, however, Fitz-Boodle attributes to him the by now familiar modes of Jew-speak.

> 'If, my Lord', said Herr Moses, counting out the gold fredericks to me, 'you intend to shtay in our town, I hope my daughtersh and I vill have shometimsh de pleasure of your high vell-born shoshiety.'
>
> (IV, 263)

Ridicule of the Jewish banker's pronunciation is, however, relativized in Fitz-Boodle's account by similar ridicule levelled at the speech of a Gentile friend to whom "Jew" means "Old Clothes Merchant" and who is proof against the charms of Jewish maidens. It is he who tells Fitz-Boodle about the sharp practice for which the Löwe family has become notorious; he does so in a lisping upper-class accent which is as ridiculous in its way as the distorted speech many Victorians imputed to Jews.

> 'Don't you thee, my good fwiend,' continued he, 'how wegularly thethe people have been doing you? I tell you their chawacterth are known all over the town. There'th not a thtudent in the place but can give you a hithtory of the family. Löwe ith an infarnal old uthuwer, and hith daughterth wegular manthwapth. At the Thtar, where I dine with the officerth of the garrithon, you and Minna are a thtantard joke. Captain Heerpauk wath caught himself for near six weekth; young Von Twommel wath wemoved by hith fwiends; old Colonel Blitz wath at one time tho nearly gone in love with the elder,

that he would have had a divorce from hith lady. Among the thtudenth the mania hath been jutht the thame. Whenever one wath worth plucking, Löwe uthed to have him to hith houthe and wob him, until at latht the wathcal'th chawacter became tho well known, that the thtudentth in a body have detherted him, and you will find that not one of them will dance with hith daughterth, handthome ath they are. Go down to Godesberg to-night and thee.'

(IV, 273)

Jew-speak, like everything else in Thackeray, must be seen in context.

It is hardly surprising, nevertheless, that "Miss Löwe" caused offence in the Anglo-Jewish community. One of the members of that community complained to the publishers of *Fraser's Magazine* and drew a reply from Fitz-Boodle at the beginning of his next adventure, entitled "Dorothea", in January 1843.

The most indignant of the manuscript critiques came from a member of the Hebrew persuasion. And what do you think is the opinion of this Lion of Judah? Simply that George Savage Fitz-Boodle is a false name, assumed by some coward, whose intention it is to insult the Jewish religion! He says that my history of the Löwe family is a dastardly attack upon the people! How is it so? If I say that an individual Christian is a rogue, do I impugn the professors of the whole Christian religion? Can my Hebrew critic say that a Hebrew banker never cheated in matters of exchange, or that a Hebrew was never guilty of a roguery? If so, what was the gold-dust robbery, and why is Ikey Solomons at Botany Bay? No; the Lion of Judah may be a good lion, but he is a deucedly bad arguer,—nay, he is a bad lion, he roars before he is hurt. Be calm, thou red-maned desert-roarer, the arrows of Fitz-Boodle have no poison at their tip, and are shot only in play.

I never wished to attack the Jewish nation, far from it; I have three bills now out; nor is he right in saying that I have made a dastardly statement, which I have given under a false name; just the contrary, my name is, as everybody knows, my real name—it is the *statement* which is false, and I confess there is not one word of truth in it—I never knew, to my knowledge, any Hirsch or Löwe in my life; I never was with Minna Löwe; the adventures never did occur at Bonn. Is my friend now satisfied? Let him remember, in the first place, that the tale is related of individuals, and not of his people at large; and in the second place, that the statement is not true. If *that* won't satisfy him, what will?

(IV, 281–2)

Fitz-Boodle returns to this defence a little later, when he attributes envy to British journalists who had joined the "Lion of Judah" in condemning "Miss Löwe".

This disgusting unanimity of sentiment at first annoyed me a good deal, for I was pained to think that success so soon bred envy, and

that the members of the British press could not bear to see an
amateur enter the lists with them, and carry off laurels for which they
had been striving long years in vain. Is there no honesty left in the
world? I thought. And the thought gave me extreme pain, for, though
(as in the Hebrew case above mentioned) I love occasionally to
disport with the follies and expose the vices of individuals, to attribute envy to a whole class is extremely disagreeable to one whose
feelings are more than ordinarily benevolent and pure.

(IV, 282)

The irony of that last sentence is patent, for no-one who followed
Fitz-Boodle's adventures so far will think his feelings "more than
ordinarily benevolent and pure"; he would be a less interesting
creation if that were so. He seems sincere enough, however, when
he says to his Jewish critic:

Rabbi, let us part in peace! Neither thee nor thy like would George
Fitz-Boodle ever willingly harm—neither thee nor any bearded nor
unbearded man. If there be no worse rogues in Jewry, the people is
more lucky than the rest of the world, and the fact is good to be
known.

(IV, 282)

Here, for once, Fitz-Boodle seems to be speaking unequivocally for
Thackeray himself.

The defence against the charge of Jew-baiting which Fitz-Boodle
has here offered has three main heads: (i) that "Miss Löwe" strikes
at individuals, not "nations"; (ii) that these individuals are invented; (iii) that in real life there undoubtedly are dishonest Jews
("Why is Ikey Solomons at Botany Bay?"), but that Jews may
count themselves more fortunate than other people if the rogues
among them are no worse than the Löwe family. Not all Thackeray's
critics will feel satisfied with Fitz-Boodle's defence; they may feel
that generalizations about Jewish bankers and money-changers
were insufficiently relativized and that remarks like Fitz-Boodle's
"his two large, swollen red lips . . . had the true Israelitish coarseness" go well beyond the characterization of an unpleasant individual. It might also be said, in mitigation, that even through Fitz-
Boodle's insensitivity Thackeray makes his readers feel the pain
and humiliation Minna Löwe experiences when she is demonstra-
tively ostracized on the dance-floor by the assembled Gentile
company. But Thackeray, it appears, ultimately came to be dissatisfied with this story; for when the "Fitz-Boodle Papers" were
reprinted in Volume IV of his *Miscellanies* (London 1857), "Miss
Löwe" was one of the items he omitted.

V

"Miss Löwe" is not the only sad chronicle of Fitz-Boodle's tribulations in love during his stay in Germany. Another such episode is recorded in a piece headed "Dorothea", which acutely observes in nineteenth-century Germany that pride in the antiquity of the Germanic "race" which was later to be perverted to such terrible ends. Dorothea's father, we read, introduced the young Fitz-Boodle

> to his *Gattin*, his Leocadia (the fat woman in blue), 'as a young world-observer, and worthy art-friend, a young scion of British Adel, who had come to refresh himself at the Urquellen of his race, and see his brethren of the great family of Hermann.'
>
> (IV, 291)

Nor did the row over "Miss Löwe" prevent Thackeray from bringing Fitz-Boodle back to *Fraser's Magazine* for a second series of adventures. From March to November 1843 Fitz-Boodle figured as narrator of a number of stories brought together under the general heading "Men's Wives". One of these stories, "The Ravenswing", is said to have been written "a long time since"' (IV, 461); it was probably written well before 1843 and revised for inclusion in the Fitz-Boodle saga. The central character, Morgiana Crump, is the good-natured daughter of a publican and becomes an accomplished singer; her fine head of black hair must be held responsible for the cognomen that gives the story its title. Three suitors aspire to her hand and heart: Mr Woolsey, a partner in a fashionable tailoring firm; Mr. Eglantine, a Bond Street wig-maker, hairdresser and perfumer; and Captain Walker, a handsomely moustachioed speculator and man about town. Walker, we learn, lives near Eglantine's business premises, in Windsor Chambers, where his neighbours include "the celebrated attorneys Kite and Levison." The name of Levison's partner suggests the sharp nature of the attorneys' practice. Walker's association with Jews goes well beyond mere proximity to Levison; he can be seen

> walking arm-in-arm with such gentlemen as my Lord Vauxhall, the Marquess of Billingsgate, or Captain Bluff; and at the same time nodding to young Moses, the dandy bailiff; or Loder, the gambling-house keeper; or Aminadab, the cigar-seller in the Quadrant.
>
> (IV, 347)

These nodding acquaintances, which suggest so much of Captain Walker's life style, occupy three professions associated with Jews in Victorian England; by wedging Loder between the young "dandy bailiff" Moses and the tobacco merchant Aminadab Thackeray suggests a close business relationship between them. Though the name Loder appears elsewhere as that of a disreputable Gentile gambler, Captain Loder, it is not beyond the bounds of possibility that the gambling-house keeper Loder might himself be Jewish, that he had shed his former name for a more English-sounding one of whose subliminal suggestions ("loaded" dice!) he was unaware. There is, in fact, a good deal of tactical name changing in "The Ravenswing", involving not only Jews but also English Gentiles like Mr Eglantine (whose original name no-one knows) and Captain Walker himself. Eglantine is said, by his rival Woolsey, to be "in the hands of the Jews" (IV, 345); an assertion confirmed by the story-teller Fitz-Boodle.

> If the truth must be told, he loved pleasure, and was in the hands of the Jews. He had been in business twenty years: he had borrowed a thousand pounds to purchase his stock and shop; and he calculated that he had paid upwards of twenty thousand pounds for the use of the one thousand, which was still as much due as on the first day when he entered business. He could show that he had received a thousand dozen of champagne from the disinterested money-dealers with whom he usually negotiated his paper. He had pictures all over his 'studios,' which had been purchased in the same bargains. If he sold his goods at an enormous price, he paid for them at a rate almost equally exorbitant. There was not an article in his shop but came to him through his Israelite providers; and in the very front shop itself sat a gentleman who was the nominee of one of them, and who was called Mr. Mossrose. He was there to superintend the cash account, and to see that certain instalments were paid to his principals, according to certain agreements entered into between Mr. Eglantine and them.
>
> (IV, 350)

Eglantine refers to one of his money-lenders as "the Minories man" (IV, 353)—a way of suggesting the Jewishness of a character by means of a topographical location which Thackeray also favours in others of his works.

Between Eglantine and the man he is forced to employ as his business associate no love is lost; Mossrose's claim to be regarded as an "artist" in his profession of hair-dresser and perfumer is scornfully dismissed: "'*He* an artist? . . . Why, he's only a disguised bailiff! Mossrose indeed! the chap's name's Amos, and he sold oranges before he came here.'" (IV, 350). By converting *Amos* into *Mos*rose Thackeray is calling up subliminal memories of a play which assumes great thematic importance later in the story: *A Midsummer Night's Dream*, where *musk*rose and eglantine are mentioned in close proximity (Act II, scene 2, line 252). Mossrose, for his part, heartily despises Eglantine and looks forward to the day "when he would become the proprietor of the shop. And take Eglantine for a foreman"; for then "it would be *his* turn to sneer and bully, and ride the high horse." (IV, 350)

The scenes in which Mossrose appears show him as a surly fellow, given to exchanges such as the following, in which he reminds Captain Walker that the transmogrification of Amos into Mossrose matched that of the name "Hooker" (which Walker's evangelical father had given him in memory of the great theologian, but which was also a cant term for a thief) into the more respectable, more aristocratic-sounding, "Howard".

'Is Eglantine at home, Mr. Mossrose?' said Walker to the foreman, who sat in the front shop.
'Don't know—go and look' (meaning go and be hanged); for Mossrose also hated Mr. Walker.
'If you're uncivil I'll break your bones, Mr. *Amos*,' says Mr. Walker, sternly.
'I should like to see you try, Mr. *Hooker* Walker,' replies the undaunted shopman, on which the captain, looking several tremendous canings at him, walked into the back room or 'studio.'
(IV, 351)

One of the reasons why Mossrose can react to the threat to break his bones in the way we here see him do is revealed in a later exchange of the same type, which begins with Walker's attempts (for reasons of his own) to placate his enemy.

'A good morning to you, Mr. Mossrose,' said Captain Walker. 'Why, sir, you look as fresh as your namesake,—you do, indeed, now, Mossrose.'
'You look ash yellow ash a guinea,' responded Mr. Mossrose, sulkily. He thought the captain was hoaxing him.
'My good sir,' replies the other, nothing cast down, 'I drank rather too freely last night.'
'The more beast you!' said Mr. Mossrose.
'Thank you, Mossrose; the same to you,' answered the captain.
'If you call me a beast I'll punch your head off!' answered the young man, who had much skill in the art which many of his brethren practise.
'I didn't, my fine fellow,' replied Walker; 'on the contrary, you—'
'Do you mean to give me the lie?' broke out the indignant Mossrose, who hated the agent fiercely, and did not in the least care to conceal his hate.
In fact, it was his fixed purpose to pick a quarrel with Walker, and to drive him, if possible, from Mr. Eglantine's shop. 'Do you mean to give me the lie, I say, Mr. Hooker Walker?'
'For Heaven's sake, Amos, hold your tongue!' exclaimed the captain, to whom the name of Hooker was as poison; but at this

moment, a customer stepping in, Mr. Amos exchanged his ferocious aspect for a bland grin, and Mr. Walker walked into the studio.
(IV, 362)

"The art which many of his brethren practise" is boxing, of course; and Thackeray builds on the theme he here strikes up when he names Mossrose's uncle—whom we will soon meet again as keeper of the Cursitor Street sponging-house—Mr Bendigo. For a Victorian readership the mere mention of this name would recall one of the most famous boxing matches of the early nineteenth century: a match fought on Skipworth Common on 3 April 1838 between the boxer who called himself "Bendigo" and one William Caunt, whom he had defeated on an earlier occasion but who now challenged him for the championship. Although the ultimate honours went to Caunt this time, Bendigo lost none of his popularity—he even had an Australian goldfield and mining town named after him by immigrant or transported admirers. His real name was William Thompson; but since he was one of three sons born at one birth, he and his brothers became known as Shadrach, Meshach and Abednego. He styled himself "Abednego of Nottingham" in 1835, and very soon became known to the sporting public as "Bendigo". He was a Protestant Dissenter and not a Jew; but since his adopted name was based on that of a character in the Old Testament and sounded distinctly Sephardic, Thackeray thought it appropriate to name Jewish characters after him.

The different kinds of grin with which Mossrose is credited throughout the story are no more endearing than his habit of listening at doors, discovered by Mr Woolsey when he enters Eglantine's shop in order to offer his old rival an alliance against Captain Walker, the suitor Morgiana has clearly begun to favour.

> Mossrose would have heard every word of the conversation . . . had not Woolsey, opening the door, suddenly pounced on the assistant, taken him by the collar, and told him to disappear altogether into the shop, which Mossrose did, vowing he would have his revenge.
> (IV, 370)

Resentment and vengefulness, money-lending activities, and determination not to allow his new partner in the firm of Eglantine and Mossrose to be softened by Morgiana's tears into remitting Captain Walker debt for goods supplied, inevitably raise the spectre of Shylock.

> 'He did pay me in a sort of way,' reasoned the perfumer with himself—'these bonds, though they are not worth much, I took 'em for better or for worse, and I can't bear to see her crying, and to

trample on a woman in distress. Morgiana,' he added, in a loud cheerful voice, 'cheer up; I'll give you a release for your husband: I *will* be the old kind Eglantine I was.'

'Be the old kind jackass you vash!' here roared a voice that made Mr. Eglantine start. 'Vy, vat an old fat fool you are, Eglantine, to give up our just debts because a voman comes snivelling and crying to you—and such a voman, too!' exclaimed Mr. Mossrose, for his was the voice.

'Such a woman, sir?' cried the senior partner.

'Yes; such a woman—vy didn't she jilt you herself?—hasn't she been trying the same game with Baroski; and are you so green as to give up a hundred and fifty pounds because she takes a fancy to come vimpering here? I won't, I can tell you. The money's as much mine as it is yours, and I'll have it, or keep Walker's body, that's what I will.'

At the presence of his partner, the timid good genius of Eglantine which had prompted him to mercy and kindness, at once outspread its frightened wings and flew away.

'You see how it is, Mrs. W.,' said he, looking down; 'it's an affair of business—in all these here affairs of business Mr. Mossrose is the managing man; ain't you, Mr. Mossrose?'

'A pretty business it would be if I wasn't,' replied Mossrose, doggedly. 'Come, ma'am,' says he, 'I'll tell you vat I do: I take fifty per shent; not a farthing less—give me that, and out your husband goes.'

'Oh, sir, Howard will pay you in a week.'

'Vell, den let him stop at my uncle Bendigo's for a week, and come out den—he's very comfortable there,' *said Shylock with a grin.* 'Hadn't you better go to the shop, Mr. Eglantine,' continued he, and look after your business; Mrs. Walker can't want you to listen to her all day.'

Eglantine was glad of the excuse, and slunk out of the studio, not into the shop but into his parlour; where he drank off a great glass of maraschino; and sat blushing and exceedingly agitated, until Mossrose came to tell him that Mrs. W. was gone, and wouldn't trouble him any more. But although he drank several more glasses of maraschino, and went to the play that night, and to the Cider-cellars afterwards, neither the liquor, nor the play, nor the delightful comic songs at the cellars, could drive Mrs. Walker out of his head, and the memory of old times, and the image of her pale weeping face.

Morgiana tottered out of the shop, scarcely heeding the voice of Mr. Mossrose, who said, 'I'll take forty per shent' (and went back to his duty cursing himself for a soft-hearted fool for giving up so much of his rights to a puling woman).

(IV, 417–8—my italics)

But in fact, Mossrose *does* soften and offer, in the end, to reduce his demand from £ 150 to a mere £ 20; by then, however, other creditors have mobilized, and Captain Walker wanders from Cursitor Street into the Fleet prison, where he makes himself tolerably comfortable until Morgiana's singing career takes off, and he is able to hold her backers to ransom. Before that, however, Morgiana, now Walker's loving wife, has been forced to sell her magnificent hair to Eglantine and Mossrose for ready cash—a fact which enrages Woolsey, who emerges more and more clearly as the most sympathetic of the male characters in "The Ravenswing."

> As he had passed the Bower of Bloom a few days before, he saw Mossrose, who was combing out a jet-black ringlet, and held it up as if for Woolsey's examination, with a peculiar grin. The tailor did not understand the joke, but he saw now what had happened. Morgiana had sold her hair for five guineas; she would have sold her arm had her husband bidden her. On looking in her drawers it was found she had sold almost all her wearing apparel; the child's clothes were all there, however. It was because her husband talked of disposing of a gilt coral that the child had, that she had parted with the locks which had formed her pride.
> 'I'll give you twenty guineas for that hair, you infamous fat coward,' roared the little tailor to Eglantine that evening. 'Give it up, or I'll kill-you–me—'
> 'Mr. Mossrose! Mr. Mossrose!' shouted the perfumer.
> 'Vell, vatsh de matter, vatsh de row? Fight avay, my boys; two to one on the tailor,' said Mr. Mossrose, much enjoying the sport (for Woolsey, striding through the shop without speaking to him, had rushed into the studio, where he plumped upon Englantine).
> 'Tell him about that hair, sir.'
> 'That hair! Now keep yourself quiet, Mister Timble, and don't tink for to bully *me*. You mean Mrs. Valker's 'air? Vy, she sold it me.'
> 'And the more blackguard you for buying it? Will you take twenty guineas for it?'
> 'No,' said Mossrose.
> 'Twenty-five?'
> 'Can't,' said Mossrose.
> 'Hang it; will you take forty? There.'
> 'I vish I'd kep it,' said the Hebrew gentleman, with unfeigned regret. 'Eglantine dressed it this very night.'
> 'For Countess Baldenstiern, the Swedish Hambassador's lady,' says Eglantine (his Hebrew partner was by no means a favourite with the ladies, and only superintended the accounts of the concern). 'It's this very night at Devonshire' Ouse, with four hostrich plumes, lappets, and trimmings. And now, Mr. Woolsey, I'll trouble you to apologize.'
> Mr. Woolsey did not answer, but walked up to Mr. Eglantine and snapped his fingers so close under the perfumer's nose that the latter started back and seized the bell-rope. Mossrose burst out laughing, and the tailor walked majestically from the shop, with both hands stuck between the lappets of his coat.
>
> (IV, 430–1)

It will have been noticed that Mossrose, who had spoken standard English in the earlier portions of the tale, has now been saddled with a Cockney Jew-speak which in another scene makes him alternate between "pounds" and "poundsh" (IV, 414); that he enjoys *encouraging* and *watching* fisticuffs as well as engaging in them; and that his laughter is no more endearing than his earlier grins. Eglantine in fact loses his share of the Bond Street business altogether in the end, and at Fitz-Boodle's last encounter with him he keeps a seedy hairdresser's shop in a provincial back street.

The story of Captain Walker's debts brings into focus again the Cursitor Street establishment which is now managed, as we have seen, by a Jewish family called Bendigo. On reaching the lock-up after his arrest, Walker tries to bluff things out:

> When carried to Mr. Bendigo's lock-up house, he summoned that gentleman in a very haughty way, took a blank banker's cheque out of his pocket-book, and filling it up for the exact sum of the writ, orders Mr. Bendigo forthwith to open the door and let him go forth. Mr. Bendigo, smiling with exceeding archness, and putting a finger covered all over with diamond rings to his extremely aquiline nose, inquired of Mr. Walker whether he saw anything green about his face? intimating by this gay and good-humoured interrogatory his suspicion of the unsatisfactory nature of the document handed over to him by Mr. Walker.
>
> 'Hang it, sir!' says Mr. Walker, 'go and get the cheque cashed, and be quick about it. Send your man in a cab, and here's a half-crown to pay for it.' The confident air somewhat staggers the bailiff, who asked him whether he would like any refreshment while his man was absent getting the amount of the cheque, and treats his prisoner with great civility during the time of the messenger's journey.
>
> But as Captain Walker had but a balance of two pounds five and twopence (this sum was afterwards divided among his creditors, the law-expenses being previously deducted from it), the bankers of course declined to cash the captain's draft for two hundred and odd pounds, simply writing the words 'No effects' on the paper; on receiving which reply Walker, far from being cast down, burst out laughing very gaily, produced a real five-pound note, and called upon his host for a bottle of champagne, which the two worthies drank in perfect friendship and good humour.
>
> (IV, 403–4)

The elements of Jewish caricature are nearly all here—"extremely aquiline" nose, excessive finery, sly or knowing demeanour; but the atmosphere is good-natured, and neither Fitz-Boodle nor Captain Walker exhibit ill-feeling towards Bendigo or "the young Israelitish gentleman who acts as a waiter in Cursitor Street" (IV, 404). To reinforce this atmosphere of "perfect friendship and good humour" Fitz-Boodle adds, in a parenthesis readers are meant to take with a pinch of salt: "I declare for my own part (I mean, of course, that I went to visit a friend) I have dined at Mr. Aminadab's as sumptuously as at Long's" (IV, 405). Mr Bendigo presents a cheerful

countenance to his customers; when he had "no person to grin at",
Fitz-Boodle reports, he would grin "at a marble bust of Mr. Pitt
which ornamented his sideboard." (IV, 408). This raises uncomfortable memories of Mossrose's unlovable grins; and indeed, the
behaviour of Bendigo and his son towards Morgiana, who has
pawned or sold her valuables under the mistaken impression that
the sum she realized would be sufficient to secure her husband's
release, goes a long way towards justifying the reader's suspicions.

> 'Take me to him', said she to the young Hebrew who opened the
> door.
> 'To whom?' says the sarcastic youth; 'there's twenty *hims* here.
> You're precious early.'
> 'To Captain Walker, young man', replied Morgiana, haughtily,
> whereupon the youth opening the second door, and seeing Mr.
> Bendigo in a flowered dressing-gown descending the stairs, ex-
> claimed, 'Papa, here's a lady for the Captain.' 'I'm come to free him',
> said she, trembling and holding out a bundle of bank-notes. 'Here's
> the amount of your claim, sir—two hundred and twenty pounds, as
> you told me last night;' and the Jew took the notes, and grinned as he
> looked at her, and grinned double as he looked at his son, and begged
> Mrs. Walker to step into his study and take a receipt. When the door
> of that apartment closed upon the lady and his father, Mr. Bendigo
> the younger fell back in an agony of laughter, which it is impossible to
> describe in words, and presently ran out into a court where some of
> the luckless inmates of the house were already taking the air, and
> communicated something to them which made those individuals also
> laugh as uproariously as he had previously done.
>
> (IV, 407–8)

The Bendigos know perfectly well that Morgiana's sacrifice has
been in vain, since there is now a further detainer, from Eglantine
and Mossrose, against her husband; and it is noticeable that
Fitz-Boodle changes his usual "Mr. Bendigo" for a curt "the Jew"
at this unamiable moment. He soon recovers his mock-courteous
tone, however, speaking of Bendigo as "the honoured bailiff" and
exhibiting for the reader's amusement Captain Walker's doomed
attempts "to cheat the bailiff into the idea that he (Walker) was an
exceedingly respectable and wealthy man." "The London tradesman", Fitz-Boodle comments, "is one of the keenest judges of
human nature extant; and if a tradesman, how much more a
bailiff?" (IV, 409).

The sponging-house is indeed a school for cynicism; for those
who suffer in and from it are honest victims like Morgiana rather
than the adventurers and grasshopper natures who accept it as one
of the risks entailed by their way of life. Bendigo junior, who is
given to sarcastic utterance and listening at keyholes like his cousin

Mossrose, has all the makings of a cynic; but he has enough human feeling left to be appalled at Captain Walker's brutal behaviour towards the affectionate wife who has just tried to liberate him.

> Fancy how he [= Walker] clenches his fists and stands over her, and stamps and screams out curses with a livid face, growing wilder and wilder in his rage; wrenching her hand when she wants to turn away, and only stopping at last when she has fallen off the chair in a fainting fit, with a heart-breaking sob that made the Jew-boy who was listening at the keyhole turn quite pale and walk away.
>
> (IV, 410)

This shows again how important it is to see Thackeray's portrayal of Jews in the context of his portrayal of the Gentile world in which they live and into which they seek to integrate.

The suit which first lands Captain Walker in Cursitor Street is brought against him by one Benjamin Baroski—a composer and music-teacher who develops Morgiana's talents and falls in love with her. The indignant rejection of this love, when he declares it, followed by his dismissal as Morgiana's teacher, causes him to seek revenge by suing for non-payment of fees. Baroski is in fact one of the most interesting characters in the story; in important respects he anticipates Du Maurier's Svengali.

> Little Baroski is the author of the opera of *Eliogabalo*, of the oratorio of *Purgatorio*, which made such an immense sensation, of songs and ballet-musics innumerable. He is a German by birth, and shows such an outrageous partiality for pork and sausages, and attends at church so constantly, that I am sure there cannot be any foundation in the story that he is a member of the ancient religion. He is a fat little man, with a hooked nose and jetty whiskers, and coal-black shining eyes, and plenty of rings and jewels on his fingers and about his person, and a very considerable portion of his shirt-sleeves turned over his coat to take the air. His great hands (which can sprawl over half a piano, and produce those effects on the instrument for which he is celebrated) are encased in lemon-coloured kids, new, or cleaned daily. Parenthetically, let us ask why so many men, with coarse red wrists and big hands, persist in the white kid glove and wristband system? Baroski's gloves alone must cost him a little fortune; only, he says with a leer, when asked the question, 'Get along vid you; don't you know dere is a gloveress that lets me have dem very sheap?' He rides in the Park; has splendid lodgings in Dover Street; and is a member of the Regent Club, where he is a great source of amusement to the members, to whom he tells astonishing stories of his successes with the ladies, and for whom he has always play and opera tickets in store. His eye glistens and his little heart beats when a lord speaks to him; and he has been known to spend large sums of money in giving treats to young sprigs of fashion at Richmond and elsewhere. 'In my bolyticks,' he says, 'I am Consarevatiff to de bagbone.' In fine, he is a puppy, and withal a man of considerable genius in his profession.
>
> (IV, 391–2)

Small stout figure, hooked nose, "jetty" whiskers, coal-black eyes, profusion of rings and jewels, distorted speech—these are all so much part of the caricature-Jew that few readers will follow Fitz-Boodle in dismissing the thought that Baroski might be "a member of the ancient religion." What is important, however, is that neither Fitz-Boodle nor the reader can be sure; that there are no infallible signs of Jewishness; that it is possible to be mistaken about external signs that seem to point to Jewish origins; and that such uncertainties beget rumour and gossip in the social circles in which the man or woman in question moves. Even an "outrageous partiality for pork and sausages" may be a compensation phenomenon, or a sign of revolt, and therefore no proof of non-Jewish descent; and attendance at Christian worship tells nothing certain about ethnic origins, as Thackeray will forcibly show in his portrait of Sherrick in *The Newcomes*. Throughout "The Ravenswing", however, the rumour of Baroski's Jewish origins is kept alive: his rival Sir George Thrum refers to him contemptuously as "the orange boy" (IV, 432—Jewish orange importers and orange sellers were a familiar part of Thackeray's London) and the narrator teases the reader with the suggestion that there were reasons why it might be doubly inappropriate to speak of Baroski's Old Testamentarian first name—the name he shared with Disraeli—as a "Christian" name:

> Benjamin looked extremely red, it must be confessed, at being thus called by what we shall denominate his Christian name . . .
> (IV, 396)

Baroski is a dedicated teacher; besides Morgiana he has a bevy of other young female pupils headed by one Amelia Larkins.

> The prima donna of the little company was Amelia Larkins, Baroski's own articled pupil, on whose future reputation the eminent master staked his own, whose profits he was to share, and whom he had farmed, to this end, from her father, a most respectable sheriff's officer's assistant, and now, by his daughter's exertions, a considerable capitalist. Amelia is blonde and blue-eyed, her complexion is as bright as snow, her ringlets of the colour of straw, her figure—but why describe her figure? Has not all the world seen her at the theatres royal and in America under the name of Miss Ligonier?
> (IV, 394)

Here we have a collocation new in Thackeray's work, which will take centre stage in du Maurier's *Trilby*: the swarthy man with the heavy Germanic accent who develops the talent, launches the career, and corners some of the profits, of a fair-complexioned singer. Baroski's obsession, however, is with the dark-haired Morgiana, the Ravenswing, rather than the blonde Amelia; and when his thwarted love seeks revenge he has a moment of sneering triumph at an auction scene which seems like a first sketch for the more famous auction scene in Chapter XVII of *Vanity Fair*.

> Woolsey bid against Baroski for the piano, very nearly up to the actual value of the instrument, when the artist withdrew from the competition; and when he was sneering at the ruin of Mr. Walker, the tailor sternly interrupted him by saying, 'What the deuce are *you* sneering at? You did it, sir; and you're paid every shilling of your claim, ain't you?'

Unlike Svengali, however, Baroski turns out, in the end to be a thoroughly harmless little man. His English rival, Sir George Thrum, who refers to him so dismissively as "the orange boy", shows himself much cleverer at driving hard bargains (IV 432, 438). He succeeds Baroski as Morgiana's teacher, launching the Ravenswing on her career with words echoed, *mutatis mutandis*, by almost every music-teacher who takes on a pupil initially trained by someone else: "We must begin . . . by unlearning all that Mr. Baroski (of whom I do not wish to speak with the slightest disrespect) has taught you!" (IV, 433). Sir George's appearance and life-style are as different as possible from that of the earlier teacher:

> While Baroski drives a cab in the park with a very suspicious Mademoiselle Léocadie, or Amenaïde, by his side, you may see Thrum walking to evening church with his lady, and hymns are sung there of his own composition."
>
> (IV, 434).

We hear of no hymns written by Baroski; his compositions include an opera (*Héliogabale*), an oratorio (*Purgatorio*, "which made such an immense sensation"), as well as "songs and ballet-music innumerable." (IV, 391). But for all the sybaritic suggestions of the opera and the diabolic ones of the oratorio there is something pathetic about little Baroski, whom we leave comforting himself with the thought that "de liddle Rafenschwing is just as font of me as effer" (IV, 460)—one of Thackeray's many shots at rendering the accent of a German speaking English; a German, in this case, at whose pork-eating and churchgoing one has to look hard in order to assure oneself—without ever becoming really sure—that "there cannot be any foundation in the story that he is a member of the ancient religion." The nineteenth century was becoming increasingly conscious of the contributions that members—or ex-members—of the "ancient religion" were making to its musical life; and Thackeray gently reminds his readers of that, in "The Ravenswing", by passing references to the performances of John

Braham and the compositions of Henri Herz (IV, 436, 390).

As if to show, however, that the old-established custom of referring to money-lenders as "the Jews" *tout simple* was alive and well, Thackeray makes the German heroine of "The—'s Wife" (*Fraser's Magazine*, November 1843) reflect: "Money we want, Heaven knows; for my father's pay is mortgaged thrive over to the Jews, and we owe ten times as much as we can pay." (IV, 495).

vi

Thackeray, or his *alter ego* Michael Angelo Titmarsh, continued supplying London periodicals with exhibition reviews and other pieces on the fine arts in the early 1840s, and frequently used these to attack the inadequacy with which contemporary painters treated Old Testament scenes:

> Mr. [Charles] Eastlake's Hagar is beautiful as everything else by this accomplished artist; but here, perhaps, the beauty is too great, and the pain not enough. The scene is not represented in its actual agony and despair; but this is, as it were, a sort of limning to remind you of the scene; a piece of mystical poetry with Ishmael and Hagar for the theme . . .
> ("Letters on the Fine Arts. No. 4. The Royal Academy (Second Notice)", *The Pictorial Times*, 27 May 1843—II, 598)

Thackeray seems to have felt most comfortable with the kind of emblematic use of scriptural representations which had been characteristic of Hogarth and which he was himself to emulate in some of the illustrations for *Vanity Fair*. He waxes lyrical over Daniel Maclise's painting of the play-scene in *Hamlet*:

> Fancy, in the little theatre, the King asleep; a lamp in front casts a huge forked fantastic shadow over the scene—a shadow that looks like a horrible devil in the background that is grinning and aping the murder. Fancy ghastly flickering tapestries of Cain and Abel on the walls, and all this painted with the utmost force, truth, and dexterity—fancy all this, and you will have not the least idea of one of the most startling, wonderful pictures that the English school has ever produced.
> ("An Exhibition Gossip . . .", *Ainsworth's Magazine*, June 1842—II, 576)

The pictures of Cain and Abel open an archetypal perspective on what happens in Shakespeare's play.

When he comes to look at representations of Jews in more modern times Titmarsh shares, in a characteristically modified and qualified way, the pleasure his contemporaries derived from Delacroix's romantic exoticism:

'A Jewish Wedding at Tangiers' is brilliant with light and merriment;
a particular sort of merriment, that is, that makes you gloomy in the
very midst of the heyday . . .
　　　("On Men and Pictures, à propos of a Walk in the Louvre",
　　　　　　　　　　　　　Fraser's Magazine, July 1841—II, 568)

A portrait of the actress Rachel Félix, however, that exotic figure in
the midst of Paris, sat uneasily among the "ogling beauties"
depicted in surrounding paintings; we have already heard
Titmarsh's left-handed praise of its "cleverness and unlikeness"
("An Exhibition Gossip . . .", *Ainsworth's Magazine*, June 1842—II,
578).

In *Thackeray: The Uses of Adversity* G.N. Ray quotes from a letter
Thackeray received from John Forster in 1842: "I'll send you the
French Order in the course of the day. Did you think of Janin? The
bearer will bring you Herwegh." (14 March 1842—op. cit., p. 485).
This would seem to refer, as Ray recognizes, to two essays in the
Foreign Quarterly Review, "English History and Character on the
French Stage" and "George Herwegh's Poems", and to afford some
evidence that Thackeray wrote them. The essay on Herwegh,
which is of great interest because of its skilful translations from the
German, mentions two contemporaries of Jewish origin (Ludwig
Börne and August Lewald) without alluding to this origin in any
way.

> All Berlin was *fou* about [Herwegh], as it had been of Liszt three
> months before, and of Börne and Madlle. Sontag a dozen years ago.
> Nor were the triumphs of George Herwegh altogether so unsubstan-
> tial as those of some other literary lions have been; for, our informant
> states, a young, rich and handsome Berlinerinn [sic] became desper-
> ately enamoured of the republican bard, and is now a rich, hand-
> some, and happy republican's wife.
> 　　　(*The Foreign Quarterly Review*, XXXI, April 1843, p. 59)

Ludwig Börne is here simply part of the German literary and social
scene; his Jewish ancestry, even if the reviewer knew about it, need
not be mentioned.
　　The evidences which Ray adduces for Thackeray's authorship of
"George Herwegh's poems" are not available for another essay in
the *Foreign Quarterly Review*, published three months later: a discussion of Karl Gutzkow's *Briefe aus Paris* which appeared under the
title: "'Letters from Paris' by Charles Gutzkow" (loc. cit. XXXI,
April 1843). The piece is, however, sufficiently like the Herwegh
review in style and tone, to lend some substance to R.S. Garnett's
claim (in *The New Sketch Book*, London 1906) that it is indeed by
Thackeray. Here is a representative passage:

... a few weeks on the banks of the Thames is apt to send the solitary wanderer back with aversion and disgust to us insulars. Thus Henry Heine, the other day, went to enjoy sea-breezes, and study English character at Boulogne. He found a gay, proud set of demi-fashionables, who had never heard of Henry Heine, who took him in consequence for a commonplace personage without livery servants and coach and pair, and treated him *de haut en bas*. Poor Henry Heine was so susceptible and so indignant at all this, that he has become a decided foe to England and her inhabitants! He is a writer for the *Augsburg Gazette*, and there he has just published the most vitriolic diatribes against our grasping, haughty, mercantile, intolerant, and abominable spirit. In short, he joins the French cry of *Delenda est Carthago*, setting us down for Carthage. For these reasons we sincerely hope that Young Germany may stay away from us, till he acquires less susceptibility, with more years, sense, and discretion.

(lot. cit., p. 103)

This passage on Heine, which treats British "demi-fashionables" at Boulogne with what may well be thought Thackerayan irony while also excoriating Heine's generalizations, is followed by a passage in which this same reviewer appraises German and French critiques of the actress Rachel Félix.

Gutzkow is very severe upon Rachel, but seems to have taken his opinions respecting her solely from Janin. He bitterly complains of her never laughing. No one is human or has a heart, says Gutzkow, who does not laugh or betray feeling by a smile. The tragedian might reply, that the parts of Corneille's and Racine's heroines are no laughing matter. But the German critic calls the French actress (in our opinion, a woman of decided genius), stiff, made of pale bronze, without feminine softness, passion or *gemuth* (sic). He goes further than Janin taught him, however. For he extends this sweeping censure to the French in general . . .

(ibid.)

The anonymous critic, whether he be Thackeray or not, here treats Heine as a representative of "Young Germany" and Rachel as a "French actress"; it is only their juxtaposition which suggests that there is a link between them in the critic' mind—a link which can only be their Jewish origins.

In other reviews of the time we find references to Jews in lowlier occupations than those of Heine and Rachel. Reviewing a book in which a German naturalist recounts his travels, Thackeray draws on his own experiences to describe the social transmogrification English travellers of humble origin may effect at foreing courts:

we bakers' sons, or retired linendrapers, or erratic lawyers'-clerks, with a sufficient sum of money to carry us genteelly through a six-months' Continental tour, need only purchase a fancy volunteer's

uniform from some fashionable tailor in Holywell Street, and may in
our turn figure in foreign courts, dancing quadrilles with the best
duchesses at the Tuileries, or eating Sauerkraut by the side of
German counts and dukes of thirty descents.

("The German in England", V, 403)

The "fashionable tailor of Holywell Street" is, of course, a Jewish
seller of secondhand clothing who passes the cast-off garments of
the well-born and well-connected to those lower down the social
scale, or one who has similar items run up on demand without
asking awkward questions about entitlement.

The early 1840s have brought many fresh nuances into Thackeray's
depiction of Jews. He shows up the irrational bases of anti-Jewish
feeling within the German setting of "Little Spitz", and exemplifies, in "The Great Hoggarty Diamond", the ribbing Jews had to
take from Gentile colleagues and associates, and their reaction to
such jests. In the *Paris Sketch Book* he introduces Jews that trade
between England and France and shows Jewish bailiffs on holiday
hobnobbing abroad with British Gentiles who may find them fascinating but who would never admit them to social intercourse at
home. There is talk of a religious service "performed with the
greatest pomp" in a Parisian synagogue. A great actress of Jewish
origin, Rachel Félix, makes an impressive appearance, as does a
great writer of similar origin, Heinrich Heine, about whose pantheistic Saint-Simonism Titmarsh has, however, profound reservations. Other works introduce Jewish musicians, attorneys and
cigar-merchants as well as the usual sellers of old clothes, bespoke
tailors, bailiffs and financiers. Some of these are estranged from the
religion into which they were born; and Titmarsh raises doubts
about the desirability of tempting Jews, or other adherents of a
non-militant religious group, away from their forefathers' "quiet
and sober way of faith". The benefits of religious toleration are
eloquently proclaimed by "Jolly Jack". There are Jewish cheats
and time-servers, but just as many Gentile ones; and when it comes
to large-scale commercial frauds like the West Diddlesex Company, the main culprits are identified as professing Christians
without any suspicion of Jewish descent. Caricature of "Jewish"
speech is used with some discretion: it sometimes marks a difference between an older generation and its more assimilated off-
spring, sometimes a psychological moment when a character
becomes aware that his conversational partner speaks with an
accent different from his own, and sometimes there is even a
suspicion of Jewish self-caricature, Jewish "playing up" to a Gentile image. Jews are presented as shrewd financial operators, but

they are not all Rothschilds: they may miscalculate, misinterpret, or overreach themselves. In all these financial matters they are not unlike Gentile colleagues and associates who show at least as keen an interest in money as they do. The portrayal of attractive Jewish girls is elaborated (with a flash-forward to later over-ornamentation and running to fat), and loaded with sexual symbolism, while male Jews are once again portrayed as physically unattractive, addicted to dubious jewellery, and inviting caricature even when they behave courageously. It is becoming more difficult, however, to distinguish assimilated Jews like Frank Leveson from British Gentiles whose accent, clothes and occupations he shares, or to assign an artist like Boroski to the "wandering race" with any degree of certainty.

In his art-criticism Thackeray-Titmarsh shows himself quick to criticize what he conceives to be inadequacies in the painters' treatment of Old Testament subjects by referring to *Paradise Lost* as easily as to the Bible itself. The poetry and human interest inherent in Biblical narrative are confirmed and strengthened by English cultural, literary and pictorial traditions.

The reception of "Miss Löwe" placed Thackeray on the defensive against Jewish critics, concerned to argue that he portrayed individuals rather than nations or ethnic groups; but the fact that "Miss Löwe" was later omitted from the Fitz-Boodle Papers may indicate that Thackeray had become uneasy about his protagonist's generalizations about "Jew bankers", his grossly unsympathetic portrayal of the physical appearance of Jewish men, and the lack of more sympathetic Jewish characters who might introduce an element of correction and counterbalance into that story. This can only be speculation, however, for Thackeray also omitted from the same collection two stories that had autobiographical relevance, but no connection whatever with Jewish affairs. The depiction of Mossrose, the aggressive, upwardly mobile Jew with a chip on his shoulder who appears in "The Ravenswing", does little to improve matters; but in that story Thackeray tempers the unsympathetic or comic traits of the Jews he portrays by showing them subject to compassion in the face of genuine distress. The most important counterbalance, however, is provided by Thackeray's unsparing depiction of a host of unattractive and dishonest Gentiles, which allowed him to say of his less than honest Jewish characters, with some justice: "If there be no worse rogues in Jewry, the people is more lucky than the rest of the world, and the fact is good to be known."

CHAPTER 4

HIGH LIFE AND SQUALOR
(1843–1846)

> . . . as the bodily Disraeli used to be seen some years
> ago about town, arrayed in green inexpressibles with
> a gold stripe down the seams, an ivory cane, and, for
> what we know, a peacock's feather in his hat—
> Disraeli the writer in like manner assumes a magnifi-
> cence never thought of by our rigid northern
> dandies . . .
>
> (VI, 507)

> Then all the fleas in Jewry
> Jumped up and bit like fury . . .
>
> (IX, 172)

i

1843 saw the publication of

THE IRISH SKETCH BOOK

1842

BY

MR. M. A. TITMARSH

WITH NUMEROUS ENGRAVINGS ON WOOD

DRAWN BY THE AUTHOR

The dedication of this book to Charles Lever, "laying aside for
the moment the travelling title of Mr. Titmarsh", reveals for the
first time the author's true name: W.M. THACKERAY (V, 3). It
turns out to be one of his liveliest performances, affording its readers
vivid impressions of Irish landscapes, townscapes, and social
conditions, while at the same time airing its author's prejudices and
predilections in a sometimes confidently assertive, sometimes humorously self-deprecating way. In his travels through Ireland,
Titmarsh seems to have met no Jews; but Old Testament narratives and sayings spring constantly to his mind, and memories of
earlier impressions and encounters occasionally intrude. Hearing
"a little smiling German boy . . . singing a ballad of Hauff's"
reminds Titmarsh of visits to Frankfurt am Main, with its "hand-

some Jew country-houses by the Bockenheimer-Thor" (V, 127); and the "labyrinth of busy swarming poverty and squalid commerce" he encounters in the less "handsome" part of Limerick brings to mind a more familiar London scene: "St. Giles's, where Jew and Irishman side by side exhibit their genius for dirt" (V, 151). Nowhere, not even in *The Journey from Cornhill to Grand Cairo*, does Thackeray show himself as fastidiously put off by dirt and squalor as in the *Irish Sketch Book*. That the "very mouldy, dirty town" of Tuam near Galway should boast an *archbishop* strikes him as risible:

> The Most Reverend Dr. MacHale is a clergyman of great learning, talents, and honesty, but his Grace the Lord Archbishop of Tuam strikes me as being no better than a mountebank; and some day I hope even his own party will laugh this humbug down. It is bad enough to be awed by big titles at all; but to respect sham ones!—O stars and garters! We shall have his Grace the Lord Chief Rabbi next, or his Lordship the Arch-Imaum!
>
> (V, 222)

Jesters do oft prove prophets—at the time of writing the British House of Lords contains no "Arch-Imaum", but a Chief Rabbi, Lord Jakobovits, made his maiden speech there on 4 March 1988. This would not, however, have shocked Thackeray greatly; for his Irish travels convinced him of the importance of religious toleration. One significant sign of this is the favour with which he speaks of the non-denominational university recently founded in London, at a time in which the older universities still insisted on religious tests before admission (Oxford) or before proceeding to a degree (Cambridge):

> The establishing of an open college in Munster would bring much popularity to any Ministry that should accord such a boon. People would cry out, "Popery and Infidelity," doubtless, as they did when the London University was established; as the same party in Spain would cry out, "Atheism and Heresy." But the time, thank God! is gone by in England when it was necessary to legislate for *them*; and Sir Robert Peel, in giving his adherence to the National Education Scheme, has sanctioned the principle of which this so much longed-for college would only be a consequence.
>
> (V, 85)

An "open college" on the lines of University College, London, would, of course, entail the admission of Jews as well as Protestant Dissenters and Roman Catholics.

The *Irish Sketch Book* caused some justified offence to Irishmen who felt that the traveller had dwelt too much on dirt, squalor, beggary and the spinning of tall tales, and that he had viewed

Ireland (as Charles Lever, to whom the book was dedicated, complained) "through complacently Cockney eyes". Thackeray felt, however, that such criticism missed too much; that he had been at pains to depict friendliness, beauty, devotion to to duty and other virtues among the Irish men and women he had encountered; and that it failed to take into account the stress he had laid throughout on the danger of generalizing about national character. After describing "a young Edinburgh cockney", a "little pert grinning Scotchman" who exhibited "an easy self-confidence that the reader may have perhaps remarked in others of his calling and nation", the traveller feels tempted

> to enter into a dissertation upon natural characteristics: to show that the bold, swaggering Irishman is really a modest fellow, while the canny Scot is a most brazen one; to wonder why the inhabitant of one country is ashamed of it—which is in itself so fertile and beautiful, and has produced more than its fair proportion of men of genius, valour, and wit; whereas it never enters into the head of a Scotchman to question his own equality (and something more) at all;

but he immediately recollects

> that such discussions are quite unprofitable; nay, that exactly the contrary propositions may be argued to just as much length. Has the reader ever tried with a dozen of De Tocqueville's short crisp philosophic apophthegms and taken the converse of them? The one or other set of propositions will answer equally well; and it is the best way to avoid all such. Let the above passage, then, simply be understood to say, that on a certain day the writer met a vulgar little Scotchman—not that all Scotchmen are vulgar; that this little pert creature prattled about his country as if he and it were ornaments to the world—which the latter is, no doubt; and that one could not but contrast his behaviour with that of great big stalwart simple Irishmen, who asked your opinion of their country with as much modesty as if you—because an Englishman—must be somebody, and they the dust of the earth.
>
> Indeed, this want of self-confidence at times becomes quite painful to the stranger. . . .
>
> (V, 118)

No one can gather impressions of a country while on an extended tour, and remember earlier encounters with natives of that country, without grouping separate encounters and recollections in a way that suggests national, regional or ethnic peculiarities. Such groupings can never be more than provisional, however—so much depends on temperament mood, time, chance meetings, prejudice, vagaries of memory, keenness of observation and generalizing faculty . . . The caveat just quoted from Chapter X of the *Irish Sketch Book* takes account of this; but one must not overlook, in pursuing a theme so important for the present undertaking, the effect of the humorous, ironic, deliberately teasing manner of narration and commentary which is so characteristic of Thackeray. His is a style of writing which invites a "deconstructive" reading, a reading against the grain. It challenges the reader to test his own previous impressions and memories against those suggested by the book before him, to consider his own attitudes alongside those of the more or less fictional narrator.

> Next Sunday, in the county Meath, in a quiet old church lying amongst meadows and fine old stately avenues of trees, and for the benefit of a congregation of some thirty persons, I heard for the space of an hour and twenty minutes some thorough Protestant doctrine, and the Popish superstitions properly belaboured. *Does it strengthen a man in his own creed to hear his neighbour's belief abused? One would imagine so*; for though abuse converts nobody, yet many of our pastors think they are not doing their duty by their own fold unless they fling stones at the flock in the next field, and have, for the honour of the service, a match at cudgelling with the shepherd.
>
> (V, 276—my italics)

To "One would imagine so" the right reader is challenged to add: "But it is futile, and should *not* be so"; and the habit of mind encouraged by this style of writing can and should be brought to bear on passages of apparently more confident, less ironic, assertion.

ii

Thackeray's contributions to *The Foreign Quarterly Review* and the early numbers of *Punch* remained anonymous; but M.A. Titmarsh is once again made to assume responsibility for a series of art criticisms, and for the essay "Jerome Paturot, with Considerations on Novels in General". The last-named piece, which was published in *Fraser's Magazine* in September 1843, warns readers off "lugubrious" fictions like *The Bride of Lammermoor* and *Oliver Twist*, bidding them opt, instead, for such more cheerful works as *Ivanhoe* and *The Pickwick Papers*:

> with regard to *Oliver Twist*, it did very well to frighten one in numbers; but I am not going to look on at Sikes's murder and to writhe and twist under the Jew's nightmare again. No! no! give me Sam Weller and Mr. Pickwick for a continuance. Which are read most—*The Pirate* and *The Bride of Lammermoor*, or *Ivanhoe* and *Quentin Durward?*—The former may be preferred by scowling Frenchmen, who pretend to admire Lord Byron. . . .
>
> (VI, 322)

Cheerful Victorian Englishmen like Titmarsh, we are meant to think, are not likely to be seduced into the perverted taste for Byron and for fictional horrors (exemplified in their literature by the "nightmare" of Dickens's Jew) which may be good enough for the "scowling" French who had welcomed the novels of Eugène Sue. Thackeray has his tongue in his cheek here, but to a very large extent he shared the taste in art and literature which he imputed to Michael Angelo Titmarsh.

An aside in "Jerome Paturot" also reintroduces a figure familiar to Victorian theatre-goers and joy-riders: "the Jew-boy who sells oranges at the coach-door" (VI, 323). Like "the burnt-umber Malay who sweeps crossings", Titmarsh declares, such boys have a greater chance of making money by their trade than the "professional penmen" of contemporary Britain. Even allowing for humorous exaggeration, and leaving aside the subsequent career of orange boys, Titmarsh's estimate of the chances of dark-skinned crossing-sweepers seem singularly wide of the mark.

In the year in which "Jerome Paturot" and *The Irish Sketch Book* appeared, the year 1843, Thackeray took a trip to Holland, where he had his most unfortunate encounter yet with Jews or men whom he took to be Jewish. In "Notes of a Tour to the Low Countries during August 1843", which he never published, he recounts how on an evening spent in Rotterdam he had walked into a district full of "goffre and fritter shops" that he compares, to its disadvantage, with Greenwich Fair:

> The fair seemed to contain scarcely any other sort of amusement. You pass through street upon street of goffres, from one frying pan to another, until the delicious amusement begins to pall. There are some shows also to be seen by the curious but these are few in number and not so splendid in appearance as in our own dear country. Vill you go to a dancing-house? says the Jew Commissioner, and leads you through a street that looks like Wapping in a state of festivity. Immense crowding, drumming banging singing flags flying up and down the street liquor shops flowing with light, and sailors and landsmen in commotion. Three other Jew Commissioners leading three other parties of newly arrived English looking perfectly calm correct & miserable make their appearance too and enter the winged 'Paard' pretty much in company. They do not speak to one another of course, but look respectively as English always do now on meeting their countrymen, with a look that seems to say D— you. What do you do here? & so sit down in respective corners with their respective Jews. About twenty four ladies are walking up & down this saloon, dressed in all the colours of the tulip and flinging about killing glances: and in an orchestra four trumpeters are blowing out the lights with the blasts of immense waltzes.

'Vil you Valtz Sirs?' says the Jew Commissioner, and you feel inclined to knock him down for asking the question. And so starting up nothing abashed, the accomplished rascal seizes one of the ladies and whirls her round the room.

Then you are called upon to pay 3 florins for three glasses of punch: and feeling heartily ashamed of ever having been entrapped into such an abominable place are now at liberty to retire. I had expected to be introduced to a scene the humour of w^h might be somewhat broad it is true, but of a general jovial good-natured sort. A tea-party of Dowagers at Hackney could not behave with more outward correctness, nor could their virtue be more abominably dull than this cold painted leering ogling Dutch vice was. And I could not understand why the lacquais de place into whose hands the helpless traveller falls on his arrival insisted upon taking his prey into this den of vice and dullness until informed that he received half the price of the three glasses of punch w^h he was at liberty to drink too besides.

(LPP, II, 833–4)

It was not unnatural, in Thackeray's domestic circumstances, that he should have frequented brothels in London and abroad—indeed, his urethral troubles in later may have been, in part, of venereal origin. He hated this physical need, and by a well-known mechanism transferred some of his hatred and self-loathing to those who ministered to it. Is not, he asks, the very existence of such *maquereaux* an "especial satire upon us British youth" as well as "a most cruel satire upon the rascality of the world?"

To a pretty sort of wants of our English gentry is that diabolical squinting laughing brazen faced red-haired wretch . . . a purveyor. In our squeamish days his name is not to be mentioned in plain English—in French it is expressed by the name of a fish that is eaten with fennel sauce—A greater rascal the world never saw dangling at a gibbets end—a more audacious cynical impudence never belonged to any scoundrel Hebrew or Xtian. He lays bare all the rascally qualities of his heart with a great unblushing effrontery, and does not scruple not merely to be but to acknowledge himself a villain. You drive him off with kicks and foul words like a dog, & the fellow comes presently grinning back again to show you the way you have lost in the street, or to place a dish on your table. As he has established a percentage upon all the goods w^h strangers purchase from tradesmen, there is no insult w^h will induce him to let go his hold of you, until your hour of departure is fixed, and he can get money from you no more.

That man must have been more kicked and reviled in his time than an army of martyrs. His villainy is quite a curiosity so enormous and apparent it is . . . But modern politeness forbids the description of such rascals, and will only tell of a rogue whose behaviour is as modest as a Quakeress's, and whose vices won't [']raise a blush to the cheek of the most delicate female'—as the saying is.

So that the agreeable picture of the Jew Commissioner at Rotterdam must not be sketched in this place—Only he has been mentioned here order that the agreeable truth may be conveyed, that it is the crimes and debauchery of our British gentry on w^h the crimes and debauchery of this rascal fatten. He might have simply swindled in a matter of oranges or sealing wax but our vices were found to be a more profitable trade to cheat and traffic in. And every boat as it comes laden from England with pink-faced lads from college who are trying to give themselves a manly air, or young dragoons with sprouting mustachios empty brains and lacquered boots, brings this watchful villain pupils to introduce into his infernal school, whom he will excite, and corrupt as much as they can be corrupted, and whom he will rob certainly.

They talk about English morality. Psha! there is no vice in the world more open, coarse, brutal infamous than that of the English young gentleman—Take that rascal yonder as a criterion. He never thinks of fastening upon a German, and has a thorough almost English contempt for a Frenchman, but he will never leave an Englishman alone. And so *Joseph* (all commissioners are called Joseph) Good bye and go and be hanged.

(LPP, II, 835–6)

"Demoniacal", "diabolical squinting laughing brazen-faced red-haired wretch", "You drive him off with kicks and foul words like a dog", threats of gibbets and hanging—indignation coupled with self-blame, and with blame of the "open, coarse, brutal infamous" vice to which the "commissioner" panders, bring Thackeray as near as he was ever to come to medieval Jew-baiting. The familiar old images resurface: the Jew as devil, the Jew as dog, the Jew as incorrigible scoundrel who deserves to be hanged. It is, to be sure, a secularized picture; but one of Thackeray's letters to his mother adds another vital ingredient to this recapitulation of medieval Jew-baiting: the Jews as murderers of Christ. Thackeray even darkens the picture in a way no medieval Christian would have done by rejecting the Old Testament from which the Middle Ages drew three of its nine worthies and every sort of prefiguration of Christ.

> ... the Jews murdered him for questioning their exclusive claims to divine favor: for propounding another law to that w^h they had been taught to believe came to them from Jehovah especially, for setting up himself against their God—Why do I love the Saviour? (I love and adore the Blessed Character so much that I don't like to speak of it, and know myself to be such a rascal that I don't dare)—Because He is all Goodness Truth Purity—I dislike the Old Testament because it is the very contrary: because it contains no Gentleness no Humility no forgiveness—nothing but exclusiveness and pride curses and arrogance—Fancy Lot, fancy Ezekiel remonstrating with God! Fancy the Divine name used as the slaughter of the Cannanites was going on—Using the very same name, acting on the very same law the descendants of Joshua murdered the Christ. How were they to know that he was the Messiah? by his miracles?—numberless people

according to the Hebrew books performed miracles: by his doctrines? It was the very contrary of that w^h they had been taught to consider as Divine—and how could God change?—his very appearance was contrary to their belief,—that is to their interpretation of Scripture. You can't be the Messiah, they might say—The prophets tell us expressly that he is to be a King, and that Judah is to be exalted by him over all the earth—they literally interpreted the Bible, and crucified the Blessed Speaker of Truth and Love and Humility.

(LPP, II, 206—to Mrs. Carmichael-Smith, 2 August 1845)

One last medieval touch is missing from this horrendous picture— the Jew as usurer; and sure enough, "Notes of a Tour in the Low Countries" has Thackeray's variation on that theme too. He narrates an encounter with a Jewish financier who sought to educate his children to be responsible and self-reliant in money-matters:

I have given my son he said to me twenty thousand guilders to begin the world with, and for whatever more money he wants, *he pays me eight per cent*. Hence to get thirty per cent from any Gentile in need, is I have no doubt not a matter of remorse with him but of exultation. He thinks of it at night as of a good action, and tells his sons, & warns them to profit by his precious example.

(LPP, II, 837)

Here the mechanisms of prejudice are clearly seen in gear. Why should there be "no doubt" that a man must feel "exultation" at another man's need (and take grossly unfair advantage of it) because he is determined to teach his children financial self-reliance? Thackeray is drawing a moral caricature, based on unsupported presuppositions about Jewish glee at Gentile misfortunes.

The prejudices Thackeray has here aired did not prevent him from accepting the same financier's invitation to dinner.

Next day we were invited to a dinner of w^h it behoves me to speak in terms of the greatest respect. There was first a course of fish consisting of marvellous turbots salmon & soles, and then a course of meat & fowls, the whole concluding with a service of pastry w^h no doubt was as good as the courses preceding it. Here were assembled the Melchisedecs of several branches, there was Mrs Zorobabel of Amsterdam, and the two young Melchisedecs of the Hague, & Miss Aaron the Rabbis daughter, and pretty Mrs Manasseh of Leyden. All these ladies were perfectly ladylike pleasing & more than ordinarily clever. They made fun of me & Smith in the most audacious good-humoured merry way possible—of Smith I think especially, though he could not understand their joking, and as I imagined was rather inclined to assert the dignity of an English gentleman. They were fit company, I will not say for Smith & me but for the very best bred society in the world. *Their* lives are not passed in money-getting and discounting and chaffering—their husbands perform that part of the family service, and a pretty opinion must the wives have of them!

But the men—o the men! there was one a young Hebrew dandy with yellow hair, and turned up wristbands & varnished boots, who was said to be a young fellow of enormous wealth and who in the course of dinner handed a paper across the table to another guest. It was a bill of exchange. It ran me through like a carving-knife, not that I have any bills in the market, but why bring out the horrible paper at dinner? Is there no time of enjoyment sacred from it? At the sight of it the salmon turned stale, the wine became flat, the smiles of good natured Mrs Zorobabel became all of a sudden suspicious odius and malignant, as did the jokes of Mynheer Melchisedec (he had plenty of them and out of Joe Miller too for he has lived long and studied in England) and I fancied that his joking and bonhommie was a part of his business. What a number of poor devils has he entertained with those stories, many a faint sufferer has smiled as he told them, they are no more genuine stories than the books on a dentist's table are genuine books, they are decoys, vile stratagems to carry off the patients attention from the Extractor's designs upon him.

Another remark w^h I have to make about this dinner, and w^h fully excuses this criticism upon it, is the following All the while we at our end of the table were drinking the costliest wines I observed Melchisedec & his family were drinking ordinaire! Can there be any doubt about a man's intentions after that? Can we suppose for a minute that his hospitality was real? No. The dinner was a part of his business as much as a bill of exchange—I was going to say, that I would have drunk ordinaire myself than submitted to see others drinking it while I had better fare. That nonsense the reader would not probably believe—no more do I. But this I swear. I would rather at a feast that others should fare as well as I and have not the slightest respect for the giver of an entertainment who arranges matters otherwise.

(LPP, II, 837–8)

With his suspicions of the financier's intentions strengthened rather than allayed, Thackeray draws once again the by now familiar distinction between Jewish men and their ladies. It is an advance, however, on earlier presentations that these Dutch Jewish ladies, with their refinement and charming sense of humour, are found "fit company . . . for the very best bred society in the world." And even in the deepest slough of prejudice we find Thackeray's sense of fairness reasserting itself; for at the very end of the passage describing his dinner with Melchisedec a thin ray of benevolence is allowed to fall on the man whose hospitality he had found so suspect.

The only time during w^h Signor Melchisedec appeared to me in an amiable light was after dinner when we retreated to the drawing room, when the young people began to frisk and sing, when our noble young fellow with nothing Israelitish about him played admirably a

concert on the violin, when the yellow-haired dandy before mentioned shrieked most abominably to the piano a French romance
about Madame & flamme, and J'aime & même, and when Melchisedec himself sate by quite happy with a long pipe w^h he filled out
of a tortoise shell tobacco-box, not thinking of money but looking on
at the happiness of his children & family.

   Next day he came to bid us adieu, and calling down blessings on
the head of Smith told me I might have the tobacco-box a bargain,
and I bought it and have it to this day. His parting words were that I
might have the money back for it whenever I pleased. And we took
boat again and came back to Antwerp.

(LPP, II, 838)

The praise of a musician who "had nothing Israelitish about him"
is a catty touch, of course, as is the description of the singing; but
Jewish family affection comes through, and the final bargain,
concerning a tobacco-box, has evidently been a fair one.

   "Notes of a Tour in the Low Countries" contain the most
virulently anti-Jewish passages to be found in Thackeray's writings
since he had called Nathan Rothschild "a greasy-faced compound
of donkey and pig." There is, however, an important distinction:
while the Rothschild poem was published, the "Notes" remained
among Thackeray's papers, as a private record of disenchantments,
grievances and hang-ups, until later editors disinterred them. Their
suppression is as significant as the fact of their existence. The
impression of Jewish traders in the Netherlands which Thackerays
Titmarsh gives to readers of *Fraser's Magazine* ("Little Travels and
Roadside Sketches", May 1844) is, by contrast, wholly favourable.

   We were a dozen tobacco-consumers in the wagon of the train that
   brought us from Antwerp; nor did the women of the party (sensible
   women!) make a single objection to the fumigation. But enough of
   this; only let me add, in conclusion, that an excellent Israelitish
   gentleman, Mr. Hartog of Antwerp, supplies cigars for a penny
   a-piece, such as are not to be procured in London for four times the
   sum.

(VI, 482)

Such praise of Jews for supplying worth-while goods at reasonable
prices had in fact been prepared for by the last paragraph about
Melchisedec in "Notes of a Tour in the Low Countries"; but the
warm words about an "excellent Israelitish gentleman" in "Little
Travels and Roadside Sketches" come untainted by the prejudice,
hatred and contempt—pathological in part, self-condemnation
turned outwards, guilt-feelings loaded onto Jewish scapegoats—
which make the "Notes" such distressing reading.

   "Little Travels and Roadside Sketches" also contains Titmarsh's most disenchanted view of fellow travellers from his native land. The chapter headed "Ghent" contains a horrific description of their haughty behaviour, and the hatred it arouses, which culminates in the sad observation: "Of all European people, which is the nation that has the most haughtiness, the strongest prejudices, the greatest reserve, the greatest dullness? I say an Englishman of the genteel classes" (VI, 496). When one contemplates Thackeray's sometimes jaundiced or ungenerous depiction of Jews or Irishmen, or certain types of French swaggerers, one must never forget how harshly critical he could be, or allow his personae to be, of men and women of the nation, and the social sphere, to which he belonged or to which he felt himself owing allegiance.

iii

From January to December 1844 *Fraser's Magazine* published, in regular instalments, "The Luck of Barry Lyndon: A Romance of the Last Century"; a work Thackeray was later to publish, in somewhat shortened form, under the title "The Memoirs of Barry Lyndon, Esq." (*Miscellanies*, III, 1856). It is a picaresque tale whose central protagonist, a scoundrel who tells his story in the first person, begins and ends in Ireland, but spends much of his disreputable manhood as a soldier and fortune hunter in the Germany of the Seven Years' War. The reader enters a world of rogues and fools, knaves and harlots, brutes and victims, filtered through the perceptions of Barry Lyndon, who is as much rascal and brute as any of them, though he has endearing moments and does not, in the end, achieve the fortune for which he is willing to sacrifice even those nearest to him in blood and affection.

Barry begins the narrative of his disreputable life and career—what Thackeray's editorial voice calls "the candid and ingenious narrative of his virtues and defects" (VI, 245)—with a reference to Genesis in which he also shows clearly how the word "race" comes into play when a family is to be seen in historical perspective:

> Since the days of Adam there has been hardly a mischief done in this world but a woman has been at the bottom of it. Ever since ours was a family (and that must be very *near* Adam's time—so old, noble and illustrious are the Barrys, as everybody knows,) women have played a mighty part with the destinies of our race.
>
> (VI, 3)

He shows the same desire to trace his "race" back to Old Testament narratives of origin elsewhere in the book—as in his conversation with a learned German to whom he boasts of the Barry family's descent from "the ancient kings":

'From which race of kings?' said he.

'Oh!', said I (for my memory for dates was never very accurate), 'from the old ancient kings of all.'

'What? can you trace your origin to the sons of Japhet?' said he.

'Faith, I can', answered I, 'and farther too,—to Nebuchadnezzar, if you like.'

(VI, 90)

It is characteristic of Barry that he is not only remarkably vague about Biblical chronology but that he is as ready to brag about his supposed descent from a Babylonian tyrant as from characters that cut a more respectable figure in Biblical narrative. Thackeray will have counted, no doubt, on his readers' recollection of what the Bible had to say about that tyrant's sticky end.

In Ireland Barry encounters a goldsmith who, reasonably enough, shows himself unwilling to let Barry have a coveted gold-chain without ready payment; he is dignified with the appelation "a rascal Jew" for his pains (VI, 59). There is also Moses the pawnbroker, who "peaches" about Barry's financial affairs and thus sets Barry's Irish creditors at that young man's heels (VI, 61). Seeking a better fortune in Germany, Barry is press-ganged into the Prussian army along with the already mentioned Saxon student of philosophy and theology who had been snapped up by King Frederick's recruiting officers just after delivering a trial sermon in support of his candidature for a vacant living. He tells Barry how after that sermon he and the other candidates had "supped lovingly at the Blue Stag in Rumpelwitz":

> While so occupied, a waiter came in and said that a person without wished to speak to one of the reverend candidates, "the tall one." This could only mean me, for I was a head and shoulders higher than any other reverend gentleman present. I issued out to see who was the person desiring to hold converse with me, and found a man whom I had no difficulty in recognizing as one of the Jewish persuasion.
>
> '"Sir," said this Hebrew, "I have heard from a friend, who was in your church to-day, the heads of the admirable discourse you pronounced there. It has affected me deeply, most deeply. There are only one or two points on which I am yet in doubt, and if your honour could but condescend to enlighten me on these, I think—I think Solomon Hirsch would be a convert to your eloquence."
>
> '"What are these points, my good friend?" said I; and I pointed out to him the twenty-four heads of my sermon, asking him in which of these his doubts lay.
>
> 'We had been walking up and down before the inn while our conversation took place, but the windows being open, and my comrades having heard the discourse in the morning, requested me, rather peevishly, not to resume it at that period. I, therefore, moved on with my disciple, and, at his request, began at once the sermon,

for my memory is good for anything, and I can repeat any book I have read thrice.

'I poured out, then, under the trees, and in the calm moonlight, that discourse which I had pronounced under the blazing sun of noon. My Israelite only interrupted me by exclamations indicative of surprise, assent, admiration, and increasing conviction. "Prodigious!" said he;—"*Wunderschön!*" would he remark at the conclusion of some eloquent passage; in a word, he exhausted the complimentary interjections of our language, and to compliments what man is averse? I think we must have walked two miles when I got to my third head, and my companion begged I would enter his house, which we now neared, and partake of a glass of beer, to which I was never averse.

'That house, sir, was the inn at which you, too, if I judge aright, were taken. No sooner was I in the place than three crimps rushed upon me, told me I was a deserter, and their prisoner, and called upon me to deliver up my money and papers, which I did with a solemn protest as to my sacred character.

(VI, 92–3)

To find treacherous Jews in the treacherous world of *Barry Lyndon* is no occasion for surprise; but it should be said that the records of German Jewry contain no evidence to suggest that Jews acted as decoys for Prussian recruiting-officers in the way here described.

In the service of the Prussian Captain von Potzdorf Barry encounters Jews in more familiar as well as more historically warranted and explicable guise: the captain, he tells us, "was in debt, and had dealings with the Jews, to whom he gave notes of hand payable on his uncle's death." (VI, 110). Such dealings in post-obits were not uncommon either in Barry's eighteenth or in Thackeray's nineteenth century. After leaving the captain's service, Barry encounters a fellow-Irishman who turns out to be his uncle, his father's brother, who is travelling the Continent in search of opportunities to gamble and who, when the cards are favourable, lays out his money in trinkets that he sports about his person.

It's property, look you, Redmond, and the only way I have found of keeping a little about me. When the luck goes against me, why, my dear, my diamonds go to the pawnbrokers, and I wear paste. Friend Moses, the goldsmith, will pay me a visit this very day, for the chances have been against me all the week past, and I must raise money for the bank to-night.

(VI, 117)

The Irish uncle's somewhat kindlier disposition throws a more friendly light on the Jewish tradesmen and money-lenders with whom such soldiers of fortune had to do business than Barry (here known as "Redmond") had found himself able or willing to do.

After reading a *chronique scandaleuse* entitled *L'Empire, ou dix ans sous Napoléon*, by the Baron de la Mothe-Langon (Paris 1836), Thackeray inserted into his novel an episode set in Württemberg (called W- in the first and X- in the second version), in which Barry, prating of love and honour, seeks to compass the hand of a wealthy aristocratic lady by means of blackmail, swindling, and extortion. The chief instrument he plans to use in furthering his plot is the Chevalier de Magny, with whom the Princess Olivia, wife of the hereditary prince, is in love. Barry and his uncle set about exploiting Magny's passion for gambling.

> My uncle dryly said, 'Get Magny to play; never mind his paying; take his notes of hand. The more he owes the better; but, above all, make him play.'
> 'He can't pay a shilling,' answered I. 'The Jews will not discount his notes at cent per cent.'
> 'So much the better. You shall see we will make use of them,' answered the old gentleman.
>
> (VI, 142)

As so often, "the Jews" in this context simply means "money-lenders"—of any religious persuasion. The plot which we see being hatched here involves blackmailing de Magny and the indiscreet Princess Olivia into supporting Barry's claim for the hand of Countess Ida, who loves a poor ensign and whose sole qualifications for Barry's attentions are her money and her title. The two adventurers obtain notes of hand and jewels from de Magny in partial settlement of his gambling debts; and among the jewels there is one that can be traced back to the Princess Olivia.

> How we came to know the history of the emerald is simple enough. As we wanted money (for my occupation with Magny caused our bank to be much neglected), my uncle had carried Magny's trinkets to Mannheim to pawn. The Jew who lent upon them knew the history of the stone in question; and when he asked how her Highness came to part with it, my uncle very cleverly took up the story where he found it, said that the Princess was very fond of play, that it was not always convenient to her to pay, and hence the emerald had come into our hands. He brought it wisely back with him to S—; and, as regards the other jewels which the chevalier pawned to us, they were of no particular mark; no inquiries have ever been made about them to this day; and I did not only not know then that they came from her Highness, but have only my conjectures upon the matter now.
>
> (VI, 145)

Here a German Jew is depicted as operating, not only a money-lending business, but also a kind of informal information service about the provenance of outstanding jewels—necessary, no doubt, if he wants to guard himself against becoming unwittingly involved with stolen goods. The emerald is returned to de Magny, in return for his promise of support for Barry's marriage-plans; but he never restores it to the Princess Olivia, who is obviously gravely compromised by his possession of it. De Magny, Barry tells us,

> had heard, in casual intercourse with me, that my uncle and I had been beholden to Mr. Moses Löwe, the banker of Heidelberg, who had given us a good price for our valuables; and the infatuated young man took a pretext to go thither, and offered the jewel for pawn. Moses Löwe recognized the emerald at once, gave Magny the sum the latter demanded, which the chevalier lost presently at play; never, you may be sure, acquainting us with the means by which he had made himself master of so much capital. We, for our parts, supposed that he had been supplied by his usual banker, the Princess; and many rouleaux of his gold pieces found their way into our treasury, when at the court galas, at our own lodgings, or at the apartments of Madame de Liliengarten (who on these occasions did us the honour to go halves with us) we held our bank of faro.
>
> Thus Magny's money was very soon gone. But though the Jew held his jewel, of thrice the value, no doubt, of the sums he had lent upon it, that was not all the profit which he intended to have from his unhappy creditor, over whom he began speedily to exercise his authority. His Hebrew connexions at X—, money-brokers, bankers, horse-dealers, about the court there, must have told their Heidelberg brother what Magny's relations with the Princess were; and the rascal determined to take advantage of these, and to press to the utmost both victims. My uncle and I were, meanwhile, swimming upon the high tide of fortune, prospering with our cards, and with the still greater matrimonial game which we were playing; and we were quite unaware of the mine under our feet.
>
> Before a month was passed, the Jew began to pester Magny. He presented himself at X—, and asked for further interest—hush-money, otherwise he must sell the emerald. Magny got money for him; the Princess again befriended her dastardly lover. The success of the first demand only rendered the second more exorbitant. I know not how much money was extorted and paid on this unlucky emerald; but it was the cause of the ruin of us all.
>
> (VI, 156–7)

Moses Löwe, it would appear, has been transported from the nineteenth to the eighteenth century, and from George Fitz-Boodle's world into the more treacherous and dangerous one of Barry Lyndon. The extortion he there practises matches—indeed, is dwarfed by—that practiced by Barry and his uncle. Löwe is now surrounded by his "Hebrew connexions"; and these include a group not so far noticed in Thackeray's work, one that is known to have played a significant part in Germany's rural economy: Jewish horse-dealers. We had learnt earlier that Barry had come to respect the expertise of such men, but that he thought himself able to "judge a horse as well as any Jew dealer in Germany." (VI, 128).

The "ruin" of which Barry speaks is brought about by a trick that makes de Magny seem guilty of attempting to rob and murder Moses Löwe; investigation of this charge, of which he is innocent, leads to the discovery of his intrigue with Princess Olivia and ultimately to his death along with that of the indiscreet princess. Barry and his uncle are caught up in all this, first imprisoned and then expelled, and their plot of marrying into the German aristocracy comes to nothing.

The climax of this story is narrated to Barry, many years after the event, by Madame de Liliengarten, the mistress or morganatic wife of the Duke who ruled the Principality at the time of Barry's sojourn there. Her narrative introduces a new character: an arch-intriguer who had done more than any other to bring down Magny and the Princess and thus to thwart Barry's own pet scheme for attaining honour and riches. The name by which Madame de Liliengarten introduces this intriguer is that of Heinrich Heine's maternal family: van Geldern, or de Geldern.

> You remember Monsieur de Geldern, the police minister. He was of Dutch extraction, and, what is more, of a family of Dutch Jews. Although everybody was aware of this blot in his scutcheon, he was mortally angry if ever his origin was suspected; and made up for his father's errors by outrageous professions of religion, and the most austere practices of devotion. He visited church every morning, confessed once a week, and hated Jews and Protestants as much as an inquisitor could do. He never lost an opportunity of proving his sincerity, by persecuting one or the other whenever occasion fell in his way.
>
> He hated the Princess mortally; for her Highness in some whim had insulted him with his origin, caused pork to be removed from before him at table, or injured him in some such silly way; and he had a violent animosity to the old Baron de Magny, both in his capacity of Protestant, and because the latter in some haughty mood had publicly turned his back upon him as a sharper and a spy. Perpetual quarrels were taking place between them in council, where it was only the presence of his august masters that restrained the Baron from publicly and frequently expressing the contempt which he felt for the officer of police.
>
> Thus Geldern had hatred as one reason for ruining the Princess, and it is my belief he had a stronger motive still—interest. You remember whom the Duke married, after the death of his first wife?—a Princess of the house of F—. Geldern built his fine palace two years after, and, as I feel convinced, with the money which was paid to him by the F— family for forwarding the match.
>
> (VI, 160)

Here we have a new phenomenon in Thackeray's depiction of men and women of Jewish descent: the Jewish Judaeophobe, the convert who hates his former brethren and who is therefore doubly offended when someone reminds him of his family origins. It is de Geldern who organizes the attack on the man whom Madame de Liliengarten calls "the odious Löwe"; a man whom she sees turning from a bold extortioner to a "trembling Israelite" when physically threatened. The German principality is now shown to have been riddled with spies ("we all had spies on each other", Madame de Liliengarten recalls); and the police minister, naturally enough, was spy-master in chief. One of these spies was de Magny's valet, who told his master of Löwe's visits and demands.

> The man conducted the trembling Israelite out of the palace, and no sooner had seen him lodged at the house of one of his brethren, where he was accustomed to put up, than he went away to the office of his excellency the minister of police, and narrated every word of the conversation which had taken place between the Jew and his master.
>
> Geldern expressed the greatest satisfaction at his spy's prudence and fidelity. He gave him a purse of twenty ducats, and promised to provide for him handsomely, as great men do sometimes promise to reward their instruments; but you ... know how seldom those promises are kept. "Now, go and find out," said Monsieur de Geldern, "at what time the Israelite proposes to return home again, or whether he will repent, and take the money." The man went on this errand. Meanwhile, to make matters sure, Geldern arranged a play-party at my house, inviting you thither with your bank, as you may remember; and finding means, at the same time, to let Maxime de Magny know that there was to be faro at Madame de Liliengarten's. It was an invitation the poor fellow never neglected.'
>
> I remembered the facts, and listened on, amazed at the artifice of the infernal minister of police.
>
> The spy came back from his message to Löwe, and stated that he had made inquiries among the servants of the house where the Heidelberg banker lodged, and that it was the latter's intention to leave X—that afternoon. He travelled by himself, riding an old horse, exceedingly humbly attired after the manner of his people.
>
> "Johann," said the minister, clapping the pleased spy upon the shoulder, "I am more and more pleased with you. I have been thinking, since you left me, of your intelligence, and the faithful manner in which you have served me; and shall soon find an occasion to place you according to your merits. Which way does this Israelitish scoundrel take?"
>
> "He goes to R—to-night."
>
> "And must pass by the Kaiserwald. Are you a man of courage, Johann Kerner?"
>
> "Will your excellency try me?" said the man, his eyes glittering; "I served through the Seven Years' War, and was never known to fail there."

"Now, listen. The emerald must be taken from that Jew; in the very keeping it the scoundrel has committed high treason. To the man who brings me that emerald I swear I will give five hundred louis.

(VI, 161–2)

The plot, as we know, succeeds, Löwe makes the necessary confessions, roaring for mercy, and de Geldern, whom Barry has called "the infernal minister of police", moves towards a happy and prosperous retirement:

The now reigning Duke of X—himself married four years after his first wife's demise; and Geldern, though no longer police-minister, built the grand house of which Madame de Liliengarten spoke. What became of the minor actors in the great tragedy, who knows? Only *Monsieur de Strasbourg* was restored to his duties. Of the rest,—the Jew, the chamber-woman, the spy on Magny, I know nothing. Those sharp tools with which great people cut out their enterprises are generally broken in the using; nor did I ever hear that their employers had much regard for them in their ruin.

(VI, 177)

We have here an interesting instance of the way Thackeray converts action into symbol: for Madame de Liliengarten had just told Barry how Princess Olivia's husband, goaded to fury by de Geldern's revelations, had forced open a trunk containing his wife's private paper with a hunting-knife: "The point broke, and he gave an oath, but continued . . . with the broken blade . . ." (VI, 167). De Geldern, it would seem, had taken good care that he should be among the breakers rather than the broken; and his abjuration of Judaism had been the first step that took him along that road.

The final chapters of Barry Lyndon's memoirs return to the British Isles and Ireland, where his involvement with Jewish moneylenders and bill-discounters continues. "I found my cousin Ulick at Dublin, grown very fat, and very poor; hunted up by Jews and creditors . . ." (VI, 203); "I raised the money of the Jews, at an exorbitant interest . . ." (VI, 231) Money-lenders become more and more wary of him not only because of his more and more doubtful ability to repay them but also because of what Barry calls

that unlucky affair I had with Lawyer Sharp, when I made him lend me the money he brought down, and old Solomons the Jew being robbed of the bond I gave him after leaving my house . . .

(VI, 301)

This passage is glossed by the editor of Barry's memoirs, our old friend George Fitz-Boodle: "These exploits of Mr. Lyndon are not related in the narrative. He probably, in the cases above alluded to, took the law into his own hands" (VI, 301). The reader will recognize, of course, that what Barry did in Solomons's case was to imitate, as closely as circumstances warranted, what de Geldern, "the infernal minister of police", had done to Löwe. He cannot, however, compass de Geldern's good fortune, and we take our leave of him in the Fleet prison, where he writes, with wholly unjustified self-righteousness, of the many cruel persecutions, conspiracies, and slanders of which he has been a victim" (VI, 1). Before reaching the Fleet he has had to pass through a forecourt all too well known to all too many of Thackeray's characters: "carried off . . . from jail to jail, until he was lodged in the hands of Mr. Bendigo, of Chancery Lane, an assistant to the Sheriff of Middlesex, from whose house he went to the Fleet Prison." (VI, 309)

Barry Lyndon is important in the context of the present book because it illustrates so well Thackeray's use of national stereotypes in cases other than that of the Jews. Swaggering, boasting and magniloquence, drinking to excess, and a tendency to domestic disorder, are imputed to fictional Irish characters alongside more individual traits. Thackeray knows nothing, however, of more recent jokes about Irish slowness of mind; on the contrary, Barry tells of Irishmen "a great deal too sharp" for the military hierarchy of Prussia (VI, 80–81) and exhibits an astuteness in some of his dealings which confirms the tenor of such tales. The novel also shows that qualities elsewhere associated with Jews are by no means confined to them. Barry is allowed to put forward a philosophy of social climbing by foul means as well as fair:

> men so poor as myself can't afford to be squeamish about their means of getting on in life . . . the poor but aspiring must clamber up the wall, or push and struggle up the back stair, or, *pardi*, crawl through any of the conduits of the house, never mind how foul and narrow, that lead to the top
>
> (VI, 146)

and the "cormorants" who dun him for money are as likely to be Gentiles as Jews:

> I was bound up in an inextricable toil of bills and debts, of mortgages and insurances, and all the horrible evils attendant upon them. Lawyers upon lawyers posted down from London: composition after composition was made, and Lady Lyndon's income hampered almost irretrievably to satisfy these cormorants.
>
> (VI, 277)

Barry includes among these dunning lawyers an Irish firm whose name is deliberately ambiguous: "Messrs Sharp and Salmon of

Dublin" (VI, 302). "Salmon" could be an impeccably Anglo-Irish name, but it could also be a contraction and Anglicization of "Salomon"; while the name "Sharp"—characterizing the central figure in "that unlucky affair . . . with lawyer Sharp" of which we have already heard Barry speak—has no Hebrew sound to it, and looks forward significantly to *Vanity Fair*.

iv

On 11 August 1844 Thackeray entered in his diary: "Disraeli's dinner. 7 1/4 Read for B[arry] L[yndon] all the morning at the Club—then walked, a pleasant dinner at Disraelis." (LPP, II, 148). Politically, Thackeray was not of Disraeli's persuasion; he felt himself nearer to the Radicals than to either Whigs of Tories; but he clearly enjoyed social contact with Disraeli, and owned in conversation that he thought he "had great talents" (IR, I, 118). Disraeli the novelist, however, did not win his unmixed plaudits. He reviewed *Coningsby; or, The New Generation* twice in the same month: for *The Morning Chronicle* on 13 May 1844, and for *The Pictorial Times* on 25 May; and just a year later, on 13 May 1845, he reviewed *Sybil; or, The Two Nations*, again for the *Morning Chronicle*.

The tone and spirit of Thackeray's reviews of Disraeli's fiction are well conveyed by the opening of his piece in the *Pictorial Times*.

> IF this book do not become popular, what other novel has a chance? *Coningsby* possesses all the happy elements of popularity. It is personal, it is witty, it is sentimental, it is outrageously fashionable, charmingly malicious, exquisitely novel, seemingly very deep, but in reality very easy of comprehension, and admirably absurd; for you do not only laugh at the personages whom the author holds up to ridicule, but you laugh at the author too, whose coxcombries are incessantly amusing. They are quite unlike the vapid cool coxcombries of an English dandy; they are picturesque, wild, and outrageous; and as the bodily Disraeli used to be seen some years ago about town, arrayed in green inexpressibles with a gold stripe down the seams, an ivory cane, and, for what we know, a peacock's feather in his hat—Disraeli the writer in like manner assumes a magnificence never thought of by our rigid northern dandies, and astonishes by a luxury of conceit which is quite oriental. He paints his own portrait in this book in the most splendid fashion: it is the queerest in the whole queer gallery of likenesses; he appears as the greatest philosopher, the greatest poet, the greatest horseman, the greatest statesman, the greatest *roué* in the world; with all the qualities of Pitt, and Byron, and Burke, and the great Mr. Widdicomb of Batty's Amphitheatre. Perhaps one is reminded of the last-named famous individual more than of any other.
>
> (VI, 507)

The flamboyantly un-English quality, the calculated dandyism and the theatricality of this leader of Young England are emphasized, in a spirit of raillery which is mostly good-natured though there are some sharp points. Disraeli can hardly have been pleased with the parallel here drawn between his personal appearance and his literary style, or by the left-handed tributes to his showmanship. In both reviews of *Coningsby*, however, Thackeray is at pains to stress Disraeli's mastery of the literary portrait. That of Mr Rigby, for instance:

> A better portrait of a parasite has never been written since Juvenal's days, and we can fancy that even ages hence people will read this book as a singular picture of manners and society in our times.
>
> (VI, 508)

This comes from the *Pictorial Times* review; that in the *Morning Chronicle* also stresses "the intenseness of the Disraelite-*ego*" (one wonders how Disraeli liked the coinage "Disraelite" in this context), the un-English dandyism (drawing on *The Young Duke* for further evidence), and the author's command of literary portraiture based on known individuals. "We believe this gentleman", Thackeray assures readers of *The Morning Chronicle*, "to be not only a dandy but a man of genius." (*Thackeray's Contributions to the 'Morning Chronicle'*, ed. G. N. Ray, Urbana 1955, pp. 39, 41). *Coningsby* is placed in the context of the "silver fork" novels of the day when Thackeray calls this book "the fashionable novel pushed . . . to its extreme verge, beyond which all is naught" (ibid., p. 39); but what Disraeli has written, in the view of this critic, is not only a "dandy-social" novel like others of the "silver-fork" variety, but also a "dandy-political" and a "dandy-religious" one.

> Fancy a prostrate world kissing the feet of a reformer—in patent blacking; fancy a prophet delivering heavenly messages—with his hair in papers, and the reader will have our notion of the effect of the book.
>
> (ibid., p. 40)

Thackeray declares himself impressed by Disraeli's criticism of existing political parties and actual politicians, but far less so by what he feels to be the vagueness and emptiness of the Young England creed.

> We wish Sir Robert Peel joy of his Young England friends; and, admiring fully the vivid correctness of Mr. Disraeli's description of this great Conservative party, which conserves nothing, which proposes nothing, which resists nothing, which believes nothing: admire still more his conclusion, that out of this nothing a something is to be

created, round which England is contentedly to rally, and that we are one day to re-organize faith and reverence round this wretched, tottering, mouldy, clumsy, old idol.

(ibid., p. 50)

Readers, Thackeray feels, will laugh at this picture of Toryism old and new—"not only with the author, but at him" (VI, 508).

In *Barry Lyndon* Thackeray had drawn the portrait of a statesman of Jewish ancestry who scorned to be reminded of the origins of his family and who persecuted his former brethren. The author of *Coningsby* is the very opposite: although no longer a member of the Jewish community (his father had had him baptised when he was still a child), Disraeli gloried in his Jewish descent and created, in Sidonia, an idealized portrait of a Jew who was as proud of his origins as he was wise, astute urbane and powerful. Thackeray shows himself amused by some of the more highfalutin aspects of this portrait, by the term "Mosaic Arabs" which Disraeli coined as a synonym for "Jew", and by the large claims Sidonia makes for the Jewish part of the "Caucasian races" and for its overt and covert representation in the arts and politics of the modern world. These claims, he comments, are either excessive or "curious if authentic" (Ray, *Contributions*, p. 47). But, Thackeray adds, with British fairness, "in the midst of his extravagance, [we] can heartily admire the chivalrous energy of this champion of a persecuted people." (ibid., p. 49)

The vagueness of Young England's positive programme is censured once more in Thackeray's review of G.S. Smythe's *Historic Fancies* (*Morning Chronicle*, 2 August 1844), where *Coningsby* figures again as prime witness. The Old Testament suggestions inherent in "Jeremiah" (incongruously, a "Jeremiah of the clubs"!) and "the sword of destruction" are, of course, pointed and deliberate in this context.

> Such is the denunciation at first vaguely put forth by "Young England" against the "Conservative" party, whom he taunts with having nothing to conserve, not merely of their own, but of any body else's. They have no honour, no principles.
>
> So were they denounced the other day by Coningsby, the Jeremiah of the clubs; and bitterly did he scoff at every man of them as he pointed to the sword of destruction which was suspended above their heads. But still no hint was given of who were to supply their places, nor of what sort of principles were to rule the destinies of man, after their no-principle reign was over; or, if anything was hinted, it was so loosely and so vaguely, that it will probably not be understood till the prophecy is fulfilled.

(ibid., p. 57)

In another review (of Lever's *St. Patrick's Eve*, *Morning Chronicle*, 3 April 1845) Thackeray alludes to Peel's survey of Disraeli's many changes of front, and then brackets him with Frances Trollope in a condemnation of novels that take the reader too deeply into "the crabbed labyrinths of political controversy":

> Thus, too, we know that the famous author of "Coningsby," before he propounded the famous New England philosophy, had preached many other respectable doctrines, viz., the Peel doctrines, the Hume doctrines, &c.: all this Sir Robert Peel himself took the pains to explain to the House of Commons the other night, when the great philosopher alluded to called the right honourable baronet an organised hypocrite.
>
> The moral of this is (for we wish to show that newspaper critics can make morals as well as successful novelists) that as a Trollope and a Disraeli, persons of a fiery and poetical imagination, have gone astray when treading the crabbed labyrinths of political controversy; and not only gone astray, but, as it were, tripped, stumbled, broken their noses, and scratched themselves in an entirely ludicrous and undignified manner; other imaginative writers should take warning by the fate of these illustrious victims, nor venture into quagmires where they may flounder beyond their depth.
>
> (ibid., p. 72)

This favourite theme of Thackeray's is then struck up once more in the last of his reviews of Disraeli's novels: that of *Sybil* which he contributed to the *Morning Chronicle* in May 1845.

Sybil. By Mr. DISRAELI, M.P.

> It will not be the fault of the romantic writers of the present day if the public don't perceive that the times are out of joint, and want setting right very sadly. A few weeks since we had occasion to speak of Mr. Jerrold and Mr. Dickens as social regenerators. Since then Mrs. Norton's eloquent voice has been lifted up, and the "Child of the Islands" has accommodated the new doctrine to the Spenserian stanza; finally comes Mr. Disraeli, to discourse once more upon the world problem, in a three-volume parable, such as becomes a philosopher of his eastern origin.
>
> We stand already committed as to our idea of the tendency and province of the novel. Morals and manners we believe to be the novelist's best themes; and hence prefer romances which do not treat of algebra, religion, political economy, or other abstract science. We doubt the fitness of the occasion, and often (it must be confessed) the competency of the teacher.
>
> (ibid., pp. 77–8)

There is nothing underhand or unfair in the reviewer's allusion to the author's "Eastern origin"; Disraeli himself stressed it often enough, and made his Sidonia take the greatest pride in it.

Inasmuch as *Sybil* is more weighted with political theory and opinion than *Coningsby*, and less filled with "amusing, bitter sketches . . ., pleasant caricaturing or laughable malice, or Gillray grotesqueness" (ibid., pp. 78–9), Thackeray thinks it a less successful novel; but he owns himself struck by the "honesty, truth and hearty sympathy" of Disraeli's account of the sufferings which were the lot of agricultural labourers in the Hungry Forties. His portrayal of miners and factory workers is judged less satisfactory; but here too, Thackeray declares, the author of *Sybil* has performed a valuable service: he has pointed to subjects that other writers might treat with greater verisimilitude and power.

> We want a Boz from among the miners or the manufactories to detail their ways of work and pleasure—to describe their feelings, interests, and lives, public and private. Mr. Disraeli has done well to point to this mystery. Incomplete as we fancy his descriptions to be, yet they must turn the attention of his very many readers to a subject so full of novelty and wonderment. They may send travellers, in quest of sensations, to Wales or Lancashire this summer, in place of the Alps or Baden. They are not good, as we fancy, but they can do good; they are written with genuine feeling, and are worth all the fantastic Venetian and Dutch theories, to our mind.
>
> (ibid., p. 80)

Thackeray agrees with Disraeli, then, in seeing truthful, knowledgable, realistic fiction as one of the means by which the gulf between Britain's "two nations" can be bridged: the rich can be made sympathetically aware of the plight of the poor, the South can learn about the North, the clubman and the clerk about the agricultural labourer and the factory worker. He thinks the plot of *Sybil*, with its rescue of the heroine by Lord John Russell and its revelation that she is really "a baroness of forty thousand pounds a year" (ibid., p. 82), distinctly odd, as well he might; but he praises Disraeli's satiric picture of parliamentary cabals, his depiction of the "impractical selfishness" and conspiracies of the Chartists, and above all the "hundreds of subordinate personages, some of whom, especially those of the higher sort, are described we think with extraordinary skill." (ibid., p. 82). Unlike Disraeli, however, Thackeray wishes to keep out of fiction theoretical disquisitions on economic and financial management—like the system of "Dutch finance" pilloried in *Sybil*, described by Disraeli as "mortgag[ing] industry to protect property"—and party-politic-proposals for curing social ills. We would have been glad, Thackeray concludes, "to see a number of disquisitions, religious, retrospective, and prophetic, omitted" from *Sybil*:

If a man professes to write a book "in a light and unpretending form," as our author does, why introduce into it subjects both heavy and pretentious? We have a novel, and poor Lord John Russell brought in to get the heroine out of a scrape—a novel in which the Queen is brought to rescue us from "Saxon thraldom"—in which the extinct worship of the Catholic saints is regretted (with an enthusiasm which may be quite sincere, but which is as out of place here, as an Ave Mary would be in a comedy), and in which Charles the First's murder by the middle classes is introduced to account for the present misery of the poor. Charles the First's head! Mr. Gunter might just as well serve it up in sugar on a supper-table between a Charlotte Russe and a trifle.

(ibid., p. 86)

That stresses the differences between Thackeray's views on the nature of fiction and those implicit in Disraeli's novels; but given these differences, his reviews of *Coningsby* and *Sybil* are balanced and fairly argued. Since Disraeli makes great play with his own Jewishness, Thackeray has every right to comment on it. He does so with good humour, however, and anti-Jewish prejudices do not overtly affect his cogent critical assessment of Disraeli's fiction, even though it becomes clear that he cannot share Disraeli's high opinion of Jewish genius and cultural achievement.

It is worthy of note that Thackeray dined at Disraeli's house *after* the publication of these reviews. Disraeli must have known who had written them—it was impossible to keep such secrets in the small, tightly-knit *beau monde* and *monde littéraire* of the day; but he took even Thackeray's allusions to his personal life style and appearance in good part. What he was never to forgive, however, was the lampooning of his Jewish allegiances and loyalties in the later *Codlingsby*; after that parody had appeared in *Punch*, Disraeli broke off all relations with Thackeray, cut him dead when the two met face to face by accident, and took his revenge long after Thackeray's death by caricaturing him as "Elias Howle" in *Endymion*.

The views on the novelist's art which surface in the Disraeli reviews also play their part in Thackeray's discussion of Charles Lever in the columns of the *Morning Chronicle*.

When suddenly, out of the gilt pages of a pretty picture-book, a comic moralist rushes forward, and takes occasion to tell us that society is diseased, the laws unjust, . . . persons who wish to lead an easy life are inclined to [protest] . . .: I have shrewd doubts as to your competency to instruct upon all these points: at any event, I would much rather hear you on your own ground—amusing by means of amiable fiction, and instructing by kindly satire . . . eschewing questions of politics and political economy, as too deep, I will not say for your comprehension, but for your readers'; and never, from their nature, to be discussed in any, the most gilded, storybook.

(ibid., pp. 56–7)

That comes from a review of Lever's *St. Patrick's Eve*, and shows one of the objective criteria on which much of the critique of *Sybil* had been based. As for Disraeli himself—he turns up in yet another of Thackeray's *Morning Chronicle* reviews, an amusing picture of the "water cures" which drew many British sufferers to hydropathic establishments, especially in Germany, and of which Thackeray had some personal experience.

> Dowagers, senators, the dyspeptic, the gourmand fatigued by dinners, the young lady worn out by six months' inveterate balls, might find a refuge and a novelty in the native waters of Malvern which the German Abanas and Pharphars, Kissingen, Baden, and the like, may fail to supply. The great merit of the system seems that the mind is constantly occupied while the body is being healed. You are always either drying yourself or wetting yourself, or packing or unpacking, or getting hot or getting cold. These incessant labours and emotions preclude all other mental exercises. A tired lawyer will find a rattling douche tumbling down on his shoulders from a mountain a real refresher; a hipped politician, plumped in a sitz bath for a couple of hours, may sit there and reflect calmly upon the vanity of ambition and the faithlessness of parties. We can fancy Mr. Disraeli in one pail, talking quite benevolently to Sir Robert, placed on his centre of gravity in an opposite can; and the ladies will learn with pleasure that this Malvern water is the very best of cosmetics.

(ibid., p. 175)

Thackeray's fantastic image of Disraeli and Peel at the water-cure is a charming fancy, and a fine symbolic depiction of the cameraderie that could unite British politicians of different factions, whether within the same party or on opposing sides, who fought one another vigorously in parliament or in print. It will have been noticed that in elaborating this image he once again found himself driven to use a phrase from the Old Testament:

> Are not Abana and Pharpar, rivers of Damascus, better than all the waters of Israel? may I not wash in them, and be clean?

(II Kings 5, 12)

Could anything be more apt as a comment on hydropathic relief sought in Malvern on the one hand (representing the waters of Israel) and Kissingen or Baden-Baden on the other? But in order to experience the full force of Thackeray's witty parallel, we have to remember the full context of his reference, the story of the prophet Naaman and the leper whose cure was finally effected in the waters

of the Jordan. He confidently expected his readers to know the Old
Testament as well as the New.

v

Catherine Peters, in her book on *Thackeray's Universe*, rightly heads
her account of his life between 1841 and 1846 "Days of Trouble".
These were the days and years of his wife's growing insanity and of
intolerable squabbles with her termagant of a mother; of having to
leave his children with his mother and step-father in Paris instead
of making a home for them himself; of finally resigning himself,
after trying cure after cure, doctor after doctor, to the fact that his
wife's condition was irreversible. She was to survive him by over
thirty years after he had placed her in the good care of a private
family in the mid-forties. Since he had no permanent home he
travelled a good deal in these years, often in search of copy that
would sell and would help his efforts to secure a firm financial
future for his children and his mentally sick but physically sturdy
wife. He was therefore glad to accept an offer from the P. & O.
Steamship Company of free passage from London to Cairo and
back, in return for an undertaking to write a travel book about the
P. & O. route through the Mediterranean and its various ports of
call. Carlyle compared Thackeray's acceptance of this commission
with "the practice of a blind fiddler going to and fro on a penny
ferry-boat in Scotland, and playing tunes to the passengers for
half-pence" (Ray, *The Uses of Adversity*, p. 301); and though Thackeray
felt the unfairness of this comment, the gibe rankled, and produced
resentments that may be responsible for some of the ill-natured
outbursts and shifts of blame in the travel-book he eventually
produced. It was called *Notes of a Journey from Cornhill to Grand Cairo,
by way of Lisbon, Athens, Constantinople, and Jerusalem; Performed in the
Steamers of the Peninsular and Oriental Company*, and its first edition, in
1846, was so quickly exhausted that a second edition appeared in
the same year. The traveller that speaks to us is, once again,
Michael Angelo Titmarsh, who favours us with such details of his
private life as that he was blessed with thirteen sisters; but the
Dedication to Captain Samuel Lewis is signed "W.M. Thackeray",
and the postscript to the second edition ends with the initials
W.M.T.

From Cornhill to Grand Cairo has many justly celebrated set-pieces:
first impressions of Gibraltar; Smyrna and a European's thrill at
first glimpsing something of the East; the Turkish baths at Misseri's
in Pera; Telmessus and the "Ionian" experience; civilized Lebanon

and colourful Cairo—these delighted contemporaries who had recently welcomed Kinglake's *Eothen* and Warburton's *The Crescent and the Cross*, and have held their own with such modern readers as have chanced upon them. Titmarsh's disappointment with some famous sights he had particularly looked forward to—the Pyramids, for instance—have also struck a sympathetic chord in the minds of readers grateful for avoidance of travel-book platitudes and avid for a record of genuine feelings and impressions rather than "objective" descriptions of sites favoured by tourists.

These feelings and impressions are frequently uncomfortable: seasickness, bedbugs and fleas, disconcerting smells, importunate beggars, uncomfortable quarters and means of transportation, overcharging and impudence, are duly recorded along with experiences of encounters that form the delight of memory. Memories, however, can also interfere with experience: Athens is spoilt for Titmarsh by reminiscences of awful Greek lessons at school, and Jerusalem (as we shall see) by the recollection of some unloved passages in the Old Testament and some painful ones in the New. Thackeray's own disgruntlement comes out clearly in some of the diary-entries he made during the sea-voyage: "Jews and midshipmen at a dirty dinner" (30 August 1844), "All sorts of Jews, filth and oddity on board" (21 September 1844) and a similar note made at Rhodes: "The Jewish quarter horrible" (26 September 1844). (LPP, II, 151–4). Anti-Jewish feelings seem to have surfaced on this trip, reinforced, perhaps, by fellow-passengers' quips: "Mr. Smith", Thackeray reports in his diary, "amused us all with his memorable query about the Jew" (6 September 1844—LPP, II, 152). The exact nature of that "memorable query" is not recorded; but it must be clear that what was to become known as "the Jewish question" received some very dusty answers at this stage of Thackeray's life.

It is once again important, however, to set anti-Jewish feelings into their context before examining how they surface in *From Cornhill to Grand Cairo*. Jews, it will then appear, are not the only victims of Titmarsh's bad temper. He has harsh things to say about Roman Catholic and Greek Orthodox believers too. He claims to have seen "hideous brutes", "ruffians", an "ugly race" in Muslim countries, alongside Romantic knights of the desert; and wherever he goes he finds, or suspects, swindlers. At the same time Titmarsh shows himself painfully aware of the arrogance to which travelling Englishmen of the day were prone:

> ...at the Frenchmen we looked with undisguised contempt. We were ready to burst with laughter as we passed the Prince's vessel—

there was a little French boy in a French boat alongside cleaning it, and twirling about a little French mop—we thought it the most comical, contemptible French boy, mop, boat, steamer, prince— Psha! it is of this wretched vapouring stuff that false patriotism is made. I write this as a sort of homily àpropos of the day, and Cape Trafalgar, off which we lie. What business have I to strut the deck, and clap my wings, and cry "Cock-a-doodle-doo" over it? Some compatriots are at that work even now.

(IX, 102)

There is a great deal more of this, helping the reader to "place" some of Titmarsh's own outbursts and complacencies.

Jews first come into Titmarsh's mind in the context of Christian cruelty and intolerance. Visiting a royal chapel in Portugal, he finds it

decorated with much care and sumptuousness of ornament,—the altar surmounted by a ghastly and horrible carved figure in the taste of the time when faith was strengthened by the shrieks of Jews on the rack, and enlivened by the roasting of heretics. Other such frightful images may be seen in the churches of the city.

(IX, 97)

Next, Titmarsh receives a lesson in physiognomic types. Meeting the Archbishop of Beirut and that worthy's brother (who is also his chaplain), Titmarsh finds the latter "a very greasy and good-natured ecclesiastic, whom, from his physiognomy, I would have imagined to be a dignitary of the Israelitish rather than the Roman church." (IX, 103). Facial traits, then, by means of which Thackeray's contemporaries thought themselves able to identify Jews, are now seen to be common among Eastern and Mediterranean peoples—a lesson brought home again at the last port of call, Cairo, by the sight of a "jovial and fat pasha . . ., who, but for a slight Jewish cast of countenance, might have passed any day for a Frenchman." (IX, 241). There is no suggestion that the archbishop's brother, or the pasha, were of Jewish extraction. In Gibraltar, however, Titmarsh is sure enough of his ground to say that "in the Main Street the Jews predominate, and Moors abound." (IX, 108). It is in Gibraltar too that Titmarsh meets and talks with a menaced group nearer to his own time than the medieval martyrs he had pictured to himself in the Portuguese chapel: "several refugee Jews from [Mogador], who said that they were much more afraid of the Kabyles without the city, than of the guns of the French squadron, of which they seemed to make rather light." (IX, 109). All through the brief time he stays in Gibraltar, Titmarsh remain conscious of the "strange scene of noise and bustle . . . in the market-place . . . where Moors, Jews, Spaniards, soldiers were thronging in the sun." (IX, 109–10). Here Jews are clearly shown as an integral part of a colourful and harmonious whole, of a spectacle that delights the visitor. In Smyrna too he finds Jewish traders an essential part of what he calls the "poetry" of the Eastern bazaar (IX, 131). "When I got into the bazaar among this race [= "the pleasant Eastern people"], somehow I felt as if they were all friends . . . merchants . . . children . . . countrymen . . . wild swarthy Arabs, who had come in with the caravans . . . Greeks and Jews squatted and smoked, their shops tended by sallow-faced boys, with large eyes, who smiled and welcomed you in; negroes . . . in gaudy colours . . . and women, with black nose-bags and shuffling yellow slippers . . ." (IX, 132). (Describing yashmaks as "black nosebags" is a characteristically Titmarshian touch). "How fresh, easy, good-natured is all this!", Titmarsh exclaims as he surveys this friendly scene and feels memories of the *Arabian Nights* pleasurably re-evoked.

At Constantinople, "the sailing of a vessel direct for Jaffa brought a great number of passengers together, and our decks were covered with Christian, Jew and heathen." (IX, 162). This meant increased discomfort, smells, dirt—especially the latter, which Titmarsh always suspected among foreigners: the Archbishop of Beirut and his brother seemed "unwashed" and "greasy" (IX, 103) and "peasant girls with dark blue eyes" whom Byron had admired appear in Titmarsh's disenchanted recollection as "brown-faced, flat-nosed, thick-lipped dirty wenches." (IX, 127). A concordance of Thackeray's writings would show how he applied such terms as "dirty" and "greasy" to a wide variety of people, from Rhineland girls to down-at-heel English clergymen. These words are very much to the fore in what is the most physically revolting picture of a group of Jews ever to appear in Thackeray's writings. Such prominence is the more startling because the passage in question is also the first in Thackeray's writings to give an account of Jewish worship based on first-hand observation. Titmarsh observes

> several families of Jewish Rabbis, who celebrated their "feast of tabernacles" on board; their chief men performing worship twice or thrice a day, dressed in their pontifical habits, and bound with philacteries . . .
> The Jews were refugees from Poland, going to lay their bones to rest in the valley of Jehoshaphat, and performing with exceeding rigour the offices of their religion. At morning and evening you were sure to see the chiefs of the families, arrayed in white robes, bowing over their books, at prayer. Once a week, on the eve before the Sabbath, there was a general washing in Jewry, which sufficed until

the ensuing Friday. The men wore long gowns and caps of fur, or else broad-brimmed hats, or, in service time, bound on their heads little iron boxes, with the sacred name engraved on them. Among the lads there were some beautiful faces; and among the women your humble servant discovered one who was a perfect rosebud of beauty when first emerging from her Friday's toilette, and for a day or two afterwards, until each succeeding day's smut darkened those fresh and delicate cheeks of hers.

(IX, 162–3)

This passage is illustrated with a dignified drawing of a orthodox Jew in kaftan, prayer-shawl, and phylacteries:

Illustration 1

Even here, however, in the text surrounding this illustration which speaks of ancient modes of worship, handsome young men and beautiful Jewish girls, Titmarsh turns up his delicate nose at the condition of passengers who travel in less comfort than he does. There is worse, much worse, in a passage that brackets a Greek nun with these Polish Jews:

The dirt of these children of captivity exceeds all possibility of description; the profusion of stinks which they raised, the grease of their venerable garments and faces, the horrible messes cooked in the filthy pots, and devoured with the nasty fingers, the squalor of mats, pots, old bedding, and foul carpets of our Hebrew friends, could hardly be painted by Swift, in his dirtiest mood, and cannot be, of course, attempted by my timid and genteel pen. What would they say in Baker Street to some sights with which our new friends favoured

us? What would your ladyship have said if you had seen the interesting Greek nun combing her hair over the cabin—combing it with the
natural fingers, and, averse to slaughter, flinging the delicate little
intruders, which she found in the course of her investigation, gently
into the great cabin? Our attention was a good deal occupied in
watching the strange ways and customs of the various comrades of
ours.

(IX, 162)

The most outrageous passage of all is yet to come.

We had some very rough weather in the course of the passage from
Constantinople to Jaffa, and the sea washed over and over our
Israelitish friends and their baggages and bundles; but though they
were said to be rich, they would not afford to pay for cabin shelter.
One father of a family, finding his progeny half drowned in a squall,
vowed he *would* pay for a cabin; but the weather was somewhat finer
the next day, and he could not squeeze out his dollars, and the ship's
authorities would not admit him except upon payment.

(IX, 164–5)

"They were said to be rich." Titmarsh simply cannot conceive that
what these refugees from Poland were "said" to be, in accordance
with popular belief that Jews must be wealthy, might not be true;
that these representatives of the poverty-stricken Jewish masses of
Eastern Europe might have been forced to put up with squalor and
hardship because they lacked the means to relieve it. There has
been a total failure of empathy; and Titmarsh's assurance that
"this unwillingness to part with money is not only found amongst
the followers of Moses, but in those of Mahomet, and Christians
too" (IX, 164) cannot excuse his refusal to contemplate the possibility that these people really were poor. The same possibility
might lead one to see in a quite different light the behaviour of these
same emigrants when the ship stopped at its ports of call; behaviour which Titmarsh chronicles with signal lack of sympathy and
understanding.

I used to watch these Jews on shore, and making bargains with one
another as soon as they came on board; the battle between vendor
and purchaser was an agony—they shrieked, clasped hands, appealed to one another passionately; their handsome, noble faces
assumed a look of woe—quite an heroic eagerness and sadness about
a farthing.
Ambassadors from our Hebrews descended at Rhodes to buy
provisions, and it was curious to see their dealings: there was our
venerable Rabbi, who, robed in white and silver, and bending over
his book at the morning service, looked like a patriarch, and whom I
saw chaffering about a fowl with a brother Rhodian Israelite. How
they fought over the body of that lean animal! The street swarmed

with Jews: goggling eyes looked out from the old carved casements—
hooked noses issued from the low antique doors—Jew boys driving
donkeys, Hebrew mothers nursing children, dusky, tawdry, ragged
young beauties and most venerable gray-bearded fathers were all
gathered round about the affair of the hen! And at the same time that
our Rabbi was arranging the price of it, his children were instructed
to procure bundles of green branches to decorate the ship during
their feast.

(IX, 164)

Even if we ignore the game of bargaining which is played throughout the Middle East as well as in much of Eastern Europe, with its
own rules and conventions, we should surely at least consider the
possibility that these would-be settlers in the Holy Land might
have been forced by poverty, and by the need to conserve what cash
they had in order to keep body and soul together in their new
abode, to haggle as they did. But Titmarsh shows himself here at
his most prejudiced and unreasonable; and his jaundiced view
scans the whole of Jewry from Old Testament times to his own, and
comes to rest, unsympathetically, on the Jews of Rhodes:

Think of the centuries during which these wonderful people have
remained unchanged; and how, from the days of Jacob downwards,
they have believed and swindled!
    The Rhodian Jews, with their genius for filth, have made their
quarter of the noble, desolate old town, the most ruinous and
wretched of all. The escutcheons of the proud old knights are still
carved over the doors, whence issue these miserable greasy hucksters
and pedlars.

(IX, 165)

To make quite sure that the reader should not miss his intent,
Thackeray works up an entry he had made in his journal on
Saturday, 28 September 1844 ("A white squall in the morning, dire
consternation among the Jews and infidels") into a poem he
attributes to Titmarsh; a poem that has the gall to mock the
sea-sickness which added to the misery of these emigrants in their
unprotected quarters.

Strange company we harboured;
We'd a hundred Jews to larboard,
Unwashed, uncombed, unbarbered,
    Jews black, and brown, and grey;
With terror it would seize ye,
And make your souls uneasy,
To see those Rabbis greasy,
    Who did nought but scratch and pray:
Their dirty children puking,
Their dirty saucepans cooking,

> Their dirty fingers hooking
>   Their swarming fleas away.
>
> .   .   .   .
>
> .   .   .   .
>
>   Then all the fleas in Jewry
> Jumped up and bit like fury;
> And the progeny of Jacob
> Did on the main-deck wake up
> (I wot those greasy Rabbins
> Would never pay for cabins);
> And each man moaned and jabbered in
> His filthy Jewish gabardine,
> In woe and lamentation,
> And howling consternation.
> And the splashing water drenches
> Their dirty brats and wenches;
> And they crawl from bales and benches,
> In a hundred thousand stenches.
>
> (IX, 170, 172)

Religious Jews living in poverty, and the squalor this often brings with it, cannot always obey to the full the Talmud's strict injunctions of personal hygiene. To mock at the misery of such people hardly seems the act of a gentleman; yet Thackeray endorsed the poem by not only including it in every edition of *From Cornhill to Grand Cairo* which he himself sanctioned, but also reprinting it, under its title "The White Squall", in the collection of ballads that formed part of his *Miscellanies* of 1855.

In a review of *Lord Lindsay's Travels in Egypt and the Holy Land*, published in *The Times*, on 25 September 1838, Thackeray had listed among the noble Lord's qualifications for the task he had set himself "an intimate acquaintance with the book which has made the lands he visited so especially interesting to us." (loc. cit., p. 2). It is not surprising, therefore, that fragments of the Bible float into Titmarsh's head as he approaches the coast of Palestine. Among the Old Testament reminiscences that come to him we find the horse that says "Ha! Ha!" among the trumpets (IX, 100), the Hebrew prophets (IX, 179), the Judgment of Solomon (IX, 190), Jacob's trickery (IX, 165), and the meeting of Rebecca and Eliezer:

> The women, with their long blue gowns and ragged veils, came to and fro with pitchers on their heads. Rebecca had such an one when she brought drink to the lieutenant of Abraham.
>
> (IX, 197)

The chapter describing Titmarsh's experience of Jerusalem was considerably altered before publication, in order to avoid offense to

Christian readers. Jewish contemporaries, however, are not granted the same consideration. In a passage that shows little of the "shame and humility" of which it speaks, Titmarsh juxtaposes the enemies of Christ described in the Gospels with the Polish Jews of his own time whom he had so heartlessly mocked.

> That is the Mount of Olives. Bethany lies beyond it. The most sacred eyes that ever looked on this world have gazed on those ridges: it was there He used to walk and teach. With shame and humility one looks towards the spot where that inexpressible Love and Benevolence lived and breathed; where the great yearning heart of the Saviour interceded for all our race; and whence the bigots and traitors of his day led him away to kill him!
>
> That company of Jews whom we had brought with us from Constantinople, and who had cursed every delay on the route, not from impatience to view the Holy City, but from rage at being obliged to purchase dear provisions for their maintenance on shipboard, made what bargains they best could at Jaffa, and journeyed to the Valley of Jehoshaphat at the cheapest rate. We saw the tall form of the old Polish Patriarch, venerable in filth, stalking among the stinking ruins of the Jewish quarter. The sly old Rabbi, in the greasy folding hat, who would not pay to shelter his children from the storm off Beyrout, greeted us in the bazaars; the younger Rabbis were furbished up with some smartness. We met them on Sunday at the kind of promenade by the walls of the Bethlehem Gate; they were in company of some red-bearded co-religionists, smartly attired in Eastern raiment; but their voice was the voice of the Jews of Berlin, and of course as we passed they were talking about so many hundert thaler. You may track one of the people, and be sure to hear mention of that silver calf that they worship.
>
> (IX, 200–201)

From these alleged worshippers of the *silver* calf who are yet secure in their Jewish religion Titmarsh turns to the few converts Christian missionaries in Palestine have been able to make. He speaks of the sanctions the Jewish communities impose on men and women who desert the faith of their forefathers, but refuses to share Christian indignation at the kidnapping, by a Jewish community, of the Jewish wife of a convert to Christianity.

> I could not help thinking, as my informant, an excellent and accomplished gentleman of the mission, told me the story, that the Jews had done only what the Christians do under the same circumstances. The woman was the daughter of a most learned Rabbi, as I gathered. Suppose a daughter of the Rabbi of Exeter, or Canterbury, were to marry a man who turned Jew, would not her right reverend father be justified in taking her out of the power of a person likely to hurl her soul to perdition?
>
> (IX, 201)

At the same time he feels sorry for a group of such converts whom he found sitting, conspicuously, in a Jerusalem church, and he thinks of

> the scorn and contumely which attended them without, as they passed in their European dresses and shaven beards, among their grisly, scowling, long-robed countrymen.
>
> (IX, 201)

Such people, he suggests, in a passage that shows how far he is from the racially based anti-Semitism of a later age, should be "sent away to England out of the way of persecution." (IX, 201). He is strengthened in his feeling that converted Jews should find a haven in his own country by his meeting with "a Hebrew convert, the Rev. Mr. E—"; the only such convert, he adds, "whom I had the fortune to meet on terms of intimacy." Readers of *From Cornhill to Grand Cairo* are then informed that Titmarsh "never saw a man whose outward conduct was more touching, whose sincerity was more evident, and whose religious feeling seemed more deep, real, and reasonable." (XI, 202). This is indeed an admirable portrait, and one well adapted to counter that of the horrid Reverend Emilius in Trollope's "Palliser" novels.

Nevertheless the impression of squalor left by Titmarsh's Polish-Jewish shipboard companions persists in Jerusalem. "As elsewhere in the towns I have seen", he tells his readers, "the Ghetto of Jerusalem is pre-eminent in filth. The people are gathered round about the dung-gate of the city. Of a Friday you may hear their wailings and lamentations for the lost glories of their city. I think the valley of Jehoshaphat is the most ghastly sight I have seen in the world. From all quarters they come hither to bury their dead. When his time is come yonder hoary old miser, with whom we made our voyage, will lay his carcass to rest here. To do that and to claw together money, has been the purpose of that strange, long life." (IX, 201–2). All this confident talk is about a man with whom Titmarsh, by his own account, has never exchanged a single word; a man whose financial circumstances, states of mind and purposes are a closed book to him, subject only to ill-informed conjectures.

When meditating on what he should include in his chapter on Jerusalem, and what he should exclude from it, Thackeray wrote to his mother:

> I am gravelled with Jerusalem, not wishing to offend the public by a needless exhibition of heterodoxy: nor daring to be a hypocrite. I have been reading lots of books—Old Testament: Church Histories:

Travels and . . . find there was a sect in the early Church who denounced the Old Testament: and get into such a rage myself when reading all that murder and crime which the name of the Almighty is blasphemously made to Sanction: that I don't dare to trust myself to write.

(26 July 1845—LPP, II, 1845)

Yet he did write, in Titmarsh's name, a passage in which the very landscape in and and around the Holy City brings hideous memories of battles, and sacrifices, bloody deeds and terrible sufferings, recorded in "the Hebrew histories".

I made many walks round the city to Olivet and Bethany, to the tombs of the kings, and the fountains sacred in story. These are green and fresh, but all the rest of the landscape seemed to me to be *frightful*. Parched mountains, with a gray bleak olive-tree trembling here and there; savage ravines and valleys, paved with tombstones—a landscape unspeakably ghastly and desolate, meet the eye wherever you wander round about the city. The place seems quite adapted to the events which are recorded in the Hebrew histories. It and they, as it seems to me, can never be regarded without terror. Fear and blood, crime and punishment, follow from page to page in frightful succession. There is not a spot at which you look, but some violent deed has been done there: some massacre has been committed, some victim has been murdered, some idol has been worshipped with bloody and dreadful rites. Not far from hence is the place where the Jewish conqueror fought for the possession of Jerusalem. "The sun stood still, and hastened not to go down about a whole day;" so that the Jews might have daylight to destroy the Amorites, whose iniquities were full, and whose land they were about to occupy. The fugitive heathen king, and his allies, were discovered in their hiding-place, and hanged: "and the children of Judah smote Jerusalem with the edge of the sword, and set the city on fire; and they left none remaining, but utterly destroyed all that breathed."
        I went out at the Zion Gate, and looked at the so-called tomb of David. I had been reading all the morning in the Psalms, and his history in Samuel and Kings. "*Bring thou down Shimei's hoar head to the grave with blood,*" are the last words of the dying monarch as recorded by the history. What they call the tomb is now a crumbling old mosque; from which Jew and Christian are excluded alike. As I saw it, blazing in the sunshine, with the purple sky behind it, the glare only served to mark the surrounding desolation more clearly. The lonely walls and towers of the city rose hard by. Dreary mountains, and declivities of naked stones, were round about: they are burrowed with holes, in which Christian hermits lived and died. You see one green place far down in the valley: it is called En Rogel. Adonijah feasted there, who was killed by his brother Solomon, for asking for Abishag for wife. The Valley of Hinnom skirts the hill; the dismal ravine was a fruitful garden once. Ahaz, and the idolatrous kings, sacrificed to idols under the green trees there, and "caused their children to pass through the fire." On the mountain opposite, Solomon,

with the thousand women of his harem, worshipped the gods of all their nations, "Ashtoreth," and "Milcom, and Molech, the abomination of the Ammonites." An enormous charnel-house stands on the hill where the bodies of dead pilgrims used to be thrown; and common belief has fixed upon this spot as the Aceldama, which Judas purchased with the price of his treason. Thus you go on from one gloomy place to another, each seared with its bloody tradition. Yonder is the Temple, and you think of Titus's soldiery storming its flaming porches, and entering the city, in the savage defence of which two million human souls perished. It was on Mount Zion that Godfrey and Tancred had their camp: when the Crusaders entered the mosque, they rode knee-deep in the blood of its defenders, and of the women and children who had fled thither for refuge: it was the victory of Joshua over again. Then, after three days of butchery, they purified the desecrated mosque and went to prayer. In the centre of this history of crime rises up the Great Murder of all. . . .

I need say no more about this gloomy landscape. After a man has seen it once, he never forgets it—the recollection of it seems to me to follow him like a remorse, as it were to implicate him in the awful deed which was done there. Oh! with what unspeakable shame and terror should one think of that crime, and prostrate himself before the image of that Divine Blessed Sufferer!

(IX, 203–4)

Nothing lightens the gloom of this survey of early Jewish history and legend, of suffering inflicted and suffering borne. Even when more cheerful associations might have been aroused, they are thwarted by attendant circumstances:

Hard by was Rebecca's Well: a dead body was lying there, and crowds of male and female mourners dancing and howling round it.

(IX, 209–10)

The message of the New Testament, in its turn, is mocked by the behaviour of various churches and nationalities that profess to follow its teachings. They trade in relics of doubtful authenticity:

The Greeks show you the Tomb of Melchisedec, while the Armenians possess the Chapel of the Penitent Thief; the poor Copts (with their little cabin of a chapel) can yet boast the thicket in which Abraham caught the Ram, which was to serve as the vicar of Isaac; the Latins point to the Pillar to which the Lord was bound.

(IX, 207–8)

Even the Tomb of *Adam* is on view within a few yards of the Invention of the Sacred Cross! Worst of all: the Holy Sepulchre itself has been made "the least sacred spot about Jerusalem" by the rapacity of some of those who call themselves Christians: they have desecrated their Saviour's tomb with "selfishness and uncharitableness and imposture", and they have set up "idols . . . for worship" by means of a "clumsy legend" woven around the grotto in Bethlehem "where the Blessed Nativity is said to have taken place." (IX, 208–10). How much better it is to have seen such sacred spots with the mind's eye only!

> . . . you, dear M—, without visiting the place, have imagined one far finer; and Bethlehem, where the Holy Child was born, and the angels sang, "Glory to God in the highest, and on earth peace and good will towards men," is the most sacred and beautiful spot in the earth to you.
>
> (IX, 210–11)

In Titmarsh's disenchanted view, Christians in Palestine come off as badly as Jews; even the dirt is there, in a Latin convent where the traveller descries"brown-clad fathers, dirty, bearded and sallow, . . . gliding about the corridors" (IX, 212). In a Greek convent at Ramleh Titmarsh is plagued by outposts of "a vast and innumerable host of hopping and crawling things, who usually persist in partaking of the traveller's bed" as well as the unwelcome attentions of an over-familiar, facetious lay-brother, "a greasy, grinning wag." (IX, 217).

What Titmarsh counters to all this, besides English hygiene, has been well summarised by Dr R.M. Klish:

> Titmarsh believes in a simple and direct relationship with God, based on common sense, uncluttered with gaudy buildings, elaborate rites, complicated beliefs; he seems to indicate that man can worship God beneath the sky as well as beneath a church, temple or mosque roof. He remains, however, an Anglican, and in Jerusalem commends "the decent and manly ceremonial of our service" and "the sheer force of good example, pure life, and kind offices" the English religious colony at the city exhibits. Plain faith, good works—this is the yardstick he repeatedly measures other religions by in *Cornhill to Cairo.*
>
> (*Thackeray's Travel Writings*, Diss. Michigan State University, East Lansing 1974, p. 143)

He finds far too little of all this in Palestine, whose coast he is glad to leave behind, along with the Polish Jews whose presence on the P. & O. liner had so offended him.

When Titmarsh rejoins his ship in Syria, he is pleased to find it "carefully cleansed and purified", "cleared of the swarming Jews, who had infested the decks all the way from Constantinople." (IX, 219). We of the twentieth century know all too well where such dehumanizing talk may lead; but even without such knowledge, speaking of human beings in terms appropriate to vermin represents a shocking failure of imagination. Titmarsh encounters a very

different attitude from his own when he meets the Consul-General
for Syria of the United States; "a kind, worthy, simple man" who
welcomes the immigration of Jews in the firm belief

> that the prophecies of Scripture are about to be accomplished; that
> the day of the return of the Jews is at hand, and the glorification of
> the restored Jerusalem. He is to witness this—he and a favourite dove
> with which he travels; and he forsook home and comfortable
> country-house, in order to make this journey. He has no other
> knowledge of Syria but what he derives from the prophecy; and this
> (as he takes the office gratis) has been considered a sufficient reason
> for his appointment by the United States' Government. As soon as he
> arrived, he sent and demanded an interview with the Pasha; ex-
> plained to him his interpretation of the Apocalypse, in which he has
> discovered that the Five Powers and America are about to intervene
> in Syrian affairs, and the infallible return of the Jews to Palestine.
>
> (IX, 212–3)

Titmarsh, of course, has no such messianic expectations; he is
happy to be out of Jerusalem, and he looks back on his time there as
"ten days passed in a fever." (IX, 216).

Once removed from this fever-zone, the traveller can look on
Jews, once again, with a kindlier eye—as just one colourful ingredient in a bustling foreign scene. In Alexandria

> The streets are busy with a motley population of Jews and Armenians,
> slave-driving-looking Europeans, large-breeched Greeks, and well-
> shaven buxom merchants, looking as trim and fat as those on the
> Bourse or on 'Change
>
> (IX, 221)

The meat served in Cairo is of "a black uncertain sort", reminding
Titmarsh of the "flesh-pots of Egypt" the Israelites yearned for
during their trek through the desert; but there are more and more
signs of what he can recognize as civilization: "Cairo is England in
Egypt. I like to see her there, with her pluck, enterprise, manliness,
bitter ale and Harvey sauce." (IX, 231). The tone of the narrative
lightens now, though the traveller is appalled by traces left behind
after a recent public beheading (IX, 225–6), shocked by the
indecencies of an Egyptian comedian (IX, 225), and sadly confirmed in his belief that everybody cheats in the Orient (IX, 238).
In retrospect it all becomes worth while: the sorrows and discom-
forts of the journey pass away while its pleasures "remain, let us
hope, as long as life will endure." (IX, 254). In this retrospective
glow Titmarsh now sees "the Jew Rabbi, bending over his book"
along with worshippers of all the other religions he had encountered: "So each, in his fashion, and after his kind, is bowing down,

and adoring the Father, who is equal above all. Cavil not, you brother and sister, if your neighbour's voice is not like yours; only hope that his words are honest (as far as they may be), and his heart humble and thankful." (IX, 255). It must remain a matter for regret that Titmarsh did not exercise some of this charity, and show some of this humility, in the chapters which deal with the voyage from Constantinople to Jaffa, and with his impressions of the Holy Land. These fly in the face, not only of the tolerant conclusion of the book which has just been quoted, but also of such earlier professions of faith as that which ends Chapter IV:

> The Maker has linked together the whole race of man with this chain of love. I like to think that there is no man but has kindly feelings for some other, and he for his neighbour, until we bind together the whole family of Adam.
>
> (IX, 120)

A contemporary reviewer, complaining, with some justice, of the prejudiced and stereotyped picture of Ireland and the Irish which emerged from the *Irish Sketch Book*, declared that while its author could not be accused of deliberately falsifying his impressions, such impressions were nevertheless sometimes false because that author had "a *crick* in the imagination." (*The Tablet*, 13 May 1843). *From Cornhill to Grand Cairo*, for all its professions of tolerance and love, for all its praise of what binds together "the whole race of man" or "the whole family of Adam", shows a similar "crick" in its dealings with Jews.

There is, however, one further complication to be considered. In *From Cornhill to Grand Cairo* Thackeray the writer was to some degree subverted by Thackeray the illustrator: for Titmarsh's dignified drawing of a traditionally garbed Jewish patriarch at prayer is so strangely at variance with his squalid depiction of the group of Jews to whom the old man belonged that one is tempted to speak, once again, of a "dual image"—Harold Fisch's term for the complex attitudes of so many British writers to the Jews they portrayed in their works. *From Cornhill to Grand Cairo* also contains what we may recognize to be the nearest Thackeray ever came to an uncaricatured pictorial representation of the "belle juive" that haunts his writings.

But "little Mariam", the subject of this picture, is not divided from either Titmarsh or Thackeray himself by her religion, as Scott's Rebecca is from Ivanhoe; the text shows unmistakably that she is a Syrian Christian.

Illustration 2

vi

The art reviews which Thackeray's Michael Angelo Titmarsh contributed to *Fraser's* and other publications just before and just after his P. & O. Cruise continue to measure the skill and imagination of contemporary painters against the Biblical narratives and, as often as not, find them wanting. He takes note of only one painter of actual Jewish origin in these later reviews. That is Solomon Hart—and Titmarsh reckons him, facetiously, among *Irish* painters because of a fancied resemblance between Hart's "Persian gentleman smoking a *calahan*" and an Irish member of parliament (II, 626); but Hart is singled out for praise when it comes to the depiction of Jewish subjects.

> Being on the subject of Jerusalem, here may be mentioned with praise Mr. Hart's picture of a Jewish ceremony, with a Hebrew name I have forgotten. This piece is exceedingly bright and pleasing in colour, odd and novel as a representation of manners and costume, a striking and agreeable picture . . .
>
> ("Picture Gossip", II, 654–5)

The ceremony whose name Titmarsh could not remember is "Simḥat Torah", "Rejoicing in the Law"—a service marking the annual completion of the synagogue reading of the Pentateuch. When Hart exhibits paintings in the Royal Academy, Thackeray once again singles out a Jewish subject first of all:

> MR. HART's *Jessica* may be placed among the portrait class: it is beautiful, as is another female portrait . . ., in quite a different style, by the same painter . . .
>
> ("The Exhibition of the Royal Academy", *The Morning Chronicle*, 11 May 1846—Ray, *Contributions* . . ., p. 152)

Thackeray never mentions Hart's Jewish ancestry; but he conveys the impression that when Hart lights on a Jewish or Eastern subject he has a happier touch than when he attempts to convey the spirit of English history. This is how Titmarsh describes Hart's "Sir Thomas More going to Execution":

> Miss More is crying on papa's neck, pa looks up to heaven, halberdiers look fierce, etc.: all the regular adjuncts and property of pictorial tragedy are here brought into play. But nobody cares, that is the fact; and one fancies the designer himself cannot have cared much for the orthodox historical group whose misfortunes he was depicting.
>
> These pictures are like boys' hexameters at school. Every lad of decent parts in the sixth form has a knack of turning out great quantities of respectable verse, without blunders, and with scarce any mental labour; but these verses are not the least like poetry, any more than the great Academical paintings of the artists are like great painting. You want something more than a composition, and a set of costumes and figures decently posed and studied.
>
> ("Picture Gossip", II, 655)

Hart is no more blameworthy, however, than most of his Gentile English contemporaries; Charles Landseer's "Charles I before the Battle of Edgehill" is dismissed on exactly the same grounds as "Sir Thomas More going to Execution" (II, 655).

One of the skills which Thackeray frequently practised in the art reviews he attributed to Titmarsh is that of hitting two *bêtes noires* with one critical stone. He constantly ridiculed A.E. Chalon, the painter of "ogling beauties" whose engraved likenesses often adorned Victorian keepsakes and annuals. The Royal Academy Exhibition of 1844, described in "May Gambols", contained some characteristic portrait paintings by Chalon which Titmarsh promptly dubbed "delightful coxcombries". "I have found out", he adds, with his tongue firmly in his cheek, "a proper task for that gentleman, and hereby propose that he should illustrate *Coningsby*." (II, 631–2). If this remark ever came to Disraeli's notice, he will not have taken it as a compliment. Nor would he have relished Thackeray's preference of Charles de Bernard's "accurate picture of the French dandy" to the *Coningsby* brand of dandyism, which is now pronounced "intense, but not real; not English that is. It is vastly too ornamental, energetic and tawdry for our quiet habits. The author's coxcombry is splendid, gold-land, refulgent, like that of Murat rather than Brummel . . ." (quoted in R.A. Colby, *Thackeray's Canvass of Humanity*," ed. cit., p. 122).

In one of his "Letters on the Fine Arts" published in *The Pictorial Times*, Titmarsh surveys the progress of literacy and artistic appreciation in Britain, and expresses his hope that such progress will result, not only in wider fame, but also in more generous remuneration, for the nation's writers and artists.

> The poet and artist is called upon to appeal to the few no longer. His profit and fame are with the many; and do not let it be thought irreverence to put the profit and fame together. Nobody ever denies the Duke of Wellington's genius, because his Grace receives twenty thousand a year from his country in gratitude for the services rendered by him; and if the nation should take a fancy to reward poets in the same way, we have similarly no right to quarrel with the verdict.
>
> The dukedoms, twenty-thousands-a-year, Piccadilly-palaces, and the like, are not, however, pleaded for here. Miss Coutts or Mr. Rothschild have the like (or may, no doubt, for the asking), and nobody grudges the wealth, though neither ever were in the battle of Waterloo, that I know of. But let us ask, as the condition of improvement in art, if not fame and honour, at least sympathy, from the public, for the artist . . .
>
> ("Letters on the Fine Arts. No. 2. The Objections against Art Unions", *Pictorial Times*, 1 April 1843—II, 591-2)

By putting the Protestant Coutts family in the same box as the Rothschilds, Thackeray robs this passage of any anti-Jewish sting it might have held—though there may be a sly suggestion that the Rothschilds, while never *in* the battle of Waterloo, did do rather well out of that event. Titmarsh's assertion, however, that no-one grudges financiers their wealth is well in line with the respect for enterprise and entrepreneurship which characterized the early Victorians, and need have held no ironic overtones for Thackeray's first readers.

A similar juxtaposition may be found in another contribution Thackeray made to *Fraser's Magazine* after his return from the Middle East—when "Titmarsh's Carmen Lilliense" depicts a continental innkeeper's respect for the moneyed "Lord Anglais, / Like Rothschild or Sir Robert Peel" (March 1844—VII, 31). At least as important, however, in the context of the present book, is his description of a non-Jew, the journalist Laman Blanchard, in a review of Blanchard's *Sketches from Life*:

> What was better than wit in his talk was, that that it was so genial. He *enjoyed* thoroughly, and chirped over his wine with a good humour that could not fail to be infectious. His own hospitality was delightful:

there was something about it charmingly brisk, simple, and kindly. How he used to laugh! As I write this, what a number of pleasant, hearty scenes come back! One can hear his jolly, clear laughter; and see his keen, kind, beaming Jew face,—a mixture of Mendelssohn and Voltaire.

(*Fraser's Magazine*, March 1846—VI, 554–6)

Thackeray had been in Weimar when young Felix Mendelssohn-Bartholdy had also been there; but the face he is thinking of, the face that blends so well with that of Voltaire, is surely not that of young Felix, but that of his grandfather, the philosopher Moses Mendelssohn, which had become a popular subject for engravings.

Moses Mendelssohn.

Illustration 3

As for the character which went with Blanchard's "Jew face"—"it was impossible", Thackeray tells us, "to help trusting a man who was so perfectly gay, gentle, and amiable" (VI, 548).

The majority of Jewish figures that people Thackeray's writings between 1843 and 1846 are encountered beyond the shores of England. They include horse dealers, tobacco merchants, goldsmiths, pawnbrokers, moneylenders, and bankers; a minister of police, baptized, of course, in eighteenth-century Württemberg (slightly disguised as "W-" or "X-"), and a recruiting officers' decoy in eighteenth-century Prussia; Polish Jews of Thackeray's own time, emigrating to Palestine, whose mode of worship Titmarsh observes on board ship, and who offend his sense of hygiene; baptized and unbaptized Palestinian Jews; and traders in many ports along the P. & O. route. British figures that come under scrutiny range from young orange-sellers to Solomon Hart and Benjamin Disraeli, whose novels are criticized with some admiration, many reservations, and a fair amount of ridicule. Disraeli takes his place in a gallery of baptized Jews: those who, like him, proudly proclaim their origin; those who, like some converts in Palestine, slink about between two worlds in which they cannot feel at home; those who seem to have comfortably adjusted to their new Christianity; and those who, like de Geldern in *Barry Lyndon*, turn against their erstwhile co-religionists and pursue with hatred anyone that reminds them of their former allegiances. A distressing amount of anti-Jewish prejudice swims to the surface in these "days of trouble": privately, in "Notes of a Tour in the Low Countries", where mediaeval attitudes are suddenly and unexpectedly revived, and publicly, in *From Cornhill to Grand Cairo*, where Jewish behavior is subjected to pejorative interpretation while ancient notions about *foetor judaicus* are nauseatingly renewed. Titmarsh's professions of tolerance and love of the human race offer a distressing contrast with failures in empathy that lead him to speak of human beings in terms appropriate to vermin. There are compensations: hatred of persecution, which includes offers of sanctuary in England for its victims; commendation of fair trading by Jews; warm praise of cultivated Jewish women; appreciations of male handsomeness as well as female beauty among young Jews, and of a generic "keen, kind, beaming Jew face" that may be found among Christians as well in the Jewish community. We find an increasing realization that there is no such thing as an exclusively Jewish physiognomy; features thought of as "Jewish" may be found in a British Gentile like Laman Blanchard or a Christian cleric like the brother of a Lebanese archbishop. Thackeray-Titmarsh continues his reproaches of contemporary painters who fail to match the dignity and poetry of the Biblical stories they attempt to illustrate, and praises Solomon Hart for his painting of an exotic-seeming Jewish subject. When all exceptions and qualifications have been noted, however, there remains a good deal of truth in R.M. Klish's characterization of *From Cornhill to Grand Cairo*: "Thackeray wanted his narrative mask to be that of a gay companion, but, sadly, it could also be that of a bigot or a boor." (op. cit. p. 152).

CHAPTER 5

PATTERNS OF PENETRATION
(1841–1847)

> ... here, too, the Hebrews have penetrated ...
> (VIII, 64)

i

In July 1841 appeared the first number of *Punch*, described in handbills as a "Guffawgraph", a "refuge for destitute wit", an "asylum for the thousands of orphan jokes which are now wandering about" and a draft prospectus submitted to potential contributors spoke of the new journal as one to be "devoted to the emancipation of the *Jew d'esprits* all over the world and the naturalization of those alien Jonathans, whose adhence to the truth has forced them to emigrate from their native land." (M.H. Spielmann, *The History of 'Punch'*, London 1895, p. 20f). Amid the puns— including "*Jew*" for "*jeux*", underlined three times for emphasis— one notes the language of social and political concern: "refuge", "asylum", "emancipation", "naturalization" were terms that surfaced in debates on parliamentary "Jew bills". "Jonathans" were American jokes. The sub-title of the new journal (*Punch or the London Charivari*) pointed to a Parisian journal with a radical slant and a strong leaning towards graphic satire and caricature. Thackeray's earliest contributions to *Punch*, which appeared in 1842 and 1843, made little impact; but he proved a most useful contributor because he could turn his hand equally well to drawings, verses, short squibs, longer satiric pieces, and sustained series. From 1844 onwards he became one of *Punch*'s most important collaborators, who combined with the editor Mark Lemon, Douglas Jerrold, Gilbert à Beckett, John Leech and Richard Doyle to set the tone and direct the content of the increasingly popular journal, until differences with Jerrold and dislike of *Punch*'s attitude to French politics after the fall of Thackeray's *bête noire* Louis Philippe ended his regular contributions in the 1850s.

The historian of *Punch*, M.H. Spielmann, has spoken of the "merry prejudice" entertained by Leech and à Beckett against the Jewish community, adding that this was "to some extent shared ... by the kindly Thackeray and ... by Jerrold", and that it was "expressive no doubt of the general feeling of the day." Mark Lemon, whom many wrongly believed to have been of Jewish origin, "did nothing to temper the flood of . . . derision which *Punch* for a while poured upon the whole house of Israel." (Spielmann, op. cit., p. 103). This is not the place to survey the complex history of *Punch*'s dealings with the Jews in Victorian times: they ranged from angry attacks on Jewish "sweaters" in the East End to generous defence of the oppressed Jewish subjects of the Emperor of All the Russias; but Thackeray played an important part in that story, and it is with his contribution alone that this chapter will be concerned.

He began his career in what he and friends considered, at first, to be a somewhat "low" form of journalism on 18 June 1842, when his satire with a pseudo-Oriental setting, "The Legend of Jawbrahim-Beraudee", made its bow in *Punch*. This made mild fun of a now forgotten author, John Abraham Heraud, to whom he credits an interminable Biblical epic which begins with the line "Eastward of Eden lies the land of Nod" and soon sends its auditors nodding off to the sound of sub-standard Miltonics that speak of "the vision of Noah, and the Book of Enoch", and carry on with tales of "the children of Cain, of Satan, Judael, Azazael". (VII, 246). Thackeray's next contribution was a series of mock history lessons, calculated to appeal to a taste later satisfied by Gilbert à Beckett and especially Sellars and Yeastman. "Miss Tickletoby's Lectures on English History" ran in *Punch* from July to October 1842; the series was broken off because of unfavourable responses from the readership, and the editors, of *Punch*; but the editors recognized Thackeray's potential usefulness and allowed him to continue contributing comic verse and prose along with comic drawings that could be engraved on wood and inserted at strategic points in the letter press. On 20 May 1843 he supplied a drawing for a piece by Gilbert à Beckett which made fun of a popular dancing-master of the day, a Mr Nathan who was for many years Master of Ceremonies at the Rosherville Gardens, and who had conferred on himself the title "Baron" Nathan without warrant from any other authority. Beckett ridiculed this "Assumption of Aristocracy", and it is the article with this heading which Thackeray embellished with a drawing of a ragged urchin who sports a battered top-hat and hands a card to a flunkey with the words: "Give that card to your master, and say a gentleman wants to see him."

Thackeray refrains from drawing "Baron" Nathan himself, whose silhouette and effigy, drawn by other caricaturists, was to feature many times in the early volumes of *Punch*. In its context,

Illustration 1

however, his caption may be seen as a first glimmer of a later controversy in that journal as to whether the terms "Jew" and "gentleman" were compatible.

"Baron" Nathan turns up again in a piece Thackeray wrote about an impending visit of the Czar of Russia, whose treatment of the Polish people had caused much justifiable indignation in Britain.

> As to the Ladies, the Ladies Patronesses of the Polish Balls, who have determined to continue their entertainment, *Punch* blesses them. Ladies, you have acted like men! Let there be several Polish Balls this year during the Emperor's presence. *Punch* will attend them all. Yes, we will dance the Polka with Judy there; we will shut ourselves up with Baron Nathan and practise for the purpose.
> (*Punch*, VI, 8 June 1844, p. 243)

"Baron" Nathan's assumption of a title to which everyone knew he had no legal right was a show-business flourish like that which makes magicians bill themselves "Professor"; but neither Thackeray nor any other contributor to *Punch* ever suggested that as a dancing teacher he was anything but excellent. It is characteristic of Thackeray that he accompanied his piece on the Czar, which promised "Baron" Nathan an unlikely new customer, with an open letter "To Daniel O'Connell, Esq.", which asked: "We are mighty angry with Nicholas over Poland, but, until lately, has somebody else treated Ireland better?" (loc. cit., p. 248).

In 1844 Thackeray introduced, into one of his *Punch* contributions, a new sense of the word "to Jew". A song for the head of the Churchill family then residing at Blenheim Castle, to the tune of "The Good Old English Gentleman", contains the stanza:

> Lord, Lord, it is a dreadful thing to think what my sires got thro' in
> A century or so of reckless life, and made extravagant doing;
> With building, racing, dicing, eating, drinking, courting, Jewing,
> They emptied Great John Churchill's bags, and left poor me to ruin . . .
>
> (*Punch*, VI, 11 May 1844, p. 207)

The context leaves little doubt that "Jewing" here means "borrowing from money-lenders"—a meaning not recorded in the Oxford English Dictionary.

A frequent target for ribbing and leg-pulling in the early numbers of *Punch* was the tailoring firm of Moses and Son, which indulged in flamboyant advertizing that made its name synonymous with low-priced clothing. On 6 July 1844 Thackeray joined in this game with drawings for a piece called "A Hint for Moses". This invents a rival firm, Aaron & Co., and credits it with a ruse for drawing customers into its shop by employing stooges dressed up as a father and son from the country who express great delight at the goods in Aaron's windows and go to have the boy measured for a suit immediately. The two illustrations Thackeray supplied for this piece are not ill-natured by Victorian standards; the profile of the Jewish shop-keeper in the first is admittedly sharp and sly, but when he appears at full length in the measuring scene he looks elegant, friendly, and unmenacing (ill. 2 and 3).

These drawings appeared in the seventh volume of *Punch*, on 6 July 1844; a week later, on 13 July, Thackeray waxed indignant over a law-case involving gambling frauds and defalcations in which the judge had made a distinction between the "gentlemen" involved in these transactions, who were assumed to be guiltless, and the lower order with whom they had associated. "Did [that judge] ever hear", Thackeray asks, speaking from the bitter experience of his younger years, "of young men being rooked at play, and in good society too? or are blacklegs only to be found among the lower classes?"

> If gentlemen consort with rogues and swindlers, knowing them perfectly to be such, have money transactions with them, win or lose by their successful or unsuccessful roguery, it is too bad of a judge to assume that the gentlemen are spotless in honour, and the clodpoles

Illustration 2

Illustration 3

the only rascals . . . They go among those knaves and swindlers, those low-bred ruffians reeking of gin and the stable, *to make money of them*. They associate with boors and grooms, Jew gambling-house keepers, boxers and bullies, for money's sake to be sure. What else could bring such dandies into communication with such brutes? . . .

(*Punch*, VII, p. 23)

The last sentence is bitterly ironical: it was the judge who had made this distinction between innocent "dandies" and guilty "brutes". In Thackeray's eyes there is nothing to choose between "Jew gambling-house keepers" and their greedy customers, whatever their religion or ethnic origin might be.

The principle of name-calling based on false distinctions and assumed superiority obtains in politics too. In 1845, Thackeray contributed a tiny squib entitled "You're Another":

In the late debate we find the following singular charges brought by Honourable Members:—
    D'Israeli accuses Peel of being a humbug.
    Roebuck accuses D'Israeli of being spiteful.
    Sibthorp accuses Murphy of being a buffoon.
O shade of Horace! isn't it too good?

(*Punch*, VIII, 26 April 1845, p. 190)

Disraeli, Roebuck, Sibthorp, Murphy—they are all fallible actors in a human comedy that has its fill of humbug, spite and buffoonery. "Mutato nomine de te / Fabula narratur." The Whigs Thackeray knew seemed to him little better than the Tories they opposed; and in a piece entitled "Punch's Fine Art Exhibition" he comments on a spoof drawing showing "B. D'Israeli, Esquire (M.P.) strangling the Whig and Tory serpents."

This is a fine idea—and the snakes we may say are magnificently *handled*. Whether, however, the Tories are snakes, or the Whigs resemble these exceedingly venomous creatures,—we for our part decline to state. To call a gent a snake, is to *our* thinking, to say that he is no better than a reptile; and is it fair to treat the two great parties in England in this humiliating manner?
The portrait of the celebrated author of "Coningsmark", &c., is good but not in the least like him. In this the artist has shown his taste and skill.

(*Punch*, VII, 13 July 1844, p. 26) (VIII, 401–4)

The ironies and "deliberate mistakes" of this passage are capped by that last sentence, which implies that Thackeray did not find Disraeli's personal appearance, at this stage in his career, altogether appealing.

Whatever he may have thought of Disraeli's appearance, there can be no doubt that he loathed that of Louis Philippe of France, whom he caricatured frequently in ways that suggest an unattractive outside revealing a devious, petty and greedy nature. That Disraeli referred to this unloved monarch as "Ulysses", and that others saw in him a "Napoleon of Peace" (a phrase coined by Heine in 1840 which became common currency) amused Thackeray greatly.

To the Napoleon of Peace:—
. . . the wise man *par excellence* of Europe, the lauded of our Journals, the Napoleon of Peace, Ben D'Israeli's Ulysses . . . Ah, Sir! after all your doubling and shuffling, your weeping and protesting, and weary smiling—all the labours of a life to make a character—is it not a pity to be losing it in your old age? What will Europe, what will Mr. Ben D'Israeli say? . . .

(*Punch*, VII, 24 August 1844, p. 90)

He pictured with glee a subscription list designed to relieve the "distress" of which Louis Philippe had complained; a list headed by

Daniel O'Connell, Esq. .... 0½ p.
Lord Brougham .... a pair of Shepherd's plaid inexpressibles
Benjamin Sidonia, Esq. .... 2 old hats.

(*Punch*, VII, 13 July 1844, p. 32)

The last-quoted entry equates Disraeli with his own Jewish superman hero, and links both with Jewish old-clothes men.

The P. & O. cruise which had resulted in the travel book *From Cornhill to Grand Cairo* had a precipitate in *Punch* too: a series of pieces called "'Punch' in the East" which Thackeray attributed, with characteristic self-persiflage, to "Our Fat Contributor". The Fat Contributor introduces himself, on 11 January 1845, as a man who has "travelled like Benjamin D'Israeli, Ulysses, Monckton Milnes, and the eminent sages of all times" (VIII, 26) and who is therefore in a position to assert, from personal observation, that the Jews of Gibraltar are among the readers of *Punch*" (VIII, 31) and that they quote its jokes. For all his irony at Disraeli's expense, however, Thackeray had come to admire that statesman's parliamentary dexterity and thought it absurd to claim that Peel had worsted him in parliamentary debate:

Historical Parallel
The *Standard* says that Sir Robert Peel administered to Ben D'Israeli "the most terrific castigation" ever delivered by man. The *National* says Soult thrashed Wellington dreadfully at Toulouse.

(*Punch*, VII, 29 March 1845, p. 149)

and again:

For the Court Circular
Mr Benjamin D'Israeli didn't take out Master Robert Peel for an airing last week, but will do so on the very first opportunity. Master Robert is anxiously looking out for the promised holiday.

(*Punch*, VII, 12 April 1845)

In his guise of "Fat Contributor" Thackeray continued, nevertheless, to have fun with Disraeli's style, and his exaltation of his Jewish ancestry, which the spelling "D'Israeli" subtly underlines. He takes a wicked pleasure in applying the term "Mosaic Arabs" (by which Disraeli had designated that branch of the "Caucasian race" to which he assigned the Jews) to the humblest among the beasts of burden:

> Horses of the Mosaic Arab breed, I mean those animals called Jerusalem ponies by some in England, by others denominated donkeys . . . I chose the Mosaic Arab then . . .
>
> ("Punch in the East"—VIII, 42)

When this piece appeared, on 1 February 1845, Thackeray had long been back from the Eastern Journey that it recalled, and had found something new to amuse him in the London scene: a proposal to make it legal for Barristers-at-Law to tout for custom. Thackeray took this as his cue for imagining letters of application different types of barristers might compose on their own behalf, beginning with "The Genteel Canvass", following this with "the Pathetic Canvass", and ending with "The Houndsditch Canvass":

> The friends of Bartholomew Nebuchadnezzar, Esquire, Barrister-at-Law, are requested to meet at the Rose of Sharon Hotel, Holywell Street, to take measures for forwarding that gentleman's canvass for the post of Judge of the Court of Requests.
> D. Davids, Esquire, Blue Lion Square, Samuel Slomax, Esquire, Fetter Lane, Benjamin Benoni, Esquire, Holywell Street (General Outfitting Warehouse), have established branch committees at their residences, where the friends of B. Nebuchadnezzar, Esquire, are requested to attend.
>
> (*Punch*, IX, 30 August 1845, p. 104)

Names of personages and the hotel in which the meeting is proposed point back to the Old Testament—though as a Jewish name "Bartholomew Nebuchadnezzar", Christian apostle and English Fair leading up to a Babylonian king, is unthinkable outside the pages of *Punch*. The names of the signatories of the letter, however, are realistic; they show traces of Anglicization (did "Slomax" develop out of "Solomon" via "Sloman", perhaps?) common in Thackeray's London. "Benjamin Benoni", owner of a clothing emporium in Holywell Street, brings a dash of Disraeli into the usual old-clothes-and-East-End atmosphere; the streets and squares mentioned all contained Jewish business premises. The Court of Requests, a prerogative court set up by Henry VII, was in fact abolished by the Long Parliament in the 1640s and never resurrected: the Jewish petitioners are either presumed to be ignorant of this, or applying for a useful title without any actual legal duties. It should be stressed, however, that the Jewish lawyer and his supporters are satirized no more harshly than their Gentile colleagues who had also been ribbed in Thackeray's satiric piece.

The Fat Contributor re-emerges, on 11 October 1845, in the guise of "*Punch*'s Commissioner", sent on exploratory journeys, not to the Middle East, but to places in the British Isles. Prominent among these places is Brighton, whence the Commissioner sent *Punch* an illustrated report in which "Mosaic Arabs" once again figure prominently. The passage in question begins with a picture of the Commissioner—a Thackeray self-portrait, though it lacks the characteristic spectacles—on the Brighton Cliff.

Illustration 4

You meet everybody on that Cliff. For a small charge you may hire the very fly here represented; with the very horse, and the very postilion, in a pink striped chintz jacket—which may have been the cover of an arm-chair once—and straight whity-brown hair, and little washleather inexpressibles, the cheapest little caricature of a postboy eyes have ever lighted on. I seldom used to select his carriage, for the horse and vehicle looked feeble, and unequal to bearing a person of weight; but, last Sunday I saw an Israelitish family of distinction ensconced in the poor little carriage—the ladies with the most flaming polkas, and flounces all the way up; the gent in velvet waistcoat, with pins in his breast big enough once to have surmounted the door of his native pawnbroker's shop, and a complement of hook-nosed children, magnificent in attire. Their number and magnificence did not break the carriage down; the little postilion bumped up and down as usual, as the old horse went his usual pace.

How they spread out, and basked, and shone, and were happy in the sun there—those honest people! The Mosaic Arabs abound here; and they rejoice and are idle with a grave and solemn pleasure, as becomes their Eastern origin.

Illustration 5

Yes, they are shown to overload the carriage with their persons and their persons with ornaments. Yes, for Victorian readers of *Punch* "distinction" and "honest", in this context, had ironic overtones; but neither drawing nor text have anything of the animus that pervaded Titmarsh's descriptions of Polish Jews in *From Cornhill to Grand Cairo* or the anger and bite that characterize *Punch*'s occasional depiction of Jewish sweat-shops or of thief-trainers in the mould of Fagin. On the contrary; Thackeray's portrayal of the "grave and solemn pleasure" peculiar to people escaping from the everyday bustle and worry (whether in pawnshops or elsewhere) has a fully intended charm of its own.

A little later "Punch's Commissioner" encounters a Jewish visitor to Brighton who has climbed further up the ladder, further away from ancestral pawnshops—"a Hebrew dentist driving a curricle" (VIII, 57); but at the very opening of his next piece, published in *Punch* on 18 October 1845, that vision is exorcised by an initial "I" cast in the form of a cheerful Jewish old-clothes man (VIII, 58) (ill. 6).

The initial associates the "second-hand" goods in which the cheerful old man deals with the "second-rate in life" that forms the subject of the text; but no other Jews are featured in this article.

In the meantime, however, a storm seems to have broken over *Punch*'s head. Jewish visitors to Brighton, disturbed by mockery unleashed by the appearance of their "likeness" in the piece of 11 October, were leaving Brighton, and lodging-house keepers complained of the loss of custom this entailed. Thackeray parodies their

HAVE always had a taste for the second-rate in life. Second-rate poetry, for instance, is an uncommon deal pleasanter to my fancy than your great thundering first-rate epic poems. Your Miltons and Dantes are magnificent,—but a bore : whereas an ode of Horace, or a song of Tommy Moore, is always fresh, sparkling, and welcome. Second-rate claret, again, is notoriously better than first-rate wine : you get the former genuine, whereas the latter is a loaded and artificial composition that cloys the palate and bothers the reason.

Illustration 6

letters of complaint, and adds some comments of his own, in the guise of "*Punch*'s Commissioner".

> Mr. Skiver writes:—'Sir, —Your ill-advised publication has passed like a whirlwind over the lodging-houses of Brighton. You have rendered our families desolate, and prematurely closed our season. As you have destroyed the lodging-houses, couldn't you, now, walk into the boarding-houses, and say a kind word to ruin the hotels?'
> And is it so? Is the power of the Commissioner's eye so fatal that it withers the object on which it falls? Is the condition of his life so dreadful that he destroys all whom he comes near? Have I made a postboy wretched—five thousand lodging-house-keepers furious—twenty thousand Jews unhappy? If so, and I really possess a power so terrible, I had best come out in the tragic line.
>
> (VIII, 63)

"20 000" seems to be Thackeray's guess at the number of Jews living in Southern England in the mid-1840s. The "tragic line" the Commissioner resolves to pursue takes him to Shoreham, where

> the first object that struck my eye was the following scene, in the green lake there, which I am credibly informed is made of pea-soup: two honest girls were rowing about their friend on this enchanting water. There was a cloudless sky overhead—rich treats were advertised for the six frequenters of the gardens; a variety of entertainments was announced in the Hall of Amusement.—Mr. and Mrs. Aminadab (here, too, the Hebrews have penetrated) were advertised as about to sing some of their most favourite comic songs and—
> But *no*, I will *not* describe the place. What, should my fatal glance bring a curse upon it? The pea-soup lake would dry up—leaving its bed a vacant tureen—the leaves would drop from the scorched trees—the pretty flowers would wither and fade—the rockets would not rise at night, nor the rebel wheels go round—the money-taker at the door would grow mouldly and die in his moss-grown and deserted

cell.—Aminadab would lose his engagement. Why should these things be, and this ruin occur? James! pack the portmanteau and tell the landlord to bring the bill; order horses immediately—this day I will quit Brighton.

(VIII, 63–4)

The phrase to notice in this passage about Jewish music-hall artists is "here, too, the Hebrews have penetrated." What the Commissioner sees is Jews leaving their traditional abodes, penetrating further into the provinces (helped, of course, by the new railways) as well as into more fashionable districts of London or Manchester. The tone is sharper than in the piece that originally caused the offence; Thackeray's instinct, when attacked, is to counterattack vigorously. This appears particularly clearly at the end of the piece, where the Commissioner turns, not on the (presumably Christian) lodging-house keepers but on the Jews who had felt threatened by public ridicule.

> The children of Israel are in a fury too. They do not like to ride in flies, since my masterly representation of them a fortnight since. They are giving up their houses daily. You read in the Brighton papers, among the departures, '—Nebuzaradan, Esq., and family for London;' or, 'Solomon Ramothgilead, Esq., has quitted his mansion in Marine Crescent; circumstances having induced him to shorten his stay among us;' and so on. The people emigrate by hundreds; they can't bear to be made the object of remark in the public walks and drives—and they are flying from a city of which they might have made a new Jerusalem.

(VIII, 64–5)

The final joke about Brighton having nearly become a "new Jerusalem" by reason of its Jewish holiday-visitors or property-owners is a bitter one that has formed a staple of anti-Jewish comment ever since. Thackeray's Commissioner shows little sympathy with the victims of snide comments in public walks or drives which the relatively mild *Punch* cartoon had unleashed.

ii

The "Fat Contributor" and "*Punch*'s Commissioner" papers were just two related series which Thackeray contributed to *Punch* in the mid-1840s. Another series built on the earlier "Yellowplush" diaries; the valet Yellowplush speculates in railway shares, makes a fortune, and transmogrifies into "C. Jeames de la Pluche, Esq.", whose diary and letters *Punch* reprints for the delectation of its readers. The old spelling games return: "Jewly" for "July" (VIII, 381) is only incongruous, but in "I hentered the market with 20lb., specklated Jewdicious and ham what i ham" (VIII, 360) "Jewdicious" makes a sharper point about financial speculation than Jeames realizes, while "I ham that I ham" parodies the Old Testament (Exodus 3, 14) and renews the familiar association of "Jew" and "ham". "Jewdiciousness" has made Jeames a rich man who can afford to bid for an aristocratic wife in the Victorian marriage market. The union is foiled by a stock exchange crash that plunges Jeames back into a humbler sphere; he marries his first love, Lady Angelina's maid, and becomes the contented and reasonably prosperous landlord of the "Wheel of Fortune" public house.

With Jeames safely tucked away in domestic contentment, Thackeray now began to contribute to *Punch* what was to become the most celebrated of all his series: "The Snobs of England, by One of Themselves" (28 February 1846–27 February 1847, later reissued in shortened form as *The Book of Snobs*, 1848). "By One of Themselves" is important; Thackeray's spokesman, Mr Snob, not only probes the different ways in which men and women of his day meanly admired, meanly emulated, and meanly strove towards, mean things—he finds the springs that moved them to behave in this way by looking into his own mind and soul.

> It is a great mistake to judge of Snobs lightly, and think they exist among the lower classes merely. An immense percentage of Snobs I believe is to be found in every rank of this mortal life. You must not judge hastily or vulgarly of Snobs: to do so shows that you are yourself a Snob. I myself have been taken for one.
>
> (IX, 261)

In "Prefatory Remarks" for the *Punch* version of "The Snobs of England", the leaders of British society are contrasted to their disadvantage with the great lawgiver portrayed in the Pentateuch.

> . . . here I cannot help observing how very queer and peculiar the condition of our own beloved England and Ireland must be. One can fancy a great people led by Moses, or liberated by Washington, or saved by Leonidas or Alfred the Great; whereas the heroes destined to relieve *us* at present are a couple of notorious quacks, as Sir Robert and Mr. O'Connell will bear me out in asserting. This I throw out as a mere parenthetic observation, and revert to the former argument, which anybody may admit or deny.
>
> (IX, 260)

There can be little doubt that one of the politicians here described as "notorious quacks" is Disraeli, whose right to lead a great people is challenged by comparison with the greatest figure of the Old Testament as well as with Leonidas and King Alfred. When

the Snob papers were revised for their reprint in book form,
Thackeray decided to omit this whole passage. Had he come to
appreciate that even from Sir Robert Peel's perspective "notorious
quack" was hardly an apt description of Disraeli as a politician and
statesman? Be that as it may—the deletion of this passage removed
not only Mr Snob's insult to Disraeli, but also one of the clearest
instances in which the Jews of the Pentateuch—moulded by their
outstanding leader Moses—are seen as "a great people".

Jews less exalted than either Moses or Disraeli appear in a
section on "Clerical Snobs", in which Mr Snob takes a cool hard
look at a university system that gives large privileges to the titled
and the rich and sets them apart from the poorer species of student
dubbed "sizars" or "servitors".

> When this wicked and shameful distinction was set up, it was of a
> piece with all the rest—a part of the brutal, unchristian, blundering
> feudal system. Distinctions of rank were then so strongly insisted
> upon that it would have been thought blasphemy to doubt them, as
> blasphemous as it is in parts of the United States now for a nigger to
> set up as the equal of a white man. A ruffian like Henry VIII talked
> as gravely about the divine powers vested in him as if he had been an
> inspired prophet. A wretch like James I not only believed that there
> was in himself a particular sanctity, but other people believed him.
> Government regulated the length of a merchant's shoes as well as
> meddled with his trade, prices, exports, machinery. It thought itself
> justified in roasting a man for his religion, or pulling a Jew's teeth out
> if he did not pay a contribution, or ordered him to dress in a yellow
> gaberdine, and locked him in a particular quarter.
>
> Now a merchant may wear what boots he pleases, and has pretty
> nearly acquired the privilege of buying and selling without the
> Government laying its paws upon the bargain. The stake for heretics
> is gone; the pillory is taken down; Bishops are even found lifting up
> their voices against the remains of persecution, and ready to do away
> with the last Catholic Disabilities. Sir Robert Peel, though he wished
> it ever so much, has no power over Mr. Benjamin Disraeli's grinders,
> or any means of violently handling that gentleman's jaw. Jews are not
> called upon to wear badges: on the contrary, they may live in
> Piccadilly, or the Minories, according to fancy; they may dress like
> Christians, and do sometimes in a most elegant and fashionable
> manner.
>
> (IX, 317–18)

At this point the *Punch* printing of the piece (*Punch* IX, 30 May
1846, p. 521) is interrupted by a cartoon, drawn by Thackeray
himself, which introduces another version of the pork-eating Jew he
had drawn at school for the delectation of his fellow-pupils (ill. 7).

The piece on "Clerical Snobs" then ends with the words:

> Why is the poor College servitor to wear that name and that badge
> still? Because Universities are the last places into which Reform

MR. NEBUCHADNEZZAR. 'What is there for Dinner, Waiter?'
WAITER. 'Sir, a nice Leg of Pork is just come up.'
[NEBUCHADNEZZAR *sits down, and helps himself to pig, crackling, sage and onions and all.*]

Illustration 7

penetrates. But now that she can go to College and back for five shillings, let her travel down thither.

(IX, 318)

In "Thackeray as a Victorian Racialist" (*Essays in Criticism*, 20 [1970], pp. 441–5) John Sutherland has pointed to the passages just quoted as a patent example of such "racialism" directed against Jews:

Clearly, the cartoon belongs where it is. It combines the idea of poor servitor, or waiter, the rich (therefore upstart Jewish) fellow-Commoner, and the mockery of Disraeli, a convert to Christianity and therefore a pork-eater.

(loc. cit., p. 441)

I fully agree that the cartoon belongs where it is in the *Punch* version, but three considerations lead me to take a somewhat less censorious view of it than that taken by Professor Sutherland. The first is Thackeray's unequivocal condemnation, not only of medieval distinctions of rank, but also of religious intolerance and cruel treatment of Jews. The second is that the piece does not equate "servitor" and "waiter"; a waiter, in Thackeray's world, is expected to serve paying customers, and the drawing holds no suggestion that the waiter is being "humiliated" by Mr Nebuchadnezzar in the way the student "sizar" or "servitor" is by those who have perpetuated a "wicked and cruel distinction", "part of the brutal, unchristian, blundering feudal system." There is nothing in Thackeray to suggest that he thinks the employment of waiters similarly wicked and cruel, even if they are asked to serve Jews. Third and last: what the cartoon illustrates are the words immediately preceding it in the *Punch* version: "Jews . . . may dress like Christians, and do so sometimes in a most elegant and fashionable manner." Thackeray's drawing depicts a Jewish dandy, who has abandoned traditional Jewish ways sufficiently to eat pork, but whose swarthy and somewhat overdressed appearance continues to proclaim his Jewishness.

To Professor Sutherland's edition of *The Book of Snobs* (Santa Lucia, 1978, pp. 235–7) we owe an excellent survey of the way in which Thackeray helped to transform the meaning of the word "snob", which had once designated a shoemaker, then a "townsman" as opposed to a university "gownsman", then "a low vulgar fellow" or "person of low birth", into the meaning it acquired from 1845 onwards: "someone who apes, or toadies to, his social betters" or "someone who falsely claims, or overvalues, social superiority". The snobs surveyed in *Punch* by "One of Themselves" include George IV, whose claim to veneration is seen as social rather than intellectural or moral; but for the most part they belong to the upper bourgeoisie: city snobs, military snobs, university snobs, and so on. When "literary snobs" come under scrutiny, Disraeli soon puts in yet another appearance. Casting an ironical eye on the "silver fork" novelists of high life, Mr Snob commends the "delightful good company" one meets in the novels of Mrs Armitage:

> She seldom introduces you to anybody under a Marquis. I don't know anything more delicious than the pictures of genteel life in *Ten Thousand a Year*, except perhaps the *Young Duke*, and *Coningsby*. There's a modest grace about *them*, and an air of easy high fashion, which only belongs to blood, my dear Sir—to true blood.
>
> (IX, 330)

"Modest grace", this suggests, is the last quality one would associate with Disraeli's novels; and ridicule is poured once again on those theories of pure race and blood with which Disraeli sought to exalt the Jews but which anti-Semites were to find a ready weapon to turn against them. A later reference to "those foreign readers of *Punch* who, as Coningsby says, want to know the customs of an English gentleman's family" (IX, 398) insinuates that Disraeli is not the most obvious source one would go to for authentic information about what happens in the private and intimate sphere of English gentlefolk.

The words "as Coningsby says" were omitted when "The Snobs of England" piece of 1846 was transferred to *The Book of Snobs* in 1848 and to Thackeray's *Miscellanies* in 1855. The same fate befell seven whole papers from the *Punch* series because, as the author explained, "on re-perusing these papers, I have found them so stupid, so personal, so snobbish, in a word, that I have withdrawn them from the collection." Among the "stupid . . . personal 'and' . . . snobbish" sections sacrificed was that which had depicted Disraeli as a Great Britannic Literary Snob under the transparent pseudonym Ben de Minories—the Minories being an East London District with many Jewish inhabitants.

> And, finally, concerning young Ben de Minories. What right have I to hold up that famous literary man as a specimen of the Great Britannic Literary Snob? Mr. de Minories is not only a man of genius (as you are, my dear Smith, though your washerwoman duns you for her little bill), but he has achieved those advantages of wealth which you have not: and we should respect him as our chief and representative in the circles of the fashion. When the Choctaw Indians were here some time ago, who was the individual whose self and house were selected to be shown to those amiable foreigners as models of the establishment and the person of 'an English gentleman'? Of all England, De Minories was the man that was selected by Government as the representative of the British aristocracy. I know it's true. I saw it in the papers: and a nation never paid a higher compliment to a literary man.
>
> And I like to see him in his public position—a quill-driver, like one of us—I like to see him because he makes our profession *respected*. For what do we admire Shakespeare so much as for his wondrous versatility? He must have *been* everything he describes: Falstaff, Miranda, Caliban, Mark Antony, Ophelia, Justice Shallow—and so I say De Minories must know more of politics than any man, for he has been (or has offered to be) everything. In the morning of life Joseph and Daniel were sponsors for the blushing young neophyte, and held him up at the font of freedom. It would make a pretty picture! Circumstances occasioned him to quarrel with the most venerable of his godfathers, and to modify the opinions advanced in

the generosity of his youth. Would he have disliked a place under the Whigs? Even with them, it is said, the young patriot was ready to serve his country. Where would Peel be now had he known his value? I turn from the harrowing theme, and depict to myself the disgust of the Romans when Coriolanus encamped before the Porta del Popolo, and the mortification of Francis the First when he saw the Constable Bourbon opposite to him at Pavia. *Raro antecedentem, &c. deseruit pede Paena claudo* (as a certain poet remarks); and I declare I know nothing more terrible than Peel, at the catastrophe of a sinister career,—Peel writhing in torture, with Nemesis de Minories down upon him!

I know nothing in Lemprière's *Dictionary* itself more terrific than that picture of Godlike vengeance. What! Peel thought to murder Canning, did he? and to escape because the murder was done twenty years ago? No, no. What! Peel thought to repeal the Corn Laws, did he? In the first place, before Corn Bills or Irish Bills are settled, let us know who was it that killed Lord George Bentinck's 'relative'. Let Peel answer for that murder to the country, to the weeping and innocent Lord George, and to Nemesis de Minories, his champion.

I call his interference real chivalry. I regard Lord George's affection for his uncle-in-law as the most elegant and amiable of the qualities of that bereaved young nobleman—and I am proud, dear Smith, to think that it is a man of letters who backs him in his disinterested feud; that if Lord George is the head of the great English country party, it is a man of letters who is viceroy over him. Happy country! to have such a pair of saviours. Happy Lord George! to have such a friend and patron—happy men of letters! to have a man out of their ranks the chief and saviour of the nation.

(IX, 334-5)

Like many contemporaries, the Snob who smells out other Snobs conveys astonishment that someone of Disraeli's origins, who looked and behaved so unlike the traditional idea of an English gentleman, should have succeeded among the literary and political gentry of the day to such an extent that when, in 1844, some American Indians were to be shown an English gentleman's residence, it was to Disraeli's house in Grosvenor Square that they found themselves conducted. What had begun as an account of a literary career soon passes into an account of a political one. "Joseph" and "Daniel" are two of Disraeli's earliest supporters, Joseph Hume and Daniel O'Connell; but their names are here meant to recall two figures from the Old Testament too, Israelites who made their voices heard at alien courts, and who may therefore figure as Disraeli's "sponsors" in another, extended sense. The mock-comparison with Shakespeare is designed to highlight the chameleon-like qualities that enabled Disraeli to commend (or try to commend) himself to various opposing factions, to make himself indispensable to the Tory party,—to oust the old leader, and to advance himself by means of his alliance with Lord George Bentinck. There is amazement, there is also some admiration, at this astonishing performance on the part of a man who stressed his Jewish ancestry instead of trying to hide it (hence "Ben de Minories"); but the final elevation of the Great Britannic Literary Snob as an object of admiration for all literary men and as "chief and saviour" of the British nation suggests a confidence trick which Ben de Minories has played on gullible Mr Smith. The picture is completed in the chapter on "Some Respectable Snobs", where the son of the parvenu who now calls himself De Mogyns "has of course joined Young England" (IX, 294)—the Tory faction that looked to Disraeli as its leader and guide.

Another of the omitted sections, "On Whig Snobs", alludes to one of Disraeli's best-known *bon mots*, which asserted that Peel had found the Whigs bathing and had stolen their clothes.

> What ensued last week when Peel gave in his adhesion to Free Trade, and, meekly resigning his place and emoluments, walked naked out of office into private life? John Russell and Company stepped in to assume those garments which, according to that illustrious English gentleman, the Member for Shrewsbury [i.e. Disraeli], the Right Honourable Baronet had originally 'conveyed' from the Whigs, but which (according to Jones and every contributor to *Punch*) the Whigs themselves had abstracted from Richard Cobden, Charles Villiers, John Bright, and others,—what, I say, ensued? . . . Do you mean to say that *you* are to rule; and Cobden is to be held of no account? It was thus that at a contest for Shrewsbury, more severe than Mr. B. Disraeli ever encountered, one Falstaff came forward and claimed to have slain Hotspur, when the noble Harry had run him through . . .
>
> (IX, 340)

No doubt Mr Snob found it amusing, once again, that Disraeli could be thought of as "an illustrious English gentleman"; but the reference to Falstaff's false claims after the battle of Shrewsbury in the last act of *Henry IV Part I* ridicules Disraeli's political opponents rather than Disraeli himself. Shrewsbury was, of course, the constituency Disraeli represented in the House of Commons. The M.P. for Shrewsbury *is* the target in another of the omitted papers, "On Conservative or Country-Party Snobs", where he appears, with intentional incongruity, in the ranks of

> The real, original, unbending, No Surrender aristocrats; the men of the soil; our old, old leaders; our Plantagenets; our Somersets; our Disraelis . . .
>
> (IX, 345–6)

The list is then completed by "our Hudsons"—the Victorian "railway king" George Hudson, with a side-glance, perhaps, at Britain's most famous dwarf, Sir Geoffrey Hudson, immortalized in

Peveril of the Peak—and "our Stanleys": a reference Thackeray explains in the next sentence:

> They have turned out in force, and for another struggle; they have taken 'the Rupert of debate', Geoffrey Stanley, for leader, and set up their standard of 'No Surrender' on Whitebait Hill.
>
> (IX, 345)

Geoffrey Stanley, fourteenth Earl of Derby, had been dubbed "the Rupert of Debate" by Thackeray's perennial butt Edward Bulwer, Lord Lytton, after Prince Rupert, the supporter of Charles II, who figures in Scott's *Woodstock*, *Legend of Montrose*, and, once again, *Peveril of the Peak*; he had been impressed into the leadership of the Tory Party's campaign against free trade. In the ranks of "No Surrender" aristocrats such as these the Disraelis, whether scholarly father or politician son, and Hudson the Railway King, make an odd enclave indeed. As for the "Whig Snobs" promised by the heading of this piece—Mr Snob the Snobographer alleges that it is difficult to find acknowledged Whigs at all in 1846, since the Tories seemed to be doing whatever work British voters demanded of their parliamentary representatives.

> How rare it is to meet a real acknowledged Whig! Do you know one? Do you know what it is to be a Whig? I can understand a man being anxious for this measure or that, wishing to do away with the sugar duties, or the corn duties, or the Jewish disabilities, or what you will; but in that case, if Peel will do my business and get rid of the nuisance for me, he answers my purpose just as well as anybody else with any other name. I want my house set in order, my room made clean; I do not make particular inquiries about the broom and the dustpan.
>
> (IX, 348–9)

This is, in fact, the first direct public reference Thackeray has made to the much-debated question of full civil rights for professsing Jews—in particular, the removal of the religious test which made it impossible for such Jews to take their seats in parliament even if they had been duly elected. Indirectly, of course, the question had come up before, when Mr Snob reminded Jews, with some justice, of how tolerant British society was in comparison with societies elsewhere which perpetuated medieval restrictions (IX, 318). Here, however, in the piece on "Whig Snobs", he lists the remaining Jewish disabilities among "nuisances" British voters may want removed, along with duties on sugar and corn. We shall see Thackeray take up a position of his own later in this history.

Sir Robert Peel's fall from power in 26 June 1846, and Disraeli's part in that fall, were subjects that attracted a good deal of comment in *Punch* outside the "Snobs of England" series, and

Thackeray joined in this game with two squibs and a drawing.

> What will Ben Disraeli do now? The amiable creature will pine like the ivy, when his attached oak is removed from him.
> *(Punch, XI, 4 July 1846, p. 12)*

The implication is that the "ivy" has already found something else to climb up—and that it may, indeed, have contributed to the removal of the "oak" (Disraeli's political rival Peel, a fellow Tory) by choking it. Discussing a recently projected Speaking Machine— a first shot at a gramophone—Thackeray returns to Disraeli's onslaughts on Peel, which included jokes that were hardly "good natured", in the context of what Thackeray depicts as a puppet-like dependence on Disraeli's political patron Lord George Bentinck.

> The machine laughs—but we are bound to say not in a hearty and jovial manner. It is a hard, dry, artificial laugh; such as that of young Misses on the stage, when they give the genteel comedy-giggle; or of Sir Robert Peel, when he is amused by some of Mr. Disraeli's good-natured jokes against him.
> By the way, why should not Lord George Bentinck have one of these machines constructed, with a Benjamin Disraeli figure-head, and play upon it himself at once, and spare the honourable Member for Shrewsbury the bother of being his Lordship's Euphonia?
> *(Punch, XI, 22 August 1846, p. 83)*

Thackeray's drawing which accompanies this piece is droll, and by no means ill-natured; the Disraeli puppet has a rather endearing expression on its face, and its Jewish traits are not exaggerated.

Illustration 8

What sting there is in this piece about the "Euphonia" speaking machine appears further alleviated by a conclusion that turns on the satirist himself:

> By far the best part of the Euphonia is its *hiss*; this is perfect. And perhaps the fact suggests to the benevolent mind the moral that hissing is the very easiest occupation of life,—which truth is, however, beside the present question.
>
> (ibid.)

Adverse criticism, "hissing", is so much easier than doing!

In the meantime, the "Snobs of England" series continued its popular progress through the columns of *Punch*; and another paper later omitted from the book version, "On Some Political Snobs", matched "Ben de Minories" with another mock-title embodying the name of a London district with a large Jewish population when it referred to "the Baron de Houndsditch's *déjeuner* at Twickenham" as a place in the "best society" where political gossip might be heard. (IX, 336). The title "Baron" brings thoughts of a dancing teacher as well as a financier, of "Baron" Nathan and Baron de Rothschild; and the move from humble Houndsditch to aristocratic Twickenham introduces another index of social mobility, another pattern of penetration, into Thackeray's account of the Jewish community of his day.

Elsewhere in the "Snobs of England" series the Rothschilds are treated with greater respect. Under the transparent pseudonym "Scharlachschild" they figure, it is true, among the "Banking Snobs"; but their hospitality contrasts most favourably with that of mean-minded "City Snobs" in England.

> A mere gentleman may hope to sit at almost anybody's table—to take his place at my lord duke's in the country—to dance a quadrille at Buckingham Palace itself . . . —but the City Snob's doors are for the most part closed to him; and hence all that one knows of this great class is mostly from hearsay.
>
> In other countries of Europe, the Banking Snob is more expansive and communicative than with us, and receives all the world into his circle. For instance, everybody knows the princely hospitalities of the Scharlachschild family at Paris, Naples, Frankfort, &c. They entertain all the world, even the poor, at their fêtes . . .
>
> (IX, 296–7)

"On Some Country Snobs" includes another respectful mention of the Rothschilds. The passage in question ridicules the claims of a snobbish governess to social eminence:

> To hear Miss Wirt herself, you would fancy that her Papa was a

Rothschild, and that the markets of Europe were convulsed when he went into the *Gazette*.

(IX, 404)

The Rothschilds are not likely to figure as bankrupts in the Stock Exchange Gazette; they are seen as the financial wizards of Europe, and a connection with them would constitute a claim to social eminence more justifiable than that made by poor Miss Wirt.

In a humbler sphere Jews are seen, by Mr Snob, as part of a varied and colourful London scene. At the end of the section on "University Snobs", he paints a charming picture of the Reverend Mr Hugsby's son coming to town during the Long Vacation, and leaving his father's church after the service

> on Sundays, at the hour when tavern-doors open, whence issue little girls with great jugs of porter; when charity-boys walk the streets, bearing brown dishes of smoking shoulders of mutton and baked 'taters; when Sheeny and Moses are seen smoking their pipes before their lazy shutters in Seven Dials; when a crowd of smiling persons in clean outlandish dresses, in monstrous bonnets and flaring printed gowns, or in crumpled glossy coats and silks, that bear the creases of the drawers where they have lain all the week, file down High Street.
>
> (IX, 322–3)

Well, yes, the dictionary tells us that "sheeny" (origin unknown) had come into use in the early nineteenth century as an "opprobrious" term for Jews; but it would take persecution mania to see anything opprobrious in this brief glimpse of Jews enjoying the Christian sabbath along with their neighbours.

The section headed "Club Snobs" returns to the governess Miss Wirt, and shows her "performing Thalberg's last sonata . . ., totally unheeded, at the piano" (IX, 45). This brings briefly into view Sigismund Thalberg (1812–1871), a composer of salon-music and notable piano virtuoso, whose Jewish origins are neither relevant nor mentioned here. Outside the "Snobs of England" series, however, Thackeray reminds the readers of *Punch* of the English and European Jews' growing love and patronage of musical and theatrical entertainments. Under the heading "Theatrical Astronomy" he draws a swarthy beau attending a performance of *The Bohemian Girl* at Drury Lane. The young man is looking at the stage with one eye fortified by one of the eye-pieces of his opera glass while the other eye squints towards the onlooker, or towards the artist who is sketching him. (IX, 532). He is not only *attending* a theatrical spectacle; he is also conscious of *providing* one, and is keen to see what impression his elaborate waistcoat and ornamental chain, and his figure-hugging coat, are making on others.

Sudden appearance of a
star.

Illustration 9

Thackeray may have meant this drawing, which appeared in the eleventh volume of *Punch* (p. 175) illustrating a piece by another hand, as a first sketch for a section on "Theatrical Snobs" which never materialized. Instead, Radical Snobs, Irish Snobs, Party-Giving Snobs and Dining-Out Snobs pass in review, to be followed by "Some Continental Snobs"—a skit on English travellers:

> They will be at Ostend in four hours; they will inundate the Continent next week; they will carry into far lands the famous image of the British Snob. I shall not see them—but am with them in spirit; and indeed there is hardly a country in the known and civilized world in which these eyes have not beheld them.
>
> (IX, 376)

Among the travellers seen "in spirit" in this way is a group of London Jews.

> Look at honest Nathan Houndsditch and his lady, and their little son. What a noble air of blazing contentment illuminates the features of those Snobs of Eastern race! What a toilet Houndsditch's is ! What rings and chains, what gold-headed canes and diamonds, what a tuft the rogue has got to his chin (the rogue! he will never spare himself any cheap enjoyment!) Little Houndsditch has a little cane with a gilt head and little mosaic ornaments—altogether an extra air. As for the lady, she is all the colours of the rainbow: she has a pink parasol, with a white lining, and a yellow bonnet, and an emerald green shawl, and a shot silk pelisse; and drab boots and rhubarb coloured gloves; and parti-coloured glass buttons, expanding from the size of a four-penny-piece to a crown, glitter and twiddle all down the front of her gorgeous costume. I have said before, I like to look at 'the Peoples' on their gala-days, they are so picturesquely and outrageously splendid and happy.
>
> (IX, 378)

"Thackeray's buttons", John Carey has well said (*Thackeray: Prodigal Genius*, p. 47), "draw attention to the cultural gulfs that lurk within minutiae". The buttons of Nathan Houndsditch's lady are a case in point—no lady in Thackeray's own circle would dress as she does, nor would their gentlemen get themselves up in Nathan Houndsditch's flashy manner. Yet Thackeray seems to take an artist's delight in it all, and the gusto of his presentation makes the scene appear exhilarating and endearing. Who can resist their picturesque and outrageous splendour and happiness? Not the presenter, the self-confessed snob passing other, less self-conscious snobs in review. Thackeray uses the vocabulary of race here— "those Snobs of Eastern race"—which Disraeli had so insistently employed in his paean to "Mosaic Arabs" and Caucasians; but though he has nothing like the wholehearted admiration of this "Eastern race" which is characteristic of Disraeli, he accepts its representatives as an integral part of the motley crowd of British citizens. "Captain Bull", a sponging snob who follows Nathan Houndsditch and his family in this procession of "Continental Snobs", is considerably less sympathetically presented; nor have these Jewish figures any taint of "the brutal ignorant peevish bully of an Englishman" whose portrait is painted in darkest colours in "Continental Snobbery Continued" (IX, 383). Heine himself, that scourge of English travellers, has nothing more savage than this. Is not the Houndsditch family, with its "air of blazing contentment", preferable to such surly bullies of unimpeachably Gentile stock?

Thackeray's use of the term "race" in the Disraelian, the ethnic-biological sense, is the exception rather than the rule. Elsewhere in the "Snobs of England" series he uses the term in the sense of "family" ("the eldest-born of your race—IX, 273); of "class" (the English aristocracy is "a race set apart . . . who . . . hold the first rank, have the first prizes and chances in all government jobs and patronages"—IX, 273); or of both together ("Pump Quartus . . . comes out a full-blown aristocrat, and takes his seat as Baron Pumpington, and his race rules hereditarily over this nation of Snobs"—IX, 299). He also speaks, humorously, of the "black-coated race" of parsons (IX, 310), dubs those who make the Court Circular their Gospel and Burke's Peerage their Bible a "cringing race" (279), and presents himself, in his "Prefatory Remarks", as the designated chronicler of the "race" of Snobs:

> . . . they existed for years and years, and were no more known than American. But presently,—*ingens patebat tellus*,—the people became darkly aware that there was such a race. Not above five-and-twenty years since, a name, an expressive monosyllable arose to designate that race. That name has spread over England like railroads subse-

quently; Snobs are known and recognized throughout an Empire on which I am given to understand the Sun never sets. *Punch* appears at the ripe season, to chronicle their history; and THE INDIVIDUAL comes forth to write that history in *Punch*.

(IX, 261)

This last instance brings us full circle; for the humorous effect here depends on pseudo-biological suggestions which make Thackeray's series a "physiology" of Snobs, on the model of the popular French "physiologies" of the time. Thackeray may use the language of the historiographer; but his presentation of the "race" of Snobs is as surely a pseudo-Bernardian "physiology" as Balzac's *Physiologie du mariage*.

It will have been noticed that Nathan Houndsditch, that English member of an "Eastern race", is said to sport "little mosaic ornaments" (IX, 378) about his person. Elsewhere in the "Snobs of England" series, such ornaments are called "dubious jewellery" (IX, 365); and when Thackeray speaks of "Jessamy, who was conspicuous for his 'jewellery'" (IX, 325) his inverted commas strongly suggest a pun on the first syllable of the word so marked out. "Mosaic ornaments", "dubious jewellery", and "'jewellery'" *tout court* suggest one and the same thing: flashy items bought from cheapjacks which are not likely to contain much in the way of authentically precious stones or authentically precious metals.

The last appearance of Jews in the "Snobs of England" series is in the conversation of Jawkins, "a most pertinacious Club Snob." Thackeray draws him holding the *Standard* in his hand (ill. 10), and then lets his narrator tell us:

> He passes the morning swaggering about the City, in bankers' and brokers' parlours, and says:—'I spoke with Peel yesterday, and his intentions are so and so. . . .' By evening-paper time he is at the Club: 'I can tell you the opinion of the City, my lord,' says he, 'and the way in which Jones Loyd looks at it is briefly this; Rothschilds told me so themselves. In Mark Lane, people's minds are *quite* made up.' He is considered rather a well-informed man.

(IX, 456)

Rothschilds (in the plural—the firm talks through any of its members) is here taken as the most unimpeachable source of financial information to be found in mid-century London. Their insights and intentions in financial matters are as highly regarded as those of Sir Robert Peel in the field of national policy.

Thackeray ends his survey of snobs "by One of Themselves" with a hit at "mammoniacal superstition" that makes members of English society, "from the highest to the lowest", sneak and bow and cringe upwards and bully downwards.

Illustration 10

A Court system that sends men of genius to the second table, I hold
to be a Snobbish system. A Society that sets up to be polite, and
ignores Arts and Letters, I hold to be a Snobbish Society. You, who
despise your neighbour, are a Snob; you, who forget your own
friends, meanly to follow after those of a higher degree, are a Snob;
you who are ashamed of your poverty, and blush for your calling, are
a Snob; as are you who boast of your pedigree, or are proud of your
wealth.

   To laugh at such is *Mr. Punch's* business. May he laugh honestly,
hit no foul blow, and tell the truth when at his very broadest
grin—never forgetting that if Fun is good, Truth is still better, and
Love best of all.

(IX, 493)

The present book adduces enough evidence to show that Thackeray did not always live up to the ideal he here described in words
partly borrowed from St. Paul. His good resolutions were on
occasions thwarted by the effects of his narrow and sometimes cruel
upbringing, contemporary club-man and Anglo-Indian prejudg-
ments, rages induced by unfortunate encounters, and the prejudiced expectations of large sections of his readership; but the ideal
he kept before himself, in all sincerity, was a worthy one, and
deserves our respect.

iii

"On Literary Snobs" had included a brief satirical reference to *Coningsby* and *The Young Duke*; and this prepared the way for a full-scale parody of Disraeli's often extravagant early manner in the next series Thackeray contributed to *Punch*. This series ran from April until October 1847 under the title *"Punch's* Prize Novelists"; it was later edited and abbreviated for Thackeray's *Miscellanies* (Volume II, 1856) where it was renamed "Novels by Eminent Hands". Among these novels is one entitled

CODLINGSBY
BY D. SHREWSBERRY, ESQ. —

an easy recognizable reference to the title of one of Disraeli's best-known works, and to the constituency he represented in parliament. The opening of this piece brilliantly parodies Disraeli's own style and that adopted by his more didactic personages.

> The whole world is bound by one chain. In every city in the globe there is one quarter that certain travellers know and recognize from its likeness to its brother district in all other places where are congregated the habitations of men. In Teheran, or Pekin, or Stamboul, or New York, or Timbuctoo, or London, there is a certain district where a certain man is not a stranger. Where the idols are fed with incense by the streams of Ching-wang-foo; where the minarets soar sparkling above the cypresses, their reflections quivering in the lucid waters of the Golden Horn; where the yellow Tiber flows under broken bridges and over imperial glories; where the huts are squatted by the Niger, under the palm-trees; where the Northern Babel lies, with its warehouses, and its bridges, its graceful factory-chimneys, and its clumsy fanes—hidden in fog and smoke by the dirtiest river in the world—in all the cities of mankind there is One Home whither men of one family may resort. Over the entire world spreads a vast brotherhood, suffering, silent, scattered, sympathizing, *waiting*—an immense of Freemasonry. Once this world-spread band was an Arabian clan—a little nation alone and outlying amongst the mighty monarchies of ancient time, the Megatheria of history. The sails of their rare ships might be seen in the Egyptian waters; the camels of their caravans might thread the sands of Baalbec, or wind through the date-groves of Damascus; their flag was raised, not ingloriously, in many wars, against mighty odds; but 'twas a small people, and on one dark night the Lion of Judah went down before Vespasian's Eagles, and in flame, and death, and struggle, Jerusalem agonized and died. . . . Yes, the Jewish city is lost to Jewish men; but have they not taken the world in exchange?
> Mused thus Godfrey de Bouillon, Marquis of Codlingsby, as he debouched from Wych Street into the Strand. He had been to take a box for Armida at Madame Vestris's theatre. That little Armida was *folle* of Madame Vestris's theatre; and her little brougham, and her

little self, and her enormous eyes, and her prodigious opera-glass, and her miraculous bouquet, which cost Lord Codlingsby twenty guineas every evening at Nathan's in Covent Garden (the children of the gardeners of Sharon have still no rival for flowers), might be seen three nights in the week at least in the narrow, charming, comfortable little theatre. Godfrey had the box. He was strolling, listlessly, eastward; and the above thoughts passed through the young noble's mind as he came in sight of Holywell Street.

(VIII, 98–9)

This is more than just parody of a literary prose-style—it is also fair humorous comment on Disraeli's concern with the details of high life and his paeans to the world-wide brotherhood of "Mosaic Arabs". What Thackeray does in the rest of the parody is to hold Disraeli's large claims for Jewry, and his stylization of his own ideal self as the wise, wealthy and powerful Sidonia, against the lowlier forms of Anglo-Jewish life which *Punch* so often caricatured for its readers. Nathan's flowershop and Holywell Street have already brought a more prosaic world into view; what follows is one of Thackeray's street-idylls heightened by Disraelian pride of race and suddenly plunged into the caricature of Jewish speech which had served Thackeray and other humorists so often before.

The occupants of the London Ghetto sat at their porches basking in the evening sunshine. Children were playing on the steps. Fathers were smoking at the lintel. Smiling faces looked out from the various and darkling draperies with which the warehouses were hung. Ring-lets glossy, and curly, and jetty—eyes black as night—mid-summer night—when it lightens; haughty noses bending like beaks of eagles—eager quivering nostrils—lips curved like the bow of Love—every man or maiden, every babe or matron in that English Jewry bore in his countenance one or more of these characteristics of his peerless Arab race.

'How beautiful they are!' mused Codlingsby, as he surveyed these placid groups calmly taking their pleasure in the sunset.

'D'you vant to look at a nishe coat?' a voice said, which made him start; and then some one behind him began handling a masterpiece of Stultz's with a familiarity which would have made the baron tremble.

'Rafael Mendoza!' exclaimed Godfrey.

(VIII, 99)

The caricatured speech-patterns associated with the largely Ashke-nazic inhabitants of Holywell Street turn out to be a disguise for the noble and wealthy Sephardi Mendoza; so does the setting, an "awning of old clothes, tawdry fripperies, greasy spangles and battered masks" leading into "a shop as black and hideous as the entrance was foul." (VIII, 101). Thackeray's drawing at this point

shows the obviously Gentile Codlingsby accosted by the flamboyantly dressed Mendoza (those check trousers! that huge neck-tie!)
who sports a "Jewish" nose echoed not only in the pipe-smoking
shopkeeper and the playing children behind him, but also in the
doll the children play with, and the mask hung up for sale.

Illustration 11

Behind this shop, in which Mendoza helps "pretty Rachel"
persuade a customer to buy a carnival costume ("selp ma Moshesh, Mishter Lint, ve'd ask a guinea of any but you"—VIII, 105) is
a luxurious palace in which Mendoza conducts business with the
great ones of the world while spouting a parody of Disraeli's claims

of Jewish ancestry for a very large proportion of those who have
made important contributions to cultural, social and political life.
Mendoza's sister Miriam, meanwhile, sings some of the music
Mendoza attributes to Jewish composers, accompanying herself on
an ivory piano. The composers named include not only Braham
and Sloman (of all people!) but also Weber and Rossini. There are
hilarious insets to the main story, comprising a very odd boat-race
that seems to be going on in Oxford and Cambridge simulta-
neously, and a boxing match won, against a huge opponent, by
Mendoza—who had also managed to win the boat-race all by
himself, rowing a canoe presented to him by a grateful Turkey after
he had saved its monarchy at the battle of Nezeeb. A cheerful
illustration shows a Disraelian Mendoza squaring up against his
huge smiling opponent while town and gown look wonderingly on.

Illustration 12

It's all excellent fooling, given additional point by the recollection that there was indeed a Jewish prize-fighter named Mendoza,
who had entered the boxing-ring in 1784 and lived on until 1836.
Thackeray also manages to include a full-length picture of a *belle
Juive*, with humorously exaggerated Disraelian flourishes:

The Talmud relates that Adam had two wives—Zillah the dark beauty; Eva the fair one. The ringlets of Zillah were black; those of Eva were golden. The eyes of Zillah were night; those of Eva were morning. Codlingsby was fair—of the fair Saxon race of Hengist and Horsa—they called him Miss Codlingsby at school; but how much fairer was Miriam the Hebrew!

Her hair had that deep glowing tinge in it which has been the delight of all painters, and which, therefore the vulgar sneer at. It was of burning auburn. Meandering over her fairest shoulders in twenty thousand minute ringlets, it hung to her waist and below it. A light blue velvet fillet clasped with a diamond aigrette (valued at two hundred thousand tomauns, and bought from Lieutenant Vicovich, who had received it from Dost Mahomed), with a simple bird of paradise, formed her headgear. A sea-green cymar with short sleeves displayed her exquisitely moulded arms to perfection, and was fastened by a girdle of emeralds over a yellow-satin frock. Pink-gauze trousers spangled with silver, and slippers of the same colour as the band which clasped her ringlets (but so covered with pearls that the original hue of the charming little papoosh disappeared entirely) completed her costume. She had three necklaces on, each of which would have dowered a Princess—her fingers glistened with rings to their rosy tips, and priceless bracelets, bangles, and armlets wound round an arm that was whiter than the ivory grand piano on which it leaned.

(VIII, 110)

What a noise all that jewellery must have made when she played on her ivory instrument! This seductive maiden, who lights Codlingsby's cigar with a thousand pound note taken from a bundle on the precious piano, is linked—inevitably, in Thackeray's world—with *Ivanhoe*.

Rafael read his thoughts. 'We have Saxon blood too in our veins,' he said. 'You smile! but it is even so. An ancestress of ours made a *mésalliance* in the reign of your King John. Her name was Rebecca, daughter of Isaac of York, and she married in Spain, whither she had fled to the Court of King Boabdil, Sir Wilfrid of Ivanhoe, then a widower by the demise of his first lady, Rowena. The match was deemed a cruel insult amongst our people; but Wilfrid conformed, and was a Rabbi of some note at the synagogue of Cordova. We are descended from him lineally. It is the only blot upon the escutcheon of the Mendozas.'

(VIII, 110)

That recapitulates the "Proposals for a Continuation of *Ivanhoe*" which Thackeray had contributed to *Fraser's Magazine* in 1846 and which were to be elaborated in *Rebecca and Rowena*—though of course Sir Wilfrid's conversion to Judaism, and his new co-religionists' reaction to this infusion of Saxon "blood", belong to the

Disraeli parody and will be replaced, in *Rebecca and Rowena*, by Rebecca's conversion to Christianity.

"Codlingsby" ends with a series of audiences given by Mendoza. First he receives Mr Aminadab, who kisses his foot and brings him papers to sign:

> 'How is the house in Grosvenor Square, Aminadab; and is your son tired of his yacht yet?' Mendoza asked. 'That is my twenty-fourth cashier,' said Rafael to Codlingsby, when the obsequious clerk went away. 'He is fond of display, and all my people may have what money they like.'
>
> (VIII, 111).

Next comes Lord Bareacres, who is shuffled off with £10,000 dispensed to him by little Mordecai, the orange boy. There had, in fact, been previous references, in "Codlingsby", to oranges and pencils peddled around London by Jewish boys—a common sight, it would appear, in Thackeray's day. Lord Bareacres is followed into Mendoza's audience chamber by an emissary of the Czar:

> A man with a square face, cat-like eyes, and a yellow moustache, came next. He had an hour-glass of a waist, and walked uneasily upon his high-heeled boots. 'Tell your master that he shall have two millions more, but not another shilling,' Rafael said. 'That story about the five-and-twenty millions of ready money at Cronstadt is all bosh. They won't believe it in Europe. You understand me, Count Grogomoffski?'
>
> 'But His Imperial Majesty said four millions, and I shall get the knout unless—'
>
> 'Go and speak to Mr. Shadrach, in room Z 94, the fourth court,' said Mendoza good-naturedly. 'Leave me at peace, Count; don't you see it is Friday, and almost sunset?' The Calmuck envoy retired cringing, and left an odour of musk and candle-grease behind him.
>
> (VIII, 111)

Codlingsby is duly amazed to find "all the affairs of the world represented here, and Holywell Street the centre of Europe", when three peculiar knocks are heard.

> Mendoza starting up, said, 'Ha! there are only four men in the world who know that signal.' At once, and with a reverence quite distinct from his former *nonchalant* manners he advanced towards the new-comer.
>
> He was an old man—an old man evidently, too, of the Hebrew race—the light of his eyes was unfathomable—about his mouth there played an inscrutable smile. He had a cotton umbrella, and old trousers, and old boots, and an old wig, curling at the top like a rotten old pear.
>
> (VIII, 112)

If the reference to "a rotten old pear" was not explicit enough for his first readers, Thackeray's accompanying caricature made it all clear: the man who is here claimed for "the Hebrew race"—as Jenny Lind, Rossini and other worthies had been before him—is Louis Philippe of France, a monarch whom Thackeray detested but whom Disraeli had hailed as a modern Ulysses.

Illustration 13

"His Majesty is one of us", Mendoza whispers, as he shows Codlingsby out; "so is the Pope of Rome; so is . . ." A whisper conceals the rest, as Codlingsby leaves Holywell street in order to "go and fetch Fifine to the Olympic."

Thackeray's parody has concentrated on just two aspects of Disraeli's novels: his high claims for the Jewish "race", and (to a lesser extent) his depictions of the appurtenances of wealth and power. The flamboyance of Disraeli's style has been exaggerated, of course, but in a way that highlighted extravagances which were undoubtedly to be found in *Coningsby*, *Tancred*, and *The Young Duke*. Disraeli himself, it seems, did not take Thackeray's skit in good part—he broke off all social intercourse with him, passed him without greeting when they met in public, and is believed to have had Thackeray in mind when he created the malicious St. Barbe in his last novel *Endymion*. Had he also recognized Thackeray's hand in the symbolic capital depicting a Jewish damsel prancing on the battlemen of a medieval castle before some astonished de Bois Gilbert, which illustrated à Beckett's "Young Israel"—an unfriendly glance at the "Young England" movement with which Disraeli's name was so intimately associated? (IX, 543)

Illustration 14

Publications in *Punch* were anonymous, of course; but a keen eye could detect stylistic similarities, and a keen ear could pick up rumours which connected anonymously published pieces with the name of their author.

iv

"Punch's Prize Novelists" concluded, in 1847, with a parody of the now forgotten novels of G.P.R. James ('Barbazure', by G.P.R. James, Esq., etc.") in which the medieval manners evoked included, once again, the extraction of money from Jews by means of the forced extraction of teeth:

> That the Baron Raoul levied toll upon the river and mail upon the shore; that he now and then ransomed a burgher, plundered a neighbour, or drew the fangs of a Jew; that he burned an enemy's castle with the wife and children within;—these were points for which the country knew and respected the stout baron.
>
> (VIII, 130–1);

and "Crinoline", ascribed, by Thackeray, to the pen of his versatile valet turned financier turned publican and now turned writer of fashionable fiction: C. Jeames Plush. The chief figure of fun in this last "prize novel" is one "Munseer Jools": a Frenchman who gleans ludicrously inaccurate information about British high life by consorting, in London, with impecunious Frenchmen like himself, "walking round and round Lester Squarr all day, and every day with the same company, occasionally dewussified by an Oprer Chorus-singer or a Jew or two . . ." (VIII, 157), and patronizing an establishment known as the Constantinople Divan, in which two Jewish ladies, the Misses Mordecai, sold cigars:

> The Constantinople Divann is greatly used by the foring gents of Lester Squar. I never ad the good fortn to pass down Pipping's Buildings without seeing a haf-a-duzen of 'em on the threshole of the extablishment, giving the street an oppertunity of testing the odar of the Misses Mordeky's prime Avannas . . .
>
> (VIII, 159)

When Jeames essays his own description of silver fork life by describing the adventures of a "Marcus" (= marquess) and his "young Marchynesses", he finds himself driven to exclaim: "Add I the penn of the hawther of a Codlingsby himself, I coodnt dixcribe the gawjusness of their aboad" (VIII, 165). That glances at Disraeli again; but by substituting "Codlingsby" for *Coningsby* it also draws the author of "*Punch*'s Prize Novelists" and *Novels by Eminent Hands* into the good-natured fun.

In "Sketches and Travels in London"—another series that Thackeray contributed to *Punch*, where it began appearing in November 1847—returns to Jewish dealers in tobacco by referring, in the very first instalment, to Mr Alvarez, who kept a shop in the Covent Garden district. In contrast to other contributors to *Punch*, whose references to Jewish involvement in the tobacco trade tended to be satirically unfriendly, Thackeray describes Alvarez as a "stately and courteous merchant who offers you a Havanna as if you were a Grandee of the first class." (*Punch*, XIII, 20 November 1847, p. 193). A later instalment, headed "A Walk with the Curate", takes the reader to an English pawnbroker "in the passage leading to Trotter's Court", who refers his visitors to a confrère, "Mr. Tubal of Charing Cross Road." (*Punch*, XIII, 4 December 1847, p. 211). The name Tubal, of course, marks this second pawnbroker out as a Jew, like his namesake in *The Merchant of Venice*.

When some Irish Catholic bishops projected a visit to London, Thackeray created a spoof programme for the occasion, which

Punch published under the title: "The New Peers Spiritual" (*Punch*, XIII, 6 November 1847). After some fun at the expense of Lord Clarendon, the new Lord Lieutenant of Ireland, Thackeray's article concludes:

> Some difficulty is made about His Grace the Lord Chief Rabbi, who claims to take precedence of every one of the new nobles [i.e. the Roman Catholic Peers Spiritual], and from the fact that both His Grace and the Lords Quakers persist in keeping their hats on in the presence of Royalty.
>
> (loc. cit. p. 162)

Thackeray often joked about the presence of a *Catholic* "Lion of Judah" in the Upper House (eg. *Punch* VI, p. 248, and XII, p. 162); he now adds the prospect of a Lord Chief Rabbi, which has become reality in our own day. The difficulties humorously anticipated in Thackeray's piece seem not to have proved insuperable.

Thackeray's last contribution to *Punch* for the year 1847 belongs, once again, to the series "Sketches and Travels in London"; it was spread over three issues from 11 to 31 December, and bore the heading: "A Dinner in the City". Right at the beginning Thackeray introduces another of his verbal caricatures of Jewish entertainers. Where "Mr. and Mrs. Aminadab" in the "*Punch*'s Commissioner" series had followed in the comic footsteps of Sloman, "Shadrach and Meshach", in "A Dinner in the City", appear to belong to the more serious tradition of Braham. And just as Thackeray's caricature of Braham in the *National Standard* had stressed the incongruity of that singer's somewhat pot-bellied outline and his sailor's costume, so Shadrach and Meshech, elderly Hebrew gentlemen teamed with a superannuated tenor, are credited with a repertoire of religious, patriotic and rustic songs which the reader is meant to see as not wholly suited to their appearance. But if the repertoire of Shadrach, Meshech, and little Jack Oldboy is meant to raise a smile, so are other incongruities observed at this "Dinner in the City"—the public exhibition of loyal emotions by the feasting Society of Bellows-Menders, for instance:

> First, the Warden of the Worshipful Society of the Bellows-Menders proposed 'Her Majesty' in a reverential voice. We all stood up respectfully, Chisel yelling out to us to 'Charge our glasses.' The royal health having been imbibed, the professional gentlemen ejaculated a part of the National Anthem; and I do not mean any disrespect to them personally, in mentioning that this eminently religious hymn was performed by Messrs. Shadrach and Meshech, two well-known melodists of the Hebrew persuasion. We clinked our glasses at the conclusion of the poem, making more dents upon the time-worn old board, where many a man present had clinked for

George III, clapped for George IV, rapped for William IV, and was rejoiced to bump the bottom of his glass as a token of reverence for our present sovereign.

Here, as in the case of the Hebrew melophonists, I would insinuate no wrong thought. Gentlemen, no doubt, have the loyal emotions which exhibit themselves by clapping glasses on the tables. We do it at home. Let us make no doubt that the bellows-menders, tailors, authors, public characters, judges, aldermen, sheriffs, and what not, shout out a health for the Sovereign every night at their banquets, and that their families fill round and drink the same toast from the bottles of half-guinea burgundy.

(VIII, 203)

The fun poked at "Hebrew melophonists" is only one ingredient in a skit on the contrast between feasting-time in the city and the everyday habits and behaviour of these feasting Londoners.

Thackeray's verbal caricature of Jewish singers receives some additional touches when he depicts how, after the Queen-Dowager's health has been proposed, the

elderly Hebrew gentlemen before mentioned began striking up a wild patriotic ditty about the 'Queen of the Isles, on whose sea-girt shores the bright sun smiles, and the ocean roars; whose cliffs never knew, since the bright sun rose, but a people true, who scorned all foes. Oh, a people true, who scorn all wiles, inhabit you, bright Queen of the Isles. Bright Quee—Bright Quee—ee—ee—ee—ee—en awf the Isles!' or words to that effect, which Shadrach took up and warbled across his glass to Meshech, which Meshech trolled away to his brother singer, until the ditty was ended, nobody understanding a word of what it meant; not Oldboy—not the old or young Israelite minstrel his companion—not we, who were clinking our glasses—

(VIII, 204).

"Non nobis, Domine", which these "melophonists" sing, may be deemed suited to them, since it is the Latin adaptation of a Hebrew psalm; but what about the rustic madrigal which concludes their contribution to the City entertainment?

Shadrach, Meshech, and Oldboy at this began singing, I don't know for what reason, a rustic madrigal, describing, 'Oh, the joys of bonny May— bonny May—a-a-ay, when the birds sing on the spray,' &c., which never, as I could see, had the least relation to that or any other ministry, but which were, nevertheless, applauded by all present. And then the Judges returned thanks; and the Clergy returned thanks; and the Foreign Ministers had an innings (all interspersed by my friends' indefatigable melodies); and the distinguished foreigners present, especially Mr. Washington Jackson, were greeted, and that distinguished American rose amidst thunders of applause.

(VIII, 206)

The distinguished American's address is long-winded, alas, and draws more applause at its beginning than at its soporiphic end:

> I observed that, during his oration, the gentlemen who report for the daily papers, were occupied with their wine instead of their note-books—that the three singers of Israel yawned, and showed many signs of disquiet and inebriety, and that my old friend, who had swallowed the three plates of turtle, was sound asleep.
>
> (VIII, 206)

That is the last we see of these "singers of Israel" before Thackeray's account of a City dinner reaches an uncomfortable end with the prospect of a mighty hangover on the next day.

Once again there has been fun at the expense of a group of Jews—but it has been no more and no less rough than that at the expense of the feasting bellows-menders, the long-winded American, and other Gentile characters. It is all part of a human comedy in which the observer's and chronicler's part may be as tragicomic as any: "May nobody have such a headache on this happy New Year as befell the present writer on the morning after the Dinner in the City!" (VIII, 207).

In Thackeray's "Sketches and Travels in London" the dreary feasting of "A Dinner in the City" was followed, in January and February 1848, by the cheerful "A Night's Pleasure": a chronicle of delights peculiar to the Christmas and New Year season which includes a visit to a traditional pantomime that ends with a transformation scene.

> At this instant King Gorgibus, the Giants, the King's Household, with clubs and battle-axes, rushed in. Drawing his immense scimitar, and seizing the Prince by his too-prominent feature [= his nose], he was just on the point of sacrificing him, when—when, I need not say, the Fairy Bandanna (Miss Bendigo), in her amaranthine car drawn by Paphian doves, appeared and put a stop to the massacre. King Gorgibus became Pantaloon, the two Giants first and second Clowns, and the Prince and Princess (who had been, all the time of the Fairy's speech, and actually while under their father's scimitar, unhooking their dresses) became the most elegant Harlequin and Columbine that I have seen for a long day. The nose flew up to the ceiling, the music began a jig, and the two Clowns, after saying, 'How are you?' went and knocked down Pantaloon.
>
> (VIII, 219–20)

The actress whose appearance as a fairy *ex machina* gives the signal for this magic transformation is characterized as Jewish by her name; but lest memories of the Gentile boxer who popularized the name "Bendigo" should obscure his intentions, Thackeray draws a

Illustration 15

picture of the actress which shows a curly-headed charmer whose arching nose and dark tresses proclaim her origin.

There is no suggestion, however, that recognition of the actress's Jewishness did anything to impair the writer's pleasure in her performance; on the contrary, it fits in well with the pantomime's exotic glories.

In July 1848 Thackeray visited Canterbury and spent an evening and part of a day "in the artless society of some officers of the Twenty-First or Royal Scots Fusiliers" who were in garrison in that city. "Artless" that society may have been, but not without its own sources of entertainment, one of which Thackeray described to Mrs. Brookfield in a letter dated 26–28 July:

> We went to see the Wizard Jacobs at the theatre. He came up in the midst of the entertainment and spoke across the box to the young officers. He knows them in private life. They think him a good fellow.

He came up & asked them confidentially if they didn't like a trick he had just performed. 'Neat little thing isnt it the great Jacobs said—brought it over from Paris.' They go to his entertainment every night. Fancy what a career of pleasure.

(LPP II, 405)

"The Wizard Jacobs", or "Jacobs the Wizard" or "The Great Jacobs", was a Jewish entertainer named Joseph Jacobs, who was born in Canterbury in 1813 and who was noted for the travels he undertook in many countries in search of new conjuring feats that he could introduce into his act. Thackeray's account is not free of irony—he would hardly have seen visiting a conjuring show every night as a "career of pleasure"; but this is not directed against Jacobs himself or his provenance. Thackeray had come a good long way since those early days in which he could not mention Braham or Sloman without an overt or covert sneer at their Jewish origins or appearance.

Pantomimes, conjuring turns, and other such theatrical pleasure —and even the digestion-ruining high jinks of "A Dinner in the City", though there the relation was more complicated—offered a welcome respite from the everyday pursuit of money, which Thackeray, like many contemporaries, felt to be the bane of modern life; a pursuit apt to poison human relations for which the Old Testament offered an apt symbol in the dance around the Golden Calf. Thackeray used that symbol for his "science of names" in another of his *Punch* series: "Mr. Brown's Letters to his Nephew". In one of these letters, Mr Brown deplores the way *nouveaux riches* despise their old friends and associates who have not equalled their financial success, and that in which "the proudest and noblest do not think they demean themselves by crowding to Mrs. Goldcalf's parties, and strike quite openly a union between her wealth and their titles." (VIII, 307). How much a name like "Mrs Goldcalf" tells us about its bearer and the society of which she is part! It can only do so, however, because Thackeray's readers have at the back of their minds the same Old Testament imagery which enabled him to fashion that name.

It was to Mark Lemon, the editor of *Punch*, that Thackeray wrote, on 24 February 1847, a letter in which he claimed for himself the title of satirical moralist who sought to teach as well as to amuse.

What I mean applies to my own case & that of all of us—who set up as Satirical-Moralists—and having such a vast multitude of readers whom we not only amuse but teach. And indeed, a solemn prayer to God Almighty was in my thoughts that we may never forget truth &

Justice and kindness as the great ends of our profession. There's something of the same strain in Vanity Fair. A few years ago I should have sneered at the idea of setting up as a teacher at all, and perhaps at this pompous and pious way of talking about a few papers of jokes in Punch—but I have got to believe in the business, and in many other things since then. And our profession seems to me to be as serious as the Parson's own. Please God we'll be honest & kind was what I meant and all I meant. I swear nothing more.

(LPP, II, 282)

The later Thackeray was subject to fits of solemnity of this kind; but on the wrappers he designed for the part-issues of *Vanity Fair* he found a different and better way of expressing what he felt, at the height of his powers, about his art and its relation to his readership.

Illustration 16

That image of a preacher wearing the same "long-eared livery in which his congregation is arrayed" while London statues stand on their head, or ride on bronze asses instead of bronze horses, fits in better, surely, than the solemn parson-teacher sketched in the letter to Mark Lemon with the Thackeray we have met in *Punch*—the man who could satirize the "Snobs of England" but attribute that satire to "One of Themselves".

It will have been noticed that the Jewish figures Thackeray introduced in the columns of *Punch* between 1843 and 1848 are presented to the reader by at least five different personae: Mr Punch himself, who speaks when contributions are anonymous rather than pseudonymous; the Fat Contributor, who also functions as "*Punch*'s Commissioner"; Jeames, of "Yellowplush" fame; Mr Snob; and D. Shrewsberry, Esq., a transparent caricature of Disraeli. The attitude readers take to these figures, and the extent to which Thackeray winks at the reader over the shoulder of his personae, differ in each case. Mr Punch is a licensed jester who speaks truth in comic form; the Fat Contributor is benevolent but also inept, apt to panic in face of opposition, and prone to exaggerating the effect of his remarks in the real world; Jeames, who is prone to all sorts of errors of judgement, is given a literary style and a mode of spelling with which Thackeray can play some of his favourite word games; and the work attributed to D. Shrewsberry is clearly a parody of Disraeli's style and subject matter. As for Mr Snob—his narrative voice has been admirably described by Dr W.C. Howes:

> He fluctuates between his reader and his target with exactly the right amount of flexibility. Neither too self-righteous, nor too self-abasing, his every word convinces us that he both identifies with, and suffers from Snobbery. But the third, and most telling reason for the *Snob* papers' success, is that curious double perspective on the reader we are familiar with from the myth of the failed Romantic. From one viewpoint, the reader is almost beneath contempt. His pettiness, his vanity, his cruelty, arouse the satirist's anger to a white heat. Nor does Mr. Snob, for all his conviviality, ever let the heat fade. Even when celebrating his success with the public, he still lashes out at human depravity, pointing a steady finger of accusation in the reader's face:
>
> > You who despise your neighbour, are a Snob; you who forget your own friends, meanly to follow after those of a higher degree, are a Snob; you who are ashamed of your poverty, and blush for your calling, are a Snob; as are you who boast of your pedigree, or are proud of your wealth.
>
> But if, viewed from this perspective, the reader is part of the problem, viewed from another, he is part of the solution. Throughout the *Snob* papers, Mr. Snob thinks of his reader as a companion in satire, not quite so familiar with the road, perhaps, but a companion nonetheless. The "beloved reader and writer" pursue "mutual reflections," at times with "playfulness and sentiment," at others, with shared outrage and disgust. If the reader is exposed for belonging to the world the individual flees, he also becomes the Other with whom that

individual must reintegrate to avoid solipsism. In *The Snobs of England*, Thackeray blends both portraits, finding in the process a perfect balance between contempt and respect. More importantly, the reader accepts this composite picture of himself as a true one, and by reading on, confesses, like the satirist, to being a Snob and a brother.

(*Reforming the Mirrored Muse: Thackeray the Victorian Satirist,*
Diss. Princeton, 1980, pp. 166–7)

It is Mr Snob who most tellingly inserts the Jews he describes into the context of Victorian society—a context in which the faults and foibles he imputes to them are seen to be connected with, and often dwarfed by, those of their Gentile contemporaries.

The Jewish figures Thackeray introduced into his contributions to *Punch* between 1842 and 1848 were headed, as has now been shown, by the Rothschilds—presented as universally respected sources of sound financial information—and by Disraeli. We have seen Disraeli's appearance lampooned, and his political ascent watched with wonder and some scepticism: is he a humbug? a chameleon? a megaphone for the interests represented by Lord George Bentinck? an upstart pretending to a place of honour equal to that of a Plantagenet or a Somerset? His literary style has been caricatured along with his large claims for the Jewish branch of the "Caucasian race" and his fascination by the appurtenances of high life. No other individual of Jewish ancestry looms anything like as large in these *Punch* pieces; but as a quip about "old hats" and the Holywell Street scene of *Codlingsby* make clear, his connections with humbler British Jews have never been lost to sight. Among these the tailoring firm of Moses and Son has been ribbed about its aggressive advertising; but Thackeray avoided denigrating the goods they sell and had no truck with the charge, brought against this firm by other contributors to *Punch*, that their success is based on sweated labour. "Baron" Nathan appeared as another master of self-advertisement; he has also been shown as a master of his craft, however, and his snobbish arrogation of the baronial title is presented as a showbusiness flourish or amiable eccentricity. His namesake, the Nathan who runs the flower-shop in the West End of London, clearly gives good service, as do the Misses Mordecai and the amiable cigar merchant Mendoza. Thackeray's contributions to *Punch* include friendly references to humble Jewish traders enjoying a peaceful Sunday alongside their Christian neighbours— the name "Sheeny" given to one of these Jews seemed patronizing rather than insulting in its context. Offence was given, however, to Jewish holiday-makers in Brighton by the verbal and graphic portrait painted of them by Mr Punch's Commissioner, who suggested that they combined penny-pinching (by overloading a hired carriage) with ostentation (by overloading their persons with ornaments). The Commissioner has pretended to take flight before their wrath, only to encounter Jews again ("Here, too, the Hebrews have penetrated") at a music hall. Their performance found no more favour in the "Commissioner's" eyes than that of the superannuated singers of "A Dinner in the City"; but Miss Bendigo, who impersonates a fairy in a London pantomime, and the conjurer Jacobs, satisfied her audiences in a way that seemed wholly justified to *Punch*'s emissary. In Thackeray's contributions to *Punch* Jews appeared as spectators as well as performers at theatrical entertainments, as travellers abroad, as overdressed dandies *à petit pied*, as barristers-at-law with hangers-on and supporters all belonging to the Jewish community, as dentists, as gambling-house keepers, and—of course—as old clothes men. Mr Snob told us of the progress in toleration which gives Sir Robert Peel no power over Disraeli's grinders, and which enables Jews to live in Piccadilly as well as the Minories and to dress according to their own taste; he did so with tongue-in-cheek humour, but with none of the nastiness that informed Carlyle's comments on this same progress. In front of Rothschild's house at Hyde Park Corner, Froude tells us, Carlyle remarked:

> I do not mean that I want King John back again, but if you ask me which mode of treating these people to have been the nearest to the will of the Almighty about them—to build them palaces like that, or to take the pincers for them, I declare for the pincers.

Imagining himself King John with Baron Rothschild on the bench before him, Froude continues, Carlyle said:

> "Now, Sir, the State requires some of these millions you have heaped together with your financial work. "You won't? very well"—and the speaker gave a twist with his wrist—"No." "Now will you?"—and then another twist, till the millions were yielded.
> (Quoted M.F. Modder, *The Jew in the Literature of England to the End of the Nineteenth Century*, Philadelphia 1944, pp. 171–2)

We know, by now, that Thackeray had his "cricks" and that he was apt to conceive aversions and resentments which released prejudices instilled in him by early upbringing and confirmed by much of the company he kept in later years. But though the fun he made of Jewish penetration into new offices, new professions and new places of abode was not always of the gentlest, and though the medieval notion of pulling Jewish teeth to extract Jewish money fascinated him as much as it did Carlyle, he never showed anything like the reactionary sadism here exhibited by that curmudgeonly and incurably prejudiced genius.

CHAPTER 6

REBECCA AT THE FAIR
(1847–1848)

Ah! *Vanitas Vanitatum*! which of us is happy in this
world? Which of us has his desire? or, having it, is
satisfied?

(XI, 878)

Thackeray had begun his work for *Punch* with some misgivings: "a
very low paper", he called it, adding, however, that he liked the
pay and the opportunity "for unrestrained laughing sneering kick-
ing and gambadoing." (to Mrs Carmichael-Smyth, 11 June
1842–LPP II, 54). His first series for the periodical had not been
judged a success; the editors let Thackeray know this and he
thereupon wrote a somewhat huffy letter to the publishers, Brad-
bury and Evans: "I wish that my writings had the good fortune to
please everyone; but all I can do, however, is to do my best, which
has been done, in this case, just as much as if I had been writing for
a more dignified periodical." (27 September 1842—LPP II, 82).
Gradually, however, he had got more into the spirit of *Punch*, and at
weekly meetings around the famous Mahogany Table he had been
able to help mould editorial policy to accord with his own developing taste and art. The contributions surveyed in the preceding
chapter, and their discussion around the *Punch* table, had helped
him develop narrative strategies and a satiric view of life which
were to stand him in good stead when he returned to the writing of
novels. He began towards the end of 1844 or the beginning of 1845
to jot down chapters of a work entitled *Pen and Pencil Sketches of
English Society*. Publication, in twenty monthly parts, started in
1847, by which time the title had been changed to *Vanity Fair. Pen
and Pencil Sketches of English Society*; and in 1848 the work appeared in
book form under its definitive title: *Vanity Fair. A Novel without a
Hero*.

Vanity Fair was recognized, from the first, as a masterpiece of
English fiction. Few novels have been more extensively discussed
and analyzed. Thackeray himself began the process by comment-
ing on his own creation in a number of letters and conversations.
On 2 July 1847, while the monthly parts were still coming out, he
wrote to his mother, who was sure to recognize his reference to

Ephesians 2, 12 though not to approve the comment her son made on a hallowed phrase: "Dont you see how odious all the people are in the book (with exception of Dobbin)—behind whom all there lies a dark moral I hope. What I want is to make a set of people living without God in the world (only that is a cant phrase) greedy pompous mean perfectly self-satisfied . . ." (LPP, II, 309). Thackeray promises that Amelia would, in the end, be saved by love; but when the final parts appeared, Amelia's "salvation" turned out as doubtful as that of any of the others. In a further letter, addressed this time to G.H. Lewes, Thackeray declared himself "aware of the dismal roguery w^h goes all through the Vanity Fair story", adding that his object had been "to make everybody engaged, engaged in the pursuit of Vanity" (6 March 1848—LPP, II, 354). To Robert Bell he wrote, on 3 September 1848: "my object . . . is to vindicate, in cheerful terms, that we are for the most part an abominably foolish and selfish people 'desperately wicked' and all eager after vanities", adding, characteristically: "Good God, don't I see (in that may-be cracked and warped looking glass in which I am always looking) my own weaknesses, wickednesses lusts follies shortcomings?" (LPP, II, 423). The book edition of 1848 shows the preacher in his fool's cap descended from the tub he had mounted in the illustration reproduced earlier, leaning against a box of puppets and contemplating his own face in a cracked mirror (ill. 1).

In the scramble after money and goods and bankable reputations in which most of the characters are caught up they inevitably encounter Jews engaged in the same activities; indeed Professor Kathleen Tillotson has remarked, in *Novels of the Eighteen-Forties* (corrected edition, Oxford 1961, p. 236), that the name of the central character, Rebecca Sharp, hints at "racial astuteness". In Thackeray's own work Becky Sharp had been preceded, as a confidence trickster who uses sexuality as one important means to compass her ends, by the *Juive fatale* Minna Löwe. The sexually alluring aura that had come to surround Scott's Rebecca also counted for something in this case, but it combined with associations derived more directly from the Old Testament—from the story of the Rebecca whom Isaac loved, and who tricked her dying husband into diverting his blessing from Esau to Jacob.

The most unpleasant feature of the "Miss Löwe" story had been the spectacle of Minna's husband and father using her beauty to lure male customers into sending more money their way than they would have done without this attraction. In *Vanity Fair* we see Rawdon Crawley acquiescing in the same game: "It is very likely that this worthy couple never absolutely conspired and agreed

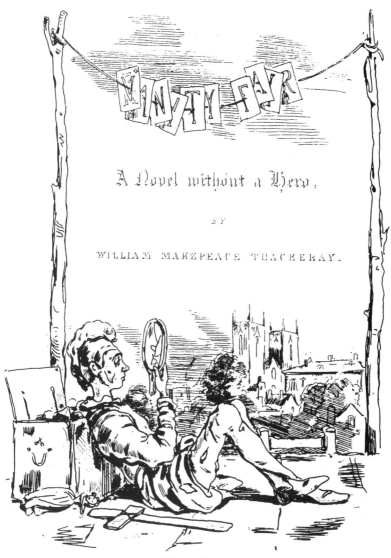

Illustration 1

together in so many words: the one to cajole the young gentleman whilst the other won his money at cards: but they understood each other perfectly well . . ." (XI, 354). Thackeray is playing fair: if Becky and Rawdon can combine their forces in this way, then what we saw in "Miss Löwe" cannot be regarded as specifically Jewish misdeeds.

Among the pupils of Miss Pinkerton's Academy surrounding

Becky and Amelia in the opening chapter is "Miss Swartz, the rich woolly-haired mulatto from St. Kitts" who dissolves in such a passion of tears at Amelia's imminent departure "that they were obliged to send for Dr. Floss, and half tipsify her with sal volatile" (XI, 7). Later on the tender-hearted Miss Swartz turns up again, as a wealthy heiress whom George Osborne's father prefers to Amelia as a prospective daughter-in-law. Old Osborne and his daughters make much of her, for "people in Vanity Fair fasten on to rich folk quite naturally" (XI, 248), while George finds her "ludicrous or odious" (XI, 250):

> 'Marry that mulatto woman?' George said, pulling up his shirt-collars. 'I don't like the colour, sir. Ask the black that sweeps opposite Fleet Market, sir. *I'm* not going to marry a Hottentot Venus.'
>
> (XI, 259)

Thackeray has much fun in describing poor Miss Swartz's outrageous taste in prodigious feathers, amber-coloured satin, turquoise bracelets, countless rings, flowers, "and all sorts of tags and gim-cracks, about as elegantly decorated as a she chimney-sweep on May-Day." (XI, 252). "Poor Swartz was seated in a place where Emmy had been accustomed to sit. Her bejewelled hands lay sprawling in her amber satin lap. Her tags and ear-rings twinkled, and her big eyes rolled about . . ." (XI, 255). To make sure the reader misses nothing of the grotesqueness intended, Thackeray draws the good-natured heiress for us, twice within the same chapter (ill. 2 and 3).

That this is an important stage leading to Thackeray's much grosser depiction of a "mulatto" in *Philip* has often been recognized; what is usually forgotten, however, is that he saddles Miss Swartz with a progenitor who is reputed to be Jewish. "Her father", George informs Amelia, "was a German Jew—a slave-owner they say—connected with the Cannibal Islands in some way or other." (XI, 246). The element of rumour and uncertainty is clearly signalled. When George rejects this heiress and marries Amelia, Miss Swartz is courted by George's money-grubbing father and then won by an epileptic Scottish nobleman; she becomes the Honourable Mrs. Rhoda McMull, with a prospect that her son will inherit the title Viscount Castletoddy and will take over the Castletoddy estates which his mother's fortune had "disengaged" (XI, 582). Her father's taste in dark ladies seems to have roamed further than Rhoda's mother; for later on in *Vanity Fair* we meet "Mr. Swartz, the woolly-headed gentleman, and half-brother to the Honourable Mrs. McMull", receiving the education of an

Illustration 2

Illustration 3

English gentleman alongside little Georgie Osborne (XI, 718). Rhoda McMull herself, meanwhile, appears to have learnt the ways of Vanity Fair; she neglects Amelia when she is poor, but "comes thundering over from Hampton Court, with flowing yellow liveries", "as impetuously fond . . . as ever" when her friend's fortunes are restored.

> Miss Swartz would have liked her always if she could have seen her. One must do her that justice. But, *que voulez vous?*—in this vast town one has not the time to go and seek one's friends; if they drop out of the rank they disappear, and we march on without them. Who is ever missed in Vanity Fair?
>
> (XI, 781)

Rhoda may be grotesque, and she may be weak and pliable enough to behave in the way other members of the society to which she now belongs tell and show her; but she is sufficiently good-natured to keep a little more of the reader's sympathy than many more malicious, clever and hard-hearted denizens of Vanity Fair who are impeccably "white" and demonstrably Gentile.

Rhoda Swartz is the most prominent character with a Jewish connection to appear in this "novel without a hero"; she is introduced to show how traditional prejudices are set aside, in this money-orientated society, when large sums are at stake. Her elevation to Castletoddy illustrates that "cash-nexus" which Carlyle imputed to human relations in Victorian England. She is later joined in high society by one of Thackeray's *belles Juives*, who appears, appropriately, *à l'Orientale* in a charade:

> 'Bid the slave-merchant enter,' says the Turkish voluptuary with a wave of his hand. Mesrour conducts the slave-merchant into my lord's presence: he brings a veiled female with him. He removes the veil. A thrill of applause bursts through the house. It is Mrs. Winkworth (she was a Miss Absolom) with the beautiful eyes and hair. She is in a gorgeous oriental costume; the black braided locks are twined with unnumerable jewels; her dress is covered over with gold piastres. The odious Mahometan expresses himself charmed by her beauty. She falls down on her knees, and entreats him to restore her to the mountains where she was born, and where her Circassian lover is still deploring the absence of his Zuleikah. No entreaties will move the obdurate Hassan. He laughs at the notion of the Circassian bridegroom. Zuleikah covers her face with her hands, and drops down in an attitude of the most beautiful despair. There seems to be no hope for her, when—when the Kislar Aga appears.
>
> The Kislar Aga brings a letter from the Sultan. Hassan receives and places on his head the dread firman. A ghastly terror seizes him, while on the negro's face (it is Mesrour again in another costume) appears a ghastly joy. 'Mercy! mercy!' cries the Pasha: while the Kislar Aga, grinning horribly, pulls out—a *bow-string*.

The curtain draws just as he is going to use that awful weapon. Hassan from within bawls out, 'First two syllables'—and Mrs. Rawdon Crawley, who is going to act in the charade, comes forward and compliments Mrs. Winkworth on the admirable taste and beauty of her costume.

(XI, 644–5)

In the end "Mrs. Rawdon Crawley" (who was, of course, Becky Sharp) outshines the one-time Miss Absolom:

As for poor Mrs. Winkworth, and her long hair and great eyes, which had made such an effect at the commencement of the evening; where was she now? Nowhere in the race. She might tear her long hair and cry her great eyes out; but there was not a person to heed or to deplore the discomfiture.

(XI, 653)

What is so important in the present context about the charade scene in which Mrs. Winkworth figures is that it brings out clearly the sadistic element which Sartre has diagnosed in Gentile admiration of the *belle Juive*: "There is in the words 'belle Juive' a very special sexual signification, one quite different from that contained in the words 'beautiful Romanian', 'beautiful Greek', or 'beautiful American', for example. This phrase carries an aura of rape and massacre . . . the special works which are given over to accounts of flagellation reserve a place of honour for the Jewess." (Jean-Paul Sartre, *Anti-Semite and Jew*, New York 1948, pp. 48–9). Like Scott's Rebecca, this Eastern Beauty with her lovely eyes, black braided locks, gorgeous Oriental costume covered with gold coins, and innumerable jewels, is only saved from violation in the nick of time. Her forced unveiling, her attitude of "beautiful despair" before an obdurate pasha intent on compelling her to serve his pleasure, are an important part of her appeal—an appeal John Carey has rightly linked with Thackeray's fondness for harem imagery and for ballets like *La Bayadère* which "gave Western man a chance of feeling like the masterful voluptuaries of the Orient, with girls exhibiting themselves at his command." (*Thackeray: Prodigal Genius*, pp. 106–7).

Other Jews appear in *Vanity Fair* in socially less exalted roles. They supply services as shopkeepers; Nathan's flower emporium proves useful to Jos Sedley when he wants to buy bouquets impartially for his sister Amelia and for Becky Sharp, who is trying, with some initial success, to "entangle" him. (XI, 44). Jos was, in fact, to have come up against another Jewish character soon after the flower-buying expedition—on the unfortunate outing to Vauxhall which put paid, for the time being, to Becky's hopes of marrying him. George Osborne finds the company's dignity impaired by

Jos's drunken invitation to the plebeians around him to "take a share of his punch", and the reader was to have been shown George "just on the point of knocking down a Hebrew gentleman from the Minories, who proposed to take advantage of this invitation" but who then saved himself by a timely retreat (E.F. Harden, *The Emergence of Thackeray's Serial Fiction*, London 1979, p. 23). Before publication the "Hebrew gentleman from the Minories" disappeared from the text, to be replaced by "a gentleman in top-boots"; but the plate showing "Mr. Joseph in a State of Excitement" which still accompanies Chapter 6 in illustrated editions shows George confronting what is clearly meant to be a "Hebrew gentleman".

Illustration 4

Jews appear next as agents or middlemen, and dealers in second-hand furniture, who frequent auction sales at which, in John Carey's felicitous formulation, "objects . . . withdraw into a stark commercial dimension from the clutches of people who want to cherish or humanize them" (*Thackeray: Prodigal Genius*, ed. cit., pp. 59–60). The narrator of *Vanity Fair* himself calls auctions an "exhibition . . . which Satire and Sentiment can visit arm-in-arm together" (XI, 200). When old Mr Sedley is bankrupted and his goods are auctioned off to pay his debts, the hall of his house in Russell Square, we are told, "swarms with dingy guests of oriental countenance who thrust printed cards into your hands and offer to bid" (XI, 201). A small inset picture shows one of these "dingy guests" accosting Becky and Rawdon Crawley as potential customers:

Illustration 5

When the auctioneer warms to his task he turns to Jewish bidders, "satirizing Mr. Davids for his sluggishness; inspiriting Mr. Moss into action"—and reproving this same Mr Moss for his levity when the picture of Jos Sedley sitting on an elephant comes under the hammer.

> 'Shall we say twenty guineas for this work of art?—fifteen, five, name your own price. The gentleman without the elephant is worth five pound.'
> 'I wonder it aint come down with him,' said a professional wag, 'he's any how a precious big one;' at which (for the elephant-rider was represented as of a very stout figure) there was a general giggle in the room.
> 'Don't be trying to deprecate the value of the lot, Mr. Moss,' Mr. Hammerdown said; 'let the company examine it as a work of art—the attitude of the gallant animal quite according to natur' . . .'
>
> (XI, 202).

Mr Moss as "professional wag" shows the Jewish flair for entertainment penetrating the auction-room as well as the music-hall.

The scene in which this happens is illustrated by a plate which depicts a startled young man between two coarse-featured swarthy bidders sporting what Thackeray and his readers thought of as a "Jewish" nose.

Illustration 6

Dobbin, it appears, and Becky too, have engaged Jewish middle-men to bid for them:

> The Hebrew aide-de-camp in the service of the officer at the table bid against the Hebrew gentleman employed by the elephant purchasers, and a brisk battle ensued over this little piano, the combatants being greatly encouraged by Mr. Hammerdown.
> At last, when the competition had been prolonged for some time, the elephant captain and lady desisted from the race; and the auctioneer said:—'Mr. Lewis, twenty-five', and Mr. Lewis's chief thus became the proprietor of the square piano . . .

(XI, 205)

Having made use of these instruments, however, Becky looks back at the "dingy visitors" to Russell Square, and says to her husband:

> 'Look at them with their hooked beaks,' Becky said, getting into the buggy, her picture under her arm in great glee. 'They're like vultures after a battle.'
> 'Don't know. Never was in action, my dear. Ask Martingale; he was in Spain, aide-de-camp to General Blazes.'
> 'He was a very kind old man, Mr. Sedley,' Rebecca said; 'I'm really sorry he's gone wrong.'
> 'O stockbrokers—bankrupts—used to it, you know,' Rawdon replied, cutting a fly off the horse's ear.
>
> (XI, 210)

"Vultures after a battle" is one of many instances in which Thackeray prepares by an image what will soon become incident: in this case the battle of Waterloo, in which Rawdon will take part and George will meet his death. The image, however, has a thrust of its own; the idea of Jewish "vultures" which Becky has here introduced to characterize her sense of Jews hovering around commodities at an auction will, alas, recur in similar contexts in Thackeray's later fiction.

In one of her Introductions to the "Biographical Edition" of her father's works, Anne Thackeray Ritchie recalls a drawing in which Thackeray humorously alluded to the conventional representation of Jewish old clothes men that he had so often employed in his caricatures. The drawing, intended for *Vanity Fair* but never included in any edition, showed "Becky at the Fancy Fair selling to Dobbin with two or three hats fitted on to his head and shoulders" (*Biog. Edn.*, I, xxviii). What prompted this picture must have been its incongruity: Dobbin, the true gentleman of *Vanity Fair*, reduced by Becky to the semblance of a slop seller! In the end Thackeray probably decided that the picture was not thematically significant (or technically accomplished?) enough to figure among the published illustrations, and it was left, along with many others, for the private amusement of his family and friends.

Old clothes men proper do not, in fact, figure in this novel; but its picture of Vanity Fair would not have been complete without the familiar troupe of Jewish money-lenders (with Old Testamentarian names like "Moses" and "Levy", XI, 365) and sheriff's officers enforcing laws on arrest and imprisonment for debt that were still in force in the early nineteenth century—the period in which the book is set. "A comfortable inn in Brighton is better than a spunging house in Chancery Lane", Becky tells her apprehensive husband; "think of those two aides de camp of Mr. Moses who watched our lodging for a week" (XI, 305). An illustration ensures

Illustration 7

that the reader recognizes these "aides de camp" as co-religionists of their principal.

"In consequence of the repeated visits of the gentlemen whose portraits have been taken in a preceding page", the narrator adds, "Rawdon and his wife did not go back to their lodgings at Brompton . . . Rebecca had an opportunity of seeing them as she skirted that suburb on her road to old Mrs. Sedley's house at Fulham . . ." (XI, 315). Rawdon now laments his reckless behaviour before marriage to Becky made him conscious of family responsibilities:

> 'Hang it,' he would say (or perhaps use a still stronger expression out of his simple vocabulary), 'before I was married I didn't care what bills I put my name to, and so long as Moses would wait or Levy would renew for three months, I kept on never minding. But since I'm married, except renewing of course, I give you my honour I've not touched a bit of stamped paper.'
>
> (XI, 365)

Inevitably, however, the "stamped paper" of his IOUs catches up with him; and Becky takes it upon herself to settle Rawdon's affairs by offering a compromise. This she does with great success, making use of Jewish lawyers acting for Jewish creditors:

> . . . she was empowered to offer, she brought the Colonel's creditors unanimously to accept her proposals, and purchased with fifteen hundred pounds of ready money, more than ten times that amount of debts.

Mrs. Crawley employed no lawyer in the transaction. The matter was so simple, to have or to leave, as she justly observed, that she made the lawyers of the creditors themselves do the business. And Mr. Lewis representing Mr. Davids, of Red Lion Square, and Mr. Moss acting for Mr. Manasseh of Cursitor Street (chief creditors of the Colonel's), complimented his lady upon the brilliant way in which she did business, and declared that there was no professional man who could beat her.

(XI, 463)

Here, in a chapter significantly entitled "How to Live Well on Nothing a Year", Professor Tillotson's suggestion that Rebecca Sharp's name hints at "racial astuteness" has a good deal of force.

One of the means by which Becky proves able to keep what position she has in society is running up debt upon debt by not paying her tradesmen's bills; another is her association with the dissolute Marquis of Steyne, whom Thackeray based on an original Disraeli had also portrayed, under a different name, in *Coningsby*. This association requires the absence of Rawdon on one crucial night. On that night, Rawdon finds himself followed home from a fashionable gathering at which Becky had scored a social and personal triumph, by "two gentlemen" whom an accompanying picture shows us as different in type: one of them sports the "Jewish" features familiar from Thackeray's picture of the auction scene, while the other has a Greek profile that sorts ill with his inelegantly wrinkled trouser-legs (ill.8).

The accompanying text reads:

When they [= Rawdon Crawley and his friend Mr Wenham] had walked down Gaunt Square a few score of paces, one of the men came up, and touching Rawdon on the shoulder, said, 'Beg your pardon, colonel, I vish to speak to you most particular.' The gentleman's acquaintance gave a loud whistle as the latter spoke, at which signal a cab came clattering up from those stationed at the gate of Gaunt House—and the aide de camp ran round and placed himself in front of Colonel Crawley.

That gallant officer at once knew what had befallen him. He was in the hands of the bailiffs. He started back, falling against the man who had first touched him.

'We're three on us—it's no use bolting,' the man behind said.

'It's you, Moss, is it?' said the colonel, who appeared to know his interlocutor. 'How much is it?'

'Only a small thing,' whispered Mr. Moss, of Cursitor Street, Chancery Lane, and assistant officer to the Sheriff of Middlesex— 'one hundred and sixty-six, six and eight-pence, at the suit of Mr. Nathan.'

'Lend me a hundred, Wenham, for God's sake,' poor Rawdon said—'I've got seventy at home.'

Illustration 8

'I've not got ten pounds in the world,' said poor Mr. Wenham—
'Good night, my dear fellow.'

'Good night,' said Rawdon ruefully. And Wenham walked away—
and Rawdon Crawley finished his cigar as the cab drove under
Temple Bar.

(XI, 654)

Rawdon's arrest enables Thackeray to give a more detailed inven-
tory of the Cursitor Street sponging-house and its inhabitants than
any that had gone before, and to introduce not only the proprietor's
son ("a little pink-eyed Jew-boy", a "ruddy-headed youth") and
his daughter ("a dark-eyed maid in curl-papers", with easy manners) but also to give the reader specimens of the proprietor's
Cockney-Jewish language which is free of the phonetic distortions
passing as "Jewish" speech that we have heard Thackeray employ
on previous occasions. The passage is worth quoting at length.

> Friend Rawdon drove on then to Mr. Moss's mansion in Cursitor
> Street, and was duly inducted into that dismal place of hospitality.

Morning was breaking over the cheerful house-tops of Chancery Lane as the rattling cab woke up the echoes there. A little pink-eyed Jew-boy, with a head as ruddy as the rising morn, let the party into the house, and Rawdon was welcomed to the ground-floor apartments by Mr. Moss, his travelling companion and host, who cheerfully asked him if he would like a glass of something warm after his drive.

The colonel was not so depressed as some mortals would be, who, quitting a palace and a *placens uxor*, find them selves barred into a spunging-house, for, if the truth must be told, he had been a lodger at Mr. Moss's establishment once or twice before. We have not thought it necessary in the previous course of this narrative to mention these trivial little domestic incidents: but the reader may be assured that they can't unfrequently occur in the life of a man who lives on nothing a year.

Upon his first visit to Mr. Moss, the colonel, then a bachelor, had been liberated by the generosity of his aunt; on the second mishap, little Becky, with the greatest spirit and kindness, had borrowed a sum of money from Lord Southdown, and had coaxed her husband's creditor (who was her shawl, velvet gown, lace pocket-handkerchief, trinket, and gimcrack purveyor, indeed) to take a portion of the sum claimed, and Rawdon's promissory note for the remainder: so on both these occasions the capture and release had been conducted with the utmost gallantry on all sides, and Moss and the colonel were therefore on the very best of terms.

'You'll find your old bed, colonel, and everything comfortable,' that gentleman said, 'as I may honestly say. You may be pretty sure its kep aired, and by the best of company, too. It was slep in the night afore last by the Honourable Capting Famish, of the Fiftieth Dragoons, whose mar took him out, after a fortnight, jest to punish him, she said. But, Law bless you, I promise you, he punished my champagne, and had a party ere every night—reglar tip-top swells, down from the clubs and the West End—Capting Ragg, the Honourable Deuceace, who lives in the Temple, and some fellers as knows a good glass of wine, I warrant you. I've got a Doctor of Diwinity upstairs, five gents in the coffee-room, and Mrs. Moss has a tably-dy-hoty at half-past five, and a little cards or music afterwards, when we shall be most happy to see you.'

'I'll ring, when I want anything,' said Rawdon, and went quietly to his bedroom. He was an old soldier, we have said, and not to be disturbed by any little shocks of fate. A weaker man would have sent off a letter to his wife on the instant of his capture. 'But what is the use of disturbing her night's rest?' thought Rawdon. 'She won't know whether I am in my room or not. It will be time enough to write to her when she has had her sleep out, and I have had mine. It's only a hundred-and-seventy, and the deuce is in it if we can't raise that.' And so, thinking about little Rawdon (whom he would not have know that he was in such a queer place), the colonel turned into the bed lately occupied by Captain Famish, and fell asleep. It was ten o'clock when he woke up, and the ruddy-headed youth brought him, with conscious pride, a fine silver dressing-case, wherewith he might perform the operation of shaving. Indeed Mr. Moss's house, though somewhat dirty, was splendid throughout. There were dirty trays, and wine-coolers *en permanence* on the sideboard, huge dirty gilt cornices, with dingy yellow satin hangings to the barred windows which looked into Cursitor Street—vast and dirty gilt picture-frames surrounding pieces sporting and sacred, all of which works were by the greatest masters; and fetched the greatest prices, too, in the bill transactions, in the course of which they were sold and bought over and over again. The Colonel's breakfast was served to him in the same dingy and gorgeous plated ware. Miss Moss, a dark-eyed maid in curl papers, appeared with the teapot, and, smiling, asked the Colonel how he had slep? and she brought him in the *Morning Post*, with the names of all the great people who had figured at Lord Steyne's entertainment the night before. It contained a brilliant account of the festivities, and of the beautiful and accomplished Mrs. Rawdon Crawley's admirable personifications.

After a lively chat with this lady (who sat on the edge of the breakfast table in an easy attitude displaying the drapery of her stocking and an ex-white satin shoe, which was down at heel), Colonel Crawley called for pens and ink, and paper; and being asked how many sheets, chose one which was brought to him between Miss Moss's own finger and thumb. Many a sheet had that dark-eyed damsel brought in; many a poor fellow had scrawled and blotted hurried lines of entreaty, and paced up and down that awful room until his messenger brought back the reply.

(XI, 668–70)

The cameraderie of the sponging-house, where Jew and Gentile meet in an enforced proximity decreed by the law of the land, in a strange aura of mutual respect, has never been better portrayed. Having written his appeal to Becky, Rawdon settles down in reasonable comfort, smoking a cigar in the by now familiar court-yard "railed in like a cage", with bars overhead and walls all around. Later on he joins Mr Moss's "tably-dy-hoty", presided over by Mrs Moss and

> served at the appointed hour of half-past five, when such of the gentlemen lodging in the house as could afford to pay for the banquet, came and partook of it in the splendid front parlour before described, and with which Mr. Crawley's temporary lodging communicated, when Miss M. (Miss Hem, as her papa called her,) appeared without the curl-papers of the morning, and Mrs. Hem did the honours of a prime boiled leg of mutton and turnips, of which the Colonel ate with a very faint appetite. Asked whether he would 'stand' a bottle of champagne for the company, he consented, and the ladies drank to his 'ealth, and Mr. Moss, in the most polite manner 'looked towards him.'
>
> In the midst of this repast, however, the door-bell was heard,— young Moss of the ruddy hair, rose up with the keys and answered the summons, and coming back, told the Colonel that the messenger

had returned with a bag, a desk and a letter, which he gave him. 'No ceramony, Colonel, I beg,' said Mrs. Moss with a wave of her hand, and he opened the letter rather tremulously.

(XI, 671–2)

Ceremonial pledging "in the most polite manner" is deliberately contrasted with dropped 'h's and distorted foreign terms ("'ealth', "tably-dy-hoty") to show the Moss family's aspirations towards English gentility together with the distance they still have to travel before achieving it. Rawdon is right to be tremulous, of course; for Becky pretends, in her letter, to have fallen at the "odious knees" of Mr Nathan, Rawdon's Jewish creditor, weeping and crying—but nothing, she claims, would "mollify the horrid man." "He would have all the money, he said, or keep my poor *monstre* in prison." (XI, 672). None of this is true, of course; Becky has the means to free her husband, but it suits her book to keep him out of the way for the night. Thackeray here shows her employing the well-known device of blaming the Jew for one's own hard-heartedness—an easy thing, because all one needs to do is to appeal to a preexisting prejudicial stereotype. Dickens shows the same device in action in *Our Mutual Friend*, where Riah has to bear a stigma that properly belongs to Fledgeby. The next picture Thackeray draws for his novel, however, shows young Moss admitting another visitor, Lady Crawley, to whom Rawdon had appealed after Becky turned him down:

Illustration 9

The elegant young man here depicted in the narrow space between the front-door and the entrance to the sponging-house proper lets Lady Crawley in "with a knowing look", locking the outer door after her before opening the inner one to admit her to the prisoner. Lady Crawley takes pity on Rawdon; Mr Moss's bills are settled, "perhaps to the disappointment of that gentleman, who had counted on having the colonel as his guest over Sunday at least" (XI, 673–4); and Rawdon is free to surprise Becky at her tête-à-tête with Lord Steyne. Moss's disappointment may of course be put down to financial considerations; but we are free to surmise, too, that he genuinely enjoys the company of the English gentlemen whom reduced circumstances and the laws relating to debt bring into his shabby-genteel domain.

Rawdon is not the only character in *Vanity Fair* to be beset by Jewish creditors and bailiffs. The family of Becky's enemy Lady Bareacres finds itself in the same predicament.

> One of Lady Gaunt's carriages went to Hill Street for her Ladyship's mother, all whose equipages were in the hands of the bailiffs, whose very jewels and wardrobe, it was said, had been seized by those inexorable Israelites. Bareacres Castle was theirs, too, with all its costly pictures, furniture, and articles of vertu—the magnificent Vandykes; the noble Reynolds pictures; the Lawrence portraits, tawdry and beautiful, and, thirty years ago, deemed as precious as works of real genius; the matchless Dancing Nymph of Canova, for which Lady Bareacres had sat in her youth—Lady Bareacres splendid then, and radiant in wealth, rank, and beauty—a toothless, bald, old woman now—a mere rag of a former robe of state. Her lord, painted at the same time by Lawrence, as waving his sabre in front of Bareacres Castle, and clothed in his uniform as Colonel of the Thistlewood Yeomanry, was a withered, old, lean man in a great-coat and a Brutus wig: slinking about Gray's Inn of mornings chiefly, and dining alone at clubs.
>
> (XI, 614–15)

In Thackeray's world it is the sad fate of cherished commodities to fall into the hands of those for whom they are only commodities rather than family heirlooms or works of art with a family connection. Lady Bareacre's celebrated diamonds too, we learn, which had played a memorable part in Becky's triumph over her enemy during the confusion that followed the battle of Waterloo, had undergone "a famous seizure" by her creditors. (XI, 618). Nevertheless, the Bareacres family continues to live in the style to which it has become accustomed; we take our leave of them as they embark for a continental holiday on a steamboat, where

> the great grandee Bareacres family sat by themselves near the wheel, stared at everybody, and spoke to no one. Their carriages, embla-

zoned with coronets, and heaped with shining imperials, were on the foredeck; locked in with a dozen more such vehicles: it was difficult to pass in and out amongst them: and the poor inmates of the fore-cabin had scarcely any space for locomotion.

(XI, 784)

Among these less favoured passengers, among artists, couriers, *femmes de chambre* and grooms Thackeray introduces "a few magnificently attired gentlemen from Houndsditch, who brought their own provisions"—whether for reasons of dietary purity, or to save money, or both, is left to our speculation. These "Hebrew gentlemen" join the chattering and smoking couriers in inspecting the carriages being transported across the Channel; and they help the reader solve the riddle of Lord Bareacre's ability to pay the expenses of this family excursion. "The Hebrew gentlemen knew how he got it. They knew what money his lordship had in his pocket at that instant, and what interest he paid for it, and who gave it him." (XI, 784–5).

After that, the gentlemen from Houndsditch fade out of the picture; but the reader follows Jos Sedley into Germany, where he waits upon "the English Consul at the Free City of Judenstadt" (XI, 787). Judenstadt, "Jews' City", is Frankfurt, of course, with its famous ghetto ("Judengasse") from which the even more famous Rothschild family emerged into European finance and society. That family appears in the background of *Vanity Fair* as it had done in so many other of Thackeray's writing "It was wonderful", we read of the broken, bankrupt Mr Sedley, "to hear him talk about millions, and agios, and discounts, and what Rothschild was doing, and Baring Brothers." (XI, 484); and Sedley's old clerk remembers how he had "seen the first men in London shaking hands with Mr. S—"—"He'd known him in times when Rothschild might be seen on 'Change with him any day . . . "(XI, 579–80). Once again, Rothschild appears as an unshakable pillar of financial stability as well as a personification of the riches that the whole of Vanity Fair agreed in pursuing. On this occasion, however, there is a little more to it than that. "Agios", as John Sutherland points out in his edition of *Vanity Fair* (Oxford 1983, p. 929), are premiums payable for the exchange of one kind of money or currency into another. Sedley's ruin is brought about by speculating in international exchange, especially in French stock and currency; and this is a field in which he could not hope to compete with the Rothschilds, who had houses in Paris as well as London, and whose international connections gave them access to information wholly beyond the reach of the ordinary British merchant. Old Osborne's trade in tallow was a much safer bet.

The action of *Vanity Fair* takes place, for the most part, in the period of the Regency and the reign of Thackeray's *bête noire*, King George IV—an age in which British Jews made a name for themselves as prizefighters. One of the most celebrated of these was Samuel Elias, known as "Dutch Sam", whom we encounter in *Vanity Fair* when young Jim Crawley, animated by claret,

> described the different pugilistic qualities of Molyneux and Dutch Sam, offered playfully to give Lady Jane the odds upon the Tutbury Pet against the Rottingdean man, or take them, as her ladyship chose . . .
>
> (XI, 430)

Dutch Sam also appeared in a footnote which was deleted from the novel after its first edition. It referred to the as yet unregenerated Rawdon Crawley:

> If anybody considers this an overdrawn picture of a noble and influential class of persons, I refer them to contemporaneous histories—such as Byron's Memoirs, for instance; in which popular illustration of Vanity Fair you have the morals of Richelieu and the elegance of Dutch Sam.
>
> (XI, 885)

From this and other *obiter dicta* one may infer that Thackeray had little sympathy with Byron and little appreciation of pugilistic elegance.

After her separation from Rawdon Becky Sharp is encountered in mixed company. In Germany she travels from one gambling resort to the next, associating with the "little colony of English raffs" that is to be found in such places:

> men whose names Mr. Hemp the officer reads out periodically at the Sheriffs' Court—young gentlemen of very good family often, only that the latter disowns them; frequenters of billiard-rooms and estaminets, patrons of foreign races and gaming-tables. They people the debtors' prisons—they drink and swagger—they fight and brawl—they run away without paying—they have duels with French and German officers—they cheat Mr. Spooney at *écarté*—they get the money, and drive off to Baden in magnificent britzkas—they try their infallible martingale, and lurk about the tables with empty pockets, shabby bullies, penniless bucks, until they can swindle a Jew banker with a sham bill of exchange, or find another Mr. Spooney to rob.
>
> (XI, 822–3)

That neatly inverts the anti-Jewish stereotype found in "Miss Löwe" and elsewhere: it is now the "Jew banker" who is marked out as a victim to be fleeced by these raffish visitors from England. Do they perhaps consider him fair game because of the popular notion that he would cheat *them* if he could?

In search of greater respectability among the expatriate English on the Continent, Becky sings sweetly in church, reads tracts and discourses on them, and paints hand-screens "for the conversion of the Pope and the Jews" (XI, 818); but

> Whenever Becky made a little circle for herself with incredible toils and labour, somebody came and swept it down rudely, and she had all her work to begin over again. It was very hard: very hard; lonely and disheartening. (ibid.)

She seems happiest when she can fall back among Bohemians like those among whom her earliest days had been passed. In Pumpernickel Jos finds her at

> the very top of the house, above the first-floor rooms where some travelling pedlars had lived, and were exhibiting their jewellery and brocades; above the second-floor apartments occupied by the *état major* of the gambling firm; above the third-floor rooms, tenanted by the band of renowned Bohemian vaulters and tumblers; and so on to the little cabins of the roof, where, among students, bag-men, small tradesmen, and country-folks, come in for the festival, Becky had found a little nest;—as dirty a little refuge as ever beauty lay hid in.
>
> Becky liked the life. She was at home with everybody in the place, pedlars, punters, tumblers, students and all. She was of a wild, roving nature, inherited from father and mother, who were both Bohemians, by taste and circumstance; if a lord was not by, she would talk to his courier with the greatest pleasure; the din, the stir, the drink, the smoke, the tattle of the Hebrew pedlars, the solemn, braggart ways of the poor tumblers, the *sournois* talk of the gambling-table officials, the songs and swagger of the students, and the general buzz and hum of the place had pleased and tickled the little woman, even when her luck was down, and she had not wherewithal to pay her bill. How pleasant was all the bustle to her now that her purse was full of the money which little Georgy had won for her the night before!
>
> (XI, 830–1)

The tattle of Hebrew pedlars, their exhibition of the jewellery and brocades which is their stock in trade, are an integral part of this disreputable but lively scene, for which Thackeray himself expressed a strong liking. In a conversation with John Esten Cooke, whom he met during his visit to Virginia in 1856, he is reported to have said:

> I like Becky . . . Sometimes I think I have some of her tastes. I like what are called Bohemians, and fellows of that sort . . . You see how I made Becky prefer them, and that sort of life, to the fine society she moved in. Perhaps you remember where she comes down in the world toward the end of the book, and associates with people of all sorts, Bohemians and the rest, in their garrets . . . I like that part of the book. I think that part is well done.
>
> (IR, II, 260)

Jos Sedley "rescues" Becky from such company and takes her back to England, where (it would appear) she speedily helps him to his grave. After that we hear no more of association with Jewish pedlars; Becky now "hangs about Bath and Cheltenham, where a strong party of excellent people consider her to be a most injured woman", and where she "busies herself in works of piety" (XI, 877).

The singer Giuditta Pasta and the pianist and composer Henri (or Heinrich) Herz are mentioned in passing in *Vanity Fair* (XI, 638, 131), but nothing is made of their Jewish origin, of which Thackeray may indeed have been unaware. Herz, whose compositions had figured in "The Ravenswing" and *Fitzboodle* as exercises budding musicians used for practice, figures in *Vanity Fair* as a purveyor of showy pieces and techniques that have an honoured place in the well-bred young lady's repertoire of husband-hunting devices:

> Has the beloved reader, in his experience of society, never heard similar remarks by good-natured female friends; who always wonder what you *can* see in Miss Smith that is so fascinating; or what *could* induce Major Jones to propose for that silly insignificant simpering Miss Thompson, who has nothing but her wax-doll face to recommend her? What is there in a pair of pink cheeks and blue eyes forsooth? these dear Moralists ask, and hint wisely that the gifts of genius, the accomplishments of the mind, the mastery of *Mangnall's Questions*, and a ladylike knowledge of botany and geology, the knack of making poetry, the power of rattling sonatas in the Herz-manner, and so forth, are far more valuable endowments for a female, than those fugitive charms which a few years will inevitably tarnish. It is quite edifying to hear women speculate upon the worthlessness and the duration of beauty.
>
> (XI, 131)

Whether the "Mr. Polonius of Coventry Street", from whom Becky pretends she has hired jewels given to her by Lord Steyne, is meant to be Jewish we never find out; his name derives from *Hamlet*, of course, but may also hint at Polish origins. Jewellery is often connected with Jews in Thackeray's world, not only because of the phonic echo, but also because of the famous line in Pope's *Rape of the Lock* which Lord Steyne is made to apply to Becky decked out in her precious finery:

> As he bowed over her he smiled, and quoted the hackneyed and beautiful lines . . . about Belinda's diamonds, 'which Jews might kiss and infidels adore.'
>   'But I hope your lordship is orthodox,' said the little lady, with a toss of her head.
>
> (XI, 604)

The "celebrated jewel" which Steyne himself wears on his fore-finger is significantly called the "Jew's eye" diamond. "Jew's eye", we know, was a proverbial expression for something highly valued; but Thackeray is also, surely, signalling his awareness of the strong representation of Jews in the international diamond trade as well as in that humbler traffic in jewellery and brocade in which the pedlars with whom Becky shared quarters in Pumpernickel are said to be engaged. As has often been said, it is an essential feature of Thackeray's art to scatter hints, to work in half-tones and tiny suggestive brush strokes, rather than spell everything out. We learn that George Osborne goes to see Edmund Kean's famous perfor-mance of Shylock at half-price (XI, 316, 321); but of the perfor-mance itself, which broke with several traditional ways of presenting the Jew of Venice and made him sympathetic, we hear nothing at all. Thackeray wants to suggest a symbolic connection between Shylock's way with money and the ways of George Osbor-ne's father; and a sympathetic Shylock would not have served his purpose.

In *Thackeray and the Form of Fiction*, John Loofbourow has analyzed the crucial scene in which Rawdon confronts Becky and Lord Steyne in the following terms:

> In the discredited context of criminal romance, a farcical Satan and a melodramatic Eve have played the primordial scene for laughs. The Fallen Becky—"wretched woman" ... "brilliants on her breast which Steyne had given her" ... "'I am innocent'" ... "all covered with serpents, and rings, and baubles." Steyne, the Tempter— "hanging over the sofa" ... "grinding his teeth" ... "fury in his looks." The "bald forehead" of this second-rate serpent is bruised by the clumsy Adam, Rawdon—"Steyne wore the scar to his dying day." In the parodic context, this biblical sequence is a moral nightmare; its dramatic integration is a mature achievement, but the precision of its satiric effects is the result of Thackeray's early parody of criminal fiction.
>
> (op. cit., Princeton 1963, p. 26)

Not everyone would agree that Rawdon's finest hour—and in one respect Becky's too—is a scene played "for laughs". What is indisputable, however, is Thackeray's symbolism here—part of a whole network of emblems and symbols in which, once again, characters and incidents from the Old Testament play an essential part. When old Osborne, angry at his son's disregard of his wish that he should marry the wealthy Rhoda Swartz and not the impoverished Amelia Sedley, takes down the family Bible and obliterates George's name from the family register inscribed on its fly-leaf, we are told: "There was a frontispiece to the volume representing Abraham sacrificing Isaac" (XI, 284). Here, as in the later passage in which Amelia parts with George junior, "no angel has intervened. The child is sacrificed." (XI, 629). Mr Osborne also owns a time-piece which features the sacrifice of Iphigenia; but as John Sutherland has shown, this powerful symbolic object had originally been meant to depict a (somewhat less apt) scene from the Old Testament: Jephtha sacrificing his daughter. (*Thackeray at Work*, London 1974, pp. 11–17). Elsewhere in the novel, classical and Old Testament figures, symbols and prefigurations work harmoniously together; when Becky marries and tames Rawdon Crawley, the narrator comments:

> Is his case a rare one? and don't we see every day in the world many an honest Hercules at the apron-strings of Omphale, and great whiskered Samsons prostrate in Delilah's lap?
>
> (XI, 190)

Here classical and Biblical reference combine and reinforce one another. The Samson and Delilah image recurs at strategic points to reinforce our sense of the relationship between Rawdon and Becky:

> "*I'll* make your fortune", she said; and Delilah patted Samson's cheek.
> "You can do anything", he said, kissing the little hand.
>
> (XI, 199)

and again:

> He was beat and cowed into laziness and submission. Delilah had imprisoned him and cut his hair off, too. The bold and reckless young blood of ten years back was subjugated, and was turned into a torpid, submissive, middle-aged , stout gentleman.
>
> (XI, 444)

That's Samson at the mill, with slaves; but when Rawdon surprises Becky with Lord Steyne he rouses himself to destructive fury, as Samson did in the house of Dagon. That he has just emerged from his Cursitor Street imprisonment reinforces the Biblical parallel.

Abraham's intended sacrifice of Isaac comes into view once again when the widowed and impoverished Amelia decides to hand over her son to the wealthy relatives who could provide him with better chances in life, and a more luxurious existence, than she is able to do; but it is coupled with another Biblical exemplum that offers a closer analogy to poor Amelia's situation:

> That night Amelia made the boy read the story of Samuel to her, and how Hannah, his mother, having weaned him, brought him to Eli the

High Priest to minister before the Lord. And he read the song of gratitude which Hannah sang: and which says, Who it is who maketh poor and maketh rich, and bringeth low and exalteth—how the poor shall be raised up out of the dust, and how, in his own might, no man shall be strong. Then he read how Samuel's mother made him a little coat, and brought it to him from year to year when she came up to offer the yearly sacrifice. And then, in her sweet simple way, George's mother made commentaries to the boy upon this affecting story. How Hannah, though she loved her son so much, yet gave him up because of her vow. And how she must always have thought of him as she sat at home, far away, making the little coat; and Samuel, she was sure, never forgot his mother: and how happy she must have been as the time came (and the years pass away very quick) when she should see her boy, and how good and wise he had grown. This little sermon she spoke with a gentle solemn voice, and dry eyes, until she came to the account of their meeting—then the discourse broke off suddenly, the tender heart overflowed, and taking the boy to her breast, she rocked him in her arms, and wept silently over him in a sainted agony of tears.

(XI, 625)

That "sainted agony of tears", alas, is an earnest of the religiose sentimentality which some of the Victorian reading public relished; but when one regards the context of this and other such passages in Thackeray's writings, one will usually find that he has truthfully presented circumstances which permit a more sober view.

The more closely we look at *Vanity Fair*, the more instances obtrude themselves of Thackeray's use of Old Testament images and references, often joined with deliberate incongruity to more modern, secular ones, to convey to the reader the feel of his characters, their relationships, and their mental horizons. Take the surprise of the school bully when young Dobbin confronts him in defense of one of his puny victims:

Fancy our late monarch George III. when he heard of the revolt of the North American colonies; fancy brazen Goliath when little David stepped forward and claimed a meeting; and you have the feelings of Mr. Reginald Cuff. . . .

(XI, 53)

The cab driver who takes Becky and old Sir Pitt to London is a "Jehu" (XI, 85); Becky reports in her letter to Amelia that Sir Pitt calls his brother Bute "as tough as old what dyecallum—old Methusalem" (XI, 66); an ancient nobleman is named "Lord Methuselah" (XI, 138); and when Becky flatters her rough-hewn husband and seeks to smooth out some of his edges, the narrator glosses her behaviour with an ominous reference to the thirty-ninth chapter of Genesis:

Who has not seen a woman hide the dulness of a stupid husband, or coax the fury of a savage one? We accept this amiable slavishness, and praise a woman for it; we call this petty treachery truth. A good housewife is of necessity a humbug; and Cornelia's husband was hoodwinked, as Potiphar was—only in a different way.

(XI, 208)

The conjunction of classical and Biblical history in that last sentence is wholly characteristic of Thackeray's art.

Jealously critical of other women's elegance the Misses Osborne comfort themselves with the reflection that "there are things, look you, of a finer texture than fur or satin, and all Solomon's glories, and all the wardrobe of the Queen of Sheba" (XI, 136); while their brother George, for his part, feels himself an Ahasuerus in his relations with the impoverished Amelia: "He would be generous-minded, Sultan as he was and raise up this kneeling Esther and make a queen of her" (XI, 236). Lady Southdown's tracts ('A Voice from the Flames', 'A Trumpet-warning to Jericho', 'Flesh-pots Broken; or, the Converted Cannibal') bristle with Old Testament allusions, as do her letters, like that to the Reverend Lawrence Grills, "exhorting that gentleman to save the brand who 'honoured' the letter", i.e., Becky Sharp, "from the burning" (XI, 534—cf. Zechariah 3, 2). Mrs Bute Crawley, as a clergy-man's wife, has a similarly allusive epistolary manner: "Mr. Crawley's brother, the Baronet, with whom we are not, alas! upon those terms of *unity* in which it *becomes brethren to dwell . . .*" (XI, 116) and her conversation too is larded with Biblical unction:

". . . as long as Nature supports me, never, never, Mr. Clump, will I desert the post of duty. Others may bring that grey head with sorrow to the bed of sickness (here Mrs. Bute, waving her hand, pointed to one of old Miss Crawley's coffee-cloured fronts, which was perched on a stand in the dressing-room), but I will never quit it . . ."

(XI, 231).

Mrs. Bute's unction is doubly odious because of the cupidity which it seeks to mask; but the incongruous conjunction between Genesis 42, 38 and modern "fronts", which exposes Mrs. Bute's insincerity, becomes delightfully gay when Thackeray reintroduces it into a bantering conversation between Peggy O'Dowd and her husband the Major:

"Mrs. Captain Magenis has made up, though her treatment of me would bring me gray hairs with sorrow to the grave!"
"And you with such a beautiful front of black, Peggy, my dear", the Major cried.

(XI, 329)

Biblical quotation moves into yet another tonality when the embittered Mrs. Sedley unjustly reproaches Amelia by saying that she, Mrs. Sedley, had obeyed the Fifth Commandments more faithfully than her daughter: "I was too glad to honour my father and mother, that I might live long in the land, and to be useful, and not to mope all day in my room and act the fine lady . . ." (XI, 487). The reference to Exodus 20, 12 does nothing to mitigate Mrs. Sedley's aggrieved whine. Becky plays the Biblical allusion game as deftly as anyone—witness her coaxing of Rawdon, when she seeks to calm a rage against his family that seemed all too likely to annihilate altogether prospects already injured by his imprudent marriage: ". . . you were in such a fury you were ready to murder your brother, *you wicked Cain you*, and what good would have come of remaining angry?" (XI, 470—my italics). Even old Sir Pitt joins in the game when he twits Lady Jane about he husband's piety: "Does he read ee very long sermons, my dear? Hundredth Psalm, Evening Hymn, hay, Pitt?" (XI, 501). The "joyful noise" of the hundredth Psalm intrudes strangely into what Thackeray has rightly called "A Cynical Chapter".

The narrator of *Vanity Fair*, though he is not a named character like Michael Angelo Titmarsh, has a personality of his own which appears most clearly in the games he plays with his readers, who find themselves addressed singly or in groups throughout the novel: "You, friendly reader" "these, brother, are our secret", "be cautious then, young ladies", "O brother wearers of motley" and so on. It is this narrator who tells us that Lord Steyne's "race"—i.e. his ancient family—was afflicted with a "mysterious taint of the blood" that expressed itself in insanity: "The pride of the race was *struck down as the firstborn of Pharaoh*" we read, and learn that Steyne sought to stifle his dark presentiments, "to lay the horrid bedside ghost", in "*Red Seas* of wine and jollity" (XI, 595–6). Lord Steyne's "august portals", the narrator fancies, with yet another of his allusions to happenings in the Garden of Eden, are "guarded by grooms of the chamber with flaming silver forks with which they prong all those who have not the right of the *entrée*"—which is as deft a transposition of the sublime into the ridiculous, the concerns of all mankind into those of a small self-opinionated coterie sustained by snobbery, as any we will find in this masterly humorous epic. The play on "entry" and "*entrée*", with its gourmet suggestions, is a particularly happy and characteristic touch. (XI, 633). The parody of Genesis prepares for the more serious use of Garden of Eden imagery in the confrontation between Rawdon, Becky, and Lord Steyne, whose analysis by Loofbourow has already been quoted, and it leads over to the Reverend Thurifer's dire warnings which combine Corinthians 13, 1 with 1 Kings 9, 18 and 2 Chronicles 8, 4 and add a dash of Ecclesiastes for good measure:

> Ah, ladies!—ask the Reverend Mr. Thurifer if Belgravia is not a sounding brass, and Tyburnia a tinkling cymbal. These are vanities. Even these will pass away. And some day or other (but it will be after our time, thank goodness,) Hyde Park Gardens will be no better known than the celebrated horticultural outskirts of Babylon; and Belgrave Square will be as desolate as Baker Street, or Tadmor in the wilderness.
>
> (XI, 634)

Here the voice of one of the novel's passing parade of characters can be clearly heard within that of the narrator addressing a female readership with guarded irony, reminding readers of the "vanity" theme that runs through this great work from the title-page onwards.

The "wilderness" theme broached in the reference to Tadmor is caught up again soon afterwards by ironic reflections on the various types of accommodation necessary to those who want to make life in Vanity Fair tolerable to themselves and others—reflections whose mock *captatio benevolentiae* is enhanced by allusions to Deuteronomy 32, 10 and Genesis 18, 12:

> If every person is to be banished from society who runs into debt and cannot pay—if we are to be peering into everybody's private life, speculating upon their income, and cutting them if we don't approve of their expenditure—why, what a howling wilderness and intolerable dwelling Vanity Fair would be! every man's hand would be against his neighbour . . .
>
> (XI, 642)

When Jos takes Becky away from her Bohemian nest in Pumpernickel and brings her back to England, we encounter yet another Old Testament image: "Jos's tent and pilau were pleasant to this little Ishmaelite—at least for a while" (XI, 856). And throughout this great novel, whose title derives from Bunyan who had himself drawn on the Bible for the names of his allegorical places and personages, we can hear the words of the Old Testament Preacher which ring out loud and clear, in their Vulgate form, in the final paragraph:

> Ah! *Vanitas Vanitatum!* which of us is happy in this world? Which of us has his desire? or, having it, is satisfied?—come, children, let us shut up the box and the puppets, for our play is played out.
>
> (XI, 878)

All this combines, of course, with manifold references to the New Testament, allusions to the wickedness of Herod, Dives and Lazarus, the Prodigal Son, and the words of St. Paul—but these are less ubiquitous than those to the older parts of the English Bible. Apart from a phrase or two from the Vulgate, Thackeray's Bible is the English version authorized by King James I; and when Miss Pinkerton claims that one of her charges has a command of the language in which the Old Testament was originally written, the reader is clearly invited to disbelieve her. Unlike Latin and Greek, Hebrew is an occult language known only to dedicated Orientalists—and (perhaps) Jews. (XI, 89, 147).

In its King James version, finally, the Bible is glimpsed throughout Vanity Fair as a physical object. It is prominently present in the Osborne household, where its flyleaf serves as a family genealogy from which the son who displeases old Osborne is ceremoniously struck out, and where it stands, symbolically, besides the Peerage (XI, 281 *et passim*). The Osborne's "great scarlet Bible and Prayer Book" has its counterpart in the "great gilt book laid on the table" in the house of the younger Sir Pitt Crawley when the family and domestics assemble for prayer; at other times it has its appointed place in Sir Pitt's study, among "the locked account books, desks, and despatch boxes . . . , the *Quarterly Review*, and the *Court Guide*, which all stood as if on parade awaiting the inspection of their chief" (XI, 678). Jos Sedley, in his sad last days, also keeps a Bible handy, and offers to kiss it in pledge of his belief in the virtue of a wife of whom he is mortally afraid and who (if we can believe the picture titled "Becky's Second Appearance in the Character of Clytemnestra") is preparing to kill him. (XI, 873–5).

Vanity Fair is remarkable, in the context of the present book, for its symbolic charade sequence, which throws so much light on the appeal the "beautiful Jewess" held for Thackeray—the appeal of a helpless, menaced beauty that contrasts with the Clytemnestra aspect of the protagonist who is here given the Biblical name Scott had appropriated for his influential version of the *belle Juive*: Rebecca. The novel is remarkable, too, for its combination of reputedly Jewish and certain black ancestry in Rhoda Swartz and her insertion into the British aristocracy by the power of money. It introduces into Thackeray's fiction jocular Jews who pick up bargains at auctions, a sharp-featured group featured in Thackeray's drawings which prepares for Becky Sharp's description of them as birds of prey. It anticipate the Fledgeby-Riah mechanism which Dickens was to employ in *Our Mutual Friend* some sixteen years later: the mechanism whereby a Gentile shifts the blame for his or her hard-heartedness onto a Jew. It elaborates earlier descriptions of the Cursitor Street personnel (though one asks oneself whether the elegant young man who lets Lady Crawley into the house can really be identical with what the text describes as "a little pink-eyed Jew-boy, with a head as ruddy as the rising morn"); and it depicts with fresh detail the strange cameraderie of the sponging-house along with its peculiar combination of dinginess and (thanks to the objects left as pledges) magnificence. It abandons the cruder varieties of "Jew-speak", allowing Jewish bailiffs to speak very much as other nineteenth-century cockneys seem to have done: "I vish to speak to you most particular", for instance, or "we're three on us". The Regency atmosphere of the book is helped along by references to a Jewish prize-fighter; but the rest of Thackeray's cast—financiers, lawyers with Jewish clients and hangers-on, shop-keepers and pedlars—remains much as before. In the three years between the first jottings for *Vanity Fair* and its appearance in book form Thackeray's private expressions of distaste for the Old Testament remained as uncompromising as ever:

> I dislike the Old Testament because it is very contrary: because it contains no Gentleness no Humanity no forgiveness—Fancy Lot, fancy Ezekiel remonstrating with God!
> (to Mrs Carmichael-Smyth, 2 August 1845—LPP, II, 205)

Three years later he calls the same book a "horrid story of hatred murder bigotry and persecution" and lists in particular the episodes of bears eating up little children for quizzing Elisha's bald head and Joshua receiving "Divine orders to slaughter man woman & child":

> St. Stephen was pelted to death by Old Testaments; & Our Lord was killed like a felon by the law he came to repeal.
> (to Mrs Jane Brookfield, 19–22 December 1848—LPP II, 473–4)

But however much he might consciously dislike the Old Testament, however distorted might be his view of its legislation and of Jesus's attitude to it—the *whole* Bible was inescapably part of his own heritage, and his artist's temperament could not help responding positively to its poetic beauty, unforgettable characters, and symbolic force.

CHAPTER 7

THE WORLD OF ALDERMAN MOSES
(1848–1851)

> ". . . we are unjustly persecuted, and yet . . . we don't
> complain: . . . we are unjustly treated, and yet . . . we
> don't threaten to rebel, or call foul names, or incite to
> hatred and fury against those who do us wrong."
>
> *(Punch*, Vol. XXI (1851), p. 123)

i

Thackeray's next novel, a *Bildungsroman* entitled

THE HISTORY OF PENDENNIS
HIS FORTUNES AND MISFORTUNES, HIS FRIENDS
AND GREATEST ENEMY

came out in twenty-four parts between mid-1848 and 1850. A
book-version, simply entitled *The History of Pendennis*, followed in
1850 as a double-decker. In both cases the name which appeared
on the title-page was Thackeray's own, not that of Titmarsh or
some other *persona*. The novel has many autobiographical features,
reproducing stages of development and realms of experience
through which Thackeray himself had passed in earlier years and
incorporating recent incidents and encounters. At the same time it
offers a keen observer's record of changes in English society from
the Georgian to the Victorian age: a society in which "rank",
"degree", "station" and "class" (all key-words within the novel
itself) continue to count for a great deal; in which notions of what
makes a "gentleman" or a "lady" are passionately held and
debated; but also one which tempers pride of descent with increasing social mobility. The chief engine of such mobility is money, of
course; and colonial expansion, technological progress and commercial enterprise offered the middle classes welcome opportunities
to enrich themselves and thereby to advance up the social ladder.

> Under the title of the Begum, Lady Clavering's fame began to spread
> in London before she herself descended upon the capital, and as it
> has been the boast of Delolme, and Blackstone, and all panegyrists of
> the British Constitution, that we admit into our aristocracy merit of
> every kind, and that the lowliest-born man, if he but deserve it, may
> wear the robes of a peer, and sit alongside of a Cavendish or a
> Stanley: so it ought to be the boast of our good society, that haughty
> though it be, naturally jealous of its privileges, and careful who shall

be admitted into its circle, yet, if an individual be but rich enough, all barriers are instantly removed, and he or she is welcomed, as from her wealth he merits to be. This fact shows our British independence and honest feeling—our higher orders are not such mere haughty aristocrats as the ignorant represent them: on the contrary, if a man have money they will hold out their hands to him, eat his dinners, dance at his balls, marry his daughters, or give their own lovely girls to his sons, as affably as your commonest *roturier* would do.

(XII, 468)

Thackeray's tone is ironic, especially when he makes his narrator speak of "British independence and honest feeling" in this context; but the passage also represents a clear-eyed recognition and acceptance of a social fact which was making the English branch of the Rothschild family more and more respectable in Victorian eyes.

In 1848, during one of his visits to Germany, Thackeray had a close encounter with a member of that famous family: Lady Louisa de Rothschild, wife of Sir Anthony de Rothschild of Grosvenor Place. They met on a Rhine steamer and took to one another, despite the fact that Thackeray did not conceal his anti-Jewish prejudices. Lady Louisa recorded in her diary:

The second, but greater charm of our journey was Mr. Thackeray's presence. Strange enough, we made acquaintance directly and he remained with us the whole day. We talked of literature, drawings, Jews, of whom he has a bad opinion, politics, etc., and we parted very good friends—at least I fancy so. He seems a good and an honest man, with a kind heart, notwithstanding a large fund of satire. I like him better than his books.

(IR, II, 361).

Lady Louisa's daughter Constance, later Lady Battersea, was still a child; but she too retained a vivid recollection of that meeting. Thackeray, it appears, took her up in his arms, poised her on his shoulders, and walked up and down the deck telling her fairy stories. This encounter did more than anything else to remind Thackeray of the Jewish background of the New Testament and the images of Christian worship based on it—images of universal human passions and concerns. He writes, in *Pendennis*:

The maternal passion is a sacred mystery to me. What one sees symbolized in the Roman churches in the image of the Virgin Mother with a bosom bleeding with love, I think one may witness (and admire the Almighty bounty for) every day. I saw a Jewish lady, only yesterday, with a child at her knee, and from whose face towards the child there shone a sweetness so angelical, that it seemed to form a sort of glory round both. I protest I could have knelt before her too, and adored in her the Divine beneficence in endowing us with the maternal *storgè*, which began with our race and sanctifies the history of mankind.

(XII, 25)

The illustration which accompanies this tribute lacks even the last vestige of the caricature element which Rowlandson and Cruikshank, Leech and Doyle, as well as Thackeray himself, had introduced into the portrayal of Jewish women and children.

Illustration 1

By connecting Catholic worship of Virgin and Christchild with the narrator's venerational attitude towards "a Jewish lady . . . and a child at her knee" Thackeray points, for once, to the Jewish origins of Jesus himself. Here something of the lustre of "the wisest and best of all teachers we know of, the untiring Comforter and Consoler" (XII, 799) reflects back onto the Jewish people, while the Jewish mother here described is bathed in the same religiose light in which this novel so often envelops Pendennis's mother Helen.

In the passage about the Jewish mother and her child which has just been quoted the phrase "our race" clearly refers to the human race as a whole. What is true of this solemn context applies to more humorous contexts too—as when Pendennis exclaims:

> 'Ye gods! how rapidly we live and grow! In nine months, Mr. Paxton grows you a pine-apple as large as a portmanteau, whereas a little one, no bigger than a Dutch cheese, took three years to attain his majority in old times; and as the race of pine-apples, so is the race of man . . .'

(XII, 571)

Elsewhere Thackeray uses the term "race" to embrace the English and Irish customers of the *Back Kitchen* club which holds its convivial meetings in the Fielding's Head inn:

As they sat thus in friendly colloquy, men of all sorts and conditions entered and quitted the house of entertainment; and Pen had the pleasure od seeing as many different persons of his race as the most eager observer need desire to inspect. Healthy country tradesmen and farmers . . . squads of young apprentices and assistants . . . rakish young medical students . . . young university bucks . . . handsome young guardsmen and florid bucks from the St. James's Street clubs . . . senators English and Irish . . . even members of the House of Peers.

(XXI, 385)

The term also occurs, of course, in the sense in which Thackeray, so often uses it—that of "family" ("Sir Francis Clavering, the representative of an ancient race, who had sat for their own borough of Clavering time out of mind in the House"—XII, 557); and humorously again, it is made to circumscribe a profession and one of its sub-divisions. The final sentence of Chapter XXXIV speaks of the "race" of literary men (XII, 440), while the penultimate sentence of the following chapter introduces a "race" of savagely humorous reviewers that is becoming extinct (XII, 346). Nothing could be further from Disraeli's assumptions of racial purity and superiority than Thackeray's usage in *Pendennis*.

Some of the physical traits which Thackeray in some contexts associates with Jews appear in this novel in his verbal and graphic representation of a theatre manager who descends from London to the provinces in search of handsome actresses (ill. 2).

He was a tall and portly gentleman with a hooked nose and a profusion of curling brown hair and whiskers; his coat was covered with the richest frogs, braiding, and velvet. He had under-waist-coats, many splendid rings, jewelled pins and neck-chains.

(XII, 156)

The manager's name is given as "Mr. Dolphin", and there is no rumour that he might be Jewish or of Jewish origin. Such origins are not to be as easily deduced from physical appearance as caricaturists like to make out; and the ethnic provenance or religious affiliation of such characters as Mr Polonius in *Vanity Fair* and Mr Dolphin in *Pendennis* are left in the same kind of obscurity which they might have in real life.

The next overtly Jewish character to flit across the stage of *Pendennis* belongs to a humbler sphere, but is again presented without rancour.

. . . as for the reader's humble servant, having but a small carpet-bag, I got up on the outside of the omnibus, and sat there very contentedly between a Jew pedlar smoking bad cigars, and a gentleman's servant taking care of a poodle-dog, until we got our fated

Illustration 2

complement of passengers and boxes, when the coachman drove
leisurely away. *We* weren't in a hurry to get to town. Neither one of us
was particularly eager about rushing into that near smoking
Babylon, or thought of dining at the Club that night, or dancing at
the Casino.

(XII, 201)

There is humour, of course, in the unlikely supposition that a
mid-nineteenth-century Jewish pedlar could possibly consider
"dining at the Club" or "dancing at the Casino", and the bad
cigars the man smokes might not be too pleasant on the nostrils;
but the narrator and his two companions are brothers under the
skin; they share some of the same aversions, and the narrator's
"we" can fitly include them all. There is an atmosphere of contented making-do in this passage which transmits some of its
contentment to the reader.

If Thackeray's illustration is a guide, then the duns that besiege

Illustration 3

Pendennis at his university lodgings may include at least one Jewish creditor (ill. 3).

But *is* the figure in the right foreground meant to be Jewish? The text says nothing about it, and what would in earlier works have been taken for infallible signs of Jewishness is again and again imputed to figures that have, as far as we know, no Jewish ancestry at all. It is remarkable how many of the characters in this novel over-ornament their person: the gambler Bloundell, who arouses Major Pendennis's suspicion by the quantity of rings and jewellery he wears (XII, 227); Colonel Altamont, "he of the many rings", who appears "gorgeously attired with chains, jewellery, and waistcoats" (XII, 480–1); and the young valet Lightfoot, whom the smitten Mrs. Bonner decks out with "lavish ornaments", making his person glitter "with pins, rings, shirt-studs, and chains and seals, purchased at the good creature's expense" (XII, 845). The French chef Mirobolant, who turns up "adorned with many ringlets and chains", is a particularly interesting case in point; Thackeray's drawing of him shows a hooked nose, dark beard and curls, and expressive hand-gestures, which silently reinforce the point he had already made with his verbal and graphic representation of Mr Dolphin, the manager from London.

Illustration 4

Another way in which this novel leads us to question stereotyped notions of Jews is by dispelling the idea that in the England here depicted moneylending is a Jewish monopoly. That Jews do, for historically understandable reason, engage in this business is beyond doubt; but before introducing a Jewish negotiator of bills Thackeray shows us a host of Gentile characters—Campion the lawyer, Finch, the Blondel family, the valet Morgan—who seek to profit by the eagerness of their contemporaries to obtain ready cash even at extortionate rates of interest. This provides a context for a character who first turns up in the disreputable company of the man who calls himself Colonel Altamont. Altamont tells Captain Strong of an encounter with "young Moss" at a gaming club which he calls an "infernal thieves' den" (XII, 545); and this prepares the reader for an appearance of the same character, under his full name Moss Abrams, in the entourage of the weak and surly Sir Francis Clavering, who prefers such gambling haunts to fashionable gatherings at Gaunt House.

> Sir Francis Clavering made his appearance, and skulked for a while about the magnificent rooms; but the company and the splendour which he met there were not to the baronet's taste, and after tossing off a tumbler of wine or two at the buffet, he quitted Gaunt House for the neighbourhood of Jermyn Street, where his friends Loder, Punter, little Moss Abrams, and Captain Skewball were assembled at the familiar green table. In the rattle of the box, and of their agreeable conversation, Sir Francis's spirits rose to their accustomed point of feeble hilarity.
>
> (XII, 773)

"Little Moss Abrams" keeps Gentile company, and would seem to be no more and no less disreputable than Loder, Punter and Skewball; indeed, the adjective which describes his small stature makes him endearing rather than menacing. Besides being a gambler, little Moss is also a financial middleman. When the horse Altamont had backed in the Derby comes in at thirty to one, the lucky winner finds himself besieged by a crowd of would-be advisers on what to do with his winnings; these include Tom Driver, Jack Holt, Jack Rackstraw, Tom Fleet, and, bringing up the rear

> little Moss Abrams, [who] entreated the colonel not to listen to these absurd fellows with their humbugging speculations, but to invest his money in some good bills which Moss could get for him, and which would return him fifty per cent. as safe as the Bank of England.
>
> (XII, 773)

The "little" Jew—small in physical stature, as many Ashkenazi Jews were, and lowly in social status—appears among English Gentiles engaged in exactly the same self-serving business as they; and he is seen, in the end, to be equally unsuccessful, for Altamont resists all blandishments. As the book nears its conclusion, however, another note creeps in:

> Sir Francis Clavering, who had pledged his word and his oath to his wife's advisers to draw or accept no more bills of exchange, and to be

content with the allowance which his victimized wife still awarded him, had managed to sign his respectable name to a piece of stamped paper, which the baronet's friend, Mr. Moss Abrams, had carried off, promising to have the bill 'done' by a party with whose intimacy Mr. Abrams was favoured. And it chanced that Strong heard of this transaction at the place where the writings had been drawn,—in the back parlour, namely, of Mr. Santiago's cigar-shop, where the Chevalier was constantly in the habit of spending an hour in the evening.

'He is at his old work again,' Mr. Santiago told his customer. 'He and Moss Abrams were in my parlour. Moss sent out my boy for a stamp. It must have been a bill for fifty pound. I heard the baronet tell Moss to date it two months back. He will pretend that it is an old bill, and that he forgot it when he came to a settlement with his wife the other day. I dare say they will give him some more money now he is clear.' A man who has the habit of putting his unlucky name to 'promises to pay' at six months, has the satisfaction of knowing, too, that his affairs are known and canvassed, and his signature handed round, among the very worst knaves and rogues of London.

(XII, 805–6)

Money-lenders' patter—having the bill "done" by going to another "party"—is ironically topped by the narrator's mock-formality: "with whose intimacy Mr. Abrams was favoured." Little Moss, who here abets Sir Francis Clavering's stratagem of dating the bill two months back in order to deceive Lady Clavering (to whom Sir Francis had sworn a solemn oath not to sign such bills again) appears more sinister than before. The narrator reckons him "among the worst knaves and rogues in London"; Major Pendennis calls him an "exceedingly disreputable person" (XII, 813); and Sir Francis himself—who is, admittedly, anything but an unimpeachable witness—adds his voice to the chorus by confessing to misgivings about "that bill of Abrams": "The little dam scoundrel, I know he'll do me in the business—he always does—" (XII, 816). Major Pendennis helps Sir Francis to "take up" the bill in question, in return for Sir Francis's agreement to give up his parliamentary seat and thus clear the way for Arthur Pendennis to enter the House of Commons; and all is sweetness and light again when

> Mr. Moss Abrams arrived with the proceeds of the baronet's bill, from which his own handsome commission was deducted and out of the remainder Sir Francis 'stood' a dinner at Greenwich to his distinguished friend, and passed the evening gaily at Vauxhall.
> (XII, 817)

Sir Francis, who trades in his parliamentary seat for money to settle his debts, is surely a greater scoundrel than busy little Moss.

In the meantime another character in the story, Captain Strong, has incurred financial difficulties; his "paper" is said to be of no

Illustration 5

value, and he is besieged in his lodgings by creditors and by two figures whose likenesses Thackeray draws for us (ill. 5).

This patient pair, introduced as "aides-de-camp" of a Mr Marks (XII, 831), besieges Strong in his chambers for weeks, forcing him to go in and out by means of a dangerous manoeuvre that involves a water-pipe and a neighbour's window. He is delivered from such indignity by Colonel Altamont, who "takes up" Mark's bill and settles with Strong's other creditors.

The world depicted in *Pendennis* is, once again, full of tradesmen who can be identified as Jewish by their names or by the location of their business premises. Holywell houses "slop-sellers" and "dealers in dingy furniture, and bedding suggestive of anything but sleep" (XII, 531), just as Wardour Street harbours suppliers of bric-a-brac and paintings that will pass for ancestral portraits. Miss Fotheringay the actress wears at her breast "a locket which he [= Arthur Pendennis] had bought of Mr. Nathan in High Street, with the last shilling he was worth, and a sovereign borrowed from Smirke." (XII, 76). The High Street in question is a provincial one, located in the town of Chatteris. At Oxbridge, where young Pendennis becomes, for a brief moment, a leader of fashion, "Simon, the jeweller, was known to sell no less than two gross of Pendennis pins, from a pattern which the young gentleman had selected in his shop." (XII, 219). To show her gratitude to a physician who had helped to cure her son, Helen Pendennis, herself a doctor's widow, determines to present to Dr Goodenough

the silver-gilt vase, the jewel of the house, and the glory of the late
John Pendennis, preserved in green baize, and presented to him at
Bath by the Lady Elizabeth Firebrace, on the recovery of her son, the
late Sir Anthony Firebrace, from the scarlet fever. Hippocrates,
Hygeia, King Bladud, and a wreath of serpents surmount the cup to
this day; which was executed, in their finest manner, by Messrs.
Abednego, of Milsom Street; and the inscription was by Mr. Birch,
tutor to the young baronet.
   This priceless gem of art the widow determined to devote to
Goodenough, the preserver of her son . . .

(XII, 664)

Here Jews appear, not as the snappers-up of cherished commodities, but as craftsmen who manufacture them—though it must be
admitted that the ironic way in which Thackeray's narrator describes what seems to Helen Pendennis a "priceless gem of art"
throws a somewhat dubious light on Messrs Abednego's "finest
manner" and on the taste that admires what they produce.

At the lower end of the world of entertainment "Conkey Sam"
the prizefighter delights his public when he faces a challenger at the
"Three-cornered Hat" in St. Martin's Lane (XII, 494), while at the
upper end the best-known Jewish composer of the day appears as a
purveyor of arias that can be detached from the operas for which
they were written and sung by amateurs as impromptu party
pieces. When "the disreputable Mr. Bloundell", whom Arthur
Pendennis had nicknamed "Captain Macheath", wants to show off
his fine voice, he does so not by singing an air from *The Beggar's
Opera*, but by "trolling out"

the chorus from *Robert the Devil*, an opera then in great vogue, in
which chorus many of the men joined, especially Pen, who was in
very high spirits, having won a good number of shillings and half-
crowns at the vingt-et-un . . .

(XII, 231)

The music they all sing is, of course, by Giacomo Meyerbeer, the
diabolic title of whose opera fulfils a symbolic function in this
chapter entitled "Rake's Progress":

From that night Pen plunged into the delights of the game of hazard
as eagerly as it was his custom to pursue any new pleasure . . .
(XII, 231)

Such dangerous excitements Thackeray knew all too well from his
own experience.

The *Ivanhoe* constellation again plays its part in *Pendennis*, where
Pen stands between Laura and Blanche; this is made explicit when

Blanche is likened, in Chapter LXV, to "Rowena going to see Ivanhoe." (XII, 846). And when Thackeray needs a metaphor for sexual excitement to match his siren and mermaid metaphors for sexual allure he chooses a wild horse-ride towards the object of the young man's love. The horse enlisted for this purpose is "Pen's mare, Rebecca (she was named after Pen's favourite heroine, the daughter of Isaac of York)." (XII, 30).

These variations on figures created by Walter Scott had been matched, in *Vanity Fair*, by variations on figures Disraeli had based on real life models; Lord Monmouth and Mrs Guy Flouncey in *Coningsby* might be seen as first sketches of Lord Steyne and Becky Sharp. Philip Collins (IR, I. 22) has noted verbal echoes of Disraeli in *Pendennis*: "At school, friendship is a passion . . ." (*Coningsby*, Book I, ch. 9) "What passions our friendships were in those old days!" (*Pendennis*, XII, 220); but Pendennis also makes fun of novels like Disraeli's *The Young Duke*:

> Pen began to laugh—'It is as cheap for a novelist to create a duke as to make him a baronet', he said. 'Shall I tell you a secret, Miss Amory? I promoted all my characters at the request of the publisher. The young duke was only a baron when the novel was first written; his false friend the viscount was a simple commoner, and so on with all the characters in the story.'
> 'What a wicked, satirical, pert young man you have become! *Comme vous voilà formé!*' said the young lady.
>
> (XII, 513)

Pendennis's *Walter Lorraine*, the narrator explains, appeared at a time "when the novel called 'the fashionable' was in vogue among us; and Warrington did not fail to point out . . . how Pen was a man of the very first fashion himself, and received at the houses of some of the greatest personages in the land." (XII, 524). Pen's novel thus caters for a taste which Disraeli had fostered by means of his early life-style as well as his fiction.

In its endeavours to "follow out, in its progress, the development of the mind of a worldly and selfish, but not ungenerous or unkind of truth-avoiding man" (XII, 800), *Pendennis* introduces a series of conversations between the eponymous hero and his friend Warrington in which the subject of toleration plays an important part. Arthur Pendennis sees the 1830s as a time when "the fiercest reformers grow calm . . . the loudest Radicals become dumb, quiescent placemen: the most fervent Liberals, when out of power, become humdrum Conservatives, or downright tyrants, or despots in office. Look at Thiers, look at Guizot, in opposition and in place! Look at the Whigs appealing to the country, and the Whigs in power! . . . they submit to circumstances which are stronger than they—move as the world marches towards reform, but at the world's pace (and the movements of the vast body of mankind must needs be slow.)'' (XII, 795–6). Warrington disdains the "wait and see" attitude his friend here advocates and this leads him to the subject of toleration, and of freedom for the expression of divergent opinions.

> 'You would have sacrificed to Jove', Warrington said, 'had you lived in the time of the Christian persecutions.'
>
> 'Perhaps I would', said Pen, with some sadness. 'Perhaps I am a coward,—perhaps my faith is unsteady; but this is my own reserve. What I argue here is that I will not persecute. Make a faith or a dogma absolute, and persecution becomes a logical consequence; and Dominic burns a Jew, or Calvin an Arian, or Nero a Christian, or Elizabeth or Mary a Papist or Protestant; or their father both or either, according to his humour; and acting without any pangs of remorse,—but, on the contrary, with strict notions of duty fulfilled. Make dogma absolute, and to inflict or to suffer death becomes easy and necessary; and Mahomet's soldiers shouting "Paradise! Paradise!" and dying on the Christian spears, are not more or less praiseworthy than the same men slaughtering a townful of Jews, or cutting off the heads of all prisoners who would not acknowledge that there was but one Prophet of God.'
>
> (XII, 797–8)

Warrington characterizes this speech, in which his friend twice adduces the persecution of Jews to show the dangers of wanting to remould the world according to one's own most cherished beliefs, as a "confession of general scepticism", and adds:

> You are six-and-twenty years old, and as blasé as a rake of sixty. You neither hope much, nor care much, nor believe much. You doubt about other men as much as about yourself. Were it made of such *pococuranti* as you, the world would be intolerable; and I had rather live in a wilderness of monkeys, and listen to their chatter, than in a company of men who denied everything.'
>
> 'Were the world composed of Saint Bernards or Saint Dominics, it would be equally odious,' said Pen; 'and at the end of a few score years would cease to exist altogether.
>
> (XII, 768)

It will not have escaped the reader that Warrington's "wilderness of monkeys" invokes the shade of Shylock, and does so in a sympathetic context. Shortly afterwards Pendennis confesses himself a "Sadducee": "I take things as I find them, and the world and the Acts of Parliament of the world, as they are . . . and if you hear of any good place under Government, I have no particular scruples that I know of, which would prevent me from accepting your offer."

(XII, 802). A later conversation between Pendennis and Warrington then picks up the threads of this first one. Warrington begins
with a quotation from *Henry IV, Part II* (Act V, scene 3), asking:

> 'And under which king does Bezonian speak or die?' asked War-
> rington. 'Do we come out as Liberal Conservative, or as Government
> man, or on our own hook?'
>
> 'Hem! There are no politics now; every man's politics, at least, are
> pretty much the same. I have not got acres enough to make me a
> Protectionist; nor could I be one, I think, if I had all the land in the
> county. I shall go pretty much with Government, and in advance of
> them upon some social questions which I have been getting up
> during the vacation;—don't grin, you old cynic, I *have* been getting
> up the Blue Books, and intend to come out rather strong on the
> Sanitary and Colonization questions.'
>
> 'We reserve to ourselves the liberty of voting against Government,
> though we are generally friendly. We are, however, friends of the
> people *avant tout*. We give lectures at the Clavering Institute, and
> shake hands with the intelligent mechanics. We think the franchise
> ought to be very considerably enlarged; at the same time we are free
> to accept office some day, when the House has listened to a few crack
> speeches from us, and the Administration perceives our merit.'
>
> 'I am not Moses,' said Pen, with, as usual, somewhat of me-
> lancholy in his voice. 'I have no laws from Heaven to bring down to
> the people from the mountain. I don't belong to the mountain at all,
> or set up to be a leader and reformer of mankind. My faith is not
> strong enough for that; nor my vanity, nor my hypocrisy, great
> enough. I will tell no lies, George, that I promise you; and do no more
> than coincide in those which are necessary and pass current, and
> can't be got in without recalling the whole circulation. Give a man at
> least the advantage of his sceptical turn. If I find a good thing to say
> in the House, I will say it; a good measure, I will support it; a fair
> place, I will take it, and be glad of my luck. But I would no more
> flatter a great man than a mob; and now you know as much about my
> politics as I do. What call have I to be a Whig? Whiggism is not a
> divine institution. Why not vote with the Liberal Conservatives?
> They have done for the nation what the Whigs would never have
> done without them. Who converted both?—the Radicals and the
> country outside. I think the *Morning Post* is often right, and *Punch* is
> often wrong. I don't profess a call, but take advantage of a chance.
> *Parlons d'autre chose.*'

(XII, 896–7)

In this passage it is the contrast with the Biblical Moses which
brings out to the full Pendennis's lax and tolerant political creed in
the age of the Reform Bill, the age of the railway, the age in which
the old gentry was being replaced, as Major Pendennis saw it, "by
a parcel of damned cotton-spinners and utilitarians, and young
sprigs of parsons with their hair combed down their backs . . ."
(XII, 872). "For the past two years", the narrator adds, "[Major

Pendennis] had begun to perceive that his day was wellnigh over, and that the men of the new time had begun to reign." (XII, 873).

The allusion to the character and rôle of Moses is only one of many respectful references to the Old Testament and its Apocrypha to be found in *Pendennis*, whose characters are frequently shown to be reading their Bibles or quoting from them. John Loofbourow has pinpointed, in *Thackeray and the Form of Fiction*, one set of references that has a *leitmotif* function in this novel: he shows how powerful a rôle a mock-Arcadia plays in the early chapters of *Pendennis*, and how Thackeray introduces, into this Arcadian idyll, ominous references to Adam and the Primal Fall: "the fruit of that awful Tree of Life which, from the beginning, has tempted all mankind" (XII, 319—cf. XII, 489 and 916). Such allusions, scattered throughout the novel, reach their climax in Chapter LXXIII where Pen discovers Foker and Blanche in intimate converse and learns what was contained in the mysterious package he had earlier seen in Foker's hand:

> It was opened, and curled round the white satin cushion within was, oh, such a magnificent serpentine bracelet, with such a blazing ruby head and diamond tail!
>
> (XII, 935)

This is, of course, a comic variation of the discovery scene in *Vanity Fair* in which serpentine ornaments had played a similar symbolic part.

ii

From 1847 onwards Thackeray competed with Dickens by offering the public an annual Christmas Book. This series he attributed, once again, to M.A. Titmarsh: but the drawing of that worthy which accompanied the first of these books, *Mrs. Perkins's Ball*, bears for once no resemblance to Thackeray's own well-known features (X, 10). Another drawing shows a singularly maladroit dancer with a comically determined expression, "dancing like a true Briton and with the charming gaiety and abandon of our race" (X, 57), and this caricature of "our [British] race" takes its place in a succession of other national caricatures which include "M. Canaillard, Chevalier of the Legion of Honour" and "Lieutenant Baron de Bobwitz" and have as their apogee a particularly grandiloquent, bumptious and drunken Irishman, the Mulligan of Ballymulligan, who causes mayhem wherever he goes. In the midst of all the comic upsets we encounter a few sly references to the Old Testament; critics, we are told, have opined that Mr Hicks's *Ararat* is "a stupendous epic" and that his *Megatheria* constitutes "a magnificent contribution to our *pre-Adamite* literature" (X, 34—my italics); and a Miss Jonas is named as a pretentious party-giver who hires the grocer George Grundsell to serve at her gatherings by saying to her page: "'Vincent, send the butler', or 'send Desborough to me'; by which name she chooses to designate G.G." (X, 69). Another Biblical name is borne by Lord Methuselah; but

MRS. TROTTER, MISS TROTTER, MISS TOADY, LORD METHUSELAH

Illustration 6

though his portrait might be mistaken for a Jewish caricature, there is no suggestion that he is anything but a lecherous old English nobleman in a curly wig. Whether the bailiff shown "in possession", drinking a pot of beer and smoking a pipe, is to be thought of as Jewish, the text of *Our Street* does not tell us; but this essay in London topography reintroduces the indubitably Jewish marginal

THE MAN IN POSSESSION

Illustration 7

men familiar from *Vanity Fair* when it speaks of the "crowd of shabby Jews about the steps" of a house inhabited, until the inevitable crash, by a suspiciously elegant widowed lady whose dubious sources of income prove, in the end, insufficient to sustain the lavish life-style which had made her a by-word among the street's respectable matrons. *Our Street* (1848) is also graced by the presence of a courier and gentleman's gentleman who is rumoured to be an Irish Jew:

> Mr. Sinbad is a foreigner, speaking no known language, but a mixture of every European dialect—so that he may be an Italian brigand, or a Tyrolese minstrel, or a Spanish smuggler, for what we know. I have heard say that he is neither of these, but an Irish Jew.
> He wears studs, hair-oil, jewellery, and linen shirt fronts, very finely embroidered but not particular for whiteness. He generally appears in faded velvet waistcoats of a morning, and is always

perfumed with stale tobacco. He wears large rings on his hands, which look as if he kept them up the chimney.

He does not appear to do anything earthly for Clarence Bulbul, except to smoke his cigars, and to practise on his guitar. He will not answer a bell, nor fetch a glass of water, nor go of an errand, on which, *au reste*, Clarence dares not send him, being entirely afraid of his servant, and not daring to use him, or to abuse him, or to send him away.

(X, 103)

A few pages later the rumour of Mr Sindbad's provenance is taken as true, and Clarence Bulbul's servant has become "that Irish Jew courier":

When we go to see him [=Clarence Bulbul who has "written an Eastern book of considerable merit"], that Irish Jew courier, whom I have before had the honour to describe, looks up from the novel which he is reading in the ante-room, and says, 'Mon maître est au Divan,' or, 'Monsieur trouvera Monsieur dans son sérail,' and relapses into the Comte de Monte Christo again.

(X, 122)

Despite the respectable front presented by his portrait Mr Sindbad

Illustration 8

hardly sounds like the ideal servant. The eponymous family of *The Kickleburys on the Rhine* (1850) appear to have had better luck with a courier named Hirsch. This is a name Thackeray had bestowed on a Jewish character in "Miss Löwe", and we may well surmise that this courier is also meant to be Jewish, although nothing is said of his antecedents or connections (ill. 9).

At the opening of *The Kickleburys on the Rhine*, Titmarsh encounters "Jews, with Sunday papers and fruit" on board ship; but these are carefully distinguished from the less appetizing "bearded foreign visitors to England, who always seem to decline to shave or wash themselves on the day of the voyage, and on the eve of quitting our country appear inclined to carry away as much as possible of its soil on their hands and linen." (X, 229). This directs

HIRSCH AND THE LUGGAGE

Illustration 9

away from Jews the opprobrium that had been cast in their direction by the shipboard chapters of *From Cornhill to Grand Cairo*. As for the Shylock of Dr Birch's school—a usurous lender of sixpences whose strong trading instincts ensure that at the end of every half year he returns home richer than he came, "with his purse full of money"—he is called Bullock and he is indubitably Gentile (*Dr. Birch and his Young Friends*, 1849, X, 190–1).

Thackeray's characters or narrators are apt to use Old Testament terminology when they speak of warring against, or triumphing over, philistine opponents; and when *The Kickleburys on the Rhine* was adversely reviewed in *The Times* and yet made a healthy profit, Thackeray rejoiced that "the Lord has delivered my enemy into my hands" (LPP, II, 751). Here, for once, he is speaking in his own person; and his use of Old Testament phraseology is given a special edge by his mistaken belief that the reviewer of *Kickleburys* was

Samuel Phillips—the critic of Jewish extraction who had compared *Pendennis* and *David Copperfield* in *The Times* of 11 June 1851 in a way that left no doubt of his strong preference for Dickens. Thackeray never forgave Phillips, and drew a posthumous verbal portrait of him that will be quoted later in the present book. In January 1851 Thackeray prefixed an essay to *Kickleburys* which introduced a brief reference to Holywell Street Jews:

> Suppose you and I had to announce the important news that some writers published what are called Christmas books; that Christmas books are so called because they are published at Christmas: and that the purpose of the authors is to try and amuse people. Suppose, I say, we had, by the sheer force of intellect, or by other means of observation or information, discovered these great truths, we should have announced them in so many words. And there it is that the difference lies between a great writer and a poor one; and we may see how an inferior man may fling a chance away. How does my friend of the *Times* put these propositions? 'It has been customary,' says he, 'of late years for the purveyors of amusing literature to put forth certain opuscules, denominated Christmas books, with the ostensible intention of swelling the tide of exhilaration, or other expansive emotions, incident upon the exodus of the old or the inauguration of the new year.' That is something like a sentence; not a word scarcely but's in Latin, and the longest and handsomest out of the whole dictionary. That is proper economy—as you see a buck from Holywell Street put every pinchbeck pin, ring, and chain which he possesses about his shirt, hands, and waistcoat, and then go and cut a dash in the Park, or swagger with his order to the theatre. It costs him no more to wear all his ornaments about his distinguished person than to leave them at home. If you can be a swell at a cheap rate, why not? And I protest, for my part, I had no idea what I was really about in writing and submitting my little book for sale, until my friend the critic, looking at the article, and examining it with the eyes of a connoisseur, pronounced that what I had fancied simply to be a book was in fact 'an opuscule denominated so-and-so, and ostensibly intended to swell the tide of expansive emotion incident upon the inauguration of the new year.' I can hardly believe as much even now—so little do we know what we really are after, until men of genius come and interpret.
> ("An Essay on Thunder and Small Beer", 1851—X, 223)

It is hard to escape the conclusion that the description of the "buck from Holywell Street" is meant as a pinprick for Samuel Phillips.

One of Thackeray's most delightful works, the "fireside pantomime" *The Rose and the Ring*, first issued as a "Christmas Book" in 1855, draws for some of its imagery and incident on Nathan's ring parable in *Nathan der Weise* (X, 497) and the trial scene of *The Merchant of Venice* (X, 454–5); but none of this brings Jewish characters even to the periphery of a story that treats a knowledge of Hebrew, once again, as a sign of extreme and most unlikely learning (X, 322, 324, 339). Among Thackeray's Christmas Books there is one, however, in which Jewish characters take the very centre of the stage. I am referring, of course, to *Rebecca and Rowena*, which first appeared in December 1850 with a Preface by its putative author, M.A. Titmarsh, dated December 20 1849. This book, with its illustrations by Richard Doyle, completed a project Thackeray had adumbrated in a diary entry of 11 August 1841 (LPP, II, 33) and had then begun to elaborate in *Fraser's Magazine* in 1846, under the title "Proposals for a Continuation of *Ivanhoe*". The thrust of this developing work is felt to the full at the end of *Rebecca and Rowena*, where Titmarsh confesses, in words to which we know Thackeray to have wholeheartedly subscribed:

> I grew to love Rebecca, that sweetest creature of the poet's fancy, and longed to see her righted.
>
> (X, 572)

Titmarsh's "Proposals for a Continuation of 'Ivanhoe'" were addressed to Alexandre Dumas, whom he challenged to do for Sir Walter Scott what he had done for himself in the sequels that followed the success of *The Three Musketeers*. Titmarsh presented Dumas with "notes" for this project in the *Fraser's Magazine* piece, and then worked these up himself when he found himself hard-pressed for a Christmas Book after a severe bout of illness. The result was *Rebecca and Rowena*, which Titmarsh, in his Preface, terms "a little play of nonsense", a "harmless jingle of the cap and bells" (X, 497), and which he calls, in a later passage, "a Christmas farce" (X, 567).

With his usual insight into Thackeray's relation to the literary genres he inherited and parodied, John Loofborouw has shown how *Rebecca and Rowena* "purposefully inverts the formal romance relationships and creates a nascent pattern of its own":

> Here, dark Rebecca is the heroine, blond Rowena a character part. Ivanhoe is a mutation of the romance hero, pacific and introverted instead of aggressive and conformist; King Richard is a buffoon, the clown a social crusader. This inversion of chivalric axioms repatterns the subsequent action. The crusade is a scene of inefficient butchery rather than of chivalrous virtue. Ivanhoe's ultimate marriage (to Rebecca) is a union of melancholy and anonymity, rather than the fairy-tale consummation of conventional romance.
>
> (*Thackeray and the Form of Fiction*, Princeton 1963, p. 41)

Insinuating "the reality of contemporary Victorianism beneath the mask of chivalric romance" (op. cit., p. 39), Thackeray "caricatures the irreproachable Victorian lady" he had lauded in *Pendennis* by means of a contrast between Rebecca, daughter of Isaac of York, whom Titmarsh describes as "admirable . . . tender . . . heroic . . . beautiful", and Rowena, "that vapid, flaxen-headed creature who is, in my humble opinion, unworthy of Ivanhoe, and unworthy of her place as heroine." (X, 501).

> Must the disinherited knight, whose blood has been fired by the suns of Palestine, and whose heart has been warmed in the company of the tender and beautiful Rebecca, sit down contented for life by the side of such a frigid piece of propriety as that icy, faultless, prim, niminy-piminy Rowena? Forbid it, fate! forbid it, poetical justice!
>
> (ibid.)

Titmarsh then describes the sort of dance Rowena is likely to have led poor Ivanhoe after their marriage, constantly casting Rebecca in his teeth and making snide remarks about his championship of Jews. She has accepted, and wears, the diamonds and rubies which Rebecca, "the poor, gentle victim" (X, 503), laid at her feet at the end of Scott's novel; but as for Rowena's "Come and live with me as a sister"—"Rebecca knew in her heart that her ladyship's proposition was what is called *bosh* (in that noble Eastern language with which Wilfrid the Crusader was familiar), or fudge, in plain Saxon." (X, 504). Titmarsh gives us a specimen of the kind of curtain-lectures Rowena might have directed towards Ivanhoe after their marriage:

> For instance, if Gurth, the swine-herd, who was now promoted to be a gamekeeper and verderer, brought the account of a famous wild boar in the wood, and proposed a hunt, Rowena would say, 'Do, Sir Wilfrid, persecute these poor pigs—you know your friends the Jews can't abide them!' Or when, as it oft would happen, our lion-hearted monarch, Richard, in order to get a loan or a benevolence from the Jews, would roast a few of the Hebrew capitalists, or extract some of the principal rabbis' teeth, Rowena would exult and say, 'Serve them right, the misbelieving wretches! England can never be a happy country until every one of these monsters is exterminated!'
>
> (ibid.)

This mixture of mockery of Hebrew, Walter Scott medievalism, and modern anti-capitalism ("capitalist" had been a key-term in Disraeli's *Sybil*) is as characteristic of the teasing tone of this "Christmas farce" as the ironic use of the term "benevolent" in this context. With such a wife Ivanhoe becomes as tired of England as his royal master Richard I, "who always quitted the country when he had squeezed from his loyal nobles, commons, clergy and Jews, all the money which he could get" (X, 505). Middle Ages and

nineteenth century meet again when Ivanhoe crosses the Channel
("From Calais Sir Wilfrid of Ivanhoe took the diligence across
country") and when Titmarsh confesses that he can't do battle-
scenes in the style of Walter Scott, who manages to transform "the
most savage and bloodstained characters of history" into "amiable,
jovial companions, for whom one has a hearty sympathy."
(X, 531). One character in particular whom Titmarsh is unable to
transform in this way is King John, whose murder of Prince Arthur
a "hero of romance" like Ivanhoe would surely have prevented had
he not been kept away by a fever,

> tied down in his bed as crazy as a Bedlamite, and raving ceaselessly
> in the Hebrew tongue, which he had caught up during a previous
> illness in which he was tended by a maiden of that nation, about a
> certain Rebecca Ben Isaacs, of whom, being a married man, he never
> would have thought, had he been in his sound senses. During this
> delirium, what were politics to him, or he to politics? King John or
> King Arthur were entirely indifferent to a man who announced to his
> nurse-tenders, the good hermits of Chalus before mentioned, that he
> was the Marquis of Jericho, and about to marry Rebecca the Queen
> of Sheba.
>
> (X, 545)

"Rebecca *Ben* [= son of !] Isaacs" shows up the writer's ignorance
of the Hebrew language, which is here facetiously compared to an
infection that can be "caught up". That the slang-word "bosh"
had earlier been credited to this infectious language compounds the
joke. Together with the deliberate mixture of medieval and modern
(Isaac*s* belongs to modern times, of course) all this sorts well with
the general air of deliberate anachronism and farce, into which, at
the end of the passage just quoted, the Old Testament is also
dragged. To make up for his inactivity over Prince Arthur, Ivanhoe
returns to England and helps his fellow-nobles to force King John
to sign Magna Charta—"that famous and palladium of our liber-
ties at present in the British Museum, Great Russell Street,
Bloomsbury" (X, 545). Rowena conveniently dies, but not before
extracting from Ivanhoe the promise "that you never will marry a
Jewess!" (X, 551).

Having placed Rowena's son, young Cedric, at school "at the
Hall of Dotheboyes, in Yorkshire" (X, 551—shades of *Nicholas
Nickleby!*), Sir Wilfrid takes up arms against the infidels by enlisting
with the Knights of St. John:

> The only fault that the great and gallant, though severe and ascetic
> Folko of Heydenbraten, the chief of the Order of St. John, found with
> the melancholy warrior, whose lance did such good service to the

cause, was, that he did not persecute the Jews as so religious a knight should. He let off sundry captives of that persuasion whom he had taken with his sword and his spear, saved others from torture, and actually ransomed the two last grinders of a venerable rabbi (that Roger de Cartright, an English knight of the order, was about to extort from the elderly Israelite) with a hundred crowns and a gimmal ring, which were all the property he possessed. Whenever he so ransomed or benefited one of this religion, he would moreover give them a little token or a message (were the good knight out of money) saying. 'Take this token, and remember this deed was done by Wilfrid the Disinherited, for the services whilome rendered to him by Rebecca, the daughter of Isaac of York!' So among themselves, and in their meetings and synagogues, and in their restless travels from land to land, when they of Jewry cursed and reviled all Christians, as such abominable heathens will, they nevertheless excepted the name of the Desdichado, or the doubly-disinherited as he now was, the Desdichado-Doblado.

(X, 552)

Here Titmarsh ironically adopts the perspective of Heydenbraten (= "roasting of heathens") while insinuating more enlightened attitudes towards such medieval-sadistic treatment of Jews. Since illness did not allow Thackeray to illustrate *Rebecca and Rowena* himself, he had entrusted the work to Richard Doyle, who produced a somewhat gloating picture of the tooth-pulling incident (ill. 11) as well as a light-hearted frontispiece in which the figures of Wamba, Ivanhoe, Rebecca and a remarkably merry Isaac of York cavort as in a holiday pantomime:

Illustration 10

Isaac of York has flourished, in Thackeray's tale, among the Moorish conquerors of Spain, where the Jews had a brief golden age. He has settled in Valencia, the Moors' last stronghold:

Illustration 11

Besides the Turks who inhabited it, there dwelt within its walls great
store of those of the Hebrew nation, who were always protected by
the Moors, during their unbelieving reign in Spain; and who were, as
we very well know, the chief physicians, the chief bankers, the chief
statesmen, the chief artists and musicians; the chief everything under
the Moorish kings. Thus it is not surprising, that the Hebrews,
having their money, their liberty, their teeth, their lives, secure under
the Mahometan domination, should infinitely prefer it to the Christian sway, beneath which they were liable to be deprived of every one
of these benefits.

(X, 566)

It is as an ambassador from Valencia that Isaac encounters Ivanhoe once again. Thackeray resists the temptation of putting nineteenth-century "Jew-speak" into his mouth; he permits Isaac a
dignified mode of speech with Old Testament colouration. To

Ivanhoe's great sorrow he announces that his daughter Rebecca is dead—a misleading piece of information explained in a flashback that shows Rebecca rejecting Moorish and Jewish suitors and finally announcing that she had turned Christian. In presenting Jewish aspirants to Rebecca's hand, Titmarsh allows strong elements of farce to return to his tale as well as unmistakable references to the Jewish communities of London in Thackeray's own day.

> . . . there are men in Jewry who admire beauty, and as I have even heard, appreciate money too, and Rebecca had such a quantity of both, that all the most desirable bachelors of the people were ready to bid for her. Ambassadors came from all quarters to propose for her. Her own uncle, the venerable Ben Solomons, with a beard as long as a Cashmere goat, and a reputation for learning and piety which still lives in his nation, quarrelled with his son Moses, the red-haired diamond merchant of Trebizond, and his son Simeon, the bald bill-broker of Bagdad, each putting in a claim for their cousin. Ben Minories came from London, and knelt at her feet: Ben Jochanan arrived from Paris, and thought to dazzle her with the latest waistcoats from the Palais Royal: and Ben Jonah brought her a present of Dutch herrings, and besought her to come back, and be Mrs. Ben Jonah at the Hague.
>
> Rebecca temporized as best she might. She thought her uncle was too old. She besought dear Moses and dear Simeon not to quarrel with each other, and offend their father by pressing their suit. Ben Minories, from London, she said was too young, and Jochanan from Paris, she pointed out to Isaac of York, must be a spendthrift, or he would not wear those absurd waistcoats. As for Ben Jonah, she said she could not bear the notion of tobacco and Dutch herrings—she wished to stay with her papa, her dear papa. In fine, she invented a thousand excuses for delay, and it was plain that marriage was odious to her. The only man whom she received with anything like favour, was young Bevis Marks, of London, with whom she was very familiar. But Bevis had come to her with a certain token that had been given to him by an English knight who saved him from a faggot to which the ferocious Hospitaller Folko of Heydenbraten was about to condemn him. It was but a ring, with an emerald in it, that Bevis knew to be sham, and not worth a groat. Rebecca knew about the value of jewels too; but, ah! she valued this one more than all the diamonds in Prester John's turban. She kissed it; she cried over it; she wore it in her bosom always; and when she knelt down at night and morning, she held it between her folded hands on her neck. . . .
> Young Bevis Marks went away finally no better off than the others; the rascal sold to the King of France a handsome ruby, the very size of the bit of glass in Rebecca's ring; but he always said, he would rather have had her, than ten thousand pounds, and very likely he would, for it was known she would at once have a plum to her fortune.

(X, 567–8)

Red-haired diamond merchants and bald bill-brokers, tobacco dealers and goat-bearded rabbis, the Minories and Bevis Marks, all point to Thackeray's own England rather than the European continent in the Middle Ages. The family council that considers Rebecca's behaviour deepens the farcical element—"all the jewelled heads of all the old ladies in council, all the beards of the family wagged against her—it must have been an awful sight to witness" (X, 568); but Rebecca herself, "helping the sick and needy of her people", is exempted from the general ridicule. To the sentence: "the poor blessed her, wherever they knew her, and many benefited by her who guessed not whence her gentle bounty came" the 1850 edition of *Rebecca and Rowena* adds a footnote: "Although I am writing but a Christmas farce, I hope the kind-hearted reader will excuse me for saying that I am thinking of the beautiful life and death of Adelaide the Queen". (X, 567).[1] It is this Rebecca who announces to her shocked family that she has turned Christian, who is imprisoned by them—pitied only by "her cousin and father's clerk, little Ben Davids"—and declared dead. In describing all this, Titmarsh shows himself no more sympathetic to what he sees as Jewish intolerance than he had been to Christian persecution of other faiths; and he has now furnished his explanation of Isaac's announcement, to Ivanhoe, that his imprisoned daughter was dead. It was indeed a custom in orthodox Jewry to mourn as dead a child that converted to another faith.

What happens from now on is not a rescue but a devaluation of Scott's touching heroine; for what made Scott's Rebecca heroic was surely her steadfast refusal to leave the community of her persecuted people for that of its persecutors. Having told us that Isaac was a curmudgeon who not only imprisoned but also half starved his daughter for some four years, Titmarsh has her liberated in the wake of Christian conquerors who murdered her father in a medieval pogrom related in pantomime style.

> Who, attracted to the Jewish quarter by the shrieks of the inhabitants who are being slain by the Moorish soldiery, and by a little boy by the name of Ben Davids, who recognizes the knight by his shield, finds Isaac of York *égorgé* on a threshold and clasping a large back-kitchen key? Who but Ivanhoe—who but Wilfrid? 'An Ivanhoe to the rescue,' he bellows out: he has heard that news from little Ben Davids which makes him sing. And who is it that comes out of the house—trembling—panting—with her arms out—in a white dress—with her hair down—who is it but dear Rebecca! Look, they rush

---

[1] Adelaide of Saxe-Meiningen, wife of William IV, died in 1849.

together, and Master Wamba is waving an immense banner over them, and knocks down a circumambient Jew with a ham, which he happens to have in his pocket. . . .

(X, 572)

Here the aura of rape and murder that clings to the *belle Juive* and adds to her sexual attractiveness becomes plain as never before. But to think that Scott's Rebecca could join the Christian conquerors amid such scenes—"and a better Christian than Rebecca now was never said her catechism" (X, 572)—hardly amounts to a "righting" of the wrongs allegedly done to this "sweetest creature of the poet's fancy" at the end of *Ivanhoe*. Thackeray seems to have felt this himself, for the deliberately created atmosphere of anachronistic farce and Christmas pantomime darkens into melancholy at the end of both the "Continuation of 'Ivanhoe'" and *Rebecca and Rowena*:

> That she and Ivanhoe were married follows of course; for Rowena's promise extorted from him was, that he would never wed a Jewess. Married I am sure they were, and adopted little Cedric, whose father had drunk away all his fortune; but I don't think they had any other children, or were subsequently very boisterously happy. Of some sorts of happiness melancholy is a characteristic, think these were a solemn pair, and died rather early.
>
> > 'Ah, L'heureux temps que celui de ces fables! . . .
> > Le raisonner aujourd'hui s'accrédite,
> > On court, hélas! après la vérité!
> > Ah, croyez-moi, l'erreur a son mérite.'
>
> With which remarks from Voltaire
> > I have the honour to be,
> > M. the Marquis' most devoted admirer,
> > > > M.A. TITMARSH.
> > > ("Continuation . . .", 1846 — X, 493)

> That she and Ivanhoe were married follows of course; for Rowena's promise extorted from him was, that he would never wed a Jewess, and a better Christian than Rebecca now was never said her Catechism. Married I am sure they were, and adopted little Cedric; but I don't think they had any other children, or were subsequently very boisterously happy. Of some sort of happiness melancholy is a characteristic, and I think these were a solemn pair, and died rather early.
>
> > (*Rebecca and Rowena*, 1850 — X, 572)

To make a "Christmas farce" out of such material as religious intolerance, and the torture or murder of human beings for the sake of their religious allegiances, was a risky undertaking, and Thackeray cannot be said to have succeeded in it, for all the incidental fun to be derived from his verbal caricatures and farcical anachronisms. As for the figure of Rebecca, the greatest *belle Juive* of English literature whom Titmarsh wished to rescue from an injustice done to her by her creator—is there not far more dignity in Scott's heroine, who chooses to leave England in order to cleave to, and to aid, her persecuted people, than in Titmarsh's renegade, who rushes into the arms of her lover in the midst of a massacre of Jews by Christians and then turns into an exemplary Catechism-saying Christian wife? It is to Thackeray's credit that the melancholy note at the end of Titmarsh's tale suggests some unease at what he had done.

iii

While writing *Pendennis* and various Christmas Books, Thackeray continued to send drawings, squibs, poems and humorous prose-pieces to *Punch*. Sometimes his contributions deviated into serious-ness, as when Thackeray speaks—like Heine before him—of the strange terror inspired in him by iconoclastic Parisian entertain-ments. A piece entitled "Two or Three Theatres in Paris", pub-lished on 24 February 1849, describes the audience at popular playhouses: "They laugh at religion, they laugh at chastity, they laugh at royalty, they laugh at the Republic most pitilessly of all." How different *Punch* would look if it were produced in Paris rather than London!

> Sir, these funny pieces at the plays frightened me more than the most bloodthirsty melodrama ever did, and inspired your humble servant with a melancholy which is not to be elicited from the most profound tragedies. There is something awful, infernal almost, I was going to say, in the gaiety with which the personages of these satiric dramas were dancing and shrieking about among the tumbled ruins of ever so many ages and traditions. I hope we shall never have the air of "God Save the King" set to ribald words amongst us—the mysteries of our religion, or any man's religion, made the subject of laughter, or of a worse sort of excitement. In the famous piece of *La Propriété c'est le Vol*, we had the honour to see Adam and Eve dance a polka, and sing a song quite appropriate to the costume in which they figured. Every-body laughed and enjoyed it—neither Eve nor the audience ever thought about being ashamed of themselves, and, for my part, I looked with a vague anxiety up at the theatre roof, to see that it was not falling in, and shall not be surprised to hear that Paris goes the way of certain other cities some day. They will go on, this pretty little painted population of Lorettes and Bayadères, singing and dancing, laughing and feasting, fiddling and flirting, to the end, depend upon it. But enough of this theme: it is growing too serious—let us drop the curtain.
>
> (VIII, 473–4)

Thackeray had himself parodied Genesis in the "Snobs" series — "First the world was made: then, as a matter of course, Snobs" (IX, 261); and he was fond of noting that Adam and Eve afforded painters a welcome opportunity of facing their public with figures wearing "very little costume indeed" (VIII, 432); but the sexually charged persiflage of Adam and Eve in French theatres transformed Paris into Sodom and Gomorrha in the eyes of *Punch*'s ironic, repelled and fascinated correspondent.

To the long list of personae whose first person narratives masked him over the years—including Titmarsh, Wagstaff, Solomons junior, Mr. Snob, Mr. Spec, the Fat Contributor and *Punch*'s Commissioner—Thackeray added an "intelligent fogey" (VIII, xiv) in 1849, when he began the series he entitled "Mr. Brown's Letters to his Nephew". Uncle Brown laces his epistles with admonitory allusions to Samson and Delilah (VIII, 334, 338); agrees with most other characters in Thackeray's repertoire that knowledge of Hebrew is as esoteric a knowledge as one could possibly have (VIII, 330); and shows commendable sympathy with the City banker who votes for Lionel Rothschild as his member of parliament in defiance not only of the Test Acts but also of a formidable aristocratic mother-in-law (VIII, 330). In 1850 Mr Brown is joined in the columns of *Punch* by a somewhat similar character who presents himself as a retired army surgeon able to remember the follies of his youth; social slights rankle in him (as they did in Thackeray himself) but an emblematic initial suggests that he has reached a level of tranquility which equals that of Diogenes in his tub (VIII, 347). Since he has arrived at an age of prose rather than poetry, he calls himself the proser; but it is no surprise to learn, from a sub-title, that Thackeray has given him the name "Solomon", thus making him a namesake of the reputed author of Ecclesiastes, the Old Testament book from which he, like Thackeray himself, likes to quote:

THE PROSER
ESSAYS AND DISCOURSES BY DR. SOLOMON PACIFICO

The surname of this new character indicates the "fogy"'s pacific or pacified nature; but it also held powerful associations for mid-nineteenth century readers to which he himself refers when he speaks of "the affairs of a celebrated namesake of mine." (VIII, 368). That namesake is David Pacifico (1784–1854), commonly known as Don Pacifico, a British subject born in Gibraltar and resident in Athens who professed the Jewish religion and whose house had been sacked in a riot with strong anti-Jewish overtones in 1847. The British government, headed by Palmerston, held the Greek government responsible for this violation of the rights of a British subject; and when Don Pacifico's claims for compensation were disallowed, a British fleet blockaded Piraeus, seizing some 200 Greek ships and holding them until Pacifico had been indemnified. Challenged in parliament about taking such actions on behalf of a Jew who was not even born in the British Isles, Palmerston defended himself in a famous *civis Romanus* speech which asserted the principle that no British subject, whether "of Jewish persuasion" or not, should suffer outrage without being avenged. Since Don Pacifico's given name was David, *Solomon* Pacifico becomes a kind of "Pacifico Junior" or "Son of Pacifico" as well as a namesake of the preacher of Ecclesiastes.

Having named his new character, Thackeray draws a portrait of him which shows what Pacifico himself calls "my aquiline countenance".

Illustration 12

There is a strong resemblance between Pacifico's features and those of the Jewish pedlar whom Thackeray had drawn for *Punch* in 1848 (IX, 567—see Illustration 13 below); but what the Pacifico portrait calls most to mind is the "keen, kind, beaming Jew face", an amalgam of Voltaire and Mendelssohn, which Thackeray had noticed in the non-Jewish Laman Blanchard (VI, 555). Dr Pacifico is made to use some of Thackeray's own favourite Old Testament allusions; but in what he tells us of his career, his mode of living, and his opinions on a variety of issues there is nothing to suggest that this new Pacifico shares the religious affiliations of his celebrated name-sake.

The Pacifico series had been preceded, in *Punch*, by a conversation piece that featured among its characters a "Mr. Dizzy" who is easily recognizable as Benjamin Disraeli. "An After-Dinner Conversation" (29 April 1848—VIII, 442–6) finds Mr Benjamin Dizzy in conversation with Colonel Sibby (based on one of *Punch*'s favourite butts, the arch-conservative Colonel Sibthorp, M.P.), with Mr Y. Doodle, a gentleman from Philadelphia, and with Mr Cuffee, a Chartist delegate. Mr Dizzy harps on his Oriental descent; when the American mistakes olives for pickles, Mr Dizzy seizes the opportunity to claim first-hand acquaintance with that olive tree which had served St. Paul as a symbol for Israel's place in the scheme of salvation (Romans 11, 15–27): "I have seen it, Sibby, lining the bleak hill sides of my native Syrian hills . . ." He is also fond of Old Testament imagery: "His Royal Highness [= Prince Albert] is, so to speak, only an august ceremony. He is attendant upon the Ark of the Monarchy; we put that out of danger when commotions menace us." He presents himself as guardian and judge of British tradition: "we grovel in old world ceremonies and superstitions of which we are too stupid to see the meaning, the folly, or the beauty." Disraeli's manner, uniting the orotund and the witty, is well caught, but there is little political content in the piece except justified ridicule of Chartist demands for *annual* parliaments and Republican demands for the abolition of the British monarchy. Dizzy puts a cash-value on the institutions he defends: "If in this country we were to have an election every year, a struggle for the President's chair every three years, men taking advantage of the excitement of the day, and outbidding each other on the popular cry, we should lose in mere money, ten times as much as the Sovereign costs us." The adjective "mere" indicates, however, that Dizzy is deliberately putting it in the lowest terms; that he is perfectly well aware of considerations that go beyond the counting-house. And looking across to France, where a revolution has just swept Louis Philippe from power, Mr Dizzy is made to repeat Disraeli's famous characterization of that devious monarch as a modern Ulysses: "They have already spent two hundred millions of our money in getting rid of old Ulysses." (VIII, 445). This links on to "The Worst Cut of All", another squib with which Thackeray had greeted Louis Philippe's fall from power (*Punch*,

XIV, 1848, p. 100); instead of attracting Disraeli's admiration Louis Philippe now attracts his pity; and "they say this cut up the Ex-King more than any other of his mishaps." Thackeray glances at the March Revolution in other contributions too. He sends in a spoof news-item in which Baron James, the head of the French branch of the Rothschild family, follows Louis Philippe into his English exile; under the heading "A Club in Uproar" he reports:

> *Saturday, Five o'clock*. Jawkins has just come from the City. The French Rothschild has arrived. He escaped in a water-butt as far as Amiens, whence he went in a coffin. A *fourgon* contain[ing] two hundred and twenty-two thousand two hundred sovereigns, and nine-and-fourpence in silver, was upset in the Rue Saint Denis . . .
>
> (*Punch*, XIV, 1848, p. 95)

There is equal glee in imagining the indignities to which the (reputedly) richest man in the world is subjected, and in reckoning up the coins, down to the last fourpence, that might fit into a French baggage-waggon. In a piece headed "A Dream of the Future", Thackeray imagines an England transformed into a Republic led by the later Lord Houghton in the guise of Citizen Monckton Milnes, whose Minister of the Interior will be that great survivor, Citizen Benjamin Disraeli. (*Punch*, XIV, 1848, p. 107). This is by no means the last we hear of Disraeli, whose career Thackeray followed with fascination. In a contribution headed "Mr. Seesaw's Conduct in Parliament during the Late Debates" (*Punch*, XIX, 6 July 1850, p. 132), he ridicules an M.P. who listens to Sir Robert Peel's speech during an all-night debate with admiration, then leaves the Chamber to look over his own notes "whilst Mr. Disraeli was speaking in the cool dawn before St. Margaret's Church", and who finds, on his return, that the government has had a majority of 46. Here as elsewhere, Disraeli is treated with respect as an important British statesman. It is on Mr Seesaw and not on Disraeli that ridicule falls; just as it falls on M. Gobemouche, the imaginary correspondent of a Parisian journal, who informs his readers that Benjamin Disraeli is the author of *The Curiosities of Literature* and the *Letters of Junius*, and talks similar nonsense about Disraeli's political affiliations and an accident in which his carriage had recently been involved. (*Punch*, XX, 10 May 1851, p. 198).

The only other famous Jewish name Thackeray drops in *Punch* in these years just after the revolutions of 1848 is that of Mendelssohn. This time the context leaves no doubt that it is Felix Mendelssohn-Bartholdy and not his grandfather Moses who is so honoured; for Thackeray commends the overture of the Grand Comic Christmas Pantomime for 1848 by asserting that "it is not difficult music to understand, like that of your Mendelssohns and Beethovens." ("A Night's Pleasure", *Punch*, XIV, 1848, p. 29).

Elsewhere in *Punch* humbler Jews show up in Thackeray's contributions. He illustrates a piece entitled "Rogues and Revolutions", written by another contributor and containing no mention of Jews, with a picture of a Jewish pedlar:

Illustration 13

The implication appears to be that the pedlar sells inferior goods; but the smiling pedlar seems second cousin to the charming "fogy" Solomon Pacifico, and his conjunction with cheerful country-customers makes an idyllic picture. Nor is there malice in Thackeray's spoof of the advertisements of the tailoring firm E. Moses and Son, "Mr. Smith and Moses", in which Louis Philippe, shorn of his side-whiskers and under the pseudonym Smith, is measured for a suit:

'I've look'd upon many a palace before,
But splendour like this, love, I never yet sor!'
This party exclaimed. 'What a great sum of mon-
ey it sure must have cost Messrs. Moses and Son!'

In the language of France his good lady replied,
'This house is well known through the universe wide;
And you, my dear Philip, to seed having run,
Had better refit with E. Moses and Son.'

E. Moses stepped forth with a bow full of grace,
Inviting the couple to enter his place:

Illustration 14

He thought they were poor—but the poor are not done,
And the rich are not fleeced by E. Moses and Son.

'What clothes can I serve you to-day, my good man?
E. Moses exclaimed: 'You shall pay what you can;
The peer or the peasant, we suit every one;
Republicans true are E. Moses and Son.'

.   .   .   .
.   .   .   .

The clothes when complete we direct in a hurry—
'—Smith, Esquire, at Prince Leopold's, Claremont, in Surrey.'
The cloth was first-rate, and the fit such a one
As only is furnished by Moses and Son.

As he paces the valley or roams in the grove,
All cry, 'What a very respectable cove!'
How changed in appearance from him who late run
From Paris to refuge with Moses and Son.

(VIII, 199–200)

The impression left by this piece and its illustration, published in
Punch on 25 March 1848, is that Jews offer a useful service and look
pleasantly cheerful while they are doing so. Three years later a

poem laced with stage Irish, in which Thackeray has a Mr Molony laud the Crystal Palace with Biblical comparisons—

> This Palace tall,
> This Cristial Hall,
> Which Imperors might covet,
> Stands in High Park
> Like Noah's Ark,
> A rainbow bint above it—

lists the products of this same Jewish tailoring firm among the wonders of the Great Exhibition:

> There's taypots there,
> And cannons rare;
> There's coffins filled with roses;
> There's canvas tints,
> Teeth insthrumints,
> And shuits of clothes by Moses.
>
> ("Mr. Molony's Account of the Crystal Palace", *Punch*, 26 April 1851—VII, 159, 162)

"Shuits" adds a touch of "Jew-speak" to Molony's stage Irish. Contributors to *Punch* frequently made fun of the extravagant rhymed advertisements with which the Victorian public's attention was drawn to those "shuits of clothes by Moses" that had attracted Mr Molony's admiration; and Thackeray had joined in this game when he published, on 22 February 1851, "A Plan for a Prize Novel, in a Letter from the eminent Dramatist BROWN to the eminent Novelist SNOOKS". "Fiction", Brown is made to write, with a glance at the puffery of Moses and Son, "advocates all sorts of truths and causes—doesn't the delightful bard of the Minories find Moses in everything?" Why, then—could England not adopt a plan hatched by "a French literary gentleman, M. Emanuel Gonzales", and smuggle advertisements into silver fork novels?

> . . . as to tailors, milliners, bootmakers, &c., how easy to get a word for them! 'Amramson, the tailor, waited upon Lord Paddington, with an assortment of his unrivalled waistcoats, or clad in that simple but aristocratic style of which Schneider alone has the secret . . .'

The names suggest that the waistcoat maker is Jewish, the tailor German; and readers are left to conjecture that M. Emanuel Gonzales, whose plan had come to light when he and an advertisement agent fell out about a question of money, might be of Marrano origin. (VIII, 175–7).

Old Testament names crop up fitfully in Thackeray's contributions to *Punch*; sometimes to designate ancient Israelites whose story holds a moral for a later day (like "silly Samson shorn" in "The Yankee Volunteers", IX, 69), more often to suggest the ethnic and religious affiliations of figures like "Messrs. Aminadab and Nebuchadnezzar", whom Lord Swellmore sees at his club "on pecuniary business" ("Poor Puggy", *Punch*, XXI, 18 October 1851, p. 167), or Rabbi Jehoshaphat from Jerusalem, whom Lady Nimrod lures to a reception along with "Monsieur Sansgêne, the eminent socialist refugee" and "the Archbishop Mealypotatoes, *in partibus infidelium*, and in purple stockings" ("The Lion Huntress of Belgravia", VIII, 510). Lady Nimrod, of course, has her name simply because she is a *huntress* of "lions" for her salon; there is no suggestion that she is to be thought of as owing greater allegiance to the Old Testament than to the New. But when Thackeray makes the prize-fighter Bendigo, whose real name was *William* Thompson, sign himself *"Benjamin* Bendigo" in a letter suggesting he be made "Purfessor of Sulf-defense", he may once again be suggesting a line of tradition that runs from the Jewish pugilists of the Regency to the boxers of the Victorian Age ("Science at Cambridge", VIII, 458–9).

Thackeray's ubiquitous Jewish process-servers and bailiffs turn up again in a piece he contributed to the issue of *Punch* which appeared on 5 April 1851. It bore the title "If Not—Why Not?". Here Thackeray protests against the lenient way in which liberal-minded members of parliament were inclined to characterize Irish debtors who took the law into their own hands. Such M.P.s applied to Ireland criteria they would never accept in England:

> In England, a landlord would most probably want his rent at the half-year, and if he waited four years, and then distrained for it, it is probable that his officer would not be fired upon by two hundred of the tenant's friends, assembled on a rising ground, with their picquets in advance. Nor would an English member for a Devonshire borough, let us say, hearing that such a disturbance had taken place in Yorkshire, rise up and ask the Home Secretary whether the conduct of the Sheriff's officer was "fair" towards those misguided Yorkshire folks—as a Munster gentleman spoke about Ulstermen the other day. Here, as yet, rent is considered to be fair, and it is not thought to be altogether unfair that a man should have to pay it. If my landlord were not to get his quarter and to put a distress into my house (both of which may Fate forbid!) the rest of the inhabitants of the street would not turn out with double-barrelled guns to shoot Mr. Levi or Mr. Sloman. If Levi and Sloman came unarmed, saved with their writ, and were fired upon by two hundred men, no English Member would inquire in Parliament, why a regiment was not sent with Messrs. L. & S., and ask if the sending them unaccompanied was "fair" upon my two hundred friends, armed with pike and gun.

> If Levi and Sloman were shot by my two hundred friends, people would use a stronger term than "misguided" to describe the ten score champions . . .
>
> (*Punch*, XX, 5 April 1851, p. 135)

Sheriff's officers and bailiffs are not likely to be loved, but they are a social institution, enforcing generally sanctioned property rights, performing a service required of them by law, and are therefore to be protected against all assaults—whether they be Jews or non-Jews, in England or in Ireland, and whether the writer (who signs himself "Hibernis Hibernior") is involved or not. It will be remembered that a family called Sloman did indeed keep the sponging-house in Cursitor Street in the mid-nineteenth century.

The most interesting of the many references to Jews in the pieces Thackeray contributed to *Punch* between 1848 and 1851 occur in "A Case of Ingratitude", published in Volume XXI on 13 September 1851. This is an allegorical piece along the lines of Swift's *Tale of a Tub*; it features Alderman Moses, who sits in Worship Street, and before whom "a person by the name of John Henry Newboy" is brought up. Newboy is charged by an old shopkeeper called "Mrs. Church" with obstructing her trade and with "indecent and riotous behaviour". "Newboy", of course, is J.H. Newman, "Mrs. Church" the Church of England, and a rival shopkeeper named "Mrs. Hills" the Church of Rome. "Alderman Moses" must then be the lawgiver of the Old Testament, who is here given modern traits that expose him to taunts about "Old Clothes"; but what is so remarkable about the treatment of this figure is the fact that the Church of England is made to recognize his jurisdiction to the extent of citing Newman before this alderman's chair, and that Thackeray pens for him a concluding speech which shows tolerance and dignity in equal measure. Old Lady Church has complained that Newboy, her late foreman, had published libels against her business, which is that of a robe-maker and haberdasher with a shop in Westminster and another, larger one in St. Paul's, and that he had caricatured her in the most ludicrous manner.

> Alderman Moses checked this unseemly jocularity and said: "Mr. Newboy, it may suit you to make fun of old Mrs. Church; but you will please remember that there are other people besides her whom some folks consider ridiculous; and I should say that this tone of levity does not become you towards an old lady who acted towards you as a mother. As for you, Mrs. Church, I don't see how I can help you: and you must remember that you have been calling Mrs. Hills names all your life, and very ugly names too. I've nothing to do with the dispute between your shops; and can neither prevent Mrs. Hills from selling her garments, or you from vending yours." A voice here,

in the crowd, crying out, "Clo! Clo!" in a jocular tone, the worthy Alderman said, "Yes, if it is a question about clothes, you know that our people have the *real* old clothes—that we are unjustly treated, and yet that we don't complain: that we are persecuted, and yet that we don't threaten to rebel, or call foul names, or utter falsehoods, or incite to hatred and fury against those who do us wrong." And another case being called both parties left the court, perfectly dissatisfied.

(loc. cit., pp. 122–3)

That neither of the parties should be satisfied is in the nature of the case; but it is refreshing to find Thackeray discounting those legends of the Jews' thirst for revenge for past injuries which were trotted out whenever a Jewish Disabilities Bill came before parliament, and having his Jew, clothed in the dignity of an alderman, give Christians a lesson in mutual tolerance and forbearance. London's first Jewish alderman, it should be remembered, David Salomons, had been elected in 1847, just four years before "A Case of Ingratitude" appeared in *Punch*.

iv

Between 1847 and 1851 Thackeray formed ever closer ties with the Reverend William Brookfield and his wife Jane—but his excessive devotion to the latter, with whom he had fallen deeply in love, and Brookfield's jealousy, caused a rift in the relationship which widened, ultimately, into a break. Some of Thackeray's liveliest letters were written to Jane Brookfield during their halcyon period of friendship; and it is not surprising to find that his expressions of distaste for the Old Testament now went to Jane rather than to his fundamentalist mother, Mrs Carmichael-Smyth, for whose sake he had earlier suppressed "heretical" remarks in the "Jerusalem" chapter of *From Cornhill to Grand Cairo*. We have already met the intemperate passage from a letter to Mrs Brookfield which begins with abuse of the Old Testament as "a horrid story of hatred murder bigotry and persecution" and ends with references to the Crucifixion and the stoning of Stephen (19–22 December 1848—LPP, II, 473–5). The fate of St. Stephen seems to have been much in his mind in these years; on 1 May 1851, writing to Mrs Brookfield about ceremonies inaugurating the Great Exhibition, he relates how "while the Archbishop was saying his prayer beginning with Paternoster (which sounded in that wonderful throng inexpressibly sweet and awful) three Romish priests were staring about with opera glasses: which made me feel as angry as the Jews who stoned Stephen." (ibid., 768). This passage expresses at once

Thackeray's continuing horror of Old Testamentarian punishments, his familiarity with the New Testament (Acts 7, 54–60), his aversion to Roman Catholic clerics at a time when Newman was beckoning Englishmen towards their Church, and his liking for the "via media" of the Church of England. In the letters to Jane Brookfield this "via media" theology implies a "return to Jesus"; for "I should like to see before I die, and think of it daily more and more, the commencement of Jesus Christ's Christianism in the world; where I am sure people may be made a hundred times happier than in its present forms—Judaism, asceticism, Bullarism; I wonder—will He come again and tell it us?" (LPP, II, 475). This was written in 1848; three years later, when "A Case of Ingratitude" appeared in *Punch*, Thackeray seems to have come to think rather better of modern Judaism, and to have conceived a respect for Moses which he would always withhold from Joshua and from those who persecuted Jesus and his disciples. If Alderman Moses is anything to go by, then Christians need not fear that the elevation of modern Jews to judicial authority held any threat of return to Old Testamentarian punishments.

Thackeray's letters continue to impress the Old Testament and its Apocrypha into the service of colourful, immediately comprehensible expression:

> After dinner I went to a ball at the Prefecture of Police—the most splendid apartments I ever saw in my life, such lights pillars marble hangings carving and gilding. *I'm sure King Belshazzar could not have been more magnificently lodged.* There must have been fifteen hundred people: of whom I did not know a single soul. I am surprised that the people did not faint in the saloons wh. were *like burning fiery furnaces*, but there they were dancing and tripping away—ogling & flirting and I suppose not finding the place a bit inconveniently warm.
>   (to Mrs Brookfield, 4–5 February 1849—LPP, II, 502)
>   (my italics).

Thackeray's correspondent can hardly have missed his insinuation that Paris was the modern Babylon, and that its high-living élite might one day meet the fate of its earlier counterpart described in the Book of Daniel, or that it might ultimately find itself in a place rather more inconveniently warm than a Paris ballroom with none of the divine protection from heat enjoyed by Shadrach, Meshach and Abednego. Old Testament stylizations and allusions may suggest character; to that of Carlyle, for instance, Thackeray and many of his contemporaries thought them particularly appropriate. "Carlyle", Thackeray wrote to James Spedding on 5 January 1850, "tossed Reeve and gored yea as a bull he chased him and horned

him . . . (LPP II, 628); and to Kate Perry he said later in the same
year that Carlyle "was a bully—attack him with persiflage and he
is silenced, in fact Carlyle is no longer the Prophet he used to be
considered—I remember his palmy days when his words were
manna to the Israelites" (Kate Perry's diary for 1850—LPP I,
cviii). The Israelites, in that quotation, are clearly Carlyle's British
admirers and disciples.

Socially Thackeray mingled more and more, in these years, with
Israelites of a more literal kind. The acquaintance he had struck up
with Lady Louisa Rothschild during their common journey down
the Rhine in 1848 led to further contacts with her famous family.
He met Baron James in Paris, and wrote breezily to Mrs Brookfield
on 1–2 February 1849: "I am come home very tired and sleepy
from the Opera where my friend Jim Rothschild gave me a place in
his box." (LPP, II, 493). Back in London he attended what he
called "a grand dinner in Jewry":

> Then at 8 o'clock a grand dinner in Jewry. Mrs Montefiore 2 young
> Israelites her sons, Sir A. Rothschild Sir I.L. Goldsmid Lady G &
> Miss G about to marry Mr Nat. Montefiore. Is it not a pretty name?
> The prétendue pleasant looking clever and well bred—a very plain
> but pleasant Hierosolymite lady to go down to dinner with sister to
> Lady Rothschild . . .
> (To Mrs Brookfield, 1–2 March 1950—LPP, II, 644–5)

In this way Henrietta Montefiore, her sons Joseph and Nathaniel,
Sir Anthony Rothschild (husband of Lady Louisa), Sir Isaac Lyon
Goldsmid, his wife Lady Isabel and their daughter Emma joined
Thackeray's widening circle of Jewish acquaintances, and he finds
a new jocular alternative for the word "Jewish"—"a very plain but
pleasant *Hierosolymite* lady . . ." He notes the clannish interconnec-
tions of this cousinhood: "they are all each others' uncles cousins
wives nieces & so" and finds that they form a peculiar enclave in
fashionable society: "The Christians were in a minority". The
women, it appears, pleased him more than the men ("the women as
I've said to you very nice"); and he is very open about what
attracts him most to their company: "My! what a fine dinner what
plate and candelabra what a deal of good things and sweet meats
especially wonderful" (ibid., p. 645). Thackeray was, and remained, a gourmet, and liked friends who could offer him a good
dinner—and he also enjoyed being lionized. Letters to Jane Brookfield record calls on Lady Louisa Rothschild (e.g. 27 April 1849);
he came to know and like Baron Lionel de Rothschild; and his
growing involvement with the English branch of this famous family
is charted in such notations as: "To-day Shakespeare's birthday at

the Garrick Club, dinner and speech—lunch Madame Lionel Rothschild ball Lady Waldegrave. She gives the finest balls in London and I've never seen one yet . . . Thursday Sir Anthony Rothschild . . . (to Mrs Brookfield, 26–30 April 1850, LPP, II, 352). What is so interesting here is that Thackeray is willingly, indeed eagerly, entering the social orbit of the immediate descendants of his two main Jewish butts in *The National Standard*: Nathan Mayer Rothschild and John Braham. Frances, Countess Waldegrave (1821–1879), the celebrated hostess whose ball Thackeray is about to attend, was John Braham's daughter. In the years to come, he would count it an honour to be in her company. On 9–12 January 1851 he will write to Mrs Brookfield about his attendance at Lady Sandwich's ball in Paris:

> Everybody was there—Thiers Molé and the French Sosiatee: and lots of English. The Castlereaghs . . . Ld Normanby & wife . . . Lady Waldegrave—all sorts of world—if I want the reign of pleasure it is here . . .
>
> (LPP, II, 731)

When he is in Paris again, two years later, his new friend Sarah Baxter receives a similar recital:

> I have just come out of the height of good society, Lady Cowley, Lady Sandwich, Lady Waldegrave, Lord Bath . . .
> (3 November 1853 — LPP, III, 316)

and an entry in a later diary (21 April 1858) reveals that he kept up his social connection with Lady Waldegrave in London too.

In 1849 Thackeray, his mother and a lady of their acquaintance visited the house of Julius Benedict, an important figure in English musical life of the time whose Jewish ancestry was well-known despite his early baptism into the Protestant Church (LPP II, 621); and in these same years the Anglo-Jewish family of Francis Henry Goldsmid swam into Thackeray's benevolent ken because they maintained friendly, neighbourly, hospitable relations with his friend Bryan Waller Procter ("Barry Cornwall"), his wife Anne, and their children (LPP II, 514–15). A discordant note crept in, however, when Thackeray encountered another member of the same family. On 3 November 1849 we find him writing to Mrs. Brookfield: "I saw Albert Goldsmid's weak aquiline beak and purple hair on the pier, and we greeted each other without the least cordiality." (LPP, IV, 422). Count de Rossi, the husband of the celebrated singer Henriette Sontag, fared only a little better— Thackeray found him "a most uninteresting Israelite" (to Mrs Ritchie, 2 February 1849, LPP, II, 499). Worst of all, however, was

Thackeray's view of potential bidders whom he encountered in Gore House when Lady Blessington's effects came under the hammer:

> Snobs looking at the furniture — foul Jews, odious bombazeen women . . . — brutes keeping their hats on in the kind old drawing rooms . . . Ah it was a strange sad picture of Wanaty Fair . . .
> (To Mrs Brookfield, 4 May 1849 — LPP, II, 532)

This "dismal scene" in Gore House recalls the auction in old Sedley's house described in *Vanity Fair*, and looks forward to a similar scene in *The Newcomes*. In all three Jews are conspicuouly present.

The letter to Jane Brookfield in which Thackeray jokingly called Baron James "my friend Jim Rothschild" (1–2 February 1849) was written just after Thackeray had returned from the opera. These were the years of Giacomo Meyerbeer's greatest fame in both Paris and London, and in this as in other matters Thackeray, now a literary lion, followed the fashion. To Mrs. Brookfield he writes, on 1 July 1849: "I wish instead of going to bed you had gone to the Huguenots: it was the finest thing in the world." (LPP, II, 557). On 4 July he goes to the Royal Italian Opera House to hear another Meyerbeer opera, *Le Prophète*, and he is so impressed that he goes to hear the same work again on 13 July (to Mrs. Brookfield, 13 July 1850—LPP, II, 680–1). From all this it appears that while *Robert le Diable* had left him sceptical, *Les Huguenots* and *Le Prophète* roused his enthusiasm in a way that contrasts strikingly with Heine's disenchanted view of Meyerbeer's later works, whose permanent value is still in dispute.

Like many afficionados of ethnic humour, Thackeray liked to hear stories involving Irishmen and Jews, either separately or together. "My brother-in-law", he reports to Anne Procter on 25 July 1848, "has just told me a story about his servant Sweeny, and a white and blue livery he has bought of a Jew for this carrotty-headed Irish rapporee which is wonderful to listen to . . ." (LPP, II, 402). As a gifted mimic of accents Thackeray no doubt relished the brogue in which his Irish brother-in-law could tell such stories—and one may speculate that a gifted story-teller would not miss the chance to caricature the speech of the Jewish clothes-merchant who figured in this tale. In his letters Thackeray also continued to play the phonetic spelling games he had made famous in the Yellowplush Papers, in which the word "Jew" replaced the French word for the deity: "O, mong Jew", he writes to Henry Brookfield on 18 October 1848, when he felt despondent over what he felt to be a decline in his writing-powers after *Vanity Fair*, "but I wish Pendennis were better . . ." (LPP, II, 441–2). We shall see later, however, what long-lasting resentments rankled in him when Samuel Phillips expressed similar doubts about the merits of *Pendennis*.

The period that has just been surveyed, 1848 to 1851, is remarkable for Thackeray's sympathetic portrayal of a Jewish mother and her child, for his implicit recognition of the right of City of London businessmen to elect a Rothschild to represent them in the Commons, and for a parable featuring a wise and dignified Jewish alderman whose name points back to the lawgiver of the Old Testament. Rebecca's conversion to Christianity may be felt, in the circumstances described in *Rebecca and Rowena*, to diminish her stature; but her marriage to Ivanhoe is given sufficient authorial approval to show how far Thackeray is from "racial" anti-Judaism. Gentile characters are increasingly credited with traits which formed part of traditional verbal and graphic caricatures of Jews; not all Jews exhibit recognizable features emphasized by British satirists; who is of Jewish origin and who is not may not always be easy to tell, and therefore becomes a subject for speculation and rumour. Money-lenders, shopkeepers, goldsmiths, pawnbrokers and pedlars appear much as before, but are mostly portrayed without rancour; Jewish sheriff's officers are defended as institutions sanctioned by law whose persons should be inviolate; and when Moses & Son swim into view, they do so in the context of an amused reference to their rhymed advertisements and without any suggestion that their success is based on sweated labour. Disraeli continues to fascinate—he is depicted with amusement but also with a good deal of respect. Persecutions of Jews are cited with abhorrence, in contexts advocating tolerance; and apparently intolerant behaviour attributed to a Jewish family is held up to scorn along with similar behaviour by Gentiles. The importance of the Bible—Old Testament as well as New—in English culture is attested by a plethora of references not quoted in the present survey, though criticism of Old Testament Judaism continues unabated in Thackeray's letters. Letters and diary entries show mostly pleasant contacts with Jews whose wealth had enabled them to enter the charmed circle of fashionable society, but also revulsion at the sight of Jewish agents and bric-à-brac dealers prospecting for bargains before the auction of Lady Blessington's possessions at Gore House. The prevailing tone, however, is set by Alderman Moses's proclamation of the civic peacefulness, the lack of rancour, characteristic of Britain's Jewish citizens even when they felt themselves disadvantaged.

This is the last period in which Thackeray contributed more than an occasional piece to *Punch*, whose genial editor, Mark Lemon, lent his features to *Punch*'s representations of John Bull but was thought, by some who knew him, to have been of Jewish origin. Rival papers, M.H. Spielmann tells us, "would taunt him with his Jewish descent" (*The History of Punch*, p. 255), and R.G.G. Price (*A History of Punch*, London 1957, p. 27) wrongly maintains that Lemon was indeed "of Jewish extraction". Thackeray's relations with Lemon were, on the whole, harmonious; but they did have their ups and downs, with Thackeray complaining, occasionally, of some of the company in which his *Punch* pieces were made to appear, and Lemon telling Mark Hatton that Thackeray was the only man on the *Punch* staff with whom he was not on thoroughly easy terms (IR, II, 325). Neither in his letters, however, nor in his recorded conversations, did Thackeray ever so much as hint that he believed Lemon to be of Jewish descent—a sure sign that he gave no credence to contrary rumours. As the case of Samuel Phillips so clearly shows, this was something Thackeray was always likely to bring up when someone irritated him.

CHAPTER 8

BEYOND THE COUNTING-HOUSE
(1852–1857)

> " . . . I honour and reverence him more now he ain't
> got a shilling in his pocket, than ever I did when we
> thought he was a-rolling in money."
>
> (XIV, 950)

i

In their several ways the historical novel *The History of Henry Esmond* (1852) and the book version of Thackeray's lectures on *The English Humourists of the Eighteenth Century* (1853) paint pictures of eighteenth-century life into which Jews intrude very little. When Lord Castlewood advises young Henry to "keep clear of women", a *belle Juive* comes briefly into view, to be followed by a shuddering reference to Henry's formidable aunt, whom the Viscount endows with an Old Testament cognomen:

> 'Take my counsel, Harry Esmond, and keep clear of women. Since I have had anything to do with the jades, they have given me nothing but disgust. I had a wife at Tangier, with whom, as she couldn't speak a word of my language, you'd have thought I might lead a quiet life. But she tried to poison me, because she was jealous of a Jew girl. There was your aunt, for aunt she is—aunt Jezebel, a pretty life your father led with *her*, and here's my lady . . .'
>
> (XIII, 104)

The novel speaks of "marriage oaths sworn before all the parsons, cardinals, ministers, muftis and rabbins in the world" (XIII, 118), and the lectures maintain that Swift's sermons "have scarcely any Christian characteristics: they might be preached from the steps of a synagogue or the floor of a mosque or the box of a coffee-house almost . . ." (XIII, 490); but in both cases Judaism figures simply as one of the world's religions whose difference from the Christianity the Dean of St. Patrick's should have propagated would be known to Thackeray's readers and audiences. In *Henry Esmond* the call "Old Clo'", which the nineteenth-century associated with itinerant Jewish dealers, becomes a punning nickname for Frank Castlewood's German wife Clotilda, who is older than her husband (XIII, 327), and the expression "a Jewish price"—suggesting an outrageously high one—reflects ingrained prejudices (XIII, 384).

There is no suggestion that Mr Graves, the silversmith accused of asking such a price, is to be thought of as actually being of Jewish origin. Those who are said to take advantage of Dick Steele's monetary insouciance are as likely to be Christians as Jews:

> Mr. Addison was perfectly right in getting the money which was his, and not giving up the amount of his just claim, to be spent by Dick upon champagne and fiddlers, laced clothes, fine furniture, and parasites, Jew and Christian, male and female, who clung to him.
> (XIII, 204).

Henry Esmond, who narrates his own life story, has his social and political prejudices; but where he speaks in his own person instead of reporting the sayings of other characters he never implies that Jews deal less fairly than Christians. This novel is also distinguished by a plethora of well-integrated references to the old Testament, particularly the stories of Jacob, Esau and Rachel which are shown to prefigure many of its relationships and incidents. Prefigurations, comparisons and passing references to Old Testament figures, stories and precepts, along with others to the parables and figures of the New, and often joined to classical allusions, helped Thackeray to communicate easily with an audience whose cultural background resembled his own. They saved him pages of description and explanation while also conjuring up images poetic in themselves and hallowed by the veneration in which the Bible was traditionally held—though he left his readers in no doubt that Scripture could be cited for purposes other than religious uplift, and that Scriptural allusions could chime in with a host of literary references that include Shakespeare, Cervantes, Fielding, the Arabian Nights, and popular writers like Pierce Egan. They all help to determine those shifting perspectives of Esmond's autobiographical narrative to which many commentators have rightly directed attention.

Thackeray was justifiable proud of *Henry Esmond*, which he had planned and executed as a whole instead of placing it before his readers in monthly parts. His dismay was all the greater, therefore, when he found *Esmond* attacked in *The Times* as a work by (it is true) a "distinguished novelist", but one "whose very breath of life is the atmosphere in which he lives, and whose most engaging quality is his own natural style"—a novelist, therefore, whose attempt at writing a historical novel was bound to be "suicidal". The reviewer also objected strongly to the relationship between Esmond and Lady Castlewood, the fostermother who becomes his wife. Like other such contributions this review, published in *The Times* on 22

December 1852, was anonymous; but the grapevine which operated swiftly in the literary coteries of Victorian London informed
Thackeray that the reviewer's name was Samuel Phillips, and that
he was of Jewish origin. This was the same reviewer whom he had
once wrongly suspected of that adverse notice of *The Kickleburys on
the Rhine* which sparked of his satirical essay on "Thunder and
Small Beer"; when he had found out—from Phillips himself—that
the latter was not the author of the offending piece, he had written
him a polite letter apologising for the mistake and expressing the
wish that "our people"—men of letters—would soon learn "to be
civil to one another and conduct their controversies fairly and with
honest courtesy" (*LPP* II, 751–2). The *Esmond* review, however,
was authentic Phillips, like that on *Pendennis* by the same reviewer;
and Thackeray's resentment comes out in a letter to his publisher
George Smith whose "bitter and complex irony" has been noted by
E.F. Harden in the essay from which my text is taken:

> The 'Times', I think, is very good, & contains a great deal of praise
> that I like very much; besides it gives me this satisfaction that the
> critic of 'Esmond' contradicts the critic of 'Pendennis'; and I should
> like some day, to set them nose to nose.
>
> ("The Writing and Publication of *Esmond*", *Studies in the Novel* 13,
> 1981, p. 86)

"Nose to nose", of course, is a not too oblique reference to Phillip's
Jewishness. In this same letter to Smith Thackeray links Phillips's
strictures on *Esmond* with similar ones by John Forster and calls
into question their qualifications as arbiters of social and literary
elegance:

> Its [*sic*] fine to see both 'Times' & 'Examiner' giving hints to me on
> good-breeding; & to think of the natural & inherited elegance of
> those two Professors of politeness. And how can I help my morality,
> with wh. my friend Samuel quarrels?
>
> (*ibid.*)

In later years Thackeray came to focus his resentment on Phillips's
review, "a slasher" which "absolutely stopped" the sales of *Esmond*
(*LPP* IV, 125); and this rankling hostility kept alive anti- Jewish
feelings which we shall see coming unexpectedly to the fore in the
novelist's otherwise more tolerant later years.

ii

The Newcomes. Memoirs of a Most Respectable Family first appeared in
twenty-three monthly parts from October 1853 until August 1855,
and was reissued in two bound volumes published separately in

1854 and 1855. A one-volume edition, shorn of its illustrations and slightly abridged, followed in 1864. Arthur Pendennis, the central figure of the novel that bears his name, turns up in *The Newcomes* as narrator and editor; characters and institutions from Thackeray's previous fictions (Major Pendennis, Becky Sharp, the Diddlesex Insurance Office) make guest appearances; and there are references also to characters from *Oliver Twist*, notably Mr Bumble, Nancy and, of course, Fagin:

> Miss Nancy and Fagin again were summoned before this little company to frighten and delight them. I dare say even Fagin and Miss Nancy failed with the widow, so absorbed was she with the thoughts of the victory she had just won . . .
>
> (XIV, 502)

Like Balzac, Thackeray is creating a common world for his fictional figures, linking them by social contacts or by consanguineity; but through the reading he allows his characters he also admits into that world creations by his greatest English rival. His illustrator, John Leech, goes a step further: he brings Bumble bodily into the lives of the Newcomes, Lady Kew, and Charles Honeyman, by depicting him chasing away a ragged urchin from the fashionable doors of Lady Whittlesea's Chapel from which the congregation is just emerging (XIV, 585).

The novel is set in a nineteenth century which sees "chimneys and smoky atmosphere" invading rural England, mills erected on river banks, dyes and cinders polluting streams, railways increasing mobility, and solid bankers vying for business with less than respectable speculators. It shows a family of Methodists and Dissenters migrating South from obscure origins in a Northern town, making money in trading and banking, moving towards the religious centre and taking its place in a society that may despise its "low" connections (Lord Farintosh says of Clive Newcome that he is "a painter by trade—his uncle is a preacher—his father is a horse-dealer, and his aunt lets out lodgings and cooks the dinner"—XIV, 565) but has to recognize that the possession of a great deal of money confers respectability. Through the mouths of characters who may be thought to have an insight into such matters Thackeray conveys the impression that the French nobility is "incomparably better than that of any except two or three families in England" (XIV, 746); that "except the Gaunts, the Howards, and one or two more, there is scarcely any good blood in England . . . As a rule, nobody is of a good family" (XIV, 685); and that what passes in England for an aristocrat is often just "an

English snob, with a coat of arms bought yesterday, or stolen out of Edmonton, or a pedigree purchased from a peerage maker." (XIV, 746). This is the ironic context within which the speaking name of the *Newcome* family must be seen.

The novel opens with an emblematic capital—drawn by Richard Doyle but suggested and approved by Thackeray—which depicts a group of children gathered around one of their number who has decked himself out in the paraphernalia of the Jewish old-clothes man: three hats piled on top of one another on his head, and a sack slung over his shoulder:

THE NEWCOMES.

CHAPTER I.

THE OVERTURE—AFTER WHICH THE CURTAIN RISES UPON A DRINKING CHORUS.

CROW, who had flown away with a cheese from a dairy window, sate perched on a tree looking down at a great big frog in a pool underneath him. The frog's hideous large eyes were goggling out of his head in a manner which appeared quite ridiculous to the old black-a-moor, who watched the splay-footed slimy wretch with that peculiar grim humour belonging to crows. Not far from the frog a fat ox was browsing ; whilst a few lambs frisked about the meadow, or nibbled the grass and buttercups there.

Who should come in to the farther end of the field but a wolf?

Illustration 1

The symbolic intention is clear: all story-telling may be seen as a kind of "dressing up in old clothes" (XIV, 4), for

> What stories are new? All types of characters march through all fables: tremblers and boasters; victims and bullies; dupes and knaves; long-eared Neddies giving themselves leonine airs; Tartuffes wearing virtuous clothing; lovers and their trials, their blindness, their folly and constancy.
>
> (XIV, 5)

Into the fable proper of *The Newcomes* Jews enter first in the guise of entertainers. John Braham, subject of one of Thackeray's earliest published caricatures, is to be seen and heard in D.F.E. Auber's comic opera *Fra Diavolo*, and the "frolic evening" inaugurated by his performance can be pleasurably ended "by partaking of supper and song at the 'Cave of Harmony'" (XIV, 7). The chief entertainer at this supper club, a predecessor of the Victorian music hall, is "Young Nadab"—a recognizable portrait of the *improvisatore* Sloman whose performances the young Thackeray had so much enjoyed, and who had hurt his feelings by refusing an invitation to dinner. *The Newcomes* gives us a good idea of the kind of turn for which Sloman was famous.

> . . . that mischievous little wag, little Nadab the Improvisatore (who had just come in), began to mimic [Colonel Newcome], feeling his imaginary whiskers, after the manner of the stranger, and flapping about his pocket-handkerchief in the most ludicrous manner.
>
> (XIV, 8).

The manager of the place "checked this ribaldry by sternly looking towards Nadab"; but the Colonel takes it all in good part, and shows himself so delighted by Nadab's performance at a later stage in the entertainment that he invites him to dine with him—an invitation the latter may well have considered cancelled when the Colonel is repelled by Captain Costigan's drunken goings-on and stalks out of the Cave of Harmony in high dudgeon. What happens before Costigan disrupts the party is described as follows:

> And now young Nadab, having been cautioned, commenced one of those surprising feats of improvisation with which he used to charm audiences. He took us all off, and had rhymes pat about all the principal persons in the room: King's pins (which he wore very splendid), Martin's red waistcoat, etc. The Colonel was charmed with each feat, and joined delighted with the chorus—'Ritolderol ritolderol ritolderolderay' (bis). And when, coming to the Colonel himself, he burst out —
>
> 'A military gent I see—And while his face I scan, I think you'll all agree with me—He came from Hindostan. And by his side sits laughing free—A

youth with curly head, I think you'll all agree with me—That he was best
in bed.
Ritolderol,' etc.

—the Colonel laughed immensely at this sally, and clapped his son,
young Clive, on the shoulder. 'Hear what he says of you, sir? Clive,
best be off to bed, my boy—ho, ho! No, no. We know a trick worth
two of that. "We won't go home till morning, till daylight does
appear." Why should we? Why shouldn't my boy have innocent
pleasure? I was allowed none when I was a young chap, and the
severity was nearly the ruin of me. I must go and speak with that
young man—the most astonishing thing I ever heard in my life.
What's his name? Mr. Nadab? Mr. Nadab, sir, you have delighted
me. May I make so free as to ask you to come and dine with me
to-morrow at six? Colonel Newcome, if you please, Nerot's Hotel,
Clifford Street. I am always proud to make the acquaintance of men
of genius, and you are one, or my name is not Newcome!'

'Sir, you do me hhonour,' says Mr. Nadab, pulling up his shirt-
collar, 'and perhaps the day will come when the world will do me
justice,—may I put down your hhonoured name for my book of
poems?'

'Of course, my dear sir,' says the enthusiastic Colonel; 'I'll send
them all over India. Put me down for six copies, and do me the favour
to bring them to-morrow when you come to dinner.'

(XIV, 10–11)

The portrait is friendly, the man's charm and artistry (of a humble
kind, it is true, though the simple Colonel takes him for a genius)
communicate themselves to the reader, and his uncertainties over
the letter "h", like his eagerness to gain subscribers for his poetry,
seem endearingly human (though they also show that he lacks the
easy manners of an English gentleman).

Jews next turn up, *in absentia* as it were, as objects of missionary
zeal: pious Evangelical ladies seek "to awaken the benighted
Hottentot to a sense of the truth, to convert Jews, Turks, Infidels
and Papists . . ." while their money-making husbands "grew weary
of the prayer-meetings . . . yawned over the sufferings of the negroes, and wished the converted Jews at Jericho" (XIV, 20–21). A
few pages later we meet the pious Mrs. Newcome, née Sophia
Alethea Hobson, driving home in a fine carriage drawn by no less
fine bay horses, bathed in the remembrance of "a most interesting
breakfast at Roehampton (where a delightful Hebrew convert had
spoken, oh! so graciously!)" (XIV, 30). The "graciousness" Mrs
Newcome here attributes to the convert no doubt includes the idea
that he has been a recipient of divine grace. The theme of Hebrew
converts will assume importance later in the novel; for the present
Thackeray counterpoints it by showing anti-Jewish mockery directed by a clubman at the respectably Gentile banker Barnes

Newcome, whom the narrator, Pendennis, describes as "a lad with scarce a beard to his chin, that would pursue his bond as rigidly as Shylock." (XIV, 82). When young Barnes Newcome enters Bay's Club, "goodnatured Charley Heavyside" greets him with the words:

> How-dy-do, Barney . . . How are the Three per Cents, you little beggar? I wish you'd do me a bit of stiff; and just tell your father, if I may overdraw my account I'll vote with him—hanged if I don't.'
>
> Barnes orders absinthe-and-water, and drinks: Heavyside resuming his elegant raillery. 'I say, Barney, your name's Barney, and you're a banker. You must be a little Jew, hey? Vell, how mosh vill you to my little pill for?'
>
> 'Do hee-haw in the House of Commons, Heavyside,' says the young man with a languid air. 'That's your place: you're returned for it.' (Captain the Honourable Charles Heavyside is a member of the legislature, and eminent in the House for asinine imitations which delight his own, and confuse the other party.) 'Don't bray here. I hate the shop out of shop hours.'
>
> (XIV, 82)

Barnes's languid air conceals a sharp and brutal mind; in the role of villain of the piece he is rivalled, in *The Newcomes*, only by the "Campaigner", perhaps the most dreadful mother-in-law in English fiction. It is surely significant that of all the Gentile characters in this novel it should be Barnes who is mocked as a crypto-Jew by Heavyside and likened to Shylock by Pendennis. The Gentile Englishman Barnes *is* what Jews were often *said to be* by their enemies. No less significant is the fact that Thackeray now places the exaggerated mockery of Jewish speech in which he had himself indulged in earlier years into the mouth of the crude Heavyside— Pendennis's report of the modes of speech characteristic of the Jewish figures he introduces into his narrative will tend to be more subtle.

Another entertainer, in a higher cultural bracket than "Young Nadab", comes into Colonel Newcome's sights in the eighth chapter of the novel. At one of Mrs Newcome's "At Homes" the Colonel asks the Reverend Charles Honeyman who "the Jew with the beard" might be whom he sees talking to a cavalry officer in a white waistcoat. "The Jew with the beard, as you call him", Honeyman replies, "is Herr von Lungen, the eminent hautboy-player." (XIV, 105). Whether Herr von Lungen is really Jewish may be doubted; it is not so easy to tell Jews from non-Jews, especially when a certain social level has been passed, and when the observer has the naïveté of the Colonel. At Brighton, Pendennis has no difficulty in picking out, from the goodnatured, colourful crowd along the promenade, "young Nathan and young Abrams, already bedizened in jewellery, and rivalling the sun in oriental splendour". (XIV, 117). Going down the scale of entertainment whose top rung is occupied by Herr von Lungen and whose middle is held by Young Nadab we come, once again, to a Jewish prize fighter; a flashback to the 1820s introduces the "fine manly old English custom" called "bruising", which offers young gentlemen eager for such spectacles the chance of going "to Moulsey to see the Slasher punch the Pet's head, or the Negro beat the Jew's nose to a jelly." (XIV, 137). It is no accident, of course, that a nose is mentioned when a Jewish boxer comes into view; a long caricature tradition had made that feature a prime distinguishing mark, and that gives a sadistic relish to the prospect of seeing it pounded to jelly. To counterpoint this brutal picture Pendennis shows us J.J. Ridley, the most important artist-figure in *The Newcomes*, lost in dreams of the gentle Jewish beauty threatened by, but ultimately saved from, rape and murder: Rebecca of York, Thackeray's own favourite fictional heroine. J.J. is rudely awakened from his dream by his parents' threat of apprenticing him to a tailor instead of allowing him to seek training for a career in the visual arts; but we must surely imagine Rebecca to be one of the imperilled maidens rescued by a parfit gentle knight in the illustration subscribed "J.J. in Dreamland" (ill. 1(a)).

The Newcomes, like *Rebecca and Rowena*, was not illustrated by Thackeray himself. The task devolved, once again, as we have seen, upon Richard Doyle, the 'wayward artist" (XIV, 1030) with whom he corresponded, to whom he suggested ideas, and of whose work he seems to have approved, with some reservations, after his initial doubts had been overcome.

It is now time to look at the most important and most complex of all the Jewish characters Thackeray introduced into his novels. The weak, vain, dandified preacher Charles Honeyman has been helped, by Colonel Newcome, to acquire "that elegant and commodious chapel, known as Lady Whittleseas, Denmark Street, Mayfair." (XIV, 38)—a location likely to bring in the kind of fashionable congregation to whom Honeyman's anodyne elegance might appeal. One of his congregants speculates on the value of this living: "A thousand a year, beside the rent of the wine-vaults below the chapel." The congregant's wife thinks he is joking; but he convinces her that he is not. There *are* wine-vaults under the chapel:

'I saw the name, Sherrick and Co.; offices, a green door, and a brass plate. It's better to sit over vaults with wine in them than

Illustration 1(a)

coffins. I wonder whether it's the Sherrick with whom Kew and Jack
Belsize had that ugly row?'

'What ugly row?—don't say ugly row. It is not a nice word to hear
the children use. Go on, my darlings. What was the dispute of Lord
Kew and Mr. Belsize, and this Mr. Sherrick?'

'It was all about pictures, and about horses, and about money, and
about one other subject which enters into every row that I ever heard
of.'

'And what is that, dear?' asks the innocent lady, hanging on her
husband's arm, and quite pleased to have led him to church and
brought him thence. 'And what is it that enters into every row, as you
call it, Charles?'

'A *woman*, my love,' answers the gentleman, behind whom we have been in imagination walking out from Charles Honeyman's church on a Sunday in June. . .

(XIV, 149)

Of course it *is* the same Sherrick; and eventually we meet him, not only as the tenant of the vaults under the Chapel—where he deals in wines and bills of exchange while Christian doctrine is preached overhead—but also as the landlord from whom Colonel Newcome rents his house in Fitzroy Square. A deleted passage, quoted by Leela Kapai in *A Study of William Makepeace Thackeray's 'The Newcomes'* (Diss. Harvard 1975, pp. 98–9) describes the social occasion on which the Fitzroy Square rental agreement was first mooted:

> Mr. Sherrick asked these gentlemen to dinner at St. John's Wood where they met Lord Bareacres. General O—[illegible] of the Portugese service. Philip Barnes Lord Kew's brother all gentlemen of rank and station and Mr. Bogs the celebrated singer T.R.D.L. & T.R.C.Q. & Galpin the delightful tenor. They had a very pleasant evening a great deal of after dinner music though the Colonel steadfastly refused to sing. Clive was not of this dinner. He and his friend Ridley finding better amusement at the play.
> Well, The result of this new acquaintance was that Mr. Sherrick having a large and comodious house no. 120 Fitzroy Sq. to let on very reasonable terms, Colonel Newcome & Binnie agreed to take it between them, & Mr. Sherrick stocked their cellar.

The house in Fitzroy Square had previously been occupied by an unprosperous ladies' school run by one Madame Latour,

> an exile from her native country (Islington was her birthplace, and Grigson her paternal name), and an outlaw at the suit of Samuel Sherrick: that Mr. Sherrick whose wine-vaults undermine Lady Whittlesea's Chapel where the eloquent Honeyman preaches.
> The house is Mr. Sherrick's house. Some say his name is Shadrach, and pretend to have known him as an orange-boy, afterwards as a chorus-singer in the theatres, afterwards as secretary to a great tragedian. I know nothing of these stories. He may or he may not be a partner of Mr. Campion, of Shepherd's Inn: he has a handsome villa, Abbey Road, St. John's Wood, entertains good company, rather loud, of the sporting sort, rides and drives very showy horses, has boxes at the Opera whenever he likes, and free access behind the scenes: is handsome, dark, bright-eyed, with a quantity of jewellery, and a tuft to his chin; sings sweetly sentimental songs after dinner. Who cares a fig what was the religion of Mr. Sherrick's ancestry, or what the occupation of his youth? Mr. Honeyman, a most respectable man surely, introduced Sherrick to the Colonel and Binnie.
> Mr. Sherrick stocked their cellar with some of the wine over which Honeyman preached such lovely sermons. It was not dear; it was not bad when you dealt with Mr. Sherrick for wine alone. Going into his

market with ready money in your hand, as our simple friends did, you were pretty fairly treated by Mr. Sherrick.

(XIV, 212)

The image of Samuel Sherrick "undermining" Lady Whittlesea's Chapel is as grotesquely sinister as that of the fastidious Honeyman preaching lovely sermons "over" Sherrick's wine is grotesquely comic. Doubts about his name, his origins, and the scope of his present interests and activities ("Some say . . . I know nothing of these stories . . . He may or he may not be . . .") underline his status as a mysterious outsider who is brought into "respectable" company by his money and possessions, however obtained. His putative rise from orange seller to partnership in Campions, a firm of solicitors whom we know, from *Pendennis*, to have acted in the main as a money-lending concern, and thence to a handsome villa in a good district, showy horses and a box at the opera, is the Victorian equivalent of a Horatio Alger story; but Pendennis stresses, throughout his account, a penchant towards the theatrical which will play an important part in Sherrick's later activities. His change of name (if change there has been) from Shadrach to Sherrick is well prepared for by the metamorphosis of Miss Grigson of Islington into Madame Latour of Fitzroy Square; professional and social reasons for effecting changes of this kind operated outside as well as inside the Jewish community. There are various pointers to his Jewish origins in Pendennis's description of his outward appearance; but none of these are infallible, and Richard Doyle's visual recreations of Thackeray's verbal hints also stop well short of the Jewish caricatures he indulges in elsewhere. Sherrick's entry into respectable society—as opposed to the "good company, rather loud, of the sporting sort" in which he feels most at home, and the backstairs association due to his money-lending activities—is largely effected through his connection with the fashionable Reverend Honeyman. Doyle glosses this connection by showing Honeyman as a puppet on a string manipulated by Sherrick: the elaboration of an image Thackeray had used when he depicted Miss Swartz as a black doll in Becky's hands (ill. 2).

But the final sentence in the passage about the house in Fitzroy Square (XIV, 212) which has been quoted above is surely not ironic. The progress of the novel will indeed show that Sherrick, the archetypal speculator is, within his lights and the moral parameters of the society in which he has to make his way, a decent and fairminded man—the very opposite of the outwardly more "respectable" but inwardly much less gentlemanly Barnes Newcome.

Fred Bayham, Clive Newcome's eccentric but socially sensitive

Illustration 2

friend, declares himself unable, at one point, to accept any invitation that would bring him into Sherrick's company; but the Colonel and Clive do invite Sherrick, as does Honeyman, who is in love with Sherrick's daughter and forced to buy bad wines from a future father-in-law who is also one of his many creditors. It is at one of Honeyman's social gatherings that we meet him again ("a dark gentleman, with a tuft to his chin, and splendid rings and chains") together with his family.

> The dark gentleman's wife and daughter were the other two ladies invited by our host. The elder was splendidly dressed. Poor Mrs. Mackenzie's simple gimcracks, though she displayed them to the most advantage, and could make an ormolu bracelet go as far as another woman's emerald clasps, were as nothing compared to the other lady's gorgeous jewellery. Her fingers glittered with rings innumerable. The head of her smelling-bottle was as big as her husband's gold snuff-box, and of the same splendid material. Our ladies, it must be confessed, came in a modest cab from Fitzroy Square; these arrived in a splendid little open carriage with white ponies, and harness all over brass, which the lady of the rings drove with a whip that was a parasol. Mrs. Mackenzie, standing at Honeyman's window, with her arm round Rosey's waist, viewed this arrival perhaps with envy. 'My dear Mr. Honeyman, whose are those beautiful horses?' cries Rosey, with enthusiasm.
> The divine says with a faint blush—'It is—ah—it is Mrs. Sherrick and Miss Sherrick who have done me the favour to come to luncheon.'
>
> (XVI, 289)

In this scene Sherrick shows himself a good-natured companion; instead of taking offence at Warrington's condemnation of the quality of the wine he had supplied, he "roared with laughter" (XIV, 289–90) and thus set the whole company at smiling ease. He also appears, however, as a heavy husband:

Mrs. Sherrick was silent during the meal, looking constantly up at her husband, as if alarmed and always in the habit of appealing to that gentleman, who gave her, as I thought, knowing glances and savage winks, which made me augur that he bullied her at home.

(XIV, 290)

In a later scene Sherrick shows himself anxious to repress his wife's naive eagerness to reveal family secrets; but when the reader is taken into Sherrick's home, the atmosphere is one of domestic peace and harmony, contrasting refreshingly with the domestic strife in the household of the wretched Barnes Newcome.

Mrs Sherrick's origins seem even more mysterious than those of her husband. Before her marriage, she had been an opera singer, Elizabeth Folthorpe, who

> after three years of brilliant triumphs at the Scala, the Pergola, the San Carlo, the opera in England, forsook her profession, rejected a hundred suitors, and married Sherrick, who was Mr. Cox's lawyer, who failed, as everybody knows, as manager of Drury Lane.
>
> (XIV, 293)

"Brilliant triumphs", "a hundred suitors"—that sounds very much like Mrs Sherrick's own version of her career. Was Sherrick really a "lawyer", or was he just the money-lending arm of the firm of Campions, Shepherd's Inn? Reliance on gossip and hearsay is one of the means Thackeray uses to convey the atmosphere in which the social life he depicts is carried on. As for "Elizabeth Folthorpe" —was that a stage name, before which Mrs Sherrick had borne another, less English one? Is her taste in conspicuous jewellery theatrical, or is it akin to that of the Jewish tradespeople whom "*Punch's* Commissioner" had observed in Brighton? We do not find out, and Doyle's portrayal of her Roman-nosed profile leaves us in doubt. To the narrator she seems a "very kind and harmless, but vulgar woman" whose gloves are "new, of the best Paris make," and whose daughter's undoubted beauty is slightly aided by cosmetics.

> Miss Sherrick was exceedingly handsome: she kept the fringed curtains of her eyes constantly down; but when she lifted them up towards Clive, who was very attentive to her (the rogue never sees a handsome woman, but to this day he continues the same practice)— when she looked up and smiled, she was indeed a beautiful young creature to behold—with her pale forehead, her thick arched eyebrows, her rounded cheeks, and her full lips slightly shaded,—how shall I mention the word?—slightly pencilled, after the manner of the lips of the French governess, Mademoiselle Lenoir.
>
> (XIV, 290)

Sherrick, who has become enough of a Victorian husband to forbid his wife to appear on the public stage after her marriage, welcomes her performances in private company

> and now with her daughter, who possesses a noble contralto voice, she takes her place royally at the piano, and the two sing so magnificently that everybody in the room, with one single exception [i.e. Mrs Mackenzie, the "Campaigner"], is charmed and delighted . . . Miss Sherrick looks doubly handsome as she sings.

(XIV, 293)

Richard Doyle has drawn the scene for us: Clive Newcome sits at the piano to the right of Miss Sherrick, lost in admiration, while Pendennis stands a little to the left just behind her, with eyeglasses and features that clearly suggest a younger version of Thackeray himself.

Illustration 3

Little Rosie Mackenzie, the Reverend Charles Honeyman, and George Warrington also appear in the foreground; in the background one recognises Mrs Mackenzie and a shadowy, smirking, hirsute figure rather unlike Pendennis's description of Sherrick but probably meant to suggest his presence.

When Sherrick invites his tenant Colonel Newcome and his son Clive to take wine with him at "our place in Regent's park", the Colonel is a little wary. "It was easy to see", he says to Clive, "that the man is not quite a gentleman", immediately adding, however: "I don't care what a man's trade is, Clive. Indeed, who are we [i.e. the *arriviste* Newcome family] to give ourselves airs upon that subject?" He warns Clive to beware of falling "into designing hands", of taking up with "rogues" that "may lead you into mischief", but goes on to say, with justice: "Mr Sherrick has been a good and obliging landlord; and a man who sells wine may certainly give a friend a bottle." (XIV, 294). There is dramatic irony here, of course, for the Colonel does indeed fall into designing hands and brings ruin not only on himself but on many who trusted him; but he will never have cause to number Sherrick among the rogues who bring him down.

Sherrick's invitation to the Newcomes gives the reader a first taste of his mode of speech.

> 'How do you like the house in Fitzroy Square? Anything wanting doing there? I'm a good landlord to a good tenant. Don't care what I spend on my houses. Lose by 'em sometimes. Name a day when you'll come to us; and I'll ask some good fellows to meet you. Your father and Mr. Binnie came once. That was when you were a young chap.—They didn't have a bad evening, I believe. You just come and try us—I can give you as good a glass of wine as most, I think,' and he smiles, perhaps thinking of the champagne which Mr. Warrington had slighted. 'I've ad the close carriage for my wife this evening,' he continues, looking out of window at a very handsome brougham which has just drawn up there. 'That little pair of horses steps prettily together, don't they? Fond of horses? I know you are. See you in the park; and going by our house sometimes. The colonel sits a horse uncommonly well: so do you, Mr. Newcome. I've often said: "Why don't they get off their horses and say Sherrick, we're come for a bit of lunch and a glass of sherry?" Name a day, sir. Mr. P., will you be in it?'

> (XIV, 294)

There is some ingratiating flattery here, as well as some half deprecating self-advertisement, and speech-habits ("I've ad", "Mr. P.") which confirm the Colonel's judgment "not quite a gentleman"; but this racy, lively mode of speaking is equally far from the much too sophisticated, allusive speech of Ikey Solomons Junior and the crude Jew-speak of some of Thackeray's early verbal caricatures. It is a credible version of how a man migh talk who has had little formal education and has made his way up the social ladder by way of the theatre, the fringes of law-practice, sporting associates, and a wine business whose transactions go well beyond the sale of alcoholic beverages.

The extent of these transactions becomes clearer when Charles Honeyman's popularity declines, Lady Whittlesea's Chapel loses its fashionable clientèle, and Honeyman is arrested at the suit of another Jewish character, Moss, who causes him to be transported to the sponging-house in Cursitor Street which seems now to be in the hands of Lazarus, Moss's brother-in-law. Fred Bayham, who had earlier refused to meet Sherrick socially, enlightens Clive about his uncle Honeyman's affairs.

> He has mortgaged his chapel to Sherrick, I suppose you know, who is master of it, and could turn him out any day. I don't think Sherrick is a bad fellow. I think he's a good fellow; I have known him do many a good turn to a chap in misfortune. He wants to get into society: what more natural? That was why you were asked to meet him the other day, and why he asked you to dinner. I hope you had a good one. I wish he'd ask me.
>
> (XIV, 322)

The change is startling. Bayham confirms what the reader comes to appreciate more and more: that Sherrick is a fundamentally decent sort, and that to dine with him is anything but a disgrace; but he also underlines the symbolic force of what is happening here when he goes on to say:

> Then Moss has got Honeyman's bills, and Moss's brother-in-law in Cursitor Street has taken possession of his revered person. He's very welcome. One Jew has the chapel, another Hebrew has the clergy-man. It's singular, ain't it? Sherrick might turn Lady Whittlesea into a synagogue and have the Chief Rabbi into the pulpit, where my uncle the Bishop has given out the text.
>
> (XIV, 322)

"I like the Hebrew, sir", Bayham adds, and goes on to show how Sherrick, far from turning the Chapel into a synagogue, has tried to help Honeyman manage it along Christian lines. It appears, how-ever, that his first efforts in this direction were clumsy; unfamiliar with the complexities of Christian worship and social compatibility in Victorian England he induced Honeyman to engage, "regardless of expense", a choir-master from Hampstead who turned out to be "the lowest of the low church . . . a red-haired dumpy man, who gasped at his h's and spoke with a Lancashire twang"—hardly a man to get on with the fastidious, southern, High Church Honey-man. Predictably, "he and Honeyman used to fight like cat and dog in the vestry: and he drove away a third part of the congregation."

(XIV, 323). Sherrick's first venture into church management has not been a success, and the failure of Lady Whittlesea's Chapel, made universally visible by Honeyman's incarceration in Lazarus's sponging-house, is therefore hastened rather than retarded by Sherrick's interference.

Honeyman's friends and relations combine to bale him out; and as they do so, Pendennis confirms Bayham's estimate of Sherrick's decency but, at the same time, his inability to understand that religion may be something other than a subject for commercial speculation. "The history of Lady Whittlesea's Chapel, Mayfair", Juliet McMaster has rightly said,

> is a study of religion as a commercial venture. Its patron saint seems to have been a society belle; its owner is a Jewish wine-merchant; its foundation is his wineshop; and its preacher is a genteel Chadband, the Reverend Charles Honeyman. Honeyman can synthesize religious fervour and convey it in calculated eloquence which he turns to good account; and his crocodile tears are current coin in certain circles of sentimental ladies. He is a kind of religious gigolo, who can excite them with his cultivated air of spirituality.
>
> (*Thackeray. The Major Novels*, Toronto 1971, p. 159)

A long speech of Sherrick's, reported by Pendennis, adds many subtle touches to earlier accounts of his career and the outlook formed by his contacts with various levels of Victorian society, culminating in his association with the "religious gigolo" Honeyman.

> Into Mr. Sherrick's account we had no need to enter. That gentleman had acted with perfect fairness by Honeyman. He laughingly said to us, 'You don't imagine I would lend that chap a shilling without security? I will give him fifty or a hundred. Here's one of his notes, with What-do-you-call-'em's—that rum fellow Bayham's—name as drawer. A nice pair, ain't they? Pooh! I shall never touch 'em. I lent some money on the shop overhead,' says Sherrick, pointing to the ceiling (we were in his counting-house in the cellar of Lady Whittlesea's Chapel), 'because I thought it was a good speculation. And so it was at first. The people liked Honeyman. All the nobs came to hear him. Now the speculation ain't so good. He's used up. A chap can't be expected to last for ever. When I first engaged Mademoiselle Bravura at my theatre, you couldn't get a place for three weeks together. The next year she didn't draw twenty pounds a week. So it was with Pottle and the regular drama humbug. At first it was all very well. Good business, good houses, our immortal bard, and that sort of game. They engaged the tigers and the French riding people over the way; and there was Pottle bellowing away in my place to the orchestra and the orders. It's all a speculation. I've speculated in about pretty much everything that's going: in theatres, in joint-stock jobs, in building-ground, in bills, in gas and insurance companies,

and in this chapel. Poor old Honeyman! I won't hurt him. About that other chap I put in to do the first business—that red-haired chap, Rawkins—I think I was wrong. I think he injured the property. But I don't know everything, you know. I wasn't bred to know about parsons—quite the reverse. I thought, when I heard Rawkins at Hampstead, he was just the thing. I used to go about, sir, just as I did to the provinces, when I had the theatre—Camberwell, Islington, Kennington, Clapton, all about, and hear the young chaps. Have a glass of sherry; and here's better luck to Honeyman. As for that Colonel, he's a trump, sir! I never see such a man. I have to deal with such a precious lot of rogues, in the City and out of it, among the swells and all, you know, that to see such a fellow refreshes me; and I'd do anything for him. You've made a good thing of that *Pall Mal Gazette!* I tried papers too; but mine didn't do. I don't know why. I tried a Tory one, moderate Liberal, and out-and-out uncompromising Radical. I say, what d'ye think of a religious paper, the *Catechism*, or some such name? Would Honeyman do as editor? I'm afraid it's all up with the poor cove at the chapel.' And I parted with Mr. Sherrick, not a little edified by his talk, and greatly relieved as to Honeyman's fate.

(XIV, 328–9)

The cash nexus, it would seem, is tying the Christian religion to the Golden Calf. What warms us to Sherrick, however, is first, that he articulates frankly what more devious characters would hide; and secondly, that he responds to the simple goodness of Colonel Newcome with affection and respect. There can be little doubt, however, that a sentence like "one Jew has the chapel, another Hebrew has the clergyman" has chilling implications, and throws a strange light on the missionary activities in which earlier generations of the Newcomes had engaged. Is the English church falling into the hands of those whose own Christianity is, to say the least, suspect? Do Honeyman and Sherrick together constitute the sort of threat the Reverend Emilius is seen to pose in Trollope's *The Eustace Diamonds*? Will the "delightful Hebrew convert" who had "spoken, oh! so graciously" at Roehampton (XIV, 30) one day succeed Charles Honeyman? And if so—what sort of Christianity would he be likely to propagate? Does his "graciousness" really imply that Heaven's grace had descended on him, or will he merely have a honeyed tongue, like Honeyman himself?

It is, in fact, Fred Bayham who helps Sherrick to a better understanding of how the fortunes (though not, perhaps, the spiritual integrity) of Lady Whittlesea's Chapel might be improved. He confesses to having had financial dealings with "that miscreant Sherrick" (said humorously, without malice) and has given him advice which worked so well that Sherrick sent Bayham "a few

dozen of wine—without any stamped paper on my part in return."
(XIV, 580). "It chanced", Bayham tells Clive,

> soon after your departure for Italy, that going to his private residence
> respecting a little bill to which a heedless friend had put his hand,
> Sherrick invited me to partake of tea in the bosom of his family. I was
> thirsty—having walked in from Jack Straw's Castle at Hampstead,
> where poor Kitely and I had been taking a chop—and accepted the
> proffered entertainment. The ladies of the family gave us music after
> the domestic muffin—and then, sir, a great idea occurred to me. You
> know how magnificently Miss Sherrick and the mother sing? They
> sang Mozart, sir. Why, I asked of Sherrick, should those ladies who
> sing Mozart to a piano, not sing Handel to an organ?
> '"Dash it, you don't mean a hurdy-gurdy?"
> '"Sherrick," says I, "you are no better than a heathen ignoramus.
> I mean, why shouldn't they sing Handel's Church Music, and
> Church Music in general, in Lady Whittlesea's Chapel? Behind the
> screen up in the organ-loft, what's to prevent 'em? By Jingo! Your
> singing-boys have gone to the Cave of Harmony[1]; you and your choir
> have split—why should not these ladies lead it?" He caught at the
> idea. You never heard the chants more finely given—and they would
> be better still if the congregation would but hold their confounded
> tongues. It was an excellent though a harmless dodge, sir: and drew
> immensely, to speak profanely. They dress the part, sir, to
> admiration—a sort of nunlike costume they come in: Mrs. Sherrick
> has the soul of an artist still—by Jove, sir, when they have once smelt
> the lamps, the love of the trade never leaves 'em. The ladies actually
> practised by moonlight in the Chapel, and came over to Honeyman's
> to an oyster afterwards. The thing took, sir. People began to take
> box—seats, I mean, again:—and Charles Honeyman, easy in his
> mind through your noble father's generosity, perhaps inspired by
> returning good fortune, has been preaching more eloquently than
> ever. He took some lessons of Husler, of the Haymarket, sir. His
> sermons are old, I believe; but so to speak, he has got them up with
> new scenery, dresses, and effects, sir. They have flowers, sir, about
> the buildin'—pious ladies are supposed to provide 'em, but *entre nous*,
> Sherrick contracts for them with Nathan, or some one in Covent
> Garden.
>
> (XIV, 580–1)

The scene in which Bayham gives Sherrick this Machiavellian
advice has been illustrated by Richard Doyle with a delightful
drawing—in a format dictated by Sherrick's long legs—showing
the Sherricks and their lapdog *en famille* (ill. 4).

To make the commercial nature of the whole enterprise complete, Bayham has got up a campaign against Honeyman for

---

[1] These choirboys' transition from chapel to music-hall is an inverse image of
Sherrick's progress from theatre to chapel.

Illustration 4

"Popish practices" which gives him free publicity and sends paying customers with High Church (or Newmanesque) leanings to the returbished Lady Whittlesea's Chapel. "That property", Bayham concludes, with another ominous phrase, "is a paying one to the incumbent, *and to Sherrick over him.*" (XIV, 582)

His curiosity whetted by Bayham's account, Clive goes to see and hear the changes for himself. "He attended punctually on the next Sunday, and in the incumbent's pew, whither the pew woman conducted him, sat Mr. Sherrick in great gravity, with large gold pins, who handed him at the anthem a large, new, gilt hymn-book." (XIV, 582). Thackeray's mastery of satiric characterization by means of ornaments and objects of use is well in evidence here, aided by an equal mastery of prose-rhythms—particularly marked in the succession of stressed monosyllables which describe the most salient objects here, the "large gold pins" and the "large, new, gilt hymn-book." Pendennis finds Sherrick using his uncommonly good voice to support the musical part of a service that Bayham had characterized in theatrical terms—his main function, however, is aptly described as that of an "impresario of the establishment" (XIV, 582–3). He sees to the Chapel's decorations, ranging from "the produce of the market-gardener" to a Flemish painted window over which Sherrick had haggled with a Jewish bric-à-brac dealer in Wardour Street. The window, we are told, gave Honeyman's chapel "a look of the Gothic hall at Rosherville" (XIV, 588). Sherrick even instructs the incumbent of Lady Whittlesea's to cough—for "the women like a consumptive parson, sir!" (XIV, 588). He speaks of the preacher's performance "as a manager would speak of a successful tragedian." "Was it not disrespectful",

Pendennis asks, and answers himself immediately: "Let us pardon Sherrick: he had been in the theatrical way" (XIV, 583). And was not Honeyman in the theatrical way too? This is the spirit in which Sherrick engages and dismisses Honeyman's supporting cast ("That Irishman was no go at all . . . got rid of him—let's see, at Michaelmas"), and sees to its costumes. It was he, no doubt, who helped his wife and daughter select the "nun-like" garments in which they do their operatic warbling of Handel's church music (XIV, 581). After such a performance, Sherrick paces up and down the aisle, rattling coins in his pockets, saying

> Capital house, Mr. Newcome, wasn't it? I counted no less than fourteen nobs. The Princess of Montecontour and her husband, I suppose, that chap with the beard, who yawns so during the sermon. I'm blessed, if I didn't think he'd have yawned his head off. Countess of Kew, and her daughter; Countess of Canterton, and the Honourable Miss Fetlock—no, Lady Fetlock. A Countess's daughter is a lady, I'm dashed if she ain't. Lady Glenlivat and her sons; the most noble the Marquis of Farintosh, and Lord Enry Roy; that makes seven—no, nine—with the Prince and Princess.—Julia, my dear, you came out like a good un to-day. Never heard you in finer voice.
>
> (XIV, 584)

The sermons preached in this setting are Honeyman's responsibility—Sherrick notes audience reactions ("I'm blessed if I didn't think [the Prince de Montecontour would] have yawned his head off") but does not otherwise interfere. What these sermons are like may be gauged from one which Pendennis and Clive heard from Honeyman in 1842, just after the young Duke of Orléans, eldest son of Louis Philippe, had had a fatal accident.

> In the sermon Charles dropped the twang with the surplice, and the priest gave way to the preacher. He preached short stirring discourses on the subjects of the day. It happened that a noble young prince, the hope of a nation, and heir of a royal house, had just then died by a sudden accident. Absalom, the son of David, furnished Honeyman with a parallel. He drew a picture of the two deaths, of the grief of kings, of the fate that is superior to them. It was, indeed, a stirring discourse, and caused thrills through the crowd to whom Charles imparted it. 'Famous, ain't it?' says Sherrick, giving Clive a hand when the rite was over. 'How he's come out, hasn't he? Didn't think he had it in him.'
>
> (XIV, 583)

If Sherrick speaks of Honeyman as if he were an actor, he is justified not only by the fact that he, Sherrick, had been "in the theatrical way", but also by the very nature of Honeyman's performances, with his carefully dressed hair, his effectively arranged

High Church costume, his "odour of millefleur", his voice training by a Haymarket thespian, and his studied attitudes: "When the music began, he stood with head on one side, and two slim fingers on the book as composed as a statue in a mediaeval niche." (XIV, 582) And it does seem that Honeyman's initial performances satisfied some of the expectations which a fashionable congregation brought to a church service.

The story of David and Absalom hardly fits that of Louis Philippe and the Duke of Orléans; but the good-natured Sherrick ladies are greatly moved by it. Mrs Sherrick had lost one of her own children, and is reminded of that loss; and the name of David's son had another personal association for her.

> 'You know his mother was an Absalom,' the good wife continues, pointing to her husband. 'Most respectable diamond merchants in—'
> 'Hold your tongue, Betsy, and leave my poor old mother alone; do now,' says Mr. Sherrick darkly.
>
> (XIV, 587)

That gives us a rare glimpse of Sherrick's antecedents, together with a no less revealing glimpse of his anxiety—understandable in view of the ecclesiastical entrepreneurship in which we see him engaged—to have his Jewish connections brought up as little as possible. But the "great black eyes" with which his daughter, "the handsome Julia", enchants her male acquaintances may well be a heritage from the Absalom side of the family; they help her win, in the end, the hand and heart of the Reverend Honeyman with whom she is touchingly, naively, uncritically in love. Clive Newcome, Arthur Pendennis and others visit the Sherricks, and spend a pleasant evening in their company, enabling Clive to learn something more about his host's money transactions. Sherrick has just announced that he has seen some portraits Clive had "done up" at the exclusive Albany Street Barracks,

> and remarking that his guest looked rather surprised at the idea of his being in such company, Sherrick said, 'What, you think they are too great swells for me? Law bless you, I often go there. I've business with several of 'em; had with Captain Belsize, with the Earl of Kew, who's every inch the gentleman—one of nature's aristocracy, and paid up like a man. The Earl and me has had many dealings together.'
>
> (XIV, 592)

Clive is subsequently engaged to draw a portrait of Julia Sherrick, producing "a famous likeness" with which the Sherricks and Charles Honeyman are delighted. Sherrick is once again shown to be genuinely fond of Colonel Newcome, of whom he speaks in a rough and ready but respectful way—"The best feller—excuse my calling him a feller—but he is, and a good one too." (XIV, 584). It is Colonel Newcome who ultimately prevails on Sherrick to let his daughter marry Honeyman.

Sherrick is presented as a speculator and adventurer, an outside practitioner, a guerrila among English merchants with more straightforward business interests (XIV, 822); but his good nature and fairmindedness come out more and more clearly as the Colonel slides into financial disaster. Sherrick warns Colonel Newcome against the "respectable" merchants and bankers—including the Colonel's own nephew Barnes—who are speeding him on his obstinate way to ruin; and when the Colonel won't listen, he tries to alert others to the dangers ahead, asking them to use their influence to make him disentangle himself, before it is too late, from the Indian bank in which he has invested his own fortune and that of others near and dear to him. The Colonel uses Sherrick to bolster up his credit; and like Honeyman before him, he is forced to take Sherrick's inferior wines in part payment of a loan. To show his obligation, he invites Sherrick and his wife (now described, by Pendennis, as a "very kind and harmless, but vulgar woman") to the entertainments he gives to more and more dubious company:

> Mr Sherrick and his wife appeared at those parties, at which the proprietor of Lady Whittlesea's Chapel made himself perfectly familiar. Sherrick cut jokes with the master of the house, which the latter received with a very grave acquiescence; he ordered the servants about, addressing the butler as 'Old Corkscrew,' and bidding the footman, whom he loved to call by his Christian name, to 'look alive.' He called the Colonel 'Newcome' sometimes, and facetiously speculated upon the degree of relationship subsisting between them now that his daughter was married to Clive's uncle, the Colonel's brother-in-law. Though I dare say Clive did not much relish receiving news of his aunt, Sherrick was sure to bring such intelligence when it reached him; and announced, in due time, the birth of a little cousin at Boggley Wollah, whom the fond parents designed to name 'Thomas Newcome Honeyman.'
>
> (XIV, 897)

> A brisk little chattering attorney, very intimate with Sherrick, with a wife of dubious gentility, was another constant guest. He enlivened the table by his jokes, and recounted choice stories about the aristocracy, with certain members of whom the little man seemed very familiar. He knew to a shilling how much this lord owed—and how much the creditors allowed to that marquis. He had been concerned with such and such a nobleman, who was now in the Queen's Bench. He spoke of their lordships affably and without their titles—calling upon 'Louisa, my dear,' his wife, to testify to the day when Viscount Tagrag dined with them, and Earl Bareacres sent them the pheas-

ants. F. B. [= Fred Bayham], as sombre and downcast as his hosts now seemed to be, informed me demurely that the attorney was a member of one of the most eminent firms in the City—that he had been engaged in procuring the Colonel's parliamentary title for him—and in various important matters appertaining to the B. B. C. [= Bundelcund Banking Company]; but my knowledge of the world and the law was sufficient to make me aware that this gentleman belonged to a well-known firm of money-lending solicitors, and I trembled to see such a person in the home of our good Colonel. Where were the generals and the judges? Where were the fogies and their respectable ladies? Stupid they were, and dull their company; but better a stalled ox in their society, than Mr. Campion's jokes over Mr. Sherrick's wines.

(XIV, 898–9)

Sherrick now seems to belong to "these darkling people" whose association with the Colonel Clive watches with an apprehension that thickens, on occasions, into "a dreadful panic and ghastly terror" (XIV, 897). We learn that Sherrick and the attorney have advised the Colonel to give expensive parties to advertise his financial solvency, and even to stand for parliament to gain additional respectability in the eyes of investors (to say nothing of benefiting from parliamentary immunity). In these circumstances Bayham finds his old suspicions of Sherrick returning:

'Do you know how much that [parliamentary] contest cost?' asks F.B. 'The sum, sir, was awful! and we have ever so much of it to pay. I came up twice from Newcome myself to Campion and Sherrick about it. I betray no secrets—F.B., sir, would die a thousand deaths before he would tell the secrets of his benefactor!—But, Pendennis, you understand a thing or two. You know what o'clock it is, and so does yours truly, F.B., who drinks your health. *I* know the taste of Sherrick's wine well enough. F.B., sir, fears the Greeks and all the gifts they bring. Confound his Amontillado! I had rather drink this honest malt and hops all my life than ever see a drop of his abominable golden sherry. Golden? F.B. believes it *is* golden—and a precious deal dearer than gold too'—and herewith, ringing the bell, my friend asked for a second pint of the just-named and cheaper fluid.'

(XIV, 900)

But Sherrick has nothing at all to do with the Bundelcund Bank, Rummun Loll, and "that complicated, enormous, outrageous swindle" (XIV, 900) which brings the Colonel down. On the contrary, he advises the Colonel, according to his lights, at first how he might possibly ride the storm, and then how to minimize his losses. When the Colonel says "he has been very kind and good, Sherrick" (XIV, 912) the reader can only assent. In the end Sherrick too is a victim—in a neat reversal of the cliché that has the

Jew ruining the improvident aristocrat, Sherrick is ruined by his dealings with an unscrupulous young nobleman. Pendennis recalls:

On one occasion, having business in the City, I there met Mr. Sherrick. Affairs had been going ill with that gentleman—he had been let in terribly, he informed me, by Lord Levant's insolvency—having had large money transactions with his lordship. 'There's none of them so good as old Newcome,' Mr. Sherrick said with a sigh; 'that was a good one—that was an honest man if ever I saw one—with no more guile, and no more idea of business than a baby. Why didn't he take my advice, poor old cove?—he might be comfortable now. Why did he sell away that annuity, Mr. Pendennis? I got it done for him when nobody else perhaps could have got it done for him—for the security ain't worth two-pence if Newcome wasn't an honest man;—but I know he is, and would rather starve and eat the nails off his fingers than not keep to his word, the old trump. And when he came to me, a good two months before the smash of the bank, which I knew it, sir, and saw that it must come—when he came and raised three thousand pounds to meet them d—d electioneering bills, having to pay lawyers, commission, premium, life-insurance—*you* know the whole game, Mr. P.—I as good as went down on my knees to him—I did—at the North and South American Coffee-house, where he was to meet the party about the money, and said, "Colonel, don't raise it—I tell you, let it stand over—let it go in along with the bankruptcy that's a-coming,"—but he wouldn't, sir—he went on like an old Bengal tiger, roaring about his honour; he paid the bills every shilling—infernal long bills they were—and it's my belief that, at this minute, he ain't got fifty pounds a year of his own to spend. I would send him back my commission—I would by Jove—only times is so bad, and that rascal Levant has let me in. It went to my heart to take the old cock's money—but it's gone—that and ever so much more—and Lady Whittlesea's Chapel too, Mr. P. Hang that young Levant.'
(XIV, 916–9)

Sherrick, we now know, has lost even Lady Whittlesea's Chapel, and the Reverend Honeyman and his handsome Julia are going abroad to try their luck elsewhere. Sherrick himself, however, tries to repair his shattered fortunes in England: Pendennis watches him run "across the street after some other capitalist who was entering the Diddlesex Insurance Office" (XIV, 919). An ominous name indeed, more ominous still for those who know, from *The History of Samuel Titmarsh and the Great Hoggarty Diamond*, what ultimately happened to the Diddlesex enterprise. When we catch our last glimpse of Sherrick, we hear him speak once more, with patent sincerity, of his continuing fondness for Colonel Newcome, who now insists—against Sherrick's advice—on handing over every shilling of his military pension to his creditors.

'Ah! what a good man that is,' says Mr. Sherrick with tears in his eyes, 'what a noble fellow, sir! He would die rather than not pay

every farthing over. He'd starve, sir, that he would. The money ain't
mine, sir, or if it was do you think I'd take it from the poor old boy?
No, sir; by Jove I honour and reverence him more now he ain't got a
shilling in his pocket, than ever I did when we thought he was
a-rolling in money.'

(XVI, 950)

The worst that can be said of Sherrick is that he gives the game
away; he openly admits the crass commercialism that rules the
society in which the Newcomes achieve affluence and respectability. Sherrick is not a "gentleman"; but he is credited with finer
instincts and a better heart than many of those whose right to that
title no social arbiter of the Victorian age would have dared to
dispute. That modern readers are likely to see the man he so much
admires as an obstinate old fool who ruins others as well as himself
in no way affects this estimate of Sherrick's good nature.

Sherrick's daughter, who enchants and marries Honeyman, is
treated with a good deal of irony, but her attractiveness is never in
doubt—Clive's painterly exclamations about "that splendid Miss
Sherrick" ("What a head!—a regular Titian!") offer sufficient proof
(XIV, 314). If the handsome Julia seems rather dull, Clive has his
answer ready: "What you call dullness I call repose. Give me a
calm woman, a slow woman—a lazy majestic woman ... Why
shouldn't the Sherrick be stupid, I say? About great beauty there
should always reign a silence ..." (XIV, 315). After painting
Julia's portrait, however, Clive returns to a more vividly exciting
belle Juive, exhibiting a picture of "Sir Brian the Templar carrying
off Rebecca." (XIV, 696). Here the menaced beauty re-exerts her
charm, and the picture is not only praised by the *Pall Mall Gazette*
and other journals, but is actually bought by a dealer.

It is no accident, of course, that Thackeray should list, among
the musical delights which Julia offers to patrons of Lady Whittlesea's under her father's management, compositions by a composer of Jewish origin: Felix Mendelssohn-Bartholdy (XIV, 588).
Another Jewish composer, Meyerbeer, figures in a more worldly
context: his *Robert le Diable* supplies a simile that characterizes the
gossip of two ancient frequenters of the *haute monde*:

Old scandals woke up, old naughtinesses rose out of their graves, and
danced, and smirked, and gibbered again, like those wicked nuns
whom Bertram and Robert le Diable evoke from their sepulchres
while the bassoon performs a diabolical incantation ...

(XIV, 414)

The supporting cast of *The Newcomes* also includes the composer
and pianist Ignaz Moscheles, who was of German-Jewish extrac-

tion and had made his home in London (XIV, 340) as well as a gaggle of tradesmen, some of whom we have already encountered: Sherrick provides wines of variable quality, Messrs. Soap and Isaac sell painting materials, flowers may be bought at Nathans, diamonds are stocked and sold by Samuels and Absalom, miscellaneous goods of all kinds may be had from Moss in Wardour Street, where money is also lent and bills are negotiated. In Soho, dancing is taught by "Professor" Levison, whose daughters greet Clive Newcome "with an admiring ogle from their great black eyes." (XIV, 222). At Levison's you can not only learn to dance the polka, but you can also buy negus at a shilling a glass. (XIV, 266). If you don't pay your debts, you may land in Lazarus's lock up in Cursitor Street, whose proprietor may take a liking to you, as he does to Mr Honeyman. 'If he hadn't a got out', says Mr Lazarus, with an intrusive "a" that is a far subtler indication of such a man's manner of speaking than Thackeray's early caricatures of Jew-speak,

> 'if he hadn't a got out time enough, I'd a let him out for Sunday, and sent one of my men with him to show him the way ome, you know; for when a gentleman behaves as a gentleman to me, I behave as a gentleman to him.'
>
> (XIV, 329)

Once again the portrait of an inconvenient Jew (for who likes to be locked up for debt? Doyle even draws him or one of his "men" as an ogre carrying Honeyman off!) is lightened by a touch of good nature and an appreciation of gentlemanliness in others.

Illustration 5

And if Pendennis fastidiously shrinks from the dirt and grease of the Cursitor Street establishment (XIV, 325), he dwells no less insistently on the "dirty" gloves habitually worn by Mrs. Hobson Newcome (XIV, 92, et passim) and the "scarcity of soap" among the Bohemian youth of Paris (XIV, 273).

No such insalubriousness now mars our view of the English Rothschilds; they appear in the background of *The Newcomes* as exemplars of a safe, self-confident and trustworthy capitalism. Major Pendennis, we learn,

> who kept naturally but a very small account with Hobsons', would walk into the parlour and salute the two magnates who governed there with the ease and gravity of a Rothschild.
>
> (XIV, 53)

All the characters mentioned so far belong to the British scene; when Thackeray's people travel abroad, they encounter Jews again, and meet them on an unaccustomed footing of social equality along with foreign nationals of all kinds. To Lord Kew's parties at Baden "the English were invited, and the Russians were invited; the Spaniards and Italians, Poles, Prussians, and Hebrews; all the motley frequenters of the place, and the warriors in the Duke of Baden's army." (XIV, 444). They also encounter, however the self-same prejudices they know so well from home: "my brother the Abbé", says M. de Florac to Clive when he meets him at Baden, "though the best of Christians, is a Jew upon certain matters . . ." (XIV, 351). As the OED puts it: " . . . a name of opprobrium or reprobation; *spec.* applied to a grasping or extortionate money-lender or usurer, or a trader who drives hard bargains or deals craftily."

"I have seen for the first time the engravings of Newcomes some of wʰ I like very much indeed", Thackeray wrote to Percival Leigh on 12 April 1854. "Why, Doyle ought to bless the day that put the etching needle in his hand. I'm sure he'll be able to do great things with it. He does beautifully and easily what I wanted to do and can't . . . Some of the wood-blox have been awfully mangled in the engravings, but Gandish and young Moss (in 2 places) are admirable." (LPP, III, 362). Here is the first of these illustrations praised by Thackeray; it shows Gandish's school of art in Soho, with the teacher, Gandish, at the back, and in the foreground, from left to right, J.J. Ridley, Clive Newcome, "young Moss", and Bob Grimes (ill. 6).

"Young Moss" may well be identical with the mysterious "Mr. Moss" queried in Thackeray's diary entry of 20 May 1844 (LPP II, 140); into the text of *The Newcomes* he irrupts in the following way:

> There was a young Hebrew amongst the pupils, upon whom his brother-students used playfully to press ham sandwiches, pork sausages, and the like. This young man (who has risen to great wealth subsequently, and was bankrupt only three months since) actually

Illustration 6

bought cocoa-nuts, and sold them at a profit amongst the lads. His pockets were never without pencil-cases, French chalk, garnet brooches, for which he was willing to bargain. He behaved very rudely to Gandish, who seemed to be afraid before him. It was whispered that the Professor was not altogether easy in his circumstances, and that the elder Moss had some mysterious hold over him. Honeyman and Bayham, who once came to see Clive at the studio, seemed each disturbed at beholding young Moss seated there (making a copy of the Marsyas). 'Pa knows both those gents,' he informed Clive afterwards, with a wicked twinkle of his Oriental eyes. 'Step in, Mr. Newcome, any day you are passing down Wardour Street, and see if you don't want anything in our way.' (He pronounced the words in his own way, saying: 'Step id, *Bister* Doocob, ady day idto Vordor Street,' etc.) This young gentleman could get tickets for almost all the theatres, which he gave or sold, and gave splendid accounts at Gandish's of the brilliant masquerades. Clive was greatly diverted at beholding Mr. Moss at one of these entertainments, dressed in a scarlet coat and top-boots, and calling out, 'Yoicks! Hark forward!' fitfully to another Orientalist, his younger brother, attired like a midshipman. Once Clive bought a half-dozen of theatre tickets from Mr. Moss, which he distributed to the young fellows of the studio. But, when this nice young man tried further to tempt him on the next day, 'Mr. Moss,' Clive said to him with much dignity, 'I am very much obliged to you for your offer, but when I go to the play, I prefer paying at the doors.'

(XIV, 228)

As this passage shows, Moss is never a solo figure; behind him we see his father, the money-lender and dealer in general goods who supplied the Flemish painted window for Honeyman's chapel and some of the money that helps tide Gandish over temporary embarrassments, and "another Orientalist, his younger brother." The incongruity of seeing high-spirited young "Hebrews" or "Orientalists" impersonate English hunting-squires or sailors underline Pendennis's sense of their exotic difference from his own kind; and young Moss's adenoidal utterances represent yet another attempt at caricaturing "Jewish" speech. Clive's visitors are "disturbed" at seeing this wheeler-dealer figure, "with a wicked twinkle in his Oriental eyes", at a London art school; and the fact that the picture he is copying depicts someone being *flayed* will hardly have served to make this vision less disturbing. One notices again the ragging (with pork sausages and the like) to which fellow students subjected such young men, who had to develop a fairly tough hide to avoid constant hurt to their feelings; Moss's insolence to Gandish may be seen as a kind of compensation phenomenon. Noticeable too is the stress on the young man's aptitude for trade in anything from coconuts to theatre tickets—an aptitude that runs in the family and for which there are clear historical and social reasons; and the ironic juxtaposition of the parenthetical remark that he later rose to great wealth with the announcement of his recent bankruptcy. The inference that the bankruptcy is as fraudulent as the fires in "The Great Hoggarty Diamond" is hard to resist.

The ragging of young Moss at Gandish's is taken up again a few pages later when Pendennis describes the caricatures these art students make of one another: crossing eyes, lengthening noses, and so on. "Little Bobby Moss" (only now do we learn young Moss's first name), "the young Hebrew artist from Wardour Street, was delineated with three hats and an old clothes bag." (XIV, 231). But the ragging is good-natured, or at least meant to be so, and Clive Newcome's cameraderie with Bobby Moss brings him together with other young Jews, to the marked displeasure of his cousin Barnes.

'If that young man goes on as charmingly as he has begun,' Clive's cousin, Barnes Newcome, said of his kinsman, 'he will be a paragon.

I saw him last night at Vauxhall in company with young Moss, whose father does bills and keeps the bric-à-brac shop in Wardour Street. Two or three other gentlemen, probably young old-clothes-men, who had concluded for the day the labours of the bag, joined Mr. Newcome and his friend, and they partook of rack-punch in an arbour. He is a delightful youth, cousin Clive, and I feel sure he is about to be an honour to our family.'

(XIV, 232)

To place this ironic speech into its proper context we have to remember that Barnes is the most loathsome character in the whole book, and that we have heard him ragged by fellow-members of his club for pursuing, along with his family, the sort of profits derived from manipulation of money and credit which was associated with Jews in so many English minds. No wonder that he wants to dissociate himself and the significantly named *Newcome* family from those who make a living by "doing bills" and keeping a shop.

When young Moss next appears in *The Newcomes*, it is as "a Mosaic youth, profusely jewelled, and scented at once with tobacco and Eau de Cologne", to whom Clive cedes the stall ticket he had bought for a benefit evening at Drury Lane after he had been disillusioned by the difference between the principal dancer's radiant appearance on the stage and her far less attractive appearance in private life. "'Paid five pounds to see that woman?'", young Moss had said; "'I could have took you behind the scenes'" (or rather, "'beide the seeds'") "'and showed her to you for dothing.'" (XIV, 248). It is at this stage that the reader encounters Doyle's second drawing of young Moss of which Thackeray had so emphatically approved (ill. 7).

Now Thackeray introduces a somewhat ominous passage:

Illustration 7

Did he take Clive behind the scenes? Over this part of the young gentleman's life, without implying the least harm to him—for have not others been behind the scenes; and can there be any more dreary object than those whitened and raddled old women who shudder at the slips?—over this stage of Clive Newcome's life we may surely drop the curtain.

(XIV, 248)

The narrator's protestations serve to strengthen rather than to weaken his strong hint of the sexual temptations into which Moss is leading young Clive—a hint reinforced by the following chapter, in which we find Clive engaged "with dice, the turf, *or worse amusements*" (XIV, 256—my italics), and by a later account of goings-on behind the scenes of the Paris Opera, where "Phryne and Aspasie" hold brief sway (XIV, 407). Did young Moss procure joys of the flesh for his customers as well as ornaments for their person and instruments which might make that person more attractive to the opposite sex? The capital illustration which begins Chapter XX shows Clive fingering his newly-grown whiskers; he was very proud of these, we are told, but he would have sacrificed them for Ethel Newcome's sake had he been truly in love with her. "Had he not already bought on credit the necessary implements in a fine dressing-case, from young Moss?" (XIV, 247).

Clive's whiskers were, in fact, to have played a more prominent part in the novel than appears from the finished version. Pendennis was to have observed that Clive had shaved them off, and Clive was to have explained that he had done so, in part, because he had observed how odd such excrescences looked on others.

'Do you know old Gandish called upon me three days ago with a pair of mustachios, and yesterday I saw a little fellow by the name of Moss swaggering about Brighton pier with another pair? You remember Moss?'
(E.F. Harden, *The Emergence of Thackeray's Serial Fiction*, London 1979, p. 109)

This scene was deleted before publication; in the finished novel Moss never appears in the splendour of his "mustachios", nor do readers ever have an extended chance to watch him disport himself at Brighton.

The newly elegant and persistently clean-shaven Bobby Moss quits Gandish's art school to join his father's business; he still visits Clive, seeking to make use of Clive's society connections for his business interests, but the old cameraderie has gone. Doyle shows us Moss studying the invitations displayed in Clive's room; and Thackeray has Pendennis present two conversation scenes which

Illustration 8

afford an impression of Moss's sharp trading and of behind-the-scenes dealings with the English gentry and aristocracy.

Mr. Clive, as we have said, had now begun to make acquaintances of his own; and the chimney-glass in his study was decorated with such a number of cards of invitation, as made his ex-fellow-student of Gandish's, young Moss, when admitted into that sanctum, stare with respectful astonishment. 'Lady Bary Rowe at obe,' the young Hebrew read out; 'Lady Baughton at obe, dadsig! By eyes! what a tip-top swell you're a gettid to be, Newcome! I guess this is a different sort of business to the hops at old Levison's, where you first learned the polka; and where we had to pay a shilling a glass for negus!'

'*We* had to pay! *You* never paid anything, Moss,' cries Clive, laughing; and indeed the negus imbibed by Mr. Moss did not cost that prudent young fellow a penny.

'Well, well; I suppose at these swell parties you 'ave as much champade as ever you like,' continues Moss. 'Lady Kicklebury at obe—small early party. Why, I declare you know the whole peerage! I say, if any of these swells want a little tip-top lace, a real bargain, or diamonds, you know, you might put in a word for us, and do us a good turn.'

'Give me some of your cards,' says Clive; 'I can distribute them about at the balls I go to. But you must treat my friends better than you serve me. Those cigars which you sent me were abominable, Moss; the groom in the stable won't smoke them.'

'What a regular swell that Newcome has become!' says Mr. Moss to an old companion, another of Clive's fellow-students: 'I saw him riding in the Park with the Earl of Kew, and Captain Belsize, and a whole lot of 'em—*I* know 'em all—and he'd hardly nod to me. I'll

have a horse next Sunday, and *then* I'll see whether he'll cut me or
not. Confound his airs! For all he's such a count, I know he's got an
aunt who lets lodgings at Brighton, and an uncle who'll be preaching
in the Bench if he don't keep a precious good look-out.'

'Newcome is not a bit of a count,' answers Moss's companion,
indignantly. 'He don't care a straw whether a fellow's poor or rich;
and he comes up to my room just as willingly as he would go to a
duke's. He is always trying to do a friend a good turn. He draws the
figure capitally: he *looks* proud, but he isn't, and is the best–natured
fellow I ever saw.'

'He ain't been in our place this eighteen months,' says Mr. Moss:
'I know that.'

'Because when he came you were always screwing him with some
bargain or other,' cried the intrepid Hicks, Mr. Moss's companion
for the moment. 'He said he couldn't afford to know you: you never
let him out of your house without a pin, or a box of eau-de-cologne, or
a bundle of cigars. And when you cut the arts for the shop, how were
you and Newcome to go on together, I should like to know?'

'I know a relative of his who comes to our 'ouse every three
months, to renew a little bill,' says Mr. Moss, with a grin: 'and I
know this, if I go to the Earl of Kew in the Albany, or the Honourable
Captain Belsize, Knightsbridge Barracks, *they* let me in soon enough.
I'm told his father ain't got much money.'

'How the deuce should I know? or what do I care?' cries the young
artist, stamping the heel of his blucher on the pavement. 'When I was
sick in that confounded Clipstone Street, I know the Colonel came to
see me, and Newcome too, day after day, and night after night. And
when I was getting well, they sent me wine and jelly, and all sorts of
jolly things. I should like to know how often *you* came to see me,
Moss, and what you did for a fellow?'

'Well, I kep away because I thought you wouldn't like to be
reminded of that two pound three you owe me, Hicks: that's why I
kep away,' says Mr. Moss, who, I dare say, was good-natured too.
And when young Moss appeared at the billiard-room that night, it
was evident that Hicks had told the story; for the Wardour Street
youth was saluted with a roar of queries, 'How about that two pound
three that Hicks owes you?'

(XIV, 266–8)

For all Moss's reminders about the parvenu status of the Newcomes themselves, and Hicks's defence of Clive's democratic instincts, the social gulf between the "Wardour Street youth" and his
erstwhile fellow student has grown all but impassable. Young Moss
can hope for customers from his connection with Clive, but hardly
for friendship or social intercourse on an equal footing. The "relation" of Clive's with whom Old Moss is said to have dealings and
who may soon be "preaching in the Bench", is Charles Honeyman,
who complains that he has paid Moss "thousands" in a transaction
involving, originally, £ 120 (XIV, 326); Honeyman is hardly a

reliable source in such matters, but the original loan is real enough, and Clive makes one of a party that resolves Honeyman's difficulties.

> The tradesmen of Honeyman's body were appeased; and as for Mr. Moss, when he found that the curate had no effects, and must go before the Insolvent Court, unless Moss chose to take the composition which we were empowered to offer him, he too was brought to hear reason, and parted with the stamped paper on which was poor Honeyman's signature. Our negotiation had like to have come to an end by Clive's untimely indignation, who offered at one stage of the proceedings to pitch young Moss out of window: but nothing came of this most ungentlebadlike beayviour on Noocob's part, further than remonstrance and delay in the proceedings: and Honeyman preached a lovely sermon at Lady Whittlesea's the very next Sunday.
>
> (XIV, 329)

There is a sting in Pendennis's description of the Jewish sheriff's officers and the creditors at whose suit they acted as "tradesmen of Honeyman's body" and also, of course, in his renewed mockery of young Moss's adenoidal speech in which the word "gentleman" receives its most significant distortion. Moss has now moved wholly into his father's world, and the estrangement between him and Clive is therefore complete. It is left to Sherrick, who has sympathies with both sides and a better understanding of what is gentlemanly than young Moss, to sum up the deterioration in the latter's character and practices.

> 'He's such a screw, that chap, that he'll over-reach himself, mark my words. At least, he'll never die rich. Did you ever hear of *me* screwing? No, I spend my money like a man.'
>
> (XIV, 588)

But this too has its dramatic irony: for the "over-reaching" Moss "has risen to great wealth" by the time Pendennis sets down his reminiscences (XIV, 227) while the more decent and generous Sherrick is all but ruined. Will privileges of wealth supersede privileges of rank in this instance too? Will the Moss family ultimately join the English gentry in the way the Newcome family has done? We do not know; but when we last encounter Bobby Moss it is as a "patron" of his erstwhile fellow student. In dire financial straits after the collapse of the Bundelcund Bank, Clive hawks his drawings around London, "tried picture dealers—pawnbrokers—Jews—Moss, whom you [= Pendennis] may remember at Gandish's and who gave me, for forty-two drawings, £18" (XIV, 930). Hardly a generous payment; but no-one else offered anything at all, and Clive uses Moss's money "to pay the doctor and bury our last poor little dead baby." (XIV, 930).

Clive Newcome's dealings with young Moss provide the reader with some idea of the stock carried by the Wardour Street emporium owned by Moss's parents.

> ... artful young Moss, whose parents dealt in pictures, furniture, gimcracks, and jewellery, victimized Clive sadly with rings and chains, shirt-studs and flaming shirt-pins, and such vanities, which the poor young rogue locked up in his desk generally, only venturing to wear them when he was out of his father's sight or of Mr. Binnie's . . .
>
> (XIV, 231)

In a letter to Pendennis Clive speaks disparagingly of the "confounded rings and gimcracks" which Moss's salesmanship foisted on him. (XIV, 275) Sherrick's purchase of a Flemish window for Lady Whittlesea's shows that more recherché objects could be bought at the same emporium; and the reader will suspect that Sir Francis Clavering's "old family portraits from Wardour Street" (*Pendennis*, XII, 471) had also passed through the hands of the Moss family.

Pendennis's least friendly portrayal of Jews, in *The Newcomes*, is directly inspired by Thackeray's encounter, at the forced sale of Lady Blessington's effects, with Jewish customers who kept their hats on while walking about the drawing rooms of Gore House. The scene which describes the auctioning off of Colonel Newcome's possessions, after the collapse of the Bundelcund Bank, embodies some of Thackeray's distaste at such forced dispersal of treasured possessions.

> Bills are up in the fine new house. Swarms of Hebrew gentlemen with their hats on are walking about the drawing-rooms, peering into the bed-rooms, weighing and poising the poor old silver cocoa-nut tree, eyeing the plate and crystal, thumbing the damast of the curtains, and inspecting ottomans, mirrors, and a hundred articles of splendid trumpery. There is Rosey's boudoir which her father-in-law loved to ornament—there is Clive's studio with a hundred sketches—there is the Colonel's bare room at the top of the house, with his little iron bedstead and ship's drawers, and a camel trunk or two which have accompanied him on many an Indian march, and his old regulation sword, and that one which the native officers of his regiment gave him when he bade them farewell. I can fancy the brokers' faces as they look over this camp wardrobe, and that the uniforms will not fetch much in Holywell Street. There is the old one still, and that new one which he ordered and wore when poor little Rosey was presented at court. I had not the heart to examine their plunder, and go amongst those wreckers. F.B. used to attend the sale regularly, and report its proceedings to us with eyes full of tears. 'A fellow laughed at me,'

says F. B., 'because when I came into the dear old drawing-room I took my hat off. I told him that if he dared say another word I would knock him down.' I think F. B. may be pardoned in this instance for emulating the office of auctioneer.

(XIV, 903)

The ironic "gentlemen" is contradicted by the dehumanizing "swarms"—a dehumanization carried further by Richard Doyle when he makes the initial A of the following chapter into a branch that carries a Jewish vulture—translating into visual terms what Becky Sharp had verbalized after the auction-scene in *Vanity Fair*.

Illustration 9

"The poor old silver cocoa-nut tree" weighed and poised by these Jewish agents and dealer is what Barbara Hardy has rightly called the "Golden Bowl" of *The Newcomes* (*The Exposure of Luxury*, London 1972, p. 153): a complex symbol of Victorian commerce and enterprise, presented to Colonel Newcome in the heyday of his fortunes, fulfilling its function of bearing candles and pickles on his dinner table, around which he assembles less and less respectable guests as his fortunes dwindle. In the auction scene it joins the Colonel's other personal effects in sinking to the status of a mere commodity, labelled "Lot 70" in Doyle's illustration, where it is surrounded by a crowd of potential customers that includes only one recognizably Gentile face (ill. 10).

These "wreckers" in search of "plunder", whose faces Pendennis imagines as they speculate that the Colonel's uniforms "will not fetch much in Holywell Street", appear to show some respect for the tokens of his valour:

> When the sale of Colonel Newcome's effects took place, a friend of the family bought in for a few shillings those two swords which had hung, as we have said, in the good man's chamber, and for which no single broker present had the heart to bid.

(XIV, 915)

Illustration 10

Pendennis's very mode of expression here, imputing a human heart to brokers whom Doyle had shown as birds of prey, counteracts some of the dehumanizing suggestion of the earlier text and drawing, which have in any case to be seen in the context of the novel's larger patterns of imagery.

The predatory theme is announced at the very beginning of the novel in the Overture which presents a mixture of animals from familiar animal fables, all envying one another and jostling for position. Animal imagery persists throughout the text, reinforcing through metaphor the fierceness of the struggle for advantage exposed in narrative action and commentary. Lady Kew is seen as an eagle, hunting down prey for her granddaughter, while Mrs. Mackenzie appears as a boa constrictor ready to swallow her own child. With her mother, Rosey is like a "bird before a boa-constrictor, doomed—fluttering, fascinated" (ch. 73). As for Clara Pulleyn, she is a "poor little fish" whose only "duty" is to be devoured (ch. 28). Such cannibalistic motifs sharpen the predatory theme, identifying the sinister basis for so many of the relationships in this world. The note is sounded in different tones, struck lightly in Ethel's casual remark that "Barnes was ready to kill me and eat me" (ch. 28) and more heavily in the repellent image of society women as "ghouls feasting on the fresh corpse of a reputation" (ch. 31).

(Ina Ferris, *William Makepeace Thackeray*, Boston 1983, pp. 86–7)

In this picture of a predatory society the Jewish snappers-up of bargains at a forced auction form only one tiny item, whose capacity to give offence lies more in Doyle's illustrations than in Thackeray's text.

The most ubiquitous of the many images describing the predatory society of *The Newcomes* is that of the marriage market, against which Ethel protests indirectly when she pins a "Sold" label onto her dress and directly when she speaks of the "humiliation" involved in being "bandied about from bidder to bidder, and offered for sale to a gentleman who will not buy me" (XIV, 504). The multitude of references to this market, in which Jews are involved along with their Gentile neighbours (though Sherrick's daughter, interestingly enough, manages to marry for love), finds its climax in Pendennis's exclamation after the disastrous end of Barnes Newcome's marriage:

> O Hymen Hymenæe! The bishops, beadles, clergy, pew-openers, and other officers of the temple dedicated to Heaven under the invocation of St. George, will officiate in the same place at scores and scores more of such marriages: and St. George of England may behold virgin after virgin offered up to the devouring monster, Mammon (with many most respectable female dragons looking on)—may see virgin after virgin given away, just as in the Soldan of Babylon's time, but with never a champion to come to the rescue!
>
> (XIV, 776)

Here classical allusions and images from the heroic folklore of Christian England knit seamlessly with images of Mammon worship that derive, of course, from Matthew 6, 24 and Luke 16, 9–11.

Jews had first appeared in *The Newcomes*, where they occupy a more central and prominent place than in any of Thackeray's previous novels, as potential objects of conversion, or as "delightful Hebrew convert[s]." Clive Newcome is as unmoved, however, as his Protestant ancestors would have been, by a miracle of conversion to which his attention is drawn during his travels in Italy. He writes to Pendennis:

> 'I wish it were not so,' writes Clive, in one of the letters wherein he used to pour his full heart out in those days. 'I see these people at

their devotions, and envy them their rapture. A friend, who belongs
to the old religion, took me, last week, into a church where the Virgin
lately appeared in person to a Jewish gentleman, flashed down upon
him from heaven in light and splendour celestial, and, of course,
straightway converted him. My friend bade me look at the picture,
and, kneeling down beside me, I know prayed with all his honest
heart that the truth might shine down upon me too; but I saw no
glimpse of heaven at all, I saw but a poor picture, an altar with
blinking candles, a church hung with tawdry strips of red and white
calico.'

(XIV, 464)

Yet Clive respects the simple religiosity of his Catholic friend far
more than the theatrical uplift the congregants of Lady Whittlesea's Chapel derive from the partnership between Honeyman and
Sherrick. Honeyman's sermon on David and Absalom (XIV, 583)
may move the simple Mrs Sherrick; but it is so presented by
Pendennis that the reader cannot but feel it to be ultimately
absurd. David's moving expression of grief for Absalom may indeed offer a parallel to that felt at the death of "a noble young
prince, the hope of a nation, and heir of a royal house"; but the
political background is so utterly different, suggestions of rebellion
and internecine warfare are so alien to anything Honeyman may be
thought to intend, and the circumstances of Absalom's death are so
remote from the accidental death the sermonizer has in mind, that
one's final impression must be one of incongruity.

The world of *The Newcomes* is once again, full of Bibles: not only
in Honeyman's chapel, and the chapel of Grey Friars School, but
also in the various homes into which the reader is introduced. It
figures as the "gilt book" from which Sir Brian Newcome reads
"for three or four minutes in a measured cadence" to the assembled
household at the chiming of the eight o' clock bell each morning
(XIV, 185); as a treasured old tome into which good old Sarah
Mason puts her spectacles when her reading is interrupted (XIV,
196) and which is replaced, in the course of the novel, by a
"splendid Bible with the large print, and the affectionate inscription, from Thomas Newcome to his dearest old friend" (XIV, 197);
as a book in which Pendennis seeks out consolatory texts (XIV,
959); and as one which occupies a prominent place in Colonel
Newcome's humble room when he becomes a Poor Brother of the
Grey Friars Foundation (XIV, 983, 984). Throughout the novel
Thackeray returns, again and again, to his favourite New Testament passages: the figure of Jesus, "whose earthly life was divinely
sad and tender" (XIV, 961), is accompanied by the Good Samaritan and the Man Fallen among Thieves, the Prodigal Son, the Wise

and Foolish Virgins, Dives and Lazarus, the sinner whose transgressions were forgiven *quia multum amavit* (XIV, 1006), and the lilies of the field arrayed like Solomon in his glory. When Colonel Newcome's judgment of men becomes clouded by rage and resentment, the narrator appeals to a higher authority:

> the Judge who sees not the outward acts merely, but their causes, and views not the wrong alone, but the temptations, struggles ignorance of erring creatures, we know has a different code to ours—to ours, who fall upon the fallen, who fawn upon the prosperous so, who administer our praises and punishments so prematurely, who now strike so hard, and, anon, spare so shamelessly.
>
> (XIV, 807)

This fits the Old Testament as well as the New; and the Old Testament is in fact well to the fore, in *The Newcomes*, as a source of moral imperatives—through repeated allusions to the Decalogue —and as a means of characterizing a mental set. The pious dissenters who erect their "serious paradise" at Clapham are doubly characterized when the narrator tells us that "in Egypt itself there were not more savoury fleshpots than at Clapham" (XIV, 19, 23); and Colonel Newcome's simple piety expresses itself in appropriate Biblical quotations. "Scarsdale is gone now, sir'', we hear him say, "and is where the wicked cease from troubling and the weary are at rest . . ." (XIV, 953–cf. Job 3, 17); while Mme d'Ivry's all-too-romantic imagination transforms Pentateuch narratives into operatic plots:

> She describes, as if she had herself witnessed the catastrophe, the passage of the Red Sea: and, as if there were no doubt of the transaction, an unhappy love-affair between Pharaoh's eldest son and Moses's daughter. At Cairo, *à propos* of Joseph's granaries, she enters into a furious tirade against Putiphar, whom she paints as an old savage, suspicious and a tyrant.
>
> (XIV, 405–6)

In a novel whose central figure is a young painter it will not be surprising to find many references to the use of Biblical subjects in the pictorial arts. Clive claims to see in the impeccably Gentile Ethel Newcome a possible model for the *belles Juives* or *Juives fatales* of the Old and New Testaments (adding a dash of Diana for good measure):

> By Jove, how handsome she is! How she turns with her long neck, and looks at you from under those black eyebrows! If I painted her hair, I think I should paint it almost blue, and then glaze over with lake. It *is* blue. And how finely her head is joined on to her shoulders!'—And he waves in the air an imaginary line with his

cigar. 'She would do for Judith, wouldn't she? Or how grand she would look as Herodias's daughter sweeping down a stair—in a great dress of cloth-of-gold like Paul Veronese—holding a charger before her with white arms, you know—with the muscles accented like that glorious Diana at Paris—a savage smile on her face and a ghastly solemn gory head on the dish—I see the picture, sir, I see the picture!' and he fell to curling his mustachios—just like his brave old father.

(XIV, 314)

And the decline of beauty becomes painfully obvious when the woman who had once been a favourite model for Venus dwindles into one for the Witch of Endor (XIV, 469).

Thackeray and his narrator constantly find prefigurations, ironic contrasts, parallels, and emotionally charged expressions in the Old Testament. Honeyman's surplice becomes an "ephod" (XIV, 56); "if he had lived to be as old as Jahaleel [Pendennis means "Jehalelel", no doubt, 2 Chronicles 29, 12] a boy could still have cheated him" (XIV, 327); a "stalled ox" in the company of the most stupid of English fogeys is found preferable to "Mr. Campion's jokes over Mr. Sherrick's wines" (XIV, 899–cf. Proverbs 15, 17). The words of Ecclesiastes are as prominent and applicable here as they are in so many of Thackeray's writings: "Vanitas vanitatum" (XIV, 594), "nothing new under the sun" (XIV, 594). Genesis illuminates problems and conditions fundamental to all human life: "With the very first page of the human story do not love, and lies too, begin?" (XIV, 5); and again:

Time was when the Colonel himself would have viewed his kinsman more charitably, but fate and circumstance had angered that originally friendly and gentle disposition; hate and suspicion had mastered him, and if it cannot be said that his new life had changed him, at least it had brought out faults for which there had hitherto been no occasion, and qualities latent before. Do we know ourselves, or what good or evil circumstance may bring from us? Did Cain know, as he and his younger brother played round their mother's knee, that the little hand which caressed Abel should one day grow larger, and seize a brand to slay him? Thrice fortunate he, to whom circumstance is made easy: whom fate visits with gentle trial, and kindly Heaven keeps out of temptation.

(XIV, 836)

What is so interesting here is that the illumination is mutual: the reference to Cain helps us to understand the change in Colonel Newcome, but what happens to the Colonel also helps us towards a new understanding of the Biblical story of Cain and Abel. In *The Newcomes* Thackeray spells out more clearly than ever before one of the most important ways in which a nineteenth-century novelist might use Biblical narrative:

> No people are so ready to give a man a bad name as his own kinsfolk; and having made him that present, they are ever most unwilling to take it back again. If they give him nothing else in the days of his difficulty, he may be sure of their pity, and that he is held up as an example to his young cousins to avoid. If he loses his money they call him poor fellow, and point morals out of him. If he falls among thieves, the respectable Pharisees of his race turn their heads aside and leave him penniless and bleeding. They clap him on the back kindly enough when he returns, after shipwreck, with money in his pocket. How naturally Joseph's brothers made salaams to him, and admired him, and did him honour, when they found the poor outcast a prime minister, and worth ever so much money! Surely human nature is not much altered since the days of those primeval Jews. We would not thrust brother Joseph down a well and sell him bodily, but—but if he has scrambled out of a well of his own digging, and got out of his early bondage into renown and credit, at least we applaud him and respect him, and are proud of Joseph as a member of the family.
>
> (XIV, 62)

That illustrates what might be called the "straight" or "parallel" use of Biblical tales: "those primeval Jews" are not strange exotics but close kin to men and women of other climes and other times, exemplification of human nature and human actions that may be observed in modern Britain as easily as in ancient Palestine, once allowances have been made for outward trappings that change in different ways in different cultures. Superimpositions like

> I pace this broad Baden walk as the sunset is gilding the hills round about, as the orchestra blows its merry tunes, as the happy children laugh and sport in the alleys, as the lamps of the gambling-palace are lighted up, as the throngs of pleasure-hunters stroll, and smoke, and flirt, and hum: and wonder sometimes, is it the sinners who are the most sinful? Is it poor Prodigal yonder amongst the bad company, calling black and red and tossing the champagne; or brother Strait-lace that grudges his repentance? Is it downcast Hagar that slinks away with poor little Ishmael in her hand; or bitter old virtuous Sarah, who scowls at her from my demure Lord Abraham's arm?
>
> (XIV, 360)

are entirely serious; but there is humour in locutions like "the Ezekiel of Clackmannon" (XIV, 93) or the appellation "this Nimrod" bestowed on de Florac (XIV, 755); there is self-caricature when Lord Kew and John Binnie apply the story of Susanna and the Elders to their own case (XIV, 240, 783); and the reader is asked to recognize that Serjeant Rowland's recourse to Genesis is pure hogwash:

In the . . . trial in the Court of Queen's Bench, how grandly Serjeant
Rowland stood up for the rights of British husbands! with what
pathos he depicted the conjugal paradise, the innocent children
prattling round their happy parents, the serpent, the destroyer,
entering into that Belgravian Eden . . .

(XIV, 773)

Serjeant Rowland's way with Scripture is paralleled by Barnes
Newcome's during his ill-fated election campaign, where an opponent takes him to task for "trying to come the religious dodge"
(XIV, 847); but it also leads over to another use of Biblical stories
exemplified, in the early pages of *The Newcomes*, by a phrase like
"that stifling garden of Eden" (XIV, 22). What matters here is
contrast rather than parallel—the kind of contrast which is well to
the fore in the 'Overture" to the whole work, where Thackeray
anticipates what might be an unfriendly critic's verdict on the
"farrago of old fables" which this overture retells and which will be
taken up by a coda at the end:

I think I see such a one—a Solomon that sits in judgment over us
authors and chops up our children.

(XIV, 4)

The point of the original Judgment of Solomon is, of course, that it
prevents such chopping up—what seems a parallel or prefiguration is
in reality a contrast which makes the modern critic seem doubly
injudicious. In defending his fables against such onslaughts,
Thackeray insists, once again, on the unchanging relevance of tales
which may use animal disguises but speak to us across centuries
and civilizations about the essential nature of man: "asses in lions'
manes roared in Hebrew; and sly foxes flattered in Etruscan; and
wolves in sheep's clothing gnashed their teeth in Sanscrit, no
doubt." (XIV, 5). Colonel Newcome, like Thackeray himself it
would seem, thought of the Hebrew language as something
esoteric, for specialists only, not part of a gentleman's education:
"Mrs Newcome", a typical utterance runs, " . . . had no more idea
of a joke than I have of Hebrew" (XIV, 50); but Thackeray leaves
his readers in no doubt that the Horatian "de te fabula narratur" is
as applicable to tales originally told in Hebrew as it is to those told
in other great languages of humanity's past and present.

In his valuable book on *The Language of Thackery* (London 1878,
p. 27), K.C. Phillips has shown how subtly the author of *The
Newcomes* uses tiny, almost unnoticeable Biblical allusions to control his readers' attitude to his characters. The virtues of Jack

Belsize, for instance, are hinted at by a passing reference to the feeding of Elijah (1 Kings 17, 6):

> As for Jack Belsize; how he lived; how he laughed; how he dressed himself so well, and looked so fat and handsome; how he got a shilling to pay for a cab or a cigar; what ravens fed him; was a wonder to all.
> (XIV, 366)

That reference to Elijah's ravens may serve to qualify suspicions Thackeray's readers have been taught to entertain of anyone who contrives to live well on nothing a year, and to suggest that there is something in his life that deserves divine favour. Dr Phillipps confesses himself less taken by what he calls "surface pastiche" of the Old Testament in *The Newcomes*:

> So Thomas Newcome, and Clive the son of Thomas, had wrath in their hearts against Barnes, their kinsman, and desired to be revenged upon him, and were eager after his undoing, and longed for an opportunity when they might meet him, and put him to shame.
> (XIV, 838)

What K. C. Phillipps omits to mention is that Thackeray's narrator adds a sentence which "places" his pastiche: "When men are in this frame of mind, a certain personage is said always to be at hand to help them and give them occasion for indulging in their pretty little passion" (loc. cit.); and that the pastiche is but one example out of many of Thackeray's use of Biblical "tone" for varying artistic purposes. *Bibelton* may help to characterize Charles Honeyman, who uses it in a letter to extract money for the lease of Lady Whittlesea's Chapel from Colonel Newcome:

> Am I blessed with gifts of eloquence to thrill and soothe, to arouse the sluggish, to terrify the sinful, to cheer and convince the timid, to lead the blind groping in darkness, and to trample the audacious sceptic in the dust?
> (XIV, 38)

It may be used with deliberate frivolity: "Forget not the humble boots", says Clive to J.J. Ridley, "so shall he bless us when we depart" (XIV, 388). The narrator resorts to it with solemnity at emotional climaxes:

> Ah, pangs of hearts torn asunder, passionate regrets, cruel, cruel partings! Shall you not end one day, ere many years; when the tears shall be wiped from all eyes, and there shall be neither sorrow nor pain?
> (XIV, 336)

descending at times into the embarrasingly religiose:

She was silent too for a while. I could see she was engaged where pious women ever will betake themselves in moments of doubt, of grief, of pain, of separation, of joy even, or whatsoever other trial. They have but to will, and as it were an invisible temple rises round them; their hearts can kneel down there; and they have an audience of the great, the merciful, untiring Counsellor and Consoler.

(XIV, 755)

The Scriptural tone becomes more insistent towards the end of the novel, where it is sustained by a number of quotations and near-quotations from the Old Testament. The process begins with the Founder's Day service at which Pendennis first sees Colonel Newcome among the black-coated pensioners of Grey Friars and listens with new appreciation to three verses from Psalm 37 that Thackeray cites in full:

23. The steps of a good man are ordered by the Lord: and he delighteth in his way.
24. Though he fall, he shall not be utterly cast down: for the Lord upholdeth him with his hand.
25. I have been young, and now am old: yet have I not seen the righteous forsaken, nor his seed begging their bread.

(XIV, 952–3)

Other Old Testament citations follow: notably one from Job 3, 17—"where the wicked cease from troubling, and the weary are at rest" (XIV, 953); and they are saved from being a mere religiose embellishment in the service of sentimental uplift by discussions such as the following between the pious Laura and the more sceptical Pen:

'That is a beautiful psalm, Pen, and those verses which you were reading when you saw him, especially beautiful.'
'But in the presence of eighty old gentlemen, who have all come to decay, and have all had to beg their bread in a manner, don't you think the clergyman might choose some other psalm?' asks Mr. Pendennis.
'They were not forsaken *utterly*, Arthur', says Mrs. Laura, gravely: but rather declines to argue the point raised by me; namely, that the selection of that especial thirty-seventh psalm was not complimentary to those decayed old gentlemen.
'*All* the psalms are good, sir,' she says, 'and this one, of course, is included,' and thus the discussion closed.

(XIV, 957)

Thackeray himself, we know, did not think *all* the Psalms good; he had even spoken, at one time, of their "cut-throat imprecations"; but it is surely significant that at what he clearly intended to be one of the emotional climaxes of his work he should have given such a prominent place to poems whose English wording keeps closely to that of their great Hebrew originals.

iii

Although, as has been seen earlier, Thackeray contributed only a handful of articles to *Punch* after 1851, this did include one more brief series in 1854—a series that rounds off his contributions neatly, for like his very first ("The Legend of Jawbrahim Heraudee", 18 June 1842) it has a mock-Oriental setting and flavour. Its title reads:

IMPORTANT FROM THE SEAT OF WAR
Letters from the East by our own Bashi-Bozouk

and it ran in *Punch* for seven instalments from 24 June until 14 July. The "Bashi-Bozouk", though invested with Turkish dignities, is in fact an Irish mercenary called Mick Mulligan—one of Thackeray's many Irish spinners of tall tales whose foundations in reality have to be divined through a cloud of prevarication and self-dramatizing. Having served in the Russian army first, Mulligan goes over to the Turks, making forays against his erstwhile Russian employers during the Crimean War. From a campaign in the Balkans he brings home treasures which include

> 'A gold bowl, a picture frame ditto ditto, and a silver arm-chair which Spiridion was intrumental in procuring for me from the abbot of the Armenian Convent hard by. I shall value these at even more than the bazaar price, as they were the means of saving the reverend man's life: indeed, I should have hanged him had he not given them up.'
> 'A bag of loose diamonds, emeralds, and a silver soup-ladle of English manufacture given to me with the the grateful tear of a Jewish family.'
>
> (VIII, 593)

What is here said about the way the abbot's treasure was obtained allows us to guess the true portent of the Jewish family's tears. And sure enough—the very next despatch "from the seat of war" begins:

> Some jealous scoundrels (I suspect the envious malignity of a couple of English officers, who are making themselves very officious here) have been complaining of the plundering propensities of my Bashi-Bozouks. In an angry interview with H.E. Mussa Pasha this morning, I repelled the accusation with scorn, and challenged both the English officers for the honour of our corps.—N.B. The Turks do not understand the practice of civilized European gentlemen: and Mussa

Pasha said, "Suppose Captain B. shoots you, will that prove you did not take the Jew merchant's silver soup-ladle and diamonds?—Go and shoot as many Russians as you please, Mulligoon Ferik! but let us hear no more of plundering." It is in vain to expect in half-educated men the refinement and delicate feelings of gentlemen with a long line of ancestry. The enemy made three attacks this evening on Arab Tabia. As I brought in a prisoner, though very much mutilated, Major-General Count Swigamoff, who led the last attack, His Excellency Mussa Pasha was pleased to compliment me, said he would send my name to the Commander-in-Chief for decoration, and look over the affair of the Jew, who was making a deuce of a disturbance.

(VIII, 594)

Extortion from Jews goes on in 1854 as it did in the Middle Ages described in *Ivanhoe*; the one difference is that Jews have a chance of obtaining redress if, like those encountered by the Bashi-Bozouk, or like Don Pacifico, they make "a deuce of a disturbance." Even so Mulligan assures us that in the end an English officer declares his conduct "overlooked . . . in consequence of my gallantry." (VIII, 597). How much credence one can give to this last statement is left unclear; what is wholly believable, however, is that some other rogues cheated Mulligan out of his ill-gotten gains in the end, leaving him with nothing but "a boot-jack, an old coat, and a pair of very old trousers." (VIII, 597).

Thackeray wrote only one more recorded piece for *Punch* after the "Seat of War" letters: "A Second Letter to an Eminent Person" was printed on 23 September 1854. He continued, however, to attend the famous "*Punch* Dinners" at which the contents of the journal were discussed; and Henry Silver's diary records how he helped to find a subject for the "large cut", the political cartoon filling a whole page, on 2 March 1859.

'Talking of cuts, Mark, how about the Large one?' Thackeray suggests Lawyer, Doctor, and Schoolmaster, standing in a row as prize boys, and Dizzy presenting them with votes. I propose Diz trying to launch a lop-sided 'Reform' ship, with the title 'Will it Swim?' Mark suggests D. joining hands of artisan and yeoman, giving each of them a vote. Thackeray thinks of workman coming among gentlemen of Parliament and asking, 'What have you done for *me?*'

(IR, II, 323)

This is by no means the only instance from the early 1850s which shows that Disraeli continued to fascinate Thackeray even after the former had broken off all social contact between them. Lewis Melville, in his pioneering *Life of William Thackeray* (London 1899) quotes from two speeches of this period that show the respect Thackeray felt for Disraeli despite all reservations, and despite the characteristic irony and chaff of his tone. The first of these speeches, written in 1851 and entitled "Authors and Their Patrons", calls on his fellow authors to take proper pride in their work:

> I see along this august table gentlemen . . . whom I should never have called my friends but for the humble literary labours I have been engaged in. And therefore, I say, don't let us be pitied any more. As for pity being employed upon authors, especially if you will but look at the novelists of the present day, I think you will see it is altogether out of the question to pity them. We will take, in the first place, if you please, a great novelist who is the great head of a great party in a great assembly in this country. When this celebrated man went into his county to be proposed to represent it, and he was asked on what interest he stood, he noble said he stood on his *head*. And who can question the gallantry and brilliancy of that eminent crest of his? and what man will deny the great merit of Mr. Disraeli?
>
> (Melville, op. cit., II, 159)

In a second speech, delivered at a Royal Literary Fund dinner in 1852, Thackeray speaks of

> . . . a literary hero who, at twenty years of age, astonished the world with his brilliant story of *Vivian Grey*; who, in a little time afterwards, and still in a youthful period of his life, amazed and delighted the public with the Wondrous Tale of *Alroy*; who, presently following up the course of his career and the development of his philosophical culture, explained to a breathless and listening world the great Caucasian mystery; who, quitting literature, then went into politics, met, faced, and fought, and conquered, the great political giant and great orator of those days; who subsequently led thanes and earls to battle, and caused reluctant squires to carry his lance; and who, but the other day, went in a gold coat to kiss the hand of his Sovereign as Leader of the House of Commons and Chancellor of Her Majesty's Exchequer. What a hero that will be for some future novelist, and what a magnificent climax for the third volume of his story!
>
> (Melville, op. cit., II, 164–5)

One can almost see the twinkle in Thackeray's eye and hear the ironic inflection of his voice when he speaks of "the great Caucasian mystery" and the "breathless and listening world" to which it was "explained"; but there is respect too, respect *quand même*, in this survey of Disraeli's achievements. What we have heard Henry Silver say about Thackeray's suggestions for a "large cut", or full page cartoon, about Disraeli, also shows a kindly rather than a dismissively censorious attitude towards that strange, gifted statesman's activities.

iv

The subject of the Hebrew scriptures crops up prominently in a letter Thackeray wrote to his daughter Anne some time in 1852.

> ... if M. Gossaint argues that because Our Lord quotes the Hebrew Scriptures therefore the Scriptures are of direct divine composition: you may make yourself quite easy; and the works of a reasoner who would maintain an argument so monstrous need not I should think occupy a great portion of your time. Our Lord not only quoted the Hebrew writings (drawing illustrations from everything familiar to the people among whom He taught, from their books poetic and historic, from the landscape round about, from the flowers the children the beautiful works of God) but he contradicted the Old Scriptures flatly; told the people that he brought them a new commandment—and that new commandment was not a complement but a contradiction of the Old—a repeal of a bad unjust law on their Statute books w^h he would suffer to remain there no more. It has been said an eye for an eye &c But *I* say to you no such thing *Love* your enemies &c It could not have been right to hate your enemies on Tuesday and to love them on Wednesday. What is right must always have been right: before it was practised as well as after. And if such and such a Commandment delivered by Moses was wrong—depend on it, it was not delivered by God: and the whole question of complete inspiration goes at once.
>
> (LPP III, 94)

Such misrepresentation of Jesus's complex attitude to the Hebrew Scriptures and the Mosaic Law, and such devaluation of Old Testament ethics, are all too familiar from Thackeray's earlier polemics against his mother's Biblical fundamentalism. The letter to Anne, however, goes on to assert that the cause of much evil and cruelty in the world will be removed once men have jettisoned the idea that the Bible—not just the Old Testament but "the Book called the Bible"—was written "under the direct dictation of God."

> the misfortune of dogmatic belief is that the first principle granted that the Book called the Bible is written under the direct dictation of God for instance—that the Catholic Church is under the direct dictation of God and solely communicates with him—that Quashimaboo is the direct appointed priest of God & so forth—pain, cruelty, persecution, separation of dear relatives, follow as a matter of course. What person possessing the secret of Divine Truth by w^h she or he is assured of Heaven and w^h idea she or he worships as if it was God, but must pass nights of tears and days of grief and lamentation if persons naturally dear cannot be got to see this necessary truth? Smith's truth being established in Smiths mind as the Divine one, persecution follows as a matter of course—Martyrs have roasted all over Europe—all over Gods world—upon this dogma—Granted that you possess the real truth; it is just that you extirpate heretics, and lies that might poison the minds of yet unborn generations: and you

have as good a right to hang a man for breaking the law and doubting the 39 Articles the Romish religion the Turkish or any you like, as you have to destroy him for any other public treason. A man who steals my purse steals trash, but a man who takes away from my children their Koran, their Jewel, their trust in Mahomet the Prophet takes what is infinitely more precious, their faith and their chances of Paradise hereafter—away with him—impale him Allah il Ullah and Mahomet is the Prophet of God

(LPP, III, 94–5)

After moving away, in this passage, from Biblical Jews to Roman Catholics and Muslims, Thackeray modulates back to his favourite theme of the unacceptable cruelties of the Old Testament narratives.

Did you hear the Chapter of the Sunday before last about Jehu murdering the Priests of Baal? The Lord says Cut away Jehu, the Lord says Murder them Jehu Smite smash run them through the body Kill 'em old and young—Do you believe the Lord directly gave any such orders: or that a chief of an Eastern race, devout, alone, worshipping one God, and finding his people perverted by idolators his neighbours determined to make an end of his enemy by slaughtering the priests who led them.

(LPP, III, 95)

The passages to which Thackeray here alludes (2 Kings 11, 17–20 and 2 Chronicles 23, 16–21) are once again seen as exempla, as prefigurations of what happens in later history: "The Lord ordered Robespierre to set the guillotine up, a Jehu Napoleon to slaughter the people before St Roche just in the same way" (loc. cit.). Thackeray then concludes his instruction to his daughter by saying:

You may read the Hebrew scriptures rationally or literally as you like. To my mind Scripture only means a writing and Bible means a Book. It contains Divine Truths: and the history of a Divine Character: but imperfect but not containing a thousandth part of Him—and it would be an untruth before God were I to hide my feelings from my dearest children: as it would be a sin, if having other opinions and believing literally in the Mosaic writings, in the 6 days cosmogony, in the serpent and apple and consequent damnation of the human race, I should hide them; and not try to make those I loved best adopt opinions of such immense importance to them. And so God bless my darlings and teach us the Truth. Every one of us in every fact, book, circumstance of life sees a different meaning & moral and so it must be about religion. But we can all love each other and say Our Father.

(LPP, III, 95–6)

A decent, humane conclusion—though few Christian theologians would agree with Thackeray's simplistic view of the relation of Jesus to the Old Testament, and many who have read their Bible with closer attention than he ever did will deplore his silence about ancient Israel's prophetic concern for universal social justice.

Most of Thackeray's letters to his daughters were not, of course, as solemn as this. He plays word-games with them, including those Yellowplush spelling-games we have so often noted in earlier pages: "Mrs. Cole has another little girl Bong Jew is she never going to stop?" (to Anne and Harriet Thackeray, 6 August 1852—LPP, III, 63). To Mrs Carmichael-Smyth, who saw these letters, substitution of "Jew" for "Dieu" must have seemed blasphemous; but it was the letter to Anne denying the divine inspiration of the Bible which roused her most vigorous protest. Thackeray countered by once again opposing his mother's view of the Scriptures' status.

> My dearest Mammy. I must write you a line, and kiss my dearest old Mother, though we differ ever so much about the Old Testament. What a deal of heart-burning & unkindness what division between friends has that book caused!—It can't be otherwise with your views regarding it, what can you do but deplore the error of those who won't receive it—what can I, but say my say too, & trust in God if I'm wrong—Trust if I'm wrong? It would be mistrust & a sort of Atheism in me to doubt for a moment that He will be good to me and all creatures—and if I kneel down & pray to God with my children, I must tell them too as reverently & carefully as I can what my views are upon this most awful of all subjects—It wasn't I that taught Nanny to beat her little hands on the picture of Abraham and Isaac. I wish that we could have the comfort of believing together: but, in all opinion, we are made different: and I must follow my truth though it's not my dear old Mother's—with this advantage over you that my conviction leads me to no sorrow or distrust about yours; You don't like the people I like nor the opinions I like nor the books I like—I don't like what you like—Ah me—our minds are no more alike than our noses: and each must follow his own.
>
> (4 January 1853—LPP, III, 168)

Not surprisingly, this explanation failed to satisfy Mrs Carmichael-Smyth. Why, for one thing, did not Thackeray tell his little daughter that Abraham did *not* sacrifice Isaac, who lived on to a ripe old age? Her son returned to the attack, however, in another letter, dated 26 February 1853.

> When as a child I used to sit on my mothers knee and hear her tell the story of Joseph & his brethen I received her ideas with her embraces Heaven bless them & their sacred memory!—but at 42 years old having opinions of my own, I choose to act by them—and when my dearest old mother carries off my children to a French parson who bids them receive as Divine facts, the Israelitish murders, the Mosaic cosmogony, &c—I must say, My dears—Listen to this old gentleman with perfect respect and to the fondest grandmother in the world with every reverence and affection: but it is right I should tell you that

those Hebrew books w^h they read as direct communications from Heaven I read but as histories upon a wrong belief in w^h has been founded an immense deal of the misery and persecution of the world, of wretchedness bitterness division in families—& that were you to adopt M. Monod's opinions & the logical consequences resulting from them; there would be division & wretchedness in our family. I speak my opinion. It is my duty: as it is your's and Monod's. I give you carte blanche to tell your religious views: but I utter mine—You are not afraid of the Bishop of Rome why should I be afraid of the Bishop of Geneva? In the meanwhile I know that the result of my religious calculation is quite diff^t to the sum as you work it out, and that my dear old Mother is unhappy. The unhappiness is the consequence of *your* religion not mine: and one of the reasons why I am a Protestant still (you & the Reformers left off protesting at the Reformation), is that religion as you hold it makes you miserable. I protest against the claims arrogance cruelties of the Church of Jerusalem as well as agst the Church of Rome—I think and believe Our Lord Jesus Christ protested against it. He is my Lord as well as your's. Divine, though I don't accept the Athanasian definition; though because he alluded to the books of the nation amongst whom he was born, I don't believe God ordered the Israelites to butcher Canaan; though I read but as a book what you receive as an Oracle; and though I think St Paul was mistaken.

(LPP, III, 217–8).

We need no deep psychologist to tell us that what this letter shows—for all the loving terms in which it is written—is how firmly Thackeray's revulsion against the Old Testament is bound up with attempts to free himself from the influence of his mother's overpowering personality. What he ultimately wants from her is loving recognition of his independence, based on an agreement to differ. In a letter to Mrs Carmichael-Smyth dated 25–28 March 1853, he imagines himself and his mother meeting "in a better place" beyond the grave and hearing her say to him: "Well my dear I think I made myself needlessly unhappy about you and those Mosaic books when we were below yonder." (LPP, III, 246); and two years later on 22 April 1855, he writes to her again: "Chapter and verse divide my dearest mother and me; but nature is stronger than print; and God over all, may Who bless all parents and children." (LPP, III, 440).

v

Some of the letters which have just been quoted were written in the United States of America, where Thackeray had toured with his lectures on the English Humourists from November 1852 to April 1853. In the two years that followed he moved to 26 Onslow Square in Brompton, a house in which he completed the last (and the most perenially delightful) of his Christmas Books (*The Rose and the Ring. A Fireside Pantomime for Great and Small Children*, 1854); wrote an unsuccessful comedy, *The Wolves and the Lamb* (1854—first published 1869), in which we find John the butler instructing Mary the maid that pork "is the hanimal which Jews ab'or" (XVII, 6); completed *The Newcomes*; and composed the lectures on *The Four Georges*, with which he left for a second tour of the United States that kept him out of England from 28 October 1855 until 18 May 1856. During this second tour he felt less happy and less well than during the first; indeed, his worsening health was largely responsible for his setting out at all, for he was anxious to earn enough money to leave his daughters comfortably off, and to ensure the maintenance of his mentally ill wife, if he were to die. His discomfort comes out clearly in passages such as the following, describing a trip from Savannah to New Orleans:

> 1500 miles of railway—one endless swamp of pines, sand, loghouses, niggers, in dirty cars, amongst dirty passengers, spitting, chewing, cutting their guns with their pen-knives, the young ones cursing outrageously—not unfriendly in the main—The hotel life is disgusting, rows all night, gongs banging at all hours to the dirty meals, knives down everybody's throat, dirty bucks straddling over the balconies in their dirty boots as high as their heads . . .
>
> (LPP III, 587)

Such sensitivity to foreign dirt and un-English table manners recalls, and helps to place, Thackeray's reaction to Polish Jews during his earlier journey to the Near and Middle East.

Thackeray's writings did not find as friendly a reception in the London *Times* as in many other contemporary publications; and as has already been seen, the critic on whose influence Thackeray blamed that relatively unfriendly welcome was the Jewish-born Samuel Phillips. In the autumn of 1854 the novelist found himself sitting opposite Phillips in a railway carriage, and the two men sat silently, without any sign of recognition, throughout their journey. A few days later Thackeray learnt that Phillips had died; but even death could not stifle resentments that break out in no less than three letters in which he felt impelled to recount this sequence of events. He found it impossible, he tells his correspondents, to give Phillips credit for sincerity—how could a man be sincere who had abandoned the religious allegiances he had inherited? Phillips was a "Hebrew renegade", a Jew who "supported the Protestant interest", who "lied himself out of Abraham's bosom" and had thereby lost his spiritual hold. How could such a man be anything but "a corrupt judge delivering wilfully dishonest sentences", "taking

God's name in vain" by tagging his pieces "with Scripture and the psalms"? He may have been "very good to his family; a very kind man"; yet in Thackeray's eyes he was anything but respectable. All this resentment poured out of Thackeray in two letters to Anne Procter (17 and 24 October 1854—LPP, III, 393–5), adding up to what he himself called "a savage assault upon the late Samuel Phillips"; an assault renewed in a letter to John Blackwood (30 December 1854—LPP, III, 407–8) which records the silent encounter in the railway carriage along with Thackeray's thoughts while it was in progress. He speaks of Phillips—with whom Dickens also had his differences—as

> that poor Hebrew whom you used to patronize (and who paid you back gratefully the poor rogue!) [and who] used to bring out careful *dampers* upon my books in the Times: which did them I believe a great deal of mischief—Only 3 days before his death I was in a railway carriage with him and [Mowbray] Morris—& thought to myself 'O you humbug! If I were to kotoo to you ever so little: to ask you to dinner and put you between two Lords; I know you would serve me a warm blanket next time instead of a wet one'—but I never could abide the man or speak to him: & I couldn't have cringed to him not for 20 columns of puff in the Times . . .
>
> (loc. cit.)

There is nothing in Phillips's life to suggest that he was the kind of toady Thackeray suspected him to be, or that his criticism of the writers he discussed was anything but the honest expression of (occasionally questionable) views. The outbursts about Phillips show the strength of prejudices that lay latent or buried much of the time; and it is surely significant that in all three of the letters which contain them the unloved critic's Jewish origins are prominently mentioned. "That Jew", "Hebrew renegade", "poor Hebrew"—the personal feud with a man to whom Thackeray had never spoken at all ("I never could abide the man or speak to him") is suffused with, and conditioned by, transpersonal enmities.

And yet, and yet . . . Thackeray is no continental ideologue, and irritation with Phillips did not make him into an indiscriminate Judaeophobe. He is perfectly happy to have his beloved daughters taught by Jewish teachers; when they need German lessons Mrs Carmichael-Smyth is asked to secure the services of Dr Kalisch, 57 rue des Petites Écuries (10 October 1855—LPP, III, 479, 482). On board ship, bound for America, he finds revulsions stirred by the voyage from Cornhill to Cairo to some degree reanimated, and tells two correspondents of encounters with "Jews of Poland and Almayne" whom he thinks "both odious and amusing" (to Mrs

Elliot and Kate Perry, 22 October 1855—LPP, IV, 44); but he also "cawicachawed" (= caricatured) a "funny little Jew" without malice, to the delight of the ship's captain who looked over his shoulder. (LPP, III, 482).

Illustration 11

In Philadelphia Thackeray meets "a Jew . . . I like very much" (LPP, III, 536); in New Orleans he was pleased to make the acquaintance of Judah Philip Benjamin, who was to become Attorney General and Secretary of State in the Confederate Cabinet (LPP, III, 581); and when he returned to England he gladly spent a convivial evening in the company of "a very pleasant and well-educated Jew", though he unfortunately drank more port than was good for his already very precarious health, and was ill the next day (LPP, III, 653–4; LPP, IV, 445–7). He kept up social relations with the Goldsmid family with whom he dined occasionally (to Mrs. F.H. Goldsmid, 26 April 1855) and remained on friendly visiting terms with the English Rothschilds—a letter of 16 August 1852 (LPP, III, 69) shows him dining at their mansion of Gunnersbury Park at Acton. His diary records amicable encounters with members of the Rothschild family between 1854 and 1863 (LPP, III, 675; LPP, IV, *passim*); and extant letters from this period include a particularly cordial one to Lady Louisa, written from Aberdeen where he was lecturing on the Hanoverian kings:

> Dear Lady Rothschild—I hope you know that I am murdering the Georges in Scotland and never heard of your beautiful party till the flowers were all dead, the dancers all in bed, the candles all out, one supper all eaten, the ices all melted, and the plate all locked up.
> How long this business of George-killing is to last I don't know, but I

have months yet of the House of Brunswick before me. Heaven bless them; I never thought my late gracious Sovereign would put so many 100 £ in the pockets of—Yours always to command

W.M. Thackeray.

What a fine wedding you had in your family! What a parasol! What a pretty bride!—we met them all at Aix-la-Chapelle last autumn, and I think we all liked each other. I know I did.

(LPP, IV, 30)

The wedding to which Thackeray refers is that celebrated on 4 March 1857 between Baron Alphonse de Rothschild and his cousin Leonora; and the "parasol" of which he speaks must be the *ḥuppah*, the canopy traditionally held over the bride and bridegroom at Jewish weddings. "I think we all liked each other. I know I did" is as cordial an expression as we will find anywhere in the letters which the usually undemonstrative Thackeray sent to men and women outside the charmed circle of his family and closest friends.

All this need not mean much—Thackeray made no mystery out of his liking for the company of people who possessed fine books and pictures, parks, town and country houses, good cooks and good cellars (J. Carey, *Thackeray: Prodigal Genius*, p. 25). The Rothschilds were, by any reckoning, an exceptional family, and we have all met Judaeophobes who claim that some of their best friends are Jews. What is remarkable about Thackeray, however, is that despite the kinds of prejudice which come out in the letters about poor Samuel Phillips and elsewhere, his political credo included the granting of full civil and political rights to Britain's Jewish citizens.

The clearest expression of this may be found in some notes for a speech to the Administrative Reform Association which Thackeray jotted down in 1855. The slogan "Administrative Reform" was often credited to Disraeli; but Thackeray is careful to distinguish his own views from those of Tory and Whig politicians alike.

It is true that the R. H. Mr Disraeli informed us that he invented the phrase Administration Reform, & that had we only been blessed with Lord Derbys Gov^t A R we should have had; but admitting that we are the God children of the Member for Buckinghamshire, & thanking that affectionate sponsor for the name w^h he gave us at our baptism, it may be doubted whether an A R administered by the gentlemen who distinguished themselves by purifying the public service of the admiralty; who purified elections by employing the exemplary Rt. Honorable W B is precisely that kind of Reform w^h this Association desires. I fear that we dont want Godpapa's party to manage for us—and as for the Whigs, our Guardians it must be confessed that aristocratic body is by no means inclined to own us.

(LPP, III, 679)

The programme he sketches after this introduction includes support for a parliamentary bill which would "give the peaceful useful alien letters of naturalization" (LPP, III, 680); and he derides the House of Lords for its obstinate upholding of religious discrimination.

> By those big-wigs the people were kept for years & years out of rights w^h are acquired and historical now:—the Catholics were kept out of their citizenship for years & years:—that modicum of Justice called the Reform Bill was kept back for years & years:—and, at this very minute, as Lord John Russel ruefully confessed the other day it is by that assembly of Lords that our Jewish fellow-citizens are kept out of their seats in the house of commons. There stand Lordships before the door and confront our Jewish fellow-citizens nose to nose— Justice and reason, and tried citizenship, and intelligence, and peaceful behaviour, and the assent of the whole country besides back the Jewish claims but my lords block the door up, and—unless he chooses to come here, Baron Rothschild has no place where he can exert his eloquence.
>
> (LPP, III, 682)

"Our Jewish fellow-citizens", "tried citizenship", "intelligence", "peaceful behaviour"—the tributes ring out loud and clear, though Thackeray would not be Thackeray if he could resist the caricature touch that has the Lords confront Jewish aspirants to parliament "nose to nose." And though the removal of Jewish political disabilities does not specifically figure in Thackeray's addresses to the electors of Oxford when he stood for parliament in 1857, the platform on which he fought is fully compatible with that discernable in the Reform Association speech.

> I would use my best endeavours not merely to enlarge the Constituencies, but to popularize the Government of this Country. With no feeling but that of good will towards the leading Aristocratic Families who are administering the chief offices of the State, I believe that it could be benefited by the skill and talents of persons less aristocratic, and that the country thinks so likewise.
> I think that to secure the freedom of Representation, and to defend the poor voter from the chance of intimidation, the Ballot is the best safeguard we know of, and would vote most hopefully for that measure. I would have the Suffrage emended in nature, as well as in numbers; and hope to see many Educated Classes represented who have now no voice in Elections,
> (From Thackeray's printed "Address to the Electors of Oxford",
> 9 July 1857)

Later on, as has often been noted, Thackeray moved more towards the political Right; but as we shall see, nothing he says of Jews in his *Cornhill* days gives grounds for believing that he ever changed his mind about the justice of their claim to become members of the

British parliament and to enjoy the same rights as their non-Jewish compatriots in all other spheres of lawful endeavour.

vi

In 1855 Thackeray sketched out a course of lectures on the Hanoverian kings of England which he delivered in the U.S.A. during 1855 and 1856, and in England and Scotland during 1856 and 1857. They were then published in the *Cornhill Magazine* during 1960 and came to rest, at last, in book form under the title: *The Four Georges. Sketches of Manners, Morals, Court and Town Life* in 1861. In the lecture devoted to George III, Thackeray lambasts religious prejudice and persecution in terms that recall formulations in letters to his daughters and his mother. The indictment includes religiously motivated persecution of Jews in a Spain dominated by the Inquisition:

> I believe it is by persons believing themselves in the right that nine-tenths of the tyranny of this world has been perpetrated. Arguing on that convenient premiss, the Dey of Algiers would cut off twenty heads of a morning; Father Dominic would burn a score of Jews in the presence of the Most Catholic King, and the Archbishops of Toledo and Salamanca sing Amen. Protestants were roasted, Jesuits hung and quartered at Smithfield, and witches burned at Salem, and all by worthy people, who believed they had the best authority for their actions.
>
> (XIII, 770)

English Jews do not swim into focus until Thackeray reaches the Regency and the reign of George IV. First comes a Jewish prize fighter: the Prince Regent is shown at a boxing match at Moulsey, where "the black man was beating Dutch Sam the Jew" (XIII, 792). Next come the money brokers: when the Prince Regent graces the gaming tables with his presence, the audience is told, "Jews waited outside to purchase his notes of hand" (XIII, 799). The moral decay of the Regency is shown lingering on among gamblers of a later epoch; Thackeray recalls a famous trial of 1837 in which a peer of the realm was found guilty of cheating at whist:

> Since that day, when my Lord's shame was made public, the gaming-table has lost all its splendour. Shabby Jews and blacklegs prowl about racecourses and tavern parlours, and now and then inveigle silly yokels with greasy packs of cards in railroad cars; but Play is a deposed goddess, her worshippers bankrupt, and her table in rags.
>
> (XIII, 799–800)

In Thackeray's unsympathetic depiction of George IV the company of Jews in which he appears is mostly sordid; but it is no more so than that of Gentile parasites and hangers-on.

The manuscript of the first of these lectures, preserving the text delivered in the U.S.A. and now kept in the Pierpont Morgan Library, introduces Old Testament parallels that were omitted from the published versions. Thackeray reminded his American audiences of court festivities towards the end of the reign of Charles II as he had found them described in Evelyn's diary; here, he commented, "we seem to see that Court by a light as gastly [sic] as those wh. burned at the death feast of Belshazzar." Yet another Old Testament parallel, combining reminiscences of a library treasure and of the Hanoverian kings' indulgences of the flesh, failed to surface in the printed versions:

> Among the curiosities at the Hanover Library they show you the Book of Esther in MS. Esther was not an unpopular character in Hanover—the ladies whom, in place of his deposed wife, the Prince delighted to honour were many & much respected. Ahasuerus the I Ahasuerus II, Ahasuerus III.—The first Royal Georges & their father Ernest Augustus had quite royal notions regarding marriage, and Louis XIV & Charles II scarce distinguished themselves more at Versailles & St. James than these German Sultans in their little city on the banks of the Leine.
>
> (Pierpont Morgan Library, New York, MA 474)

The beauty and grace of the Biblical Esther might have seemed too flattering an image to fit easily into Thackeray's conception of the Hanoverian court; the printed version of *The Four Georges* offers, therefore, a less complimentary parallel, describing the Countess of Platen, who seems to have served as a model for the Countess Gruffanuff of *The Rose and the Ring*, as the Elector's "old painted Jezebel of a mistress" (XIII, 714).

In the present context, two further features of these lectures deserve to be stressed. One of these is the lecturer's explicit warning against tribal prejudices, as he finds them in polemics accompanying the Napoleonic wars.

> We prided ourselves on our prejudices; we blustered and bragged with absurd vainglory; we dealt to our enemy a monstrous injustice of contempt and scorn; we fought him with all weapons, mean as well as heroic. There was no lie we would not believe; no charge of crime which our furious prejudice would not credit. I thought at one time of making a collection of the lies which the French had written against us, and we had published against them during the war: it would be a strange memorial of popular falsehood.
>
> (XIII, 776)

The other is the most sustained examination since the *Punch* series on the Snobs of England of the British notion of what makes a gentleman. The lecture on George IV ridicules the title "The First Gentleman of Europe" bestowed on Beau Brummel's Fat Friend, and laments the decay of an older gentlemanly ideal, an ideal found realized in the life of Nelson's friend Cuthbert Collingwood:

> I think, since Heaven made gentlemen, there is no record of a better one than that. Of brighter deeds, I grant you, we may read performed by others; but where of a nobler, kinder, more beautiful life of duty, of a gentler, truer heart? Beyond dazzle of success and blaze of genius, I fancy shining a hundred and a hundred times higher the sublime purity of Collingwood's gentle glory. His heroism stirs British hearts when we recall it. His love, and goodness, and piety make one thrill with happy emotion. As one reads of him and his great comrade going into the victory with which their names are immortally connected, how the old English word comes up, and that old English feeling of what I should like to call Christian honour!
>
> (XIII, 806)

But when, at the conclusion of *The Four Georges*, Thackeray tries to spell out more fully what it is that makes a true gentleman in modern times, he describes something more easily fostered in Victorian England than in the rakish atmosphere of the Regency; something, moreover, which was not the sole prerogative of English Christians:

> Which was the most splendid spectacle ever witnessed,—the opening feast of Prince George in London, or the resignation of Washington? Which is the noble character for after-ages to admire,—yon fribble dancing in lace and spangles, or yonder hero who sheaths his sword after a life of spotless honour, a purity unreproached, a courage indomitable, and a consummate victory? Which of these is the true gentleman? What is it to be a gentleman? Is it to have lofty aims, to lead a pure life, to keep your honour virgin; to have the esteem of your fellow-citizens, and the love of your fireside; to bear good fortune meekly; so suffer evil with constancy; and through evil or good to maintain truth always? Show me the happy man whose life exhibits these qualities, and him we will salute as gentleman, whatever his rank may be; show me the prince who possesses them, and he may be sure of our love and loyalty.
>
> (XIII, 811)

There is no more talk now of the "old English feeling" of specifically "Christian honour"; there is now no reason why the "Jewish fellow-citizens" lauded in the Administrative Reform Association speech should not strive towards, and attain, this ideal alongside others who worship Heaven according to their lights, alongside other subjects of the young Queen Victoria with whose praise *The Four Georges* ends:

The heart of Britain still beats kindly for George III—not because he was wise and just, but because he was pure in life, honest in intent, and because according to his lights he worshipped Heaven. I think we acknowledge in the inheritrix of his sceptre a wiser rule and a life as honourable and pure; and I am sure the future painter of our manners will pay a willing allegiance to that good life, and be loyal to the memory of that unsullied virtue.

(XIII, 811)

In the reign of this gracious First Lady, the lecturer wants his audience to feel, a new gentlemanly ideal was taking shape and had a chance to flourish.

The period bounded by *Henry Esmond* at one end and *The Four Georges* at the other exhibits the full complexity of Thackeray's depiction of Jews ancient and modern, and of Judaism. Irrational prejudices linger, to surface especially at moments of stress—when a revered lady's possessions are auctioned off, when he comes face to face with a critic who has reviewed one of his books less than favourably. Stereotypes of Jewish tradesmen and financiers persist, but are countered by more sympathetic or more subtly differentiated portraits—notably those of Sherrick and his family in *The Newcomes*. Thackeray's view of the Hebrew Bible comes, more and more, to resemble Balaam's view of the Israelites when he went out to curse but stayed to praise—denunciations in Thackeray's letters are constantly contradicted by the evidence of his novels and lectures. The poems present a similar picture: witness "The Idler", appropriately published in *The Idler Magazine of Fiction* in March 1856, which uses the Old Testament notion of "Tophet" as a near-equivalent of "Hades" and places the Biblical Solomon and the Elizabethan Sir Philip Sidney side by side as exemplars of wisdom and chivalry respectively, with whom the "fogyfied old sinner" who speaks in the poem refuses to vie (VII, 205, 206). Above all: despite his prejudices and the accesses of rage that could bring them out, Thackeray never wavered in his abhorrence of religious persecution and discrimination. He did not often formulate political programmes—but in one of his rare ventures onto this slippery ground he voiced the demand for full civic equality of British Jews, including the right to hold parliamentary office without submitting to baptism. Indeed, one of the reasons he gives for his recoil from Phillips is that the latter had abandoned the religious allegiances of his forefathers; that he had been willing, to use Heine's famous phrase, to pay the price of baptism for his entrance-ticket to European culture.

CHAPTER 9

EVER WONDERFUL
(1857–1863)

... that ever-wonderful Jews' quarter ...
(XVII, 458)

i

In November 1857 Thackeray published the first instalment of a novel once again set in the eighteenth century: a sequel to *Henry Esmond*, set in America as well as in England, entitled *The Virginians. A Tale of the Last Century*. Monthly parts continued to come out until October 1859; and the book edition appeared in two volumes, dated 1858 and 1859 respectively. The central protagonists, George and Harry Warrington, are Henry Esmond's American grandsons, who have been on different sides during the American War of Indpendence; among other characters from the earlier novel that reappear is Beatrix Esmond, now Baroness Bernstein.

The (very occasional) presentation of Jews in this novel runs mainly along well-worn lines. Harry Warrington's English cousin William mistakes Harry for "a bailiff, a confounded pettifogging bum-bailiff" when he first meets him: "Gad! I thought it was Nathan come to nab me." (XV, 17–18). Nathan never appears; but later in the novel we do meet colleagues of his who are called Nadab (XV, 847) and Amos (XV, 505 et passim). A special feature of *The Virginians* is that the Jewish sheriff's officers appear in tandem with Roman Catholic Irish colleagues; and one of the most memorable of these scenes shows a posse of such bailiffs intruding on a church service in order to serve a writ on the Esmond family's domestic chaplain, ironically named Sampson. The Irish members of the team spread "a rich fragrance of whisky" wherever they go. Have all these strangers come to pay homage to the Reverend Sampson's interpretation of the Church of England creed?

> A man may be a heretic, but possess genius: these Catholic gentlemen have come to pay homage to Mr. Sampson.
> Nay, there are not only members of the old religion present, but disciples of a creed still older. Who are those two individuals with hooked noses and sallow countenances who worked into the church, in spite of some little opposition on the part of the beadle? Seeing the greasy appearance of these Hebrew strangers, Mr. Beadle was for

denying them admission. But one whispered into his ear, 'We wants to be conwerted, gov'nor!' another slips money into his hand,—Mr. Beadle lifts up the mace with which he was barring the doorway, and the Hebrew gentlemen enter. There goes the organ! the doors have closed. Shall we go in, and listen to Mr. Sampson's sermon, or lie on the grass without?

Preceded by that beadle in gold lace, Sampson walked up to the pulpit, as rosy and jolly a man as you could wish to see. Presently, when he surged up out of his plump pulpit cushion, why did his reverence turn as pale as death? He looked to the western church-door—there, on each side of it, were those horrible Hebrew Carya-tides. He then looked to the vestry-door, which was hard by the rector's pew, in which Sampson had been sitting during the service, alongside of their ladyships his *patronesses*. Suddenly, a couple of perfumed Hibernian gentlemen slipped out of an adjacent seat, and placed themselves on a bench close by that vestry-door and rector's pew, and so sat till the conclusion of the sermon, with eyes meekly cast down to the ground. How can we describe that sermon, if the preacher himself never knew how it came to an end?

Nevertheless, it was considered an excellent sermon. When it was over, the fine ladies buzzed into one another's ears over their pews, and uttered their praise and comments. Madame Walmoden, who was in the next pew to our friends, said it was bewdiful, and made her dremble all over. Madame Bernstein said it was excellent. Lady Maria was pleased to think that the family chaplain should so distinguish himself. She looked up at him, and strove to catch his reverence's eye, as he still sat in his pulpit: she greeted him with a little wave of the hand and flutter of her handkerchief. He scarcely seemed to note the compliment; his face was pale, his eyes were looking yonder, towards the font, where those Hebrews still re-mained. The stream of people passed by them—in a rush, when they were lost to sight,—in a throng—in a march of twos and threes—in a dribble of one at a time. Everybody was gone. The two Hebrews were still there by the door.

(XV, 397)

The Jewish bailiffs are seen through Mr Sampson's eyes, and for him they are indeed "horrible"; but other perspectives also prevail, notably that of the beadle, to whom they pretend a wish for conversion when their "greasy" appearance tempts him to shut the door in their faces. "We wants to be conwerted, gov'nor" adds a new twist to Thackeray's presentation of the tricks bailiffs might employ to seize hold of the debtor they have come to arrest, as well as a fresh notation of nineteenth-century East London speech, here put into the mouth of eighteenth-century Jews. But then: these Jewish sheriff's officers seem in any case to belong to early nine-teenth rather than mid-eighteenth century England.

While the Irish bailiffs single out a victim in Mr Sampson's congregation, their Jewish colleagues make for the reverend gentleman himself. "Like the fabled opossum", who, "when he spied the unerring gunner from his gum-tree, said: 'It's no use, major, I will come down'", the Reverend Sampson gives himself up to his pursuers whose names we now learn.

> 'At whose suit, Simons?' he sadly asked. Sampson knew Simons, they had met many a time before.
> 'Buckleby Cordwainer,' says Mr. Simons.
> 'Forty-eight pound and charges, I know,' says Mr. Sampson, with a sigh. 'I haven't got the money. What officer is there here?' Mr. Simons's companion, Mr. Lyons, here stepped forward, and said his house was most convenient, and often used by gentlemen, and he should be most happy and proud to accommodate his reverence.
> Two chairs happened to be in waiting outside the chapel. In those two chairs my Lady Maria Esmond and Mr. Sampson placed themselves, and went to Mr. Lyons's residence, escorted by the gentlemen to whom we have just been introduced.
>
> (XV, 401)

Harry Warrington too lands in a Jewish bailiff's lock-up, recognizably the same we have so often encountered in fiction with a nineteenth-century setting: "that horrible den in Cursitor Street" (XV, 553). His brother George comes to his rescue, accompanied by Harry's black servant Gumbo, who is represented with what Thackeray might have thought a degree of affection, but also a patronizing condescension harder to take in the twentieth century than it may have been in the nineteenth.

> Poor Gumbo knows the way to the bailiff's house well enough. Again the bell is set ringing. The first door is opened to George and his negro; then that first door is locked warily upon them, and they find themselves in a little passage with a little Jewish janitor; . . .
>
> (XV, 505)

"A little Jewish janitor"—does not this sound more endearing than previous characterizations of the young Cerberuses of the Cursitor Street door? The janitor stares as his flaring tallow torch lights up a second Mr Warrington, then unlocks an inner door, allowing George to penetrate into "a small apartment which went by the name of Mr. Amos's office." There he encounters Colonel Lambert, who had also come to help Harry out of his predicament; and between them they have Harry released to the accompaniment of Mr Amos's protestations:

> 'Nay, your honours, I have done my best to make the young gentleman comfortable; and knowing your honour before, when you came to bail Captain Watkins, and that your security is perfectly good,—if your honour wishes, the young gentleman can go out this very night, and I will make it all right with the lawyer in the morning,' says

Harry's landlord, who knew the rank and respectability of the two gentlemen who had come to offer bail for his young prisoner.

(XV, 506)

Mr Amos's speech differs in nothing but obsequiousness from that of other characters in those sections of *The Virginians* which are set in eighteenth-century England. In the American sections of the novel it is a negro butler, and not a Jewish bailiff, who bears the name Nathan; but the many references to Jews of the Old Testament that will be examined later are supplemented, at the opening of Chapter XI, by an emblematic capital depicting Shylock whetting his knife:

Illustration 1

The heading of this chapter reads: "Wherein the two Georges prepare for Blood"; and Shylock is here used as an emblem for bloodthirsty vengefulness in the same way that other pictorial capitals use Othello as an emblem for bloodthirsty jealousy.

Chapter XLV, significantly headed "In which Harry finds two *Uncles*" (my italics), takes Thackeray's protagonist into "a certain pawnbroker's shop in St. Martin's Lane"—an establishment depicted in the capital that opens the chapter (ill. 1(a)).

Neither this illustration nor the text it introduces suggests that the pawnbroker should be thought of as Jewish, though Thackeray traces the path that leads from his door to the Cursitor Street sponging house. But capitals, whether emblematic or more straightforwardly illustrative, represent only one of the ways in which the novelist glosses his narrative. He also allows his nineteenth-century narrator a good deal of direct commentary that compares the

Illustration 1(a)

period in which the story is set with that in which it is told and in which it was first read. One of these commentaries introduces Disraeli in a wholly respectful context.

> As for your book-learning, O respectable ancestors (though, to be sure, you have the mighty Gibbon with you), I think you will own that you are beaten, and could point to a couple of professors at Cambridge and Glasgow who know more Greek than was to be had in your time in all the universities of Europe, including that of Athens, if such an one existed. As for science, you were scarce more advanced than those heathen to whom in literature you owned yourselves inferior. And in public and private morality? Which is the better, this actual year 1858, or its predecessor a century back? Gentlemen of Mr. Disraeli's House of Commons! has every one of you his price, as in Walpole's or Newcastle's time,—or (and that is the delicate question) have you almost all of you had it? Ladies, I do not say that you are a society of Vestals—but the chronicle of a hundred years since contains such an amount of scandal, that you may be thankful you did not live in such dangerous times. No: on my conscience I believe that men and women are both better; not only that the Susannahs are more numerous, but that the Elders are not nearly so wicked. Did you ever hear of such books as *Clarissa, Tom Jones, Roderick Random*; paintings by contemporary artists, of the men and women, the life and society, of their day? Suppose we were to describe the doings of such a person as Mr. Lovelace, or my Lady Bellaston, or that wonderful 'Lady of Quality' who lent her memoirs to the author of *Peregrine Pickle*. How the pure and outraged Nineteenth Century would blush, scream, run out of the room, call away the young ladies, and order Mr. Mudie never to send one of that odious author's books again!

(XV, 424–5)

There is irony here, of course, for we know how Thackeray chafed under the restraints that allowed him so much less freedom in depicting human sexuality than Fielding or Smollett had; but his preference for Disraeli's House of Commons over that of Walpole, for parliament after the Reform Act over what had been there before, is well attested. Whether he really agreed with his narrator that there were fewer Susannahs and that the Elders they encountered were less wicked must remain in doubt. What is not in doubt, however, is that *The Virginians* once again demonstrates how important a part the Bible plays in Thackeray's narrative art—a subject which will be more fully pursued in a moment.

When he is led to comment on the welcome "the fashionable world" extends to Harry Warrington in his days of affluence, and on Harry's reaction to that welcome, Thackeray's narrator speaks as a nineteenth-century man of letters looking back on the clearer class-divisions he perceives in the eighteenth.

> Our Virginian was very grand, and high and mighty, to be sure; but, in those times, when the distinction of ranks yet obtained, to be high and distant with his inferiors brought no unpopularity to a gentleman. Remember that, in those days, the secretary of state always knelt when he went to the king with his dispatches of a morning, and the undersecretary never dared to sit down in his chief's presence. If I were secretary of state (and such there have been amongst men of letters since Addison's days) I should not like to kneel when I went in to my audience with my dispatch-box. If I were under-secretary, I should not like to have to stand, whilst the Right Honourable Benjamin or the Right Honourable Sir Edward looked over the papers. But there is a *modus in rebus*: there are certain lines which must be drawn: and I am only half pleased, for my part, when Bob Bowstreet, whose connexion with letters is through Policemen X and Y, and Tom Garbage, who is an esteemed contributor to the *Kennel Miscellany*, propose to join fellowship as brother literary men, slap me on the back, and call me old boy, or by my Christian name.
>
> (XV, 442–3)

"The Right Honourable Benjamin" is, of course, Disraeli, and "the Right Honourable Sir Edward" is Bulwer Lytton, who had become a baronet in 1837 and had reentered the House of Commons in 1852, where he soon afterwards succeeded Lord Stanley as Secretary for the Colonies. A man of letters of Thackeray's stature, the comment suggests, would think it an indignity to have to stand at attention before authors like Bulwer and Disraeli, in the House of Commons or anywhere else—but there is no suggestion that mandatory servility before a statesman and writer of Jewish origin would be more humiliating than the same servility before an impeccably Christian one. It is also obvious that neither Disraeli

nor Bulwer Lytton—of whose contributions to literature Thackeray
had come to think more highly in his later years—are to be thought
of as belonging to the same gutter category as the journalistic hacks
"Bob Bowstreet" and "Tom Garbage".

"Bowstreet", in the passage just quoted, stands for the haunt of
the crime reporter, much as "Cursitor Street", throughout Thackeray's fiction, stands for the meeting place of bailiff, lock-up keeper
and impecunious debtor. Cursitor Street is also one of several
locations which serve, in *The Virginians* as elsewhere, to indicate a
presumption of Jewishness—other examples are Duke's Place, with
its famous synagogue ("our revered Captain had dealings with the
gentlemen of Duke's Place"—XV, 906), and the Minories, also in
the East End of London ("his play debts and little transactions in
the Minories"—XV, 979). All these cases are linked, of course, by
the idea of money-lending and debt. The "bird of prey" image,
however, which in *Vanity Fair* and elsewhere had been applied to
Jews, is reserved, in *The Virginians*, for aristocratic Gentiles eager to
secure the dying Baroness Bernstein's inheritance: "They looked
greedily at us . . .they were hungry for the prey" (XV, 882).

Among the most memorable features of *The Virginians* may be
reckoned its consistent demythologizing, in the grand satiric portrait
of the grossly selfish and worldly Sir Miles Warrington, of sentimental notions about "the Grand Old English Country Gentleman". This is only one of several illusions about English life and
character that come under scrutiny; but it would appear, at the
same time, that travel in the United States—particularly their
southern portions—had made Thackeray more race-conscious than
before. We now find him speaking, not only of the "race" of
women, toad-eaters and footmen, or the "race" of the Warringtons
(meaning their family), but also of "gently nurtured men and
women of Anglo-Saxon race" (XV, 6), of the "negro race" (or the
"negro people") and of the "race" of Red Indians. The novel leaves
its readers in little doubt that the non-white races are to be thought
of as inferior, though black Gumbo is treated to condescending
affection because he fulfils the role of faithful servant to his white
master, and though the cruelties laid at the Red Indians' door are
occasionally matched by those of their fairer-skinned adversaries.

The Bible plays a prominent part in the lives, and the speech, of
the characters Thackeray introduces into *The Virginians*. Clergymen
in America and in England are shown at their task of propagating
Holy Writ and their parishioners fill their discourse with Scripture
phrases and allusions. Books of Psalms are found in bedrooms
(XV, 132), psalms are sung and recited in church (XV, 465), and

snatches of them are heard by passers-by, animating and reanimating reverent feelings:

> There came a great burst of music from people in the chapel hard by,
> as she was speaking. . . I can never forget the tune of that psalm. I
> have heard it all through my life. My wife has touched it on her
> harpsichord, and her little ones have warbled it. Now, do you
> understand, young people, why I love it so? Because 'twas the music
> played at our *amoris redintegratio*. Because it sang hope to me, at the
> period of my existence the most miserable . . .
>
> (XV, 807)

This passage is particularly interesting because it shows how
music helps the words of the Psalmist to linger in the hearer's
consciousness, and how religious feelings mingle with the ordinary
concerns of an individual's life. That such concerns may also
impede religious uplift, Thackeray would be the last to deny; at any
given church service

> very likely the maidservant is thinking of her sweetheart: the grocer is
> casting about how he can buy that parcel of sugar. . . the clerk who
> calls out the psalm has his daughter in trouble, and drones through
> his responses scarcely aware of their meaning: the very moment the
> parson hides his face on his cushion, he may be thinking of that bill
> which is coming due on Monday . . .
>
> (XV, 464–5)

That does not make such people hypocrites in Thackeray's
world; they have to live on this earth, and make their way in a
society which does not allow one to be heavenly-minded most of
one's time.

The Bibles that appear in the narrative of *The Virginians* are also
made to fulfil a worldly task: they serve as family chronicles as well
as repositories of God's word and aids to devotion. ". . . didn't they
show me the Family Bible, where all your names are down, and the
dates of your birth?" (XV, 183). "They both married, as I see by
the note in the Family Bible . . ." (XV, 792). Such chronicles do
not contain only welcome information: "Do you know how old the
woman is?", Baroness Bernstein demands of George, as she asks
him to help prevent the "absurd marriage of Lady Maria Esmond
to his brother Harry. "I can tell you, though she has torn the first
leaf out of the family Bible at Castlewood" (XV, 561).

No novel of Thackeray's, in fact, is fuller of Biblical presences
than *The Virginians*. The Prodigal Son and the various characters
that figure in the Good Samaritan parable appear alongside Dives
and Lazarus, the Woman Taken in Adultery, and repentant sin-
ners of various kinds; the Epistle to Titus is invoked by one of the

characters to enjoin obedience to husbands (XV, 910); but it is the Old Testament which is most often and most colourfully invoked. Such invocations are of six main kinds.

The first set of references to the Old Testament and its Apocrypha is prefigurative in a variety of ways. The angels and serpents of Genesis, and the Garden of Eden itself, prefigure the struggle of wordliness and spirituality in modern society:

> I am not sure that some worldly views might not suit even with Mrs. Lambert's spiritual plans (for who knows into what pure Eden, though guarded by flaming-sworded angels, worldliness will not creep?)
>
> (XV, 723)

That Eden could not, in the long run, content an ever-striving mankind is borne out by the experience of George Warrington:

> There came a period of my life, when having reached the summit of felicity I was quite tired of the prospect I had there: I yawned in Eden, and said, 'Is this all? What, no lions to bite? no rain to fall? no thorns to prick you in the rose-bush when you sit down?—only Eve, for ever sweet and tender, and figs for breakfast, dinner, supper, from week's end to week's end!'
>
> (XV, 905)

Forbidden fruit is as alluring as ever to young and old: young George Warrington, indulging his love of the theatre, "had the satisfaction of thinking that his mother only half approved of plays and playhouses, and of feasting on fruits forbidden at home" (XV, 661), while the aged Baroness Bernstein, hiding or painting her grey hair, clings to the world with her crutch: "For fourscore years she had moved on it, and eaten of the tree, forbidden and permitted . . ." (XV, 876). The Fall of Man, as recounted in Genesis, can serve as alibi or excuse as well as prefiguration; Lord Castlewood glosses his less than admirable life-style with "a very pleasant sardonical discourse upon the fall of man, and his faults, and shortcomings . . ." (XV, 765). Prefigurative functions are also fulfilled by the emblematic beasts of the Bible ("Maria Esmond, who had advanced to her brother like a raging lion, now sat down at his feet like a gentle lamb"—XV, 481); the idolatrous worship recorded in Exodus ("You shall go to church to-morrow morning, and see how the whole congregation will turn away from its books and prayers, to worship the golden calf in your person"—XV, 251); Naaman's devotion to his native Syria (" . . .the habitual insolence of Englishmen towards all foreigners, all colonists, all folk who dare to think their rivers as good as our Aban and Pharpar. . ." —XV, 890); and Ruth's trusting submission: "Theo . . . placed . . .

he entire trust in me—murmuring those sweet words of Ruth that must have comforted myriads of tender hearts in my dearest maiden's plight; that whither I would go she would go, and that my people should be hers" (XV, 834). The last-quoted instance is particularly significant: it show Thackeray's appreciation of the way in which the example, indeed the very words, of a character in the Old Testament may give strength and courage to those who see their own lives, and their own problems, prefigured by them.

As in Thackeray's earlier novels, the very names of the characters may suggest prefiguration; but contrast is here as important as parallel. "Rachel is by no means weeping for her children, and has every desire to be comforted", George Warrington says bitterly about his mother (XV, 82); and the many references to the Biblical Samson and his heroic exploits against the Philistines serve to underline the unheroic nature of his near-namesake, the Reverend Sampson (XV, 149, 372, 392 *et passim*). Thackeray is always glad to exploit, for satiric purposes, the contrast between epic or heroic incidents recounted in the Old Testament and far less exalted modern avatars—as when he has his narrator tell us of the inability of a "red sea" of claret to drown modern man's blue devils (XV, 907); and he is no less adept at satirizing the less than honourable conduct of an ostensibly religious-minded person by adducing some Biblical parallel such a character might adduce to justify his or her peccadilloes. Of the Dowager Lady Warrington George Warrington says, wrily: "No doubt she thought there was no harm in spoiling the Philistines: for she made us pay unconscionably for the goods she left behind in our country house . ." (XV, 903).

This last example, like George Warrington's earlier comment on the contrast between the Biblical Rachel and her modern namesake, leads over to another way in which Thackeray uses Old Testament allusions or quotations in *The Virginians*: as a means of conveying the narrator's, or the characters', estimate of the worth of their fellow men and women. An obvious example of this is the narrator's account of General Wolfe's victory and death on the Plains of Abraham:

> . . . at the time when we first heard of Wolfe's glorious deeds upon the Plains of Abraham—of that army marshalled in darkness and carried silently up the midnight river—of those rocks scaled by the intrepid leader and his troops—of that miraculous security of the enemy, of his present acceptance of our challenge to battle, and of his defeat on the open plain by the sheer valour of his conqueror—we were all intoxicated in England by the news. The whole nation rose up and felt itself stronger for Wolfe's victory . . . People did not deplore the dead warrior, but admired his *euthanasia*. Should James Wolfe's

friends weep and wear mourning, because a chariot had come from the skies to fetch him away? Let them watch with wonder, and see him departing, radiant; rising above us superior.

(XV, 789–90)

The beauty and nobility of Wolfe's death, his "euthanasia", is here likened to the ascension of a prophet, a legendary comforter and saviour, who was borne up to heaven in a chariot of fire (cf. 2 Kings 2, 11). Conversely, Harry Warrington, on the Republican side in the American War of Independence, cuts off a speech prepared by the Reverend Hagan, who sought to invoke the authority of George III:

'I am too busy to listen to speeches. And as for King George, he has henceforth no more authority in this country than King Nebuchadnezzar.'

(XV, 958)

No doubt Hagan, and the reader, is meant to envisage poor King George in the likeness of the Babylonian king driven from the society of men, eating grass as oxen, his body wet with the dew of heaven, till his hairs were grown like eagle's feathers, and his nails like birds' claws (Daniel 4, 33). The Hanoverian kings' raddled German mistresses are not only predictably compared to Jezebel, but also ironically dignified with a phrase from the Book of Esther (Esther 6,6) which introduces a more satiric note: ". . .the lady whom the king delighted to honour . . . the good-natured old Jezebel" (XV, 828); "don't tread on the robe of the lady whom the king delights to honour" (XV, 329); "the lady whom His Majesty, George the Second, of Great Britain, France and Ireland, Defender of the Faith, delighted to honour" (XV, 518). The Book of Esther, in fact, becomes a more palpable presence by means of a painting: "the noble picture of 'Esther before Ahasuerus' painted by Tintoret" (XV, 594) which George Warrington notices in Kensington Palace alongside Titian's Venus and Rubens's "St. Francis adoring the infant Saviour". Such emblematic, symbolic, characterizing use of paintings recalls—and was probably suggested by—the works of Hogarth.

A third way in which the Old Testament enters the world of *The Virginians* is as a source of still binding commandments. The central role in this is obviously played by the Decalogue: "Might I, as a son, be equally able to answer for myself, and to show, when the Great Judge demanded the question of me, whether I had done my own duty, and honoured my father and mother!" (XV, 824). ". . . and of course the good folk said, that having made free with the seventh commandment, I was inclined to break the sixth. . ." (XV,

571). "Why, Jack, I protest you are swearing again! This morning, 'twas the Sixth Commandment you wanted to break; and now ..." (XV, 752). But though in *The Virginians*, as elsewhere, Thackeray's characters frequently refer themselves and others to the Decalogue, the novels tend to look for valuable moral precepts in the direction of the New Testament rather than the Old.

Thackeray also continues to find, in the locutions of the Old Testament as in those of the New, a welcome means of establishing easy communion with his readers in face of a shared cultural heritage. A coachman becomes a "grumbling Jehu" (XV, 879), a watchful servant an "Abigail" (XV, 814), a painted old woman—as always—a "Jezebel":

> that painted High Dutch Jezebel (XV, 329) the good-natured old Jezebel laying her hand upon the boy's curly pate ... (XV, 828) I intend to say of every woman that she is chaste and handsome ... of Xantippe, that she has a sweet temper; of Jezebel, that he colour is natural; ... What? a word against the spotless Messalina? ...
> (XV, 364)

In this last, characteristically ironic, example we have classical reminiscences joined to Biblical ones; a conjunction that is as common in Thackeray as conjunction with English literature, particularly with Milton or (as in the following instance) with Shakespeare:

> Who wants to survive into old age after abdicating all his faculties one by one, and be sans teeth, sans eyes, sans memory, sans hope, sans sympathy? How fared it with those patriarchs of old who lived for their nine centuries, and when were life's conditions so changed that, after three-score years and ten, it became a vexation and a burden?
> (XV, 655)

This bitter reflection on post-Biblical old age, which draws on Genesis and *As You Like It*, is prompted by a contemplation of Baroness Bernstein, who had been the beautiful Beatrix Esmond and in whom "the cold snow [had struck] down from the head and [checked] the glow of feeling." That in *The Virginians* as elsewhere in Thackeray Methuselah is cited as a standard of extreme longevity (XV, 256, 831) can almost go without saying. And when we hear Thackeray's narrator ask "Happy? Who is happy? What good is a stalled ox for dinner every day, and no content therewith?", then the stylized Biblical language, and the overt reference to Proverbs 15, 17, may well be felt to anchor his words in traditional wisdom, and to lend them a weight and an authority which transcend those any particular speaker could possibly give them unaided on some particular occasion in modern times.

Thackeray's fifth use of Biblical phrases and allusions brings us back to his already mentioned way of characterizing the speech, and through it the mental world, of the figures that play a part in his tale. He allows us to listen in on sermons, first from Mr Ward, who seeks to propagate in Virginia the doctrines he learnt from his British teacher Whitfield and whose discourse is said to have been

> about Naaman the Syrian, and the pride he had in his native rivers of Abana and Pharpar, which he vainly imagined to be superior to the healing waters of Jordan—the moral being, that he, Ward, was the keeper and guardian of the undoubted waters of Jordan, and that the unhappy conceited boys must go to perdition unless they came to him.
>
> (XV, 49)

and to eavesdrop on divine worship as conducted by the more easygoing Mr Sampson, the Church of England's equivalent of a worldly French abbé:

> The clergyman, a tall, high-coloured, handsome young man, read the service in a lively, agreeable voice, giving almost a dramatic point to the chapters of Scripture which he read.
>
> (XV, 148)

While Ward, we are told, is apt to make long speeches even out of his pulpit "interspersed with many of his usual Scripture phrases" (XV, 51), Sampson is more likely to quote Shakespeare than the Bible when he is not formally preaching. Home prayers, naturally enough, incorporate Old as well as New Testament locutions—Mr Lambert, for instance, is found praying with his family and servants "that Heaven would lighten their darkness and defend them from the perils of the night, and . . . that it would grant the supplication of those two or three gathered together" (XV, 331–2; cf. 2 Samuel 22, 29, Matthew 18, 20). This is just one example out of many in which we find Thackeray's characters drawing strength, consolation or confirmation from recollections of the Scriptures; but they may also draw self-reproach from the same source. Madam Esmond shows herself "disturbed, because my eldest born is a *disobedient son* and an *unkind brother*—because he has an estate, and my poor Harry, bless him, but *a mess of pottage*" (XV, 38–41) and is later heard to exclaim:

> 'My fault hath been, and I own it, that my love was centred upon you, perhaps to the neglect of your elder brother . . .I turned from Esau, and I clung to Jacob. And now I have my reward. . . .
>
> (XV, 896)

Even the least pious characters will occasionally "[dress their] worldliness out in phylacteries" (XV, 794): Lord Castlewood, for instance, who

> did not conceal his ... natural want of courage. 'I dare say you respect me no more than I respect myself, George,' he would say, in his candid way, and begin a very pleasant sardonical discourse upon the fall of man ...
>
> (XV, 765)

or Jack Morris, who warns Harry Warrington that Lord March would play him

> 'for every acre you have in Virginia ... And for all your tobacco, and for all your spices, and for all your slaves, and for all your oxen and asses, and for everything that is yours'
>
> (XV, 263);

or Baroness Bernstein:

> 'I am but seventy-six. But what a wreck, my dear: and isn't it cruel that our time should be so short?'
> Here my wife has to state the incontrovertible proposition that the time of all of us is short here below.
> 'Ha!' cried the Baroness, 'did not Adam live near a thousand years, and was not Eve beautiful all the time? I used to perplex Mr. Tusher with that—poor creature! What have we done since, that our lives are so much lessened, I say?'
>
> (XV, 876–7)

Perplexing the pious, as the Baroness here recalls doing to her first husband who became a bishop, is one of the pleasures the worldly find in quoting Scripture. The pious do not always take this in good part; witness this exchange between Colonel Esmond and his daughter:

> 'Say what you will, dear sir, I can *not* believe that this fiddling is work for persons of fashion.'
> 'And King David who played the harp, my dear?'
> 'I wish my papa would read him more, and not speak about him in that way,', said Mrs. Warrington.
>
> (XV, 32)

George Warrington not only enjoys referring his and his friends' life-experience to that recorded by the Hebrews as well as the Greeks ("we argued that the Virginian Squire was under female domination—as Hercules, Samson, and *fortes multi* had been before him"—XV, 900), but also likes to introduce, into his conversation, sly allusions to Biblical characters and incidents which less quick-witted or Scripturally versed partners are apt to miss:

'You should moderate your expressions, cousin, regarding the dear countess and my lord, your brother, Mr. Warrington resumed. 'Of you they always speak most tenderly. Her ladyship has told me everything.'

'What, *everything?*' cries Will, aghast.

'As much as women ever *do* tell, cousin. She owned that she thought you had been a little *épris* with her. What woman can help liking a man who has admired her?'

'Why, she hates you, and says you were wild about her, Mr. Warrington!' says Mr. Esmond.

'*Spretae injuria formae*, cousin!'

'For me—what's for me?' asks the other.

'I never did care for her, and hence, perhaps, she does not love me. Don't you remember that case of the wife of the captain of the guard?'

'Which guard?' asks Will.

'My Lord Potiphar,' says Mr. Warrington.

'Lord Who? My Lord Falmouth is Captain of the Yeomen of the Guard, and my Lord Berkeley of the Pensioners. My Lord Hobart had 'em before. Suppose you haven't been long enough in England to know who's who, cousin!' remarks Mr. William.

But Mr. Warrington explained that he was speaking of a captain of the guard of the King of Egypt, whose wife had persecuted one Joseph for not returning her affection for him. On which Will said that, as for Egypt, he believed it was a confounded long way off, and that, if Lord Whatd'ye-call's wife told lies about him, it was like her sex, who he supposed were the same everywhere.

(XV, 768–9)

Thackeray indulges, occasionally, in the game of pitting the dignity of a Scriptural phrase against the comicality of the character who uses it—especially when it is spoken in what passes in these novels for an Irish accent. An Irishman who tells wildly exaggerated, blood-curdling stories about himself and his family ("Every crime which you can think of; the entire Ten Commandments broken in a general smash") is thus made to deform Genesis 42, 38: "Me brother Tim had brought his fawther's gree hairs with sorrow to the greeve; me brother Mick had robbed the par'sh church repaytedly . . ." (XV, 392). Baroness Bernstein's mental and moral world is brightly illuminated when we hear her equate "Joseph" with "simpleton" (XV, 289, yet another allusion to the Potiphar story, so important in Fielding as well as Thackeray); and the reader is surely meant to think meanly of the intellectual and moral penetration of Gumbo when he commends the one incident in the Old Testament narrative which Thackeray himself detested more than any other: "Gumbo, dressing his master for dinner, talked about Elisha (of whom he had heard the chaplain read in the morning), 'and his bald head and de boys who call um names, and de bars eat em up, and serve um right,' says Gumbo" (XV,

774—cf. 2 Kings 2, 23). Comic-book "darkie" speech, like the stage-Irish so frequent in Thackeray's fiction, is another means of making the English reader feel superior to the character who so "deforms" his language.

One last use of Old Testament quotations and allusions remains to be noticed. The phrase "vine and fig-tree" (Deuteronomy 8, 8, Psalm 105, 33, Job 2, 22 and especially Jeremiah 5, 17) occurs early in *The Virginians*, when George Warrington bitterly glosses George Warrington's "When we have given the French a sufficient drubbing, I shall return to repose under my own vine and fig-tree" (XV, 82); this becomes a *leitmotif* in the novel when George's own return to his Virginian estates and the domestic contentment he finds there is narrated in a chapter headed "Under Vine and Fig-Tree" (XV, 979ff.). The variations Thackeray plays, in the course of the Virginians, on the stories of the Fall of Man, of Joseph, of Samson and of Esther fulfil a similar *leitmotif* function.

Adam and Eve, the Garden of Eden and its Forbidden Tree, Methuselah, Sarah, Jacob and Esau, Mother Rachel, Joseph and the Potiphars, the Red Sea, the Golden Calf, the Decalogue, Samson and Delilah (XV, 372), the spoiling of the Philistines, Jephtha's daughter (XV, 817), David and Goliath (XV, 718) as well as King David the Psalmist, Naaman the Syrian, Jehu and Abigail, Elijah and Elisha, the children who cried "Go up, thou bald head", Jezebel, Ruth, Esther and Ahasuerus, Susanna and the Elders, the bulls of Bashan (XV, 284, 616), the phrasing of the Psalms, of Solomon the Preacher, and of the Prophets of Israel, become vivid presences in *The Virginians*, bringing with them a world of colourful incident, poetry and—on occasions— spirituality. None of this prevented Thackeray, however, from continuing his polemic against his mother's view of the Deity's actions and purposes with regard to the Jewish people:

> Was [Heaven] specially concerned in punishing chastising trying blessing, smashing saving those Jews, who were under the tower of Siloam when it fell? A brick may have knocked a just man's brains out: and a beam fallen so as to protect a scoundrel who happened to be standing under. The bricks and beams fell according to the laws which regulate bricks in tumbling . . .
> (to Mrs Carmichael-Smyth, February 1859 - LPP, IV, 128)

The reference here is to Luke 13, 4–5; and Thackeray is invoking the New Testament along with Newtonian laws of gravity and with aleatory rules of chance to counteract what he thought his mother's exaggerated ideas about the Jews as a "chosen" people.

ii

In 1859 Thackeray accepted the editorship of the *Cornhill Magazine*, which henceforth became the main outlet for his serial fiction, his essays and occasional papers, and the printed versions of his lectures. "The Four Georges" appeared there in 1860; so did the first of his "Roundabout Papers", entitled "On a Lazy, Idle Boy", as well as a poem whose very title, "Vanitas Vanitatum", places it under the aegis of the Old Testament.

> How spake of old the Royal Seer?
>   (His text is one I love to treat on.)
> This life of ours, he said, is sheer
>   *Mataiotes Mataioteton.*
>
> O Student of this gilded Book,
>   Declare, while musing on its pages,
> If truer words were ever spoke
>   By ancient or by modern sages?
> .   .   .   .
> .   .   .   .
>
> Though thrice a thousand years are past
>   Since David's son, the sad and splendid,
> The weary King Ecclesiast,
>   Upon his awful tablets penned it,—
>
> Methinks the text is never stale,
>   And life is every day renewing
> Fresh comments on the old, old tale
>   Of Folly, Fortune, Glory, Ruin.
>
> Hark to the Preacher, preaching still!
>   He lifts his voice and cries his sermon,
> Here at St. Peter's of Cornhill,
>   As yonder on the Mount of Hermon:
>
> For you and me to heart to take
>   (O dear beloved brother readers)
> To-day as when the good King spake
>   Beneath the solemn Syrian cedars.

                                                 (VII, 96–8)

This long poem is the most eloquent tribute Thackeray was ever to pay to an Old Testament text and its putative author; a tribute all the more powerful because the poet takes account of objections that might be and have been made against this text, and still feels able to assert its truth and the undying value of the book of Ecclesiastes from which it comes.

The first of Thackeray's prose fictions to be serialized in the *Cornhill Magazine* was *Lovel the Widower* (January—June 1860): a fascinating but now unjustly neglected short novel based on the

comedy *The Wolves and the Lamb* which no-one had wanted to stage
and which was to achieve only two recorded performances in its
author's life-time—private ones in the house at 2, Palace Green,
Kensington into which he moved in 1862 and where he died at the
end of the following year.

Lovel the Widower is narrated by Mr Batchelor, a friend of the
eponymous hero: a gentle and well-meaning man who finds himself
maligned as an extortionate creditor and protests that "it was hard
of Mrs. Prior to represent me in the character of Shylock to the
Master of Boniface" (XVII, 91). When he falls in love, he sees his
beloved as Scott's Rebecca and an importunate suitor as Brian de
Bois Guilbert, but he himself lacks Ivanhoe's self-confidence and
ability to act resolutely in moments of stress and crisis.

> I was just *going* to run in—and I didn't. I was just going to rush to
> Bessy's side to clasp her (I have no doubt) to my heart: to beard the
> whiskered champion who was before her, and perhaps say, 'Cheer
> thee—cheer thee, my persecuted maiden, my beauteous love—my
> Rebecca! Come on, Sir Brian de Bois Guilbert, thou dastardly
> Templar! It is I, Sir Wilfred of Ivanhoe.' (By the way, though the
> fellow was not a *Templar*, he was a *Lincoln's Inn man*, having passed
> twice through the Insolvent Court there with infinite discredit.) But I
> made no heroic speeches. There was no need for Rebecca to jump out
> of the window and risk her lovely neck. How could she, in fact, the
> French window being flush with the ground-floor? And I give you my
> honour, just as I was crying my war-cry, couching my lance, and
> rushing *à la recousse* upon Sir Baker, a sudden thought made me rein
> in my galloping (metaphorical) steed, and spare Baker for that time.
>   (XVII, 151-2)

Scott's Jewish heroine here represents the archetypal maiden in
distress, a subject for daydreams of valour for whose realization the
modern period offers few opportunities. Even when such an opportunity presents itself, however, Mr Batchelor is unable to seize it;
someone else rushes in and effects the rescue he dreamed about. At
times this Prufrock *avant la lettre* laments his lonely state, comparing
himself, with self-caricaturing pathos, to the Wandering Jew:

> Oh! alone, alone, alone! Why, Fate! didst ordain that I should be
> companionless? Tell me where the Wandering Jew is, that I may go
> and sit with him. . . .
>   (XVII, 176)

but he rightly reflects that he might have had a bullying wife, and
ten children to bring up on £ 420 a year (XVII, 152); and he might
have added that Ivanhoe's own marriages did not turn out altogether happily, if *Rebecca and Rowena* is to be believed.

Lovel the Widower affords Thackeray's readers another glimpse of

his most complex and interesting Jewish character: Sherrick, whose
original name may have been Shadrach and whose mother was the
daughter of a diamond merchant who bore the family name Absalom. Sherrick's associate, here as in *The Newcomes*, is Charles
Honeyman; but instead of running Lady Whittlesea's Chapel
between them, they here own a moribund literary journal called
Museum which Honeyman persuades Mr Batchelor to purchase.
This is as autobiographically relevant as Thackeray's depiction of
dreadful mothers-in-law: what happens to Mr Batchelor in the case
of *Museum* closely resembles what happened to Thackeray in the
case of the *National Standard*. Might the character of Sherrick be
based on someone involved in that transaction? The mysterious Mr
Goldshede perhaps?

> My college friends had a joke at my expense (a very small joke serves
> to amuse those port-wine-bibbing fogies, and keeps them laughing for
> ever so long a time)—they are welcome, I say, to make merry at my
> charges—in respect of a certain bargain which I made on coming to
> London, and in which, had I been Moses Primrose purchasing green
> spectacles, I could scarcely have been more taken in. *My* Jenkinson
> was an old college acquaintance, whom I was idiot enough to
> imagine a respectable man: the fellow had a very smooth tongue, and
> sleek, sanctified exterior. He was rather a popular preacher, and used
> to cry a good deal in the pulpit. He, and a queer wine-merchant and
> bill-discounter, Sherrick by name, had somehow got possession of
> that neat little literary paper, the *Museum*, which perhaps, you
> remember; and this eligible literary property my friend Honeyman,
> with his wheedling tongue, induced me to purchase. I bear no malice:
> the fellow is in India now, where I trust he pays his butcher and
> baker. He was in dreadful straits for money when he sold me the
> *Museum*. He began crying when I told him some short time after-
> wards that he was a swindler, and from behind his pocket-
> handkerchief sobbed a prayer that I should one day think better of
> him; whereas my remarks to the same effect produced an exactly
> contrary impression upon his accomplice, Sherrick, who burst out
> laughing in my face, and said, 'The more fool you.' Mr. Sherrick was
> right. He was a fool, without mistake, who had any money-dealing
> with him; and poor Honeyman was right, too; I don't think so badly
> of him as I did. A fellow so hardly pinched for money could not resist
> the temptation of extracting it from such a greenhorn. I dare say I
> gave myself airs as editor of that confounded *Museum*, and proposed
> to educate the public taste, to diffuse morality and sound literature
> throughout the nation, and to pocket a liberal salary in return for my
> services. I dare say I printed my own sonnets, my own tragedy, my
> own verses (to a Being who shall be nameless, but whose conduct has
> caused a faithful heart to bleed not a little). I dare say I wrote
> satirical articles, in which I piqued myself upon the fineness of my
> wit, and criticisms, got up for the nonce, out of encyclopaedias and
> biographical dictionaries; so that I would be actually astounded at
> my own knowledge. I dare say I made a gaby of myself to the world:

pray, my good friend, hast thou never done likewise? If thou hast never been a fool, be sure thou wilt never be a wise man.

I think it was my brilliant *confrère* on the first floor (he had pecuniary transactions with Sherrick, and visited two or three of her Majesty's metropolitan prisons at that gentleman's suit) who first showed me how grievously I had been cheated in the newspaper matter.

(XVII, 73–4)

It is the sentimental Honeyman, not the realistic and humorous Sherrick, who persuades the greenhorn to buy a dubious property, leaving his partner in the background until, after the event, that partner points out what a hard and valuable lesson the whole transaction should have taught Mr Batchelor. There is no hint here of the presumptive Jewish ancestry of this wine merchant and bill-broker who has agents conducting pecuniary transactions with imprisoned debtors—this could be known only by those who re- member the part Sherrick played in *The Newcomes*. As the body of his fiction grew, however, Thackeray could rely more and more on his readers' recollection of earlier novels and could build up a world of interconnected families, friends and enemies which recalls that of Balzac and anticipates that of Trollope.

iii

In a book of reminiscences entitled *Some Experiences of a Barrister's Life* (quoted LPP IV, 59), William Ballantine describes a carica-ture Thackeray had drawn of some acquaintances and fellow members of a gentlemen's club: "Robbins was represented wounded by thieves and assisted by some good Samaritans, also portrayed, while Albert Smith, the Pharisee of the parable, was passing scornfully on the other side." The parable of the man fallen among thieves was one of Thackeray's favourite New Testament passages; he used it many times, drew a pictorial capital which embodied it, made it figure ironically in one of his last illustrations for *Vanity Fair*, and incorporated it into the full title of a novel that began to appear in the *Cornhill* in January 1861. This novel, published in book-form in 1862, was called

THE
ADVENTURES OF PHILIP
ON HIS WAY THROUGH THE WORLD
SHEWING
WHO ROBBED HIM, WHO HELPED HIM,
AND WHO PASSED HIM BY.

Over and over again, in the course of this novel, the narrator alludes to this same New Testament parable, playing a number of variations on it—nowhere more forcibly than in Chapter VIII, where it is accompanied by a familiar phrase from the Old Testament (Exodus 20, 5 and 34, 7; Numbers 14, 18; Deuteronomy 5, 9).

> If somebody or some Body of savants would write the history of the harm that has been done in the world by people who believe themselves to be virtuous, what a queer, edifying book it would be, and how poor oppressed rogues might look up! Who burns the Protestants?—the virtuous Catholics to be sure. Who roasts the Catholics?—the virtuous Reformers. Who thinks I am a dangerous character, and avoids me at the club?—the virtuous Squaretoes. Who scorns? who persecutes? who doesn't forgive?—the virtuous Mrs. Grundy. She remembers her neighbour's peccadilloes to the third and fourth generation; and, if she finds a certain man fallen in her path, gathers up her affrighted garments with a shriek, for fear the muddy, bleeding wretch should contaminate her, and passes on.
>
> (XVI, 103)

In his justly famous article headed "Thackeray's Recantation" (*PMLA* LXXVII, 1962 pp. 586–94), J.E. Baker has forcefully argued that in *Philip* the original meaning of the New Testament parable evoked on the very title page has been perverted, because if the parallel were to hold, Thackeray would have had to make the mulatto Woolcomb give the help which those whom Philip thinks of as "his own people" had refused. The distressing racism of Thackeray's either patronising or hostile treatment of black or Asian characters, including his mockery of the Abolitionist slogan "Am I not a Man and a Brother?", cannot be gainsaid; it should not be overlooked, however, that some of Philip's "helpers" *are* found among the socially disadvantaged, wounded or despised— modern equivalents of the Samaritan of the parable—but that Thackeray refuses to believe that the good impulses and actions of the "Samaritans" are wholly denied to "Levites".

> Because they are born gentlemen and ladies of good degree, are in easy circumstances, and have a generous education, it does not follow that they are heartless and will turn their back on a friend.
>
> (XVI, 539)

He would surely have sympathized with the stand taken by the great American lawyer Clarence Darrow who justified taking on the unpopular task of defending the wealthy murderers Leopold and Loeb by saying that the rich were entitled to as fair a trial as the poor.

Juliet McMaster, in her brilliant essay on the terrifying subtext of *Philip*, makes another important point in defence of the novelist's way with his favourite New Testament parable. "Thackeray is concerned here", she writes, "less with class alignments than with familial ones. Both the thieves and the uncharitable Levites are generally of the traveller's own tribe—Dr. Firmin, the Twysdens and the Ringwoods; while those who aid him are those on whom he has no direct claim—the Pendennises, Madame de Smolensk, and Dr. Goodenough" ("Funeral Baked Meats: Thackeray's Last Novel", *Studies in the Novel*, North Texas State University, XIII, 1981, p. 154). Pendennis's and Phillip's experiences lead them to add a rider to the New Testament parable, to recognise the possibility of righteous insiders as well as righteous outsiders. The Old Testament Decalogue is treated in a similar way: while recognizing these commandments as foundations of ethical behaviour (XVI, 131, 407), Pendennis is ready to add riders and extensions to them. We are commanded to honour our parents; Pendennis is ready to agree, but he adduces a case where "a parent [has] forgotten to honour her daughter" in order to indict Philip's father:

> Suppose there is some reason which prevents Philip from loving his father—that the doctor has neglected to cleanse the boy's heart, and by carelessness and indifference has sent him erring into the world. If so, woe be to that doctor!
>
> (XVI, 62)

Thackeray's readiness, occasionally distressing to his modern readers, to accept some of the prejudices of his society—reinforced by Anglo-Indian relatives, and by friends in the southern states of the USA—is cut across, here and elsewhere, by his conviction that hallowed maxims must be subjected to rational scrutiny and the test of experience.

New Testament references—to the Good Samaritan, the Prodigal Son, the widow's mite, the widow's cruse, the figure of Jesus and the Lord's prayer he enjoined on his followers, to Matthew 6, 27 and Matthew 7, 3—are once again shadowed by a plethora of allusions to the figures of the Old Testament. None of these acquire such central importance as the figures in the Good Samaritan parable; but four pairs of them, at least, assume considerable thematic significance. These are Abraham and Isaac (XVI, 555); Nathan reproaching King David (XVI, 395–6) (ill. 2).
Samson in the toils of Delilah (XVI, 157, 397–8, 525–6); and Judith and Holofernes (XVI, 558) (ill. 3).

The "Judith" image is introduced in connection with the chloroforming of the blackmailing villain of the piece, Tufton Hunt; and Juliet McMaster, in the essay already cited, has analyzed the way in which this "Judith" parallel fits in with what she rightly regards as "the major stratum of interest" in this novel, "erupting recur-

WHAT NATHAN SAID UNTO DAVID

Illustration 2

rently into the cooler world of social accommodation": "the panic and hatred within, the irrational fantasies and suppressed desperation that find their strangled expression in gestures and images" (loc. cit., p. 136).

The blackmailer who is put out of action by "the Little Sister", that Victorian parlour version of Judith and Delilah, is a Christian

JUDITH AND HOLOFERNES

Illustration 3

clergyman; and it is he, not the privileged narrator, who speaks of
his German creditors as "wicked Jews" and designates the creditors of another Englishman stranded in Frankfurt "Philistines":

> 'Dr. Luther's hymn! *Wein, Weib[er] und Gesang*, to be sure! cries the
> clergyman, humming the tune. 'I learned it in Germany myself—
> passed a good deal of time in Germany, Captain Gann—six months
> in a specially shady place—*Quod* Strasse, in Frankfort-on-the-

Maine—being persecuted by some wicked Jews there. And there was another poor English chap in the place, too, who used to chirp that song behind the bars, and died there and disappointed the Philistines.'

(XVII, 122)

Significantly enough, it is this same drunken, greasy, dirty, disreputable but clearly Gentile clergyman who consciously assumes the role of Shylock: "'No, I'll have my bond!' And he gave a tipsy imitation of Shylock, and lurched back into his chair, and laughed." (XVI, 575). Hunt is also, of course, the miserable totally unheroic Holofernes against whom the Little Sister plays Judith for the sake of Philip's financial and social salvation.

Hunt's creditors in London include Jacobs the moneylender (XVI, 156); and the bailiffs who move in on Dr Firmin are nightmare figures out of Cursitor Street. "'My poor father'". Philip tells Pendennis, "'had ruin written in his face: and when those bailiffs made their appearance in Parr Street yesterday, I felt as if I had known them before. I had seen their hooked beaks in my dreams.'" (XVI, 202). This birds-of-prey image recurs in yet another of Thackeray's auction-scenes:

> . . . when Firmin's furniture came to be sold, it was a marvel how little his creditors benefited by the sale. Contemptuous brokers declared there never was such a shabby lot of goods. A friend of the house and poor Philip bought in his mother's picture for a few guineas; and as for the doctor's own state portrait, I am afraid it went for a few shillings only, and in the midst of a roar of Hebrew laughter. I saw in Wardour Street, not long after, the doctor's sideboard, and what dealers cheerfully call the sarcophagus cellaret. Poor doctor! his wine was all drunken; his meat was eaten up; but his own body had slipped out of the reach of the hook-beaked birds of prey.
>
> (XVI, 206)

What is so painful here is that fond memories and associations which have accumulated around possessions count for nothing any more. Objects revert to their material state "in the midst of a roar of Hebrew laughter." And the same people who at forced auctions run the exhibits down in order to acquire them as cheaply as possible conduct auctions of their own at which they run up the objects they want to sell:

> [Philip's] purchases were not always lucky. For example, he was sadly taken in at an auction about a little pearl ornament. Some artful Hebrews at the sale conspired and ran him up, as the phrase is, to a price more than equal to the value of the trinket.
>
> (XVI, 461)

Here we see commodities on their way upwards again, aspiring towards the associations that will cluster around them when their purchaser hands them to a beloved recipient.

While the buyers at the auction are undoubtedly Jews, no ethnic provenance is suggested when Pendennis tells his readers of "dangerous financiers" to whom Dr Firmin had resorted and who had thus come into possession of "numberless lately-signed bills" (XVI, 202). Readers of Thackeray's novels may well think of Jews in this connection, however, when they recollect how often he had presented Jewish money-lenders and middle-men elsewhere; and they may also remember his many portrayals of Jewish bailiffs and sheriff's officers when they hear Philip refer (in one of the letters he is said to have written "to his present biographer") to creditors "as insatiable as any usurer, and as hard as any bailiff" (XVI, 271).

Among the Jewish traders who swim into Pendennis's ken in *Philip* are old-clothes men and bric-à-brac dealers who have moved into what was once the haunt of the London *beau monde*.

> Why shall not one moralize over London, as over Rome, or Baalbec, or Troy town? I like to walk among the Hebrews of Wardour Street, and fancy the place, as it once was, crowded with chairs and gilt chariots, and torches flashing of the hands of the running footmen. I have a grim pleasure in thinking that Golden Square was once the resort of the aristocracy, and Monmouth Street the delight of the genteel world. What shall prevent us Londoners from musing over the decline and fall of city sovereignties, and drawing our cockney morals? As the late Mr. Gibbon meditated his history leaning against a column in the Capitol, why should not I muse over mine, reclining under an arcade of the Pantheon? Not the Pantheon at Rome, in the Cabbage Market by the Piazza Navona, where the immortal gods were worshipped,—the immortal gods who are now dead; but the Pantheon in Oxford Street, ladies, where you purchase feeble pomatums, music, glassware, and baby-linen; and which has its history too. Have not Selwyn, and Walpole, and March, and Carlisle figured there? Has not Prince Florizel flounced through the hall in his rustling domino, and danced there in powdered splendour? and when the ushers refused admission to lovely Sophy Baddeley, did not the young men, her adorers, draw their rapiers and vow to slay the doorkeepers; and, crossing the glittering blades over the head of the enchantress, make a warlike triumphal arch for her to pass under, all flushed, and smiling, and perfumed, and painted? The lives of streets are as the lives of men, and shall not the street-preacher, if so minded, take for the text of his sermon the stones in the gutter? That you were once the resort of the fashion, O Monmouth Street! by the invocation of blessed St. Giles shall I not improve that sweet thought into a godly discourse, and make the ruin edifying?
>
> (XVI, 17)

Florizel, of course, is the young crown prince who later became George IV; and what Thackeray depicts here is part of the evolution of London, which included the metamorphosis of Monmouth Street into the row of cheap clothing establishments that Cruikshank had depicted with such verve, over twenty years earlier, for the "Meditations in Monmouth-Street" of Dickens's *Sketches by Boz*.

Illustration 4

Dickens had drawn a distinction between Holywell Street, where "the red-headed and red-whiskered Jews .... forcibly haul you into their squalid houses, and thrust you into a suit of clothes, whether you will or not", and Monmouth Street, where "a peace-

able and retiring race" waits within shops and dwellings for customers and comes forth into the world to take the air in the dusk
and coolness of evening. "Through every alteration and every
change, Monmouth Street has still remained the burial-place of
fashions; and such, to judge from all present appearances, it will
remain until there are no more fashions to bury." Dickens stresses
continuity within change, and then flies off into fantasy in which
the clothes exhibited for sale take on a life of their own, transport-
ing Boz into the lives of those who may once have worn them.
Thackeray stresses change and degeneration, and no wings of
fantasy bear him beyond Monmouth Street in its present state, as
he focuses on one particular establishment, whose exhibits he
terms, with characteristically Thackerayan humour, a "museum"
of turned old clothes:

> See, in the embrasure of the window, where you sat looking to the
> stars and nestling by the soft side of your first-love, hang Mr. Moses's
> museum of turned old clothes, very cheap; of worn old boots, be-
> draggled in how much and how many people's mud; a great bargain.
> See! along the street, strewed with flowers once mayhap—a fight of
> beggars for the refuse of an apple-stall, or a tipsy basket-woman,
> reeling shrieking to the station. O me! O my beloved congregation! I
> have preached this stale sermon to you for ever so many years. O my
> jolly companions, I have drunk many a bout with you and always
> found *vanitas vanitatum* written on the bottom of the pot!
>
> (XVI, 18)

As so often before, the words of the Hebrew Preacher conclude
Thackeray's, or his narrator's, reflections on the vicissitudes of
Vantity Fair. This should not be overstressed, however—we must
also give due weight to the opening words of the passage on
changing London which has already been quoted: "*I like to walk
among the Hebrews of Wardour Street. . . .*" (XVI, 17—my italics).

The higher rag-trade comes into view later in Thackeray's novel.

> You must know, ladies, that when Philip's famous ship of dollars
> arrived from America, Firmin had promised his wife that baby
> should have a dear delightful white cloak trimmed with the most
> lovely tape, on which poor Charlotte had often cast a longing eye as
> she passed by the milliner and curiosity shops in Hanway Yard,
> which I own, she loved to frequent. Well: when Philip told her that
> his father had sent home forty pounds, or what not, thereby deceiving
> his fond wife, the little lady went away straight to her darling shop in
> the Yard— (Hanway Yard has become a street now, but ah! it is
> always delightful)—Charlotte, I say, went off, ran off to Hanway
> Yard, pavid with fear lest the darling cloak, should be gone, found
> it—oh, joy!—still in Miss Isaacson's window; put it on baby straight-

way then and there; kissed the dear infant, and was delighted with the effect of the garment, which all the young ladies at Miss Isaacson's pronounced to be perfect; and took the cloak away on baby's shoulders, promising to send the money, five pounds, if you please, next day. And in this cloak baby and Charlotte went to meet papa when he came home; and I don't know which of them, mamma or baby, was the most pleased and absurd and happy baby of the two.

(XVI, 505)

Miss Isaacson, the Jewish shopkeeper of Hanway Yard, is clearly rendering a valuable service to the community, in an atmosphere wholly free from Holywell Street sordidness.

Jewish names more famous than that of Miss Isaacson reappear in the pages of *Philip*. One of these is only suggested when the facetious Lord Ascot refers to a cigar "given to my father by the Duke of Medina Sidonia" (XVI, 88)—which brings Disraeli's super-Jew Sidonia into proximity to the cigar-trade in which so many Victorian Jews engaged. Another is more overtly introduced in the course of a description of how the Little Sister's father, "Captain" Gann, enriched the musical parts of a chapel service.

Mr. Gann . . . brought a rich, though somewhat worn, bass voice to bear upon the anthems and hymns at the chapel. His style was more florid than is general now among church singers, and, indeed, had been acquired in a former age and in the performance of rich Bachanalian chants, such as delighted the contemporaries of our Incledons and Brahams.

(XVI, 68)

Here John Braham (1774–1856), of whose Jewish antecedents Thackeray had made such cruel fun in the *National Standard*, is named alongside the Gentile Charles Benjamin Incledon (1763–1826) among "our" singers who delighted British audiences of an earlier time. No ethnic distinctions are made or hinted at. And just as the piece on Braham in the *National Standard* had a companion piece on Rothschild, so Rothschild's name appears alongside that of Braham in *Philip*. It does so in a paean to the art and activity of a gifted painter.

To be a painter, and to have your hand in perfect command, I hold to be one of life's *summa bona*. The happy mixture of hand and head work must render the occupation supremely pleasant. . . Here is occupation: here is excitement: here is struggle and victory: and here is profit. Can man ask more from fortune? Dukes and Rothschilds may be envious of such a man.

(XVI, 75)

"Our Incledons and Brahams", "Dukes and Rothschilds"—the Gentile and the (baptized) Jewish singer, the hereditary aristocracy and the (unbaptized) aristocracy of money, now appear on equal footing, with no Jew's harp or Old Clothes symbolism to distinguish the one from the other. That associations of Jewishness cling to the name Rothschild Thackeray would be the last to deny; but his Pendennis thinks it neither necessary nor desirable to draw attention to these in the invidious manner of the *National Standard*.

iv

"Thorns in the Cushion", one of the "Roundabout Papers" Thackeray published in the *Cornhill Magazine* between 1861 and 1863, contains a memorable defence of a Jewish painter who contributed to the Pre-Raphaelite movement in England: Simeon Solomon. (1840–1905). His discussion of one of Solomon's paintings exhibited in the Royal Academy in 1860 contains a characteristically Thackerayan elaboration of an incident related in the Old Testament, together with a defence of the kind of realism in art to which the Pre-Raphaelites aspired.

> . . . one of the pictures I admired most at the Royal Academy is by a gentleman on whom I never, to my knowledge, set eyes. This picture is No. 346, *Moses*, by Mr. S. Solomon. I thought it had a great intention. I thought it finely drawn and composed. It nobly represented, to my mind, the dark children of the Egyptian bondage, and suggested the touching story. My newspaper says: 'Two ludicrously ugly women, looking at a dingy baby, do not form a pleasing object;' and so good-bye, Mr. Solomon. Are not most of our babies served so in life? and doesn't Mr. Robinson consider Mr. Brown's cherub an ugly, squalling little brat? So cheer up, Mr. S.S. It may be the critic who discoursed on your baby is a bad judge of babies. When Pharaoh's kind daughter found the child, and cherished and loved it, and took it home, and found a nurse for it, too, I dare say there were grim, brick-dust-coloured chamberlains, or some of the tough, old, meagre, yellow princesses at court, who never had children themselves, who cried out, 'Faugh! the horrid little squalling wretch!' and knew he would never come to good; and said 'Didn't I tell you so?' when he assaulted the Egyptian.
> Never mind then, Mr. S. Solomon, I say, because a critic pooh-poohs your work of art—your Moses—your child—your foundling. Why, did not a wiseacre in *Blackwood's Magazine* lately fall foul of *Tom Jones*? O hypercritic! So, to be sure, did good old Mr. Richardson, who could write novels himself—but you, and I, and Mr. Gibbon, my dear sir, agree in giving our respect, and wonder, and admiration, to the brave old master.

(XVII,399–400)

The "touching story" of the "dark children of the Egyptian bondage" is brought nearer to a Victorian readership when "grim, brick-dust coloured chamberlains" and "tough, old, meagre, yellow princesses" at Pharaoh's court are made to speak with the voice of Simeon Solomon's—and Fielding's—nineteenth-century detractors. The adjective "brick-dust-coloured" would seem peculiarly appropriate in its context: the story of Israel in Egypt in which brick-making plays such a prominent part.

As for the title "A Thorn in the Cushion"—that is explained in the final paragraphs of the essay containing Simeon Solomon's defence, where Thackeray speaks, in his own person, of the thorny editorial chair he had recently begun to occupy in the offices of the *Cornhill Magazine*, and then widens the argument to take in enemies he had made by writing his novels in the only way he could.

> In the little history of *Lovel the Widower* I described, and brought to condign punishment, a certain wretch of a ballet-dancer, who lived splendidly for awhile on ill-gotten gains, had an accident, and lost her beauty, and died poor, deserted, ugly, and every way odious. In the same page, other little ballet-dancers are described, wearing homely clothing, doing their duty, and carrying their humble savings to the family at home. But nothing will content my dear correspondents but to have me declare that the majority of ballet-dancers have villas in the Regent's Park, and to convict me of 'deliberate falsehood'. Suppose, for instance, I had chosen to introduce a red-haired washerwoman into a story? I might get an expostulatory letter saying, 'Sir, In stating that the majority of washerwomen are red-haired, you are a liar! and you had best not speak of ladies who are immeasurably your superiors.' Or suppose I had ventured to describe an illiterate haberdasher? One of the craft might write to me, 'Sir, In describing haberdashers as illiterate, you utter a wilful falsehood. Haberdashers use much better English than authors.' It is a mistake, to be sure. I have never said what my correspondents say I say. There is the text under their noses, but what if they choose to read it their own way? 'Hurroo, lads! Here's for a fight. There's a bald head peeping out of the hut. There's a bald head! It must be Tim Malone's.' And whack! come down both the bludgeons at once.
>
> Ah me! we wound where we never intended to strike; we create anger where we never meant harm; and these thoughts are the Thorns in our Cushion.
>
> (XVII, 404–5)

The questions Thackeray raises here are important in the context of the present book. When are individuals, or groups, justified in thinking a fictional portrayal offensive? Is a character portrayed as an individual, or in such a way that readers must think him or her as a typical representative of his group? What is the cumulative effect of a large number of grotesque or unsympathetic individuals whom the writer unmistakably assigns to a given group? It all depends on the context, of course—whether the particular group pilloried is the only one so treated, or whether others are also satirized or lashed; whether there are any balancing factors, such as sympathetic portrayals of members of a given group in other passage or other works. Dickens came to feel the force of such questions when he created Riah as a conscious counterblast to Fagin; how Thackeray faced them in practice is the subject of the present book and will be considered more fully in its conclusion.

Is it an accident that after raising these questions in "A Thorn in the Cushion" Thackeray opens his next Roundabout Paper with the portrayal of a bailiff who might, but need not, be Jewish? He calls him "Mr. Nab"—a reference to his profession, but also a possible contraction of "Aminadab" or "Nadab", in the way "Braham" contracts "Abraham", and "Sloman" looks back to "Solomon".

> When the bailiffs are after a man, they adopt all sorts of disguises, pop out on him from all conceivable corners, and tap his miserable shoulder. His wife is taken ill; his sweetheart, who remarked his brilliant, too brilliant appearance at the Hyde Park review, will meet him at Cremorne, or where you will. The old friend who has owed him that money these five years will meet him at so-and-so and pay. By one bait or other the victim is hooked, netted, landed, and down goes the basket-lid. It is not your wife, your sweetheart, your friend, who is going to pay you. It is Mr. Nab the bailiff. *You* know——you are caught. You are off in a cab to Chancery Lane.
>   You know, I say? *Why* should you know? I make no manner of doubt you never were taken by a bailiff in your life. I never was. I have been in two or three debtors' prisons, but not on my own account. Goodness be praised! I mean you can't escape your lot; and Nab only stands here metaphorically as the watchful, certain, and untiring officer of Mr. Sheriff Fate.
>
>   (XVII, 406–7)

Punch, and Thackeray's novels, had accustomed Victorian readers to see sheriff's officers as Jewish; but Thackeray makes no such identification here. In view of the symbolic function the bailiff figure is made to serve on this occasion it was clearly better not to insist on the officer's ethnic provenance.

If one remembers Thackeray's unpleasant view of Jewish touts and pimps—or Dutch touts and pimps whom he took for Jews—in the "Notes" recording his "Tour of the Low Countries" in 1843, which remained unpublished in his own life-time, one can only think what he says in the paper entitled "A Roundabout Journey. Notes of a Week's Holiday" (November 1860) to be most pleasantly restrained:

> As we drove through the old city [of Rotterdam] at night, how it swarmed and hummed with life! What a special clatter, crowd, and

outcry there was in the Jewish quarter, where myriads of young ones were trotting about the fishy street! Why don't they have lamps? We passed by canals seeming so full that a pailful of water more would overflow the place. The *laquais de place* calls out the names of the buildings: the town-hall, the cathedral, the arsenal, the synagogue, the statue of Erasmus. . .

(XVII, 450)

This is one of the few places in which Thackeray takes notice of a synagogue; there is no record of his ever having been inside one. If his reaction to the bustling Jewish quarter of Rotterdam is restrained, that to the corresponding quarter in Amsterdam is positively enthusiastic:

> Amsterdam is as good as Venice, with a superadded humour and grotesqueness, which gives the sight-seer the most singular zest and pleasure. A run through Pekin I could hardly fancy to be more odd, strange, and yet familiar. This rush, and crowd, and prodigious vitality—this immense swarm of life—these busy waters, crowding barges, swinging drawbridges, piled ancient gables, spacious markets teeming with people—that ever-wonderful Jews' quarter—that dear old world of painting and the past, yet alive, and throbbing, and palpable—actual, and yet passing before you swiftly and strangely as a dream! Of the many journeys of this Roundabout life, that drive through Amsterdam is to be specially and gratefully remembered.
>
> (XVII, 458)

No doubt Rembrandt's paintings of Dutch Jews has had their effect on Thackeray; but what most strikes us here is Mr. Roundabout's delight in the "prodigious vitality", the "immense swarm of life" which the traveller encounters everywhere in Amsterdam and which makes the Jewish quarter too "ever wonderful". Even the grotesque element (to which Thackeray always responded) adds to a feeling of "singular zest and pleasure" which makes this description of a holiday in the Low Countries so refreshingly different from the trip through the same regions recorded in the "Notes" he had penned some twenty-seven years before.

The Roundabout Paper entitled "Ogres" (August 1861) includes a passing reference to the Rothschilds as pillars of financial stability and respectability who may be cited, along with the Baring brothers, and without their knowledge and authority, by less stable and less respectable practitioners in the City of London.

> Now, there are ogres in City courts who lure you into their dens. About our Cornish mines I am told there are many most plausible ogres, who tempt you into their caverns and pick your bones there. In a certain newspaper there used to be lately a whole column of advertisements from ogres who would put on the most plausible, nay,

piteous appearance, in order to inveigle their victims. You would read, 'A tradesman, established for seventy years in the City, and known, and much respected by Messrs. N. M. Rothschild and Baring Brothers, has pressing need for three pounds until next Saturday. He can give security for half a million, and forty thousand pounds will be given for the use of the loan,' and so on.

(XVII, 524)

When Mr Roundabout has to think, in "De Finibus" (1862), of two men who are utterly "different, in my mind's eye", the names he immediately remembers are those of "Lord Palmerston and Mr. Disraeli" (593). And when he has to recall, in "On a Pear Tree" (1862), an example of mutual benevolence and beneficence, he retells a story that features an unnamed Jew residing in New York. The story opens with an Englishman—"Laërtes let us call him"—who is "at present in exile, having been compelled to fly from remorseless creditors."

Laërtes fled to America, where he earned his bread by his pen. I own to having a kindly feeling towards this scapegrace, because, though an exile, he did not abuse the country whence he fled. I have heard that he went away taking no spoil with him, penniless almost; and on his voyage he made acquaintance with a certain Jew; and when he fell sick, at New York, this Jew befriended him and gave him help and money out of his own store, which was but small. Now, after they had been awhile in the strange city, it happened that the poor Jew spent all his little money, and he too fell ill, and was in great penury. And now it was Laërtes who befriended that Ebrew Jew. He fee'd doctors; he fed and tended the sick and hungry. Go to, Laërtes! I know thee not. It may be thou art justly *exul patriae*. But the Jew shall intercede for thee, thou not, let us trust, hopeless Christian sinner.

(XVII, 613)

This portrayal of Christian and Jew giving and receiving friendship and charity is as benevolent as anything in Richard Cumberland's *The Jew* or Lessing's *Die Juden*; indeed, this tale of mutual benefit and help is more pleasing than apologetics like Maria Edgeworth's *Harrington* in which a preternaturally virtuous Jew bestows all the benefits and Christians accept them gratefully or grudgingly.

"De Juventute" (1860), in which the aging Mr Roundabout looks back on his youthful pleasures, includes *Ivanhoe* (together with *Quentin Durward*) among early literary delights (XVII, 431); and "On a Peal of Bells" (1862) contrasts the ever-youthful Rebecca with aging women of her "Orient race":

Rebecca, daughter of Isaac of York, I have loved thee faithfully for forty years! Thou wert twenty years old (say) and I but twelve, when I knew thee. At sixty odd, love, most of the ladies of thy Orient race

have lost the bloom of youth, and bulged beyond the line of beauty;
but to me thou art ever young and fair, and I will do battle with any
felon Templar who assails thy fair name.

(XVII, 608)

Like Disraeli, Thackeray uses the term "race" to indicate the
ethnic origin of Jews; but here he uses it in a neutral way, without
asserting either the superiority of "Mosaic Arabs" in Disraeli's
manner or the inferiority of a people that includes the unnamed
American Jew of "On a Pear Tree". That he knew feelings of racial
superiority cannot be denied—his utterances on blacks, in his
letters and in some of his published writings, alternate between the
patronizing and the denigratory. He remains an enemy, however,
of religious or racial persecution; and he includes in the paper
entitled "On a Hundred Years Hence" (1861) a version of the
Sweeney Todd story which exhibits some of the mechanism by
which blood-libels—stories of ritual murder—were able to gain
credence among the gullible from medieval to modern times.

Well, yesterday at dinner Jucundus was good enough to tell me a
story about myself, which he had heard from a lady of his acquaintance, to whom I send my best compliments. The tale is this. At nine
o'clock on the evening of the 31st of November last, just before
sunset, I was seen leaving No. 96, Abbey Road, St. John's Wood,
leading two little children by the hand, one of them in a nankeen
pelisse, and the other having a mole on the third finger of his left
hand (she thinks it was the third finger, but is quite sure it was the
left hand). Thence I walked with them to Charles Boroughbridge's,
pork and sausage man, No. 29, Upper Theresa Road. Here, whilst I
left the little girl innocently eating a polony in the front shop, I and
Boroughbridge retired with the boy into the back parlour, where
Mrs. Boroughbridge was playing cribbage. She put up the cards and
boxes, took out a chopper and a napkin, and we cut the little boy's
little throat (which he bore with great pluck and resolution), and
made him into sausage-meat by the aid of Purkis's excellent sausage-
machine. The little girl at first could not understand her brother's
absence, but, under the pretence of taking her to see Mr. Fechter in
Hamlet, I led her down to the New River at Sadler's Wells, where a
body of a child in a nankeen pelisse was subsequently found, and has
never been recognized to the present day. And this Mrs. Lynx can
aver, because she saw the whole transaction with her own eyes, as she
told Mr. Jucundus.

I have altered the little details of the anecdote somewhat. But this
story is, I vow and declare, as true as Mrs. Lynx's. Gracious goodness! how do lies begin? What are the averages of lying?

(XVII, 502–3)

Jews are not mentioned, the slanderers' motives are not exposed;
but anyone who knows the history of the ritual murder charges

levelled against Jews, and the terrible persecutions to which they gave rise, will find Thackeray's indictment through ridicule applicable to such widespread and baseless calumnies. In his conscious mind Thackeray was a true heir of the European Enlightenment; but his preconscious or subconscious self was always near the surface, ready to seize occasions for challenging and invading the realm of his reason.

In all the "Roundabout Papers" so far discussed, Jewish characters are peripheral. They move into the centre, however, in two others that have now to be considered.

The first of these is entitled "The Notch on the Axe—A Story à la Mode", which ran in the *Cornhill Magazine* from April to June 1862 and in which Thackeray contributes his mite to the Wandering Jew stories which Eugène Sue had made newly popular. For the physical appearance of his Wandering Jew, Mr Roundabout directs his readers' attention to a capital he had drawn for an earlier paper ("On a Joke I once heard from the late Thomas Hood", December 1860)—a design Thackeray had copied from an old spoon:

Illustration 5

The Wandering Jew now calls himself Mr Pinto, and Mr Roundabout notes that he is much the worse for wear: he has false teeth, a glass eye, and a wooden leg; and that he speaks all languages with an equally foreign accent. His English is fairly represented by "I wore a beard den; I am shafed now; perhaps you tink I am a spoon" (XVII, 567); and "I have apartments in many cities. I lock dem up, and do not carry mosh logish." (XVII, 568). "Mosh logish" for "much luggage" recalls Thackeray's earlier attempts to create a mode of Jew-speak; but when Mr Roundabout hears Mr Pinto pronounce "did" as "dit", he concludes that although his name seems to point to a Portuguese origin, he must be a German —an allusion, perhaps, to the important German filiations of the Wandering Jew legend, and to the difference, increasingly perceived in Victorian England, between Sephardic and Ashkenazic Jews. Mr Roundabout, we find, is relieved to see that the mark left by Mr Pinto's wooden leg on the dusty floor is not cloven (thus dismissing the ancient popular identification of Jew and devil); but the glass eye is credited with the power to reinforce the natural eye's hypnotic force. (XVII, 569). One remembers what Thackeray had once said of Goethe's piercing and brilliant eyes:

> I felt quite afraid before them, and recollect comparing them to the eyes of the hero of a certain romance called *Melmoth the Wanderer*, which used to alarm us boys thirty years ago; eyes of an individual who had made a bargain with a Certain Person, and at extreme old age retained these eyes in all their awful splendour.
>
> ("Reminiscences of Weimar and Goethe"—X, 632)

Mr Pinto turns out to be a connoisseur of pictures and painters, speaking familiarly of Reynolds and Angelica Kaufmann; he cites Shakespeare and Wilkie Collins; he has been a prisoner of the Moors and a victim of the Inquisition; and he strongly hints at his identity with the notorious David Rizzo.

> 'Jack Wilkes said the handsomest man in London had but half an hour's start of him. And without vanity, I am scarcely uglier than Jack Wilkes. We were members of the same club at Medmenham Abbey, Jack and I, and had many a merry night together. Well, sir, I—Mary of Scotland knew me but as a little hunch-backed music-master; and yet, I think, *she* was not indifferent to her David Riz—and *she* came to misfortune. They all do—they all do!'
> 'Sir, you are wandering from your point!' I said, with some severity.
>
> (XVII, 581)

To accuse the Jew of "wandering" from the point is delicious piece of Thackerayan dramatic irony. When Mr Pinto confesses to having felt the tender passion on occasion, Mr Roundabout gives a most unflattering overall view of his present appearance.

> In truth, I was thinking, if girls fall in love with this sallow, hooked-nosed, glass-eyed, wooden-legged, dirty, hideous old man, with the sham teeth, they have a queer taste. *That* is what I was thinking.
>
> (ibid.)

It appears that he had lived, at one time, at Baden-Baden in great splendour; but now he is holed up in dusty London chambers, and his dress is said to be "as shabby as an old-clothes-man's" (XVII,

574). Even the Wandering Jew cannot escape the mental mechanism which made Victorian Englishmen think of old clothes whenever a Jew crossed their path. When Mr Pinto is challenged, however, to produce "a cheque with a known signature" to establish his financial credentials, he performs a feat that calls up very different associations.

> I saw a hand come quivering down from the ceiling—a very pretty hand, on which was a ring with a coronet, with a lion rampant gules for a crest. *I saw that hand take a dip of ink and write across the paper.* Mr. Pinto then, taking a grey receipt stamp out of his blue leather pocket-book, fastened it on to the paper by the usual process; and the hand then wrote across the receipt-stamp, went across the table and shook hands with Pinto, and then, as if waving him an adieu, vanished in the direction of the ceiling.
>   There was the paper before me, wet with the ink. There was the pen which THE HAND had used. Does anybody doubt me? *I have that pen now.* A cedar stick of a not uncommon sort, and holding one of Gillott's pens. It is in my inkstand now, I tell you. Anybody may see it. The handwriting on the cheque, for such the document was, was the writing of a female. It ran thus:—'London, midnight, March 31, 1862. Pay the bearer one thousand and fifty pounds. Rachel Sidonia. To Messrs. Sidonia, Pozzosanto, and Co., London.'
>   'Noblest and best of women!' said Pinto, kissing the sheet of paper with much reverence; 'my good Mr. Roundabout, I suppose you do not question *that* signature?'
>   Indeed, the house of Sidonia, Pozzosanto, and Co. is known to be one of the richest in Europe, and as for the Countess Rachel, she was known to be the chief manager of that enormously wealthy establishment. There was only one little difficulty, *the Countess Rachel died last October.*
>
>   (XVII, 577)

"Sidonia", of course, is a creation of Disraeli's, which joins and idealizes traits taken from Disraeli himself and from members of the Rothschild family; but the Countess Rachel—whose Biblical name Thackeray had once used for one of his favourite heroines—is Thackeray's own addition to the Sidonia saga.

Mr Pinto, we are led to believe, does not wish to give positive clues to his true identity; he therefore breaks off his account of sufferings at the hands of the Inquisition as soon as the word "Jew" is about to be pronounced:

> 'Ah, tenez! when we marched to the terrible stake together at Valladolid—the Protestant and the J -- But away with memory!'
>   (XVII, 578)

He does, however, hint at past commerce with King Solomon:

I could tell her [Blanche, the woman he loved], an I would, the
watchword never known but to one woman, the Saban queen, which
Hiram breathed in the abysmal ear of Solomon. . . . Was strong
Sampson not as weak as I? Was Solomon the Wise much better when
Balkis wheedled him? I said to the king --- But enough of that . . .
(XVII, 579)

All this, surely, makes it unlikely that he can be identical with the
shoemaker of Jerusalem whom Jesus condemned to live until the
Second Coming. Thackeray's Wandering Jew—who can trace
nursery legends to their Sanscrit source and whisper legends of the
Egyptian magi (XVII, 579)—seems to have been around since the
beginning of time.

When, ultimately, Mr Pinto vanishes, Mr Roundabout is naturally anxious to cash the Sidonia cheque for which he had given
his golden snuff-box; and with this purpose in mind he enters the
great banking house of Manasseh in Duke Street. Here Thackeray
falls back into his old manner and brings together many of the
elements of the Jewish comedy he had presented in earlier writings:
banking and diamonds, the name Abednego, "aquiline beaks", red
whiskers, funny speech, excited gestures and shrieks, and suggestions about "fencing" stolen goods.

As the clock struck ten I was at the counter and laid down my
cheque.
The gentleman who received it, who was one of the Hebrew
persuasion, as were the other two hundred clerks of the establishment, having looked at the draft with terror in his countenance, then
looked at me, then called to himself two of his fellow clerks, and queer
it was to see all their aquiline beaks over the paper.
'Come, come!' said I, 'don't keep me here all day. Hand me over
the money, short, if you please!' for I was, you see, a little alarmed,
and so determined to assume some extra bluster.
'Will you have the kindness to step into the parlour to the partners?' the clerk said, and I followed him.
'What, *again?*' shrieked a bald-headed, red-whiskered gentleman,
whom I knew to be Mr. Manasseh. 'Mr. Salathiel, this is too bad!
Leave me with this gentleman, S.' And the clerk disappeared.
'Sir,' he said, 'I know how you came by this; the count de Pinto
gave it you. It is too bad! I honour my parents; I honour *their* parents;
I honour their bills! But this one of grandma's is too bad—it is, upon
my word, now! She've been dead these five-and-thirty years. And this
last four months she has left her burial-place and took to drawing on
our 'ouse! It's too bad, grandma; it is too bad!' and he appealed to
me, and tears actually trickled down his nose.
'Is it the Countess Sidonia's cheque or not?' I asked, haughtily.
'But, I tell you, she's dead! It's a shame!—it's a shame!—it is,
grandmamma!' and he cried, and wiped his great nose in his yellow

pocket-handkerchief. 'Look year—will you take pounds instead of guineas? She's dead, I tell you! It's no go! Take the pounds—one tausand pound!—ten nice, neat, crisp hundred-pound notes, and go away vid you, do!'

'I will have my bond, sir, or nothing,' I said; and I put on an attitude of resolution which I confess surprised even myself.

'Wery vell,' he shrieked, with many oaths, 'then you shall have noting—ha, ha, ha!—noting but a policeman! Mr. Abednego, call a policeman! Take that, you humbug and impostor!' and here, with an abundance of frightful language which I dare not repeat, the wealthy banker abused and defied me.

Au bout du compte, what was I to do, if a banker did not choose to honour a cheque drawn by his dead grandmother? I began to wish I had my snuff-box back. I began to think I was a fool for changing that little old-fashioned gold for this slip of strange paper.

Meanwhile the banker had passed from his fit of anger to a paroxysm of despair. He seemed to be addressing some person invisible, but in the room: 'Look here, ma'am, you've really been coming it too strong. A hundred thousand in six months, and now a thousand more! The 'ouse can't stand it; it *won't* stand it, I say! What? Oh! mercy, mercy!'

As he uttered these words, A HAND fluttered over the table in the air! It was a female hand: that which I had seen the night before. That female hand took a pen from the green baize table, dipped it in a silver inkstand, and wrote on a quarter of a sheet of foolscap on the blotting-book, 'How about the diamond robbery? If you do not pay, I will tell him where they are.'

What diamonds? what robbery? what was this mystery? That will never be ascertained, for the wretched man's demeanour instantly changed. 'Certainly, sir;—oh, certainly,' he said, forcing a grin. 'How will you have the money, sir? All right, Mr. Abednego. This way out.'

'I hope I shall often see you again,' I said; on which I own poor Manasseh gave a dreadful grin, and shot back into his parlour.

(XVII, 587–8)

This ghost-story with a Jewish cast receives its Thackerayan twist when it is Mr Roundabout, the Gentile customer, who speaks with the voice of Shylock: "I will have my bond, sir . . ." In the end the whole adventure turns out to have been a dream, brought on by the reading of an adventure novel—Sue's *Le Juif Errant*, no doubt; "but between ourselves", Mr Roundabout confesses to the reader,

> this Pinto, who fought at the Colosseum, who was nearly being roasted by the Inquisition, and sang duets at Holyrood, I am rather sorry to lose him after three little bits of Roundabout Papers. *Et vous?*
>
> (XVII, 589)

The half-promise at the end of "The Notch on the Axe" that the Wandering Jew would celebrate a return engagement in the columns of the *Cornhill Magazine* is fulfilled by "Autour de mon

Chapeau"—one of the last of the Roundabout Papers, published in February 1863. Its opening capital depicts a dignified, bearded man carrying the sack and wearing the three hats of the old clothes men that thronged the pages of *Punch*; the topmost one is Napoleon's hat, with an "N" that forms the first letter of the opening word "Never".

Illustration 6

NEVER have I seen a more noble tragic face. In the centre of the forehead there was a great furrow of care, towards which the brows rose piteously. What a deep solemn grief in the eyes! They looked blankly at the object before them, but through it, as it were, and into the grief beyond.

(XVII, 635)

From here Mr Roundabout launches into a discussion of grief which returns, after a while, to the figure depicted and described at the outset.

That man of whom I said that his magnificent countenance exhibited the noblest tragic woe. He was not of European blood. He was handsome, but not of European beauty. His face white—not of a Northern whiteness: his eyes protruding somewhat, and rolling in their grief. Those eyes had seen the Orient sun, and his beak was the eagle's. His lips were full. The beard, curling round them, was unkempt and tawny. The locks were of a deep, deep coppery red. The hands, swart and powerful, accustomed to the rough grasp of the wares in which he dealt, seemed unused to the flimsy artifices of the bath. He came from the Wilderness, and its sands were on his robe, his cheek, his tattered sandal, and the hardy foot it covered.

And his grief—whence came his sorrow? I will tell you. He bore it in his hand. He had evidently just concluded the compact by which it became his. His business was that of a purchaser of domestic raiment. At early dawn—nay, at what hour when the city is alive—do we not all hear the nasal cry of 'Clo'? In Paris, *Habits Galons, Marchand d'habits*, is the twanging signal with which the wandering merchant makes his presence known. It was in Paris I saw this man. Where else have I not seen him? In the Roman Ghetto—at the Gate of David, in his fathers' once imperial city. The man I mean was an itinerant vendor and purchaser of wardrobes—what you call an . . . Enough! You know his name.

On his left shoulder hung his bag; and he held in that hand a white hat, which I am sure he had just purchased, and which was the cause of the grief which smote his noble features. Of course I cannot particularize the sum, but he had given too much for that hat. He felt he might have got the thing for less money. It was not the amount, I am sure it was the principle involved. He had given fourpence (let us say) for that which threepence would have purchased. He had been done: and a manly shame was upon him, that he, whose energy, acuteness, experience, point of honour, should have made him the victor in any mercantile duel in which he should engage, had been overcome by a porter's wife, who very likely sold him the old hat, or by a student who was tired of it. I can understand his grief. Do I seem to be speaking of it in a disrespectful or flippant way? Then you mistake me. He had been outwitted. He had desired, coaxed, schemed, haggled, got what he wanted, and now found he had paid too much for his bargain. You don't suppose I would ask you to laugh at that man's grief? It is you, clumsy cynic, who are disposed to sneer, whilst it may be tears of genuine sympathy are trickling down this nose of mine. What do you mean by laughing? If you saw a wounded soldier on the field of battle, would you laugh? If you saw a ewe robbed of her lamb, would you laugh, you brute? It is you who are the cynic, and have no feeling: and you sneer because that grief is unintelligible to you which touches my finer sensibility. The OLD CLOTHES' MAN had been defeated in one of the daily battles of his most interesting, chequered, adventurous life.

Have you ever figured to yourself what such a life must be? The pursuit and conquest of twopence must be the most eager and fascinating of occupations. We might all engage in that business if we would. Do not whist-players, for example, toil, and think, and lose their temper over sixpenny points? They bring study, natural genius, long forethought, memory, and careful historical experience to bear upon their favourite labour. Don't tell me that it is the sixpenny points, and five shillings the rub, which keeps them for hours over their painted pasteboard. It is the desire to conquer. Hours pass by. Night glooms. Dawn, it may be, rises unheeded; and they sit calling for fresh cards at the Portland, or the Union, while waning candles sputter in the sockets, and languid waiters snooze in the ante-room. Sol rises. Jones has lost four pounds; Brown has won two; Robinson lurks away to his family house and (mayhap, indignant) Mrs. R. Hours of evening, night, morning, have passed away whilst they have been waging this sixpenny battle. What is the loss of four pounds to

Jones, the gain of two to Brown? B. is, perhaps, so rich that two pounds more or less are as naught to him; J. is so hopelessly involved that to win four pounds cannot benefit his creditors, or alter his condition; but they play for that stake: they put forward their best energies: they ruff, finesse (what are the technical words, and how do I know?) It is but a sixpenny game if you like; but they want to win it. So as regards my friend yonder with the hat. He stakes his money: he wishes to win the game, not the hat merely. I am not prepared to say that he is not inspired by a noble ambition. Caesar wished to be first in a village. If first of a hundred yokels, why not first of two? And my friend the old clothes' man wishes to win his game, as well as to turn his little sixpence.

(XVII, 636–8)

The old clothes merchant is an avatar of the Wandering Jew, encountered in Paris, in Rome, and in London; the suggestion of inadequate washing recurs here as it did in "The Notch on the Axe", as does the bird-of-prey beak (an eagle's, this time, not a vulture's—the difference is significant!); but instead of the grotesque ugliness of Mr Pinto, we find a handsome, fascinating face of Oriental cast. The old clothes man's concerns may seem petty to those more fortunately placed than he; but the griefs and passions excited by the "sixpenny battle" he has to fight day in, day out, are none the less genuine for that, and Mr Roundabout describes them with humorous sympathy. In the end, as Mr Roundabout addresses a well-meant caution to "my friend the old clothes' man", the perspective widens to include all humanity.

In this delightful, wholesome, ever-novel twopenny game, there is a danger of excess, as there is in every other pastime or occupation of life. If you grow too eager for your twopence, the acquisition or the loss of it may affect your peace of mind, and peace of mind is better than any amount of twopences. My friend, the old clothes' man, whose agonies over the hat have led to this rambling disquisition, has, I very much fear, by a too eager pursuit of small profits, disturbed the equanimity of a mind that ought to be easy and happy. 'Had I stood out', he thinks, 'I might have had the hat for three-pence', and he doubts whether, having given fourpence for it, he will ever get back his money. My good Shadrach, if you go through life passionately deploring the irrevocable, and allow yesterday's transactions to embitter the cheerfulness of to-day and to-morrow—as lieve walk down to the Seine, souse in, hats, body, clothes-bag and all, and put an end to your sorrow and sordid cares. Before and since Mr. Franklin wrote his pretty apologue of the Whistle have we not all made bargains of which we repented, and coveted and acquired objects for which we have paid too dearly? Who has not purchased his hat in some market or other? There is General M'Clellan's cocked hat for example: I dare say he was eager enough to wear it, and he has learned that it is by no means cheerful wear. There were the

military beavers of Messeigneurs of Orleans: they wore them gal-
lantly in the face of battle; but I suspect they were glad enough to
pitch them into the James River and come home in mufti. Ah, *mes
amis! à chacun son schakot!*

(XVII, 643–4)

It may well be thought that Mr Roundabout has little idea of what
it means to scratch a living, to be utterly dependent on small profits
to fight for which would only be a game to the prosperous readers of
the *Cornhill Magazine*. What he gives his readers here, however, is a
pointer towards the depiction of the Jew as representative man—
towards Leopold Bloom and his many successors in the British and
American novel. In his Table Talk of 14 August 1833, Coleridge
had said:

> The two images farthest removed from each other which can be
> comprehended under one term, are, I think, Isaiah—"Hear, O
> heavens, and give ear, O earth!"—and Levi of Holywell Street—
> "Old Clothes!"—both of them Jews, you'll observe.

Thackeray, whose veneration of Isaiah was less absolute than
Coleridge's, has brought the two disparate images together in his
pictorial initial—which depicts a face fit for Isaiah surmounted by
the three hats that seem to come from a *Punch* cartoon of Holywell
Street—and has gestured towards their reconciliation in a text that
makes the old clothes man's concerns stand for wider concerns of
humanity. It was left to George Eliot—who felt the contrast drawn
by Coleridge as keenly as anyone—to try for a full-scale reconciliation. The poor scholar Mordecai, who voices Zionist aspirations in
Daniel Deronda, might indeed be seen as an all too voluble attempt
to create an Isaiah of Holywell Street.

v

The early reading matter which Thackeray recalls in the "Roundabout Papers" includes not only the ubiquitous *Ivanhoe* (XVII,
434) and the novels of Dumas, but also Pierce Egan's *Life in London:
or, The Day and Night Scenes of Jerry Hawthorn and his elegant Friend,
Corinthian Tom* (1824—with illustrations by Cruikshank). In "De
Juventute", first published in *Fraser's Magazine* in October 1860,
Mr Roundabout recalls his early acquaintance with Egan's Tom
and Jerry:

> So the game of life proceeds, until Jerry Hawthorn, the rustic, is fairly
> knocked up by all this excitement and is forced to go home, and the
> last picture represents him getting into the coach at the White Horse
> Cellar, he being one of six inside; whilst the sailor mounts the roof;

whilst the Jews hang round with oranges, knives, and sealing-wax; whilst the guard is closing the door. Where are they now, those sealing-wax vendors? . . .

(XVII, 434)

That last question shows Thackeray's sense that the life-style and business methods of English Jews were changing. Though old clothes men, as "Autour de mon Chapeau" may serve to suggest, were still a familiar sight, pedlars were becoming rarer in the London streets, vanishing along with the old coach stations. Possibly they were becoming rarer in the countryside too—though Mr Roundabout, whose ladies shop at Shoolbred's (XVII, 513), is too urban a creature to speak of that with authority:

I wonder, whether those little silver pencil-cases with a movable almanac at the butt-end are still favourite implements with boys, and whether pedlars still hawk them about the country? Are there pedlars and hawkers still, or are rustics and children grown too sharp to deal with them?

("Tunbridge Toys", September 1860
—XVII, 413)

When a fence, a receiver of stolen diamonds, is introduced in a piece published in August 1863, there is no hint of a suggestion that he might be Jewish ("On a Medal of George the Fourth"—II, 662), and as we have seen, bailiffs and presenters of unwelcome bills of exchange are now given punning, English-sounding names like "Nab" or "Nabbam" (XVII, 406–7) rather than Old Testament names like Moses or Abednego. Even Jewish prizefighters seem to belong to the past; it is only Beau Brummel, as a down-at-heel old man who outlived his time, who remembers "Dutch Sam, the boxer" (XVII, 622).

vi

Thackeray's own contributions to the *Cornhill Magazine* should not be seen in isolation from the work he accepted, or commissioned, between August 1859, when he took on the editorship, and March 1862, when he resigned it. His daughter Anne made her debut there with an essay entitled "Little Scholars" which takes an affectionate and admiring view of Jewish charity schools in East London (March 1860, pp. 549–559)—an essay of which her father fondly and proudly approved. Nor was this the only contribution that brought Jews into the Victorian reader's view. A first instalment of a biography of Hogarth (March 1860, p. 267) retells the anecdote of young Hogarth's inability—"faute de quoi?"—to buy a coveted horn-handled three-bladed penknife "which the Hebrew youth in Duke's Place offered him at the price of twentypence"; a second instalment sketches in the historical background, reminding readers who had in more recent times sympathized with the Jews of Damascus that in Hogarth's day the Jews of Ferrara had had to defend themselves against the charge "that they have sacrificed a child at Easter à la Hugh of Lincoln" (loc. cit., p. 428); and a third paper in the same series waxes indignant at the dramatization of Hogarth's *The Harlot's Progress* under the title *The Jew Decoyed; or a Harlot's Progress*:

> It is worthy of observation that the perverse and depraved taste of the town took it as rather a humorous thing that the courtezan, splendidly kept by a Hebrew money-lender, should decoy and betray her keeper. *The Jew Decoyed.* Ho! ho! it was a thing to laugh at. Who sympathizes with M. Géronte in the farce . . .?
>
> (June 1860, pp. 717–718)

The writer goes on to compare those who relished such Jew-baiting to children who torture animals. A series on crime and judicial practice in contemporaryEngland (running from July to December 1860) presents readers with a glossary of thieves' slang that contains no terms deriving from Yiddish or Hebrew; the only Jewish involvement in crime which it depicts concerns a Barney Fence or Ikey Solomons type named Moses who is shown cheating the thieves for whom he acts as fence (loc. cit.). Elsewhere contributors to the *Cornhill* may be seen chipping away at Jewish stereotypes. A scientific correspondent with Darwinian leanings enlivens the fifth of his "Studies in Animal Life" with an attack on the notion that so long as Jews marry Jews there must be a "perpetuation of . . . Jewish types" in which "the tenth generation adds nothing to the evidence of the first, nor the ten-thousandth to the tenth." (May 1860, p. 601). "I conceive the doctrine of Fixity of Species", the writer concludes, "to be altogether wrong." (ibid., p. 605). In November 1861 an essay on "National Character" carries the argument to another plane by criticizing, from a historical standpoint, the extrapolation of permanent Jewish characteristics from a reading of the Old and New Testaments. This cannot do justice even to the many groups and sub-groups of Jews that inhabited Palestine during some fifteen centuries of early history—how much less to the Jews of modern Britain! The author does believe, however, that most Jews will be found to have two characteristics: "ardent love of material prosperity" and "strong family and personal affections"; and he rebukes his contemporaries for insisting so much on the first and so little on the second (loc. cit., pp. 595–6).

When Disraeli comes into question in contributions to the *Cornhill* during Thackeray's editorship, he does so as a member of the British political and literary establishment, with none of the constant allusions to his Jewish ancestry in which *Punch* liked to engage. In November 1861 an essay on the principles of Physiognomy discusses Disraeli's description of Peel's face and facial expression at some length because "Mr. Disraeli is a good observer" (loc. cit., p. 579); while an article on "Liberalism" speaks of Disraeli's novels in the same breath as those of Dickens, Kingsley and Mrs Gaskell (January 1862, p. 77). The last issue Thackeray himself saw through the press, that of March 1862, contains an instalment of a series built around the adventures of three Victorian Englishmen called Brown, Jones and Robinson, which shows the Gentile Robinson able to teach Sloman, the Jewish "official consignee" of a now bankrupt haberdashery business, some advertising tricks the latter would never have thought of by himself (pp. 294, 300–301). And while some of the characters in the *Cornhill* most popular serialization, Anthony Trollope's *Framley Parsonage*, speak of moneylenders as "the Jews" in the old-established way, and though Disraeli's Sidonia (who had been saddled with a far from respectable descendant in *Barchester Towers*) is treated as a joke in this new novel of 1861, it is surely remarkable that Trollope's plot, which turns on bills of exchange obtained by dubious manoeuvres that ultimately cause bailiffs to move into the parsonage of the title, bestows the functions of moneylender and bailiff on non-Jewish Englishmen. Stereotyped notions persist; but they are found, increasingly, to need adjustment and correction as more and more readers and contributors come into social contact with their Jewish compatriots and contemporaries. It may also be surmised that a popular publication like the *Cornhill Magazine* attracted Jewish readers and subscribers whose susceptibilities would have to be considered.

vii

Thackeray's correspondence, during his last years on earth, continued his by now fixed habit of speaking about his own life and its concerns in mostly familiar Scriptural phrases.

> I hope we may both of us live so long as to outlive all chances of paragraphs in large print: decent prosy people under our vine and fig-tree: playing at whist of nights: looked up to in the parish: respected by the neighbouring tradesmen . . .
>
> (to an unknown correspondent, 1861, LPP
> IV, 254—cf. Micah 4, 4)

[My daughters] are both of them beginning to bewail their Virginity
in the mountains: and seem to be much excited because Ella Merivale who is only 17 has had 3 or 4 lovers already and is doubting
between 2 who are imploring her . . .

(to Mrs Carmichael-Smith, 5 July 1862,
LPP IV, 272—cf. Judges 11, 38)

These were the years when Bishop William Colenso began to
publish a series of papers in which he examined the Pentateuch and
the Book of Joshua and questioned the historical accuracy and
traditional authorship of these and other canonical text. Thackeray, who had taken little discernible notice of the German and
German-inspired "higher criticism" of the Bible which fascinated
George Eliot and her circle, found himself drawn to Colenso's
watered-down critique, and vented his glee in an impromptu
limerick whose barb was directed mainly against Bishop Samuel
Wilberforce, disrespectfully known as "Soapy Sam".

This is the bold bishop Colenso
Whose heresies seem to offend so,
    Quoth Sam of the Soap,
    Bring fagot and roap,
For we know he ain't got no friends, Oh!

(G.N. Ray, *Thackeray. The Age
of Wisdom*, London 1958, p. 368)

Given Thackeray's views on the Old Testament, it is hardly
surprising that he began by concurring wholeheartedly with Colenso's views: "Thackeray defends Colenso & denies the Creation in 6
Days", Henry Silver notes in his diary; "Jonah & sun standing still
he views as fables." (Ray, loc. cit.) His daughter Anne reports on
his renewed protests about treating the Bible "as if it was God
Almighty", and on the way this refusal to accept Scriptural authority now extended to the New Testament along with the Old:

It is perfectly preposterous the way they go on about a collection of
oriental fables & histories. Papa said I think that St John was a
gentleman that he liked the Epistle of St James the best. That it
would almost seem as if the simplicity & stupidity of the disciples had
been purposely exaggerated in order by this simple artifice to
heighten the superiority of the Personage whom they surrounded.
They could not understand the plainest things. They were always
asking stupid questions.

(Ray, loc. cit.)

Yet by 2 December 1863, Henry Silver tells us, Thackeray had
changed his mind and started arguing for the truth-value of Genesis. A week later he reverted to this topic; he confessed himself
puzzled by the Higher Criticism which had reached him so late

and in such weakened form, and dismissed the questions it raised with a *Quien sabe?* (cf. J.Y.T. Greig, *Thackeray. A Reconsideration*, London 1950, pp. 1–2). These are his last recorded words on the subject of the Bible's authority—a subject he had so often broached in discussions with his mother and with friends more orthodox and less sceptical than he could ever be. There is no reason to doubt, however, the sincerity of the religious feelings Thackeray expressed throughout his life—nowhere more memorably than in a diary-entry dated Saturday, 8 March 1862, when he moved into the house he had built for himself in Palace Green, Kensington:

> I pray Almighty God that the words I write in this house may be pure and honest; that they be dictated by no personal spite, unworthy motive, or unjust greed for gain; that they may tell the truth as far as I know it; and tend to promote love and peace amongst men, for the sake of Christ our Lord.
>
> (Biographical Edition, XI, xxxviii)

That, in essence, is Thackeray's vision of how a Christian life might be lived in the midst of Vanity Fair.

viii

When the debates about Colenso's Biblical criticism began to interest him, Thackeray had already vacated the thorny cushions of the *Cornhill* editorial chair. His brief but commercially very successful tenure of that chair had brought into the open a shift to the political Right which Thackeray had undergone since the days of the Administrative Reform Association. In *Thackeray. The Age of Wisdom* G.N. Ray has documented this shift towards conservatism:

> In 1861 he accepted an essay from James Fitzjames Stephen, which anticipates many of the points in that author's forcible polemic against liberalism and popular government in his *Liberty, Equality, Fraternity* of 1873. When its boldness alarmed George Smith, Thackeray argued: "The article is a very moderate sensible plea for an aristocratic government, and shows the dangers of democracy quite fairly . . .The politics of gentlemen are pretty much alike. Since 48 in France, and esp. since America, I for one am very much inclined to subscribe to Stephen's article." [Letter dated 9 October 1861].
>
> (op. cit., pp. 312–13)

What the position of Jews would have to be in an aristocratically governed Britain Thackeray does not spell out; but since the aristocracy envisaged includes an aristocracy of talent as well as a hereditary one, there is no reason to suppose that he had changed his mind about granting political rights to Britain's Jewish citizens equal to those of their Christian neighbours. He certainly never proposed reintroducing the religious tests—or any ethnic substitute for them—which had kept Lionel Rothschild out of parliament until 1858.

Thackeray died in December 1863, on a day on which he had looked forward to dining with his neighbours at Palace Green, Kensington, the family of Ernest Leopold Benzon. He had just published an essay in *Cruikshank's Gallery*, in which he alluded to Cruikshank's campaign against the demon Drink by saying that the great caricaturist refused to have any truck with the odious god Bacchus: "the wicked idol is smashed like Bel and Dagon" (II, 719—cf. Jeremiah 50, 2 and 1 Samuel 5, 3–4). *The Autographic Mirror* (Vol. II, London 1864, p. 161) published, posthumously, a drawing of Isaac D'Israeli by Thackeray, which shows none of the caricaturistic distortions or exaggerations of traits felt to be "Jewish" to which *Punch* and other publications had accustomed Victorian readers (ill. 7).

The *Cornhill Magazine* also had some posthumous publishing to do. The ballad "Mrs. Katherine's Lantern", addressed to Dickens's daughter Kate, tells of an apparently worthless object bought from a Jewish trader in an unattractive neighbourhood:

'COMING from a gloomy court,
Place of Israelite resort,
This old lamp I've brought with me.
Madam, on its panes you'll see
The initials K and E.'

'An old lantern brought to me?
Ugly, dingy, battered, black!'
(Here a lady I suppose
Turning up a pretty nose) —
'Pray, sir, take the old thing back.
I've no taste for *bric-à-brac*.'

(VII, 101—January 1867)

The lady's objections are countered, however, by the giver of the lamp, who makes it testify to former times and former owners, and—in a more melancholy vein—to his own vanished youth. Cherished objects, reduced to mere commodities when death or the vicissitudes of life have forced their owners to relinquish them, pass through Jewish hands into those of owners who know how to re-endow them with personal associations and personal values.

"Mrs. Katherine's Lantern" had been preceded in the *Cornhill* by another posthumous publication: the unfinished novel *Denis Duval*, which appeared in instalments that ran from March to June 1864. The eponymous hero of this novel, an exciting tale of adven-

Illustration 7

tures set in the eighteenth century, is a descendant of French
Huguenots who have become "trusty and loyal subjects of the
British crown" (XVII, 199). They remain duly grateful to those
who once offered much-needed shelter from persecution:

> They settled at Winchelsea, in Sussex, where there has been a French
> church ever since Queen Bess's time, and the dreadful day of Saint

> Bartholomew. Three miles off, at Rye, is another colony and church of our people: another *fester Burg* [sic!], where, under Britannia's sheltering buckler, we have been free to exercise our fathers' worship, and sing the songs of our Zion.
>
> (XVII, 199–200)

The songs of Zion at the end of a passage that also quotes from Luther's most famous hymn make the Jews archetypes of all who claim freedom of worship as a basic human right. They bring to mind those Psalms which we are shown, elsewhere in the story, to have played an essential part in the young Denis's education. In his piously Protestant family circle a chapter is read from Grand-father's "great Bible"at morning and evening prayers (XVII, 233); he remembers his mother reading "our great German Bible" (XVII, 244) and recalls "my book for reading the German was Doctor Luther's Bible" (XVII, 265). When a kindly clergyman helps to absolve him from a trumped up charge of theft, he finds himself taken to church for a thanksgiving in which the Psalms come, once again, into play:

> As we read the last psalm appointed for that evening service, I remember how the good man, bowing his own head, put his hand upon mine; and we recited together the psalm of thanks to the Highest who had respect unto the lowly, and who had stretched forth His hand upon the furiousness of my enemies, and whose right hand had saved me.
>
> (XVII, 299)

"Out of the Depths", the title of Chapter IV of *Denis Duval*, derives, of course, from Psalm 130. The forbidden tree, Eve, and the serpent, make their expected appearance when Madame de Saverne, hearing of feasts, balls and theatrical entertainments her stern husband forbids to attend,

> began to have a wicked longing to go, as Madame's first ancestress had for the fruit of the forbidden tree. Is not the apple always ripe on that tree, and does not the tempter for ever invite you to pluck and eat?
>
> (XVII, 216)

In this passage with unmistakable ironic overtones the tempter takes the form of a "a lively little waiting-maid, whose bright eyes loved to look into neighbours' parks and garden" from which she brings news of pleasures of which Count de Saverne's pastor and pious relatives talk "as if the fires of Gomorrah [sic] were ready to swallow up" all who partook of them (XVII, 216). "What happened", Denis asks, "where the wicked spirit was whispering 'Eat', and the tempting apple hung within reach?" (XVII, 217). Mme.

de Saverne succumbs, of course, sneaks out to a comedy and a ball, and is drawn into the orbit of an evil much more insidious than that about which Denis, with Thackeray guiding his hand, had been able to play his irony:

> Wherever the poor thing moved I fancy those ill-omened eyes of La Motte glimmering upon her out of the darkness. Poor Eve,—not lost quite, I pray and think,—but that serpent was ever trailing after her, and she was to die poisoned in its coil.
>
> (XVII, 222)

Here the sinister La Motte appears as a serpent more deadly than that which tempted Eve; later on, however, Denis sees "a *Cain mark*, as it were, on the unhappy man" (XVII, 249) and La Motte himself, after he has killed the Count de Saverne in a duel, falls "to weeping and crying that the curse—the curse of Cain—was upon him". The Protestant rector who hears these lamentations is quite unmoved, however, and returns to the image of the archetypal tempter in a more folk-like than Biblical form: "My good boy, . . . thy friend the chevalier was the most infernal scoundrel I ever set eyes on, and I never looked at his foot without expecting to see it was cloven" (XVII, 263).

In no other novel of Thackeray's do the characters speak as frequently, and as habitually, in Old Testament terms as in this last, unfinished one. We find the Count de Saverne confronting a Cardinal with Nathan's monitory parable (2 Samuel 12, 1–7): "Where is my lamb that you have taken from me?" What corresponds to the taking of the lamb, in this case, is the reception of two Protestant ladies into the Catholic Church, without the knowledge, and against the wishes, of their husband and father; and it is surely striking that Thackeray derives the recrimination "with those Scripture phrases which M. de Saverne ever had at his command" from the Old Testament whose authority all Christian factions continued to acknowledge (XVII, 226–7). Such authority adheres especially to the Decalogue, explicitly invoked by various characters in *Denis Duval* (XVII, 235, 255, 266), while others speak as habitually in Old Testament phrases as M. de Saverne himself: "She whipped the little prince with a scorpion", "They . . . made me eat the bread of humiliation" (XVII, 229, 305) and so on. Even jokes have a Biblical tinge in this novel, as when the narrator recalls a saying about "the famous General James Wolfe, the glorious conqueror of Quebec:

> A macaroni guardsman, speaking of Mr. Wolfe, asked, 'Was he a Jew? Wolfe is a Jewish name.' 'Certainly', says Mr. S-lw-n, "Mr. Wolfe was the *Height of Abraham*.'
>
> (XVII, 200)

The joke may not be of the best—but the reference to Jews which is here ascribed to George Augustus Selwyn is not malicious.

When a usurer appears in *Denis Duval* he is, significantly, not a Jew, but "a church elder, who lends money *à la petite semaine*, and at great interest" (XVII, 252), while the one Jewish character Thackeray introduces into the part of his tale which he found time to finish before his death is hard-working and sympathetic. When Midshipman Duval becomes a gentleman, "and in a fair way to be an officer in his Majesty's navy", he repairs to a Jewish tailor to bespeak some uniforms that would suit his new status and dignity.

> My uniforms were ready in a very short time. Twenty-four hours after they were ordered Mr. Levy brought them to our inn, and I had the pleasure of putting them on; and walked on the Parade, with my hat cocked and my hanger by my side, and mother on my arm. Though I was perfectly well pleased with myself, I think she was the prouder of the two.
>
> (XVII, 327–8)

The uniforms obviously fit, and there are no complaints. How Mr Levy managed to have them ready in so short a time we are not told; but he was clearly providing a valuable service much appreciated by his young customer.

In the last chapter Thackeray completed before his death Denis Duval enters the British navy. The American revolution is still going on, and Denis hears his beloved rector. Dr Barnard, exhort his congregation to be loyal and testify "to the authority of Caesar"—a welcome reminder of the New Testament allusions which accompany the more numerous Old Testament ones in this novel. "War", the rector teaches, "is not altogether evil":

> "We English of the present day are the better for Crécy, and Agincourt, and Blenheim. I do not grudge the Scots their day at Bannockburn, nor the French their Fountenoy. Such valour proves the manhood of nations. When we have conquered the American rebellion, as I have no doubt we shall do, I trust it will be found that these rebellious children of ours have comported themselves in a manner becoming our English race, that they have been hardy and resolute, merciful and moderate . . ."
>
> (XVII, 312–3)

"Our English race", the pastor says, but he is speaking to a congregation in which there are parishioners of French ancestry, like Denis himself. There is national pride here, but it is not narrowly exclusive; even in this context the term "race" has the overtones of "family" which we have heard so often when Thackeray introduced the term into his writings—and one can marry into, or be adopted by, a family, without having been born into it. When the good rector stresses, as we have just heard him do, the virtues of mercy and moderation, we recall, not only Dr Barnard's words and actions throughout the novel, but also Denis's account of how he had come to be a member of Dr Barnard's congregation in the first place: "I was made to become a member of the Church of England, because mother took a huff at our French Protestants, who would continue persecuting her for harbouring the Papists . . ." (XVII, 265). Religious persecution is as abhorrent to Thackeray as to the more symphathetic characters in his books; and though he indubitably harboured feelings of racial differences, and the Victorian Anglo-Indian's patronizing sense of superiority over people of darker skin; though he was much concerned, in his later work, with "the gently nurtured man or woman of Anglo-Saxon race" (*The Virginians* XV, 6)—especially with Englishmen who sustained a gentlemanly ideal in a society increasingly held together, as Carlyle had complained, by the cash nexus—despite all this there can be no doubt that Thackeray's publicly expressed view of his Jewish fellow citizens had become more respectful and less acerbic than it had been in the period of the *National Standard* with which this study began.

CONCLUSION

Rabbi, let us part in peace!
Neither thee nor thy like
would George Fitz-Boodle
ever willingly harm . . .

(IV, 282)

In his Preface to the book-version of *Pendennis*, Thackeray asks the reader to judge writers as they do those whose society they frequent for a long time: "not by one speech, or by one mood or opinion, but by the tenor of [their] general bearing and conversation." Speaking in his own person, the person of the man who had just signed the Dedication of his book "W.M. Thackeray", he suggests the kind of questions we should ask of a writer: "Is he honest? Does he tell the truth in the main? Does he seem actuated by a desire to find out and speak it?" He himself, he confides, "found many thousands more readers than [he] ever looked for":

> I have no right to say to these, You shall not find fault with my art, or fall asleep over my pages; but I ask you to believe that this person writing strives to tell the truth. If there is not that, there is nothing.
> (XII, xxxv–xxxvi)

The experience of Jews which Thackeray conveys in his writings was not gained by conscious expeditions in search of knowledge; he did not study Jewish history or Jewish religious documents other than the Old Testament, he did not seek instruction from Jewish scholars or set out to acquire a variety of Jewish informants. It is no accident that whenever there is talk of the Hebrew language in Thackeray writings, the reader finds himself assured that the character or narrator could not possibly be expected to know what it was really like. Thackeray relied on casual contacts, which threw him into the company of Jewish money-lenders or gamblers, brought him to artists' studios, art-galleries, theatres and music-halls, made him the customer of a variety of traders and shop-keepers, made him the fellow traveller of Jews on ship-board, in coaches and railway compartments, and brought him encounters at *tables d'hôte* as well as in less salubrious establishments. He observed Jews, along with other denizens and holiday makers in the streets of London and Brighton; and when he became a literary lion his social rounds included the wealthy "Cousinhood" of the Roth-schilds and the Goldsmids. But it is precisely this which makes Thackeray's depictions, presentations and discussions so interest-ing: for he was a sharp observer of whatever swam into his ken; he had a feel for the middle-class sentiment of his time; he was steeped in the literary and cultural traditions of the educated Englishman of the day; and with his novels, his essays, his lectures, his reviews and his highly important work for *Punch* he influenced public taste and public views all the more powerfully because, for all his criticism of the society he knew, he shared many of its prejudices and preconceptions. The truth he sought to tell by means of his ironic art, an art mediated through spokesmen that ranged from Titmarsh's closeness to his creator to Barry Lyndon's utter remote-ness from him, an art in which words were reinforced and supple-mented by graphic images, was truth to experience—an experience sharper than that of the majority of his first readers, but not too remote from it. The readers he demanded had to be alert to nuances of irony, alternations of engagement and detachment; he addressed them frequently, in ways examined by Michael Lund in *Reading Thackeray*, and challenged them to measure their own complexity of experience against the view of life that emerged from his works.

The writings discussed in the present book mention rabbis on several occasions and allow passing glimpses of Jewish modes of worship, but show nothing of Jewish communal organization or relationships between the Sephardic and Ashkenazic branches of English Jewry. Jews appear almost exclusively in their interaction with a Gentile society in which they formed a tiny minority. They appear as old clothes men, pedlars, travelling salesmen, pawn-brokers, moneylenders, money-changers, and bankers of varying degrees of eminence and respectability. We encounter a dentist on holiday, an election agent, an upwardly mobile clerk in an insur-ance office, and a partner in a wig-making business. There are artists' models, pugilists, entertainers of various kinds in supper-room, theatre and opera house, and backstage hangers-on as well as spectators. We encounter Jews as theatrical costumiers, dance-hall managers and customers in London's East End, and dancing-teachers. Jews keep lodging houses, billiard rooms and gambling establishments, and they frequent various venues at which betting and gambling takes place. They haunt auctions in search of bar-gains, often as agents for customers who do not want to be seen bidding on their own behalf. They conduct rigged auctions at which prices are jacked up by means of bogus bids. Jewish boys sell

oranges and pencils about the streets—goods imported or bought
in by their parents and other co-religionists. Thackeray's characters have dealings with Jewish goldsmiths, diamond merchants,
owners of ready-made, bespoke or second-hand clothes shops and
millinery stores, purveyors of flowers, tobacco, artists' materials,
bric-à-brac and miscellaneous goods that range from jewellery to
Flemish painted windows. Jews are seen experimenting with novel
kinds of advertising. Some operate beyond the law—"Jewish fires"
and bankruptcies are suspect; but Ikey Solomons junior seems to
have said good-bye to fencing and the other illegal activities for
which his namesake was notorious, and to aspire to authorship and
public honours. On the right side of the law we find an alderman,
some lawyers on the fringes of their profession, and a good number
of sheriff's officers or sponging-house keepers. The work of Jewish
writers, composers and painters comes into view as an integral part
of the nineteenth century's artistic life. Outside the British isles
Jews are encountered in capacities similar to those observed in
England, but also as a (baptized) minister of police and a recruiting officer's decoy in eighteenth-century Germany; as a plantation
and slave owner; as touts, guides and agents for foreign visitors;
and as fellow tourists. We hear of eminent contemporaries: Benjamin
Disraeli and his father; the Rothschilds, Montefiores and Goldsmids; Meyerbeer, Mendelssohn, Herz and Moscheles; Heine;
Simeon Solomon; Solomon Hart; Braham; Sloman; Don Pacifico;
"Dutch Sam".

Thackeray is very conscious of topographical distribution. His
writings take ample notice, therefore, not only of trades and professions he sees Jews espousing in his life-time, but also of their
topographical mobility—from London to the provinces (particularly to Brighton), and within the capital from Houndsditch and
Duke's Place to Piccadilly and the more rural as well as affluent
Twickenham.

As the present book has tried to show throughout, however,
Thackeray's fictional presentation of Jews owes a great deal to
literary tradition as well as to direct observation and experience of
life. Charles Macklin's Little Shadrach, Samuel Foote's Abednego
Potiphar, Moses Manasses and Nebuchadnezzar Zebulon, provided models of nomenclature used by other Victorian writers
besides Thackeray—Catherine Gore, for instance, has a novel
called *Abednego, the Moneylender*. These names stem from the Bible,
of course; and the importance of the Authorized Version, which
had made the Old and New Testaments, along with their Apocrypha, part of the British literary heritage as well as the nation's

devotional life, can hardly be over-estimated in an assessment of Thackeray's writings, and will therefore be touched again in this concluding chapter. He makes emblematic use of the figure of Shylock, reintroduces, elaborates, and plays variations on, Isaac of York and Rebecca, looks with a shudder towards a Fagin whom he sees as a composite creation by Dickens and Cruikshank, mocks Wordsworth's Jewish sympathies in an early work and Disraeli's self-dramatizing creation of super-Jews in several later ones, looks back to Dibdin and Cumberland in his "Roundabout" tale of Jewish generosity and to Sheridan's Moses (in *The School for Scandal*) for the more friendly varieties of his Cursitor Street types, draws on German legends and a sensational novel by Eugène Sue for his Wandering Jew figures, and evolves a type of adenoidal Jew-speak which owes something to the traditions of the English stage, as do his redhaired and over-ornamented Jewish characters. His predominantly realistic art has no overt use, for the more extravagant and damaging stereotypes of earlier literature, from Chaucer's "Prioress's Tale" to Marlowe and Nashe, which had perpetuated conceptions of Jews as Anti-Christ, devil, poisoner, ritual murderer, desecrator and super-villain; but as Charles Lamb testified in his essay on "Imperfect Sympathies", these lived on into the nineteenth century as often buried or half-buried fears. They surface occasionally in Thackeray's unpublished papers, and may be felt as pressures in his published work. It is, however, characteristic of his art that when, in "The Notch on the Axe", he uses the well-known stereotype of the Jew as sorcerer and sage, he does so in order to play a humorous game with it.

Though some of Thackeray's onomastic procedures undoubtedly derive from literary tradition, the names he gives his Jewish characters form a system he has made his own. For humorous purposes, or to mark a character as alien or strange, Thackeray bestows on his people names culled from the Bible, but never, or rarely, adopted by modern Jews: Nebuchadnezzar, or Ahasuerus, or Abednego, or Aminadab, or Nebuzaradan, or Solomon Ramothgilead. "Ahasuerus" occupies a special place in this system—for it was the name German legend had bestowed on the Wandering Jew. Other names used by Thackeray are more verisimilitudinous: English Jews did indeed bear Biblical names like Moses, Manasseh, Mordecai, Nathan, or Levy. Often such names were Anglicized by having a patronymic affixed—Thackeray has Isaacs, Abrams, Solomonson among his nineteenth-century cast, and achieves humorous anachronistic effects in *Rebecca and Rowena* by naming a medieval Jew Ben Davids. Sometimes Anglicization is

achieved by contraction—Solomon becomes Sloman; sometimes by
the addition of one letter and the change of another—Levi becomes
Lewis; sometimes by more radical adaptation—Shadrach becomes
Sherrick. "Nabb" or "Nab", a speaking name for a bailiff, may also
figure as a contraction of Aminadab. The name Moss, which occurs
frequently, may be thought of as a decapitation of Amos or a
squashing of Moses; it may also be expanded to a (Jewish) Mossrose to match a (Gentile) Eglantine. The (reputedly German) Jew
who marries a black woman is symbolically named Swartz, a name
which then describes the children who inherit it. German Jews bear
either Biblical names or heraldic ones, like Löwe (out of Levi?) and
Hirsch. Silberschmidt, in *The Great Hoggarty Diamond*, has clearly
been named in order to recall the Anglo-Jewish Goldsmid cousinhood, just as Scharlachschild is meant to recall the Rothschilds.
Sidonia is taken over directly from Disraeli, and other names with
an Iberian sound—Alvarez, Mendoza, Pinto—suggest a Sephardic
or Marrano provenance. Mendoza, moreover, recalls that boxing
prowess of British Jews to which Thackeray so often alludes. The
given names prefixed to surnames such as these are usually Biblical: Benjamin (particularly useful in Thackeray's contexts because
it was Disraeli's, and because when abbreviated to "Ben" it could
suggest a Hebrew patronymic), Moses, Nathan, Rebecca, Rachel;
but the younger generation often bears names common among
their Gentile compatriots: Minna Löwe, Bobby Moss, Frank Leveson. Sometimes Thackeray indicates the provenance of his characters by giving them the names of London districts largely inhabited
by Jews: Ben de Minories, for instance, or Nathan Houndsditch;
this is only one of the ways in which his works convey information
about districts and streets in which Jews lived and traded: Holywell
Street, Cursitor Street, Hanway Yard, Wardour Street, Duke's
Place, Bevis Marks (with its synagogue) and many more.

In Thackeray's writings, the words "Jew" and "Jews" are used
as nouns in five main senses. They describe (i) members of a Jewish
community or adherents of the Jewish religion; (ii) men and
women who have abjured that religion, usually by means of baptism, but who are still felt, or still feel themselves, to retain an
ethnic relationship with the Jewish people, or the Jewish community in a given country; (iii) the Biblical people from whom modern
Jews claim descent, or are felt to be descended ("those primeval
Jews"); (iv) moneylenders; (v) men and women suspected of sharp
trading or of being excessively keen on the acquisition of money. In
this last, pejorative sense, it is occasionally used by Thackeray's
characters, but never by the author speaking in his own person.

"Jew" may be extended, when gender demands it, to "Jewess"; it is used as part of a compound expression like "Jew-boy", "a Jew banker", "a Jew pedlar"; and Thackeray also uses it as a verb ("Jewing" in the sense of "having recourse to money-lenders"). The adjective "Jewish" is neutrally descriptive when applied to a person ("a little Jewish janitor"), but can become pejorative when transferred: "Jewish fires" are fires suspected of having been deliberately started for the sake of collecting insurance, just as "Mosaic" jewellery is paste. "Mosaic" is one of several more or less humorous alternatives to "Jewish": its most obviously comic use in Thackeray is in the term "Mosaic Arabs" which Disraeli had applied to Jews in all seriousness but which seemed irresistibly funny to the writers and readers of *Punch*. Other alternatives are "Hebrew" and "Hebrews" ("a Hebrew", "my Hebrew critic", "a Hebrew banker", "their Hebrew connections") or "Israelite" and "Israelitish" ("a little red-haired Israelite", "trembling Israelite", "an Israelitish gentleman", "the Israelitish Church", and so on). "Ebrew Jew" derives directly from Shakespeare, and is as facetious as "Orientalist" to denote what Thackeray calls elsewhere "a member of the ancient religion", or "a gentleman of the Hebrew persuasion". "Gentleman" is usually ironic in such expressions; Jewish "ladies" appear more frequently in unironic contexts than their male counterparts. This may be seen as a Thackerayan extension of a literary tradition which made Abigails, Jessicas and Rebeccas more civilized than the Jewish males in whose company they appeared. The Victorian ideal of the gentleman presupposed a standard of English education most of the Jews whom Thackeray encountered had not had the chance to acquire, and a degree of leisure more easily found among Jewish women than their busy menfolk, once a certain standard of affluence had been reached. He does, however, indulge in circumlocutions like "a very pleasant but plain Hierosolomyte lady", where the word "Jewish" is ostentatiously skirted in a mock-solemn way.

Sometimes Thackeray indicates that his figures are Jewish simply by the names he gives them—a character named "Sheeny" is not likely to be anything else, nor is "Mr Levy the tailor"; or by mentioning the district from which they come ("the two gentlemen from Houndsditch"). He also invents facetious appellations for Jews who criticized his more unflattering presentations of their fellows; these ranged from "stag of Israel" to "red-maned desert roarer". This last expression is particularly telling. As a comic variation on a dignified Biblical term ("Lion of Judah") it links modern Jews with their forebears of the Old Testament. By its mention of the desert it parodies Disraeli's "Mosaic Arabs" and insinuates that English Jews have more affinities with the Middle East than with full-blooded Britons. "Red-maned" recalls the red-haired Jews caricatured on the English stage from medieval times onwards and given unfriendly mention in *Sketches by Boz*. And the total image of the red-maned roarer constitutes a Grandvillean caricature of the man who had dared to censure some aspect of Thackeray's writing. It was dangerous to criticize Thackeray; early slights and difficulties had made him hypersensitive, and he was apt to hit back vigorously with every literary weapon at his command. It was always better for him to get the aggression out of his system than to let it fester as it clearly did in the case of Samuel Phillips's critique of *Pendennis* and *Henry Esmond*.

Thackeray never uses "the Jew" as a collective noun (as in "The Jew in Literature" or "The Jew in History"). Besides "Jews", "Israelites", "Hebrews" and other terms already listed, he offers his readers "the Jewish nation", "the people" (or, parodistically, "the peoples"), "Jewry", "wandering race" and "Eastern race". In this last connection it should be remembered, however, that "race" in the sense of "ethnic provenance" is comparatively rare in Thackeray; he more often uses this word as a synonym of "family" in the wide sense—embracing all generations of a given family, past, present and future. He even speaks of the "race"of Whig Snobs (IX, 342)! "The human race" takes this usage to its farthest limits; and Thackeray reminds his readers more than once of their common ancestry and common membership of the family of Adam. Talk of "race" in the ethnic or tribal sense brought to Victorian minds mainly Disraeli's claims for the innate superiority of the race to which he believed the Jews to belong—claims which Thackeray, like his fellow-contributors to *Punch*, found fit subject only for ridicule.* This is not to say, of course, that Thackeray was a stranger to feelings of ethnic superiority: his partly patronizing and partly denigratory treatment of blacks, in his fiction and in his letters, affords ample evidence of prejudices he shared with many other Anglo-Indians, and indeed with many other Victorians of his class. He gradually shed the notion that a Jew's ordained place in British society was that of the old clothes man or the pawnbroker; but he never ceased to insinuate that a black man or a "mulatto" who was neither a servant nor a crossing sweeper usurped a place on the social ladder to which he had no right. Here common

---

* See *Appendix*.

membership of the family of Adam came up against its limits; and the abolitionists' slogan "Am I not a man and a brother?" roused him either to denial or to parody. Nothing about Thackeray's art and view of life, however, is ever as simple as selected facts might make it appear; for he showed himself keenly aware of unjustified British arrogance in the face of foreigners, and with an insider's knowledge combined with an intelligent artist's more detached view he often scourged the failings of those who set the tone in British society during the Regency, the reign of George IV and William IV, and the early years of the Victorian age of which he had the high hopes expressed at the end of *The Four Georges*.

In answer to complaints about bias in his writings Thackeray maintained that what he depicted in his fiction was individuals— and invented individuals at that!—and that no general conclusions about groups or classes should be drawn from such depictions. What this ignores is the cumulative effect within a single work and within an author's work as a whole: when Irishmen, for instance, are again and again shown to be addicted to drink and tall tales, as they are in Thackeray, a type or stereotype inevitably emerges from the separate individuals depicted. One work after another introduces Jewish characters behaving in roughly similar ways; when all allowances for deliberately distorted perspectives and unreliable narrators have been made, a steady view of certain types and classes of Jews, of certain kinds of economic or sartorial behaviour, of speech-patterns and common physiognomic features, must inevitably emerge. Many of Thackeray's verbal and visual portrayals deliberately invoke stereotypes. His swarthy hook-nosed faces, his triple-hatted old clothes men, his contrast between beautiful Jewish girls and their less than attractive male relatives, draw on a stock of images available to other artists and writers. The preceding pages of the present book will have shown, however, how often Thackeray's works play significant variations on these stereotypes, inverting or subverting them—as when he makes a "levanting" British Lord plunge poor Sherrick into ruin where the usual prejudiced notion would have demanded the opposite. Instead of showing predatory Jews corrupting Gentile society, as revenge, perhaps, for past injuries, Thackeray's work shows a predominantly Gentile society exhibiting predatory behaviour at every level and forcing such behaviour on anyone who has not inherited wealth and who wants to make his way towards social position and esteem. The Vanity Fair in which Jewish characters find themselves is not of their making and is not conducive to Christian virtues—it is to the credit of Sherrick, and the anonymous Jew of Mr Roundabout's touching tale of mutual help, that they remain as essentially decent as they are shown to be.

In one of his letters Thackeray referred to the persecutors of Jesus as "Old Testaments"; but much of his conscious dislike of the Jewish Bible may be traced back, not to purely theological factors, but to his struggle to free himself from his beloved mother's oppressive literalism and fundamentalism, as well as from the lingering influence of bullying teachers and preachers *in loco patris*. Yet the Old Testament remained an indelible part of his cultural heritage, filling his writings with incidents, figures, locutions from the Jewish Scriptures in the linguistic dress fashioned for it by Tyndale and the compilers of the King James Bible. Like most of his contemporaries he could introduce Old Testament names and places as part of the common English language, as when he speaks of a Jehu, or an Abigail, or a Jezebel, or a Babel of tongues—but he would often revitalize these by recalling their original context or merging them with non-Biblical material in such coinages as "Jezebella". He drew on the Old Testament freely in his "science of names", making "Lord Methuselah" bid for a young girl in the marriage market of society's Vanity Fair, or having his characters recall the wooing of the Biblical figure after whom Rachel Castlewood was named, or searching Old Testament and Apocrypha—as many of his contemporaries did too—to find names with a humorously outlandish sound for Jewish characters not simply called Nathan or Moses. He again and again characterized his personages, and the social and religious groupings to which they belonged, by the amount, the kind, the correctness, and the provenance, of the Biblical quotations or allusions they used. He lent characters and incidents archetypal or symbolic resonances by referring them to Biblical prefigurations. The serpent ornaments that played a crucial part in important scenes of *Vanity Fair* and *Pendennis* provide an obvious example, but there are less obvious ones like the reference to Colonel Newcome's "wandering forty years through the world" after parting from his beloved Léonore. Thackeray and his narrators use direct quotations from the Old Testament, or words and constructions recalling the Psalms, for controlling the emotional temperature and tonality of the work in question: "Ah, pangs of hearts torn asunder, passionate regrets, cruel partings! Shall you not end one day, ere many years; when the tears shall be wiped from all eyes, and there shall be no more sorrow nor pain?" (XIV, 336). The stories of Abraham, Samson, Esther, Ruth or Judith act as leitmotifs in individual novels, fulfilling structural functions analyzed earlier; but allusions to and quotations from the Old Testament also bind together the whole of Thackeray's work, essays, stories, novels, letters. References to the Ecclesiast's "Vanity of Vanities" are as ubiquitous as those to the New Testament parable of the Good Samaritan and the Man fallen among Thieves. Such references, to be sure, recall their original context in the Scriptures; but this is constantly felt to have been enriched by their subsequent use in English literature—in Bunyan, who transformed the Hebrew preacher's generalized vanities into Vanity Fair, or in Milton, whose classic depiction of man's first disobedience and his fall supplements and overlays the account in Genesis from which it derives. Last but by no means least: Thackeray is always ready to add riders or impose limitations—riders and limitations whose full effect depend on readers able to recall the provenance of the original axiom. Michael Lund, in the important study of Thackeray's relation to his readership which has already been mentioned, has rightly pointed, in this connection, to a typical "but" in the "overture" of *The Newcomes*: "There may be nothing new under and including the sun; *but* it looks fresh every morning, and we rise with it to toil, hope, scheme, laugh, struggle, love, suffer, until the night comes and quiet. And then will wake Morrow and the eyes that look on it; and so *da capo*" (*Reading Thackeray*, Detroit 1988, p. 108–XIV, 5).

Like his many references to Shakespeare, Cervantes, Fielding, Horace, the Arabian Nights, and once popular writers like Pierce Egan, Thackeray's Biblical images, quotations and allusions helped him communicate easily with an audience whose cultural background resembled his own. By appealing to shared experience they saved him many pages of description and explanation while also conjuring up images poetic in themselves and hallowed by the veneration in which the Bible—Old Testament as well as New—was traditionally held. He could play on that veneration negatively as well as positively, shocking his readers by the unholy application some of his personages made of Scriptural allusion, or forcing them to face the human, all-too-human realities portrayed in a Bible of whose use in private and public worship he constantly reminded his public, and which came to him mediated by many of his predecessors in English literature. In defiance of Matthew 5, 17 he thought the Old Testament's teaching superseded by the New; but his professed dislike of the Jewish Scriptures—whose psychological roots are so easy to discern—never inhibited him from using the story of Rachel, or of Samson, as readily for his purposes as that of the Prodigal Son or the Good Samaritan, or from acknowledging the towering greatness of the Biblical Moses. His sense that the people called Moses, or Moss, or Mossrose whom he portrayed in various lowly occupations in nineteenth-century England formed a piquant or ludicrous contrast with such Biblical forebears he shared with many of his contemporaries, from Coleridge onwards; but the figure of Alderman Moses suggests that there may be continuities too—that ancient virtues might be reanimated when social circumstances and enlightened legislation permitted it.

In Thackeray's depiction of Jews there is much that remains permanent; a clear line runs from his early caricatures of Jewish speech and behaviour to the Duke Street banking-house scene in "The Notch on the Axe." But no-one can read his writings in chronological order without becoming aware of a double movement. One is above ground, as it were: a steady augmentation of favourable features in his portrayal of Jews, beginning with the Jewish mother and child of *Pendennis*, gathering force with the Sherrick family, and ending with the helpful and efficient tailor of *Denis Duval*. The other movement can be most clearly observed in documents Thackeray did not publish or suppressed after their first publication, though it inevitably has its effect on the rest of his work: the re-activation of ancient prejudices and superstitions by some sudden shock, like the encounter with touts in "Notes of a Tour in the Low Countries" which brings back medieval images of Jewish devils, usurers and corrupters; the culture-shock of his first sight of Polish Jews, reanimating notions of *foetor judaicus* exploded by Sir Thomas Browne; the spectacle of Jewish dealers with their hats on in Lady Blessington's desecrated drawing room, reviving dehumanizing notions of Jews as birds of prey; the silent confrontation with Samuel Phillips, the "Jewish renegade" who had articulated doubts about *Pendennis* that Thackeray himself secretly harboured, which strengthened suspicions about the efficacy of baptism to "improve" the nature of Jews who submitted to it. I strongly suspect that the action of "Miss Löwe" is also based on an unfortunate encounter—an attempt, perhaps, to find an equivalent of Scott's Rebecca in real life which leads to the transformation of *belle juive* into *juive fatale*, a decoy used by sordid financial manipulators. A later encounter with the erstwhile *belle juive* as a fat and over-ornamented Jewish matron also revives the idea that Jewish beauties are *beautés de diable* whose attractions fade fast once they have caught their man. It must not be forgotten, however, that "Notes of a Tour in the Low Countries" was never published by Thackeray himself and that he suppressed "Miss Löwe" after its first appearance in print, along with his reanimation of the *Judensau* image in his *National Standard* poem about Nathan Rothschild.

Thackeray's prayer, written down in the last year of his life and recorded by Follett Synge, "that he might never propagate his own prejudices or pander to those of others" (IR, II, 354), was as deeply felt as the lament he attributed to his pen in a poem first published in 1853:

> I've writ the foolish fancy of his brain;
> The aimless jest that, striking, hath caused pain;
> The idle word that he'd wish back again.
>
> (VII, 64)

It should be remembered, moreover, that even when his powers of empathy failed him most thoroughly, as they did in his depiction of his journey to the Holy Land, he was apt to introduce compensatory features: his drawing of a bearded Polish Jew at prayer has a dignity wholly free from caricature elements, and the Titmarsh of *From Cornhill to Grand Cairo* is allowed, for once, to notice handsome male Jews as well as beautiful female ones among his Polish fellow travellers. His privately expressed loathing of the Old Testament—his denunciations of the very Israelites with whom the Puritans who sanctioned the re-admission of Jews into Britain had so readily identified and who were held up to his admiration by his fundamentalist mother—was constantly undercut, as we have seen so many times, by his sensitive response to the poetry, the human truth, and the symbolic force, of the Jewish Scriptures. And no personal shock, no failure of empathy, no deep-seated prejudice made him ever waver in his abhorrence of religious persecution or oppose the process of Jewish emancipation which went on in his life-time—a process which brought Britain's Jews from the status of permitted alien residents in the time of George III to the achievement of full civic rights in that of Queen Victoria.

From the vantage point of twentieth-century Europe it is salutary to look back on Thackeray's depiction of Jews and Judaism in order to see what pitfalls he avoided. Richard Doyle may draw Sherrick manipulating Honeyman like a puppet, and Thackeray's image of Sherrick's wine-vaults "undermining" Honeyman's chapel suggest analogies with T.S. Eliot's notorious image of the Jew who is "underneath the lot"—but *The Newcomes* never show the Jews as a serious threat to the British character and way of life. What threat there is comes from within. Sherrick manages Lady Whittlesea's Chapel like a theatre because pastors like Honeyman and his fashionable Mayfair flock have lost all true feeling for the spirituality of Christian worship and the difference between the Church of England liturgy and operatic performances. The great swindlers in

Thackeray's works—those who launch and manage the great Diddlesex speculation or the Bundelcund Bank—are not Jewish; the Diddlesex people, indeed, make a great show of their Christian piety. The sharp Jewish business men and the Jewish crooks that people Thackeray's fiction are comparatively small-time operators. There are no equivalents, in his writings, of Trollope's Melmotte, Lopez, or Emilius; and the Rothschilds, once Lionel and James had succeeded Nathan Mayer, are always mentioned with respect.

Nor does Thackeray show undue fears about possible admixture of Jewish and English blood: the marriage between Honeyman and Julia Sherrick has clear authorial approval, as has that of Ivanhoe and Rebecca in *Rebecca and Rowena*—though it is to be noted that this last union remains childless, and that we never see Gentile Englishwomen marrying Jewish men—as they do happily in the Prague of Trollope's *Nina Balatka*, but disastrously in the England of *The Way We Live Now*. Where the "Victorian racialism" imputed to Thackeray by John Sutherland shows up most nakedly is in his treatment of the intermarriage of white with black or partly black; the most unpleasant pages in his later writings are undoubtedly those in which a stream of racial insults is directed, with implied authorial approval, at the "quadroon" or "mulatto" Woolcomb who marries an English lady. Here personal hang-ups joined contemporary cultural prejudice: Thackeray was an Anglo-Indian ("an outsider", Nina Ferris has called him, "who looked very much like an insider") with dark-skinned half-sisters of whom he was ashamed.

When Thackeray found himself confronted with the compositions of Meyerbeer or Mendelssohn, the writings of Heine, or the paintings of Simeon Solomon, he judged them according to aesthetic or moral criteria, without being tempted to assign them to some inferior specious because their begetters were Jewish. He does, of course, notoriously stress the Jewishness of Benjamin Disraeli—but that was inevitable because Disraeli's novels foreground the Jewish theme and claim a pre-eminence for the Jewish "race" which goes beyond all reasonable measure. Even here, however, Thackeray finds much to admire: though he offended Disraeli by ridicule of his early dandyism and his Jewish hobby horse, he is by no means niggard of praise for the art of literary portraiture exhibited in *Coningsby* and *Sybil*. And if some ancient prejudice was suddenly confirmed or re-activated by an unfortunate experience—as the notion of *foetor judaicus* was in the encounter with Polish Jews described in *From Cornhill to Grand Cairo*—Thackeray was fairminded enough to observe similar phenomena outside the Jewish community and levelheaded enough to notice that his own Jewish acquaintances did not offend Gentile sensitivities in the same way.

The early drawings of Jews, reproduced in Chapter 1 from Thackeray's journal and the *National Standard*, show his gift of catching a physiognomic likeness in caricature and of caricaturing dress (Miss Absaloms) and body-stance (Braham); his endeavours, in the tradition of Hogarth, to combine caricature of individuals with emblematic and symbolic elements (Rothschild's and Braham's mock coats of arms, the figures and buildings behind the worthies represented in the foreground); and his indebtedness to vigorous English traditions of personal caricature going back to Gillray (see especially the figure on the left in Thackeray's drawing of three female opera singers). His happy knack of suggesting physiognomic expression with just a few strokes of pen or pencil is well represented by the figure of the pawnbroker in Chapter 2; this also shows clearly the debt the whole *Dionysius Diddler* sequence owes to Rodolphe Toepffer, whose art was greatly admired in Weimar while Thackeray was there. Chapter 3 shows the congruence between George Cruikshank's caricatures of Jews which Thackeray (who had been Cruikshank's pupil for a while) singles out for praise, and the verbal suggestions he supplied for the exercise of Cruikshank's art. He found in Cruikshank that combination of precise and loving observation of the minutiae of ordinary contemporary life with caricature elements which characterized his own early work and which was to make him such a powerful force in *Punch*. The dignified picture of a bearded Jew, worshipping God on shipboard in the traditional garb of prayer-shawl and phylacteries, is free of Cruikshankian elements, however, and forms a surprising contrast with Thackeray's verbal assault on Polish Jews in the work in which this wood-engraving appears (*From Cornhill to Grand Cairo*). It exemplifies an almost schizophrenic disjunction of visual appreciation of patriarchal venerability from olfactory recoil—an unfeigned recoil which recalls the German expression for deep-seated animosity: "Ich kann ihn nicht riechen." The portrait of the Syrian Christian Mariam, in this same work, is also the nearest Thackeray ever came to a visual representation of his ideal "belle Juive"; for the illustrator of *Rebecca and Rowena* was Richard Doyle and not the author himself.

Doyle, along with Archibald Henning and John Leech, helped to mould the lay-out and imagery of *Punch*, whose sub-title, *The London Charivari*, indicated the indebtedness of Punch to Parisian models provided by Daumier, Grandville, and Philipon. Thackeray had paid his own artistic homage to Daumier in *Flore et Zéphir*; many of

his personal caricatures (notably those of Louis Philippe) are
modelled on images perfected by Philipon's team; but his characteristic techniques call for engraving on wood and copper or steel
rather than for the lithography which Daumier raised to such
heights. His *Punch* caricatures of Jews show the influence of Doyle
and Leech rather than his French contemporaries. They fall into
three main categories. The first—the majority—depicts cheerful
individuals and groups, with luxuriant hair or beards, and with
obligatory long noses descending towards a smiling, or contentedly
smoking, mouths drawn with a single sinuous line. The second
shows overdressed, thick-lipped bearded creatures, drawn with less
sympathetic gusto though never with the viciousness of some of
Leech's cartoons of Jews—Chapter 5 showed two examples, Mr
Nebuchadnezzar ordering pork, and an unnamed spectator at a
theatre-performance who looks through one eye piece of his opera
glasses while his unoccupied eye squints towards the beholder. The
third group of Thackeray's *Punch* drawings is concerned with
Disraeli. His representation of that statesman as a mechanical doll
controlled by Lord George Bentinck is not grossly caricatured;
except for the ringlets of hair "Jewish" features are not overempha-
sized, and the doll wears an over-alert expression—suggested by
raised eyebrows and wide-open eyes—which seems rather endearing; but Disraeli, of course, for all his devotion to Lord George,
could hardly have relished the idea of appearing as the great man's
puppet. In the *Codlingsby* illustrations, on the other hand, Mendoza
is given pronouncedly "Jewish" features, with nose and dark hair
creating the main effect, as well as outrageously flamboyant costumes featuring boldly chequered trousers and conspicuous ornamental pins; these caricatures have just enough suggestions of the
younger, dandified Disraeli to remind viewers of the latter's tendency to introduce idealized self-portraits into his novels. The
expressions on the caricatured Mendoza's face are never malevolent, however; they exhibit benevolence, good-natured pugnacity
(in the boxing scene) and alert deference (when facing Louis
Philippe).

   One of the features of the *Punch* style which Thackeray developed
with especial success was the pictorial initial. This could embody a
visual impression of a character or narrator (as in the example from
"The Proser" reproduced in Chapter 7); or it could introduce an
emblematic, symbolic element, as in the medieval battlement scene
in the penultimate illustration of Chapter 5. By the time he came to
write *Vanity Fair*, Thackeray had fully absorbed the *Punch* style
(which, indeed, he had helped to form). He was now able to

combine the emblematic, symbolic, Hogarthian element of his art—shown in the "Fool" pictures reproduced in Chapters 5 and 6—with more straightforward illustrations set into the text or separated out as a full-page engraving. In *Vanity Fair* Thackeray's pictorial Jews tend to confront Gentiles nose to nose: witness the gentleman from the Minories startled by George Osborne's pugnacity; Becky facing a tout at the Sedley auction, with Rawdon Crawley in attendance; a Jewish bidder at that auction, with an aggressively jutting lower lip, thrusting his face at a youth who seems literally taken aback; a bulbous-nosed bailiff facing Rawdon and laying an arresting hand on his sleeve while his colleague blocks his way from the other side; and the small inset which shows the young janitor of the Cursitor Street sponging-house ushering a hesitant Lady Crawley into its inner sanctum.

Pendennis brings a significant development. The Jewish mother and child in the first illustration reproduced in Chapter 7 shows no vestige of the caricature to which Jewish characters had so far always tempted Thackeray. There can be little doubt that this is connected, not only with Thackeray's personal encounters with affluent English Jews, but also with that idealizing urge which John Carey so deplores in the later Thackeray and which shows itself in his characterizations of Helen and Laura Pendennis no less than in that of this unnamed Jewish mother. At the same time characters depicted with the hirsute, swarthy, hook-nosed, over-dressed appearance of Thackeray's earlier Jewish caricatures are theatrical folk like Mr Dolphin or Latin foreigners like Mirobolant who are not designated as Jewish in the novel's text.

After *Pendennis*, Thackeray increasingly allowed other artists to illustrate his fiction, though he kept some control over their work, suggesting possibilities and criticizing designs. The image of the little round-shouldered Jew on a camp-stool reproduced in Chapter 8, shows his undiminished power of lightning caricature and characterization, while the portrait of Isaac D'Israeli in Chapter 9 represents a most sympathetic view of a man of letters at slippered ease by his own fire-side, with his beloved books beside him. D'Israeli's features are at once pensive and animated, and their "Jewishness" is no way exaggerated. While writing *Philip*, Thackeray suggested Old Testament captions for Frederick Walker's drawings ("What Nathan said unto David"; "Judith and Holofernes") which gave an archetypal dimensions to these naturalistic representations of scenes from his novel; and he also supplied many of the pictorial initials, including a cowering Shylock, scowling with his knife at the ready, as an emblem for dangerous vengefulness.

The Shylock initial, which recalls Devrient's assumption of that part rather than Kean's, shows how readily ancient fears of the malevolent Jew, the patriarch wielding the knife, the seeker of vengeance for past wrongs, could irrupt into consciousness even in the enlightened nineteenth century—there is, after all, a well-known line that leads from the Jew of Malta and the Jew of Venice to Fagin and Svengali. The Shylock initial from *Philip* forms an instructive contrast with the initial from "Autour de mon chapeau" reproduced in Chapter 9, which combines the *Punch* convention of the three hats and the bag of old clothes flung over the shoulder with the depiction of a handsome, noble-featured, Jewish face, a patriarchal countenance that inspires veneration rather than fear. What we have here, of course, at the very end of Thackeray's life, is another instance of that "dual vision" which had been such a striking feature of the British conception of the Jew since the time in which a red-wigged, usurous, murderous, blasphemous Judas Ischariot appeared on popular stages that on other occasions presented dignified impersonations of Old Testament worthies.

Thackeray's emblematic depiction of Shylock, and the many references in his fiction to Abraham's willingness to sacrifice Isaac, represent his closest approach to those ancient fears and demonologies which found their most potent—though by no means their most elaborate—Victorian expression in *Oliver Twist*. But though nothing in his work corresponds to the loving and knowledgeable (if occasionally tiresome) depiction of Jews in *Daniel Deronda*, Thackeray is by no means the "racialist" anti-Semite as whom some of his modern critics have depicted him. He finds much to laugh at in the Jews he portrayed with pen and pencil, and much to deplore; but he also finds a good deal of cheerfulness, useful service, and fair dealing. He took an artist's delight in the differences he perceived, or thought he perceived, between Jews and Gentile Englishmen, and never thought of demanding complete assimilation, the giving up of religious and cultural differences, as the price of emancipation. If the cultural gap was too great, as it seems to have been in the case of the Polish Jews encountered on shipboard in *From Cornhill to Grand Cairo*, he was apt to mantle his instinctive recoil in unfair suppositions; and one manuscript he took care never to publish shows him projecting hatred of his own sexual needs onto Dutch touts he took for Jews who offered to minister to them. It is a sign, however, of the ever-growing integration of Jews into British society that in the 1850s he found no cultural gap worth mentioning when he visited the Rothschilds or Lady Waldegrave—the direct descendants of two men whose alienness, whose Jewish unassimilability, he had pilloried only two decades before. He had sufficient respect for the resilience of the British society of his day to recognize that its Jewish component constituted no threat to it, and a sufficiently clear view of that society's vices to see that the faults popularly attributed to Jews, and undoubtedly exhibited by some members of the Jewish community, were faults that could be equally well found in impeccably Gentile Christians. He never advocated or defended the persecution or political disadvantaging of Jews, and came more and more to accept their presence as a sometimes objectionable, sometimes amusing, sometimes admirable part of the social scene of which he was such a gifted chronicler. His sympathies with the Jewish people always remained imperfect; but Anne Thackeray's essay "Little Scholars", and her father's proud approval of it, suggest that they gradually became less so. This may help to explain why Thackeray stood away from what Froude called Carlyle's "true Teutonic aversion" to the Jewish people and approached the position of Hazlitt, who saw the "emancipation" of the Jews as "but a natural step in the progress of civilization", and that of Macaulay, who advocated such emancipation as a necessary part of what he thought the best and wisest of his contemporaries should work for: "blotting out from the statute-book the last traces of intolerance." Indeed, one of Thackeray's late essays, composed after his turn to a more conservative view of life, specifically commends the way in which Macaulay "backs and applauds freedom struggling for its own" ("Nil Nisi Bonum", February 1860–xvii, 364–5). The readers of the *Cornhill Magazine*, for whom this essay was written, could not fail to recall that Jewish emancipation played an important part in these struggles.

That he could never rid his mind, or his writings, of stereotypical notions inherited from the past and transmitted by education, some types of religious teaching, stage conventions, reading-matter of many levels of sophistication and appeal, the formulae of caricature, peer-group talk and many other forms of social osmosis—and that such notions could colour his view of the Jews' function and behaviour in the nineteenth-century society which he so keenly observed—Thackeray would have been the last to deny. He always remained conscious of limitations he had indicated to his mother when he wrote to her, on 21 August 1844, that the book he intended to base on his travels to the East could only describe "that cockney part which I shall see", and to Dr John Brown, when he told him, on 11 May 1848: "I hope I may be able to tell truth always, and see it aright, according to the eyes which God Almighty gives me"

(*Biographical Edition* V, xxxvi; VI, xxxvii). Bayard Taylor summed it up best when he wrote, in an article first published in 1864, of Thackeray's "honesty, his proud, almost defiant candour, his ever-present, yet shrinking tenderness, and that sadness of the moral sentiment which the world persisted in regarding as cynicism." This impression, Taylor continued, "deepened with further acquaintance and was never modified. Although he belonged to the sensitive, irritable genus, his only manifestations of impatience which I remember were when that which he had written with a sigh was interpreted as a sneer. When so misunderstood, he scorned to set himself right. 'I have no brain above the eyes', he was accustomed to say; 'I describe what I see.' He was quick and unerring in detecting the weaknesses of his friends, and spoke of them with a tone of disappointment sometimes bordering on exasperation; but he was equally severe upon his own shortcomings. He allowed no friend to think him better than his own deliberate estimate made him. I have never known a man whose nature was so immovably based on truth" (*IR*, II, 265).

In Thackeray's fiction Jews are marginal men and women in a double sense: most of them appear at the margins of British society of which they or their descendants seek to become a more integral part; and they figure only in the margins of all his novels and most of his short stories and essays. His novels add to Victorian literature no supervillains like Fagin or Svengali; no superheroes like Sidonia or figures of supervirtue and supergenerosity like the Montenero of Maria Edgeworth (who sought, in *Harrington*, to make up for Jewish bug-bear figures in her earlier fiction, as Smollett had done in *Ferdinand Count Fathom* and Dickens was to do in *Our Mutual Friend*); no figures whom the very name of the novel announces to be of dominant interest and importance, like Daniel Deronda. But this is precisely how he experienced them in life: moving briefly into his ken, unpleasantly (as Miss Löwe does in the early version of the *Fitz-Boodle Papers*); pleasantly (like the younger Rothschilds who are invoked in the novels as pillars of financial solidity and furnish the model for an uplifting encounter with a mother and child); or—most frequently—with more mixed effects, affording the same sort of sardonic amusement with which he so often depicted his Gentile contemporaries at home and abroad. One such character, indeed, the archetypal marginal man Sherrick, becomes a valid critic of a society in which a Barnes Newcome and a Bobby Moss can flourish while a Colonel Thomas Newcome sees his fortune in ruins. No dispassionate survey of the evidence assembled in this book could fail to conclude that prejudice and animus sometimes distorted Thackeray's view in a way they did not distort that of a Hazlitt or a Robert Browning, and that the brilliant visual apprehension of the superficies of life which guided his imagination was not always supplemented by reflective penetration to deeper truths—a failing which he himself, characteristically, recognized and exaggerated when he denied that he had a brain above the eyes. It should also conclude, however, that the delight in the variety of human existence which went with his satirist's apprehension of folly and wickedness left him as little, after some early follies and indiscretions that he scorned to republish, as his desire not to fly into a passion with the characters that peopled his fiction, and to convey as faithful a simulacrum of life as could be obtained from the cracked looking glass in which the sad jester of *Vanity Fair* surveyed his own features and the world behind them.

APPENDIX

Punch's Comments on the "Unity of Race" Movement

To Mr. Punch

"SIR,

"I wish you would do something to put a stop to that ridiculous movement towards "Unity of Race", wherein half the people of Europe are going to loggerheads. In Schleswig-Holstein there are the Scandinavian and Teutonic elements of the population, as they are called, quarreling and cutting each others' throats. In another direction, the Sclavenic breed is longing to be at the Teutons. The Austrian and Italian folks are at variance, and even the Neapolitans must needs fall out with Sicilians. It is unnecessary to mention the wrong-headed Celts in Ireland, burning with envy, and hatred, and malice, and all uncharitableness towards the Saxons. By and bye, I suppose the fingers of Highland and Lowland Scotch will itch for internecine war. Why can't they fuse? Why can't they mingle? Why can't they put their horses together? I declare, *Mr. Punch*, that this mania for asserting Unity of Race puts me in bodily fear. When I examine the composition of my own anatomy, what do I find? Why, that I am partly Ancient Briton, with a cross of the Roman, a good deal of the Saxon, a spice of the Dane, a bit of the Norman, and a touch of the Lombard and the Fleming into the bargain.

"If this madness should prove contagious, who knows but that a squabble will arise between my constituent atoms? The Belgian, Lombard, and Danish particles of my blood will separate from each other; my Saxon muscles will detach themselves from my Norman bones; and there will be a breach between my ancient British forehead and my Roman nose. The consequence will be, that I shall go to pieces, or fall a victim to spontaneous combustion. Pray arrest this nonsensical Unity of Race movement if you can. If you cannot, at least endeavour to give it a right direction. Just remind the contending nations of the fact that they are all descended from ADAM; and persuade them to amalgamate in one common stock on the strength of it.

"Your constant reader,
"JOHN BULL."

(*Punch*, XV [1848–9], p. 93)

SELECT BIBLIOGRAPHY

I. Editions

The Oxford Thackeray ed. G. Saintsbury, 17 vols., London 1908 (quoted throughout, unless another source is specifically named).

The Works of William Makepeace Thackeray, with biographical introductions by his daughter, Anne Ritchie (the Biographical Edition), 13 vols., London 1898–99.

The Works of William Makepeace Thackeray, with biographical introductions by Lady Ritchie (the Centenary Biographical Edition), 26 vols., London 1910–11.

The Letters and Private Papers of William Makepeace Thackeray, ed. G.N. Ray, 4 vols., Cambridge (Mass.) 1945–6 (cited as *LPP*).

Letters of Anne Thackeray Ritchie, with 42 additional letters from her father, William Makepeace Thackeray, ed. H. Ritchie, London 1942.

Mr. Thackeray's Writings in "The National Standard" and "Constitutional", compiled by W.T. Spencer (London 1899).

W.M. Thackeray: Contributions to the "Morning Chronicle", ed. G.N. Ray, Urbana 1955.

W.M. Thackeray: Stray Papers. Being Stories, Reviews, Verses and Sketches (1921–1847), ed. L. Melville, London 1901.

Thackerayana. Notes & Anecdotes, illustrated by Nearly Six Hundred Sketches by William Makepeace Thackeray, depicting Humorous Incidents in his School Life, and Favourite Scenes and Characters in the Books of his Every-day Reading, ed. J. Grego, London 1875.

W.M. Thackeray: The New Sketch Book. Essays Collected from the Foreign Quarterly Review, ed. R.S. Garnett, London 1906.

Thackeray: Interviews and Recollections, ed. P. Collins, 2 vols., London 1983 (cited as *IR*).

Of the important critical edition of Thackeray issued by Garland Publishing under the general editorship of P.L. Shillingsburg the following volumes were published when the manuscript for the present book was completed:

The History of Henry Esmond, ed. E.F. Harden, New York 1989.

Vanity Fair, ed. P.L. Shillingsburg, New York 1989.

I have also consulted, with profit, the following editions of individual works:

Vanity Fair, ed. G. and K. Tillotson (London 1963), and ed. J.A. Sutherland (Oxford 1984).

Barry Lyndon, ed. M.J. Anisman (New York 1970), and ed. A. Sanders (Oxford 1984).

Henry Esmond, ed. J.A. Sutherland and M. Greenfield (Harmondsworth 1970).

Pendennis, ed. D. Hawes (Harmondsworth 1972).

The Book of Snobs, ed. J.A. Sutherland (Santa Lucia 1978).

The Roundabout Papers, ed. J.E. Wells (New York 1925).

II. Bibliographies

Van Duzer, H.S., *A Thackeray Library*, augmented edition, Port Washington 1965.

Flamm, D., *Thackeray's Critics: An Annotated Bibliography of British and American Criticism*, North Carolina 1966.

Olmsted, J.C., *Thackeray and his Twentieth-century Critics*, New York 1977.

Goldfarb, S., *W.M. Thackeray: An Annotated Bibliography, 1976–1987*, New York 1989.

III. Critical, Historical and Textual Studies Consulted:

Anderson, G.K., *The Legend of the Wandering Jew*, Providence 1965.
Baker, J.E., "Thackeray's Recantation", *PMLA* 77 (1962).
Bernt, P.W., *Thackeray and the Irish. A Study in Victorian Prejudice* Diss. Nebraska 1979.
Bitton-Jackson, L., *The Jewish Woman in Christian Literature*, New York 1982.
Bloch, M., "La Femme juive dans le roman et au théatre", *Revue des études juives*, 24 (1892).
Broich, U., *Ironie im Prosawerk W.M. Thackerays*, Bonn 1958.
Brookfield, C. and F., *Mrs. Brookfield and her Circle*, London 1905.
Brown, T., *Disraeli the Novelist*, London 1981.
Buchanan-Brown, J., *The Illustrations of William Makepeace Thackeray* Newton Abbot 1979.
Cabot, F.C., "The Two Voices of Thackeray's *Catherine*", *Nineteenth Century Fiction*, 28 (1974).
Canham, S., "Art and the Illustrations of *Vanity Fair* and *The New-Comes*", *Modern Language Quarterly*, 43 (1982).
Carey, J., *Thackeray: Prodigal Genius*, London 1977.
Chancellor, E.B., *The London of Thackeray: Being Some Account of the Haunts of Thackeray's Characters*, London 1923.
Chancey, C.L., "Thackeray and the Plight of the Victorian Satirist", *English Studies* (Amsterdan), 49 (1968).
Chesterton, G.K., *Thackeray* (in the *Masters of Literature* series), London 1909.
Cline, C.L., "Disraeli and Thackeray", *Review of English Studies*, 19 (1942).
Coates, J., "Handling Change. A Study of Thackeray's Techniques of Presenting Social and Personal Change in *Pendennis*", *Durham University Journal* 1982.
Cohen, J.R., *Charles Dickens and his Original Illustrators*, Columbus (Ohio) 1980.
Cohen, S.M., and P.E. Hyman (ed.), *The Jewish Family. Myths and Reality*, New York and London 1986.
Colby, R.A., "*Catherine*: Thackeray's Credo", *Review of English Studies*, 15 (1964).
Colby, R.A., *Thackeray's Canvass of Humanity*, Ohio 1979.
Colby, R.A., (ed.), *Thackeray* issue of *Studies in the Novel*, North Texas State University, 1981.
Costerus: Essays in English and American Language and Literature, Volume II: Thackeray, ed. P.L. Shillingsburg, Amsterdam 1974.
Cowen, A. and R., *Victorian Jews through British Eyes*, Oxford 1986.
Davies, P.G., "The Miscegenation Theme in the Works of Thackeray", *Modern Language Notes* 76 (1961).
Dodds, J.W., *Thackeray. A Critical Portrait*, New York 1941.
Dodds, J.W., *The Age of Paradox. A Biography of England 1841–1851*, New York 1952.
Eberhard, W., *Fontane und Thackeray*, Heidelberg 1975.
Elwin, M., *Thackeray: A Personality*, London 1932.
Endelman, T.M., *The Jews of Georgian England, 1714–1830*, Philadelphia 1979.
Ennis, L., *Thackeray: The Sentimental Cynic*, Evanston 1950.
Ferris, I.G., *Fictions by Pendennis. Narrative and Self in Thackeray's Later Novels*, Diss. University of California, Los Angeles 1975.
Ferris, I.G., *William Makepeace Thackeray* (*Twayne's English Authors*), Boston 1983.
Ferris, I.G., "Realism and the Discord of Ending: The Example of Thackeray", *Nineteenth Century Fiction* 38 (1984).
Fiedler, L.A., "What Can We Do About Fagin? The Jew-Villain in Western Tradition", *Commentary*, May 1949.
Fisch, H., *Jerusalem and Albion. The Hebraic Factor in Seventeenth-Century Literature*, London 1964.
Fisch, H., *The Dual Image. A Study of the Jew in English Literature*, London 1971.
Fisher, J.L., *Thackeray's Moral Landscape: The Aesthetic Principles of William Makepeace Thackeray*, Diss. Illinois University, Urbana 1980.

Fisher, J.L., "The Aesthetics of the Mediocre: Thackeray and the Visual Arts", *Victorian Studies* 26 (1982).

Fisher, J.L., "Siren and Artist. Contradiction in Thackeray's Aesthetic Ideal", *Nineteenth Century Fiction* 39 (1985).

Gaer, J., *The Legend of the Wandering Jew*, New York 1961.

Garrett-Goodyear, J., "Stylized Emotions, Unrealized Selves, Expressive Characterization in Thackeray", *Victorian Studies* 22 (1979).

Gilmour, R., *The Idea of the Gentleman in the Victorian Novel*, London 1981.

Gilmour, R., *Thackeray: Vanity Fair (Studies in English Literature*, 74) London 1982.

Gneiting, T.T., "The Pencil's Role in *Vanity Fair*", *Huntington Library Quarterly* 1976.

Golden, C.J., *The Victorian Illustrated Book*, Diss. Michigan 1986.

Gombrich, E.H., *Art and Illusion. A Study in the Psychology of Pictorial Representation*, London 1959.

Goodell, M.M., *Three Satirists of Snobbery: Thackeray, Meredith, Proust*, Hamburg 1939.

Gould, C.G., *Thackeray and the Death of Innocence in Victorian Fiction*, Diss. New York University 1986.

Greene, D.J., "Becky Sharp and Lord Steyne. Thackeray or Disraeli?" *Nineteenth Century Fiction* 16 (1961).

Greig, J.Y.T., *Thackeray: A Reconsideration*, London 1950.

Griffiths, P., and L.R.M. Strachan, "Ikey Solomons, Junior", *Notes and Queries* 174 (1938).

Gulliver, H.S., *Thackeray's Literary Apprenticeship*, Valdosta 1934.

Handley, G., *Vanity Fair (Penguin Master Studies)*, Harmondsworth 1985.

Harden, E.F., *The Emergence of Thackeray's Serial Fiction*, London 1979.

Hardy, B., *The Exposure of Luxury. Radical Themes in Thackeray*, London 1972.

Harvey, J.R., *Victorian Novelists and their Illustrators*, London 1970.

Hawari, R., *A Study of the Exotic East in the Works of W.M. Thackeray, With Reference to the Cult of the Oriental in 18th and 19th Century England*, Diss. London 1967.

Hawari, R., "Thackeray's Oriental Reading", *Revue de littérature comparée* 48 (1975).

Hawes, D., "Thackeray and the *National Standard*", *Review of English Studies* 23 (1972).

Hewett, O.B., *Strawberry Fair. A Biography of Frances, Countess Waldegrave, 1821–1879*, London 1956.

Hollingsworth, K., *The Newgate Novel, 1830–1847: Bulwer, Ainsworth and Thackeray*, Detroit 1963.

Howes, W.C., *Reforming the Mirrored Muse. Thackeray the Victorian Satirist*, Diss. Princeton 1980.

Hurst, H., Ironischer und sentimentaler Realismus bei Thackeray, Hamburg 1938.

Iser, W., *Der implizite Leser*, Munich 1972.

Kapai, L., *A Study of W.M. Thackeray's "The Newcomes"*, Diss. Howard University, Washington D.C., 1975.

Kaufmann, R.F. *The Relationship between Illustration and Text in the Novels of Dickens, Thackeray, Trollope and Hardy*, Diss. New York University 1974.

Kileen, J.E.M., *Type and Anti-Type: A Study of the Figure of the Jew in Popular Literature of the First Half of the Nineteenth Century*, Diss. Canterbury, N.Z., 1972.

Kleis, J.C., "Dramatic Irony in Thackeray's *Catherine*: The Function of Ikey Solomons, Esq., Junior", *Victorian Newsletter* 33 (1968).

Klish, R.M., *Thackeray's Travel Writings*, Diss. Michigan State Univ. 1974.

Kollse, A.-M., *Disraeli, Dickens und Thackeray in ihrer Stellung zur englisch-aristokratischen Gesellschaftsschicht*, Diss. Hamburg 1949.

Krishnaswami, P.R., *In Thackeray's Workshop*, Madras 1956.

Landa, M.J., *The Jew in Drama*, New York 1927.

Las Vergnas, R., *William Makepeace Thackeray. L'homme, le penseur, le romancier*, Paris 1932.

Lipman, V.D., *Social History of the Jews in England, 1850–1950*, London 1954.
Lipman, V.D. (ed.), *Three Centuries of Anglo-Jewish History. A Volume of Essays*, Cambridge 1961.
Loofbourow, J., *Thackeray and the Form of Fiction*, Princeton 1964.
Lund, M.C., *Indifferent Monitors. Character and Narration in Dickens and Thackeray*, Diss. Emory University, 1973.
Lund, M.C., *Reading Thackeray*, Detroit 1988.
McKendy, T.F., *"Catherine", "Punch's Prize Novelists" and "Vanity Fair": Thackeray as Parodist*, Diss. Michigan 1974.
McMaster, J., *Thackeray: The Major Novels*, Manchester 1971.
McMaster, J. and R.D., *The Novel from Sterne to James. Essays on the Relation of Literature to Life*, London 1981.
Mandel, O., *Annotations to "Vanity Fair,"* Washington 1981.
Meisel, M., *Realizations. Narrative, Pictorial and Theatrical Arts in Nineteenth Century England*, Princeton 1983.
Melville, L., *The Life of William Makepeace Thackeray*, London 1899.
Melville, L., *The Thackeray Country*, London 1905.
Merivale, H., and F.T. Marzials, *Life of William Makepeace Thackeray*, London 1891.
Merritt, J.D., "The Novelist St. Barbe in Disraeli's *Endymion*. Revenge on Whom?" *Nineteenth Century Fiction* 23 (1968).
Meyer, W., *Der Wandel des jüdischen Typus in der englischen Literatur*, Diss. Marburg 1912.
Modder, M.F., *The Jew in the Literature of England to the End of the Nineteenth Century*, Philadelphia 1944.
Monsarratt, A. *An Uneasy Victorian. Thackeray the Man, 1811–1863*, London 1980.
Mudge, I.G., and M.E. Sears, *A Thackeray Dictionary*, New York 1910.
Mueller, J.L., *Thackeray's Critical and Aesthetic Principles*, Diss. Harvard 1973.
Naman, A.A., *The Jew in the Victorian Novel. Some Relationships between Prejudice and Art*, New York 1980.
Neale, R.H., *The Characterizations of Thackeray's Narrators*, Diss. University of California, Berkeley 1975.
Painting, D.E., "Thackeray v. Disraeli", *Quarterly Review* 302 (1964).
Panitz, E.L., *The Alien in their Midst: Images of Jews in English Literature*, E. Brunswick N.J., 1981.
Patai, R., and J. Wing, *The Myth of the Jewish Race*, New York 1975.
Peters, C., *Thackeray's Universe. Shifting Worlds of Imagination and Reality*, London 1987.
Phillipps, K.C., "Thackeray's Proper Names", *Neuphilologische Mitteilungen* 75 (1974).
Phillipps, K.C., *The Language of Thackeray*, London 1978.
Poliakov, L., *The History of Anti-Semitism*. Vol. III: *From Voltaire to Wagner*, transl. M. Kochan, London 1975.
Polk, J.R., *Thackeray, "Punch", and the Victorian Burlesque Convention*, Diss. Harvard 1968.
Pollard, A., (ed.), *Thackeray's "Vanity Fair". A Case Book*, London 1978.
Popowski, D.J., *Preliminary Sketches. The Short Tale in Dickens and Thackeray*, Diss. Bowling Green State University 1974.
Price, R.G.G., *A History of "Punch"*, London 1957.
Puschmann-Nalenz, B., "Unscrewing the Old Framework of Society". Zur gesellschaftlichen Hierarchie in *"Vanity Fair"*, *Germanisch-romanische Monatsschrift*, N.F. 27 (1979).
Ray, G.N., *The Buried Life. A Study of the Relation between Thackeray's Fiction and his Personal History*, London 1952.
Ray, G.N., *Thackeray: The Uses of Adversity (1811–1846)*, London 1955.
Ray, G.N., *Thackeray: The Age of Wisdom (1847–1863)*. London 1958.
Ray, G.N., *The Illustrator and the Book in England, 1790–1914*, Oxford 1976.

Rawlins, J.P., *Thackeray's Novels: A Fiction that is True*, Berkeley 1974.

Ricks, C., *T.S. Eliot and Prejudice*, London 1988.

Ritchie, Lady A., Biographical Introductions to *The Works of William Makepeace Thackeray*, 13 vols., London 1898–09.

Ritchie, Lady A., Biographical Introductions to the "Centenary Edition" of *The Works of William Makepeace Thackeray*, 26 vols., London 1910–11.

Rosa, M.W., *The Silver Fork School. Novels of Fashion preceding "Vanity Fair"*, New York 1936.

Rosenberg, E., *From Shylock to Svengali. Jewish Stereotypes in English Fiction*, Stanford 1960.

Roth, C., *A History of the Jews in England*, Third edn., Oxford 1964.

Rubin, A., *Images in Transition. The English Jew in English Literature, 1660–1830*, Westport, Conn, 1984.

Salbstein, M.C.N., *The Emancipation of the Jews in Britain*, Rutherford N.J. 1982.

Salerno, N.A., "*Catherine*: Theme and Structure", *American Imago* 18 (1961).

Sartre, J.P., *Anti-Semite and Jew*, transl. G.J. Becker, New York 1948.

Schaffer, E.S., "*Kubla Khan*" *and "The Fall of Jerusalem". The Mythological School in Biblical Criticism and Secular Literature, 1770–1880*, Cambridge 1975.

Schiff, E., *From Stereotype to Metaphor. The Jew in Contemporary Drama*, Albany, N.Y., 1982.

Schwarz, D.R., *Disraeli's Fiction*, London 1979.

Silverman, J.H., *The World of Thackeray's Novels*, Diss. University of Pennsylvania 1982.

Sudrann, J., "The Philosopher's Property: Thackeray and the Use of Time", *Victorian Studies* 10 (1967).

Spielmann, M.H., *The History of "Punch"*, London 1895.

Spielmann, M.H., *The Hitherto Unidentified Contributions of W.M. Thackeray to "Punch"*, London 1899. (G.N. Ray has provided an essential supplement to this in *The Times Literary Supplement*, 1 January 1949.)

Stevens, J., "Thackeray's *Vanity Fair*", *Review of English Studies* VI (1965) (see also: *Costerus*, above).

Stevenson, L., *The Showman of Vanity Fair. The Life of William Makepeace Thackeray*, second edition, New York 1968.

Strauss, H.A., and C. Hoffmann (eds.), *Juden und Judentum in der Literatur*, Munich 1985.

Studies in the Novel. Special Number: W.M. Thackeray, ed. R. Colby, Denton 1981.

Sutherland, J.A., "Thackeray as a Victorian Racialist", *Essays in Criticism* 20 (1970).

Sutherland, J.A., *Thackeray at Work*, London 1974.

Sutherland, J.A., *The Longman Companion to Victorian Fiction*, London 1988.

Szladits, L.L., and H. Simmonds, *Pen and Brush. The Author as Artist* (Berg Collection Exhibition Catalogue) New York 1969.

Taine, H., *Histoire de la littérature anglaise* (Vol. V: *Les contemporains*), Paris 1897.

Taube, M., "Thackeray and the Reminiscential Fiction", *Nineteenth Century Fiction* 18 (1963).

Tillotson, G., *Thackeray the Novelist*, Cambridge 1954.

Tillotson, G., *A View of Victorian Literature*, Oxford 1978.

Tillotson, G., and D. Hayes (eds.), *Thackeray, The Critical Heritage*, London 1968.

Tillotson, K., *Novels of the Eighteen-Forties*, corrected edition, Oxford 1961.

Trachtenberg, J., *The Devil and the Jews. The Medieval Conception of the Jew and its Relation to Modern Anti-Semitism*, New Haven 1943.

Trollope, A., *William Makepeace Thackeray* (*English Men of Letters* series), London 1879.

Van Cleave, M.E., *A Necessary Alliance. A Study of the Relation of Author, Narrator and Reader in Thackeray's Fiction*, Diss. Oregon 1978.

Varcoe, G., *The Intrusive Narrator. Fielding, Thackeray and the English Novel*, Diss. Uppsala 1972.

Wall, S., *Trollope and Character*, London 1988.
Welsh, A. (ed.), *Thackeray. A Collection of Critical Essays*, Englewood Cliffs 1968.
Wheatley, J.H., *Patterns in Thackeray's Fiction*, Cambridge (Mass) 1969.
White, E.M., "Thackeray's Contributions to *Fraser's Magazine*", (*Victorian Studies* 19 (1986).
Winner, V.H., "Thackeray and Richard Doyle, the 'Wayward Artist'", Harvard Library Bulletin 26 (1978).

Notes

R.D. McMaster's *Thackeray's Cultural Frame of Reference: Allusion in 'The Newcomes'* (London 1991) was published too late for inclusion. Its chapter on Thackeray's use of the Bible to appeal to a "religiously knowledgeable, middle-class, Victorian-readership" (pp. 43–52) confirms and usefully supplements my observations on this subject.

INDEX

BRILL'S SERIES
IN JEWISH STUDIES